Nine
Plays
of
the
Modern
Theater

NINE PLAYS OF THE MODERN THEATER

With an Introduction by Harold Clurman, ed.

Grove Press, Inc.　　New York

[c1981]

First Evergreen Edition 1981
Second Printing 1982
ISBN: 0-394-17411-9
Library of Congress Catalog Card Number: 79-52121

LIBRARY OF CONGRESS CATALOGING IN PUBLICATION DATA

Main entry under title:

Nine plays of the modern theater.

   CONTENTS: Clurman, H.   Introduction. — Beckett, S.   Waiting for Godot. — Brecht, B.   The Caucasian chalk circle. [etc.]
   1. Drama — 20th century. I. Clurman, Harold, 1901 — PN6112.N56
808.82′04   79-52121   ISBN   0-394-17411-9 pbk.

Manufactured in the United States of America

GROVE PRESS, INC., 196 West Houston Street, New York, N.Y. 10014

Contents

INTRODUCTION

by

Harold Clurman

Vladimir, the more "philosophical" of the two vagrants in Beckett's *Waiting for Godot,* stiffens their morale by asking, ". . . what's the good of losing heart now? We should have thought of it a million years ago, in the nineties!" What does this mean in the play's context? What were the nineties that these bewildered blighters should recall them with regret? It was perhaps a time when they had not yet entered upon their agony. It was a time of certainty, a beautiful time–or so it seemed to them and to most of their contemporaries.

In 1882 Nietzsche had pronounced God dead. The mass of men who did not read Nietzsche were not yet affected by his devastating affirmation. In 1865, Ibsen, presumably an athiest, wrote *Brand,* in which God is very real to its protagonist. Faith in those days, though under attack, still resisted. And even in the nineties God was still in his heaven and there was peace on Earth. Disturbed by doubt during the twenties, the world was nevertheless giddily livable and hectically "safe." The destruction of old idols was an intellectual's game.

The Second World War all but demolished the age-old fortress of belief sustained by the idea of God. For what is God, apart from its sacred meaning, but the concept of a coherent order, a hierarchy of values which either rationally or transcendantally illuminates the chaos of existence. Without the support of such a structure life becomes a desert plain without a clear path, direction, or destination; it makes no "sense." Even iconoclasm becomes pointless. Humans become blind mice. Or so it appeared to many people of sensibility and probing minds. The noblest of them could hardly affirm anything more than that they were desperately pining for an answer, a "Godot," which might save them.

The nine plays included in this volume are not only modern by date —1944 to 1975—but in their dramatization of the dilemma. Though each may differ from the other in literary and theatrical quality, in personality or style, they nearly all confront a common concern, the same spiritual situation. While each expresses an individual consciousness and temperament, all move toward a unity in which we may discern a por-

vii

trait of our day. What, in any case, is incontrovertible is that they are among the most representative plays of our era.

Whatever topical material they employ, all of them aim at a universality of meaning. None is strictly realistic. It is only a seeming paradox that while most of them have been lumped as "pessimistic," they are generally comedies, often quite funny. But where nothing is sure, where everything is put in question, when as in *Godot* the difference of one season from another is nothing but the addition of a leaf to a hitherto lone tree, a sad note will prevail. Beckett called his play a tragicomedy, as Dürrenmatt did with *The Visit*.

The exception to the "nihilistic" aspect of the pieces collected here is Bertolt Brecht's *The Caucasian Chalk Circle*. It is perhaps telling that it was written in California in 1944 when the author, though in exile, was hopeful with the impending defeat of nazism of a better day to come. But a much more operative factor in Brecht's optimism was that he believed in an order in human history. For him, Marxism establishes a coherence and order in the dialectics of experience.

Still, Brecht's Marxism (barely acceptable in the Soviet Union) and the moment when *The Caucasian Chalk Circle* was written do not precisely explain the play's healthy ebullience. There is in Brecht a peasant-like robustness of humor, a quizzical wisdom of which his frequent use of earthy proverbs is a sign. Speaking of the Governor's Wife who during the turmoil of a rebellion wantonly loses sight of her baby that is found and cared for by Nina, the baby's nurse, a woman in the crowd comments, "Nina takes it more to heart than the mistress. . . . They [the rich] even have to have their weeping done for them."

The Caucasian Chalk Circle is a fable which never departs from a primitive simplicity. Its ribaldries are gentle, its overall tone light-hearted and cleansing. Its "music" is yea saying. "Fearful is the seductive power of goodness," the Singer (or chorus) tells us; and at another point "in the bloodiest times, there are kind people." Contrary to his reputation, except for a few didactic plays, Brecht's plays are not propaganda unless we consider a morality play like *Everyman* to be propaganda. The climactic scene of *The Circle* is very much a folk jest. The moral is summed up in the Singer's serene envoi, ". . . you who have listened to the Story of the Chalk Circle, take note of what men of old have concluded: that what there is shall go to those who are good for it, children to the motherly that they prosper, carts to good drivers that they be driven well, the valley to the waterers that it yield fruit."

There is another respect in which Brecht is contemporary and pre-eminent: his work is cast in unequivocally *theatrical* form. Along with poetically inspired dialogue he employs song and musical accompaniment, innovative scenic inventions rarely found in the drama which runs from Ibsen through to the German expressionists. Brecht's formal means, which mark a return to classic modes—he said "Japanese"—and a new kind of direction (demanded by the texts themselves), have influenced a large area of contemporary stagecraft, whatever their "ideology."

With *Waiting for Godot,* written in 1948 and first produced in Paris in 1952, we come to the seminal play of the period, indeed its masterpiece. In it the era of dismay and discouragement finds its most incisive and poignant theatrical expression. Its opening line and image set the key for the whole parable. As one of the tramps sits on a low mound "in the midst of nothingness" trying in vain to pull off his boot which pinches painfully, he murmurs "nothing to be done," to which Vladimir concurs, "I am beginning to come around to that opinion." But he adds more thoughtfully, "That is man all over for you, blaming on his boots the fault of his feet."

There is, for all the repetitiousness, hardly a wasted word or an insignificant allusion in the entire play. This terseness is characteristic not only of Beckett but of much of the writing in contemporary drama —often carried to the point of nearly total silence. In Beckett's case the effect, with a few sudden eruptions of anguished verbiage, mounts to an incantatory eloquence.

In the encompassing void and in the absence of meaningful event, each of the men is isolated within his own hurt; yet both feel a desperate need to cling together. Nothing is left to them but to wait for some redeeming agent, a "Godot." They thrash about, they speak of going on but they do not move. "Let's not do anything, it's safer." They contemplate suicide, but even this becomes a matter for ridicule. "Let's wait till we hear where we stand," they decide.

Godot may be salvation. But not God. If he were, Beckett has explained, he would have said so. There is nevertheless a religious core to the play. The theologian Paul Tillich has written, "The god who is absent as an object of faith is present in the sense of restlessness which asks the question of the meaning of existence." So it is in "Godot." "To all mankind they were addressed, those cries for help still ringing in our ears! But at this place, at this moment of time all mankind is us...."

Mankind has lost its rights because, Vladimir asserts, "we got rid of them." Social revolution in which others find the "answer" appears to be of little avail. The two men see Pozzo a "boss" or master-figure driving

Lucky, his slave, like a packhorse. The slave is mute, and only when forced to speak emits a torrent of clichés. And when the situation is reversed and Pozzo becomes a blinded slave, he is driven by Lucky, his former victim. There is little or no progress, Pozzo maintains on Beckett's behalf. "Let us not speak ill of our generation, it is not any unhappier than its predecessors. Let us not speak well of it either. Let us not speak of it at all," and adds judiciously, "it is true the population has increased."

What then is to be done? Practically nothing, it would seem. "Let us converse calmly, since we cannot keep silent." But human beings cannot keep silent. Nor can Beckett for all his resolve to do so. The play's constriction of grim humor suddenly bursts into a passionate outburst in which we may find a trace of healing: "What are we doing here, *that* is the question. And we are blest in this, that we happen to know the answer. Yes, in this immense confusion, one thing alone is clear. We are waiting for Godot to come. . . . We are not saints, but we have kept our appointment. How many people can boast as much?"

Thus Beckett, a prophet despite himself, proclaims nobility in trying to find a true response to the question posed by the death of God. *Waiting for Godot* may be viewed as a challenge addressed to our baffled minds and wracked souls.

It is also a poem and more than that a consummate theater piece. It is replete with scenic metaphors to visualize and give body to the dramatist's thought and feeling. The means are minimal and in this the work achieves a new kind of classicism.

The Swiss playwright Friedrich Dürrenmatt in *The Visit*, written in 1956, banks the metal of European dramatic ore and puts it to rich theatrical use. Many currencies become negotiable coin in a new synthesis. There are in this play fragments of German expressionism, of French existentialism, of Pirandello, and perhaps even of the Mark Twain of *The Man Who Corrupted Hadleyburg*. With macabre humor, a strain of quasi-romantic sentiment and transparent symbolism, the play tells us that everything may be bought, including justice. There is in it the fascination of the horror story, a shrewd melodrama in which a multimillionairess, an old lady whose very limbs are held together by steel and stone, after an absence of many years comes to venge herself on the man and the townsfolk who wronged her in her native village. She is Nemesis equipped with immense industrial and financial power. "The world turned me into a whore," she says, "I shall turn the world into a brothel." The dramatization of the process is the play's effective spine.

But there is more to the play than that—a special "twist." Nemesis in this instance is justified. The lady in question was abandoned by the man who seduced her in her innocence so that he might make a monetarily advantageous marriage. Pathos is introduced by a touching scene in which she and the man who betrayed her recall the purity of their early love. But it is this man whom she plans to have murdered by bribing the members of the impoverished town with the bequest of collective and individual fortunes. In the end the victim himself consents to his fate. Here all is hypocrisy: the community pretends that in accepting the bribe it is the instrument of a just retribution in killing the seducer for the crime of his youth, and then extends its hypocrisy to regarding the act as a kind of justice.

Modern civilization as a blazing bawdyhouse is what Jean Genet projects in frenetically exaultant prose and a sort of lurid mysticism in *The Balcony,* which dates from 1958. Genet is a "saint" of evil: he embraces it in our stead as a sort of punishment and curse. There is surely no reformist intent on his part, yet if we take it as Genet means us to, his play terrifies and stuns. It is "a true image of a false spectacle." The Balcony (the place itself) is the name of a brothel in which very ordinary citizens —most of them petty functionaries—enact their dreams of power or self-abasement as bishops, judges, generals, executioners. As a dream house it is also to a degree a work of art where the repressed desires and the drives of commonplace people reap gratification from their sordid sublimation. It is a "secret theater." And as such, like all art, it offers consolation. The house is threatened by a people's rebellion in which everything is to go up in flames in final dissolution.

The revolution which surrounds The Balcony fails; its symbolic leader, Chantal, herself formerly a whore who has escaped the brothel, is shot. The chief of police in a pact with Irma, The Balcony's madam, crowns her as the new queen to replace the deposed one. He himself will become the head of the new state whose triumphant insignia will be a penis! And the brothel's clients, who previously had only played the roles of bishop, judge, etc., will actually serve in those capacities under the new government. There is little to choose between the rulers the people have turned out and the new incumbents. It is all, Genet tells us, a matter of Nomenclature, that is, of advertised labels, publicity, the "media"! *The Balcony* is an infernal condemnation of society: Genet is a poet of the Last Judgment. He is also an extraordinarily imaginative, albeit occasionally overcomplex and confusing, theater artist. He ends the play with a bitterly ironic admonition: "You must go home where everything—you can be quite sure—will be falser than here."

Though Pinter avows a major debt to Beckett, there is a palpable difference between them. Pinter is much more "realistic": his plays are imbued by a local English atmosphere. The very weather permeates them—cold and damp making for a peculiar seediness. Then, too, Pinter's technique is that of melodrama and the mystery thriller. A mounting tension of impending doom grips us. Both these elements are conveyed in sharp strokes of dialogue composed of a workaday vocabulary.

The dis-ease in Pinter is not the same as in Beckett. Beckett's world has a certain negative purity: his characters are suspended in an airless air. In Pinter all is puzzlement, a kind of helpless groping for intelligibility; the characters hardly know what is happening to them. This ambiguity is couched in concrete words the very banality of which becomes chilling. A deathlike mist hovers over every action. Take, for instance, the final moments of *The Birthday Party*. Something terrible is about to occur. Benighted, Stanley, the central figure, is being removed somewhere; to what destination, for what reason, by whose command? We are not informed. The point is that he is being *taken away* by the strangest of strangers, themselves virtual cretins. We are in a bleak void of schizophrenia. Beckett is wholly expressive; Pinter suggests that expression has become all but incommunicative.

Though to Ionesco, Brecht is as much to be abjured as the *Boulevard* ("commercial") theater because Brecht is "political" and what is worse, Marxist, the fact is that in *Rhinoceros* at least, Ionesco implies a social purpose. It is an anticonformist cartoon. There is much of the same disquiet here as in most of the leading playwrights of the postwar generation and certain traits of mystification, but *Rhinoceros* is a comedy sustained by gags, vaudevillesque stunts, and Marx Brothers jocularity.

Ionesco's target is such a catch phrase as "We must move with the times." Systematically pursued, it makes everything ugly and ultimately dangerous; it transforms humans into "rhinoceroses." Its dominance explains the totalitarian push and why "the world's gone sick." Like the little fellow Berenger, the play's antihero, Ionesco insists "I'm not capitulating." But in *Rhinoceros* Ionesco's resistance is not grave but soft, like a man upset by too demanding and tumultuous an environment who yearns for homey ease and comfort.

Because Poland has for centuries been a subject nation, its theater has to a considerable degree perfected a style of grotesquerie and invidious farce with subversive political connotations sparked by bitter though seemingly innocuous jokes. The disguise is what underlies the foolery of Mrozek's *Tango*.

Speaking for the author, a character says, "Don't you realize that tragedy isn't possible anymore?" Tragedy requires the recognition of a "god," an order widely accepted as sacrosanct, a sustaining ideal. It is our increasing awareness that this hardly exists anymore which must be the premise for an appreciation of the plays under discussion. But if so, Mrozek asks, what then? "Tragedy impossible, farce a bore—what's left but experiments?" Perhaps this explains much of today's avant-garde theater. What Mrozek is saying in his cockeyed comedy is that Poland especially is stumbling or falling between all the stools.

A late comer in the "field" is Tom Stoppard's 1966 *Rosencrantz and Guildenstern Are Dead*. They are the boys from Wittenberg called to spy on Hamlet for objectives they cannot fathom, to an end they cannot anticipate. The play is the cleverest in the present collection. In a most engaging theatrical form the removal in time and place fosters a stagey glamor—it seizes upon a Beckett-like theme—men lost in an incomprehensible world—and makes it delectably witty.

The plot line is saddening, but the trimmings are jocular. On the one hand, we hear the blithe anarchism of "Generally speaking, things have gone about as far as they can possibly get when they have got about as bad as they reasonably get"; on the other hand, we are treated to the foreboding of "We follow directions—there's no *choice* involved. The bad end unhappily, the good unluckily. That is what tragedy means." But for all its dire implications, the play is chiefly bright-minded entertainment.

Its virtue is not in its import but in its writing. It is bedecked with well-turned quips: "Life is a gamble, at terrible odds—if it were a bet you wouldn't take it." The man's mouthpiece amuses and dazzles.

Last we come to our United States. This is only natural. America is the youngest of the great countries, often inspired or infected by Europe. David Mamet's 1975 *American Buffalo* breaks away from the tradition in our native drama which runs through O'Neill, Odets, Williams, to a play reminiscent of, though unlike, Pinter.

It is very much *our* play. A good part of its meaning is in its speech. The characters express themselves in the debris of our language: words and sentences have become eroded. (In part this explains the occasional obscurity in narrative development.) If the play finally achieves eloquence it is through the inarticulate. No ideas or statements are ever completed, conversation is chiefly carried on in a series of muddled or explosive ejaculations. One often doubts whether the characters themselves know what they want to say. Hardly anything is fulfilled. There is something about the characters and their values as effaced as the American buffalo in the old coins. We perceive only their lineaments.

Yet they are people with feelings, intensified by their very muddle. The guy called Teach speaks of himself as a businessman, but he is the most thoroughly confused of the three. Repressed or undeveloped in his emotions he is terrifying. (We might learn from him something of gangster psychology.) It is he nevertheless who stridently voices the frustration and distress of the general condition—far less exceptional than we are wont to suppose. With a preface and a coda of obscenities, and a weapon ready to destroy the junk shop which is the three characters' collective haven, he cries out, "The Whole Entire World. There is no law. There is no Right and Wrong. The World is Lies. There is no Friendship." In this hysterical blast he speaks for everyone, everyone exacerbated by our present state. No wonder then that Teach and the many like him need a gun—to relax, to make themselves comfortable!

Still, astonishingly, friendship does exist among the three men who brawl, insult, and hurt one another: a friendship of physical connection, a spastic reaching out for solace, even a dumb loyalty. "I am sorry," says the least knowing of them, the shop's apprentice, for having messed up a planned robbery, and is forgiven by his lumbering boss with, "That's all right."

One further observation: where there is little aim motivated by high purpose, psychology becomes rudimentary, thinking is deprived of complexity, emotions sapped of subtlety. There can be little possible action except for the satisfaction of almost infantile cravings and speech itself loses definition. Everything tends toward stylization and abstraction. From all this ensues shortness of breath. Plays with such characteristics often seem little more than expanded sketches. They are like people with no place to go.

This bespeaks no rejection. The merit of the dramatists who write such plays is that they make vivid what is happening to us and, unintentionally in most cases, warn us of our peril. We can understand them correctly only if we share with them their sense of the present day and the societies from which they and their plays emerge and which produce them.

Nine
Plays
of
the
Modern
Theater

The
Caucasian
Chalk
Circle

by
Bertolt Brecht

Revised English Version
by Eric Bentley

CHARACTERS

Old Man *on the right*

Peasant Woman *on the right*

Young Peasant

A Very Young Worker

Old Man *on the left*

Peasant Woman *on the left*

Agriculturist Kato

Girl Tractorist

Wounded Soldier

The Delegate *from the capital*

The Singer

Georgi Abashwili, *the Governor*

Natella, *the Governor's wife*

Michael, *their son*

Shalva, *an adjutant*

Arsen Kazbeki, *a fat prince*

Messenger *from the capital*

Niko Mikadze *and* Mika Loladze, *doctors*

Simon Shashava, *a soldier*

Grusha Vashnadze, *a kitchen maid*

Old Peasant *with the milk*

Corporal *and* Private

Peasant *and his wife*

Lavrenti Vashnadze, *Grusha's brother*

Aniko, *his wife*

Peasant Woman, *for a while Grusha's mother-in-law*

Jussup, *her son*

Monk

Azdak, *village recorder*

Shauwa, *a policeman*

Grand Duke

Doctor

Invalid

Limping Man

Blackmailer

Ludovica

Innkeeper, *her father-in-law*

Stableboy

Poor Old Peasant Woman

Irakli, *her brother-in-law, a bandit*

Three Wealthy Farmers

Illo Shuboladze *and* Sandro Oboladze, *lawyers*

Old Married Couple

> Soldiers, Servants, Peasants, Beggars, Musicians, Merchants, Nobles, Architects

The time and the place: After a prologue, set in 1945, we move back perhaps 1000 years.

The action of The Caucasian Chalk Circle *centers on Nuka (or Nukha), a town in Azerbaijan. However, the capital referred to in the prologue is not Baku (capital of Soviet Azerbaijan) but Tiflis (or Tbilisi), capital of Georgia. When Azdak, later, refers to "the capital" he means Nuka itself, though whether Nuka was ever capital of Georgia I do not know: in what reading I have done on the subject I have only found Nuka to be the capital of a Nuka Khanate.*

The word "Georgia" has not been used in this English version because of its American associations; instead, the alternative name "Grusinia" (in Russian, Gruziya) has been used.

The reasons for resettling the old Chinese story in Transcaucasia are not far to seek. The play was written when the Soviet chief of state, Joseph Stalin, was a Georgian, as was his favorite poet, cited in the Prologue, Mayakovsky. And surely there is a point in having this story acted out at the place where Europe and Asia meet, a place incomparably rich in legend and history. Here Jason found the Golden Fleece. Here Noah's Ark touched ground. Here the armies of both Genghis Khan and Tamerlane wrought havoc.

—E.B.

PROLOGUE

Summer, 1945.

Among the ruins of a war-ravaged Caucasian village the members of two Kolkhoz villages, mostly women and older men, are sitting in a circle, smoking and drinking wine. With them is a DELEGATE *of the State Reconstruction Commission from Nuka.*

PEASANT WOMAN, *left* (*pointing*): In those hills over there we stopped three Nazi tanks, but the apple orchard was already destroyed.

OLD MAN, *right*: Our beautiful dairy farm: a ruin.

GIRL TRACTORIST: I laid the fire, Comrade.

Pause.

DELEGATE: Nuka, Azerbaijan S.S.R. Delegation received from the goat-breeding Kolkhoz "Rosa Luxemburg." This is a collective farm which moved eastwards on orders from the authorities at the approach of Hitler's armies. They are now planning to return. Their delegates have looked at the village and the land and found a lot of destruction. (*Delegates on the right nod.*) But the neighboring fruit farm—Kolkhoz (*to the left*) "Galinsk"—proposes to use the former grazing land of Kolkhoz "Rosa Luxemburg" for orchards and vineyards. This land lies in a valley where grass doesn't grow very well. As a delegate of the Reconstruction Commission in Nuka I request that the two Kolkhoz villages decide between themselves whether Kolkhoz "Rosa Luxemburg" shall return or not.

5

OLD MAN, *right*: First of all, I want to protest against the time limit on discussion. We of Kolkhoz "Rosa Luxemburg" have spent three days and three nights getting here. And now discussion is limited to half a day.

WOUNDED SOLDIER, *left*: Comrade, we haven't as many villages as we used to have. We haven't as many hands. We haven't as much time.

GIRL TRACTORIST: All pleasures have to be rationed. Tobacco is rationed, and wine. Discussion should be rationed.

OLD MAN, *right* (*sighing*): Death to the fascists! But I will come to the point and explain why we want our valley back. There are a great many reasons, but I'll begin with one of the simplest. Makinä Abakidze, unpack the goat cheese. (*A peasant woman from right takes from a basket an enormous cheese wrapped in a cloth. Applause and laughter.*) Help yourselves, Comrades, start in!

OLD MAN, *left* (*suspiciously*): Is this a way of influencing us?

OLD MAN, *right* (*amid laughter*): How could it be a way of influencing you, Surab, you valley-thief? Everyone knows you'll take the cheese and the valley, too. (*Laughter.*) All I expect from you is an honest answer. Do you like the cheese?

OLD MAN, *left*: The answer is: yes.

OLD MAN, *right*: Really. (*Bitterly.*) I ought to have known you know nothing about cheese.

OLD MAN, *left*: Why not? When I tell you I like it?

OLD MAN, *right*: Because you can't like it. Because it's not what it was in the old days. And why not? Because our goats don't like the new grass as they did the old. Cheese is not cheese because grass is not grass, that's the thing. Please put that in your report.

OLD MAN, *left*: But your cheese is excellent.

OLD MAN, *right*: It isn't excellent. It's just passable. The new grazing land is no good, whatever the young people may say. One can't live there. It doesn't even smell of morning in the morning. (*Several people laugh.*)

DELEGATE: Don't mind their laughing: they understand you. Comrades, why does one love one's country? Because the bread tastes better there, the air smells better, voices sound stronger, the sky is higher, the ground is easier to walk on. Isn't that so?

OLD MAN, *right*: The valley has belonged to us from all eternity.

SOLDIER, *left*: What does *that* mean—from all eternity? Nothing belongs to anyone from all eternity. When you were young you didn't even belong to yourself. You belonged to the Kazbeki princes.

OLD MAN, *right*: Doesn't it make a difference, though, what kind of trees stand next to the house you are born in? Or what kind of neighbors you have? Doesn't that make a difference? We want to go back just to have you as our neighbors, valley-thieves! Now you can all laugh again.

OLD MAN, *left* (*laughing*): Then why don't you listen to what your neighbor, Kato Wachtang, our agriculturist, has to say about the valley?

PEASANT WOMAN, *right*: We've not said all we have to say about our valley. By no means. Not all the houses are destroyed. As for the dairy farm, at least the foundation wall is still standing.

DELEGATE: You can claim State support—here and there —you know that. I have suggestions here in my pocket.

PEASANT WOMAN, *right*: Comrade Specialist, we haven't come here to haggle. I can't take your cap and hand you another, and say "This one's better." The other one might *be* better, but you *like* yours better.

GIRL TRACTORIST: A piece of land is not a cap—not in our country, Comrade.

DELEGATE: Don't get mad. It's true we have to consider a piece of land as a tool to produce something useful, but it's also true that we must recognize love for a particular piece of land. As far as I'm concerned, I'd like to find out more exactly what you (*to those on the left*) want to do with the valley.

OTHERS: Yes, let Kato speak.

KATO (*rising; she's in military uniform*): Comrades, last winter, while we were fighting in these hills here as Partisans, we discussed how, once the Germans were expelled, we could build up our fruit culture to ten times its original size. I've prepared a plan for an irrigation project. By means of a cofferdam on our mountain lake, 300 hectares of unfertile land can be irrigated. Our Kolkhoz could not only cultivate more fruit, but also have vineyards. The project, however, would pay only if the disputed valley of Kolkhoz "Rosa Luxemburg" were also included. Here are the calculations. (*She hands* DELEGATE *a briefcase.*)

OLD MAN, *right*: Write into the report that our Kolkhoz plans to start a new stud farm.

GIRL TRACTORIST: Comrades, the project was conceived during days and nights when we had to take cover in the mountains. We were often without ammunition for our half-dozen rifles. Even finding a pencil was difficult. (*Applause from both sides.*)

OLD MAN, *right*: Our thanks to the Comrades of Kolkhoz "Galinsk" and all those who've defended our country! (*They shake hands and embrace.*)

PEASANT WOMAN, *left*: In doing this our thought was that our soldiers––both your men and our men—should return to a still more productive homeland.

GIRL TRACTORIST: As the poet Mayakovsky said: "The home of the Soviet people shall also be the home of Reason"!

The delegates excluding the OLD MAN *have got up, and with the* DELEGATE *specified proceed to study the Agriculturist's drawings. Exclamations such as:* "Why is the altitude of fall 22 meters?"—"This rock will have to be blown up"—"Actually, all they need is cement and dynamite"—"They force the water to come down here, that's clever!"

A VERY YOUNG WORKER, *right* (*to* OLD MAN, *right*): They're going to irrigate all the fields between the hills, look at that, Aleko!

OLD MAN, *right*: I'm not going to look. I knew the project would be good. I won't have a pistol pointed at me!

DELEGATE: But they only want to point a pencil at you!

Laughter.

OLD MAN, *right* (*gets up gloomily, and walks over to look at the drawings*): These valley-thieves know only too well that we in this country are suckers for machines and projects.

PEASANT WOMAN, *right*: Aleko Bereshwili, you have a weakness for new projects. That's well known.

DELEGATE: What about my report? May I write that you will all support the cession of your old valley in the interests of this project when you get back to your Kolkhoz?

PEASANT WOMAN, *right*: I will. What about you, Aleko?

OLD MAN, *right* (*bent over drawings*): I suggest that you give us copies of the drawings to take along.

PEASANT WOMAN, *right*: Then we can sit down and eat. Once he has the drawings and he's ready to discuss them, the matter is settled. I know him. And it will be the same with the rest of us.

Delegates laughingly embrace again.

OLD MAN, *left*: Long live the Kolkhoz "Rosa Luxemburg" and much luck to your horse-breeding project!

PEASANT WOMAN, *left*: In honor of the visit of the delegates from Kolkhoz "Rosa Luxemburg" and of the Specialist, the plan is that we all hear a presentation of the Singer Arkadi Tscheidse.

Applause. GIRL TRACTORIST *has gone off to bring the* SINGER.

PEASANT WOMAN, *right*: Comrades, your entertainment had better be good. It's going to cost us a valley.

PEASANT WOMAN, *left*: Arkadi Tscheidse knows about our discussion. He's promised to perform something that has a bearing on the problem.

KATO: We wired Tiflis three times. The whole thing nearly fell through at the last minute because his driver had a cold.

PEASANT WOMAN, *left*: Arkadi Tscheidse knows 21,000 lines of verse.

OLD MAN, *left*: He's hard to get. You and the Planning Commission should persuade him to come north more often, Comrade.

DELEGATE: We are more interested in economics, I'm afraid.

OLD MAN, *left* (*smiling*): You arrange the redistribution of vines and tractors, why not songs?

Enter the SINGER *Arkadi Tscheidse, led by* GIRL TRACTORIST. *He is a well-built man of simple manners, accompanied by* FOUR MUSICIANS *with their instruments. The artists are greeted with applause.*

GIRL TRACTORIST: This is the Comrade Specialist, Arkadi.

The SINGER *greets them all.*

DELEGATE: Honored to make your acquaintance. I heard about your songs when I was a boy at school. Will it be one of the old legends?

SINGER: A very old one. It's called "The Chalk Circle" and comes from the Chinese. But we'll do it, of course, in a changed version. Comrades, it's an honor for me to entertain you after a difficult debate. We hope you will find that the voice of the old poet also sounds well in the shadow of Soviet tractors. It may be a mistake to mix different wines, but old and new wisdom mix admirably. Now I hope we'll get something to eat before the performance begins—it would certainly help.

VOICES: Surely. Everyone into the Club House!

While everyone begins to move, DELEGATE *turns to* GIRL TRACTORIST.

DELEGATE: I hope it won't take long. I've got to get back tonight.

GIRL TRACTORIST: How long will it last, Arkadi? The Comrade Specialist must get back to Tiflis tonight.

SINGER (*casually*): It's actually two stories. An hour or two.

GIRL TRACTORIST (*confidentially*): Couldn't you make it shorter?

SINGER: No.

VOICE: Arkadi Tscheidse's performance will take place here in the square after the meal.

And they all go happily to eat.

1

THE NOBLE CHILD

As the lights go up, the SINGER *is seen sitting on the floor, a black sheepskin cloak round his shoulders, and a little, well-thumbed notebook in his hand. A small group of listeners—the chorus—sits with him. The manner of his recitation makes it clear that he has told his story over and over again. He mechanically fingers the pages, seldom looking at them. With appropriate gestures, he gives the signal for each scene to begin.*

SINGER:

> In olden times, in a bloody time,
> There ruled in a Caucasian city—
> Men called it City of the Damned—
> A Governor.
> His name was Georgi Abashwili.
> He was rich as Croesus
> He had a beautiful wife
> He had a healthy baby.
> No other governor in Grusinia
> Had so many horses in his stable
> So many beggars on his doorstep
> So many soldiers in his service
> So many petitioners in his courtyard.
> Georgi Abashwili—how shall I describe him to you?
> He enjoyed his life.
> On the morning of Easter Sunday
> The Governor and his family went to church.

At the left a large doorway, at the right an even larger

13

gateway. BEGGARS *and* PETITIONERS *pour from the gateway, holding up thin* CHILDREN, *crutches, and petitions. They are followed by* IRONSHIRTS, *and then, expensively dressed, the* GOVERNOR'S FAMILY.

BEGGARS AND PETITIONERS:

—Mercy! Mercy, Your Grace! The taxes are too high.
—I lost my leg in the Persian War, where can I get . . .
—My brother is innocent, Your Grace, a misunderstanding . . .
—The child is starving in my arms!
—Our petition is for our son's discharge from the army, our last remaining son!
—Please, Your Grace, the water inspector takes bribes.

One servant collects the petitions. Another distributes coins from a purse. Soldiers push the crowd back, lashing at them with thick leather whips.

SOLDIER: Get back! Clear the church door!

Behind the GOVERNOR, *his* WIFE, *and the* ADJUTANT, *the* GOVERNOR'S CHILD *is brought through the gateway in an ornate carriage.*

CROWD:

—The baby!
—I can't see it, don't shove so hard!
—God bless the child, Your Grace!

SINGER (*while the crowd is driven back with whips*):

For the first time on that Easter Sunday, the people
    saw the Governor's heir.
Two doctors never moved from the noble child, apple
    of the Governor's eye.

Even the mighty Prince Kazbeki bows before him at
the church door.

The FAT PRINCE *steps forwards and greets the* FAMILY.

FAT PRINCE: Happy Easter, Natella Abashwili! What a
day! When it was raining last night, I thought to myself, gloomy holidays! But this morning the sky was
gay. I love a gay sky, a simple heart, Natella Abashwili. And little Michael is a governor from head to
foot! Tititi! (*He tickles the* CHILD.)

GOVERNOR'S WIFE: What do you think, Arsen, at last
Georgi has decided to start building the east wing.
All those wretched slums are to be torn down to make
room for the garden.

FAT PRINCE: Good news after so much bad! What's the
latest on the war, Brother Georgi? (*The* GOVERNOR
indicates a lack of interest.) Strategical retreat, I
hear. Well, minor reverses are to be expected. Sometimes things go well, sometimes not. Such is war.
Doesn't mean a thing, does it?

GOVERNOR'S WIFE: He's coughing. Georgi, did you hear?
(*She speaks sharply to the* DOCTORS, *two dignified
men standing close to the little carriage.*) He's
coughing!

FIRST DOCTOR (*to the* SECOND): May I remind you, Niko
Mikadze, that I was against the lukewarm bath? (*To
the* GOVERNOR'S WIFE:) There's been a little error
over warming the bath water, Your Grace.

SECOND DOCTOR (*equally polite*): Mika Loladze, I'm
afraid I can't agree with you. The temperature of the
bath water was exactly what our great, beloved
Mishiko Oboladze prescribed. More likely a slight
draft during the night, Your Grace.

GOVERNOR'S WIFE: But do pay more attention to him. He looks feverish, Georgi.

FIRST DOCTOR (*bending over the* CHILD): No cause for alarm, Your Grace. The bath water will be warmer. It won't occur again.

SECOND DOCTOR (*with a venomous glance at the* FIRST): I won't forget that, my dear Mika Loladze. No cause for concern, Your Grace.

FAT PRINCE: Well, well, well! I always say: "A pain in my liver? Then the doctor gets fifty strokes on the soles of his feet." We live in a decadent age. In the old days one said: "Off with his head!"

GOVERNOR'S WIFE: Let's go into church. Very likely it's the draft here.

The procession of FAMILY *and* SERVANTS *turns into the doorway. The* FAT PRINCE *follows, but the* GOVERNOR *is kept back by the* ADJUTANT, *a handsome young man. When the crowd of* PETITIONERS *has been driven off, a young dust-stained* RIDER, *his arm in a sling, remains behind.*

ADJUTANT (*pointing at the* RIDER, *who steps forward*): Won't you hear the messenger from the capital, Your Excellency? He arrived this morning. With confidential papers.

GOVERNOR: Not before Service, Shalva. But did you hear Brother Kazbeki wish me a happy Easter? Which is all very well, but I don't believe it did rain last night.

ADJUTANT (*nodding*): We must investigate.

GOVERNOR: Yes, at once. Tomorrow.
They pass through the doorway. The RIDER, *who has waited in vain for an audience, turns sharply round and, muttering a curse, goes off. Only one of the*

*palace guards—*SIMON SHASHAVA—*remains at the. door.*

SINGER:

The city is still.
Pigeons strut in the church square.
A soldier of the Palace Guard
Is joking with a kitchen maid
As she comes up from the river with a bundle.

*A girl—*GRUSHA VASHNADZE—*comes through the gateway with a bundle made of large green leaves under her arm.*

SIMON: What, the young lady is not in church? Shirking?

GRUSHA: I was dressed to go. But they needed another goose for the banquet. And they asked me to get it. I know about geese.

SIMON: A goose? (*He feigns suspicion.*) I'd like to see that goose. (GRUSHA *does not understand.*) One must be on one's guard with women. "I only went for a fish," they tell you, but it turns out to be something else.

GRUSHA (*walking resolutely toward him and showing him the goose*): There! If it isn't a fifteen-pound goose stuffed full of corn, I'll eat the feathers.

SIMON: A queen of a goose! The Governor himself will eat it. So the young lady has been down to the river again?

GRUSHA: Yes, at the poultry farm.

SIMON: Really? At the poultry farm, down by the river . . . not higher up maybe? Near those willows?

GRUSHA: I only go to the willows to wash the linen.

SIMON (*insinuatingly*): Exactly.

GRUSHA: Exactly what?

SIMON (*winking*): Exactly that.

GRUSHA: Why shouldn't I wash the linen by the willows?

SIMON (*with exaggerated laughter*): "Why shouldn't I wash the linen by the willows!" That's good, really good!

GRUSHA: I don't understand the soldier. What's so good about it?

SIMON (*slyly*): "If something I know someone learns, she'll grow hot and cold by turns!"

GRUSHA: I don't know what I could learn about those willows.

SIMON: Not even if there was a bush opposite? That one could see everything from? Everything that goes on there when a certain person is—"washing linen"?

GRUSHA: What does go on? Won't the soldier say what he means and have done?

SIMON: Something goes on. Something can be seen.

GRUSHA: Could the soldier mean I dip my toes in the water when it's hot? There's nothing else.

SIMON: There's more. Your toes. And more.

GRUSHA: More what? At most my foot?

SIMON: Your foot. And a little more. (*He laughs heartily.*)

GRUSHA (*angrily*): Simon Shashava, you ought to be ashamed of yourself! To sit in a bush on a hot day and wait till a girl comes and dips her legs in the river!

And I bet you bring a friend along too! (*She runs off.*)

SIMON (*shouting after her*): I didn't bring any friend along!

As the SINGER *resumes his tale, the* SOLDIER *steps into the doorway as though to listen to the service.*

SINGER:

> The city lies still
> But why are there armed men?
> The Governor's palace is at peace
> But why is it a fortress?
> And the Governor returned to his palace
> And the fortress was a trap
> And the goose was plucked and roasted
> But the goose was not eaten this time
> And noon was no longer the hour to eat:
> Noon was the hour to die.

From the doorway at the left the FAT PRINCE *quickly appears, stands still, looks around. Before the gateway at the right two* IRONSHIRTS *are squatting and playing dice. The* FAT PRINCE *sees them, walks slowly past, making a sign to them. They rise: one goes through the gateway, the other goes off at the right. Muffled voices are heard from various directions in the rear:* "To your posts!" *The palace is surrounded. The* FAT PRINCE *quickly goes off. Church bells in the distance. Enter, through the doorway, the Governor's family and procession, returning from church.*

GOVERNOR'S WIFE (*passing the* ADJUTANT): It's impossible to live in such a slum. But Georgi, of course, will only build for his little Michael. Never for me! Michael is all! All for Michael!

The procession turns into the gateway. Again the ADJUTANT *lingers behind. He waits. Enter the wounded* RIDER *from the doorway. Two* IRONSHIRTS *of the Palace Guard have taken up positions by the gateway.*

ADJUTANT (*to the* RIDER): The Governor does not wish to receive military news before dinner—especially if it's depressing, as I assume. In the afternoon His Excellency will confer with prominent architects. They're coming to dinner too. And here they are! (*Enter three gentlemen through the doorway.*) Go to the kitchen and eat, my friend. (*As the* RIDER *goes, the* ADJUTANT *greets the* ARCHITECTS.) Gentlemen, His Excellency expects you at dinner. He will devote all his time to you and your great new plans. Come!

ONE OF THE ARCHITECTS: We marvel that His Excellency intends to build. There are disquieting rumors that the war in Persia has taken a turn for the worse.

ADJUTANT: All the more reason to build! There's nothing to those rumors anyway. Persia is a long way off, and the garrison here would let itself be hacked to bits for its Governor. (*Noise from the palace. The shrill scream of a woman. Someone is shouting orders. Dumbfounded, the* ADJUTANT *moves toward the gateway. An* IRONSHIRT *steps out, points his lance at him.*) What's this? Put down that lance, you dog.

ONE OF THE ARCHITECTS: It's the Princes! Don't you know the Princes met last night in the capital? And they're against the Grand Duke and his Governors? Gentlemen, we'd better make ourselves scarce. (*They rush off. The* ADJUTANT *remains helplessly behind.*)

ADJUTANT (*furiously to the Palace Guard*): Down with those lances! Don't you see the Governor's life is threatened?

The IRONSHIRTS *of the Palace Guard refuse to obey.*

They stare coldly and indifferently at the ADJUTANT
and follow the next events without interest.

SINGER:

O blindness of the great!
They go their way like gods,
Great over bent backs,
Sure of hired fists,
Trusting in the power
Which has lasted so long.
But long is not forever.
O change from age to age!
Thou hope of the people!

Enter the GOVERNOR, *through the gateway, between
two* SOLDIERS *armed to the teeth. He is in chains.
His face is gray.*

Up, great sir, deign to walk upright!
From your palace the eyes of many foes follow you!
And now you don't need an architect, a carpenter will
    do.
You won't be moving into a new palace
But into a little hole in the ground.
Look about you once more, blind man!

The arrested man looks round.

Does all you had please you?
Between the Easter Mass and the Easter meal
You are walking to a place whence no one returns.

The GOVERNOR *is led off. A horn sounds an alarm.
Noise behind the gateway.*

When the house of a great one collapses
Many little ones are slain.
Those who had no share in the *good* fortunes of
    the mighty

Often have a share in their *mis*fortunes.
The plunging wagon
Drags the sweating oxen down with it
Into the abyss.

The SERVANTS *come rushing through the gateway in panic.*

SERVANTS (*among themselves*):

—The baskets!
—Take them all into the third courtyard! Food for five days!
—The mistress has fainted! Someone must carry her down.
—She must get away.
—What about us? We'll be slaughtered like chickens, as always.
—Goodness, what'll happen? There's bloodshed already in the city, they say.
—Nonsense, the Governor has just been asked to appear at a Princes' meeting. All very correct. Everything'll be ironed out. I heard this on the best authority . . .

The two DOCTORS *rush into the courtyard.*

FIRST DOCTOR (*trying to restrain the other*): Niko Mikadze, it is your duty as a doctor to attend Natella Abashwili.

SECOND DOCTOR: My duty! It's yours!

FIRST DOCTOR: Whose turn is it to look after the child today, Niko Mikadze, yours or mine?

SECOND DOCTOR: Do you really think, Mika Loladze, I'm going to stay a minute longer in this accursed house on that little brat's account? (*They start fighting. All one hears is:* "You neglect your duty!" *and* "Duty, my foot!" *Then the* SECOND DOCTOR *knocks the* FIRST *down.*) Go to hell! (Exit.)

Enter the soldier, SIMON SHASHAVA. *He searches in the crowd for* GRUSHA.

SIMON: Grusha! There you are at last! What are you going to do?

GRUSHA: Nothing. If worst comes to worst, I've a brother in the mountains. How about you?

SIMON: Forget about me. (*Formally again:*) Grusha Vashnadze, your wish to know my plans fills me with satisfaction. I've been ordered to accompany Madam Abashwili as her guard.

GRUSHA: But hasn't the Palace Guard mutinied?

SIMON (*seriously*): That's a fact.

GRUSHA: Isn't it dangerous to go with her?

SIMON: In Tiflis, they say: Isn't the stabbing dangerous for the knife?

GRUSHA: You're not a knife, you're a man, Simon Shashava, what has that woman to do with you?

SIMON: That woman has nothing to do with me. I have my orders, and I go.

GRUSHA: The soldier is pigheaded: he is running into danger for nothing—nothing at all. I must get into the third courtyard, I'm in a hurry.

SIMON: Since we're both in a hurry we shouldn't quarrel. You need time for a good quarrel. May I ask if the young lady still has parents?

GRUSHA: No, just a brother.

SIMON: As time is short—my second question is this: Is the young lady as healthy as a fish in water?

GRUSHA: I may have a pain in the right shoulder once in a while. Otherwise I'm strong enough for my job. No one has complained. So far.

SIMON: That's well known. When it's Easter Sunday, and the question arises who'll run for the goose all the same, she'll be the one. My third question is this: Is the young lady impatient? Does she want apples in winter?

GRUSHA: Impatient? No. But if a man goes to war without any reason and then no message comes—that's bad.

SIMON: A message will come. And now my final question . . .

GRUSHA: Simon Shashava, I must get to the third courtyard at once. My answer is yes.

SIMON (*very embarrassed*): Haste, they say, is the wind that blows down the scaffolding. But they also say: The rich don't know what haste is. I'm from . . .

GRUSHA: Kutsk . . .

SIMON: The young lady has been inquiring about me? I'm healthy, I have no dependents, I make ten piasters a month, as paymaster twenty piasters, and I'm asking —very sincerely—for your hand.

GRUSHA: Simon Shashava, it suits me well.

SIMON (*taking from his neck a thin chain with a little cross on it*): My mother gave me this cross, Grusha Vashnadze. The chain is silver. Please wear it.

GRUSHA: Many thanks, Simon.

SIMON (*hangs it round her neck*): It would be better to go to the third courtyard now. Or there'll be difficulties. Anyway, I must harness the horses. The young lady will understand?

GRUSHA: Yes, Simon.

They stand undecided.

SIMON: I'll just take the mistress to the troops that have stayed loyal. When the war's over, I'll be back. In two weeks. Or three. I hope my intended won't get tired, awaiting my return.

GRUSHA:

Simon Shashava, I shall wait for you.
Go calmly into battle, soldier
The bloody battle, the bitter battle
From which not everyone returns:
When you return I shall be there.
I shall be waiting for you under the green elm
I shall be waiting for you under the bare elm
I shall wait until the last soldier has returned
And longer
When you come back from the battle
No boots will stand at my door
The pillow beside mine will be empty
And my mouth will be unkissed.
When you return, when you return
You will be able to say: It is just as it was.

SIMON: I thank you, Grusha Vashnadze. And good-bye!

He bows low before her. She does the same before him. Then she runs quickly off without looking round. Enter the ADJUTANT *from the gateway.*

ADJUTANT (*harshly*): Harness the horses to the carriage! Don't stand there doing nothing, scum!

SIMON SHASHAVA *stands to attention and goes off. Two* SERVANTS *crowd from the gateway, bent low under huge trunks. Behind them, supported by her women, stumbles* NATELLA ABASHWILI. *She is followed by a* WOMAN *carrying the* CHILD.

GOVERNOR'S WIFE: I hardly know if my head's still on. Where's Michael? Don't hold him so clumsily. Pile the trunks onto the carriage. No news from the city, Shalva?

ADJUTANT: None. All's quiet so far, but there's not a minute to lose. No room for all those trunks in the carriage. Pick out what you need. (*Exit quickly.*)

GOVERNOR'S WIFE: Only essentials! Quick, open the trunks! I'll tell you what I need. (*The trunks are lowered and opened. She points at some brocade dresses.*) The green one! And, of course, the one with the fur trimming. Where are Niko Mikadze and Mika Loladze? I've suddenly got the most terrible migraine again. It always starts in the temples. (*Enter* GRUSHA.) Taking your time, eh? Go and get the hot water bottles this minute! (GRUSHA *runs off, returns later with hot water bottles; the* GOVERNOR'S WIFE *orders her about by signs.*) Don't tear the sleeves.

A YOUNG WOMAN: Pardon, madam, no harm has come to the dress.

GOVERNOR'S WIFE: Because I stopped you. I've been watching you for a long time. Nothing in your head but making eyes at Shalva Tzereteli. I'll kill you, you bitch! (*She beats the* YOUNG WOMAN.)

ADJUTANT (*appearing in the gateway*): Please make haste, Natella Abashwili. Firing has broken out in the city. (*Exit.*)

GOVERNOR'S WIFE (*letting go of the* YOUNG WOMAN): Oh dear, do you think they'll lay hands on us? Why should they? Why? (*She herself begins to rummage in the trunks.*) How's Michael? Asleep?

WOMAN WITH THE CHILD: Yes, madam.

GOVERNOR'S WIFE: Then put him down a moment and get my little saffron-colored boots from the bedroom. I need them for the green dress. (*The* WOMAN *puts down the* CHILD *and goes off.*) Just look how these things have been packed! No love! No understanding! If you don't give them every order yourself . . . At such moments you realize what kind of servants you have! They gorge themselves at your expense, and never a word of gratitude! I'll remember this.

ADJUTANT (*entering, very excited*): Natella, you must leave at once!

GOVERNOR'S WIFE: Why? I've got to take this silver dress—it cost a thousand piasters. And that one there, and where's the wine-colored one?

ADJUTANT (*trying to pull her away*): Riots have broken out! We must leave at once. Where's the baby?

GOVERNOR'S WIFE (*calling to the* YOUNG WOMAN *who was holding the baby*): Maro, get the baby ready! Where on earth are you?

ADJUTANT (*leaving*): We'll probably have to leave the carriage behind and go ahead on horseback.

The GOVERNOR'S WIFE *rummages again among her dresses, throws some onto the heap of chosen clothes, then takes them off again. Noises, drums are heard. The* YOUNG WOMAN *who was beaten creeps away. The sky begins to grow red.*

GOVERNOR'S WIFE (*rummaging desperately*): I simply cannot find the wine-colored dress. Take the whole pile
to the carriage. Where's Asja? And why hasn't Maro
come back? Have you all gone crazy?

ADJUTANT (*returning*): Quick! Quick!

GOVERNOR'S WIFE (*to the* FIRST WOMAN): Run! Just throw
them into the carriage!

ADJUTANT: We're not taking the carriage. And if you
don't come now, I'll ride off on my own.

GOVERNOR'S WIFE (*as the* FIRST WOMAN *can't carry everything*): Where's that bitch Asja? (*The* ADJUTANT
pulls her away.) Maro, bring the baby! (*To the*
FIRST WOMAN:) Go and look for Masha. No, first
take the dresses to the carriage. Such nonsense! I
wouldn't dream of going on horseback!

*Turning round, she sees the red sky, and starts back
rigid. The fire burns. She is pulled out by the AD-
JUTANT. Shaking, the FIRST WOMAN follows with the
dresses.*

MARO (*from the doorway with the boots*): Madam! (*She
sees the trunks and dresses and runs toward the CHILD,
picks it up, and holds it a moment.*) They left it
behind, the beasts. (*She hands it to GRUSHA.*) Hold
it a moment. (*She runs off, following the GOVERNOR'S
WIFE.*)

Enter SERVANTS from the gateway.

COOK: Well, so they've actually gone. Without the food
wagons, and not a minute too early. It's time for us
to clear out.

GROOM: This'll be an unhealthy neighborhood for quite
a while. (*To one of the WOMEN:*) Suliko, take a few
blankets and wait for me in the foal stables.

GRUSHA: What have they done with the Governor?

GROOM (*gesturing throat cutting*): Ffffft.

A FAT WOMAN (*seeing the gesture and becoming hysterical*): Oh dear, oh dear, oh dear, oh dear! Our master Georgi Abashwili! A picture of health he was, at the morning Mass—and now! Oh, take me away, we're all lost, we must die in sin like our master, Georgi Abashwili!

OTHER WOMAN (*soothing her*): Calm down, Nina! You'll be taken to safety. You've never hurt a fly.

FAT WOMAN (*being led out*): Oh dear, oh dear, oh dear! Quick! Let's all get out before they come, before they come!

A YOUNG WOMAN: Nina takes it more to heart than the mistress, that's a fact. They even have to have their weeping done for them.

COOK: We'd better get out, all of us.

ANOTHER WOMAN (*glancing back*): That must be the East Gate burning.

YOUNG WOMAN (*seeing the* CHILD *in* GRUSHA's *arms*). The baby! What are you doing with it?

GRUSHA: It got left behind.

YOUNG WOMAN: She simply left it there. Michael, who was kept out of all the drafts!

The SERVANTS *gather round the* CHILD.

GRUSHA: He's waking up.

GROOM: Better put him down, I tell you. I'd rather not think what'd happen to anybody who was found with that baby.

COOK: That's right. Once they get started, they'll kill each other off, whole families at a time. Let's go.

Exeunt all but GRUSHA, *with the* CHILD *on her arm, and* TWO WOMEN.

TWO WOMEN: Didn't you hear? Better put him down.

GRUSHA: The nurse asked me to hold him a moment.

OLDER WOMAN: She's not coming back, you simpleton.

YOUNGER WOMAN: Keep your hands off it.

OLDER WOMAN (*amiably*): Grusha, you're a good soul, but you're not very bright, and you know it. I tell you, if he had the plague he couldn't be more dangerous.

GRUSHA (*stubbornly*): He hasn't got the plague. He looks at me! He's human!

OLDER WOMAN: Don't look at *him*. You're a fool—the kind that always gets put upon. A person need only say, "Run for the salad, you have the longest legs," and you run. My husband has an ox cart—you can come with us if you hurry! Lord, by now the whole neighborhood must be in flames.

Both women leave, sighing. After some hesitation, GRUSHA *puts the sleeping* CHILD *down, looks at it for a moment, then takes a brocade blanket from the heap of clothes and covers it. Then both women return, dragging bundles.* GRUSHA *starts guiltily away from the* CHILD *and walks a few steps to one side.*

YOUNGER WOMAN: Haven't you packed anything yet? There isn't much time, you know. The Ironshirts will be here from the barracks.

GRUSHA: Coming!

She runs through the doorway. Both women go to the

gateway and wait. The sound of horses is heard. They flee, screaming. Enter the FAT PRINCE *with drunken* IRONSHIRTS. *One of them carries the Governor's head on a lance.*

FAT PRINCE: Here! In the middle! (*One soldier climbs onto the other's back, takes the head, holds it tentatively over the door.*) That's not the middle. Farther to the right. That's it. What I do, my friends, I do well. (*While with hammer and nail, the soldier fastens the head to the wall by its hair:*) This morning at the church door I said to Georgi Abashwili: "I love a gay sky." Actually, I prefer the lightning that comes out of a gay sky. Yes, indeed. It's a pity they took the brat along, though, I need him, urgently.

Exit with IRONSHIRTS *through the gateway. Trampling of horses again. Enter* GRUSHA *through the doorway looking cautiously about her. Clearly she has waited for the* IRONSHIRTS *to go. Carrying a bundle, she walks toward the gateway. At the last moment, she turns to see if the* CHILD *is still there. Catching sight of the head over the doorway, she screams. Horrified, she picks up her bundle again, and is about to leave when the* SINGER *starts to speak. She stands rooted to the spot.*

SINGER:

As she was standing between courtyard and gate,
She heard or she thought she heard a low voice calling.
The child called to her,
Not whining, but calling quite sensibly,
Or so it seemed to her.
"Woman," it said, "help me."
And it went on, not whining, but saying quite sensibly:
"Know, woman, he who hears not a cry for help
But passes by with troubled ears will never hear
The gentle call of a lover nor the blackbird at dawn

Nor the happy sigh of the tired grape-picker as the
    Angelus rings."

She walks a few steps toward the CHILD *and bends
over it.*

Hearing this she went back for one more look at the
    child:
Only to sit with him for a moment or two,
Only till someone should come,
His mother, or anyone.

Leaning on a trunk, she sits facing the CHILD.

Only till she would have to leave, for the danger was
    too great,
The city was full of flame and crying.

*The light grows dimmer, as though evening and night
were coming on.*

Fearful is the seductive power of goodness!

GRUSHA *now settles down to watch over the* CHILD
*through the night. Once, she lights a small lamp to
look at it. Once, she tucks it in with a coat. From
time to time she listens and looks to see whether
someone is coming.*

And she sat with the child a long time,
Till evening came, till night came, till dawn came.
She sat too long, too long she saw
The soft breathing, the small clenched fists,
Till toward morning the seduction was complete
And she rose, and bent down and, sighing, took the
    child
And carried it away.

She does what the SINGER *says as he describes it.*

As if it was stolen goods she picked it up.
As if she was a thief she crept away.

2

THE FLIGHT INTO
THE NORTHERN MOUNTAINS

SINGER:

> When Grusha Vashnadze left the city
> On the Grusinian highway
> On the way to the Northern Mountains
> She sang a song, she bought some milk.

CHORUS:

> How will this human child escape
> The bloodhounds, the trap-setters?
> Into the deserted mountains she journeyed
> Along the Grusinian highway she journeyed
> She sang a song, she bought some milk.

GRUSHA VASHNADZE *walks on. On her back she carries the* CHILD *in a sack, in one hand is a large stick, in the other a bundle. She sings.*

THE SONG OF THE FOUR GENERALS

> Four generals
> Set out for Iran.
> With the first one, war did not agree.
> The second never won a victory.
> For the third the weather never was right.
> For the fourth the men would never fight.
> Four generals
> And not a single man!

Sosso Robakidse
Went marching to Iran
With him the war did so agree
He soon had won a victory.
For him the weather was always right.
For him the men would always fight.
Sosso Robakidse,
He is our man!

A peasant's cottage appears.

GRUSHA (*to the* CHILD): Noontime is meal time. Now we'll sit hopefully in the grass, while the good Grusha goes and buys a little pitcher of milk. (*She lays the* CHILD *down and knocks at the cottage door. An* OLD MAN *opens it.*) Grandfather, could I have a little pitcher of milk? And a corn cake, maybe?

OLD MAN: Milk? We have no milk. The soldiers from the city have our goats. Go to the soldiers if you want milk.

GRUSHA: But grandfather, you must have a little pitcher of milk for a baby?

OLD MAN: And for a God-bless-you, eh?

GRUSHA: Who said anything about a God-bless-you? (*She shows her purse.*) We'll pay like princes. "Head in the clouds, backside in the water." (*The peasant goes off, grumbling, for milk.*) How much for the milk?

OLD MAN: Three piasters. Milk has gone up.

GRUSHA: Three piasters for this little drop? (*Without a word the* OLD MAN *shuts the door in her face.*) Michael, did you hear that? Three piasters! We can't afford it! (*She goes back, sits down again, and gives the* CHILD *her breast.*) Suck. Think of the three piasters. There's nothing there, but you *think* you're drinking, and that's something. (*Shaking her head, she sees that the* CHILD *isn't sucking any more. She gets up, walks back to the door, and knocks again.*) Open, grandfather, we'll pay. (*Softly.*) May lightning strike you! (*When the* OLD MAN *appears*:) I thought it would be half a piaster. But the baby must be fed. How about one piaster for that little drop?

OLD MAN: Two.

GRUSHA: Don't shut the door again. (*She fishes a long time in her bag.*) Here are two piasters. The milk better be good. I still have two days' journey ahead of me. It's a murderous business you have here—and sinful, too!

OLD MAN: Kill the soldiers if you want milk.

GRUSHA (*giving the* CHILD *some milk*): This is an expensive joke. Take a sip, Michael, it's a week's pay. Around here they think we earned our money just sitting on our behinds. Oh, Michael, Michael, you're a nice little load for a girl to take on! (*Uneasy, she gets up, puts the* CHILD *on her back, and walks on. The* OLD MAN, *grumbling, picks up the pitcher and looks after her unmoved.*)

SINGER:

As Grusha Vashnadze went northward
The Princes' Ironshirts went after her.

CHORUS:

How will the barefoot girl escape the Ironshirts,
The bloodhounds, the trap-setters?
They hunt even by night.
Pursuers never tire.
Butchers sleep little.

Two IRONSHIRTS *are trudging along the highway.*

CORPORAL: You'll never amount to anything, blockhead, your heart's not in it. Your senior officer sees this in little things. Yesterday, when I made the fat gal, yes, you grabbed her husband as I commanded, and you did kick him in the belly, at my request, but did you *enjoy* it, like a loyal Private, or were you just doing your duty? I've kept an eye on you blockhead, you're a hollow reed and a tinkling cymbal, you won't get promoted. (*They walk a while in silence.*) Don't think I've forgotten how insubordinate you are, either. Stop limping! I forbid you to limp! You limp because I sold the horses, and I sold the horses because I'd never have got that price again. You limp to show me you don't like marching. I know you. It won't help. You wait. Sing!

TWO IRONSHIRTS (*singing*):

Sadly to war I went my way
Leaving my loved one at her door.
My friends will keep her honor safe
Till from the war I'm back once more.

CORPORAL: Louder!

TWO IRONSHIRTS (*singing*):

When 'neath a headstone I shall be
My love a little earth will bring:
"Here rest the feet that oft would run to me
And here the arms that oft to me would cling."

They begin to walk again in silence.

CORPORAL: A good soldier has his heart and soul in it. When he receives an order, he gets a hard-on, and when he drives his lance into the enemy's guts, he comes. (*He shouts for joy.*) He lets himself be torn to bits for his superior officer, and as he lies dying he takes note that his corporal is nodding approval, and that is reward enough, it's his dearest wish. *You* won't get any nod of approval, but you'll croak all right. Christ, how'm I to get my hands on the Governor's bastard with the help of a fool like you! (*They stay on stage behind.*)

SINGER:
When Grusha Vashnadze came to the River Sirra
Flight grew too much for her, the helpless child too
    heavy.
In the cornfields the rosy dawn
Is cold to the sleepless one, only cold.
The gay clatter of the milk cans in the farmyard where
    the smoke rises
Is only a threat to the fugitive.
She who carries the child feels its weight and little
    more.

GRUSHA *stops in front of a farm. A fat* PEASANT WOMAN *is carrying a milk can through the door.* GRUSHA *waits until she has gone in, then approaches the house cautiously.*

GRUSHA (*to the* CHILD): Now you've wet yourself again, and you know I've no linen. Michael, this is where we part company. It's far enough from the city. They wouldn't want you *so* much that they'd follow you all *this* way, little good-for-nothing. The peasant woman is kind, and can't you just smell the milk? (*She bends down to lay the* CHILD *on the threshold.*) So farewell, Michael, I'll forget how you kicked me in the back all night to make me walk faster. And you can forget the meager fare—it was meant well. I'd like to have kept you—your nose is so tiny— but it can't be. I'd have shown you your first rabbit, I'd have trained you to keep dry, but now I must turn around. My sweetheart the soldier might be back soon, and suppose he didn't find me? You can't ask that, can you? (*She-creeps up to the door and lays the* CHILD *on the threshold. Then, hiding behind a tree, she waits until the* PEASANT WOMAN *opens the door and sees the bundle.*)

PEASANT WOMAN: Good heavens, what's this? Husband!

PEASANT: What is it? Let me finish my soup.

PEASANT WOMAN (*to the* CHILD): Where's your mother then? Haven't you got one? It's a boy. Fine linen. He's from a good family, you can see that. And they just leave him on our doorstep. Oh, these are times!

PEASANT: If they think we're going to feed it, they're wrong. You can take it to the priest in the village. That's the best we can do.

PEASANT WOMAN: What'll the priest do with him? He needs a mother. There, he's waking up. Don't you think we could keep him, though?

PEASANT (*shouting*): No!

PEASANT WOMAN: I could lay him in the corner by the arm-chair. All I need is a crib. I can take him into the fields with me. See him laughing? Husband, we have a roof over our heads. We can do it. Not another word out of you!

She carries the CHILD *into the house. The* PEASANT *follows protesting.* GRUSHA *steps out from behind the tree, laughs, and hurries off in the opposite direction.*

SINGER:
Why so cheerful, making for home?

CHORUS:
Because the child has won new parents with a laugh,
Because I'm rid of the little one, I'm cheerful.

SINGER:

And why so sad?

CHORUS:

Because I'm single and free, I'm sad
Like someone who's been robbed
Someone who's newly poor.

She walks for a short while, then meets the two IRON-
SHIRTS *who point their lances at her.*

CORPORAL: Lady, you are running straight into the arms
of the Armed Forces. Where are you coming from?
And when? Are you having illicit relations with the
enemy? Where is he hiding? What movements is he
making in your rear? How about the hills? How about
the valleys? How are your stockings held in position?
(GRUSHA *stands there frightened.*) Don't be scared,
we always withdraw, if necessary . . . what, blockhead? I always withdraw. In that respect at least,
I can be relied on. Why are you staring like that at
my lance? In the field no soldier drops his lance, that's
a rule. Learn it by heart, blockhead. Now, lady, where
are you headed?

GRUSHA: To meet my intended, one Simon Shashava, of the
Palace Guard in Nuka.

CORPORAL: Simon Shashava? Sure, I know him. He gave
me the key so I could look you up once in a while.
Blockhead, we are getting to be unpopular. We must
make her realize we have honorable intentions. Lady,
behind apparent frivolity I conceal a serious nature,
so let me tell you officially: I want a child from you.
(GRUSHA *utters a little scream.*) Blockhead, she understands me. Uh-huh, isn't it a sweet shock? "Then first
I must take the noodles out of the oven, Officer. Then
first I must change my torn shirt, Colonel." But away
with jokes, away with my lance! We are looking for a

baby. A baby from a good family. Have you heard of such a baby, from the city, dressed in fine linen, and suddenly turning up here?

GRUSHA: No, I haven't heard a thing. (*Suddenly she turns round and runs back, panic-stricken. The* IRONSHIRTS *glance at each other, then follow her, cursing.*)

SINGER:
Run, kind girl! The killers are coming!
Help the helpless babe, helpless girl!
And so she runs!

CHORUS:
In the bloodiest times
There are kind people.

As GRUSHA *rushes into the cottage, the* PEASANT WOMAN *is bending over the* CHILD'S *crib.*

GRUSHA: Hide him. Quick! The Ironshirts are coming! I laid him on your doorstep. But he isn't mine. He's from a good family.

PEASANT WOMAN: Who's coming? What Ironshirts?

GRUSHA: Don't ask questions. The Ironshirts that are looking for it.

PEASANT WOMAN: They've no business in my house. But I must have a little talk with you, it seems.

GRUSHA: Take off the fine linen. It'll give us away.

PEASANT WOMAN: Linen, my foot! In this house I make the decisions! "*You* can't vomit in *my* room!" Why did you abandon it? It's a sin.

GRUSHA (*looking out of the window*): Look, they're coming out from behind those trees! I shouldn't have run away, it made them angry. Oh, what shall I do?

PEASANT WOMAN (*looking out of the window and suddenly starting with fear*): Gracious! Ironshirts!

GRUSHA: They're after the baby.

PEASANT WOMAN: Suppose they come in!

GRUSHA: You mustn't give him to them. Say he's yours.

PEASANT WOMAN: Yes.

GRUSHA: They'll run him through if you hand him over.

PEASANT WOMAN: But suppose they ask for it? The silver for the harvest is in the house.

GRUSHA: If you let them have him, they'll run him through, right here in this room! You've got to say he's yours!

PEASANT WOMAN: Yes. But what if they don't believe me?

GRUSHA: You must be firm.

PEASANT WOMAN: They'll burn the roof over our heads.

GRUSHA: That's why you must say he's yours. His name's Michael. But I shouldn't have told you. (*The* PEASANT WOMAN *nods.*) Don't nod like that. And don't tremble —they'll notice.

PEASANT WOMAN: Yes.

GRUSHA: And stop saying yes, I can't stand it. (*She shakes the* WOMAN.) Don't you have any children?

PEASANT WOMAN (*muttering*): He's in the war.

GRUSHA: Then maybe *he's* an Ironshirt? Do you want *him* to run children through with a lance? You'd bawl him out. "No fooling with lances in my house!" you'd shout, "is that what I've reared you for? Wash your neck before you speak to your mother!"

PEASANT WOMAN: That's true, he couldn't get away with anything around here!

GRUSHA: So you'll say he's yours?

PEASANT WOMAN: Yes.

GRUSHA: Look! They're coming!

There is a knocking at the door. The women don't answer. Enter IRONSHIRTS. *The* PEASANT WOMAN *bows low.*

CORPORAL: Well, here she is. What did I tell you? What a nose I have! I *smelt* her. Lady, I have a question for you. Why did you run away? What did you think I would do to you? I'll bet it was something unchaste. Confess!

GRUSHA (*while the* PEASANT WOMAN *bows again and again.*): I'd left some milk on the stove, and I suddenly remembered it.

CORPORAL: Or maybe you imagined I looked at you unchastely? Like there could be something between us? A carnal glance, know what I mean?

GRUSHA: I didn't see it.

CORPORAL: But it's possible, huh? You admit that much. After all, I might be a pig. I'll be frank with you: I could think of all sorts of things if we were alone. (*To the* PEASANT WOMAN:) Shouldn't you be busy in the yard? Feeding the hens?

PEASANT WOMAN (*falling suddenly to her knees*): Soldier, I didn't know a thing about it. Please don't burn the roof over our heads.

CORPORAL: What are you talking about?

PEASANT WOMAN: I had nothing to do with it. She left it on my doorstep, I swear it!

CORPORAL (*suddenly seeing the* CHILD *and whistling*): Ah, so there's a little something in the crib! Blockhead, I smell a thousand piasters. Take the old girl outside and hold on to her. It looks like I have a little cross-examining to do. (*The* PEASANT WOMAN *lets herself be led out by the* PRIVATE, *without a word.*) So, you've got the child I wanted from you! (*He walks toward the crib.*)

GRUSHA: Officer, he's mine. He's not the one you're after.

CORPORAL: I'll just take a look. (*He bends over the crib.*)

GRUSHA *looks round in despair.*

GRUSHA: He's mine! He's mine!

CORPORAL: Fine linen!

GRUSHA *dashes at him to pull him away. He throws her off and again bends over the crib. Again looking round in despair, she sees a log of wood, seizes it, and hits the* CORPORAL *over the head from behind. The* CORPORAL *collapses. She quickly picks up the* CHILD *and rushes off.*

SINGER:
And in her flight from the Ironshirts
After twenty-two days of journeying
At the foot of the Janga-Tau Glacier
Grusha Vashnadze decided to adopt the child.

CHORUS:
The helpless girl adopted the helpless child.

GRUSHA *squats over a half-frozen stream to get the* CHILD *water in the hollow of her hand.*

GRUSHA:
Since no one else will take you, son,
I must take you.
Since no one else will take you, son,
You must take me.
O black day in a lean, lean year,

The trip was long, the milk was dear,
My legs are tired, my feet are sore:
But I wouldn't be without you any more.
I'll throw your silken shirt away
And wrap you in rags and tatters.
I'll wash you, son, and christen you in glacier water.
We'll see it through together.

*She has taken off the child's fine linen and wrapped it
in a rag.*

SINGER:
When Grusha Vashnadze
Pursued by the Ironshirts
Came to the bridge on the glacier
Leading to the villages of the Eastern Slope
She sang the Song of the Rotten Bridge
And risked two lives.

*A wind has risen. The bridge on the glacier is visible
in the dark. One rope is broken and half the bridge
is hanging down the abyss.* MERCHANTS, *two men and
a woman, stand undecided before the bridge as*
GRUSHA *and the* CHILD *arrive. One man is trying to
catch the hanging rope with a stick.*

FIRST MAN: Take your time, young woman. You won't
get across here anyway.

GRUSHA: But I *have* to get the baby to the east side. To
my brother's place.

MERCHANT WOMAN: Have to? How d'you mean, "have to"?
I have to get there, too—because I have to buy carpets
in Atum—carpets a woman had to sell because her
husband had to die. But can *I* do what I have to? Can
she? Andrei's been fishing for that rope for hours.
And I ask you, how are we going to fasten it, even if
he gets it up?

FIRST MAN *(listening)*: Hush, I think I hear something.

GRUSHA: The bridge isn't quite rotted through. I think I'll try it.

MERCHANT WOMAN: *I* wouldn't—if the devil himself were after me. It's suicide.

FIRST MAN (*shouting*): Hi!

GRUSHA: Don't shout! (*To the* MERCHANT WOMAN:) Tell him not to shout.

FIRST MAN: But there's someone down there calling. Maybe they've lost their way.

MERCHANT WOMAN: Why shouldn't he shout? Is there something funny about you? Are they after you?

GRUSHA: All right, I'll tell. The Ironshirts are after me. I knocked one down.

SECOND MAN: Hide our merchandise!

The WOMAN *hides a sack behind a rock.*

FIRST MAN: Why didn't you say so right away? (*To the others*:) If they catch her they'll make mincemeat out of her!

GRUSHA: Get out of my way. I've got to cross that bridge.

SECOND MAN: You can't. The precipice is two thousand feet deep.

FIRST MAN: Even with the rope it'd be no use. We could hold it up with our hands. But then we'd have to do the same for the Ironshirts.

GRUSHA: Go away.

There are calls from the distance: "Hi, up there!"

MERCHANT WOMAN: They're getting near. But you can't take the child on that bridge. It's sure to break. And look!

GRUSHA *looks down into the abyss. The* IRONSHIRTS *are heard calling again from below.*

SECOND MAN: Two thousand feet!

GRUSHA: But those men are worse.

FIRST MAN: You can't do it. Think of the baby. Risk your life but not a child's.

SECOND MAN: With the child she's that much heavier!

MERCHANT WOMAN: Maybe she's *really* got to get across. Give *me* the baby. I'll hide it. Cross the bridge alone!

GRUSHA: I won't. We belong together. (*To the* CHILD:) "Live together, die together." (*She sings.*)

THE SONG OF THE ROTTEN BRIDGE

Deep is the abyss, son,
I see the weak bridge sway
But it's not for us, son,
To choose the way.

The way I know
Is the one you must tread,
And all you will eat
Is my bit of bread.

Of every four pieces
You shall have three.
Would that I knew
How big they will be!

Get out of my way, I'll try it without the rope.

MERCHANT WOMAN: You are tempting God!

There are shouts from below.

GRUSHA: Please, throw that stick away, or they'll get the rope and follow me. (*Pressing the* CHILD *to her, she steps onto the swaying bridge. The* MERCHANT WOMAN *screams when it looks as though the bridge is about to collapse. But* GRUSHA *walks on and reaches the far side.*)

FIRST MAN: She made it!

MERCHANT WOMAN (*who has fallen on her knees and begun to pray, angrily*): I still think it was a sin.

The IRONSHIRTS *appear; the* CORPORAL's *head is bandaged.*

CORPORAL: Seen a woman with a child?

FIRST MAN (*while the* SECOND MAN *throws the stick into the abyss*): Yes, there! But the bridge won't carry you!

CORPORAL: You'll pay for this, blockhead!

GRUSHA, *from the far bank, laughs and shows the* CHILD *to the* IRONSHIRTS. *She walks on. The wind blows.*

GRUSHA (*turning to the* CHILD): You mustn't be afraid of the wind. He's a poor thing too. He has to push the clouds along and he gets quite cold doing it. (*Snow starts falling.*) And the snow isn't so bad, either, Michael. It covers the little fir trees so they won't die in winter. Let me sing you a little song. (*She sings.*)

THE SONG OF THE CHILD

Your father is a bandit
A harlot the mother who bore you.
Yet honorable men
Shall kneel down before you.
Food to the baby horses
The tiger's son will take.
The mothers will get milk
From the son of the snake.

3

IN THE NORTHERN MOUNTAINS

SINGER:

Seven days the sister, Grusha Vashnadze,
Journeyed across the glacier
And down the slopes she journeyed.
"When I enter my brother's house," she thought,
"He will rise and embrace me."
"Is that you, sister?" he will say,
"I have long expected you.
This is my dear wife,
And this is my farm, come to me by marriage,
With eleven horses and thirty-one cows. Sit down.
Sit down with your child at our table and eat."
The brother's house was in a lovely valley.
When the sister came to the brother,
She was ill from walking.
The brother rose from the table.

A fat peasant couple rise from the table. LAVRENTI
VASHNADZE *still has a napkin round his neck, as*
GRUSHA, *pale and supported by a* SERVANT, *enters with*
the CHILD.

LAVRENTI: Where've *you* come from, Grusha?

GRUSHA (*feebly*): Across the Janga-Tu Pass, Lavrenti.

SERVANT: I found her in front of the hay barn. She has a
baby with her.

SISTER-IN-LAW: Go and groom the mare.

48

Exit the SERVANT.

LAVRENTI: This is my wife Aniko.

SISTER-IN-LAW: I thought you were in service in Nuka.

GRUSHA (*barely able to stand*): Yes, I was.

SISTER-IN-LAW: Wasn't it a good job? We were told it was.

GRUSHA: The Governor got killed.

LAVRENTI: Yes, we heard there were riots. Your aunt told us. Remember, Aniko?

SISTER-IN-LAW: Here with us, it's very quiet. City people always want something going on. (*She walks toward the door, calling:*) Sosso, Sosso, don't take the cake out of the oven yet, d'you hear? Where on earth are you? (*Exit, calling.*)

LAVRENTI (*quietly, quickly*): Is there a father? (*As she shakes her head:*) I thought not. We must think up something. She's religious.

SISTER-IN-LAW (*returning*): Those servants! (*To* GRUSHA:) You have a child.

GRUSHA: It's mine. (*She collapses.* LAVRENTI *rushes to her assistance.*)

SISTER-IN-LAW: Heavens, she's ill—what are we going to do?

LAVRENTI (*escorting her to a bench near the stove*): Sit down, sit. I think it's just weakness, Aniko.

SISTER-IN-LAW: As long as it's not scarlet fever!

LAVRENTI: She'd have spots if it was. It's only weakness. Don't worry, Aniko. (*To* GRUSHA:) Better, sitting down?

SISTER-IN-LAW: Is the child hers?

GRUSHA: Yes, mine.

LAVRENTI: She's on her way to her husband.

SISTER-IN-LAW: I see. Your meat's getting getting cold. (LAVRENTI *sits down and begins to eat.*) Cold food's not good for you, the fat mustn't get cold, you know your stomach's your weak spot. (*To* GRUSHA:) If your husband's not in the city, where is he?

LAVRENTI: She got married on the other side of the mountain, she says.

SISTER-IN-LAW: On the other side of the mountain. I see. (*She also sits down to eat.*)

GRUSHA: I think I should lie down somewhere, Lavrenti.

SISTER-IN-LAW: If it's consumption we'll all get it. (*She goes on cross-examining her.*) Has your husband got a farm?

GRUSHA: He's a soldier.

LAVRENTI: But he's coming into a farm—a small one—from his father.

SISTER-IN-LAW: Isn't he in the war? Why not?

GRUSHA (*with effort*): Yes, he's in the war.

SISTER-IN-LAW: Then why d'you want to go to the farm?

LAVRENTI: When he comes back from the war, he'll return to his farm.

SISTER-IN-LAW: But you're going there now?

LAVRENTI: Yes, to wait for him.

SISTER-IN-LAW (*calling shrilly*): Sosso, the cake!

GRUSHA (*murmuring feverishly*): A farm—a soldier—waiting—sit down, eat.

SISTER-IN-LAW: It's scarlet fever.

GRUSHA (*starting up*): Yes, he's got a farm!

LAVRENTI: I think it's just weakness, Aniko. Would you look after the cake yourself, dear?

SISTER-IN-LAW: But when will he come back if war's broken out again as people say? (*She waddles off, shouting:*) Sosso! Where on earth are you? Sosso!

LAVRENTI: (*getting up quickly and going to* GRUSHA): You'll get a bed in a minute. She has a good heart. But wait till after supper.

GRUSHA (*holding out the* CHILD *to him*): Take him.

LAVRENTI (*taking it and looking around*): But you can't stay here long with the child. She's religious, you see.

GRUSHA *collapses.* LAVRENTI *catches her.*

SINGER:

> The sister was so ill,
> The cowardly brother had to give her shelter.
> Summer departed, winter came.
> The winter was long, the winter was short.
> People mustn't know anything.
> Rats mustn't bite.
> Spring mustn't come.

GRUSHA *sits over the weaving loom in a workroom. She and the* CHILD, *who is squatting on the floor, are wrapped in blankets. She sings.*

THE SONG OF THE CENTER

And the lover started to leave
And his betrothed ran pleading after him
Pleading and weeping, weeping and teaching:
"Dearest mine, dearest mine

When you go to war as now you do
When you fight the foe as soon you will
Don't lead with the front line
And don't push with the rear line
At the front is red fire
In the rear is red smoke
Stay in the war's center
Stay near the standard bearer
The first always die
The last are also hit
Those in the center come home."

Michael, we must be clever. If we make ourselves as small as cockroaches, the sister-in-law will forget we're in the house, and then we can stay till the snow melts.

Enter LAVRENTI. *He sit down beside his sister.*

LAVRENTI: Why are you sitting there muffled up like coach-men, you two? Is it too cold in the room?

GRUSHA (*hastily removing one shawl*): It's not too cold, Lavrenti.

LAVRENTI: If it's too cold, you shouldn't be sitting here with the child. Aniko would never forgive herself! (*Pause.*) I hope our priest didn't question you about the child?

GRUSHA: He did, but I didn't tell him anything.

LAVRENTI: That's good. I wanted to speak to you about Aniko. She has a good heart but she's very, very sensitive. People need only mention our farm and she's worried. She takes everything hard, you see. One time our milkmaid went to church with a hole in her stocking. Ever since, Aniko has worn two pairs of stockings in church. It's the old family in her. (*He listens.*) Are you sure there are no rats around? If there are rats, you couldn't live here. (*There are sounds as of dripping from the roof.*) What's that, dripping?

GRUSHA: It must be a barrel leaking.

LAVRENTI: Yes, it must be a barrel. You've been here six months, haven't you? Was I talking about Aniko? (*They listen again to the snow melting.*) You can't imagine how worried she gets about your soldier-husband. "Suppose he comes back and can't find her!" she says and lies awake. "He can't come before the spring," I tell her. The dear woman! (*The drops begin to fall faster.*) When d'you think he'll come? What do *you* think? (GRUSHA *is silent.*) Not before the spring, you agree? (GRUSHA *is silent.*) You don't believe he'll come at all? (GRUSHA *is silent.*) But when the spring comes and the snow melts here and on the passes, you can't stay on. They may come and look for you. There's already talk of an illegitimate child. (*The "glockenspiel" of the falling drops has grown faster and steadier.*) Grusha, the snow is melting on the roof. Spring is here.

GRUSHA: Yes.

LAVRENTI (*eagerly*): I'll tell you what we'll do. You need a place to go, and, because of the child (*he sighs*), you have to have a husband, so people won't talk. Now I've made cautious inquiries to see if we can find you a husband. Grusha, I *have* one. I talked to a peasant woman who has a son. Just the other side of the mountain. A small farm. And she's willing.

GRUSHA: But I *can't* marry! I must wait for Simon Shashava.

LAVRENTI: Of course. That's all been taken care of. You don't need a man in bed—you need a man on paper. And I've found you one. The son of this peasant woman is going to die. Isn't that wonderful? He's at his last gasp. And all in line with our story—a husband from the other side of the mountain! And when you met him he was at the last gasp. So you're a widow. What do you say?

GRUSHA: It's true I could use a document with stamps on it for Michael.

LAVRENTI: Stamps make all the difference. Without something in writing the Shah couldn't prove he's a Shah. And you'll have a place to live.

GRUSHA: How much does the peasant woman want?

LAVRENTI: Four hundred piasters.

GRUSHA: Where will you find it?

LAVRENTI (*guiltily*): Aniko's milk money.

GRUSHA: No one would know us there. I'll do it.

LAVRENTI (*getting up*): I'll let the peasant woman know.

Quick exit.

GRUSHA: Michael, you make a lot of work. I came by you as the pear tree comes by sparrows. And because a Christian bends down and picks up a crust of bread so nothing will go to waste. Michael, it would have been better had I walked quickly away on that Easter Sunday in Nuka in the second courtyard. Now I *am* a fool.

SINGER:

The bridegroom was on his deathbed when the bride arrived.
The bridegroom's mother was waiting at the door, telling her to hurry.
The bride brought a child along.
The witness hid it during the wedding.

On one side the bed. Under the mosquito net lies a very sick man. GRUSHA *is pulled in at a run by her future mother-in-law. They are followed by* LAVRENTI *and the* CHILD.

MOTHER-IN-LAW: Quick! Quick! Or he'll die on us before the wedding. (*To* LAVRENTI:) I was never told she had a child already.

LAVRENTI: What difference does it make? (*Pointing toward the dying man.*) It can't matter to him—in his condition.

MOTHER-IN-LAW: To him? But I'll never survive the shame! We are honest people. (*She begins to weep.*) My Jussup doesn't have to marry a girl with a child!

LAVRENTI: All right, make it another two hundred piasters. You'll have it in writing that the farm will go to you: but she'll have the right to live here for two years.

MOTHER-IN-LAW (*drying her tears*): It'll hardly cover the funeral expenses. I hope she'll really lend a hand with the work. And what's happened to the monk? He must have slipped out through the kitchen window. We'll have the whole village on our necks when they hear Jussup's end is come! Oh dear! I'll go get the monk. But he mustn't see the child!

LAVRENTI: I'll take care he doesn't. But why only a monk? Why not a priest?

MOTHER-IN-LAW: Oh, he's just as good. I only made one mistake: I paid half his fee in advance. Enough to send him to the tavern. I only hope . . . (*She runs off.*)

LAVRENTI: She saved on the priest, the wretch! Hired a cheap monk.

GRUSHA: You *will* send Simon Shashava to see me if he turns up after all?

LAVRENTI: Yes. (*Pointing at the* SICK PEASANT.) Won't you take a look at him? (GRUSHA, *taking* MICHAEL *to her, shakes her head.*) He's not moving an eyelid. I hope we aren't too late.

They listen. On the opposite side enter neighbors who look around and take up positions against the walls, thus forming another wall near the bed, yet leaving an opening so that the bed can be seen. They start murmuring prayers. Enter the MOTHER-IN-LAW *with a* MONK. *Showing some annoyance and surprise, she bows to the guests.*

MOTHER-IN-LAW: I hope you won't mind waiting a few moments? My son's bride has just arrived from the city. An emergency wedding is about to be celebrated. (*To the* MONK *in the bedroom*:) I might have known you couldn't keep your trap shut. (*To* GRUSHA:) The wedding can take place at once. Here's the license. Me and the bride's brother (LAVRENTI *tries to hide in the background, after having quietly taken* MICHAEL *back from* GRUSHA. *The* MOTHER-IN-LAW *waves him away.*) are the witnesses.

GRUSHA *has bowed to the* MONK. *They go to the bed. The* MOTHER-IN-LAW *lifts the mosquito net. The* MONK *starts reeling off the marriage ceremony in Latin. Meanwhile the* MOTHER-IN-LAW *beckons to* LAVRENTI *to get rid of the* CHILD, *but fearing that it will cry he draws its attention to the ceremony,* GRUSHA *glances once at the* CHILD, *and* LAVRENTI *waves the* CHILD's *hand in a greeting.*

MONK: Are you prepared to be a faithful, obedient, and good wife to this man, and to cleave to him until death you do part?

GRUSHA (*looking at the* CHILD): I am.

MONK (*to the* SICK PEASANT): Are you prepared to be a good and loving husband to your wife until death you do part? (*As the* SICK PEASANT *does not answer, the* MONK *looks inquiringly around.*)

MOTHER-IN-LAW: Of course he is! Didn't you hear him say yes?

MONK: All right. We declare the marriage contracted! How about extreme unction?

MOTHER-IN-LAW: Nothing doing! The wedding cost quite enough. Now I must take care of the mourners. (*To* LAVRENTI:) Did we say seven hundred?

LAVRENTI: Six hundred. (*He pays.*) Now I don't want to sit with the guests and get to know people. So farewell, Grusha, and if my widowed sister comes to visit me, she'll get a welcome from my wife, or I'll show my teeth. (*Nods, gives the* CHILD *to* GRUSHA, *and leaves. The mourners glance after him without interest.*)

MONK: May one ask where this child comes from?

MOTHER-IN-LAW: Is there a child? I don't see a child. And you don't see a child either—you understand? Or it may turn out I saw all sorts of things in the tavern! Now come on.

After GRUSHA *has put the* CHILD *down and told him to be quiet, they move over left,* GRUSHA *is introduced to the neighbors.*

This is my daughter-in-law. She arrived just in time to find dear Jussup still alive.

ONE WOMAN: He's been ill now a whole year, hasn't he? When our Vassili was drafted he was there to say good-bye.

ANOTHER WOMAN: Such things are terrible for a farm. The corn all ripe and the farmer in bed! It'll really be a blessing if he doesn't suffer too long, I say.

FIRST WOMAN (*confidentially*): You know why we thought he'd taken to his bed? Because of the draft! And now his end is come!

MOTHER-IN-LAW: Sit yourselves down, please! And have some cakes!

She beckons to GRUSHA *and both women go into the bedroom, where they pick up the cake pans off the floor. The guests, among them the* MONK, *sit on the floor and begin conversing in subdued voices.*

ONE PEASANT (*to whom the* MONK *has handed the bottle which he has taken from his soutane*): There's a child, you say! How can that have happened to Jussup?

A WOMAN: She was certainly lucky to get herself married, with him so sick!

MOTHER-IN-LAW: They're gossiping already. And wolfing down the funeral cakes at the same time! If he doesn't die today, I'll have to bake some more tomorrow!

GRUSHA: I'll bake them for you.

MOTHER-IN-LAW: Yesterday some horsemen rode by, and I went out to see who it was. When I came in again he was lying there like a corpse! So I sent for you. It can't take much longer. (*She listens.*)

MONK: Dear wedding and funeral guests! Deeply touched, we stand before a bed of death and marriage. The bride gets a veil; the groom, a shroud: how varied, my children, are the fates of men! Alas! One man dies and has a roof over his head, and the other is married and the flesh turns to dust from which it was made. Amen.

MOTHER-IN-LAW: He's getting his own back. I shouldn't have hired such a cheap one. It's what you'd expect. A more expensive monk would behave himself. In Sura there's one with a real air of sanctity about him, but of course he charges a fortune. A fifty piaster monk like that has no dignity, and as for piety, just fifty piasters' worth and no more! When I came to get him in the tavern he'd just made a speech, and he was shouting: "The war is over, beware of the peace!" We must go in.

GRUSHA (*giving* MICHAEL *a cake*): Eat this cake, and keep nice and still, Michael.

The two women offer cakes to the guests. The dying man sits up in bed. He puts his head out from under the mosquito net, stares at the two women, then sinks back again. The MONK *takes two bottles from his soutane and offers them to the peasant beside him. Enter three* MUSICIANS *who are greeted with a sly wink by the* MONK.

MOTHER-IN-LAW (*to the* MUSICIANS): What are you doing here? With instruments?

ONE MUSICIAN: Brother Anastasius here (*pointing at the* MONK) told us there was a wedding on.

MOTHER-IN-LAW: What? You brought them? Three more on my neck! Don't you know there's a dying man in the next room?

MONK: A very tempting assignment for a musician: something that could be either a subdued Wedding March or a spirited Funeral Dance.

MOTHER-IN-LAW: Well, you might as well play. Nobody can stop you eating in any case.

The musicians play a potpourri. The women serve cakes.

MONK: The trumpet sounds like a whining baby. And you, little drum, what have you got to tell the world?

DRUNKEN PEASANT (*beside the* MONK, *sings*):

There was a young woman who said:
I thought I'd be happier, wed.
But my husband is old
And remarkably cold
So I sleep with a candle instead.

The MOTHER-IN-LAW *throws the* DRUNKEN PEASANT *out. The music stops. The guests are embarrassed.*

GUESTS (*loudly*):

—Have you heard? The Grand Duke is back! But the Princes are against him.
—They say the Shah of Persia has lent him a great army to restore order in Grusinia.
—But how is that possible? The Shah of Persia is the enemy . . .
—The enemy of Grusinia, you donkey, not the enemy of the Grand Duke!
—In any case, the war's over, so our soldiers are coming back.

GRUSHA *drops a cake pan.* GUESTS *help her pick up the cake.*

AN OLD WOMAN (*to* GRUSHA): Are you feeling bad? It's just excitement about dear Jussup. Sit down and rest. a while, my dear. (GRUSHA *staggers.*)

GUESTS: Now everything'll be the way it was. Only the taxes'll go up because now we'll have to pay for the war.

GRUSHA (*weakly*): Did someone say the soldiers are back?

A MAN: I did.

GRUSHA: It can't be true.

FIRST MAN (*to a woman*): Show her the shawl. We bought it from a soldier. It's from Persia.

GRUSHA (*looking at the shawl*): They are here. (*She gets up, takes a step, kneels down in prayer, takes the silver cross and chain out of her blouse, and kisses it.*)

MOTHER-IN-LAW (*while the guests silently watch* GRUSHA): What's the matter with you? Aren't you going to look after our guests? What's all this city nonsense got to do with us?

GUESTS (*resuming conversation while* GRUSHA *remains in prayer*):

—You can buy Persian saddles from the soldiers too. Though many want crutches in exchange for them.
—The leaders on one side can win a war, the soldiers on both sides lose it.
—Anyway, the war's over. It's something they can't draft you any more.

The dying man sits bolt upright in bed. He listens.

—What we need is two weeks of good weather.
—Our pear trees are hardly bearing a thing this year.

MOTHER-IN-LAW (*offering cakes*): Have some more cakes and welcome! There are more!

The MOTHER-IN-LAW *goes to the bedroom with the empty cake pans. Unaware of the dying man, she is bending down to pick up another tray when he begins to talk in a hoarse voice.*

PEASANT: How many more cakes are you going to stuff down their throats? D'you think I can shit money?

The MOTHER-IN-LAW *starts, stares at him aghast, while he climbs out from behind the mosquito net.*

FIRST WOMAN (*talking kindly to* GRUSHA *in the next room*):
Has the young wife got someone at the front?

A MAN: It's good news that they're on their way home,
huh?

PEASANT: Don't stare at me like that! Where's this wife
you've saddled me with?

*Receiving no answer, he climbs out of bed and in
his nightshirt staggers into the other room. Trembling,
she follows him with the cake pan.*

GUESTS (*seeing him and shrieking*): Good God! Jussup!

*Everyone leaps up in alarm. The women rush to
the door.* GRUSHA, *still on her knees, turns round and
stares at the man.*

PEASANT: A funeral supper! You'd enjoy that, wouldn't
you? Get out before I throw you out! (*As the guests
stampede from the house, gloomily to* GRUSHA:) I've
upset the apple cart, huh? (*Receiving no answer, he
turns round and takes a cake from the pan which
his mother is holding.*)

SINGER:

O confusion! The wife discovers she has a husband.
By day there's the child, by night there's the husband.
The lover is on his way both day and night.
Husband and wife look at each other.
The bedroom is small.

Near the bed the PEASANT *is sitting in a high wooden
bathtub, naked, the* MOTHER-IN-LAW *is pouring water
from a pitcher. Opposite* GRUSHA *cowers with*
MICHAEL, *who is playing at mending straw mats.*

PEASANT (*to his mother*): That's her work, not yours.
Where's she hiding out now?

MOTHER-IN-LAW (*calling*): Grusha! The peasant wants you!

GRUSHA (*to* MICHAEL): There are still two holes to mend.

PEASANT (*when* GRUSHA *approaches*): Scrub my back!

GRUSHA: Can't the peasant do it himself?

PEASANT: "Can't the peasant do it himself?" Get the brush! To hell with you! Are you the wife here? Or are you a visitor? (*To the* MOTHER-IN-LAW:) It's too cold!

MOTHER-IN-LAW: I'll run for hot water.

GRUSHA: Let me go.

PEASANT: You stay here. (*The* MOTHER-IN-LAW *exits.*) Rub harder. And no shirking. You've seen a naked fellow before. That child didn't come out of thin air.

GRUSHA: The child was not conceived in joy, if that's what the peasant means.

PEASANT (*turning and grinning*): You don't look the type. (GRUSHA *stops scrubbing him, starts back. Enter the* MOTHER-IN-LAW.)

PEASANT: A nice thing you've saddled me with! A simpleton for a wife!

MOTHER-IN-LAW: She just isn't cooperative.

PEASANT: Pour—but go easy! Ow! Go easy, I said. (*To* GRUSHA:) Maybe you did something wrong in the city . . . I wouldn't be surprised. Why else should you be here? But I won't talk about that. I've not said a word about the illegitimate object you brought into my house either. But my patience has limits! It's against nature. (*To the* MOTHER-IN-LAW:) More! (*To* GRUSHA:) And even if your soldier does come back, you're married.

GRUSHA: Yes.

PEASANT: But your soldier won't come back. Don't you believe it.

GRUSHA: No.

PEASANT: You're cheating me. You're my wife and you're not my wife. Where you lie, nothing lies, and yet no other woman can lie there. When I go to work in the morning I'm tired—when I lie down at night I'm awake as the devil. God has given you sex—and what d'you do? I don't have ten piasters to buy myself a woman in the city. Besides, it's a long way. Woman weeds the fields and opens up her legs, that's what our calendar says. D'you hear?

GRUSHA (*quietly*): Yes. I didn't mean to cheat you out of it.

PEASANT: She didn't mean to cheat me out of it! Pour some more water! (*The* MOTHER-IN-LAW *pours.*) Ow!

SINGER:

> As she sat by the stream to wash the linen
> She saw his image in the water
> And his face grew dimmer with the passing moons.
> As she raised herself to wring the linen
> She heard his voice from the murmuring maple
> And his voice grew fainter with the passing moons.
> Evasions and sighs grew more numerous,
> Tears and sweat flowed.
> With the passing moons the child grew up.

GRUSHA *sits by a stream, dipping linen into the water. In the rear, a few children are standing.*

GRUSHA (*to* MICHAEL): You can play with them, Michael, but don't let them boss you around just because you're the littlest. (MICHAEL *nods and joins the children. They start playing.*)

BIGGEST BOY: Today it's the Heads-Off Game. (*To a* FAT BOY:) You're the Prince and you laugh. (*To* MICHAEL:) You're the Governor. (*To a* GIRL:) You're the Governor's wife and you cry when his head's cut off. And I do the cutting. (*He shows his wooden sword.*) With this. First, they lead the Governor into the yard. The Prince walks in front. The Governor's wife comes last.

They form a procession. The FAT BOY *is first and laughs. Then comes* MICHAEL, *then the* BIGGEST BOY, *and then the* GIRL, *who weeps.*

MICHAEL (*standing still*): Me cut off head!

BIGGEST BOY: That's my job. You're the littlest. The Governor's the easy part. All you do is kneel down and get your head cut off—simple.

MICHAEL: Me want sword!

BIGGEST BOY: It's mine! (*He gives* MICHAEL *a kick.*)

GIRL (*shouting to* GRUSHA): He won't play his part!

GRUSHA (*laughing*): Even the little duck is a swimmer, they say.

BIGGEST BOY: You can be the Prince if you can laugh. (MICHAEL *shakes his head.*)

FAT BOY: I laugh best. Let him cut off the head just once. Then you do it, then me.

Reluctantly, the BIGGEST BOY *hands* MICHAEL *the wooden sword and kneels down. The* FAT BOY *sits down, slaps his thigh, and laughs with all his might. The* GIRL *weeps loudly.* MICHAEL *swings the big sword and "cuts off" the head. In doing so, he topples over.*

BIGGEST BOY: Hey! I'll show you how to cut heads off!

MICHAEL *runs away. The children run after him.* GRUSHA *laughs, following them with her eyes. On looking back, she sees* SIMON SHASHAVA *standing on the opposite bank. He wears a shabby uniform.*

GRUSHA: Simon!

SIMON: Is that Grusha Vashnadze?

GRUSHA: Simon!

SIMON (*formally*): A good morning to the young lady. I hope she is well.

GRUSHA (*getting up gaily and bowing low*): A good morning to the soldier. God be thanked he has returned in good health.

SIMON: They found better fish, so they didn't eat me, said the haddock.

GRUSHA: Courage, said the kitchen boy. Good luck, said the hero.

SIMON: How are things here? Was the winter bearable? The neighbor considerate?

GRUSHA: The winter was a trifle rough, the neighbor as usual, Simon.

SIMON: May one ask if a certain person still dips her toes in the water when rinsing the linen?

GRUSHA: The answer is no. Because of the eyes in the bushes.

SIMON: The young lady is speaking of soldiers. Here stands a paymaster.

GRUSHA: A job worth twenty piasters?

SIMON: And lodgings.

GRUSHA (*with tears in her eyes*): Behind the barracks under the date trees.

SIMON: Yes, there. A certain person has kept her eyes open:

GRUSHA: She has, Simon.

SIMON: And has not forgotten? (GRUSHA *shakes her head.*) So the door is still on its hinges as they say? (GRUSHA *looks at him in silence and shakes her head again.*) What's this? Is anything not as it should be?

GRUSHA: Simon Shashava, I can never return to Nuka. Something has happened.

SIMON: What can have happened?

GRUSHA: For one thing, I knocked an Ironshirt down.

SIMON: Grusha Vashnadze must have had her reasons for that.

GRUSHA: Simon Shashava, I am no longer called what I used to be called.

SIMON (*after a pause*): I do not understand.

GRUSHA: When do women change their names, Simon? Let me explain. Nothing stands between us. Everything is just as it was. You must believe that.

SIMON: Nothing stands between us and yet there's something?

GRUSHA: How can I explain it so fast and with the stream between us? Couldn't you cross the bridge there?

SIMON: Maybe it's no longer necessary.

GRUSHA: It is very necessary. Come over on this side, Simon, Quick!

SIMON: Does the young lady wish to say someone has come too late?

GRUSHA *looks up at him in despair, her face streaming with tears.* SIMON *stares before him. He picks up a piece of wood and starts cutting it.*

SINGER:

So many words are said, so many left unsaid.
The soldier has come.
Where he comes from, he does not say.
Hear what he thought and did not say:
"The battle began, gray at dawn, grew bloody at noon.
The first man fell in front of me, the second behind
      me, the third at my side.
I trod on the first, left the second behind, the third
      was run through by the captain.
One of my brothers died by steel, the other by smoke.
My neck caught fire, my hands froze in my gloves,
      my toes in my socks.
I fed on aspen buds, I drank maple juice, I slept on
      stone, in water."

SIMON: I see a cap in the grass. Is there a little one already?

GRUSHA: There is, Simon. There's no keeping *that* from you. But please don't worry, it is not mine.

SIMON: When the wind once starts to blow, they say, it blows through every cranny. The wife need say no more. (GRUSHA *looks into her lap and is silent.*)

SINGER:

There was yearning but there was no waiting.
The oath is broken. Neither could say why.
Hear what she thought but did not say:
"While you fought in the battle, soldier,
The bloody battle, the bitter battle
I found a helpless infant
I had not the heart to destroy him
I had to care for a creature that was lost

I had to stoop for breadcrumbs on the floor
I had to break myself for that which was not mine
That which was other people's.
Someone must help!
For the little tree needs water
The lamb loses its way when the shepherd is asleep
And its cry is unheard!"

SIMON: Give me back the cross I gave you. Better still, throw it in the stream. (*He turns to go.*)

GRUSHA (*getting up*): Simon Shashava, don't go away! He isn't mine! He isn't mine! (*She hears the children calling.*) What's the matter, children?

VOICES: Soldiers! And they're taking Michael away!

GRUSHA *stands aghast as two* IRONSHIRTS, *with* MICHAEL *between them, come toward her.*

ONE OF THE IRONSHIRTS: Are you Grusha? (*She nods.*) Is this your child?

GRUSHA: Yes. (SIMON *goes.*) Simon!

IRONSHIRT: We have orders, in the name of the law, to take this child, found in your custody, back to the city. It is suspected that the child is Michael Abashwili, son and heir of the late Governor Georgi Abashwili, and his wife, Natella Abashwili. Here is the document and the seal. (*They lead the* CHILD *away.*)

GRUSHA (*running after them, shouting*): Leave him here. Please! He's mine!

SINGER:

The Ironshirts took the child, the beloved child.
The unhappy girl followed them to the city, the dreaded city.
She who had borne him demanded the child.

She who had raised him faced trial.
Who will decide the case?
To whom will the child be assigned?
Who will the judge be? A good judge? A bad?
The city was in flames.
In the judge's seat sat Azdak.*

---

* The name Azdak should be accented on the second syllable.—E. B.

4

THE STORY OF THE JUDGE

SINGER:

Hear the story of the judge
How he turned judge, how he passed judgment, what
kind of judge he was.
On that Easter Sunday of the great revolt, when the
Grand Duke was overthrown
And his Governor Abashwili, father of our child, lost
his head
The Village Scrivener Azdak found a fugitive in the
woods and hid him in his hut.

AZDAK, *in rags and slightly drunk, is helping an old
beggar into his cottage.*

AZDAK: Stop snorting, you're not a horse. And it won't
do you any good with the police to run like a snotty
nose in April. Stand still, I say. (*He catches the* OLD
MAN, *who has marched into the cottage as if he'd
like to go through the walls.*) Sit down. Feed. Here's
a hunk of cheese. (*From under some rags, in a chest,
he fishes out some cheese, and the* OLD MAN *greedily
begins to eat.*) Haven't eaten in a long time, huh?
(*The* OLD MAN *growls.*) Why were you running like
that, asshole? The cop wouldn't even have seen you.

OLD MAN: Had to! Had to!

AZDAK: Blue funk? (*The* OLD MAN *stares, uncomprehending.*) Cold feet? Panic? Don't lick your chops like a
Grand Duke. Or an old sow. I can't stand it. We have

71

to accept respectable stinkers as God made them, but not you! I once heard of a senior judge who farted at a public dinner to show an independent spirit! Watching you eat like that gives me the most awful ideas. Why don't you say something? (*Sharply.*) Show me your hand. Can't you hear? (*The* OLD MAN *slowly puts out his hand.*) White! So you're not a beggar at all! A fraud, a walking swindle! And I'm hiding you from the cops like you were an honest man! Why were you running like that if you're a landowner? For that's what you are. Don't deny it! I see it in your guilty face! (*He gets up.*) Get out! (*The* OLD MAN *looks at him uncertainly.*) What are you waiting for, peasant-flogger?

OLD MAN: Pursued. Need undivided attention. Make proposition . . .

AZDAK: Make what? A proposition? Well, if that isn't the height of insolence. He's making me a proposition! The bitten man scratches his fingers bloody, and the leech that's biting him makes him a proposition! Get out, I tell you!

OLD MAN: Understand point of view! Persuasion! Pay hundred thousand piasters one night! Yes?

AZDAK: What, you think you can buy me? For a hundred thousand piasters? Let's say a hundred and fifty thousand. Where are they?

OLD MAN: Have not them here. Of course. Will be sent. Hope do not doubt.

AZDAK: Doubt very much. Get out!

The OLD MAN *gets up, waddles to the door. A* VOICE *is heard offstage.*

VOICE: Azdak!

The OLD MAN *turns, waddles to the opposite corner, stands still.*

AZDAK (*calling out*): I'm not in! (*He walks to door.*) So you're sniffing around here again, Shauwa?

SHAUWA (*reproachfully*): You caught another rabbit, Azdak. And you'd promised me it wouldn't happen again!

AZDAK (*severely*): Shauwa, don't talk about things you don't understand. The rabbit is a dangerous and destructive beast. It feeds on plants, especially on the species of plants known as weeds. It must therefore be exterminated.

SHAUWA: Azdak, don't be so hard on me. I'll lose my job if I don't arrest you. I know you have a good heart.

AZDAK: I do not have a good heart! How often must I tell you I'm a man of intellect?

SHAUWA (*slyly*): I know, Azdak. You're a superior person. You say so yourself. I'm just a Christian and an ignoramus. So I ask you: When one of the Prince's rabbits is stolen, and I'm a policeman, what should I do with the offending party?

AZDAK: Shauwa, Shauwa, shame on you. You stand and ask me a question, than which nothing could be more seductive. It's like you were a woman—let's say that bad girl Nunowna, and you showed me your thigh— Nunowna's thigh, that would be—and asked me: "What shall I do with my thigh, it itches?" Is she as innocent as she pretends? Of course not. I catch a rabbit, but you catch a man. Man is made in God's image. Not so a rabbit, you know that. I'm a rabbit-eater, but you're a man-eater, Shauwa. And God will pass judgment on you. Shauwa, go home and repent. No, stop, there's something . . . (*He looks at the* OLD MAN *who stands trembling in the*

corner.) No, it's nothing. Go home and repent.
(*He slams the door behind* SHAUWA.) Now you're
surprised, huh? Surprised I didn't hand you over?
I couldn't hand over a bedbug to that animal. It
goes against the grain. Now don't tremble because
of a cop! So old and still so scared? Finish your
cheese, but eat it like a poor man, or else they'll
still catch you. Must I even explain how a poor man
behaves? (*He pushes him down, and then gives him
back the cheese.*) That box is the table. Lay your
elbows on the table. Now, encircle the cheese on the
plate like it might be snatched from you at any
moment—what right have you to be safe, huh?—
now, hold your knife like an undersized sickle, and
give your cheese a troubled look because, like all
beautiful things, it's already fading away. (AZDAK
watches him.) They're after you, which speaks in your
favor, but how can we be sure they're not mistaken
about you? In Tiflis one time they hanged a landowner, a Turk, who could prove he quartered his
peasants instead of merely cutting them in half, as
is the custom, and he squeezed twice the usual amount
of taxes out of them, his zeal was above suspicion.
And yet they hanged him like a common criminal—
because he was a Turk—a thing he couldn't do much
about. What injustice! He got onto the gallows by a
sheer fluke. In short, I don't trust you.

SINGER:

Thus Azdak gave the old beggar a bed,
And learned that old beggar was the old butcher,
     the Grand Duke himself,
And was ashamed.
He denounced himself and ordered the policeman to
     take him to Nuka, to court, to be judged.

In the court of justice three IRONSHIRTS *sit drinking.*

From a beam hangs a man in judge's robes. Enter AZDAK, *in chains, dragging* SHAUWA *behind him.*

AZDAK (*shouting*): I've helped the Grand Duke, the Grand Thief, the Grand Butcher, to escape! In the name of justice I ask to be severely judged in public trial!

FIRST IRONSHIRT: Who's this queer bird?

SHAUWA: That's our Village Scrivener, Azdak.

AZDAK: I am contemptible! I am a traitor! A branded criminal! Tell them, flatfoot, how I insisted on being tied up and brought to the capital. Because I sheltered the Grand Duke, the Grand Swindler, by mistake. And how I found out afterwards. See the marked man denounce himself! Tell them how I forced you to walk half the night with me to clear the whole thing up.

SHAUWA: And all by threats. That wasn't nice of you, Azdak.

AZDAK: Shut your mouth, Shauwa. You don't understand. A new age is upon us! It'll go thundering over you. You're finished. The police will be wiped out—poof! Everything will be gone into, everything will be brought into the open. The guilty will give themselves up. Why? They couldn't escape the people in any case. (*To* SHAUWA:) Tell them how I shouted all along Shoemaker Street (*with big gestures, looking at the* IRONSHIRTS) "In my ignorance I let the Grand Swindler escape! So tear me to pieces, brothers!" I wanted to get it in first.

FIRST IRONSHIRT: And what did your brothers answer?

SHAUWA: They comforted him in Butcher Street, and they laughed themselves sick in Shoemaker Street. That's all.

AZDAK: But with you it's different. I can see you're men of iron. Brothers, where's the judge? I must be tried.

FIRST IRONSHIRT (*pointing at the hanged man*): There's the judge. And please stop "brothering" us. It's rather a sore spot this evening.

AZDAK: "There's the judge." An answer never heard in Grusinia before. Townsman, where's His Excellency the Governor? (*Pointing to the ground.*) There's His Excellency, stranger. Where's the Chief Tax Collector? Where's the official Recruiting Officer? The Patriarch? The Chief of Police? There, there, there—all there. Brothers, I expected no less of you.

SECOND IRONSHIRT: What? *What* was it you expected, funny man?

AZDAK: What happened in Persia, brother, what happened in Persia?

SECOND IRONSHIRT: What did happen in Persia?

AZDAK: Everybody was hanged. Viziers, tax collectors. Everybody. Forty years ago now. My grandfather, a remarkable man by the way, saw it all. For three whole days. Everywhere.

SECOND IRONSHIRT: And who ruled when the Vizier was hanged?

AZDAK: A peasant ruled when the Vizier was hanged.

SECOND IRONSHIRT: And who commanded the army?

AZDAK: A soldier, a soldier.

SECOND IRONSHIRT: And who paid the wages?

AZDAK: A dyer. A dyer paid the wages.

SECOND IRONSHIRT: Wasn't it a weaver, maybe?

FIRST IRONSHIRT: And why did all this happen, Persian?

AZDAK: Why did all this happen? Must there be a special reason? Why do you scratch yourself, brother? War! Too long a war! And no justice! My grandfather brought back a song that tells how it was. I will sing it for you. With my friend the policeman. (*To* SHAUWA:) And hold the rope tight. It's very suitable. (*He sings, with* SHAUWA *holding the rope tight around him.*)

THE SONG OF INJUSTICE IN PERSIA

Why don't our sons bleed any more? Why don't our daughters weep?
Why do only the slaughterhouse cattle have blood in their veins?
Why do only the willows shed tears on Lake Urmia?
The king must have a new province, the peasant must give up his savings.
That the roof of the world might be conquered, the roof of the cottage is torn down.
Our men are carried to the ends of the earth, so that great ones can eat at home.
The soldiers kill each other, the marshals salute each other.
They bite the widow's tax money to seé if it's good, their swords break.
The battle was lost, the helmets were paid for.
Refrain: Is it so? Is it so?

SHAUWA (*refrain*): Yes, yes, yes, yes, yes it's so.

AZDAK: Want to hear the rest of it? (*The* FIRST IRONSHIRT *nods.*)

SECOND IRONSHIRT (*to* SHAUWA): Did he teach you that song?

SHAUWA: Yes, only my voice isn't very good.

SECOND IRONSHIRT: No. (*To* AZDAK:) Go on singing.

AZDAK: The second verse is about the peace. (*He sings.*)

> The offices are packed, the streets overflow with
> officials.
> The rivers jump their banks and ravage the fields.
> Those who cannot let down their own trousers rule
> countries.
> They can't count up to four, but they devour eight
> courses.
> The corn farmers, looking round fot buyers, see only
> the starving.
> The weavers go home from their looms in rags.
> *Refrain*: Is it so? Is it so?

SHAUWA (*refrain*): Yes, yes, yes, yes, yes it's so.

AZDAK:

> That's why our sons don't bleed any more, that's why
> our daughters don't weep.
> That's why only the slaughterhouse cattle have blood
> in their veins,
> And only the willows shed tears by Lake Urmia
> toward morning.

FIRST IRONSHIRT: Are you going to sing that song here in
town?

AZDAK: Sure. What's wrong with it?

FIRST IRONSHIRT: Have you noticed that the sky's getting
red? (*Turning round,* AZDAK *sees the sky red with
fire.*) It's the people's quarters on the outskirts of
town. The carpet weavers have caught the "Persian
Sickness," too. And they've been asking if Prince
Kazbeki isn't eating too many courses. This morning
they strung up the city judge. As for us we beat them
to pulp. We were paid one hundred piasters per man,
you understand?

AZDAK (*after a pause*): I understand. (*He glances shyly round and, creeping away, sits down in a corner, his head in his hands.*)

IRONSHIRTS (*to each other*): If there ever was a trouble-maker it's him.

—He must've come to the capital to fish in the troubled waters.

SHAUWA: Oh, I don't think he's a really bad character, gentlemen. Steals a few chickens here and there. And maybe a rabbit.

SECOND IRONSHIRT (*approaching* AZDAK): Came to fish in the troubled waters, huh?

AZDAK (*looking up*): I don't know why I came.

SECOND IRONSHIRT: Are you in with the carpet weavers maybe? (AZDAK *shakes his head.*) How about that song?

AZDAK: From my grandfather. A silly and ignorant man.

SECOND IRONSHIRT: Right. And how about the dyer who paid the wages?

AZDAK (*muttering*): That was in Persia.

FIRST IRONSHIRT: And this denouncing of yourself? Because you didn't hang the Grand Duke with your own hands?

AZDAK: Didn't I tell you I let him run? (*He creeps farther away and sits on the floor.*)

SHAUWA: I can swear to that: he let him run.

The IRONSHIRTS *burst out laughing and slap* SHAUWA *on the back.* AZDAK *laughs loudest. They slap* AZDAK *too, and unchain him. They all start drinking as the* FAT PRINCE *enters with a young man.*

FIRST IRONSHIRT (*to* AZDAK, *pointing at the* FAT PRINCE):
There's your "new age" for you! (*More laughter.*)

FAT PRINCE: Well, my friends, what is there to laugh about?
Permit me a serious word. Yesterday morning the
Princes of Grusinia overthrew the warmongering government of the Grand Duke and did away with his
Governors. Unfortunately the Grand Duke himself
escaped. In this fateful hour our carpet weavers, those
eternal troublemakers, had the effrontery to stir up
a rebellion and hang the universally loved city judge,
our dear Illo Orbeliani. Ts—ts—ts. My friends, we
need peace, peace, peace in Grusinia! And justice!
So I've brought along my dear nephew Bizergan
Kazbeki. He'll be the new judge, hm? A very gifted
fellow. What do you say? I want your opinion. Let
the people decide!

SECOND IRONSHIRT: Does this mean *we* elect the judge?

FAT PRINCE: Precisely. Let the people propose some very
gifted fellow! Confer among yourselves, my friends.
(*The* IRONSHIRTS *confer.*) Don't worry, my little fox.
The job's yours. And when we catch the Grand Duke
we won't have to kiss this rabble's ass any longer.

IRONSHIRTS (*among themselves*):

—Very funny: they're wetting their pants because
they haven't caught the Grand Duke.
—When the outlook isn't so bright, they say: "My
friends!" and "Let the people decide!"
—Now he even wants justice for Grusinia! But fun
is fun as long as it lasts! (*Pointing at* AZDAK.) *He*
knows all about justice. Hey, rascal, would you like
this nephew fellow to be the judge?

AZDAK: Are you asking me? You're not asking *me?!*

FIRST IRONSHIRT: Why not? Anything for a laugh!

AZDAK: You'd like to test him to the marrow, correct? Have you a criminal on hand? An experienced one? So the candidate can show what he knows?

SECOND IRONSHIRT: Let's see. We do have a couple of doctors downstairs. Let's use them.

AZDAK: Oh, no, that's no good, we can't take real criminals till we're sure the judge will be appointed. He may be dumb, but he must be appointed, or the law is violated. And the law is a sensitive organ. It's like the spleen, you mustn't hit it—that would be fatal. Of course you can hang those two without violating the law, because there was no judge in the vicinity. But judgment, when pronounced, must be pronounced with absolute gravity—it's all such nonsense. Suppose, for instance, a judge jails a woman—let's say she's stolen a corn cake to feed her child—and this judge isn't wearing his robes—or maybe he's scratching himself while passing sentence and half his body is uncovered—a man's thigh *will* itch once in a while —the sentence this judge passes is a disgrace and the law is violated. In short it would be easier for a judge's robe and a judge's hat to pass judgment than for a man with no robe and no hat. If you don't treat it with respect, the law just disappears on you. Now you don't try out a bottle of wine by offering it to a dog; you'd only lose your wine.

FIRST IRONSHIRT: Then what do you suggest, hairsplitter?

AZDAK: I'll be the defendant.

FIRST IRONSHIRT: You? (*He bursts out laughing.*)

FAT PRINCE: What have you decided?

FIRST IRONSHIRT: We've decided to stage a rehearsal. Our friend here will be the defendant. Let the candidate be the judge and sit there.

FAT PRINCE: It isn't customary, but why not? (*To the* NEPHEW:) A mere formality, my little fox. What have I taught you? Who got there first—the slow runner or the fast?

NEPHEW: The silent runner, Uncle Arsen.

The NEPHEW *takes the chair. The* IRONSHIRTS *and the* FAT PRINCE *sit on the steps. Enter* AZDAK, *mimicking the gait of the Grand Duke.*

AZDAK (*in the Grand Duke's accent*): Is any here knows me? Am Grand Duke.

IRONSHIRTS:

—*What* is he?
—The Grand Duke. He knows him, too.
—Fine. So get on with the trial.

AZDAK: Listen! Am accused instigating war? Ridiculous! Am saying ridiculous! That enough? If not, have brought lawyers. Believe five hundred. (*He points behind him, pretending to be surrounded by lawyers.*) Requisition all available seats for lawyers! (*The* IRONSHIRTS *laugh; the* FAT PRINCE *joins in.*)

NEPHEW (*to the* IRONSHIRTS): You really wish me to try this case? I find it rather unusual. From the taste angle, I mean.

FIRST IRONSHIRT: Let's go!

FAT PRINCE (*smiling*): Let him have it, my little fox!

NEPHEW: All right. People of Grusinia versus Grand Duke. Defendant, what have you got to say for yourself?

AZDAK: Plenty. Naturally, have read war lost. Only started on the advice of patriots. Like Uncle Arsen Kazbeki. Call Uncle Arsen as witness.

FAT PRINCE (*to the* IRONSHIRTS, *delightedly*): What a madcap!

NEPHEW: Motion rejected. One cannot be arraigned for declaring a war, which every ruler has to do once in a while, but only for running a war badly.

AZDAK: Rubbish! Did not run it at all! Had it run! Had it run by Princes! Naturally, they messed it up.

NEPHEW: Do you by any chance deny having been commander-in-chief?

AZDAK: Not at all! Always *was* commander-in-chief. At birth shouted at wet nurse. Was trained drop turds in toilet, grew accustomed to command. Always commanded officials rob my cash box. Officers flog soldiers only on command. Landowners sleep with peasants' wives only on strictest command. Uncle Arsen here grew his belly at *my* command!

IRONSHIRTS (*clapping*): He's good! Long live the Grand Duke!

FAT PRINCE: Answer him, my little fox: I'm with you.

NEPHEW: I shall answer him according to the dignity of the law. Defendant, preserve the dignity of the law!

AZDAK: Agreed. Command you proceed with trial!

NEPHEW: It is not your place to command me. You claim that the Princes forced you to declare war. How can you claim, then, that they—er—"messed it up"?

AZDAK: Did not send enough people. Embezzled funds. Sent sick horses. During attack, drinking in whorehouse. Call Uncle Arsen as witness.

NEPHEW: Are you making the outrageous suggestion that the Princes of this country did not fight?

AZDAK: No. Princes fought. Fought for war contracts.

FAT PRINCE (*jumping up*): That's too much! This man talks like a carpet weaver!

AZDAK: Really? Told nothing but truth.

FAT PRINCE: Hang him! Hang him!

FIRST IRONSHIRT (*pulling the* PRINCE *down*): Keep quiet! Go on, Excellency!

NEPHEW: Quiet! I now render a verdict: You must be hanged! By the neck! Having lost war!

AZDAK: Young man, seriously advise not fall publicly into jerky clipped speech. Cannot be watchdog if howl like wolf. Got it? If people realize Princes speak same language as Grand Duke, may hang Grand Duke *and Princes,* huh? By the way, must overrule verdict. Reason? War lost, but not for Princes. Princes won their war. Got 3,863,000 piasters for horses not delivered, 8,240,000 piasters for food supplies not produced. Are therefore victors. War lost only for Grusinia, which is not present in this court.

FAT PRINCE: I think that will do, my friends. (*To* AZDAK:) You can withdraw, funny man. (*To the* IRONSHIRTS:) You may now ratify the new judge's appointment, my friends.

FIRST IRONSHIRT: Yes, we can. Take down the judge's gown. (*One* IRONSHIRT *climbs on the back of the other, pulls the gown off the hanged man.*) (*To the* NEPHEW:) Now you run away so the right ass can get on the right chair. (*To* AZDAK:) Step forward! Go to the judge's seat! Now sit in it! (AZDAK *steps up, bows, and sits down.*) The judge was always a rascal! Now the rascal shall be a judge! (*The judge's gown*

is placed round his shoulders, the hat on his head.)
And what a judge!

SINGER:

And there was civil war in the land.
The mighty were not safe.
And Azdak was made a judge by the Ironshirts.
And Azdak remained a judge for two years.

SINGER AND CHORUS:

When the towns were set afire
And rivers of blood rose higher and higher,
Cockroaches crawled out of every crack.
And the court was full of schemers
And the church of foul blasphemers.
In the judge's cassock sat Azdak.

AZDAK *sits in the judge's chair, peeling an apple.*
SHAUWA *is sweeping out the hall. On one side an*
INVALID *in a wheelchair. Opposite, a young man accused of blackmail. An* IRONSHIRT *stands guard, holding the Ironshirts' banner.*

AZDAK: In consideration of the large number of cases, the Court today will hear two cases at a time. Before I open the proceedings, a short announcement—I accept. (*He stretches out his hand. The* BLACKMAILER *is the only one to produce any money. He hands it to* AZDAK.) I reserve the right to punish one of the parties for contempt of court. (*He glances at the* INVALID.) You (*to the* DOCTOR) are a doctor, and you (*to the* INVALID) are bringing a complaint against him. Is the doctor responsible for your condition?

INVALID: Yes. I had a stroke on his account.

AZDAK: That would be professional negligence.

INVALID: Worse than negligence. I gave this man money for his studies. So far, he hasn't paid me back a cent.

It was when I heard he was treating a patient free that I had my stroke.

AZDAK: Rightly. (*To a* LIMPING MAN:) And what are *you* doing here?

LIMPING MAN: I'm the patient, Your Honor.

AZDAK: He treated your leg for nothing?

LIMPING MAN: The wrong leg! My rheumatism was in the left leg, he operated on the right. That's why I limp.

AZDAK: And you were treated free?

INVALID: A five-hundred-piaster operation free! For nothing! For a God-bless-you! And I paid for this man's studies! (*To the* DOCTOR:) Did they teach you to operate free?

DOCTOR: Your Honor, it is the custom to demand the fee before the operation, as the patient is more willing to pay before an operation than after. Which is only human. In the case in question I was convinced, when I started the operation, that my servant had already received the fee. In this I was mistaken.

INVALID: He was mistaken! A good doctor doesn't make mistakes! He examines before he operates!

AZDAK: That's right: (*To* SHAUWA:) Public Prosecutor, what's the other case about?

SHAUWA (*busily sweeping*): Blackmail.

BLACKMAILER: High Court of Justice, I'm innocent. I only wanted to find out from the landowner concerned if he really *had* raped his niece. He informed me very politely that this was not the case, and gave me the money only so I could pay for my uncle's studies.

AZDAK: Hm. (*To the* DOCTOR:) You, on the other hand,

can cite no extenuating circumstances for your offense, huh?

DOCTOR: Except that to err is human.

AZDAK: And you are aware that in money matters a good doctor is a highly responsible person? I once heard of a doctor who got a thousand piasters for a sprained finger by remarking that sprains have something to do with blood circulation, which after all a less good doctor might have overlooked, and who, on another occasion made a real gold mine out of a somewhat disordered gall bladder, he treated it with such loving care. You have no excuse, Doctor. The corn merchant Uxu had his son study medicine to get some knowledge of trade, our medical schools are so good. (*To the* BLACKMAILER:) What's the landowner's name?

SHAUWA: He doesn't want it mentioned.

AZDAK: In that case I will pass judgment. The Court considers the blackmail proved. And you (*to the* INVALID) are sentenced to a fine of one thousand piasters. If you have a second stroke, the doctor will have to treat you free. Even if he has to amputate. (*To the* LIMPING MAN:) As compensation, you will receive a bottle of rubbing alcohol. (*To the* BLACKMAILER:) You are sentenced to hand over half the proceeds of your deal to the Public Prosecutor to keep the landowner's name secret. You are advised, moreover, to study medicine—you seem well suited to that calling. (*To the* DOCTOR:) You have perpetrated an unpardonable error in the practice of your profession: you are acquitted. Next cases!

SINGER AND CHORUS:

Men won't do much for a shilling.
For a pound they may be willing.

For twenty pounds the verdict's in the sack.
As for the many, all too many,
Those who've only got a penny—
They've one single, sole recourse: Azdak.

Enter AZDAK *from the caravansary on the highroad,
followed by an old bearded* INNKEEPER. *The judge's
chair is carried by a stableman and* SHAUWA. *An* IRON-
SHIRT, *with a banner, takes up his position.*

AZDAK: Put me down. Then we'll get some air, maybe even
a good stiff breeze from the lemon grove there. It
does justice good to be done in the open: the wind
blows her skirts up and you can see what she's got.
Shauwa, we've been eating too much. These official
journeys are exhausting. (*To the* INNKEEPER:) It's a
question of your daughter-in-law?

INNKEEPER: Your Worship, it's a question of the family
honor. I wish to bring an action on behalf of my son,
who's away on business on the other side the mountain. This is the offending stableman, and here's my
daughter-in-law.

Enter the DAUGHTER-IN-LAW, *a voluptuous wench.
She is veiled.*

AZDAK (*sitting down*): I accept. (*Sighing, the* INNKEEPER
hands him some money.) Good. Now the formalities
are disposed of. This is a case of rape?

INNKEEPER: Your Honor, I caught the fellow in the act.
Ludovica was in the straw on the stable floor.

AZDAK: Quite right, the stable. Lovely horses! I specially
liked the little roan.

INNKEEPER: The first thing I did, of course, was to question Ludovica. On my son's behalf.

AZDAK (*seriously*): I said I specially liked the little roan.

INNKEEPER (*coldly*): Really? Ludovica confessed the stableman took her against her will.

AZDAK: Take your veil off, Ludovica. (*She does so.*) Ludovica, you please the Court. Tell us how it happened.

LUDOVICA (*well schooled*): When I entered the stable to see the new foal the stableman said to me on his own accord: "It's hot today!" and laid his hand on my left breast. I said to him: "Don't do that!" But he continued to handle me indecently, which provoked my anger. Before I realized his sinful intentions, he got much closer. It was all over when my father-in-law entered and accidentally trod on me.

INNKEEPER (*explaining*): On my son's behalf.

AZDAK (*to the* STABLEMAN): You admit you started it?

STABLEMAN: Yes.

AZDAK: Ludovica, you like to eat sweet things?

LUDOVICA: Yes, sunflower seeds!

AZDAK: You like to lie a long time in the bathtub?

LUDOVICA: Half an hour or so.

AZDAK: Public Prosecutor, drop your knife—there on the ground. (SHAUWA *does so.*) Ludovica, pick up that knife. (LUDOVICA, *swaying her hips, does so.*) See that? (*He points at her.*) The way it moves? The rape is now proven. By eating too much—sweet things, especially—by lying too long in warm water, by laziness and too soft a skin, you have raped that unfortunate man. Think you can run around with a behind like that and get away with it in court? This is a case of intentional assault with a dangerous weapon! You are sentenced to hand over to the Court the little roan which your father liked to ride "on his son's

behalf." And now, come with me to the stables, so
the Court can inspect the scene of the crime, Ludovica.

SINGER AND CHORUS:

When the sharks the sharks devour
Little fishes have their hour.
For a while the load is off their back.
On Grusinia's highways faring
Fixed-up scales of justice bearing
Strode the poor man's magistrate: Azdak.

And he gave to the forsaken
All that from the rich he'd taken.
And a bodyguard of roughnecks was Azdak's.
And our good and evil man, he
Smiled upon Grusinia's Granny.
His emblem was a tear in sealing wax.

All mankind should love each other
But when visiting your brother
Take an ax along and hold it fast.
Not in theory but in practice
Miracles are wrought with axes
And the age of miracles is not past.

AZDAK's *judge's chair is in a tavern. Three rich*
FARMERS *stand before* AZDAK. SHAUWA *brings him*
wine. In a corner stands an OLD PEASANT WOMAN. *In*
the open doorway, and outside, stand villagers looking
on. An IRONSHIRT *stands guard with a banner.*

AZDAK: The Public Prosecutor has the floor.

SHAUWA: It concerns a cow. For five weeks, the defendant
has had a cow in her stable, the property of the
farmer Suru. She was also found to be in possession
of a stolen ham, and a number of cows belonging to
Shutoff were killed after he asked the defendant to
pay the rent on a piece of land.

FARMERS:

—It's a matter of my ham, Your Honor.
—It's a matter of my cow, Your Honor.
—It's a matter of my land, Your Honor.

AZDAK: Well, Granny, what have *you* got to say to all this?

OLD WOMAN: Your Honor, one night toward morning, five weeks ago, there was a knock at my door, and outside stood a bearded man with a cow. "My dear woman," he said, "I am the miracle-working Saint Banditus and because your son has been killed in the war, I bring you this cow as a souvenir. Take good care of it."

FARMERS:

—The robber, Irakli, Your Honor!
—Her brother-in-law, Your Honor!
—The cow-thief!
—The incendiary!
—He must be beheaded!

Outside, a woman screams. The crowd grows restless, retreats. Enter the BANDIT *Irakli with a huge ax.*

BANDIT: A very good evening, dear friends! A glass of vodka!

FARMERS (*crossing themselves*): Irakli!

AZDAK: Public Prosecutor, a glass of vodka for our guest. And who are you?

BANDIT: I'm a wandering hermit, Your Honor. Thanks for the gracious gift. (*He empties the glass which* SHAUWA *has brought.*) Another!

AZDAK: I am Azdak. (*He gets up and bows. The* BANDIT *also bows.*) The Court welcomes the foreign hermit. Go on with your story, Granny.

OLD WOMAN: Your Honor, that first night I didn't yet know Saint Banditus could work miracles, it was only the cow. But one night, a few days later, the farmer's servants came to take the cow away again. Then they turned round in front of my door and went off without the cow. And bumps as big as a fist sprouted on their heads. So I knew that Saint Banditus had changed their hearts and turned them into friendly people.

The BANDIT *roars with laughter.*

FIRST FARMER: I know what changed them.

AZDAK: That's fine. You can tell us later. Continue.

OLD WOMAN: Your Honor, the next one to become a good man was the farmer Shutoff—a devil, as everyone knows. But Saint Banditus arranged it so he let me off the rent on the little piece of land.

SECOND FARMER: Because my cows were killed in the field.

The BANDIT *laughs.*

OLD WOMAN (*answering* AZDAK's *sign to continue*): Then one morning the ham came flying in at my window. It hit me in the small of the back. I'm still lame, Your Honor, look. (*She limps a few steps. The* BANDIT *laughs.*) Your Honor, was there ever a time when a poor old woman could get a ham *without* a miracle?

The BANDIT *starts sobbing.*

AZDAK (*rising from his chair*): Granny, that's a question that strikes straight at the Court's heart. Be so kind as to sit here. (*The* OLD WOMAN, *hesitating, sits in the judge's chair.*)

AZDAK (*sits on the floor, glass in hand, reciting*):

Granny
We could almost call you Granny Grusinia

The Woebegone
The Bereaved Mother
Whose sons have gone to war.
Receiving the present of a cow
She bursts out crying.
When she is beaten
She remains hopeful.
When she's not beaten
She's surprised.
On us
Who are already damned
May you render a merciful verdict
Granny Grusinia!

(*Bellowing at the* FARMERS:) Admit you don't believe in miracles, you atheists! Each of you is sentenced to pay five hundred piasters! For godlessness! Get out! (*The* FARMERS *slink out.*) And you Granny, and you (*to the* BANDIT) pious man, empty a pitcher of wine with the Public Prosecutor and Azdak!

SINGER AND CHORUS:
And he broke the rules to save them.
Broken law like bread he gave them,
Brought them to shore upon his crooked back.
At long last the poor and lowly
Had someone who was not too holy
To be bribed by empty hands: Azdak.

For two years it was his pleasure
To give the beasts of prey short measure:
He became a wolf to fight the pack.
From All Hallows to All Hallows
On his chair beside the gallows
Dispensing justice in his fashion sat Azdak.

SINGER:
But the era of disorder came to an end.
The Grand Duke returned.

The Governor's wife returned.
A trial was held.
Many died.
The people's quarters burned anew.
And fear seized Azdak.

ADZAK's *judge's chair stands again in the court of justice.* AZDAK *sits on the floor, shaving and talking to* SHAUWA. *Noises outside. In the rear the* FAT PRINCE's *head is carried by on a lance.*

AZDAK: Shauwa, the days of your slavery are numbered, maybe even the minutes. For a long time now I have held you in the iron curb of reason, and it has torn your mouth till it bleeds. I have lashed you with reasonable arguments, I have manhandled you with logic. You are by nature a weak man, and if one slyly throws an argument in your path, you *have* to snap it up, you can't resist. It is your nature to lick the hand of some superior being. But superior beings can be of very different kinds. And now, with your liberation, you will soon be able to follow your natural inclinations, which are low. You will be able to follow your infallible instinct, which teaches you to plant your fat heel on the faces of men. Gone is the era of confusion and disorder, which I find described in the Song of Chaos. Let us now sing that song together in memory of those terrible days. Sit down and don't do violence to the music. Don't be afraid. It sounds all right. And it has a fine refrain. (*He sings.*)

THE SONG OF CHAOS

Sister, hide your face! Brother, take your knife!
The times are out of joint!
Big men are full of complaint
And small men full of joy.
The city says:

"Let us drive the mighty from our midst!"
Offices are raided. Lists of serfs are destroyed.
They have set Master's nose to the grindstone.
They who lived in the dark have seen the light.
The ebony poor box is broken.
Sesnem* wood is sawed up for beds.
Who had no bread have full barns.
Who begged for alms of corn now mete it out.

SHAUWA (*refrain*): Oh, oh, oh, oh.

AZDAK (*refrain*):
Where are you, General, where are you?
Please, please, please, restore order!

The nobleman's son can no longer be recognized;
The lady's child becomes the son of her slave-girl
The councilors meet in a shed.
Once, this man was barely allowed to sleep on the wall;
Now, he stretches his limbs in a bed.
Once, this man rowed a boat; now, he owns ships.
Their owner looks for them, but they're his no longer.
Five men are sent on a journey by their master.
"Go yourself," they say, "we have arrived."

SHAUWA (*refrain*): Oh, oh, oh, oh.

AZDAK (*refrain*):
Where are you, General, where are you?
Please, please, please, restore order!

---

* I do not know what kind of wood this is, so I have left
the word exactly as it stands in the German original. The song
is based on an Egyptian papyrus which Brecht cites as such in
his essay, "Five Difficulties in the Writing of the Truth." I
should think he must have come across it in Adolf Erman's
Die Literatur der Aegypter, 1923, p. 130 ff. Erman too gives
the word as Sesnem. The same papyrus is quoted in Karl
Jaspers' *Man in the Modern Age* (Anchor edition, pp. 18-19)
but without the sentence about the Sesnem wood.—E.B.

Yes, so it might have been, had order been neglected much longer. But now the Grand Duke has returned to the capital, and the Persians have lent him an army to restore order with. The people's quarters are already aflame. Go and get me the big book I always sit on. (SHAUWA *brings the big book from the judge's chair.* AZDAK *opens it.*) This is the Statute Book and I've always used it, as you can testify. Now I'd better look in this book and see what they can do to me. I've let the down-and-outs get away with murder, and I'll have to pay for it. I helped poverty onto its skinny legs, so they'll hang me for drunkenness. I peeped into the rich man's pocket, which is bad taste. And I can't hide anywhere—everybody knows me because I've helped everybody.

SHAUWA: Someone's coming!

AZDAK (*in panic, he walks trembling to the chair*): It's the end. And now they'd enjoy seeing what a Great Man I am. I'll deprive them of that pleasure. I'll beg on my knees for mercy. Spittle will slobber down my chin. The fear of death is in me.

Enter Natella Abashwili, the GOVERNOR'S WIFE, *followed by the* ADJUTANT *and an* IRONSHIRT.

GOVERNOR'S WIFE: What sort of a creature is that, Shalva?

AZDAK: A willing one, Your Highness, a man ready to oblige.

ADJUTANT: Natella Abashwili, wife of the late Governor, has just returned. She is looking for her two-year-old son, Michael. She has been informed that the child was carried off to the mountains by a former servant.

AZDAK: The child will be brought back, Your Highness, at your service.

ADJUTANT: They say that the person in question is passing it off as her own.

AZDAK: She will be beheaded, Your Highness, at your service.

ADJUTANT: That is all.

GOVERNOR'S WIFE (*leaving*): I don't like that man.

AZDAK (*following her to door, bowing*): At your service, Your Highness, it will all be arranged.

5

THE CHALK CIRCLE

SINGER:

> Hear now the story of the trial
> Concerning Governor Abashwili's child
> And the determination of the true mother
> By the famous test of the Chalk Circle.

Law court in Nuka. IRONSHIRTS *lead* MICHAEL *across stage and out at the back.* IRONSHIRTS *hold* GRUSHA *back with their lances under the gateway until the child has been led through. Then she is admitted. She is accompanied by the former Governor's* COOK. *Distant noises and a fire-red sky.*

GRUSHA (*trying to hide*): He's brave, he can wash himself now.

COOK: You're lucky. It's not a real judge. It's Azdak, a drunk who doesn't know what he's doing. The biggest thieves have got by through him. Because he gets everything mixed up and the rich never offer him big enough bribes, the like of us sometimes do pretty well.

GRUSHA: I *need* luck right now.

COOK: Touch wood. (*She crosses herself.*) I'd better offer up another prayer that the judge may be drunk. (*She prays with motionless lips, while* GRUSHA *looks around, in vain, for the child.*) Why must you hold on to it at any price if it isn't yours? In days like these?

98

GRUSHA: He's mine. I brought him up.

COOK: Have you never thought what'd happen when she came back?

GRUSHA: At first I thought I'd give him to her. Then I thought she wouldn't come back.

COOK: And even a borrowed coat keeps a man warm, hm? (GRUSHA *nods.*) I'll swear to anything for you. You're a decent girl. (*She sees the soldier* SIMON SHASHAVA *approaching.*) You've done wrong by Simon, though. I've been talking with him. He just can't understand.

GRUSHA (*unaware of* SIMON's *presence*): Right now I can't be bothered whether he understands or not!

COOK: He knows the child isn't yours, but you married and not free "till death you do part"—he can't understand *that*.

GRUSHA *sees* SIMON *and greets him.*

SIMON (*gloomily*): I wish the lady to know I will swear I am the father of the child.

GRUSHA (*low*): Thank you, Simon.

SIMON: At the same time I wish the lady to know my hands are not tied—nor are hers.

COOK: You needn't have said that. You know she's married.

SIMON: And it needs no rubbing in.

Enter an IRONSHIRT.

IRONSHIRT: Where's the judge? Has anyone seen the judge?

ANOTHER IRONSHIRT (*stepping forward*): The judge isn't here yet. Nothing but a bed and a pitcher in the whole house!

Exeunt IRONSHIRTS.

COOK: I hope nothing has happened to him. With any other judge you'd have as much chance as a chicken has teeth.

GRUSHA (*who has turned away and covered her face*): Stand in front of me. I shouldn't have come to Nuka. If I run into the Ironshirt, the one I hit over the head . . .

She screams. An IRONSHIRT *had stopped and, turning his back, had been listening to her. He now wheels around. It is the* CORPORAL, *and he has a huge scar across his face.*

IRONSHIRT (*in the gateway*): What's the matter, Shotta? Do you know her?

CORPORAL (*after staring for some time*): No.

IRONSHIRT: She's the one who stole the Abashwili child, or so they say. If you know anything about it you can make some money, Shotta.

Exit the CORPORAL, *cursing.*

COOK: Was it him? (GRUSHA *nods.*) I think he'll keep his mouth shut, or he'd be admitting he was after the child.

GRUSHA: I'd almost forgotten him.

Enter the GOVERNOR'S WIFE, *followed by the* ADJUTANT *and two* LAWYERS.

GOVERNOR'S WIFE: At least there are no common people here, thank God. I can't stand their smell. It always gives me migraine.

FIRST LAWYER: Madam, I must ask you to be careful what you say until we have another judge.

GOVERNOR'S WIFE: But I didn't say anything, Illo Shuboladze. I love the people with their simple straight-forward minds. It's only that their smell brings on my migraine.

SECOND LAWYER: There won't be many spectators. The whole population is sitting at home behind locked doors because of the riots in the people's quarters.

GOVERNOR'S WIFE (*looking at* GRUSHA): Is that the creature?

FIRST LAWYER: Please, most gracious Natella Abashwili, abstain from invective until it is certain the Grand Duke has appointed a new judge and we're rid of the present one, who's about the lowest fellow ever seen in judge's gown. Things are all set to move, you see.

Enter IRONSHIRTS *from the courtyard.*

COOK: Her Grace would pull your hair out on the spot if she didn't know Azdak is for the poor. He goes by the face.

IRONSHIRTS *begin fastening a rope to a beam.* AZDAK, *in chains, is led in, followed by* SHAUWA, *also in chains. The three* FARMERS *bring up the rear.*

AN IRONSHIRT: Trying to run away, were you? (*He strikes* AZDAK.)

ONE FARMER: Off with his judge's gown before we string him up!

IRONSHIRTS *and* FARMERS *tear off Azdak's gown. His torn underwear is visible. Then someone kicks him.*

AN IRONSHIRT (*pushing him into someone else*): Want a load of justice? Here it is!

Accompanied by shouts of "You take it!" *and* "Let me have him, Brother!" *they throw* AZDAK *back and forth until he collapses. Then he is lifted up and dragged under the noose.*

GOVERNOR'S WIFE (*who, during this "ballgame," has clapped her hands hysterically*): I disliked that man from the moment I first saw him.

AZDAK (*covered with blood, panting*): I can't see. Give me a rag.

AN IRONSHIRT: What is it you want to see?

AZDAK: You, you dogs! (*He wipes the blood out of his eyes with his shirt.*) Good morning, dogs! How goes it, dogs! How's the dog world? Does it smell good? Got another boot for me to lick? Are you back at each other's throats, dogs?

Accompanied by a CORPORAL, *a dust-covered* RIDER *enters. He takes some documents from a leather case, looks at them, then interrupts.*

RIDER: Stop! I bring a dispatch from the Grand Duke, containing the latest appointments.

CORPORAL (*bellowing*): Atten—shun!

RIDER: Of the new judge it says: "We appoint a man whom we have to thank for saving a life indispensable to the country's welfare—a certain Azdak of Nuka." Which is he?

SHAUWA (*pointing*): That's him, Your Excellency.

CORPORAL (*bellowing*): What's going on here?

AN IRONSHIRT: I beg to report that His Honor Azdak was already His Honor Azdak, but on these farmers' denunciation was pronounced the Grand Duke's enemy.

CORPORAL (*pointing at the* FARMERS): March them off!

(*They are marched off. They bow all the time.*) See to it that His Honor Azdak is exposed to no more violence.

Exeunt RIDER *and* CORPORAL.

COOK (*to* SHAUWA): She clapped her hands! I hope he saw it!

FIRST LAWYER: It's a catastrophe.

AZDAK *has fainted. Coming to, he is dressed again in judge's robes. He walks, swaying, toward the* IRONSHIRTS.

AN IRONSHIRT: What does Your Honor desire?

AZDAK: Nothing, fellow dogs, or just an occasional boot to lick. (*To* SHAUWA:) I pardon you. (*He is unchained.*) Get me some red wine, the sweet kind. (SHAUWA *stumbles off.*) Get out of here, I've got to judge a case. (*Exeunt* IRONSHIRTS. SHAUWA *returns with a pitcher of wine.* AZDAK *gulps it down.*) Something for my backside. (SHAUWA *brings the Statute Book, puts it on the judge's chair.* AZDAK *sits on it.*) I accept.

The Prosecutors, among whom a worried council has been held, smile with relief. They whisper.

COOK: Oh dear!

SIMON: A well can't be filled with dew, they say.

LAWYERS (*approaching* AZDAK, *who stands up, expectantly*): A quite ridiculous case, Your Honor. The accused has abducted a child and refuses to hand it over.

AZDAK (*stretching out his hand, glancing at* GRUSHA): A most attractive person. (*He fingers the money, then sits down, satisfied.*) I declare the proceedings open and demand the whole truth. (*To* GRUSHA:) Especially from you.

FIRST LAWYER: High Court of Justice! Blood, as the popular saying goes, is thicker than water. This old adage . . .

AZDAK (*interrupting*): The Court wants to know the lawyers' fee.

FIRST LAWYER (*surprised*): I beg your pardon? (AZDAK, *smiling, rubs his thumb and index finger.*) Oh, I see. Five hundred piasters, Your Honor, to answer the Court's somewhat unusual question.

AZDAK: Did you hear? The question is unusual. I ask it because I listen in quite a different way when I know you're good.

FIRST LAWYER (*bowing*): Thank you, Your Honor. High Court of Justice, of all ties the ties of blood are strongest. Mother and child—is there a more intimate relationship? Can one tear a child from its mother? High Court of Justice, she has conceived it in the holy ecstasies of love. She has carried it in her womb. She has fed it with her blood. She has borne it with pain. High Court of Justice, it has been observed that the wild tigress, robbed of her young, roams restless through the mountains, shrunk to a shadow. Nature herself . . .

ADZAK (*interrupting, to* GRUSHA): What's your answer to all this and anything else that lawyer might have to say?

GRUSHA: He's mine.

AZDAK: Is that all? I hope you can prove it. Why should I assign the child to you in any case?

GRUSHA: I brought him up like the priest says "according

to my best knowledge and conscience." I always found him something to eat. Most of the time he had a roof over his head. And I went to such trouble for him. I had expenses too. I didn't look out for my own comfort. I brought the child up to be friendly with everyone, and from the beginning taught him to work. As well as he could, that is. He's still very little.

FIRST LAWYER: Your Honor, it is significant that the girl herself doesn't claim any tie of blood between her and the child.

AZDAK: The Court takes note of that.

FIRST LAWYER: Thank you, Your Honor. And now permit a woman bowed in sorrow—who has already lost her husband and now has also to fear the loss of her child —to address a few words to you. The gracious Natella Abashwili is . . .

GOVERNOR'S WIFE (*quietly*): A most cruel fate, sir, forces me to describe to you the tortures of a bereaved mother's soul, the anxiety, the sleepless nights, the . . .

SECOND LAWYER (*bursting out*): It's outrageous the way this woman is being treated! Her husband's palace is closed to her! The revenue of her estates is blocked, and she is cold-bloodedly told that it's tied to the heir. She can't do a thing without that child. She can't even pay her lawyers! ! (*To the* FIRST LAWYER, *who, desperate about this outburst, makes frantic gestures to keep him from speaking:*) Dear Illo Shuboladze, surely it can be divulged now that the Abashwili estates are at stake?

FIRST LAWYER: Please, Honored Sandro Oboladze! We agreed . . . (*To* AZDAK:) Of course it is correct that the trial will also decide if our noble client can take over the Abashwili estates, which are rather extensive. I say "also" advisedly, for in the foreground stands the human tragedy of a mother, as Natella Abashwili very properly explained in the first words of her moving statement. Even if Michael Abashwili were not heir to the estates, he would still be the dearly beloved child of my client.

AZDAK: Stop! The Court is touched by the mention of estates. It's a proof of human feeling.

SECOND LAWYER: Thanks, Your Honor. Dear Illo Shuboladze, we can prove in any case that the woman who took the child is not the child's mother. Permit me to lay before the Court the bare facts. High Court of Justice, by an unfortunate chain of circumstances, Michael Abashwili was left behind on that Easter Sunday while his mother was making her escape. Grusha, a palace kitchen maid, was seen with the baby . . .

COOK: All her mistress was thinking of was what dresses she'd take along!

SECOND LAWYER (*unmoved*): Nearly a year later Grusha turned up in a mountain village with a baby and there entered into the state of matrimony with . . .

AZDAK: How'd you get to that mountain village?

GRUSHA: On foot, Your Honor. And he was mine.

SIMON: I'm the father, Your Honor.

COOK: I used to look after it for them, Your Honor. For five piasters.

SECOND LAWYER: This man is engaged to Grusha, High Court of Justice: his testimony is suspect.

AZDAK: Are you the man she married in the mountain village?

AZDAK (*to* GRUSHA): Why? (*Pointing at* SIMON.) Is he no good in bed? Tell the truth.

GRUSHA: We didn't get that far. I married because of the baby. So he'd have a roof over his head. (*Pointing at* SIMON.) He was in the war, Your Honor.

AZDAK: And now he wants you back again, huh?

SIMON: I wish to state in evidence . . .

GRUSHA (*angrily*): I am no longer free, Your Honor.

AZDAK: And the child, you claim, comes from whoring? (GRUSHA *doesn't answer.*) I'm going to ask you a question: What kind of child is he? A ragged little bastard? Or from a good family?

GRUSHA (*angrily*): He's an ordinary child.

AZDAK: I mean—did he have refined features from the beginning?

GRUSHA: He had a nose on his face.

AZDAK: A very significant comment! It has been said of me that I went out one time and sniffed at a rosebush before rendering a verdict—tricks like that are needed nowadays. Well, I'll make it short, and not listen to any more lies. (*To* GRUSHA:) Especially not yours. (*To all the accused:*) I can imagine what you've cooked up to cheat me! I know you people. You're swindlers.

GRUSHA (*suddenly*): I can understand your wanting to cut it short, now I've seen what you accepted!

AZDAK: Shut up! Did I accept anything from you?

GRUSHA (*while the* COOK *tries to restrain her*): I haven't got anything.

AZDAK: True. Quite true. From starvelings I never get a thing. I might just as well starve, myself. You want justice, but do you want to pay for it, hm? When you go to a butcher you know you have to pay, but you people go to a judge as if you were off to a funeral supper.

SIMON (*loudly*): When the horse was shod, the horsefly held out its leg, as the saying is.

AZDAK (*eagerly accepting the challenge*): Better a treasure in manure than a stone in a mountain stream.

SIMON: A fine day. Let's go fishing, said the angler to the worm.

AZDAK: I'm my own master, said the servant, and cut off his foot.

SIMON: I love you as a father, said the Czar to the peasants, and had the Czarevitch's head chopped off.

AZDAK: A fool's worst enemy is himself.

SIMON: However, a fart has no nose.

AZDAK: Fined ten piasters for indecent language in court! That'll teach you what justice is.

GRUSHA (*furiously*): A fine kind of justice! You play fast and loose with us because we don't talk as refined as that crowd with their lawyers

AZDAK: That's true. You people are too dumb. It's only right you should get it in the neck.

GRUSHA: You want to hand the child over to her, and she wouldn't even know how to keep it dry, she's so "refined"! You know about as much about justice as I do!

AZDAK: There's something in that. I'm an ignorant man. Haven't even a decent pair of pants on under this gown. Look! With me, everything goes on food and drink—I was educated in a convent. Incidentally, I'll fine you ten piasters for contempt of court. And you're a very silly girl, to turn me against you, instead of making eyes at me and wiggling your backside a little to keep me in a good temper. Twenty piasters!

GRUSHA: Even if it was thirty, I'd tell you what I think of your justice, you drunken onion! (*Incoherently.*) How dare you talk to me like the cracked Isaiah on the church window? As if you were somebody? For you weren't born to this. You weren't born to rap your own mother on the knuckles if she swipes a little bowl of salt someplace. Aren't you ashamed of yourself when you see how I tremble before you? You've made yourself their servant so no one will take their houses from them—houses they had stolen! Since when have houses belonged to the bedbugs? But you're on the watch, or they couldn't drag our men into their wars! You bribetaker!

AZDAK *half gets up, starts beaming. With his little hammer he halfheartedly knocks on the table as if to get silence. As* GRUSHA's *scolding continues, he only beats time with his hammer.*

I've no respect for you. No more than for a thief or a bandit with a knife! You can do what you want. You can take the child away from me, a hundred against one, but I tell you one thing: only extortioners should be chosen for a profession like yours, and men who rape children! As punishment! Yes, let *them* sit in judgment on their fellow creatures. It is worse than to hang from the gallows.

AZDAK (*sitting down*): Now it'll be thirty! And I won't go on squabbling with you—we're not in a tavern. What'd happen to my dignity as a judge? Anyway, I've lost interest in your case. Where's the couple who wanted a divorce? (*To* SHAUWA:) Bring 'em in. This case is adjourned for fifteen minutes.

FIRST LAWYER (*to the* GOVERNOR'S WIFE): Even without using the rest of the evidence, Madam, we have the verdict in the bag.

COOK (*to* GRUSHA): You've gone and spoiled your chances with him. You won't get the child now.

GOVERNOR'S WIFE: Shalva, my smelling salts!

Enter a very old couple.

AZDAK: I accept. (*The old couple don't understand.*) I hear you want to be divorced. How long have you been together?

OLD WOMAN: Forty years, Your Honor.

AZDAK: And why do you want a divorce?

OLD MAN: We don't like each other, Your Honor.

AZDAK: Since when?

OLD WOMAN: Oh, from the very beginning, Your Honor.

AZDAK: I'll think about your request and render my verdict when I'm through with the other case. (SHAUWA *leads them back.*) I need the child. (*He beckons* GRUSHA *to him and bends not unkindly toward her.*) I've noticed you have a soft spot for justice. I don't believe he's your child, but if he *were* yours, woman, wouldn't you want him to be rich? You'd only have to say he wasn't yours, and he'd have a palace and many horses in his stable and many beggars on his doorstep and many soldiers in his service and many petitioners in his courtyard, wouldn't he? What do you say—don't you want him to be rich?

GRUSHA *is silent.*

SINGER:

Hear now what the angry girl thought but did not say:

Had he golden shoes to wear
He'd be cruel as a bear
Evil would his life disgrace.
He'd laugh in my face.

Carrying a heart of flint
Is too troublesome a stint.
Being powerful and bad
Is hard on a lad.

Then let hunger be his foe!
Hungry men and women, no.
Let him fear the darksome night
But not daylight!

AZDAK: I think I understand you, woman.

GRUSHA (*suddenly and loudly*): I won't give him up. I've raised him, and he knows me.

Enter SHAUWA *with the* CHILD.

GOVERNOR'S WIFE: He's in rags!

GRUSHA: That's not true. But I wasn't given time to put his good shirt on.

GOVERNOR'S WIFE: He must have been in a pigsty.

GRUSHA (*furiously*): I'm not a pig, but there are some who are! Where did you leave your baby?

GOVERNOR'S WIFE: I'll show you, you vulgar creature! (*She is about to throw herself on* GRUSHA, *but is restrained by her lawyers.*) She's a criminal, she must be whipped. Immediately!

SECOND LAWYER (*holding his hand over her mouth*): Natella Abashwili, you promised . . . Your Honor, the plaintiff's nerves . . .

AZDAK: Plaintiff and defendant! The Court has listened to your case, and has come to no decision as to who the real mother is; therefore, I, the judge, am obliged to *choose* a mother for the child. I'll make a test. Shauwa, get a piece of chalk and draw a circle on the floor. (SHAUWA *does so.*) Now place the child in the center. (SHAUWA *puts* MICHAEL, *who smiles at* GRUSHA, *in the center of the circle.*) Stand near the circle, both of you. (*The* GOVERNOR'S WIFE *and* GRUSHA *step up to the circle.*) Now each of you take the child by one hand. (*They do so.*) The true mother is she who can pull the child out of the circle.

SECOND LAWYER (*quickly*): High Court of Justice, I object! The fate of the great Abashwili estates, which are tied to the child, as the heir, should not be made dependent on such a doubtful duel. In addition, my client does not command the strength of this person, who is accustomed to physical work.

AZDAK: She looks pretty well fed to me. Pull! (*The* GOVERNOR'S WIFE *pulls the* CHILD *out of the circle on her side;* GRUSHA *has let go and stands aghast.*) What's the matter with you? You didn't pull.

GRUSHA: I didn't hold on to him.

FIRST LAWYER (*congratulating the* GOVERNOR'S WIFE): What did I say! The ties of blood!

GRUSHA (*running to* AZDAK): Your Honor, I take back everything I said against you. I ask your forgiveness. But could I keep him till he can speak all the words? He knows a few.

AZDAK: Don't influence the Court. I bet you only know

about twenty words yourself. All right, I'll make the test once more, just to be certain. (*The two women take up their positions again.*) Pull! (*Again* GRUSHA *lets go of the* CHILD.)

GRUSHA (*in despair*): I brought him up! Shall I also tear him to bits? I can't!

AZDAK (*rising*): And in this manner the Court has determined the true mother. (*To* GRUSHA:) Take your child and be off. I advise you not to stay in the city with him. (*To the* GOVERNOR'S WIFE:) And you disappear before I fine you for fraud. Your estates fall to the city. They'll be converted into a playground for the children. They need one, and I've decided it'll be called after me: Azdak's Garden.

The GOVERNOR'S WIFE *has fainted and is carried out by the* LAWYERS *and the* ADJUTANT. GRUSHA *stands motionless.* SHAUWA *leads the* CHILD *toward her.*

Now I'll take off this judge's gown—it's got too hot for me. I'm not cut out for a hero. In token of farewell I invite you all to a little dance in the meadow outside. Oh, I'd almost forgotten something in my excitement . . . to sign the divorce decree. (*Using the judge's chair as a table, he writes something on a piece of paper, and prepares to leave. Dance music has started.*)

SHAUWA (*having read what is on the paper*): But that's not right. You've not divorced the old people. You've divorced Grusha!

AZDAK: Divorced the wrong couple? What a pity! And I never retract! If I did, how could we keep order in the land? (*To the old couple:*) I'll invite you to my party instead. You don't mind dancing with each other, do you? (*To* GRUSHA *and* SIMON:) I've got forty piasters coming from you.

SIMON (*pulling out his purse*): Cheap at the price, Your Honor. And many thanks.

AZDAK (*pocketing the cash*): I'll be needing this.

GRUSHA (*to* MICHAEL): So we'd better leave the city tonight, Michael? (*To* SIMON:) You like him?

SIMON: With my respects, I like him.

GRUSHA: Now I can tell you: I took him because on that Easter Sunday I got engaged to you. So he's a child of love. Michael, let's dance.

She dances with MICHAEL, SIMON *dances with the* COOK, *the old couple with each other.* AZDAK *stands lost in thought. The dancers soon hide him from view. Occasionally he is seen, but less and less as more couples join the dance.*

SINGER:

And after that evening Azdak vanished and was never
    seen again.
The people of Grusinia did not forget him but long
    remembered
The period of his judging as a brief golden age,
Almost an age of justice.

All the couples dance off. AZDAK *has disappeared.*

But you, you who have listened to the Story of the
    Chalk Circle,
Take note what men of old concluded:
That what there is shall go to those who are good
    for it,
Children to the motherly, that they prosper,
Carts to good drivers, that they be driven well,
The valley to the waterers, that it yield fruit.

Waiting for Godot

Tragicomedy
by
Samuel Beckett

*Translated from his original French text
by the author*

WAITING FOR GODOT was first presented (as *En Attendant Godot*) at the Théâtre de Babylone, 38 Boulevard Raspail, Paris, during the season of 1952-53. The play was directed by Roger Blin, with décor by Sergio Gerstein, and with the following cast:

ESTRAGON . . . . Pierre Latour

VLADIMIR . . . . Lucien Raimbourg

POZZO . . . . Roger Blin

LUCKY . . . . Jean Martin

A BOY . . . . Serge Lecointe

The play is in two acts

ACT ONE

A country road. A tree.

Evening.

ESTRAGON, *sitting on a low mound, is trying to take off his boot. He pulls at it with both hands, panting. He gives up, exhausted, rests, tries again. As before.*

Enter VLADIMIR.

ESTRAGON (*giving up again*): Nothing to be done.

VLADIMIR (*advancing with short, stiff strides, legs wide apart*): I'm beginning to come round to that opinion. All my life I've tried to put it from me, saying, Vladimir, be reasonable, you haven't yet tried everything. And I resumed the struggle. (*He broods, musing on the struggle. Turning to* ESTRAGON.) So there you are again.

ESTRAGON: Am I?

VLADIMIR: I'm glad to see you back. I thought you were gone for ever.

ESTRAGON: Me too.

VLADIMIR: Together again at last! We'll have to celebrate this. But how? (*He reflects.*) Get up till I embrace you.

ESTRAGON (*irritably*): Not now, not now.

VLADIMIR (*hurt, coldly*): May one inquire where His Highness spent the night?

ESTRAGON: In a ditch.

VLADIMIR (*admiringly*): A ditch! Where?

ESTRAGON (*without gesture*): Over there.

VLADIMIR: And they didn't beat you?

ESTRAGON: Beat me? Certainly they beat me.

VLADIMIR: The same lot as usual?

ESTRAGON: The same? I don't know.

VLADIMIR: When I think of it . . . all these years . . . but for me . . . where would you be . . . (*Decisively.*) You'd be nothing more than a little heap of bones at the present minute, no doubt about it.

117

ESTRAGON: And what of it?

VLADIMIR (*gloomily*): It's too much for one man. (*Pause. Cheerfully.*) On the other hand what's the good of losing heart now, that's what I say. We should have thought of it a million years ago, in the nineties.

ESTRAGON: Ah stop blathering and help me off with this bloody thing.

VLADIMIR: Hand in hand from the top of the Eiffel Tower, among the first. We were respectable in those days. Now it's too late. They wouldn't even let us up. (ESTRAGON *tears at his boot.*) What are you doing?

ESTRAGON: Taking off my boot. Did that never happen to you?

VLADIMIR: Boots must be taken off every day, I'm tired telling you that. Why don't you listen to me?

ESTRAGON (*feebly*): Help me!

VLADIMIR: It hurts?

ESTRAGON (*angrily*): Hurts! He wants to know if it hurts!

VLADIMIR (*angrily*): No one ever suffers but you. I don't count. I'd like to hear what you'd say if you had what I have.

ESTRAGON: It hurts?

VLADIMIR (*angrily*): Hurts! He wants to know if it hurts!

ESTRAGON (*pointing*): You might button it all the same.

VLADIMIR (*stooping*): True. (*He buttons his fly.*) Never neglect the little things of life.

ESTRAGON: What do you expect, you always wait till the last moment.

VLADIMIR (*musingly*): The last moment . . . (*He meditates.*) Hope deferred maketh the something sick, who said that?

ESTRAGON: Why don't you help me?

VLADIMIR: Sometimes I feel it coming all the same. Then I go all queer. (*He takes off his hat, peers inside it, feels about inside it, shakes it, puts it on again.*) How shall I say? Relieved and at the same time . . . (*He searches for the word.*) . . . appalled. (*With emphasis.*) AP-PALLED. (*He takes off his hat again, peers inside it.*) Funny. (*He knocks on the crown as though to dislodge a foreign body, peers into it again, puts it on again.*) Nothing to be done. (ESTRAGON *with a supreme effort succeeds in pulling off his boot. He peers inside it, feels about inside it, turns it upside down, shakes it, looks on the ground to see if anything has fallen out, finds nothing, feels inside it again, staring sightlessly before him.*) Well?

ESTRAGON: Nothing.

VLADIMIR: Show.

ESTRAGON: There's nothing to show.

VLADIMIR: Try and put it on again.

ESTRAGON (*examining his foot*): I'll air it for a bit.

VLADIMIR: There's man all over for you, blaming on his boots the faults of his feet. (*He takes off his hat again, peers inside it, feels about inside it, knocks on the crown, blows into it, puts it on again.*) This is getting alarming. (*Silence.* VLADIMIR *deep in thought,* ESTRAGON *pulling at his toes.*) One of the thieves was saved. (*Pause.*) It's a reasonable percentage. (*Pause.*) Gogo.

ESTRAGON: What?

VLADIMIR: Suppose we repented.

ESTRAGON: Repented what?

VLADIMIR: Oh . . . (*He reflects.*) We wouldn't have to go into the details.

ESTRAGON: Our being born?

> VLADIMIR *breaks into a hearty laugh which he immediately stifles, his hand pressed to his pubis, his face contorted.*

VLADIMIR: One daren't even laugh any more.

ESTRAGON: Dreadful privation.

VLADIMIR: Merely smile. (*He smiles suddenly from ear to ear, keeps smiling, ceases as suddenly.*) It's not the same thing. Nothing to be done. (*Pause.*) Gogo.

ESTRAGON (*irritably*): What is it?

VLADIMIR: Did you ever read the Bible?

ESTRAGON: The Bible . . . (*He reflects.*) I must have taken a look at it.

VLADIMIR: Do you remember the Gospels?

ESTRAGON: I remember the maps of the Holy Land. Coloured they were. Very pretty. The Dead Sea was pale blue. The very look of it made me thirsty. That's where we'll go, I used to say, that's where we'll go for our honeymoon. We'll swim. We'll be happy.

VLADIMIR: You should have been a poet.

ESTRAGON: I was. (*Gesture towards his rags.*) Isn't that obvious?

Silence.

VLADIMIR: Where was I . . . How's your foot?

ESTRAGON: Swelling visibly.

VLADIMIR: Ah yes, the two thieves. Do you remember the story?

ESTRAGON: No.

VLADIMIR: Shall I tell it to you?

ESTRAGON: No.

VLADIMIR: It'll pass the time. (*Pause.*) Two thieves, crucified at the same time as our Saviour. One—

ESTRAGON: Our what?

VLADIMIR: Our Saviour. Two thieves. One is supposed to have been saved and the other . . . (*He searches for the contrary of saved.*) . . . damned.

ESTRAGON: Saved from what?

VLADIMIR: Hell.

ESTRAGON: I'm going.

> *He does not move*

VLADIMIR: And yet . . . (*Pause*) . . . how is it—this is not boring you I hope—how is it that of the four Evangelists only one speaks of a thief being saved. The four of them were there—or thereabouts—and only one speaks of a thief being saved. (*Pause.*) Come on, Gogo, return the ball, can't you, once in a way?

ESTRAGON (*with exaggerated enthusiasm*): I find this really most extraordinarily interesting.

VLADIMIR: One out of four. Of the other three two don't mention any thieves at all and the third says that both of them abused him.

ESTRAGON: Who?

VLADIMIR: What?

ESTRAGON: What's this all about? Abused who?

VLADIMIR: The Saviour.

ESTRAGON: Why?

VLADIMIR: Because he wouldn't save them.

ESTRAGON: From hell?

VLADIMIR: Imbecile! From death.

ESTRAGON: I thought you said hell.

VLADIMIR: From death, from death.

ESTRAGON: Well what of it?

VLADIMIR: Then the two of them must have been damned.

ESTRAGON: And why not?

VLADIMIR: But one of the four says that one of the two was saved.

ESTRAGON: Well? They don't agree and that's all there is to it.

VLADIMIR: But all four were there. And only one speaks of a thief being saved. Why believe him rather than the others?

ESTRAGON: Who believes him?

VLADIMIR: Everybody. It's the only version they know.

ESTRAGON: People are bloody ignorant apes.

He rises painfully, goes limping to extreme left, halts, gazes into distance off with his hand screening his eyes, turns, goes to extreme right, gazes into distance. VLADIMIR *watches him, then goes and picks up the boot, peers into it, drops it hastily.*

VLADIMIR: Pah!

He spits. ESTRAGON *moves to center, halts with his back to auditorium.*

ESTRAGON: Charming spot. (*He turns, advances to front, halts facing auditorium.*) Inspiring prospects. (*He turns to* VLADIMIR.) Let's go.

VLADIMIR: We can't.

ESTRAGON: Why not?

VLADIMIR: We're waiting for Godot.

ESTRAGON (*despairingly*): Ah! (*Pause.*) You're sure it was here?

VLADIMIR: What?

ESTRAGON: That we were to wait.

VLADIMIR: He said by the tree. (*They look at the tree.*) Do you see any others.

ESTRAGON: What is it?

VLADIMIR: I don't know. A willow.

ESTRAGON: Where are the leaves?

VLADIMIR: It must be dead.

ESTRAGON: No more weeping.

VLADIMIR: Or perhaps it's not the season.

ESTRAGON: Looks to me more like a bush.

VLADIMIR: A shrub.

ESTRAGON: A bush.

VLADIMIR: A—. What are you insinuating? That we've come to the wrong place?

ESTRAGON: He should be here.

VLADIMIR: He didn't say for sure he'd come.

ESTRAGON: And if he doesn't come?

VLADIMIR: We'll come back to-morrow.

ESTRAGON: And then the day after to-morrow.

VLADIMIR: Possibly.

ESTRAGON: And so on.

VLADIMIR: The point is—

ESTRAGON: Until he comes.

VLADIMIR: You're merciless.

ESTRAGON: We came here yesterday.

VLADIMIR: Ah no, there you're mistaken.

ESTRAGON: What did we do yesterday?

VLADIMIR: What did we do yesterday?

ESTRAGON: Yes.

VLADIMIR: Why . . . (*Angrily.*) Nothing is certain when you're about.

ESTRAGON: In my opinion we were here.

VLADIMIR (*looking round*): You recognize the place?

ESTRAGON: I didn't say that.

VLADIMIR: Well?

ESTRAGON: That makes no difference.

VLADIMIR: All the same . . . that tree . . . (*Turning towards auditorium.*) that bog . . .

ESTRAGON: You're sure it was this evening?

VLADIMIR: What?

ESTRAGON: That we were to wait.

VLADIMIR: He said Saturday. (*Pause.*) I think.

ESTRAGON: You think.

VLADIMIR: I must have made a note of it. (*He fumbles in his pockets, bursting with miscellaneous rubbish.*)

ESTRAGON (*very insidious*): But what Saturday? And is it Saturday? Is it not rather Sunday? (*Pause.*) Or Monday? (*Pause.*) Or Friday?

VLADIMIR (*looking wildly about him, as though the date was inscribed in the landscape*): It's not possible!

ESTRAGON: Or Thursday?

VLADIMIR: What'll we do?

ESTRAGON: If he came yesterday and we weren't here you may be sure he won't come again to-day.

VLADIMIR: But you say we were here yesterday.

ESTRAGON: I may be mistaken. (*Pause.*) Let's stop talking for a minute, do you mind?

VLADIMIR (*feebly*): All right. (ESTRAGON *sits down on the mound.*

VLADIMIR *paces agitatedly to and fro, halting from time to time to gaze into distance off.* ESTRAGON *falls asleep.* VLADIMIR *halts finally before* ESTRAGON.) Gogo! . . . Gogo! . . . GOGO!

ESTRAGON *wakes with a start.*

ESTRAGON (*restored to the horror of his situation*): I was asleep! (*Despairingly.*) Why will you never let me sleep?
VLADIMIR: I felt lonely.
ESTRAGON: I had a dream.
VLADIMIR: Don't tell me!
ESTRAGON: I dreamt that—
VLADIMIR: DON'T TELL ME!
ESTRAGON (*gesture towards the universe*): This one is enough for you? (*Silence.*) It's not nice of you, Didi. Who am I to tell my private nightmares to if I can't tell them to you?
VLADIMIR: Let them remain private. You know I can't bear that.
ESTRAGON (*coldly*): There are times when I wonder if it wouldn't be better for us to part.
VLADIMIR: You wouldn't go far.
ESTRAGON: That would be too bad, really too bad. (*Pause.*) Wouldn't it, Didi, be really too bad? (*Pause.*) When you think of the beauty of the way. (*Pause.*) And the goodness of the wayfarers. (*Pause. Wheedling.*) Wouldn't it, Didi?
VLADIMIR: Calm yourself.
ESTRAGON (*voluptuously*): Calm . . . calm . . . The English say cawm. (*Pause.*) You know the story of the Englishman in the brothel?
VLADIMIR: Yes.
ESTRAGON: Tell it to me.
VLADIMIR: Ah stop it!
ESTRAGON: An Englishman having drunk a little more than usual proceeds to a brothel. The bawd asks him if he wants a fair one, a dark one or a red-haired one. Go on.
VLADIMIR: STOP IT!

Exit VLADIMIR *hurriedly.* ESTRAGON *gets up and follows him as far as the limit of the stage. Gestures of* ESTRAGON *like those of a spectator encouraging a pugilist. Enter* VLADIMIR. *He brushes past* ESTRAGON, *crosses the stage with bowed head.* ESTRAGON *takes a step towards him, halts.*

ESTRAGON (*gently*): You wanted to speak to me? (*Silence.* ESTRAGON *takes a step forward.*) You had something to say to me? (*Silence. Another step forward.*) Didi . . .

VLADIMIR (*without turning*): I've nothing to say to you.

ESTRAGON (*step forward*): You're angry? (*Silence. Step forward.*) Forgive me. (*Silence. Step forward.* ESTRAGON *lays his hand on* VLADIMIR's *shoulder.*) Come, Didi. (*Silence.*) Give me your hand. (VLADIMIR *half turns.*) Embrace me! (VLADIMIR *stiffens.*) Don't be stubborn! (VLADIMIR *softens. They embrace.* ESTRAGON *recoils.*) You stink of garlic!

VLADIMIR: It's for the kidneys. (*Silence.* ESTRAGON *looks attentively at the tree.*) What do we do now?

ESTRAGON: Wait.

VLADIMIR: Yes, but while waiting.

ESTRAGON: What about hanging ourselves?

VLADIMIR: Hmm. It'd give us an erection.

ESTRAGON (*highly excited*): An erection!

VLADIMIR: With all that follows. Where it falls mandrakes grow. That's why they shriek when you pull them up. Did you not know that?

ESTRAGON: Let's hang ourselves immediately!

VLADIMIR: From a bough? (*They go towards the tree.*) I wouldn't trust it.

ESTRAGON: We can always try.

VLADIMIR: Go ahead.

ESTRAGON: After you.

VLADIMIR: No no, you first.

ESTRAGON: Why me?

VLADIMIR: You're lighter than I am.

ESTRAGON: Just so!

VLADIMIR: I don't understand.

ESTRAGON: Use your intelligence, can't you?

VLADIMIR *uses his intelligence.*

VLADIMIR (*finally*): I remain in the dark.

ESTRAGON: This is how it is. (*He reflects.*) The bough . . . the bough . . . (*Angrily.*) Use your head, can't you?

VLADIMIR: You're my only hope.

ESTRAGON (*with effort*): Gogo light—bough not break—Gogo dead. Didi heavy—bough break—Didi alone. Whereas—

VLADIMIR: I hadn't thought of that.

ESTRAGON: If it hangs you it'll hang anything.

VLADIMIR: But am I heavier than you?

ESTRAGON: So you tell me. I don't know. There's an even chance. Or nearly.

VLADIMIR: Well? What do we do?

ESTRAGON: Don't let's do anything. It's safer.

VLADIMIR: Let's wait and see what he says.

ESTRAGON: Who?

VLADIMIR: Godot.

ESTRAGON: Good idea.

VLADIMIR: Let's wait till we know exactly how we stand.

ESTRAGON: On the other hand it might be better to strike the iron before it freezes.

VLADIMIR: I'm curious to hear what he has to offer. Then we'll take it or leave it.

ESTRAGON: What exactly did we ask him for?

VLADIMIR: Were you not there?

ESTRAGON: I can't have been listening.

VLADIMIR: Oh . . . Nothing very definite.

ESTRAGON: A kind of prayer.

VLADIMIR: Precisely.

ESTRAGON: A vague supplication.

VLADIMIR: Exactly.

ESTRAGON: And what did he reply?

VLADIMIR: That he'd see.

ESTRAGON: That he couldn't promise anything.

VLADIMIR: That he'd have to think it over.

ESTRAGON: In the quiet of his home.

VLADIMIR: Consult his family.

ESTRAGON: His friends.

VLADIMIR: His agents.

ESTRAGON: His correspondents.

VLADIMIR: His books.

ESTRAGON: His bank account.

VLADIMIR: Before taking a decision.

ESTRAGON: It's the normal thing.

VLADIMIR: Is it not?

ESTRAGON: I think it is.

VLADIMIR: I think so too

Silence.

ESTRAGON (*anxious*): And we?

VLADIMIR: I beg your pardon?

ESTRAGON: I said, And we?

VLADIMIR: I don't understand.

ESTRAGON: Where do we come in?

VLADIMIR: Come in?

ESTRAGON: Take your time.

VLADIMIR: Come in? On our hands and knees.

ESTRAGON: As bad as that?

VLADIMIR: Your Worship wishes to assert his prerogatives?

ESTRAGON: We've no rights any more?

Laugh of VLADIMIR, *stifled as before, less the smile.*

VLADIMIR: You'd make me laugh if it wasn't prohibited.

ESTRAGON: We've lost our rights?

VLADIMIR (*distinctly*): We got rid of them.

Silence. They remain motionless, arms dangling, heads sunk, sagging at the knees.

ESTRAGON (*feebly*): We're not tied? (*Pause.*) We're not—

VLADIMIR: Listen!

They listen, grotesquely rigid.

ESTRAGON: I hear nothing.

VLADIMIR: Hsst! (*They listen.* ESTRAGON *loses his balance, almost falls. He clutches the arm of* VLADIMIR *who totters. They listen, huddled together.*) Nor I.

Sighs of relief. They relax and separate.

ESTRAGON: You gave me a fright.

VLADIMIR: I thought it was he.

ESTRAGON: Who?

VLADIMIR: Godot.

ESTRAGON: Pah! The wind in the reeds.

VLADIMIR: I could have sworn I heard shouts.

ESTRAGON: And why would he shout?

VLADIMIR: At his horse.

Silence.

ESTRAGON (*violently*): I'm hungry!

VLADIMIR: Do you want a carrot?

ESTRAGON: It that all there is?

VLADIMIR: I might have some turnips.

ESTRAGON: Give me a carrot. (VLADIMIR *rummages in his pockets, takes out a turnip and gives it to* ESTRAGON *who takes a bite out of it. Angrily.*) It's a turnip!

VLADIMIR: Oh pardon! I could have sworn it was a carrot. (*He rummages again in his pockets, finds nothing but turnips.*) All that's turnips. (*He rummages.*) You must have eaten the last. (*He rummages.*) Wait, I have it. (*He brings out a carrot and gives it to* ESTRAGON.) There, dear fellow. (ESTRAGON *wipes the carrot on his sleeve and begins to eat it.*) Make it last, that's the end of them.

ESTRAGON (*chewing*): I asked you a question.

VLADIMIR: Ah.

ESTRAGON: Did you reply?

VLADIMIR: How's the carrot?

ESTRAGON: It's a carrot.

VLADIMIR: So much the better, so much the better. (*Pause.*) What was it you wanted to know?

ESTRAGON: I've forgotten. (*Chews.*) That's what annoys me. (*He looks at the carrot appreciatively, dangles it between finger and thumb.*) I'll never forget this carrot. (*He sucks the end of it meditatively.*) Ah yes, now I remember.

VLADIMIR: Well?

ESTRAGON (*his mouth full, vacuously*): We're not tied?

VLADIMIR: I don't hear a word you're saying.

ESTRAGON (*chews, swallows*): I'm asking you if we're tied.

VLADIMIR: Tied?

ESTRAGON: Ti-ed.

VLADIMIR: How do you mean tied?

ESTRAGON: Down.

VLADIMIR: But to whom? By whom?

ESTRAGON: To your man.

VLADIMIR: To Godot? Tied to Godot! What an idea! No question of it. (*Pause.*) For the moment.

ESTRAGON: His name is Godot?

VLADIMIR: I think so.

ESTRAGON: Fancy that. (*He raises what remains of the carrot by the stub of leaf, twirls it before his eyes.*) Funny, the more you eat the worse it gets.

VLADIMIR: With me it's just the opposite.

ESTRAGON: In other words?

VLADIMIR: I get used to the muck as I go along.

ESTRAGON (*after prolonged reflection*): Is that the opposite?

VLADIMIR: Question of temperament.

ESTRAGON: Of character.

VLADIMIR: Nothing you can do about it.

ESTRAGON: No use struggling.

VLADIMIR: One is what one is.

ESTRAGON: No use wriggling.

VLADIMIR: The essential doesn't change.

ESTRAGON: Nothing to be done. (*He proffers the remains of the carrot to* VLADIMIR.) Like to finish it?

> *A terrible cry close at hand.* ESTRAGON *drops the carrot. They remain motionless, then together make a sudden rush towards the wings.* ESTRAGON *stops halfway, runs back, picks up the carrot, stuffs it in his pocket, runs to rejoin* VLADIMIR *who is waiting for him, stops again, runs back, picks up his boot, runs to rejoin* VLADIMIR. *Huddled together, shoulders hunched, cringing away from the menace, they wait.*

> *Enter* POZZO *and* LUCKY. POZZO *drives* LUCKY *by means of a rope passed round his neck, so that* LUCKY *is the first to enter, followed by the rope which is long enough to let him reach the middle of the stage before* POZZO *appears.* LUCKY *carries a heavy bag, a folding stool, a picnic basket and a greatcoat,* POZZO *a whip.*

POZZO (*off*): On! (*Crack of whip.* POZZO *appears. They cross the stage.*

LUCKY *passes before* VLADIMIR *and* ESTRAGON *and exit.* POZZO *at the sight of* VLADIMIR *and* ESTRAGON *stops short. The rope tautens.* POZZO *jerks at it violently.*) Back!

Noise of LUCKY *falling with all his baggage.* VLADIMIR *and* ESTRAGON *turn towards him, half wishing half fearing to go to his assistance.* VLADIMIR *takes a step towards* LUCKY, ESTRAGON *holds him back by the sleeve.*

VLADIMIR: Let me go!

ESTRAGON: Stay where you are!

POZZO: Be careful! He's wicked. (VLADIMIR *and* ESTRAGON *turn towards* POZZO.) With strangers.

ESTRAGON (*undertone*): Is that him?

VLADIMIR: Who?

ESTRAGON (*trying to remember the name*): Er ..

VLADIMIR: Godot?

ESTRAGON: Yes.

POZZO: I present myself: Pozzo.

VLADIMIR (*to* ESTRAGON): Not at all!

ESTRAGON: He said Godot.

VLADIMIR: Not at all!

ESTRAGON (*timidly, to* POZZO): You're not Mr. Godot, Sir?

POZZO (*terrifying voice*): I am Pozzo! (*Silence.*) Pozzo! (*Silence.*) Does that name mean nothing to you? (*Silence.*) I say does that name mean nothing to you?

VLADIMIR *and* ESTRAGON *look at each other questioningly.*

ESTRAGON (*pretending to search*): Bozzo ... Bozzo ...

VLADIMIR (*ditto*): Pozzo ... Pozzo ...

POZZO: PPPOZZZO!

ESTRAGON: Ah! Pozzo ... let me see ... Pozzo ...

VLADIMIR: Is it Pozzo or Bozzo?

ESTRAGON: Pozzo ... no ... I'm afraid I ... no ... I don't seem to ...

VLADIMIR (*conciliating*): I once knew a family called Gozzo. The mother had the clap.

ESTRAGON (*hastily*): We're not from these parts, Sir.

POZZO (*halting*): You are human beings none the less. (*He puts on his glasses.*) As far as one can see. (*He takes off his glasses.*) Of the same species as myself. (*He bursts into an enormous laugh.*) Of the same species as Pozzo! Made in God's image!

VLADIMIR: Well you see—

POZZO (*peremptory*): Who is Godot?

ESTRAGON: Godot?

POZZO: You took me for Godot.

VLADIMIR: Oh no, Sir, not for an instant, Sir.

POZZO: Who is he?

VLADIMIR: Oh he's a . . . he's a kind of acquaintance.

ESTRAGON: Nothing of the kind, we hardly know him.

VLADIMIR: True . . . we don't know him very well . . . but all the same . . .

ESTRAGON: Personally I wouldn't even know him if I saw him.

POZZO: You took me for him.

ESTRAGON (*recoiling before* POZZO): That's to say . . . you understand . . . the dusk . . . the strain . . . waiting . . . I confess . . . I imagined . . . for a second . . .

POZZO: Waiting? So you were waiting for him?

VLADIMIR: Well you see—

POZZO: Here? On my land?

VLADIMIR: We didn't intend any harm.

ESTRAGON: We meant well.

POZZO: The road is free to all.

VLADIMIR: That's how we looked at it.

POZZO: It's a disgrace. But there you are.

ESTRAGON: Nothing we can do about it.

POZZO (*with magnanimous gesture*): Let's say no more about it. (*He jerks the rope.*) Up pig! (*Pause.*) Every time he drops he falls asleep. (*Jerks the rope.*) Up hog! (*Noise of* LUCKY *getting up and picking up his baggage.* POZZO *jerks the rope.*) Back! (*Enter* LUCKY *backwards.*) Stop! (LUCKY *stops.*) Turn! (LUCKY *turns. To* VLADIMIR *and* ESTRAGON, *affably.*) Gentlemen, I am happy to have met you. (*Before their incredulous expression.*) Yes yes, sincerely happy. (*He jerks the rope.*) Closer! (LUCKY *advances.*) Stop! (LUCKY *stops.*) Yes, the road seems long when one journeys all alone for . . . (*He consults his watch.*) . . . yes . . . (*He calculates.*) . . . yes, six hours, that's right, six hours on end, and never a soul in sight. (*To* LUCKY.) Coat! (LUCKY *puts down the bag, advances, gives the coat, goes back to his place, takes up the bag.*) Hold that! (POZZO *holds out the whip.* LUCKY *advances and, both his hands being occupied, takes the whip in his mouth, then goes back to his place.* POZZO *begins to put on his coat, stops.*) Coat! (LUCKY *puts down bag, basket and stool, advances, helps* POZZO *on with his coat, goes back to his place and takes up bag, basket and stool.*) Touch of autumn in the air this evening. (POZZO *finishes buttoning his coat, stoops, inspects himself, straightens up.*) Whip! (LUCKY *advances, stoops,* POZZO *snatches the whip from his mouth,* LUCKY *goes back to his place.*) Yes, gentlemen, I cannot go for long without the society of my likes (*He puts on his glasses and looks at the two likes.*) even when the likeness is an imperfect one. (*He takes off his glasses.*) Stool! (LUCKY *puts down bag and basket, advances, opens stool, puts it down, goes back to his place, takes up bag and basket.*) Closer! (LUCKY *puts down bag and basket, advances, moves stool, goes back to his place, takes up bag and basket.* POZZO *sits down, places the butt of his whip against* LUCKY's *chest and pushes.*) Back! (LUCKY *takes a step back.*) Further! (LUCKY *takes another step back.*) Stop! (LUCKY *stops. To* VLADIMIR *and* ESTRAGON.) That is why, with your permission, I propose to dally with you a moment, before I venture any further. Basket! (LUCKY *advances, gives the basket, goes back to his place.*) The fresh air stimulates the jaded appetite. (*He opens the basket, takes out a piece of chicken and a bottle of wine.*) Basket! (LUCKY *advances, picks up the basket and goes back to his place.*) Further! (LUCKY *takes a step back.*) He stinks. Happy days!

He drinks from the bottle, puts it down and begins to eat. Silence. VLADIMIR *and* ESTRAGON, *cautiously at first, then more boldly, begin to circle about* LUCKY, *inspecting him up and down.* POZZO *eats his chicken voraciously, throwing away the bones after having sucked them.* LUCKY *sags slowly, until bag and basket touch the ground, then straightens up with a start and begins to sag again. Rhythm of one sleeping on his feet.*

ESTRAGON: What ails him?

VLADIMIR: He looks tired.

ESTRAGON: Why doesn't he put down his bags?

VLADIMIR: How do I know? (*They close in on him.*) Careful!

ESTRAGON: Say something to him.

VLADIMIR: Look!

ESTRAGON: What?

VLADIMIR (*pointing*): His neck!

ESTRAGON (*looking at the neck*): I see nothing.

VLADIMIR: Here.

ESTRAGON *goes over beside* VLADIMIR.

ESTRAGON: Oh I say!

VLADIMIR: A running sore!

ESTRAGON: It's the rope.

VLADIMIR: It's the rubbing.

ESTRAGON: It's inevitable.

VLADIMIR: It's the knot.

ESTRAGON: It's the chafing.

They resume their inspection, dwell on the face.

VLADIMIR (*grudgingly*): He's not bad looking.

ESTRAGON (*shrugging his shoulders, wry face*): Would you say so?

VLADIMIR: A trifle effeminate.

ESTRAGON: Look at the slobber.

VLADIMIR: It's inevitable.

ESTRAGON: Look at the slaver.

VLADIMIR: Perhaps he's a halfwit.

ESTRAGON: A cretin.

VLADIMIR (*looking closer*): Looks like a goiter.

ESTRAGON (*ditto*): It's not certain.

VLADIMIR: He's panting.

ESTRAGON: It's inevitable.

VLADIMIR: And his eyes!

ESTRAGON: What about them?

VLADIMIR: Goggling out of his head.

ESTRAGON: Looks at his last gasp to me.

VLADIMIR: It's not certain. (*Pause.*) Ask him a question.

ESTRAGON: Would that be a good thing?

VLADIMIR: What do we risk?

ESTRAGON (*timidly*): Mister . . .

VLADIMIR: Louder.

ESTRAGON (*louder*): Mister . . .

POZZO: Leave him in peace! (*They turn towards* POZZO *who, having finished eating, wipes his mouth with the back of his hand.*) Can't you see he wants to rest? Basket! (*He strikes a match and begins to light his pipe.* ESTRAGON *sees the chicken bones on the ground and stares at them greedily. As* LUCKY *does not move* POZZO *throws the match angrily away and jerks the rope.*) Basket! (LUCKY *starts, almost falls, recovers his senses, advances, puts the bottle in the basket and goes back to his place.* ESTRAGON *stares at the bones.* POZZO *strikes another match and lights his pipe.*) What can you expect, it's not his job. (*He pulls at his pipe, stretches out his legs.*) Ah! That's better.

ESTRAGON (*timidly*): Please Sir . . .

POZZO: What is it, my good man?

ESTRAGON: Er . . . you've finished with the . . . er . . . you don't need the . . . er . . . bones, Sir?

VLADIMIR (*scandalized*): You couldn't have waited?

POZZO: No no, he does well to ask. Do I need the bones? (*He turns them over with the end of his whip.*) No, personally I do not need them any more. (ESTRAGON *takes a step towards the bones.*) But . . . (ESTRAGON *stops short.*) . . . but in theory the bones go to the carrier. He is therefore the one to ask. (ESTRAGON *turns towards* LUCKY, *hesitates.*) Go on, go on, don't be afraid, ask him, he'll tell you.

ESTRAGON *goes towards* LUCKY, *stops before him.*

ESTRAGON: Mister . . . excuse me, Mister . . .

POZZO: You're being spoken to, pig! Reply! (*To* ESTRAGON.) Try him again.

ESTRAGON: Excuse me, Mister, the bones, you won't be wanting the bones?

LUCKY *looks long at* ESTRAGON.

POZZO (*in raptures*): Mister! (LUCKY *bows his head.*) Reply! Do you want them or don't you? (*Silence of* LUCKY. *To* ESTRAGON.)

They're yours. (ESTRAGON *makes a dart at the bones, picks them up and begins to gnaw them.*) I don't like it. I've never known him refuse a bone before. (*He looks anxiously at* LUCKY.) Nice business it'd be if he fell sick on me!

He puffs at his pipe.

VLADIMIR (*exploding*): It's a scandal!

Silence. Flabbergasted, ESTRAGON *stops gnawing, looks at* POZZO *and* VLADIMIR *in turn.* POZZO *outwardly calm.* VLADIMIR *embarrassed.*

POZZO (*to* VLADIMIR): Are you alluding to anything in particular?
VLADIMIR (*stutteringly resolute*): To treat a man . . . (*Gesture towards* LUCKY.) . . . like that . . . I think that . . . no . . . a human being . . . no . . . it's a scandal!
ESTRAGON (*not to be outdone*): A disgrace! (*He resumes his gnawing.*)
POZZO: You are severe. (*To* VLADIMIR.) What age are you, if it's not a rude question? (*Silence.*) Sixty? Seventy? (*To* ESTRAGON.) What age would you say he was?
ESTRAGON: Eleven.
POZZO: I am impertinent. (*He knocks out his pipe against the whip, gets up.*) I must be getting on. Thank you for your society. (*He reflects.*) Unless I smoke another pipe before I go. What do you say? (*They say nothing.*) Oh I'm only a small smoker, a very small smoker, I'm not in the habit of smoking two pipes one on top of the other, it makes (*Hand to heart, sighing.*) my heart go pit-a-pat. (*Silence.*) It's the nicotine, one absorbs it in spite of one's precautions. (*Sighs.*) You know how it is. (*Silence.*) But perhaps you don't smoke? Yes? No? It's of no importance. (*Silence.*) But how am I to sit down now, without affectation, now that I have risen? Without appearing to—how shall I say—without appearing to falter. (*To* VLADIMIR.) I beg your pardon? (*Silence.*) Perhaps you didn't speak? (*Silence.*) It's of no importance. Let me see . . . (*He reflects.*)
ESTRAGON: Ah! That's better. (*He puts the bones in his pocket.*)
VLADIMIR: Let's go.
ESTRAGON: So soon?
POZZO: One moment! (*He jerks the rope.*) Stool! (*He points with his*

whip. LUCKY *moves the stool.)* More! There! (*He sits down.* LUCKY *goes back to his place.)* Done it! (*He fills his pipe.)*

VLADIMIR (*vehemently*): Let's go!

POZZO: I hope I'm not driving you away. Wait a little longer, you'll never regret it.

ESTRAGON (*scenting charity*): We're in no hurry.

POZZO (*having lit his pipe*): The second is never so sweet ... (*He takes the pipe out of his mouth, contemplates it.*) ... as the first I mean. (*He puts the pipe back in his mouth.*) But it's sweet just the same.

VLADIMIR: I'm going.

POZZO: He can no longer endure my presence. I am perhaps not particularly human, but who cares? (*To* VLADIMIR.) Think twice before you do anything rash. Suppose you go now while it is still day, for there is no denying it is still day. (*They all look up at the sky.*) Good. (*They stop looking at the sky.*) What happens in that case— (*He takes the pipe out of his mouth, examines it.*)—I'm out— (*He relights his pipe.*)—in that case— (*Puff.*)—in that case— (*Puff.*)—what happens in that case to your appointment with this ... Godet ... Godot ... Godin ... anyhow you see who I mean, who has your future in his hands ... (*Pause.*) ... at least your immediate future?

VLADIMIR: Who told you?

POZZO: He speaks to me again! If this goes on much longer we'll soon be old friends.

ESTRAGON: Why doesn't he put down his bags?

POZZO: I too would be happy to meet him. The more people I meet the happier I become. From the meanest creature one departs wiser, richer, more conscious of one's blessings. Even you ... (*He looks at them ostentatiously in turn to make it clear they are both meant.*) ... even you, who knows, will have added to my store.

ESTRAGON: Why doesn't he put down his bags?

POZZO: But that would surprise me.

VLADIMIR: You're being asked a question.

POZZO (*delighted*): A question! Who? What? A moment ago you were calling me Sir, in fear and trembling. Now you're asking me questions. No good will come of this!

VLADIMIR (*to* ESTRAGON): I think he's listening.

ESTRAGON (*circling about* LUCKY): What?

VLADIMIR: You can ask him now. He's on the alert.

ESTRAGON: Ask him what?

VLADIMIR: Why he doesn't put down his bags.

ESTRAGON: I wonder.

VLADIMIR: Ask him, can't you?

POZZO (*who has followed these exchanges with anxious attention, fearing lest the question get lost*): You want to know why he doesn't put down his bags, as you call them.

VLADIMIR: That's it.

POZZO (*to* ESTRAGON): You are sure you agree with that?

ESTRAGON: He's puffing like a grampus.

POZZO: The answer is this. (*To* ESTRAGON.) But stay still, I beg of you, you're making me nervous!

VLADIMIR: Here.

ESTRAGON: What is it?

VLADIMIR: He's about to speak.

> ESTRAGON *goes over beside* VLADIMIR. *Motionless, side by side, they wait.*

POZZO: Good. Is everybody ready? Is everybody looking at me? (*He looks at* LUCKY, *jerks the rope.* LUCKY *raises his head.*) Will you look at me, pig! (LUCKY *looks at him.*) Good. (*He puts the pipe in his pocket, takes out a little vaporizer and sprays his throat, puts back the vaporizer in his pocket, clears his throat, spits, takes out the vaporizer again, sprays his throat again, puts back the vaporizer in his pocket.*) I am ready. Is everybody listening? Is everybody ready? (*He looks at them all in turn, jerks the rope.*) Hog! (LUCKY *raises his head.*) I don't like talking in a vacuum. Good. Let me see. (*He reflects.*)

ESTRAGON: I'm going.

POZZO: What was it exactly you wanted to know?

VLADIMIR: Why he—

POZZO (*angrily*): Don't interrupt me! (*Pause. Calmer.*) If we all speak at once we'll never get anywhere. (*Pause.*) What was I saying? (*Pause. Louder.*) What was I saying?

> VLADIMIR *mimics one carrying a heavy burden.* POZZO *looks at him, puzzled.*

ESTRAGON (*forcibly*): Bags. (*He points at* LUCKY.) Why? Always hold. (*He sags, panting.*) Never put down. (*He opens his hands, straightens up with relief.*) Why?

POZZO: Ah! Why couldn't you say so before? Why he doesn't make himself comfortable? Let's try and get this clear. Has he not the right to? Certainly he has. It follows that he doesn't want to. There's reasoning for you. And why doesn't he want to? (*Pause.*) Gentlemen, the reason is this.

VLADIMIR (*to* ESTRAGON): Make a note of this.

POZZO: He wants to impress me, so that I'll keep him.

ESTRAGON: What?

POZZO: Perhaps I haven't got it quite right. He wants to mollify me, so that I'll give up the idea of parting with him. No, that's not exactly it either.

VLADIMIR: You want to get rid of him?

POZZO: He wants to cod me, but he won't.

VLADIMIR: You want to get rid of him?

POZZO: He imagines that when I see how well he carries I'll be tempted to keep him on in that capacity.

ESTRAGON: You've had enough of him?

POZZO: In reality he carries like a pig. It's not his job.

VLADIMIR: You want to get rid of him?

POZZO: He imagines that when I see him indefatigable I'll regret my decision. Such is his miserable scheme. As though I were short of slaves! (*All three look at* LUCKY.) Atlas, son of Jupiter! (*Silence.*) Well, that's that I think. Anything else?

Vaporizer.

VLADIMIR: You want to get rid of him?

POZZO: Remark that I might just as well have been in his shoes and he in mine. If chance had not willed otherwise. To each one his due.

VLADIMIR: You waagerrim?

POZZO: I beg your pardon?

VLADIMIR: You want to get rid of him?

POZZO: I do. But instead of driving him away as I might have done, I mean instead of simply kicking him out on his arse, in the goodness of my heart I am bringing him to the fair, where I hope to get a good price for him. The truth is you can't drive such creatures away. The best thing would be to kill them.

LUCKY *weeps.*

ESTRAGON: He's crying!

POZZO: Old dogs have more dignity. (*He proffers his handkerchief to* ESTRAGON.) Comfort him, since you pity him. (ESTRAGON *hesitates.*) Come on. (ESTRAGON *takes the handkerchief.*) Wipe away his tears, he'll feel less forsaken.

ESTRAGON *hesitates.*

VLADIMIR: Here, give it to me, I'll do it.

ESTRAGON *refuses to give the handkerchief. Childish gestures.*

POZZO: Make haste, before he stops. (ESTRAGON *approaches* LUCKY *and makes to wipe his eyes.* LUCKY *kicks him violently in the shins.* ESTRAGON *drops the handkerchief, recoils, staggers about the stage howling with pain.*) Hanky!

LUCKY *puts down bag and basket, picks up handkerchief and gives it to* POZZO, *goes back to his place, picks up bag and basket.*

ESTRAGON: Oh the swine! (*He pulls up the leg of his trousers.*) He's crippled me!

POZZO: I told you he didn't like strangers.

VLADIMIR (*to* ESTRAGON): Show. (ESTRAGON *shows his leg. To* POZZO, *angrily.*) He's bleeding!

POZZO: It's a good sign.

ESTRAGON (*on one leg*): I'll never walk again!

VLADIMIR (*tenderly*): I'll carry you. (*Pause.*) If necessary.

POZZO: He's stopped crying. (*To* ESTRAGON.) You have replaced him as it were. (*Lyrically.*) The tears of the world are a constant quantity. For each one who begins to weep somewhere else another stops. The same is true of the laugh. (*He laughs.*) Let us

relationship

not then speak ill of our generation, it is not any unhappier than its predecessors. (*Pause.*) Let us not speak well of it either. (*Pause.*) Let us not speak of it at all. (*Pause. Judiciously.*) It is true the population has increased.

VLADIMIR: Try and walk.

ESTRAGON *takes a few limping steps, stops before* LUCKY *and spits on him, then goes and sits down on the mound.*

POZZO: Guess who taught me all these beautiful things. (*Pause. Pointing to* LUCKY.) My Lucky!

VLADIMIR (*looking at the sky*): Will night never come?

POZZO: But for him all my thoughts, all my feelings, would have been of common things. (*Pause. With extraordinary vehemence.*) Professional worries! (*Calmer.*) Beauty, grace, truth of the first water, I knew they were all beyond me. So I took a knook.

VLADIMIR (*startled from his inspection of the sky*): A knook?

POZZO: That was nearly sixty years ago ... (*He consults his watch.*) ... yes, nearly sixty. (*Drawing himself up proudly.*) You wouldn't think it to look at me, would you? Compared to him I look like a young man, no? (*Pause.*) Hat! (LUCKY *puts down the basket and takes off his hat. His long white hair falls about his face. He puts his hat under his arm and picks up the basket.*) Now look. (POZZO *takes off his hat.*[1] *He is completely bald. He puts on his hat again.*) Did you see?

VLADIMIR: And now you turn him away? Such an old and faithful servant!

ESTRAGON: Swine!

POZZO *more and more agitated.*

VLADIMIR: After having sucked all the good out of him you chuck him away like a ... like a banana skin. Really ...

POZZO (*groaning, clutching his head*): I can't bear it ... any longer ... the way he goes on ... you've no idea ... it's terrible ... he must go ... (*He waves his arms.*) ... I'm going mad ... (*He collapses, his head in his hands.*) ... I can't bear it ... any longer ...

---

[1] *All four wear bowlers.*

Silence All look at POZZO.

VLADIMIR: He can't bear it.

ESTRAGON: Any longer.

VLADIMIR: He's going mad.

ESTRAGON: It's terrible.

VLADIMIR (*to* LUCKY): How dare you! It's abominable! Such a good master! Crucify him like that! After so many years! Really!

POZZO (*sobbing*). He used to be so kind . . . so helpful . . . and entertaining . . . my good angel . . . and now . . . he's killing me.

ESTRAGON (*to* VLADIMIR): Does he want to replace him?

VLADIMIR: What?

ESTRAGON: Does he want someone to take his place or not?

VLADIMIR: I don't think so.

ESTRAGON: What?

VLADIMIR: I don't know.

ESTRAGON: Ask him.

POZZO (*calmer*): Gentlemen, I don't know what came over me. Forgive me. Forget all I said. (*More and more his old self.*) I don't remember exactly what it was, but you may be sure there wasn't a word of truth in it. (*Drawing himself up, striking his chest.*) Do I look like a man that can be made to suffer? Frankly? (*He rummages in his pockets.*) What have I done with my pipe?

VLADIMIR: Charming evening we're having.

ESTRAGON: Unforgettable.

VLADIMIR: And it's not over.

ESTRAGON: Apparently not.

VLADIMIR: It s only beginning.

ESTRAGON: It's awful.

VLADIMIR: Worse than the pantomime.

ESTRAGON: The circus.

VLADIMIR: The music-hall.

ESTRAGON: The circus.

POZZO: What can I have done with that briar?

ESTRAGON: He's a scream. He's lost his dudeen. (*Laughs noisily.*)

VLADIMIR: I'll be back. (*He hastens towards the wings.*)

ESTRAGON: End of the corridor, on the left.

VLADIMIR: Keep my seat.

Exit VLADIMIR.

Handwritten margin note (rotated, left): Vladimir went to piss.

POZZO (*on the point of tears*): I've lost my Kapp and Peterson!

ESTRAGON (*convulsed with merriment*): He'll be the death of me!

POZZO: You didn't see by any chance—. (*He misses* VLADIMIR.) Oh! He's gone! Without saying goodbye! How could he! He might have waited!

ESTRAGON: He would have burst. *[handwritten: went to pee]*

POZZO: Oh! (*Pause.*) Oh well then of course in that case . . .

ESTRAGON: Come here.

POZZO: What for?

ESTRAGON: You'll see.

POZZO: You want me to get up?

ESTRAGON: Quick! (POZZO *gets up and goes over beside* ESTRAGON. ESTRAGON *points off.*) Look!

POZZO (*having put on his glasses*): Oh I say!

ESTRAGON: It's all over.

> *Enter* VLADIMIR, *somber. He shoulders* LUCKY *out of his way, kicks over the stool, comes and goes agitatedly.*

POZZO: He's not pleased.

ESTRAGON (*to* VLADIMIR): You missed a treat. Pity.

> VLADIMIR *halts, straightens the stool, comes and goes, calmer.*

POZZO: He subsides. (*Looking round.*) Indeed all subsides. A great calm descends. (*Raising his hand.*) Listen! Pan sleeps.

VLADIMIR: Will night never come? *[handwritten: all is well]*

> *All three look at the sky.*

POZZO: You don't feel like going until it does?

ESTRAGON: Well you see—

POZZO: Why it's very natural, very natural. I myself in your situation, if I had an appointment with a Godin . . . Godet . . . Godot . . . anyhow you see who I mean, I'd wait till it was black night before I gave up. (*He looks at the stool.*) I'd very much like to sit down, but I don't quite know how to go about it.

ESTRAGON: Could I be of any help?

POZZO: If you asked me perhaps.

ESTRAGON: What?

POZZO: If you asked me to sit down.

ESTRAGON: Would that be a help?

POZZO: I fancy so.

ESTRAGON: Here we go. Be seated, Sir, I beg of you.

POZZO: No no, I wouldn't think of it! (*Pause. Aside.*) Ask me again.

ESTRAGON: Come come, take a seat I beseech you, you'll get pneumonia.

POZZO: You really think so?

ESTRAGON: Why it's absolutely certain.

POZZO: No doubt you are right. (*He sits down.*) Done it again! (*Pause.*) Thank you, dear fellow. (*He consults his watch.*) But I must really be getting along, if I am to observe my schedule.

VLADIMIR: Time has stopped.

POZZO (*cuddling his watch to his ear*): Don't you believe it, Sir, don't you believe it. (*He puts his watch back in his pocket.*) Whatever you like, but not that.

ESTRAGON (*to* POZZO): Everything seems black to him to-day.

POZZO: Except the firmament. (*He laughs, pleased with this witticism.*) But I see what it is, you are not from these parts, you don't know what our twilights can do. Shall I tell you? (*Silence.* ESTRAGON *is fiddling with his boot again,* VLADIMIR *with his hat.*) I can't refuse you. (*Vaporizer.*) A little attention, if you please. (VLADIMIR *and* ESTRAGON *continue their fiddling,* LUCKY *is half asleep.* POZZO *cracks his whip feebly.*) What's the matter with this whip? (*He gets up and cracks it more vigorously, finally with success.* LUCKY *jumps.* VLADIMIR'S *hat,* ESTRAGON'S *boot,* LUCKY'S *hat, fall to the ground.* POZZO *throws down the whip.*) Worn out, this whip. (*He looks at* VLADIMIR *and* ESTRAGON.) What was I saying?

VLADIMIR: Let's go.

ESTRAGON: But take the weight off your feet, I implore you, you'll catch your death.

POZZO: True. (*He sits down. To* ESTRAGON.) What is your name?

ESTRAGON: Adam.

POZZO (*who hasn't listened*): Ah yes! The night. (*He raises his head.*) But be a little more attentive, for pity's sake, otherwise we'll never get anywhere. (*He looks at the sky.*) Look! (*All look at the sky except* LUCKY *who is dozing off again.* POZZO *jerks the rope.*) Will you look at the sky, pig! (LUCKY *looks at the sky.*) Good, that's enough. (*They stop looking at the sky.*) What is there so extraordinary about it? Qua sky. It is pale and luminous like any sky at this hour of the day. (*Pause.*) In these latitudes.

(*Pause.*) When the weather is fine. (*Lyrical.*) An hour ago (*He looks at his watch, prosaic.*) roughly (*Lyrical.*) after having poured forth even since (*He hesitates, prosaic.*) say ten o'clock in the morning (*Lyrical.*) tirelessly torrents of red and white light it begins to lose its effulgence, to grow pale (*Gesture of the two hands lapsing by stages.*) pale, ever a little paler, a little paler until (*Dramatic pause, ample gesture of the two hands flung wide apart.*) pppffft! finished! it comes to rest. But— (*Hand raised in admonition.*)—but behind this veil of gentleness and peace night is charging (*Vibrantly.*) and will burst upon us (*Snaps his fingers.*) pop! like that! (*His inspiration leaves him.*) just when we least expect it. (*Silence. Gloomily.*) That's how it is on this bitch of an earth.

Long silence.

ESTRAGON: So long as one knows.
VLADIMIR: One can bide one's time.
ESTRAGON: One knows what to expect.
VLADIMIR: No further need to worry.
ESTRAGON: Simply wait.
VLADIMIR: We're used to it. (*He picks up his hat, peers inside it, shakes it, puts it on.*)
POZZO: How did you find me? (VLADIMIR *and* ESTRAGON *look at him blankly.*) Good? Fair? Middling? Poor? Positively bad?
VLADIMIR (*first to understand*): Oh very good, very very good.
POZZO (*to* ESTRAGON): And you, Sir?
ESTRAGON: Oh tray bong, tray tray tray bong.
POZZO (*fervently*): Bless you, gentlemen, bless you! (*Pause.*) I have such need of encouragement! (*Pause.*) I weakened a little towards the end, you didn't notice?
VLADIMIR: Oh perhaps just a teeny weeny little bit.
ESTRAGON: I thought it was intentional.
POZZO: You see my memory is defective.

Silence.

ESTRAGON: In the meantime nothing happens.
POZZO: You find it tedious?

ESTRAGON: Somewhat.

POZZO (*to* VLADIMIR): And you, Sir?

VLADIMIR: I've been better entertained.

Silence. POZZO *struggles inwardly.*

POZZO: Gentlemen, you have been . . civil to me.

ESTRAGON: Not at all!

VLADIMIR: What an idea!

POZZO: Yes yes, you have been correct. So that I ask myself is there anything I can do in my turn for these honest fellows who are having such a dull, dull time.

ESTRAGON: Even ten francs would be a help.

VLADIMIR: We are not beggars!

POZZO: Is there anything I can do, that's what I ask myself, to cheer them up? I have given them bones, I have talked to them about this and that, I have explained the twilight, admittedly. But is it enough, that's what tortures me, is it enough?

ESTRAGON: Even five.

VLADIMIR (*to* ESTRAGON, *indignantly*): That's enough!

ESTRAGON: I couldn't accept less.

POZZO: Is it enough? No doubt. But I am liberal. It's my nature. This evening. So much the worse for me. (*He jerks the rope.* LUCKY *looks at him.*) For I shall suffer, no doubt about that. (*He picks up the whip.*) What do you prefer? Shall we have him dance, or sing, or recite, or think, or—

ESTRAGON: Who?

POZZO: Who! You know how to think, you two?

VLADIMIR: He thinks?

POZZO: Certainly. Aloud. He even used to think very prettily once, I could listen to him for hours. Now . . . (*He shudders.*) So much the worse for me. Well, would you like him to think something for us?

ESTRAGON: I'd rather he'd dance, it'd be more fun.

POZZO: Not necessarily.

ESTRAGON: Wouldn't it, Didi, be more fun?

VLADIMIR: I'd like well to hear him think.

ESTRAGON: Perhaps he could dance first and think afterwards, if it isn't too much to ask him.

VLADIMIR (*to* POZZO): Would that be possible?

POZZO: By all means, nothing simpler. It's the natural order. (*He laughs briefly.*)

VLADIMIR: Then let him dance.

Silence.

POZZO: Do you hear, hog?

ESTRAGON: He never refuses?

POZZO: He refused once. (*Silence.*) Dance, misery!

LUCKY *puts down bag and basket, advances towards front, turns to* POZZO. LUCKY *dances. He stops.*

ESTRAGON: Is that all?

POZZO: Encore!

LUCKY *executes the same movements, stops.*

ESTRAGON: Pooh! I'd do as well myself. (*He imitates* LUCKY, *almost falls.*) With a little practice.

POZZO: He used to dance the farandole, the fling, the brawl, the jig, the fandango and even the hornpipe. He capered. For joy. Now that's the best he can do. Do you know what he calls it?

ESTRAGON: The Scapegoat's Agony.

VLADIMIR: The Hard Stool.

POZZO: The Net. He thinks he's entangled in a net.

VLADIMIR (*squirming like an aesthete*): There's something about it . . .

LUCKY *makes to return to his burdens.*

POZZO: Woaa!

LUCKY *stiffens.*

ESTRAGON: Tell us about the time he refused.

POZZO: With pleasure, with pleasure. (*He fumbles in his pockets.*) Wait. (*He fumbles.*) What have I done with my spray? (*He fumbles.*) Well now isn't that . . . (*He looks up, consternation on his features. Faintly.*) I can't find my pulverizer!

ESTRAGON (*faintly*): My left lung is very weak! (*He coughs feebly. In ringing tones.*) But my right lung is as sound as a bell!

POZZO (*normal voice*): No matter! What was I saying. (*He ponders.*) Wait. (*Ponders.*) Well now isn't that . . . (*He raises his head.*) Help me!

ESTRAGON: Wait!

VLADIMIR: Wait!

POZZO: Wait!

> *All three take off their hats simultaneously, press their hands to their foreheads, concentrate.*

ESTRAGON (*triumphantly*): Ah!

VLADIMIR: He has it.

POZZO (*impatient*): Well?

ESTRAGON: Why doesn't he put down his bags?

VLADIMIR: Rubbish!

POZZO: Are you sure?

VLADIMIR: Damn it haven't you already told us?

POZZO: I've already told you?

ESTRAGON: He's already told us?

VLADIMIR: Anyway he has put them down.

ESTRAGON (*glance at* LUCKY): So he has. And what of it?

VLADIMIR: Since he has put down his bags it is impossible we should have asked why he does not do so.

POZZO: Stoutly reasoned!

ESTRAGON: And why has he put them down?

POZZO: Answer us that.

VLADIMIR: In order to dance.

ESTRAGON: True!

POZZO: True!

> *Silence. They put on their hats.*

ESTRAGON: Nothing happens, nobody comes, nobody goes, it's awful!

VLADIMIR (*to* POZZO): Tell him to think.

POZZO: Give him his hat.

VLADIMIR: His hat?

POZZO: He can't think without his hat.

VLADIMIR (*to* ESTRAGON): Give him his hat.

ESTRAGON: Me! After what he did to me! Never!

VLADIMIR: I'll give it to him. (*He does not move.*)

ESTRAGON (*to* POZZO): Tell him to go and fetch it.

POZZO: It's better to give it to him.

VLADIMIR: I'll give it to him.

> *He picks up the hat and tenders it at arm's length to* LUCKY, *who does not move.*

POZZO: You must put it on his head.

ESTRAGON (*to* POZZO): Tell him to take it.

POZZO: It's better to put it on his head.

VLADIMIR: I'll put it on his head.

> *He goes round behind* LUCKY, *approaches him cautiously, puts the hat on his head and recoils smartly.* LUCKY *does not move. Silence.*

ESTRAGON: What's he waiting for?

POZZO: Stand back! (VLADIMIR *and* ESTRAGON *move away from* LUCKY. POZZO *jerks the rope.* LUCKY *looks at* POZZO.) Think, pig! (*Pause.* LUCKY *begins to dance.*) Stop! (LUCKY *stops.*) Forward! (LUCKY *advances.*) Stop! (LUCKY *stops.*) Think!

> *Silence.*

LUCKY: On the other hand with regard to—

POZZO: Stop! (LUCKY *stops.*) Back! (LUCKY *moves back.*) Stop! (LUCKY *stops.*) Turn! (LUCKY *turns towards auditorium.*) Think!

> *During* LUCKY's *tirade the others react as follows.*
> 1) VLADIMIR *and* ESTRAGON *all attention,* POZZO *dejected and disgusted.*
> 2) VLADIMIR *and* ESTRAGON *begin to protest,* POZZO's *sufferings increase.*
> 3) VLADIMIR *and* ESTRAGON *attentive again,* POZZO *more and more agitated and groaning.*
> 4) VLADIMIR *and* ESTRAGON *protest violently.* POZZO *jumps up, pulls on the rope. General outcry.* LUCKY *pulls on the rope,*

> *staggers, shouts his text. All three throw themselves on* LUCKY *who struggles and shouts his text.*

LUCKY: Given the existence as uttered forth in the public works of Puncher and Wattmann of a personal God quaquaquaqua with white beard quaquaquaqua outside time without extension who from the heights of divine apathia divine athambia divine aphasia loves us dearly with some exceptions for reasons unknown but time will tell and suffers like the divine Miranda with those who for reasons unknown but time will tell are plunged in torment plunged in fire whose fire flames if that continues and who can doubt it will fire the firmament that is to say blast hell to heaven so blue still and calm so calm with a calm which even though intermittent is better than nothing but not so fast and considering what is more that as a result of the labors left unfinished crowned by the Acacacacademy of Anthropopopometry of Essy-in-Possy of Testew and Cunard it is established beyond all doubt all other doubt than that which clings to the labors of men that as a result of the labors unfinished of Testew and Cunard it is established as hereinafter but not so fast for reasons unknown that as a result of the public works of Puncher and Wattmann it is established beyond all doubt that in view of the labors of Fartov and Belcher left unfinished for reasons unknown of Testew and Cunard left unfinished it is established what many deny that man in Possy of Testew and Cunard that man in Essy that man in short that man in brief in spite of the strides of alimentation and defecation wastes and pines wastes and pines and concurrently simultaneously what is more for reasons unknown in spite of the strides of physical culture the practice of sports such as tennis football running cycling swimming flying floating riding gliding conating camogie skating tennis of all kinds dying flying sports of all sorts autumn summer winter winter tennis of all kinds hockey of all sorts penicilline and succedanea in a word I resume flying gliding golf over nine and eighteen holes tennis of all sorts in a word for reasons unknown in Feckham Peckham Fulham Clapham namely concurrently simultaneously what is more for reasons unknown but time will tell fades away I resume Fulham Clapham in a word the dead loss per head since the death of Bishop Berkeley being to the tune of one inch four ounce per head approximately by

and large more or less to the nearest decimal good measure
round figures stark naked in the stockinged feet in Connemara
in a word for reasons unknown no matter what matter the facts
are there and considering what is more much more grave that
in the light of the labors lost of Steinweg and Peterman it
appears what is more much more grave that in the light the
light the light of the labors lost of Steinweg and Peterman that
in the plains in the mountains by the seas by the rivers running
water running fire the air is the same and then the earth
namely the air and then the earth in the great cold the great
dark the air and the earth abode of stones in the great cold alas
alas in the year of their Lord six hundred and something the air
the earth the sea the earth abode of stones in the great deeps the
great cold on sea on land and in the air I resume for reasons unknown in spite of the tennis the facts are there but time will tell
I resume alas alas on on in short in fine on on abode of stones
who can doubt it I resume but not so fast I resume the skull
fading fading fading and concurrently simultaneously what is
more for reasons unknown in spite of the tennis on on the beard
the flames the tears the stones so blue so calm alas alas on on the
skull the skull the skull the skull in Connemara in spite of the
tennis the labors abandoned left unfinished graver still abode of
stones in a word I resume alas alas abandoned unfinished the
skull the skull in Connemara in spite of the tennis the skull alas
the stones Cunard (*Mêlée, final vociferations.*) tennis . . . the
stones . . . so calm . . . Cunard . . . unfinished . . .

POZZO: His hat!

VLADIMIR *seizes* LUCKY'S *hat. Silence of* LUCKY. *He falls. Silence.
Panting of the victors.*

ESTRAGON: Avenged!

VLADIMIR *examines the hat, peers inside it.*

POZZO: Give me that! (*He snatches the hat from* VLADIMIR, *throws it
on the ground, tramples on it.*) There's an end to his thinking!
VLADIMIR: But will he be able to walk?
POZZO: Walk or crawl! (*He kicks* LUCKY.) Up pig!
ESTRAGON: Perhaps he's dead.

VLADIMIR: You'll kill him.

POZZO: Up scum! (*He jerks the rope.*) Help me!

VLADIMIR: How?

POZZO: Raise him up!

> VLADIMIR *and* ESTRAGON *hoist* LUCKY *to his feet, support him an instant, then let him go. He falls.*

ESTRAGON: He's doing it on purpose!

POZZO: You must hold him. (*Pause.*) Come on, come on, raise him up.

ESTRAGON: To hell with him!

VLADIMIR: Come on, once more.

ESTRAGON: What does he take us for?

> *They raise* LUCKY, *hold him up.*

POZZO: Don't let him go! (VLADIMIR *and* ESTRAGON *totter.*) Don't move! (POZZO *fetches bag and basket and brings them towards* LUCKY.) Hold him tight! (*He puts the bag in* LUCKY's *hand.* LUCKY *drops it immediately.*) Don't let him go! (*He puts back the bag in* LUCKY's *hand. Gradually, at the feel of the bag,* LUCKY *recovers his senses and his fingers finally close round the handle.*) Hold him tight! (*As before with basket.*) Now! You can let him go. (VLADIMIR *and* ESTRAGON *move away from* LUCKY *who totters, reels, sags, but succeeds in remaining on his feet, bag and basket in his hands.* POZZO *steps back, cracks his whip.*) Forward! (LUCKY *totters forward.*) Back! (LUCKY *totters back.*) Turn! (LUCKY *turns.*) Done it! He can walk. (*Turning to* VLADIMIR *and* ESTRAGON.) Thank you, gentlemen, and let me . . . (*He fumbles in his pockets.*) . . . let me wish you . . . (*Fumbles.*) . . . wish you . . . (*Fumbles.*) . . . what have I done with my watch? (*Fumbles.*) A genuine half-hunter, gentlemen, with deadbeat escapement! (*Sobbing.*) Twas my granpa gave it to me! (*He searches on the ground,* VLADIMIR *and* ESTRAGON *likewise.* POZZO *turns over with his foot the remains of* LUCKY's *hat.*) Well now isn't that just—

VLADIMIR: Perhaps it's in your fob.

POZZO: Wait! (*He doubles up in an attempt to apply his ear to his stomach, listens. Silence.*) I hear nothing. (*He beckons them to approach.* VLADIMIR *and* ESTRAGON *go over to him, bend over his stomach.*) Surely one should hear the tick-tick.

VLADIMIR: Silence!

All listen, bent double.

ESTRAGON: I hear something.
POZZO: Where?
VLADIMIR: It's the heart.
POZZO (*disappointed*): Damnation!
VLADIMIR: Silence!
ESTRAGON: Perhaps it has stopped.

They straighten up.

POZZO: Which of you smells so bad?
ESTRAGON: He has stinking breath and I have stinking feet.
POZZO: I must go.
ESTRAGON: And your half-hunter?
POZZO: I must have left it at the manor.

Silence.

ESTRAGON: Then adieu.
POZZO: Adieu.
VLADIMIR: Adieu.
POZZO: Adieu.

Silence. No one moves.

VLADIMIR: Adieu.
POZZO: Adieu.
ESTRAGON: Adieu.

Silence.

POZZO: And thank you.
VLADIMIR: Thank *you.*
POZZO: Not at all.
ESTRAGON: Yes yes.
POZZO: No no.
VLADIMIR: Yes yes.

ESTRAGON: No no.

Silence.

POZZO: I don't seem to be able . . . (*Long hesitation.*) . . . to depart.
ESTRAGON: Such is life.

POZZO *turns, moves away from* LUCKY *towards the wings, paying out the rope as he goes.*

VLADIMIR: You're going the wrong way.
POZZO: I need a running start. (*Having come to the end of the rope, i.e. off stage, he stops, turns and cries.*) Stand back! (VLADIMIR *and* ESTRAGON *stand back, look towards* POZZO. *Crack of whip.*) On! On!
ESTRAGON: On!
VLADIMIR: On!

LUCKY *moves off.*

POZZO: Faster! (*He appears, crosses the stage preceded by* LUCKY. VLADIMIR *and* ESTRAGON *wave their hats. Exit* LUCKY.) On! On! (*On the point of disappearing in his turn he stops and turns. The rope tautens. Noise of* LUCKY *falling off.*) Stool! (VLADIMIR *fetches stool and gives it to* POZZO *who throws it to* LUCKY.) Adieu!

VLADIMIR ⎫
ESTRAGON ⎭ (*waving*): Adieu! Adieu!

POZZO: Up! Pig! (*Noise of* LUCKY *getting up.*) On! (*Exit* POZZO.) Faster! On! Adieu! Pig! Yip! Adieu!

Long silence.

VLADIMIR: That passed the time.
ESTRAGON: It would have passed in any case.

at least we were entertained

VLADIMIR: Yes, but not so rapidly.

Pause.

ESTRAGON: What do we do now?

VLADIMIR: I don't know.

ESTRAGON: Let's go.

VLADIMIR: We can't.

ESTRAGON: Why not?

VLADIMIR: We're waiting for Godot.

ESTRAGON (*despairingly*): Ah!

Pause.

VLADIMIR: How they've changed!

ESTRAGON: Who?

VLADIMIR: Those two.

ESTRAGON: That's the idea, let's make a little conversation.

VLADIMIR: Haven't they?

ESTRAGON: What?

VLADIMIR: Changed.

ESTRAGON: Very likely. They all change. Only we can't.

VLADIMIR: Likely! It's certain. Didn't you see them?

ESTRAGON: I suppose I did. But I don't know them.

VLADIMIR: Yes you do know them.

ESTRAGON: No I don't know them.

VLADIMIR: We know them, I tell you. You forget everything. (*Pause. To himself.*) Unless they're not the same . . .

ESTRAGON: Why didn't they recognize us then?

VLADIMIR: That means nothing. I too pretended not to recognize them. And then nobody ever recognizes us.

ESTRAGON: Forget it. What we need—ow! (VLADIMIR *does not react.*) Ow!

VLADIMIR (*to himself*): Unless they're not the same . . .

ESTRAGON: Didi! It's the other foot! (*He goes hobbling towards the mound.*)

VLADIMIR: Unless they're not the same . . .

BOY (*off*): Mister!

ESTRAGON *halts. Both look towards the voice.*

ESTRAGON: Off we go again.

VLADIMIR: Approach, my child.

Enter BOY, *timidly. He halts.*

BOY: Mister Albert . . . ?
VLADIMIR: Yes.
ESTRAGON: What do you want?
VLADIMIR: Approach!

The BOY *does not move.*

ESTRAGON (*forcibly*): Approach when you're told, can't you?

The BOY *advances timidly, halts.*

VLADIMIR: What is it?
BOY: Mr. Godot . . .
VLADIMIR: Obviously . . . (*Pause.*) Approach.
ESTRAGON (*violently*): Will you approach! (*The* BOY *advances timidly.*) What kept you so late?
VLADIMIR: You have a message from Mr. Godot?
BOY: Yes Sir.
VLADIMIR: Well, what is it?
ESTRAGON: What kept you so late?

The BOY *looks at them in turn, not knowing to which he should reply.*

VLADIMIR (*to* ESTRAGON): Let him alone.
ESTRAGON (*violently*): You let me alone. (*Advancing, to the* BOY.) Do you know what time it is?
BOY (*recoiling*): It's not my fault, Sir.
ESTRAGON: And whose is it? Mine?
BOY: I was afraid, Sir.
ESTRAGON: Afraid of what? Of us? (*Pause.*) Answer me!
VLADIMIR: I know what it is, he was afraid of the others.
ESTRAGON: How long have you been here?
BOY: A good while, Sir.
VLADIMIR: You were afraid of the whip?
BOY: Yes Sir.
VLADIMIR: The roars?
BOY: Yes Sir.
VLADIMIR: The two big men.
BOY: Yes Sir.

VLADIMIR: Do you know them?

BOY: No Sir.

VLADIMIR: Are you a native of these parts? (*Silence.*) Do you belong to these parts?

BOY: Yes Sir.

ESTRAGON: That's all a pack of lies. (*Shaking the* BOY *by the arm.*) Tell us the truth!

BOY (*trembling*): But it is the truth, Sir!

VLADIMIR: Will you let him alone! What's the matter with you? (ESTRAGON *releases the* BOY, *moves away, covering his face with his hands.* VLADIMIR *and the* BOY *observe him.* ESTRAGON *drops his hands. His face is convulsed.*) What's the matter with you?

ESTRAGON: I'm unhappy.

VLADIMIR: Not really! Since when?

ESTRAGON: I'd forgotten.

VLADIMIR: Extraordinary the tricks that memory plays!

> ESTRAGON *tries to speak, renounces, limps to his place, sits down and begins to take off his boots.*

(*To* BOY.) Well?

BOY: Mr. Godot—

VLADIMIR: I've seen you before, haven't I?

BOY: I don't know, Sir.

VLADIMIR: You don't know me?

BOY: No Sir.

VLADIMIR: It wasn't you came yesterday?

BOY: No Sir.

VLADIMIR: This is your first time?

BOY: Yes Sir.

> *Silence.*

VLADIMIR: Words words. (*Pause.*) Speak.

BOY (*in a rush*): Mr. Godot told me to tell you he won't come this evening but surely to-morrow.

> *Silence.*

VLADIMIR: Is that all?

BOY: Yes Sir.

Silence.

VLADIMIR: You work for Mr. Godot?
BOY: Yes Sir.
VLADIMIR: What do you do?
BOY: I mind the goats, Sir.
VLADIMIR: Is he good to you?
BOY: Yes Sir.
VLADIMIR: He doesn't beat you?
BOY: No Sir, not me.
VLADIMIR: Whom does he beat?
BOY: He beats my brother, Sir.
VLADIMIR: Ah, you have a brother?
BOY: Yes Sir.
VLADIMIR: What does he do?
BOY: He minds the sheep, Sir.
VLADIMIR: And why doesn't he beat you?
BOY: I don't know, Sir.
VLADIMIR: He must be fond of you.
BOY: I don't know, Sir.

Silence.

VLADIMIR: Does he give you enough to eat? (*The* BOY *hesitates.*) Does he feed you well?
BOY: Fairly well, Sir.
VLADIMIR: You're not unhappy? (*The* BOY *hesitates.*) Do you hear me?
BOY: Yes Sir.
VLADIMIR: Well?
BOY: I don't know, Sir.
VLADIMIR: You don't know if you're unhappy or not?
BOY: No Sir.
VLADIMIR: You're as bad as myself. (*Silence.*) Where do you sleep?
BOY: In the loft, Sir.
VLADIMIR: With your brother?
BOY: Yes Sir.
VLADIMIR: In the hay?
BOY: Yes Sir.

Silence.

VLADIMIR: All right, you may go.

BOY: What am I to tell Mr. Godot, Sir?

VLADIMIR: Tell him . . . (*He hesitates.*) . . . tell him you saw us. (*Pause.*) You did see us, didn't you?

BOY: Yes Sir. (*He steps back, hesitates, turns and exit running.*)

> *The light suddenly fails. In a moment it is night. The moon rises at back, mounts in the sky, stands still, shedding a pale light on the scene.*

VLADIMIR: At last!

> ESTRAGON *gets up and goes towards* VLADIMIR, *a boot in each hand. He puts them down at edge of stage, straightens and contemplates the moon.*

What are you doing?

ESTRAGON: Pale for weariness.

VLADIMIR: Eh?

ESTRAGON: Of climbing heaven and gazing on the likes of us.

VLADIMIR: Your boots, what are you doing with your boots?

ESTRAGON (*turning to look at the boots*): I'm leaving them there. (*Pause.*) Another will come, just as . . . as . . . as me, but with smaller feet, and they'll make him happy.

VLADIMIR: But you can't go barefoot!

ESTRAGON: Christ did.

VLADIMIR: Christ! What has Christ got to do with it? You're not going to compare yourself to Christ!

ESTRAGON: All my life I've compared myself to him.

VLADIMIR: But where he lived it was warm, it was dry!

ESTRAGON: Yes. And they crucified quick.

Silence.

VLADIMIR: We've nothing more to do here.

ESTRAGON: Nor anywhere else.

VLADIMIR: Ah Gogo, don't go on like that. To-morrow everything will be better.

ESTRAGON: How do you make that out?

VLADIMIR: Did you not hear what the child said?

ESTRAGON: No.

VLADIMIR: He said that Godot was sure to come to-morrow. (*Pause.*) What do you say to that?

ESTRAGON: Then all we have to do is to wait on here.

VLADIMIR: Are you mad? We must take cover. (*He takes* ESTRAGON *by the arm.*) Come on. (*He draws* ESTRAGON *after him.* ESTRAGON *yields, then resists. They halt.*)

ESTRAGON (*looking at the tree*): Pity we haven't got a bit of rope.

VLADIMIR: Come on. It's cold. (*He draws* ESTRAGON *after him. As before.*)

ESTRAGON: Remind me to bring a bit of rope to-morrow.

VLADIMIR: Yes. Come on. (*He draws him after him. As before.*)

ESTRAGON: How long have we been together all the time now?

VLADIMIR: I don't know. Fifty years maybe.

ESTRAGON: Do you remember the day I threw myself into the Rhone?

VLADIMIR: We were grape harvesting.

ESTRAGON: You fished me out.

VLADIMIR: That's all dead and buried.

ESTRAGON: My clothes dried in the sun.

VLADIMIR: There's no good harking back on that. Come on. (*He draws him after him. As before.*)

ESTRAGON: Wait!

VLADIMIR: I'm cold!

ESTRAGON: Wait! (*He moves away from* VLADIMIR.) I sometimes wonder if we wouldn't have been better off alone, each one for himself. (*He crosses the stage and sits down on the mound.*) We weren't made for the same road.

VLADIMIR (*without anger*): It's not certain.

ESTRAGON: No, nothing is certain.

> VLADIMIR *slowly crosses the stage and sits down beside* ESTRAGON.

VLADIMIR: We can still part, if you think it would be better.

ESTRAGON: It's not worth while now.

Silence.

VLADIMIR: No, it's not worth while now.

Silence.

ESTRAGON: Well, shall we go?
VLADIMIR: Yes, let's go.

They do not move.

Curtain.

Contemplating hanging themselves

ACT TWO

Next day. Same time.

Same place.

ESTRAGON's *boots front center, heels together, toes splayed.* LUCKY's *hat at same place. The tree has four or five leaves. Enter* VLADIMIR *agitatedly. He halts and looks long at the tree, then suddenly begins to move feverishly about the stage. He halts before the boots, picks one up, examines it, sniffs it, manifests disgust, puts it back carefully Comes and goes. Halts extreme right and gazes into distance off, shading his eyes with his hand. Comes and goes. Halts extreme left, as before. Comes and goes. Halts suddenly and begins to sing loudly*

VLADIMIR:
              A dog came in—

(Having begun too high he stops, clears his throat, resumes.)

              A dog came in the kitchen
              And stole a crust of bread.
              Then cook up with a ladle
              And beat him till he was dead.

              Then all the dogs came running
              And dug the dog a tomb—

(He stops, broods, resumes.)

              Then all the dogs came running
              And dug the dog a tomb
              And wrote upon the tombstone
              For the eyes of dogs to come:

              A dog came in the kitchen

And stole a crust of bread.
Then cook up with a ladle
And beat him till he was dead.

Then all the dogs came running
And dug the dog a tomb—

(He stops, broods, resumes.)

Then all the dogs came running
And dug the dog a tomb—

(He stops, broods. Softly.)

And dug the dog a tomb . . .

He remains a moment silent and motionless, then begins to move feverishly about the stage. He halts before the tree, comes and goes, before the boots, comes and goes, halts extreme right, gazes into distance, extreme left, gazes into distance. Enter ESTRAGON *right, barefoot, head bowed. He slowly crosses the stage.* VLADIMIR *turns and sees him.*

VLADIMIR: You again! (ESTRAGON *halts but does not raise his head.* VLADIMIR *goes towards him.*) Come here till I embrace you
ESTRAGON: Don't touch me!

VLADIMIR *holds back, pained.*

VLADIMIR: Do you want me to go away? (*Pause.*) Gogo! (*Pause.* VLADIMIR *observes him attentively.*) Did they beat you? (*Pause.*) Gogo! (ESTRAGON *remains silent, head bowed.*) Where did you spend the night?
ESTRAGON: Don't touch me! Don't question me! Don't speak to me! Stay with me!
VLADIMIR: Did I ever leave you?
ESTRAGON: You let me go.
VLADIMIR: Look at me. (ESTRAGON *does not raise his head. Violently.*) Will you look at me!

ESTRAGON *raises his head. They look long at each other, then suddenly embrace, clapping each other on the back. End of the embrace.* ESTRAGON, *no longer supported, almost falls.*

ESTRAGON: What a day!

VLADIMIR: Who beat you? Tell me.

ESTRAGON: Another day done with.

VLADIMIR: Not yet.

ESTRAGON: For me it's over and done with, no matter what happens. (*Silence.*) I heard you singing.

VLADIMIR: That's right, I remember.

ESTRAGON: That finished me. I said to myself, He's all alone, he thinks I'm gone for ever, and he sings.

VLADIMIR: One is not master of one's moods. All day I've felt in great form. (*Pause.*) I didn't get up in the night, not once!

ESTRAGON (*sadly*): You see, you piss better when I'm not there.

VLADIMIR: I missed you . . . and at the same time I was happy. Isn't that a queer thing?

ESTRAGON (*shocked*): Happy?

VLADIMIR: Perhaps it's not quite the right word.

ESTRAGON: And now?

VLADIMIR: Now? . . . (*Joyous.*) There you are again . . . (*Indifferent.*) There we are again . . . (*Gloomy.*) There I am again.

ESTRAGON: You see, you feel worse when I'm with you. I feel better alone too.

VLADIMIR (*vexed*): Then why do you always come crawling back?

ESTRAGON: I don't know.

VLADIMIR: No, but I do. It's because you don't know how to defend yourself. I wouldn't have let them beat you.

ESTRAGON: You couldn't have stopped them.

VLADIMIR: Why not?

ESTRAGON: There was ten of them.

VLADIMIR: No, I mean before they beat you. I would have stopped you from doing whatever it was you were doing.

ESTRAGON: I wasn't doing anything.

VLADIMIR: Then why did they beat you?

ESTRAGON: I don't know.

VLADIMIR: Ah no, Gogo, the truth is there are things escape you that don't escape me, you must feel it yourself.

ESTRAGON: I tell you I wasn't doing anything.

VLADIMIR: Perhaps you weren't. But it's the way of doing it that counts, the way of doing it, if you want to go on living.

ESTRAGON: I wasn't doing anything.

VLADIMIR: You must be happy too, deep down, if you only knew it.

ESTRAGON: Happy about what?

VLADIMIR: To be back with me again.

ESTRAGON: Would you say so?

VLADIMIR: Say you are, even if it's not true.

ESTRAGON: What am I to say?

VLADIMIR: Say, I am happy.

ESTRAGON: I am happy.

VLADIMIR: So am I.

ESTRAGON: So am I.

VLADIMIR: We are happy.

ESTRAGON: We are happy. (*Silence.*) What do we do now, now that we are happy?

VLADIMIR: Wait for Godot. (ESTRAGON *groans. Silence.*) Things have changed here since yesterday.

ESTRAGON: And if he doesn't come.

VLADIMIR (*after a moment of bewilderment*): We'll see when the time comes. (*Pause.*) I was saying that things have changed here since yesterday.

ESTRAGON: Everything oozes.

VLADIMIR: Look at the tree.

ESTRAGON: It's never the same pus from one second to the next.

VLADIMIR: The tree, look at the tree.

ESTRAGON *looks at the tree.*

ESTRAGON: Was it not there yesterday?

VLADIMIR: Yes of course it was there. Do you not remember? We nearly hanged ourselves from it. But you wouldn't. Do you not remember?

ESTRAGON: You dreamt it.

VLADIMIR: Is it possible you've forgotten already?

ESTRAGON: That's the way I am. Either I forget immediately or I never forget.

VLADIMIR: And Pozzo and Lucky, have you forgotten them too?

ESTRAGON: Pozzo and Lucky?

VLADIMIR: He's forgotten everything!

ESTRAGON: I remember a lunatic who kicked the shins off me. Then he played the fool.

VLADIMIR: That was Lucky.

ESTRAGON: I remember that. But when was it?

VLADIMIR: And his keeper, do you not remember him?

ESTRAGON: He gave me a bone.

VLADIMIR: That was Pozzo.

ESTRAGON: And all that was yesterday, you say?

VLADIMIR: Yes of course it was yesterday.

ESTRAGON: And here where we are now?

VLADIMIR: Where else do you think? Do you not recognize the place?

ESTRAGON (*suddenly furious*): Recognize! What is there to recognize? All my lousy life I've crawled about in the mud! And you talk to me about scenery! (*Looking wildly about him.*) Look at this muckheap! I've never stirred from it!

VLADIMIR: Calm yourself, calm yourself.

ESTRAGON: You and your landscapes! Tell me about the worms!

VLADIMIR: All the same, you can't tell me that this (*Gesture*) bears any resemblance to . . (*He hesitates.*) . . . to the Macon country for example. You can't deny there's a big difference.

ESTRAGON: The Macon country! Who's talking to you about the Macon country?

VLADIMIR: But you were there yourself, in the Macon country.

ESTRAGON: No I was never in the Macon country! I've puked my puke of a life away here, I tell you! Here! In the Cackon country!

VLADIMIR: But we were there together, I could swear to it! Picking grapes for a man called . . . (*He snaps his fingers.*) . . . can't think of the name of the man, at a place called . . . (*Snaps his fingers.*) . . . can't think of the name of the place, do you not remember?

ESTRAGON (*a little calmer*): It's possible. I didn't notice anything.

VLADIMIR: But down there everything is red!

ESTRAGON (*exasperated*): ɪ didn't notice anything, I tell you!

Silence. VLADIMIR *sighs deeply.*

VLADIMIR: You're a hard man to get on with, Gogo.

ESTRAGON: It'd be better if we parted.

VLADIMIR: You always say that and you always come crawling back.

ESTRAGON: The best thing would be to kill me, like the other.

VLADIMIR: What other? (*Pause.*) What other?

ESTRAGON: Like billions of others.

VLADIMIR (*sententious*): To every man his little cross. (*He sighs.*) Till he dies. (*Afterthought.*) And is forgotten.

ESTRAGON: In the meantime let us try and converse calmly, since we are incapable of keeping silent.

VLADIMIR: You're right, we're inexhaustible.

ESTRAGON: It's so we won't think. ◄— *why Talk?*

VLADIMIR: We have that excuse.

ESTRAGON: It's so we won't hear.

VLADIMIR: We have our reasons.

ESTRAGON: All the dead voices.

VLADIMIR: They make a noise like wings.

ESTRAGON: Like leaves.

VLADIMIR: Like sand.

ESTRAGON: Like leaves.

Silence.

Vladimir] never self
Estragon] reflect
not responsible
for everything

VLADIMIR: They all speak at once.

ESTRAGON: Each one to itself.

Silence.

voices ?

VLADIMIR: Rather they whisper.

ESTRAGON: They rustle.

VLADIMIR: They murmur.

ESTRAGON: They rustle.

Silence.

VLADIMIR: What do they say?

ESTRAGON: They talk about their lives.

VLADIMIR: To have lived is not enough for them.

ESTRAGON: They have to talk about it.

VLADIMIR: To be dead is not enough for them.

ESTRAGON: It is not sufficient.

Silence.

VLADIMIR: They make a noise like feathers.

ESTRAGON: Like leaves.
VLADIMIR: Like ashes.
ESTRAGON: Like leaves.

Long silence.

VLADIMIR: Say something!
ESTRAGON: I'm trying.

Long silence.

VLADIMIR (*in anguish*): Say anything at all!
ESTRAGON: What do we do now?
VLADIMIR: Wait for Godot.
ESTRAGON: Ah!

Silence.

VLADIMIR: This is awful!
ESTRAGON: Sing something.
VLADIMIR: No no! (*He reflects.*) We could start all over again perhaps.
ESTRAGON: That should be easy.
VLADIMIR: It's the start that's difficult.
ESTRAGON: You can start from anything.
VLADIMIR: Yes, but you have to decide.
ESTRAGON: True.

Silence.

VLADIMIR: Help me!
ESTRAGON: I'm trying.

Silence.

VLADIMIR: When you seek you hear.
ESTRAGON: You do.
VLADIMIR: That prevents you from finding.
ESTRAGON: It does.
VLADIMIR: That prevents you from thinking.
ESTRAGON: You think all the same.

VLADIMIR: No no, impossible.

ESTRAGON: That's the idea, let's contradict each other.

VLADIMIR: Impossible.

ESTRAGON: You think so?

VLADIMIR: We're in no danger of ever thinking any more.

ESTRAGON: Then what are we complaining about?

VLADIMIR: Thinking is not the worst.

ESTRAGON: Perhaps not. But at least there's that.

VLADIMIR: That what?

ESTRAGON: That's the idea, let's ask each other questions.

VLADIMIR: What do you mean, at least there's that?

ESTRAGON: That much less misery.

VLADIMIR: True.

ESTRAGON: Well? If we gave thanks for our mercies?

VLADIMIR: What is terrible is to *have* thought.

ESTRAGON: But did that ever happen to us?

VLADIMIR: Where are all these corpses from?

ESTRAGON: These skeletons.

VLADIMIR: Tell me that.

ESTRAGON: True.

VLADIMIR: We must have thought a little.

ESTRAGON: At the very beginning.

VLADIMIR: A charnel-house! A charnel-house!

ESTRAGON: You don't have to look.

VLADIMIR: You can't help looking.

ESTRAGON: True.

VLADIMIR: Try as one may.

ESTRAGON: I beg your pardon?

VLADIMIR: Try as one may.

ESTRAGON: We should turn resolutely towards Nature.

VLADIMIR: We've tried that.

ESTRAGON: True.

VLADIMIR: Oh it's not the worst, I know.

ESTRAGON: What?

VLADIMIR: To have thought.

ESTRAGON: Obviously.

VLADIMIR: But we could have done without it.

ESTRAGON: Que voulez-vous?

VLADIMIR: I beg your pardon?

ESTRAGON: Que voulez-vous.

VLADIMIR: Ah! que voulez-vous. Exactly.

Silence.

ESTRAGON: That wasn't such a bad little canter.
VLADIMIR: Yes, but now we'll have to find something else.
ESTRAGON: Let me see. (*He takes off his hat, concentrates.*)
VLADIMIR: Let me see. (*He takes off his hat, concentrates. Long silence.*) Ah!

They put on their hats, relax.

ESTRAGON: Well?
VLADIMIR: What was I saying, we could go on from there.
ESTRAGON: What were you saying when?
VLADIMIR: At the very beginning.
ESTRAGON: The very beginning of WHAT?
VLADIMIR: This evening . . . I was saying . . . I was saying . . .
ESTRAGON: I'm not a historian.
VLADIMIR: Wait . . . we embraced . . . we were happy . . . happy . .
   what do we do now that we're happy . . . go on waiting . . . wait-
   ing . . . let me think . . . it's coming . . . go on waiting . . . now
   that we're happy . . . let me see .   ah! The tree!
ESTRAGON: The tree?
VLADIMIR: Do you not remember?
ESTRAGON: I'm tired.
VLADIMIR: Look at it.

They look at the tree.

ESTRAGON: I see nothing.
VLADIMIR: But yesterday evening it was all black and bare. And now
   it's covered with leaves.
ESTRAGON: Leaves?
VLADIMIR: In a single night.
ESTRAGON: It must be the Spring.
VLADIMIR: But in a single night!
ESTRAGON: I tell you we weren't here yesterday. Another of your
   nightmares.
VLADIMIR: And where were we yesterday evening according to you?

ESTRAGON: How would I know? In another compartment. There's no lack of void.

VLADIMIR (*sure of himself*): Good. We weren't here yesterday evening. Now what did we do yesterday evening?

ESTRAGON: Do?

VLADIMIR: Try and remember.

ESTRAGON: Do . . . I suppose we blathered.

VLADIMIR (*controlling himself*): About what?

ESTRAGON: Oh . . . this and that I suppose, nothing in particular. (*With assurance.*) Yes, now I remember, yesterday evening we spent blathering about nothing in particular. That's been going on now for half a century.

VLADIMIR: You don't remember any fact, any circumstance?

ESTRAGON (*weary*): Don't torment me, Didi.

VLADIMIR: The sun. The moon. Do you not remember?

ESTRAGON: They must have been there, as usual.

VLADIMIR: You didn't notice anything out of the ordinary?

ESTRAGON: Alas!

VLADIMIR: And Pozzo? And Lucky?

ESTRAGON: Pozzo?

VLADIMIR: The bones.

ESTRAGON: They were like fishbones.

VLADIMIR: It was Pozzo gave them to you.

ESTRAGON: I don't know.

VLADIMIR: And the kick.

ESTRAGON: That's right, someone gave me a kick.

VLADIMIR: It was Lucky gave it to you.

ESTRAGON: And all that was yesterday?

VLADIMIR: Show your leg.

ESTRAGON: Which?

VLADIMIR: Both. Pull up your trousers. (ESTRAGON *gives a leg to* VLADIMIR, *staggers.* VLADIMIR *takes the leg. They stagger.*) Pull up your trousers.

ESTRAGON: I can't.

VLADIMIR *pulls up the trousers, looks at the leg, lets it go.* ESTRAGON *almost falls.*

VLADIMIR: The other. (ESTRAGON *gives the same leg.*) The other, pig!

(ESTRAGON *gives the other leg. Triumphantly*.) There's the wound!
Beginning to fester!

ESTRAGON: And what about it?

VLADIMIR (*letting go the leg*): Where are your boots?

ESTRAGON: I must have thrown them away.

VLADIMIR: When?

ESTRAGON: I don't know.

VLADIMIR: Why?

ESTRAGON (*exasperated*): I don't know why I don't know!

VLADIMIR: No, I mean why did you throw them away?

ESTRAGON (*exasperated*): Because they were hurting me!

VLADIMIR (*triumphantly, pointing to the boots*): There they are!
(ESTRAGON *looks at the boots*.) At the very spot where you left
them yesterday!

ESTRAGON *goes towards the boots, inspects them closely*.

ESTRAGON: They're not mine.

VLADIMIR (*stupefied*): Not yours!

ESTRAGON: Mine were black. These are brown.

VLADIMIR: You're sure yours were black?

ESTRAGON: Well they were a kind of gray.

VLADIMIR: And these are brown. Show.

ESTRAGON (*picking up a boot*): Well they're a kind of green.

VLADIMIR: Show. (ESTRAGON *hands him the boot*. VLADIMIR *inspects it,
throws it down angrily*.) Well of all the—

ESTRAGON: You see, all that's a lot of bloody—

VLADIMIR: Ah! I see what it is. Yes, I see what's happened.

ESTRAGON: All that's a lot of bloody—

VLADIMIR: It's elementary. Someone came and took yours and left you
his.

ESTRAGON: Why?

VLADIMIR: His were too tight for him, so he took yours.

ESTRAGON: But mine were too tight.

VLADIMIR: For you. Not for him.

ESTRAGON (*having tried in vain to work it out*): I'm tired! (*Pause*.)
Let's go.

VLADIMIR: We can't.

ESTRAGON: Why not?

VLADIMIR: We're waiting for Godot.

ESTRAGON: Ah! (*Pause. Despairing.*) What'll we do, what'll we do!

VLADIMIR: There's nothing we can do.

ESTRAGON: But I can't go on like this!

VLADIMIR: Would you like a radish?

ESTRAGON: Is that all there is?

VLADIMIR: There are radishes and turnips.

ESTRAGON: Are there no carrots?

VLADIMIR: No. Anyway you overdo it with your carrots.

ESTRAGON: Then give me a radish. (VLADIMIR *fumbles in his pockets, finds nothing but turnips, finally brings out a radish and hands it to* ESTRAGON *who examines it, sniffs it.*) It's black!

VLADIMIR: It's a radish.

ESTRAGON: I only like the pink ones, you know that!

VLADIMIR: Then you don't want it?

ESTRAGON: I only like the pink ones!

VLADIMIR: Then give it back to me.

ESTRAGON *gives it back.*

ESTRAGON: I'll go and get a carrot.

He does not move.

VLADIMIR: This is becoming really insignificant.

ESTRAGON: Not enough.

Silence.

VLADIMIR: What about trying them.

ESTRAGON: I've tried everything.

VLADIMIR: No, I mean the boots.

ESTRAGON: Would that be a good thing?

VLADIMIR: It'd pass the time. (ESTRAGON *hesitates.*) I assure you, it'd be an occupation.

ESTRAGON: A relaxation.

VLADIMIR: A recreation.

ESTRAGON: A relaxation.

VLADIMIR: Try.

ESTRAGON: You'll help me?

VLADIMIR: I will of course.

ESTRAGON: We don't manage too badly, eh Didi, between the two of us?

VLADIMIR: Yes yes. Come on, we'll try the left first.

ESTRAGON: We always find something, eh Didi, to give us the impression we exist?

VLADIMIR (*impatiently*): Yes yes, we're magicians. But let us persevere in what we have resolved, before we forget. (*He picks up a boot.*) Come on, give me your foot. (ESTRAGON *raises his foot.*) The other, hog! (ESTRAGON *raises the other foot.*) Higher! (*Wreathed together they stagger about the stage.* VLADIMIR *succeeds finally in getting on the boot.*) Try and walk. (ESTRAGON *walks.*) Well?

ESTRAGON: It fits.

VLADIMIR (*taking string from his pocket*): We'll try and lace it.

ESTRAGON (*vehemently*): No no, no laces, no laces!

VLADIMIR: You'll be sorry. Let's try the other. (*As before.*) Well?

ESTRAGON (*grudgingly*): It fits too.

VLADIMIR: They don't hurt you?

ESTRAGON: Not yet.

VLADIMIR: Then you can keep them.

ESTRAGON: They're too big.

VLADIMIR: Perhaps you'll have socks some day.

ESTRAGON: True.

VLADIMIR: Then you'll keep them?

ESTRAGON: That's enough about these boots.

VLADIMIR: Yes, but—

ESTRAGON (*violently*): Enough! (*Silence.*) I suppose I might as well sit down.

He looks for a place to sit down, then goes and sits down on the mound.

VLADIMIR: That's where you were sitting yesterday evening.

ESTRAGON: If I could only sleep.

VLADIMIR: Yesterday you slept.

ESTRAGON: I'll try.

He resumes his foetal posture, his head between his knees.

VLADIMIR: Wait. (*He goes over and sits down beside* ESTRAGON *and begins to sing in a loud voice.*)

> Bye bye bye bye
> Bye bye—

ESTRAGON (*looking up angrily*): Not so loud!

VLADIMIR (*softly*):

> Bye bye bye bye
> Bye bye bye bye
> Bye bye bye bye
> Bye bye . . .

ESTRAGON *sleeps.* VLADIMIR *gets up softly, takes off his coat and lays it across* ESTRAGON'S *shoulders, then starts walking up and down, swinging his arms to keep himself warm.* ESTRAGON *wakes with a start, jumps up, casts about wildly.* VLADIMIR *runs to him, puts his arms round him.*

There . . . there . . . Didi is there . . . don't be afraid . . .

ESTRAGON: Ah!

VLADIMIR: There . . . there . . . it's all over.

ESTRAGON: I was falling—

VLADIMIR: It's all over, it's all over.

ESTRAGON: I was on top of a—

VLADIMIR: Don't tell me! Come, we'll walk it off.

He takes ESTRAGON *by the arm and walks him up and down until* ESTRAGON *refuses to go any further.*

ESTRAGON: That's enough. I'm tired.

VLADIMIR: You'd rather be stuck there doing nothing?

ESTRAGON: Yes.

VLADIMIR: Please yourself.

He releases ESTRAGON, *picks up his coat and puts it on.*

ESTRAGON: Let's go.

VLADIMIR: We can't.

ESTRAGON: Why not?

VLADIMIR: We're waiting for Godot.

ESTRAGON: Ah!

VLADIMIR *walks up and down.*

Can you not stay still?

VLADIMIR: I'm cold.

ESTRAGON: We came too soon.

VLADIMIR: It's always at nightfall.

ESTRAGON: But night doesn't fall.

VLADIMIR: It'll fall all of a sudden, like yesterday.

ESTRAGON: Then it'll be night.

VLADIMIR: And we can go.

ESTRAGON: Then it'll be day again. (*Pause. Despairing.*) What'll we do, what'll we do!

VLADIMIR (*halting, violently*): Will you stop whining! I've had about my bellyful of your lamentations!

ESTRAGON: I'm going.

VLADIMIR (*seeing* LUCKY's *hat*): Well!

ESTRAGON: Farewell.

VLADIMIR: Lucky's hat. (*He goes towards it.*) I've been here an hour and never saw it. (*Very pleased.*) Fine!

ESTRAGON: You'll never see me again.

VLADIMIR: I knew it was the right place. Now our troubles are over. (*He picks up the hat, contemplates it, straightens it.*) Must have been a very fine hat. (*He puts it on in place of his own which he hands to* ESTRAGON.) Here.

ESTRAGON: What?

VLADIMIR: Hold that.

ESTRAGON *takes* VLADIMIR's *hat.* VLADIMIR *adjusts* LUCKY's *hat on his head.* ESTRAGON *puts on* VLADIMIR's *hat in place of his own which he hands to* VLADIMIR. VLADIMIR *takes* ESTRAGON's *hat.* ESTRAGON *adjusts* VLADIMIR's *hat on his head.* VLADIMIR *puts on* ESTRAGON's *hat in place of* LUCKY's *which he hands to* ESTRAGON. ESTRAGON *takes* LUCKY's *hat.* VLADIMIR *adjusts* ETRAGON's *hat on his head.* ESTRAGON *puts on* LUCKY's *hat in place of* VLADIMIR's *which he hands to* VLADIMIR. VLADIMIR *takes his hat.* ESTRAGON *adjusts* LUCKY's *hat on his head.* VLADIMIR *puts on his hat in place of* ESTRAGON's *which he hands to* ESTRAGON. ESTRAGON *takes his hat.* VLADIMIR *adjusts his hat on his head.* ESTRAGON *puts on his hat in place of* LUCKY's *which he hands*

to VLADIMIR. VLADIMIR *takes* LUCKY'S *hat.* ESTRAGON *adjusts his
hat on his head.* VLADIMIR *puts on* LUCKY'S *hat in place of
his own which he hands to* ESTRAGON. ESTRAGON *takes* VLADIMIR'S
hat. VLADIMIR *adjusts* LUCKY'S *hat on his head.* ESTRAGON *hands*
VLADIMIR'S *hat back to* VLADIMIR *who takes it and hands it
back to* ESTRAGON *who takes it and hands it back to* VLADIMIR
who takes it and throws it down.

How does it fit me?

ESTRAGON: How would I know?

VLADIMIR: No, but how do I look in it?

*He turns his head coquettishly to and fro, minces like a man-
nequin.*

ESTRAGON: Hideous.

VLADIMIR: Yes, but not more so than usual?

ESTRAGON: Neither more nor less.

VLADIMIR: Then I can keep it. Mine irked me. (*Pause.*) How shall I
say? (*Pause.*) It itched me.

He takes off LUCKY'S *hat, peers into it, shakes it, knocks on the
crown, puts it on again.*

ESTRAGON: I'm going.

Silence.

VLADIMIR: Will you not play?

ESTRAGON: Play at what?

VLADIMIR: We could play at Pozzo and Lucky.

ESTRAGON: Never heard of it.

VLADIMIR: I'll do Lucky, you do Pozzo. (*He imitates* LUCKY *sagging
under the weight of his baggage.* ESTRAGON *looks at him with
stupefaction.*) Go on.

ESTRAGON: What am I to do?

VLADIMIR: Curse me!

ESTRAGON (*after reflection*): Naughty!

VLADIMIR: Stronger!

ESTRAGON: Gonococcus! Spirochete!

Gonorrea   Siphilis

VLADIMIR *sways back and forth, doubled in two.*

VLADIMIR: Tell me to think.
ESTRAGON: What?
VLADIMIR: Say, Think, pig!
ESTRAGON: Think, pig!

Silence.

VLADIMIR: I can't!
ESTRAGON: That's enough of that.
VLADIMIR: Tell me to dance.
ESTRAGON: I'm going.
VLADIMIR: Dance, hog! (*He writhes. Exit* ESTRAGON *left, precipitately.*) I can't! (*He looks up, misses* ESTRAGON.) Gogo! (*He moves wildly about the stage. Enter* ESTRAGON *left, panting. He hastens towards* VLADIMIR, *falls into his arms.*) There you are again at last!
ESTRAGON: I'm accursed!
VLADIMIR: Where were you? I thought you were gone for ever.
ESTRAGON: They're coming!
VLADIMIR: Who?
ESTRAGON: I don't know.
VLADIMIR: How many?
ESTRAGON: I don't know.
VLADIMIR (*triumphantly*): It's Godot! At last! Gogo! It's Godot! We're saved! Let's go and meet him! (*He drags* ESTRAGON *towards the wings.* ESTRAGON *resists, pulls himself free, exit right.*) Gogo! Come back! (VLADIMIR *runs to extreme left, scans the horizon. Enter* ESTRAGON *right, he hastens towards* VLADIMIR, *falls into his arms.*) There you are again again!
ESTRAGON: I'm in hell!
VLADIMIR: Where were you?
ESTRAGON: They're coming there too!
VLADIMIR: We're surrounded! (ESTRAGON *makes a rush towards back.*) Imbecile! There's no way out there. (*He takes* ESTRAGON *by the arm and drags him towards front. Gesture towards front.*) There! Not a soul in sight! Off you go! Quick! (*He pushes* ESTRAGON *towards auditorium.* ESTRAGON *recoils in horror.*) You won't? (*He contemplates auditorium.*) Well I can understand that. Wait till I see. (*He reflects.*) Your only hope left is to disappear.

ESTRAGON: Where?

VLADIMIR: Behind the tree. (ESTRAGON *hesitates.*) Quick! Behind the tree. (ESTRAGON *goes and crouches behind the tree, realizes he is not hidden, comes out from behind the tree.*) Decidedly this tree will not have been the slightest use to us.

ESTRAGON (*calmer*): I lost my head. Forgive me. It won't happen again. Tell me what to do.

VLADIMIR: There's nothing to do.

ESTRAGON: You go and stand there. (*He draws* VLADIMIR *to extreme right and places him with his back to the stage.*) There, don't move, and watch out. (VLADIMIR *scans horizon, screening his eyes with his hand.* ESTRAGON *runs and takes up same position extreme left. They turn their heads and look at each other.*) Back to back like in the good old days. (*They continue to look at each other for a moment, then resume their watch. Long silence.*) Do you see anything coming?

VLADIMIR (*turning his head*): What?

ESTRAGON (*louder*): Do you see anything coming?

VLADIMIR: No.

ESTRAGON: Nor I.

They resume their watch. Silence.

VLADIMIR: You must have had a vision.

ESTRAGON (*turning his head*): What?

VLADIMIR (*louder*): You must have had a vision.

ESTRAGON: No need to shout!

They resume their watch. Silence.

VLADIMIR }
ESTRAGON } (*turning simultaneously*): Do you—

VLADIMIR: Oh pardon!

ESTRAGON: Carry on.

VLADIMIR: No no, after you.

ESTRAGON: No no, you first.

VLADIMIR: I interrupted you.

ESTRAGON: On the contrary.

They glare at each other angrily.

VLADIMIR: Ceremonious ape!

ESTRAGON: Punctilious pig!

VLADIMIR: Finish your phrase, I tell you!

ESTRAGON: Finish your own!

Silence. They draw closer, halt.

VLADIMIR: Moron!

ESTRAGON: That's the idea, let's abuse each other.

They turn, move apart, turn again and face each other.

VLADIMIR: Moron!

ESTRAGON: Vermin!

VLADIMIR: Abortion!

ESTRAGON: Morpion!

VLADIMIR: Sewer-rat!

ESTRAGON: Curate!

VLADIMIR: Cretin!

ESTRAGON (*with finality*): Crritic!

VLADIMIR: Oh!

He wilts, vanquished, and turns away.

ESTRAGON: Now let's make it up.

VLADIMIR: Gogo!

ESTRAGON: Didi!

VLADIMIR: Your hand!

ESTRAGON: Take it!

VLADIMIR: Come to my arms!

ESTRAGON: Your arms?

VLADIMIR: My breast!

ESTRAGON: Off we go!

They embrace. They separate. Silence.

VLADIMIR: How time flies when one has fun!

Silence.

ESTRAGON: What do we do now?
VLADIMIR: While waiting.
ESTRAGON: While waiting.

Silence.

VLADIMIR: We could do our exercises.
ESTRAGON: Our movements.
VLADIMIR: Our elevations.
ESTRAGON: Our relaxations.
VLADIMIR: Our elongations.
ESTRAGON: Our relaxations.
VLADIMIR: To warm us up.
ESTRAGON: To calm us down.
VLADIMIR: Off we go.

VLADIMIR *hops from one foot to the other.* ESTRAGON *imitates him.*

ESTRAGON (*stopping*): That enough. I'm tired.
VLADIMIR (*stopping*): We're not in form. What about a little deep breathing?
ESTRAGON: I'm tired breathing.
VLADIMIR: You're right. (*Pause.*) Let's just do the tree, for the balance.
ESTRAGON: The tree?

VLADIMIR *does the tree, staggering about on one leg.*

VLADIMIR (*stopping*): Your turn.

ESTRAGON *does the tree, staggers.*

ESTRAGON: Do you think God sees me?
VLADIMIR: You must close your eyes.

ESTRAGON *closes his eyes, staggers worse.*

ESTRAGON (*stopping, brandishing his fists, at the top of his voice*): God have pity on me!
VLADIMIR (*vexed*): And me?

ESTRAGON: On me! On me! Pity! On me!

> *Enter* POZZO *and* LUCKY. POZZO *is blind.* LUCKY *burdened as before. Rope as before, but much shorter, so that* POZZO *may follow more easily.* LUCKY *wearing a different hat. At the sight of* VLADIMIR *and* ESTRAGON *he stops short.* POZZO, *continuing on his way, bumps into him.*

VLADIMIR: Gogo!

POZZO (*clutching on to* LUCKY *who staggers*): What is it? Who is it?

> LUCKY *falls, drops everything and brings down* POZZO *with him They lie helpless among the scattered baggage.*

ESTRAGON: It is Godot?

VLADIMIR: At last! (*He goes towards the heap.*) Reinforcements at last!

POZZO: Help!

ESTRAGON: Is it Godot?

VLADIMIR: We were beginning to weaken. Now we're sure to see the evening out.

POZZO: Help!

ESTRAGON: Do you hear him?

VLADIMIR: We are no longer alone, waiting for the night, waiting for Godot, waiting for . . . waiting. All evening we have struggled, unassisted. Now it's over. It's already to-morrow.

POZZO: Help!

VLADIMIR: Time flows again already. The sun will set, the moon rise and we away . . . from here.

POZZO: Pity!

VLADIMIR: Poor Pozzo!

ESTRAGON: I knew it was him.

VLADIMIR: Who?

ESTRAGON: Godot.

VLADIMIR: But it's not Godot.

ESTRAGON: It's not Godot?

VLADIMIR: It's not Godot.

ESTRAGON: Then who is it?

VLADIMIR: It's Pozzo.

POZZO: Here! Here! Help me up!

VLADIMIR: He can't get up.

ESTRAGON: Let's go.

VLADIMIR: We can't.

ESTRAGON: Why not?

VLADIMIR: We're waiting for Godot.

ESTRAGON: Ah!

VLADIMIR: Perhaps he has another bone for you.

ESTRAGON: Bone?

VLADIMIR: Chicken. Do you not remember?

ESTRAGON: It was him?

VLADIMIR: Yes.

ESTRAGON: Ask him.

VLADIMIR: Perhaps we should help him first.

ESTRAGON: To do what?

VLADIMIR: To get up.

ESTRAGON: He can't get up?

VLADIMIR: He wants to get up.

ESTRAGON: Then let him get up.

VLADIMIR: He can't.

ESTRAGON: Why not?

VLADIMIR: I don't know.

POZZO *writhes, groans, beats the ground with his fists.*

ESTRAGON: We should ask him for the bone first. Then if he refuses we'll leave him there.

VLADIMIR: You mean we have him at our mercy?

ESTRAGON: Yes.

VLADIMIR: And that we should subordinate our good offices to certain conditions?

ESTRAGON: What?

VLADIMIR: That seems intelligent all right. But there's one thing I'm afraid of.

POZZO: Help!

ESTRAGON: What?

VLADIMIR: That Lucky might get going all of a sudden. Then we'd be ballocksed.

ESTRAGON: Lucky?

VLADIMIR: The one that went for you yesterday.

ESTRAGON: I tell you there was ten of them.

VLADIMIR: No, before that, the one that kicked you.

ESTRAGON: Is he there?

VLADIMIR: As large as life. (*Gesture towards* LUCKY.) For the moment he is inert. But he might run amuck any minute.

POZZO: Help!

ESTRAGON: And suppose we gave him a good beating the two of us?

VLADIMIR: You mean if we fell on him in his sleep?

ESTRAGON: Yes.

VLADIMIR: That seems a good idea all right. But could we do it? Is he really asleep? (*Pause.*) No, the best would be to take advantage of Pozzo's calling for help—

POZZO: Help!

VLADIMIR: To help him—

ESTRAGON: *We* help *him?*

VLADIMIR: In anticipation of some tangible return.

ESTRAGON: And suppose he—

VLADIMIR: Let us not waste our time in idle discourse! (*Pause. Vehemently.*) Let us do something, while we have the chance! It is not every day that we are needed. Not indeed that we personally are needed. Others would meet the case equally well, if not better. To all mankind they were addressed, those cries for help still ringing in our ears! But at this place, at this moment of time, all mankind is us, whether we like it or not. Let us make the most of it, before it is too late! Let us represent worthily for once the foul brood to which a cruel fate consigned us! What do you say? (ESTRAGON *says nothing.*) It is true that when with folded arms we weigh the pros and cons we are no less a credit to our species. The tiger bounds to the help of his congeners without the least reflexion, or else he slinks away into the depths of the thickets. But that is not the question. What are we doing here, *that* is the question. And we are blessed in this, that we happen to know the answer. Yes, in this immense confusion one thing alone is clear. We are waiting for Godot to come—

ESTRAGON: Ah!

POZZO: Help!

VLADIMIR: Or for night to fall. (*Pause.*) We have kept our appointment and that's an end to that. We are not saints, but we have kept our appointment. How many people can boast as much?

ESTRAGON: Billions.

VLADIMIR: You think so?

ESTRAGON: I don't know.

VLADIMIR: You may be right.

POZZO: Help!

VLADIMIR: All I know is that the hours are long, under these conditions, and constrain us to beguile them with proceedings which—how shall I say—which may at first sight seem reasonable, until they become a habit. You may say it is to prevent our reason from foundering. No doubt. But has it not long been straying in the night without end of the abyssal depths? That's what I sometimes wonder. You follow my reasoning?

ESTRAGON (*aphoristic for once*): We are all born mad. Some remain so.

POZZO: Help! I'll pay you!

ESTRAGON: How much?

POZZO: One hundred francs!

ESTRAGON: It's not enough.

VLADIMIR: I wouldn't go so far as that.

ESTRAGON: You think it's enough?

VLADIMIR: No, I mean so far as to assert that I was weak in the head when I came into the world. But that is not the question.

POZZO: Two hundred!

VLADIMIR: We wait. We are bored. (*He throws up his hand.*) No, don't protest, we are bored to death, there's no denying it. Good. A diversion comes along and what do we do? We let it go to waste. Come, let's get to work! (*He advances towards the heap, stops in his stride.*) In an instant all will vanish and we'll be alone once more, in the midst of nothingness! (*He broods.*)

POZZO: Two hundred!

VLADIMIR: We're coming!

He tries to pull POZZO *to his feet, fails, tries again, stumbles, falls, tries to get up, fails.*

ESTRAGON: What's the matter with you all?

VLADIMIR: Help!

ESTRAGON: I'm going.

VLADIMIR: Don't leave me! They'll kill me!

POZZO: Where am I?

VLADIMIR: Gogo!

POZZO: Help!

VLADIMIR: Help!

ESTRAGON: I'm going.

VLADIMIR: Help me up first, then we'll go together.

ESTRAGON: You promise?

VLADIMIR: I swear it!

ESTRAGON: And we'll never come back?

VLADIMIR: Never!

ESTRAGON: We'll go to the Pyrenees.

VLADIMIR: Wherever you like.

ESTRAGON: I've always wanted to wander in the Pyrenees.

VLADIMIR: You'll wander in them.

ESTRAGON (*recoiling*): Who farted?

VLADIMIR: Pozzo.

POZZO: Here! Here! Pity!

ESTRAGON: It's revolting!

VLADIMIR: Quick! Give me your hand!

ESTRAGON: I'm going. (*Pause. Louder.*) I'm going.

VLADIMIR: Well I suppose in the end I'll get up by myself. (*He tries, fails.*) In the fullness of time.

ESTRAGON: What's the matter with you?

VLADIMIR: Go to hell.

ESTRAGON: Are you staying there?

VLADIMIR: For the time being.

ESTRAGON: Come on, get up, you'll catch a chill.

VLADIMIR: Don't worry about me.

ESTRAGON: Come on, Didi, don't be pig-headed!

He stretches out his hand which VLADIMIR *makes haste to seize.*

VLADIMIR: Pull!

ESTRAGON *pulls, stumbles, falls. Long silence.*

POZZO: Help!

VLADIMIR: We've arrived.

POZZO: Who are you?

VLADIMIR: We are men.

Silence.

ESTRAGON: Sweet mother earth!

VLADIMIR: Can you get up?

ESTRAGON: I don't know.

VLADIMIR: Try.

ESTRAGON: Not now, not now.

Silence.

POZZO: What happened?

VLADIMIR (*violently*): Will you stop it, you! Pest! He can think of nothing but himself!

ESTRAGON: What about a little snooze?

VLADIMIR: Did you hear him? He wants to know what happened!

ESTRAGON: Don't mind him. Sleep.

Silence.

POZZO: Pity! Pity!

ESTRAGON (*with a start*): What is it?

VLADIMIR: Were you asleep?

ESTRAGON: I must have been.

VLADIMIR: It's this bastard Pozzo at it again.

ESTRAGON: Make him stop it. Kick him in the crotch.

VLADIMIR (*striking* POZZO): Will you stop it! Crablouse! (POZZO *extricates himself with cries of pain and crawls away. He stops, saws the air blindly, calling for help.* VLADIMIR, *propped on his elbow, observes his retreat.*) He's off! (POZZO *collapses.*) He's down!

ESTRAGON: What do we do now?

VLADIMIR: Perhaps I could crawl to him.

ESTRAGON: Don't leave me!

VLADIMIR: Or I could call to him.

ESTRAGON: Yes, call to him.

VLADIMIR: Pozzo! (*Silence.*) Pozzo! (*Silence.*) No reply.

ESTRAGON: Together.

VLADIMIR: }
ESTRAGON: } Pozzo! Pozzo!

VLADIMIR: He moved.

ESTRAGON: Are you sure his name is Pozzo?

VLADIMIR (*alarmed*): Mr. Pozzo! Come back! We won't hurt you!

Silence.

ESTRAGON: We might try him with other names.
VLADIMIR: I'm afraid he's dying.
ESTRAGON: It'd be amusing.
VLADIMIR: What'd be amusing?
ESTRAGON: To try him with other names, one after the other. It'd pass the time. And we'd be bound to hit on the right one sooner or later.
VLADIMIR: I tell you his name is Pozzo.
ESTRAGON: We'll soon see. (*He reflects.*) Abel! Abel!
POZZO: Help!
ESTRAGON: Got it in one!
VLADIMIR: I begin to weary of this motif.
ESTRAGON: Perhaps the other is called Cain. Cain! Cain!
POZZO: Help!
ESTRAGON: He's all humanity. (*Silence.*) Look at the little cloud.
VLADIMIR (*raising his eyes*): Where?
ESTRAGON: There. In the zenith.
VLADIMIR: Well? (*Pause.*) What is there so wonderful about it?

Silence.

ESTRAGON: Let's pass on now to something else, do you mind?
VLADIMIR: I was just going to suggest it.
ESTRAGON: But to what?
VLADIMIR: Ah!

Silence.

ESTRAGON: Suppose we got up to begin with?
VLADIMIR: No harm trying.

They get up.

ESTRAGON: Child's play.
VLADIMIR: Simple question of will-power.
ESTRAGON: And now?
POZZO: Help!
ESTRAGON: Let's go.

VLADIMIR: We can't.

ESTRAGON: Why not?

VLADIMIR: We're waiting for Godot.

ESTRAGON: Ah! (*Despairing.*) What'll we do, what'll we do!

POZZO: Help!

VLADIMIR: What about helping him?

ESTRAGON: What does he want?

VLADIMIR: He wants to get up.

ESTRAGON: Then why doesn't he?

VLADIMIR: He wants us to help him to get up.

ESTRAGON: Then why don't we? What are we waiting for?

They help POZZO *to his feet, let him go. He falls.*

VLADIMIR: We must hold him. (*They get him up again.* POZZO *sags between them, his arms round their necks.*) Feeling better?

POZZO: Who are you?

VLADIMIR: Do you not recognize us?

POZZO: I am blind.

Silence.

ESTRAGON: Perhaps he can see into the future.

VLADIMIR: Since when?

POZZO: I used to have wonderful sight—but are you friends?

ESTRAGON (*laughing noisily*): He wants to know if we are friends!

VLADIMIR: No, he means friends of his.

ESTRAGON: Well?

VLADIMIR: We've proved we are, by helping him.

ESTRAGON: Exactly. Would we have helped him if we weren't his friends?

VLADIMIR: Possibly.

ESTRAGON: True.

VLADIMIR: Don't let's quibble about that now.

POZZO: You are not highwaymen?

ESTRAGON: Highwaymen! Do we look like highwaymen?

VLADIMIR: Damn it can't you see the man is blind!

ESTRAGON: Damn it so he is. (*Pause.*) So he says.

POZZO: Don't leave me!

VLADIMIR: No question of it.

ESTRAGON: For the moment.

POZZO: What time is it?

VLADIMIR (*inspecting the sky*): Seven o'clock . . . eight o'clock . . .

ESTRAGON: That depends what time of year it is.

POZZO: Is it evening?

    Silence. VLADIMIR *and* ESTRAGON *scrutinize the sunset.*

ESTRAGON: It's rising.

VLADIMIR: Impossible.

ESTRAGON: Perhaps it's the dawn.

VLADIMIR: Don't be a fool. It's the west over there.

ESTRAGON: How do you know?

POZZO (*anguished*): Is it evening?

VLADIMIR: Anyway it hasn't moved.

ESTRAGON: I tell you it's rising.

POZZO: Why don't you answer me?

ESTRAGON: Give us a chance.

VLADIMIR (*reassuring*): It's evening, Sir, it's evening, night is drawing nigh. My friend here would have me doubt it and I must confess he shook me for a moment. But it is not for nothing I have lived through this long day and I can assure you it is very near the end of its repertory. (*Pause.*) How do you feel now?

ESTRAGON: How much longer are we to cart him around. (*They half release him, catch him again as he falls.*) We are not caryatids!

VLADIMIR: You were saying your sight used to be good, if I heard you right.

POZZO: Wonderful! Wonderful, wonderful sight!

    Silence.

ESTRAGON (*irritably*): Expand! Expand!

VLADIMIR: Let him alone. Can't you see he's thinking of the days when he was happy. (*Pause.*) *Memoria praeteritorum bonorum*—that must be unpleasant.

ESTRAGON: We wouldn't know.

VLADIMIR: And it came on you all of a sudden?

POZZO: Quite wonderful!

VLADIMIR: I'm asking you if it came on you all of a sudden

POZZO: I woke up one fine day as blind as Fortune. (*Pause.*) Sometimes I wonder if I'm not still asleep.

VLADIMIR: And when was that?

POZZO: I don't know.

VLADIMIR: But no later than yesterday—

POZZO (*violently*): Don't question me! The blind have no notion of time. The things of time are hidden from them too.

VLADIMIR: Well just fancy that! I could have sworn it was just the opposite.

ESTRAGON: I'm going.

POZZO: Where are we?

VLADIMIR: I couldn't tell you.

POZZO: It isn't by any chance the place known as the Board?

VLADIMIR: Never heard of it.

POZZO: What is it like?

VLADIMIR (*looking round*): It's indescribable. It's like nothing. There's nothing. There's a tree.

POZZO: Then it's not the Board.

ESTRAGON (*sagging*): Some diversion!

POZZO: Where is my menial?

VLADIMIR: He's about somewhere.

POZZO: Why doesn't he answer when I call?

VLADIMIR: I don't know. He seems to be sleeping. Perhaps he's dead.

POZZO: What happened exactly?

ESTRAGON: Exactly!

VLADIMIR: The two of you slipped. (*Pause.*) And fell.

POZZO: Go and see is he hurt.

VLADIMIR: We can't leave you.

POZZO: You needn't both go.

VLADIMIR (*to* ESTRAGON): You go.

ESTRAGON: After what he did to me? Never!

POZZO: Yes yes, let your friend go, he stinks so. (*Silence.*) What is he waiting for?

VLADIMIR: What you waiting for?

ESTRAGON: I'm waiting for Godot.

Silence.

VLADIMIR: What exactly should he do?

POZZO: Well to begin with he should pull on the rope, as hard as he likes so long as he doesn't strangle him. He usually responds to that. If not he should give him a taste of his boot, in the face and the privates as far as possible.

VLADIMIR (*to* ESTRAGON): You see, you've nothing to be afraid of. It's even an opportunity to revenge yourself.

ESTRAGON: And if he defends himself?

POZZO: No no, he never defends himself.

VLADIMIR: I'll come flying to the rescue.

ESTRAGON: Don't take your eyes off me.

He goes towards LUCKY.

VLADIMIR: Make sure he's alive before you start. No point in exerting yourself if he's dead.

ESTRAGON (*bending over* LUCKY): He's breathing.

VLADIMIR: Then let him have it.

With sudden fury ESTRAGON *starts kicking* LUCKY, *hurling abuse at him as he does so. But he hurts his foot and moves away, limping and groaning.* LUCKY *stirs.*

ESTRAGON: Oh the brute!

He sits down on the mound and tries to take off his boot. But he soon desists and disposes himself for sleep, his arms on his knees and his head on his arms.

POZZO: What's gone wrong now?

VLADIMIR: My friend has hurt himself.

POZZO: And Lucky?

VLADIMIR: So it is he?

POZZO: What?

VLADIMIR: It is Lucky?

POZZO: I don't understand.

VLADIMIR: And you are Pozzo?

POZZO: Certainly I am Pozzo.

VLADIMIR: The same as yesterday?

POZZO: Yesterday?

VLADIMIR: We met yesterday. (*Silence.*) Do you not remember?

POZZO: I don't remember having met anyone yesterday. But to-morrow

I won't remember having met anyone to-day. So don't count on me to enlighten you.

VLADIMIR: But—

POZZO: Enough! Up pig!

VLADIMIR: You were bringing him to the fair to sell him. You spoke to us. He danced. He thought. You had your sight.

POZZO: As you please. Let me go! (VLADIMIR *moves away.*) Up!

LUCKY *gets up, gathers up his burdens.*

VLADIMIR: Where do you go from here.

POZZO: On. (LUCKY, *laden down, takes his place before* POZZO.) Whip! (LUCKY *puts everything down, looks for whip, finds it, puts it into* POZZO's *hand, takes up everything again.*) Rope!

LUCKY *puts everything down, puts end of rope into* POZZO's *hand, takes up everything again.*

VLADIMIR: What is there in the bag?

POZZO: Sand. (*He jerks the rope.*) On!

VLADIMIR: Don't go yet.

POZZO: I'm going.

VLADIMIR: What do you do when you fall far from help?

POZZO: We wait till we can get up. Then we go on. On!

VLADIMIR: Before you go tell him to sing.

POZZO: Who?

VLADIMIR: Lucky.

POZZO: To sing?

VLADIMIR: Yes. Or to think. Or to recite.

POZZO: But he is dumb.

VLADIMIR: Dumb!

POZZO: Dumb. He can't even groan.

VLADIMIR: Dumb! Since when?

POZZO (*suddenly furious*): Have you not done tormenting me with your accursed time! It's abominable! When! When! One day, is that not enough for you, one day he went dumb, one day I went blind, one day we'll go deaf, one day we were born, one day we shall die, the same day, the same second, is that not enough for you? (*Calmer.*) They give birth astride of a grave, the light gleams an instant, then it's night once more. (*He jerks the rope.*) On!

> *Exeunt* POZZO *and* LUCKY. VLADIMIR *follows them to the edge of the stage, looks after them. The noise of falling, reinforced by mimic of* VLADIMIR, *announces that they are down again. Silence.* VLADIMIR *goes towards* ESTRAGON, *contemplates him a moment, then shakes him awake.*

ESTRAGON (*wild gestures, incorherent words. Finally*): Why will you never let me sleep?

VLADIMIR: I felt lonely.

ESTRAGON: I was dreaming I was happy.

VLADIMIR: That passed the time.

ESTRAGON: I was dreaming that—

VLADIMIR (*violently*): Don't tell me! (*Silence.*) I wonder is he really blind.

ESTRAGON: Blind? Who?

VLADIMIR: Pozzo.

ESTRAGON: Blind?

VLADIMIR: He told us he was blind.

ESTRAGON: Well what about it?

VLADIMIR: It seemed to me he saw us.

ESTRAGON: You dreamt it. (*Pause.*) Let's go. We can't. Ah! (*Pause.*) Are you sure it wasn't him?

VLADIMIR: Who?

ESTRAGON: Godot.

VLADIMIR: But who?

ESTRAGON: Pozzo.

VLADIMIR: Not at all! (*Less sure.*) Not at all! (*Still less sure.*) Not at all!

ESTRAGON: I suppose I might as well get up. (*He gets up painfully.*) Ow! Didi!

VLADIMIR: I don't know what to think any more.

ESTRAGON: My feet! (*He sits down again and tries to take off his boots.*) Help me!

VLADIMIR: Was I sleeping, while the others suffered? Am I sleeping now? To-morrow, when I wake, or think I do, what shall I say of to-day? That with Estragon my friend, at this place, until the fall of night, I waited for Godot? That Pozzo passed, with his

carrier, and that he spoke to us? Probably. But in all that what truth will there be? (ESTRAGON, *having struggled with his boots in vain, is dozing off again.* VLADIMIR *looks at him.*) He'll know nothing. He'll tell me about the blows he received and I'll give him a carrot. (*Pause.*) Astride of a grave and a difficult birth. Down in the hole, lingeringly, the grave-digger puts on the forceps. We have time to grow old. The air is full of our cries. (*He listens.*) But habit is a great deadener. (*He looks again at* ESTRAGON.) At me too someone is looking, of me too someone is saying, He is sleeping, he knows nothing, let him sleep on. (*Pause.*) I can't go on! (*Pause.*) What have I said?

He goes feverishly to and fro, halts finally at extreme left, broods. Enter BOY *right. He halts. Silence.*

BOY: Mister . . . (VLADIMIR *turns.*) Mister Albert . . .
VLADIMIR: Off we go again. (*Pause.*) Do you not recognize me?
BOY: No Sir.
VLADIMIR: It wasn't you came yesterday.
BOY: No Sir.
VLADIMIR: This is your first time.
BOY: Yes Sir.

Silence.

VLADIMIR: You have a message from Mr. Godot.
BOY: Yes Sir.
VLADIMIR: He won't come this evening.
BOY: No Sir.
VLADIMIR: But he'll come to-morrow.
BOY: Yes Sir.
VLADIMIR: Without fail.
BOY: Yes Sir.

Silence.

VLADIMIR: Did you meet anyone?
BOY: No Sir.
VLADIMIR: Two other . . . (*He hesitates.*) . . . men?
BOY: I didn't see anyone, Sir.

Silence.

VLADIMIR: What does he do, Mr. Godot? (*Silence.*) Do you hear me?
BOY: Yes Sir.
VLADIMIR: Well?
BOY: He does nothing, Sir.

Silence.

VLADIMIR: How is your brother?
BOY: He's sick, Sir.
VLADIMIR: Perhaps it was he came yesterday.
BOY: I don't know, Sir.

Silence.

VLADIMIR (*softly*): Has he a beard, Mr. Godot?
BOY: Yes Sir.
VLADIMIR: Fair or . . . (*He hesitates.*) . . . or black?
BOY: I think it's white, Sir.

Silence.

VLADIMIR: Christ have mercy on us!

Silence.

BOY: What am I to tell Mr. Godot, Sir?
VLADIMIR: Tell him . . . (*He hesitates.*) . . . tell him you saw me and
that . . .(*He hesitates.*) . . . that you saw me. (*Pause.* VLADIMIR
advances, the BOY *recoils.* VLADIMIR *halts, the* BOY *halts. With
sudden violence.*) You're sure you saw me, you won't come and
tell me to-morrow that you never saw me!

> *Silence.* VLADIMIR *makes a sudden spring forward, the* BOY
> *avoids him and exit running. Silence. The sun sets, the moon
> rises. As in Act One.* VLADIMIR *stands motionless and bowed.*
> ESTRAGON *wakes, takes off his boots, gets up with one in each
> hand and goes and puts them down center front, then goes
> towards* VLADIMIR.

ESTRAGON: What's wrong with you?
VLADIMIR: Nothing.
ESTRAGON: I'm going.
VLADIMIR: So am I.
ESTRAGON: Was I long asleep?
VLADIMIR: I don't know.

Silence.

ESTRAGON: Where shall we go?
VLADIMIR: Not far.
ESTRAGON: Oh yes, let's go far away from here.
VLADIMIR: We can't.
ESTRAGON: Why not?
VLADIMIR: We have to come back to-morrow.
ESTRAGON: What for?
VLADIMIR: To wait for Godot.
ESTRAGON: Ah! (*Silence.*) He didn't come?
VLADIMIR: No.
ESTRAGON: And now it's too late.
VLADIMIR: Yes, now it's night.
ESTRAGON: And if we dropped him? (*Pause.*) If we dropped him?
VLADIMIR: He'd punish us. (*Silence. He looks at the tree.*) Everything's dead but the tree.
ESTRAGON (*looking at the tree*): What is it?
VLADIMIR: It's the tree.
ESTRAGON: Yes, but what kind?
VLADIMIR: I don't know. A willow.

> ESTRAGON *draws* VLADIMIR *towards the tree. They stand motionless before it. Silence.*

ESTRAGON: Why don't we hang ourselves?
VLADIMIR: With what?
ESTRAGON: You haven't got a bit of rope?
VLADIMIR: No.
ESTRAGON: Then we can't.

Silence.

VLADIMIR: Let's go.

ESTRAGON: Wait, there's my belt.

VLADIMIR: It's too short.

ESTRAGON: You could hang on to my legs.

VLADIMIR: And who'd hang on to mine?

ESTRAGON: True.

VLADIMIR: Show all the same. (ESTRAGON *loosens the cord that holds up his trousers which, much too big for him, fall about his ankles. They look at the cord.*) It might do at a pinch. But is it strong enough?

ESTRAGON: We'll soon see. Here.

> *They each take an end of the cord and pull. It breaks. They almost fall.*

VLADIMIR: Not worth a curse.

> *Silence.*

ESTRAGON: You say we have to come back to-morrow?

VLADIMIR: Yes.

ESTRAGON: Then we can bring a good bit of rope.

VLADIMIR: Yes.

> *Silence.*

ESTRAGON: Didi.

VLADIMIR: Yes.

ESTRAGON: I can't go on like this.

VLADIMIR: That's what you think.

ESTRAGON: If we parted? That might be better for us.

VLADIMIR: We'll hang ourselves to-morrow. (*Pause.*) Unless Godot comes.

ESTRAGON: And if he comes?

VLADIMIR: We'll be saved.

> VLADIMIR *takes off his hat* (LUCKY'S), *peers inside it, feels about inside it, shakes it, knocks on the crown, puts it on again.*

ESTRAGON: Well? Shall we go?

VLADIMIR: Pull on your trousers.

ESTRAGON: What?

VLADIMIR: Pull on your trousers.

ESTRAGON: You want me to pull off my trousers?

VLADIMIR: Pull ON your trousers.

ESTRAGON (*realizing his trousers are down*): True. (*He pulls up his trousers.*)

VLADIMIR: Well? Shall we go?

ESTRAGON: Yes, let's go.

They do not move.

Curtain.

The
Visit

by
Friedrich Dürrenmatt

Translated by Patrick Bowles

CHARACTERS

Visitors:

Claire Zachanassian, née Wascher,
multi-millionairess,   Armenian
Oil
Her Husbands, VII-IX
Butler
Toby ⎱
Roby ⎰ gum-chewers
Koby ⎱
Loby ⎰ blind

Visited:
Ill
His wife
His son
His daughter
Mayor
Priest
Schoolmaster
Doctor
Policeman
Man One
Man Two
Man Three
Man Four
Painter
First woman
Second woman
Miss Louisa

Extras:
Station-master
Ticket Inspector
Guard
Bailiff

Distractors:
First Reporter
Second Reporter
Radio Commentator
Cameraman

PLACE: Guellen, a Smalltown

TIME: the Present

(Interval after Act Two)

ACT ONE

Clangor of railway-station bell before curtain rises to discover legend: 'Guellen'. Obviously name of small, skimpily depicted township in background: a tumbledown wreck. Equally ramshackle station-buildings may or may not be cordoned off, according to country, and include a rusty signal-cabin, its door marked 'No Entry'. Also depicted in bare outline, centre, the piteous Station Road. Left, a barren little building with tiled roof and mutilated posters on its windowless walls. A sign, at left corner: 'Ladies'. Another, at right corner: 'Gents'. This entire prospect steeped in hot autumn sun. In front of little building, a bench. On it, four men. An unspeakably ragged fifth (so are the other four) is inscribing letters in red paint on a banner clearly intended for some procession: 'Welcome Clarie'. Thunderous pounding din of express train rushing through. Men on bench show interest in express train by following its headlong rush with head movements from left to right.

MAN ONE. The Gudrun. Hamburg-Naples.

MAN TWO. The Racing Roland gets here at eleven twenty-seven. Venice-Stockholm.

MAN THREE. Our last remaining pleasure: watching trains go by.

MAN FOUR. Five years ago the Gudrun and the Racing Roland stopped in Guellen. And the Diplomat. And the Lorelei. All famous express trains.

MAN ONE. World famous.

MAN TWO. Now not even the commuting trains stop. Just two from Kaffigen and the one-thirteen from Kalberstadt.

MAN THREE. Ruined.

MAN FOUR. The Wagner Factory gone crash.

MAN ONE. Bockmann bankrupt.

MAN TWO. The Foundry on Sunshine Square shut down.

MAN THREE. Living on the dole.

MAN FOUR. On Poor Relief soup.

201

MAN ONE. Living?

MAN TWO. Vegetating.

MAN THREE. And rotting to death.

MAN FOUR. The entire township.

> (*Bell rings.*)

MAN TWO. It's more than time that millionairess got here. They say she founded a hospital in Kalberstadt.

MAN THREE. And a kindergarten in Kaffigen. And a memorial church in the Capital.

PAINTER. She had Zimt do her portrait. That Naturalistic dauber.

MAN ONE. She and her money. She owns Armenian Oil, Western Railways, North Broadcasting Company and the Hong Kong — uh — Amusement District.

> (*Train clatter. Station-master salutes. Men move heads from right to left after train.*)

MAN FOUR. The Diplomat.

MAN THREE. We were a city of the Arts, then.

MAN TWO. One of the foremost in the land.

MAN ONE. In Europe.

MAN FOUR. Goethe spent a night here. In the Golden Apostle.

MAN THREE. Brahms composed a quartet here.

> (*Bell rings.*)

MAN TWO. Bertold Schwarz invented gunpowder here.

PAINTER. And I was a brilliant student at the Ecole des Beaux Arts. And what am I doing here now? Sign-painting!

> (*Train clatter. Guard appears, left, as after jumping off train.*)

GUARD (*long-drawn wail*). Guellen!

MAN ONE. The Kaffigen commuter.

> (*One passenger has got off, left. He walks past men on bench, disappears through doorway marked 'Gents'.*)

MAN TWO. The Bailiff.

MAN THREE. Going to distrain on the Town Hall.

MAN FOUR. We're even ruined politically.

STATION-MASTER (*waves green flag, blows whistle*). Stand clear!
(*Enter from town, Mayor, Schoolmaster, Priest and Ill —
a man of near sixty-five; all shabbily dressed.*)

MAYOR. The guest of honour will be arriving on the one-
thirteen commuter from Kalberstadt.

SCHOOLMASTER. We'll have the mixed choir singing; the
Youth Club.

PRIEST. And the fire bell ringing. It hasn't been pawned.

MAYOR. We'll have the town band playing on Market Square.
The Athletics Club will honour the millionairess with a
pyramid. Then a meal in the Golden Apostle. Finances
unfortunately can't be stretched to illuminating the
Cathedral for the evening. Or the Town Hall.
(*Bailiff comes out of little building.*)

BAILIFF. Good morning, Mister Mayor, a very good morning
to you.

MAYOR. Why, Mister Glutz, what are you doing here?

BAILIFF. You know my mission, Mister Mayor. It's a colossal
undertaking I'm faced with. Just you try distraining on an
entire town.

MAYOR. You won't find a thing in the Town Hall. Apart from
one old typewriter.

BAILIFF. I think you're forgetting something, Mister Mayor.
The Guellen History Museum.

MAYOR. Gone three years ago. Sold to America. Our coffers
are empty. Not a single soul pays taxes.

BAILIFF. It'll have to be investigated. The country's booming
and Guellen has the Sunshine Foundry. But Guellen goes
bankrupt.

MAYOR. We're up against a real economic enigma.

MAN ONE. The whole thing's a Free Masons' plot.

MAN TWO. Conspired by the Jews.

MAN THREE. Backed by High Finance.

MAN FOUR. International Communism's showing its colours.
(*Bell rings.*)

BAILIFF. I always find something. I've got eyes like a hawk. I
think I'll take a look at the Treasury.
(*Exit.*)

MAYOR. Better let him plunder us first. Not after the millionairess's visit.
(*Painter has finished painting his banner.*)

ILL. You know, Mister Mayor, that won't do. This banner's
too familiar. It ought to read, 'Welcome Claire Zachanassian'.

MAN ONE. But she's Clarie!

MAN TWO. Clarie Wascher!

MAN THREE. She was educated here!

MAN FOUR. Her dad was the builder.

PAINTER. O.K., so I'll write 'Welcome Claire Zachanassian'
on the back. Then if the millionairess seems touched we
can turn it round and show her the front.

MAN TWO. It's the Speculator. Zürich-Hamburg.
(*Another express train passes. Right to left.*)

MAN THREE. Always on time, you can set your watch by it.

MAN FOUR. Tell me who still owns a watch in this place.

MAYOR. Gentlemen, the millionairess is our only hope.

PRIEST. Apart from God.

MAYOR. Apart from God.

SCHOOLMASTER. But God won't pay.

MAYOR. You used to be a friend of hers, Ill, so now it all
depends on you.

PRIEST. But their ways parted. I heard some story about it —
have you no confession to make to your Priest?

ILL. We were the best of friends. Young and hotheaded. I
used to be a bit of a lad, gentlemen, forty-five years ago. And
she, Clara, I can see her still: coming towards me through
the shadows in Petersens' Barn, all aglow. Or walking

barefoot in the Konrad's Village Wood, over the moss and the leaves, with her red hair streaming out, slim and supple as a willow, and tender, ah, what a devilish beautiful little witch. Life tore us apart. Life. That's the way it is.

MAYOR. I ought to have a few details about Madam Zachanassian for my little after-dinner speech in the Golden Apostle.

(*Takes a small notebook from pocket.*)

SCHOOLMASTER. I've been going through the old school-reports. Clara Wascher's marks, I'm sorry to say, were appalling. So was her conduct. She only passed in botany and zoology.

MAYOR (*takes note*). Good. Botany and zoology. A pass. That's good.

ILL. I can help you here, Mister Mayor. Clara loved justice. Most decidedly. Once when they took a beggar away she flung stones at the police.

MAYOR. Love of justice. Not bad. It always works. But I think we'd better leave out that bit about the police.

ILL. She was generous too. Everything she had she shared. She stole potatoes once for an old widow woman.

MAYOR. Sense of generosity. Gentlemen, I absolutely must bring that in. It's the crucial point. Does anyone here remember a building her father built? That'd sound good in my speech.

ALL. No. No one.

(*Mayor shuts his little notebook.*)

MAYOR. I'm fully prepared, for my part. The rest is up to Ill.

ILL. I know. Zachanassian has to cough up her millions.

MAYOR. Millions — that's the idea. Precisely.

SCHOOLMASTER. It won't help us if she only founds a nursery.

MAYOR. My dear Ill, you've been the most popular personality in Guellen for a long while now. In the spring, I shall be retiring. I've sounded out the Opposition: we've agreed to nominate you as my successor.

ILL. But Mister Mayor.

SCHOOLMASTER. I can confirm that.

ILL. Gentlemen, back to business. First of all, I'll tell Clara all about our wretched plight.

PRIEST. But do be careful — do be tactful.

ILL. We've got to be clever. Psychologically acute. If we make a fiasco of the welcome at the station, we could easily wreck everything else. You won't bring it off by relying on the municipal band and the mixed choir.

MAYOR. Ill's right, there. It'll be one of the decisive moments. Madam Zachanassian sets foot on her native soil, she's home again, and how moved she is, there are tears in her eyes, ah, the old familiar places. The old faces. Not that I'll be standing here like this in my shirt-sleeves. I'll be wearing my formal black and a top hat. My wife beside me, my two grandchildren in front of me, all in white. Holding roses. My God, if only it all works out according to plan!

(*Bell rings.*)

MAN ONE. It's the Racing Roland.

MAN TWO. Venice-Stockholm eleven twenty-seven.

PRIEST. Eleven twenty-seven! We still have nearly two hours to get suitably dressed.

MAYOR. Kuhn and Hauser hoist the 'Welcome Claire Zachanassian' banner. (*Points at four men.*) You others better wave your hats. But please: no bawling like last year at the Government Mission, it hardly impressed them at all and so far we've had no subsidy. This is no time for wild enthusiasm, the mood you want is an inward, an almost tearful sympathy for one of our children, who was lost, and has been found again. Be relaxed. Sincere. But above all, time it well. The instant the choir stops singing, sound the fire-alarm. And look out ...

(His speech is drowned by thunder of oncoming train. Squealing brakes. Dumbfounded astonishment on all faces. The five men spring up from bench.)

PAINTER. The Express!

MAN ONE. It's stopping!

MAN TWO. In Guellen!

MAN THREE. The lousiest —

MAN FOUR. Most poverty-stricken —

MAN ONE. Desolate dump on the Venice-Stockholm line!

STATION-MASTER. It's against the Laws of Nature. The Racing Roland ought to materialize from around the Leuthenau bend, roar through Guellen, dwindle into a dark dot over at Pückenried valley and vanish.

(Enter, right, Claire Zachanassian. Sixty-three, red hair, pearl necklace, enormous gold bangles, unbelievably got up to kill and yet by the same token a Society Lady with a rare grace, in spite of all the grotesquerie. Followed by her entourage, comprising Butler Boby, aged about eighty, wearing dark glasses, and Husband VII, tall and thin with a black moustache, sporting a complete angler's outfit. Accompanying this group, an excited Ticket Inspector, peaked cap, little red satchel.)

CLAIRE ZACHANASSIAN. Is it Guellen?

TICKET INSPECTOR. Madam. You pulled the Emergency Brake.

CLAIRE ZACHANASSIAN. I always pull the Emergency Brake.

TICKET INSPECTOR. I protest. Vigorously. No one ever pulls the Emergency Brake in this country. Not even in case of emergency. Our first duty is to our time-table. Will you kindly give me an explanation.

CLAIRE ZACHANASSIAN. It is Guellen, Moby. I recognize the wretched dump. That's Konrad's Village Wood, yonder, with a stream you can fish — pike and trout; that roof on the right is Petersens' Barn.

ILL *(as if awakening)*. Clara.

SCHOOLMASTER. Madam Zachanassian.

ALL. Madam Zachanassian.

SCHOOLMASTER. And the choir and the Youth Club aren't ready!

MAYOR. The Athletics Club! The Fire Brigade!

PRIEST. The Sexton!

MAYOR. My frock-coat, for God's sake, my top hat, my grandchildren!

MAN ONE. Clarie Wascher's here! Clarie Wascher's here!

(*Jumps up, rushes off towards town.*)

MAYOR (*calling after him*). Don't forget my wife!

TICKET INSPECTOR. I'm waiting for an explanation. In my official capacity. I represent the Railway Management.

CLAIRE ZACHANASSIAN. You're a simpleton. I want to pay this little town a visit. What d'you expect me to do, hop off your express train?

TICKET INSPECTOR. You stopped the Racing Roland just because you wanted to visit Guellen?

CLAIRE ZACHANASSIAN. Of course.

TICKET INSPECTOR. Madam. Should you desire to visit Guellen, the twelve-forty commuter from Kalberstadt is at your service. Please use it. Like other people. Arrival in Guellen one thirteen p.m.

CLAIRE ZACHANASSIAN. The ordinary passenger train? The one that stops in Loken, Brunnhübel, Beisenbach and Leuthenau? Are you really and truly asking me to go puffing round this countryside for half an hour?

TICKET INSPECTOR. You'll pay for this, Madam. Dearly.

CLAIRE ZACHANASSIAN. Boby, give him a thousand.

ALL (*murmuring*). A thousand.

(*Butler gives Ticket Inspector a thousand.*)

TICKET INSPECTOR (*perplexed*). Madam.

CLAIRE ZACHANASSIAN. And three thousand for the Railway Widows' Fund.

ALL (*murmuring*). Three thousand.

(*Ticket Inspector receives three thousand from Butler.*)

TICKET INSPECTOR (*staggered*). Madam. No such fund exists.

CLAIRE ZACHANASSIAN. Then found one.

(*The supreme Civic Authority whispers a word or two in Ticket Inspector's ear.*)

TICKET INSPECTOR (*all confusion*). Madam is Madam Claire Zachanassian? O do excuse me. Of course it's different in that case. We'd have been only too happy to stop in Guellen if we'd had the faintest notion, O, here's your money back, Madam, four thousand, my God.

ALL (*murmuring*). Four thousand.

CLAIRE ZACHANASSIAN. Keep it, it's nothing.

ALL (*murmuring*). Keep it.

TICKET INSPECTOR. Does Madam require the Racing Roland to wait while she visits Guellen? I know the Railway Management would be only too glad. They say the Cathedral portals are well worth a look. Gothic. With the Last Judgment.

CLAIRE ZACHANASSIAN. Will you and your express train get the hell out of here?

HUSBAND VII (*whines*). But the Press, poppet, the Press haven't got off yet. The Reporters have no idea. They're dining up front in the saloon.

CLAIRE ZACHANASSIAN. Let them dine, Moby, let them dine. I can't use the Press in Guellen yet, and they'll come back later on, don't worry.

(*Meanwhile Man Two has brought Mayor his frock-coat. Mayor crosses ceremoniously to Claire Zachanassian. Painter and Man Four stand on bench, hoist banner: 'Welcome Claire Zachanassi' … Painter did not quite finish it.*)

STATION-MASTER (*whistles, waves green flag*). Stand clear!

TICKET INSPECTOR. I do trust you won't complain to the

Railway Management, Madam. It was a pure misunderstanding.

(*Train begins moving out. Ticket Inspector jumps on.*)

MAYOR. Madam Zachanassian, my dear lady. As Mayor of
Guellen, it is my honour to welcome you, a child of our
native town ...

(*Remainder of Mayor's speech drowned in clatter of express
train as it begins to move and then to race away. He speaks
doggedly on.*)

CLAIRE ZACHANASSIAN. I must thank you, Mister Mayor, for
your fine speech.

(*She crosses to Ill who, somewhat embarrassed, has moved
towards her.*)

ILL. Clara.

CLAIRE ZACHANASSIAN. Alfred.

ILL. It's nice you've come.

CLAIRE ZACHANASSIAN. I'd always planned to. All my life.
Ever since I left Guellen.

ILL (*unsure of himself*). It's sweet of you.

CLAIRE ZACHANASSIAN. Did you think about me too?

ILL. Of course. All the time. You know I did, Clara.

CLAIRE ZACHANASSIAN. They were wonderful, all those days
we used to spend together.

ILL (*proudly*). They sure were. (*To Schoolmaster.*) See, Professor,
I've got her in the bag.

CLAIRE ZACHANASSIAN. Call me what you always used to
call me.

ILL. My little wildcat.

CLAIRE ZACHANASSIAN (*purrs like an old cat*). And what else?

ILL. My little sorceress.

CLAIRE ZACHANASSIAN. I used to call you my black panther.

ILL. I still am.

CLAIRE ZACHANASSIAN. Rubbish. You've grown fat. And grey.
And drink-sodden.

ILL. But *you're* still the same, my little sorceress.

CLAIRE ZACHANASSIAN. Don't be daft. I've grown old and fat as well. And lost my left leg. An automobile accident. Now I only travel in express trains. But they made a splendid job of the artificial one, don't you think? (*She pulls up her skirt, displays left leg.*) It bends very well.

ILL (*wipes away sweat*). But my little wildcat, I'd never have noticed it.

CLAIRE ZACHANASSIAN. Would you like to meet my seventh husband, Alfred? Tobacco Plantations. We're very happily married.

ILL. But by all means.

CLAIRE ZACHANASSIAN. Come on, Moby, come and make your bow. As a matter of fact his name's Pedro, but Moby's much nicer. In any case it goes better with Boby; that's the butler's name. And you get your butlers for life, so husbands have to be christened accordingly.

(*Husband* VII *bows.*)

Isn't he nice, with his little black moustache? Think it over, Moby.

(*Husband* VII *thinks it over.*)

Harder.

(*Husband* VII *thinks it over harder.*)

Harder still.

HUSBAND VII. But I can't think any harder, poppet, really I can't.

CLAIRE ZACHANASSIAN. Of course you can. Just try.

(*Husband* VII *thinks harder still. Bell rings.*)

You see. It works. Don't you agree, Alfred, he looks almost demoniacal like that. Like a Brazilian. But no! He's Greek-Orthodox. His father was Russian. We were married by a Pope. Most interesting. Now I'm going to have a look round Guellen.

(*She inspects little house, left, through jewel-encrusted lorgnette.*)

My father built this Public Convenience, Moby. Good work, painstakingly executed. When I was a child I spent hours on that roof, spitting. But only on the Gents.

(*Mixed choir and Youth Club have now assembled in background. Schoolmaster steps forward wearing top hat.*)

SCHOOLMASTER. Madam. As Headmaster of Guellen College, and lover of the noblest Muse, may I take the liberty of offering you a homely folk-song, rendered by the mixed choir and the Youth Club.

CLAIRE ZACHANASSIAN. Fire away, Schoolmaster, let's hear your homely folk-song.

(*Schoolmaster takes up tuning-fork, strikes key. Mixed choir and Youth Club begin ceremoniously singing, at which juncture another train arrives, left. Station-master salutes. Choir struggles against cacophonous clatter of train, Schoolmaster despairs, train, at long last, passes.*)

MAYOR (*despondent*). The fire alarm, sound the fire alarm!

CLAIRE ZACHANASSIAN. Well sung, Guelleners! That blond bass out there on the left, with the big Adam's apple, he was really most singular.

(*A Policeman elbows a passage through mixed choir, draws up to attention in front of Claire Zachanassian.*)

POLICEMAN. Police Inspector Hahncke, Madam. At your service.

CLAIRE ZACHANASSIAN (*inspects him*). Thank you. I shan't want to arrest anybody. But Guellen may need you soon. Can you wink a blind eye to things from time to time?

POLICEMAN. Sure I can, Madam. Where would I be in Guellen if I couldn't!

CLAIRE ZACHANASSIAN. Start learning to wink them both.

(*Policeman goggles at her, perplexed.*)

ILL (*laughing*). Just like Clara! Just like my little wildcat!

(*Slaps thigh with enjoyment. Mayor perches Schoolmaster's top hat on his own head, ushers pair of grandchildren forward. Twin seven-year-old girls, blond plaits.*)

MAYOR. My grandchildren, Madam. Hermione and Adolfina. My wife is the only one not present.

    (*Mops perspiration. The two little girls curtsy for Madam Zachanassian and offer her red roses.*)

CLAIRE ZACHANASSIAN. Congratulations on your kids, Mister Mayor. Here!

    (*She bundles roses into Station-master's arms. Mayor stealthily hands top hat to Priest, who puts it on.*)

MAYOR. Our Priest, Madam.

    (*Priest raises top hat, bows.*)

CLAIRE ZACHANASSIAN. Ah, the Priest. Do you comfort the dying?

PRIEST (*startled*). I do what I can.

CLAIRE ZACHANASSIAN. People who've been condemned to death as well?

PRIEST (*perplexed*). The death sentence has been abolished in this country, Madam.

CLAIRE ZACHANASSIAN. It may be reintroduced.

    (*Priest, with some consternation, returns top hat to Mayor, who dons it again.*)

ILL (*laughing*). Really, little wildcat! You crack the wildest jokes.

CLAIRE ZACHANASSIAN. Now I want to go into town.

    (*Mayor attempts to offer her his arm.*)

What's all this, Mister Mayor. I don't go hiking miles on my artificial leg.

MAYOR (*shocked*). Immediately, immediately, Madam. The doctor owns a car. It's a Mercedes. The nineteen thirty-two model.

POLICEMAN (*clicking heels*). I'll see to it, Mister Mayor. I'll have the car commandeered and driven round.

CLAIRE ZACHANASSIAN. That won't be necessary. Since my accident I only go about in sedan-chairs. Roby, Toby, bring it here.

(*Enter, left, two herculean gum-chewing brutes with sedan-chair. One of them has a guitar slung at his back.*)

Two gangsters. From Manhattan. They were on their way to Sing Sing. To the electric chair. I petitioned for them to be freed as sedan-bearers. Cost me a million dollars per petition. The sedan-chair came from the Louvre. A gift from the French President. Such a nice man; he looks exactly like his pictures in the newspapers. Roby, Toby, take me into town.

ROBY/TOBY (*in unison*). Yes Mam.

CLAIRE ZACHANASSIAN. But first of all to the Petersens' Barn, and then to Konrad's Village Wood. I want to take Alfred to visit our old trysting-places. In the meanwhile have the luggage and the coffin put in the Golden Apostle.

MAYOR (*startled*). The coffin?

CLAIRE ZACHANASSIAN. Yes, I brought a coffin with me. I may need it. Roby, Toby, off we go!

(*The pair of gum-chewing brutes carry Claire Zachanassian away to town. Mayor gives signal, whereon all burst into cheers which spontaneously fade as two more servants enter, bearing an elaborate black coffin, cross stage and exeunt, towards Guellen. Now, undaunted and unpawned, the fire-alarm bell starts ringing.*)

MAYOR. At last! The fire bell.

(*Populace gather round coffin. It is followed in by Claire Zachanassian's maidservants and an endless stream of cases and trunks, carried by Guelleners. This traffic is controlled by Policeman, who is about to follow it out when enter at that point a pair of little old fat soft-spoken men, both impeccably dressed.*)

THE PAIR. We're in Guellen. We can smell it, we can smell it, we can smell it in the air, in the Guellen air.

POLICEMAN. And who might you be?

THE PAIR. We belong to the old lady, we belong to the old lady. She calls us Koby and Loby.

POLICEMAN. Madam Zachanassian is staying at the Golden Apostle.

THE PAIR (*gay*). We're blind, we're blind.

POLICEMAN. Blind? O.K., I'll take you there, in duplicate.

THE PAIR. O thank you Mister Policeman, thank you very much.

POLICEMAN (*with surprise*). If you're blind, how did you know I was a policeman?

THE PAIR. By your tone of voice, your tone of voice, all policemen have the same tone of voice.

POLICEMAN (*with suspicion*). You fat little men seem to have had a bit of contact with the police.

THE PAIR (*incredulous*). Men, he thinks we're men!

POLICEMAN. Then what the hell are you?

THE PAIR. You'll soon see, you'll soon see!

POLICEMAN (*baffled*). Well, you seem cheerful about it.

THE PAIR. We get steak and ham, every day, every day.

POLICEMAN. Yeah. I'd get up and dance for that too. Come on, give me your hands. Funny kind of humour foreigners have. (*Goes off to town with pair.*)

THE PAIR. Off to Boby and Moby, off to Roby and Toby!

(*Open scene-change: façade of station and adjacent little building soar into flies. Interior of the Golden Apostle: an hotel-sign might well be let down from above, an imposing gilded Apostle, as emblem, and left to hang in mid-air. Faded, outmoded luxury. Everything threadbare, tattered, dusty and musty and gone to seed. Interminable processions of porters taking interminable pieces of luggage upstairs: first a cage, then the cases and trunks. Mayor and Schoolmaster seated in foreground drinking Schnapps.*)

MAYOR. Cases, cases, and still more cases. Mountains of them. And a little while ago they came in with a cage. There was a panther in it. A black, wild animal.

SCHOOLMASTER. She had the coffin put in a special spare room. Curious.

MAYOR. Famous women have their whims and fancies.

SCHOOLMASTER. She seems to want to stay here quite a while.

MAYOR. So much the better. Ill has her in the bag. He was calling her his little wildcat, his little sorceress. He'll get thousands out of her. Her health, Professor. And may Claire Zachanassian restore the Bockmann business.

SCHOOLMASTER. And the Wagner Factory.

MAYOR. And the Foundry on Sunshine Square. If they boom we'll all boom — my Community and your College and the Standard of Living.

(*He has called a toast; they clink glasses.*)

SCHOOLMASTER. I've been correcting the Guellen school-children's Latin and Greek exercises for more than two decades, Mister Mayor, but let me tell you, Sir, I only learned what horror is one hour ago. That old lady in black robes getting off the train was a gruesome vision. Like one of the Fates; she made me think of an avenging Greek goddess. Her name shouldn't be Claire; it should be Clotho. I could suspect her of spinning destiny's webs herself.

(*Enter Policeman. Hangs cap on peg.*)

MAYOR. Pull up a chair, Inspector.

(*Policeman pulls up a chair.*)

POLICEMAN. Not much fun patrolling in this dump. But maybe now it'll rise from the ashes. I've just been to Petersens' Barn with the millionairess and that shopkeeper Ill. I witnessed a moving scene. Both parties maintained a meditative pause, as in church. I was embarrassed. I therefore did not follow them when they went to Konrad's

Village Wood. Say, that was a real procession. The sedan-chair first, then Ill walking beside it, then the Butler, then her seventh husband last with his fishing-rod.

SCHOOLMASTER. That conspicuous consumption of husbands; she's a second Laïs.

POLICEMAN. And those two little fat men. The devil knows what it all means.

SCHOOLMASTER. Sinister. An ascent from the infernal regions.

MAYOR. I wonder what they're after, in Konrad's Village Wood.

POLICEMAN. The same as in Petersens' Barn, Mister Mayor. They're calling in on the places where their passion used to burn, as they say.

SCHOOLMASTER. Flame, flame. Remember Shakespeare: Romeo and Juliet. Gentlemen: I'm stirred. I sense the grandeur of antiquity in Guellen. I've never sensed it here before.

MAYOR. Gentlemen: we must drink a special toast to Ill — a man who's doing all a man can to better our lot. To our most popular citizen: to my successor!

(*The Hotel Apostle floats away, back into the flies. Enter the four citizens, left, with a simple, backless wooden bench, which they set down, left. Man One, with a huge, paste-board heart hanging from his neck, on it the letters A ↑ C, climbs on to the bench. The others stand round him in a half-circle, holding twigs at arm's length to designate trees.*)

MAN ONE.

We are trees, we're pine and spruce

MAN TWO.

We are beech, and dark-green fir

MAN THREE.

Lichen, moss and climbing ivy

MAN FOUR.

Undergrowth and lair of fox

MAN ONE.

Drifting cloud and call of bird

MAN TWO.

We are the woodland wilderness

MAN THREE.

Toadstool, and the timid deer

MAN FOUR.

And rustling leaves; and bygone dreams.

(*The two gum-chewing brutes emerge from background bearing sedan-chair with Claire Zachanassian, Ill at her side. Behind her, Husband VII. Butler brings up rear, leading blind pair by the hand.*)

CLAIRE ZACHANASSIAN. It's the Konrad's Village Wood. Roby, Toby, stop a moment.

BLIND PAIR. Stop, Roby and Toby, stop, Boby and Moby.

(*Claire Zachanassian descends from sedan-chair, surveys wood.*)

CLAIRE ZACHANASSIAN. There's the heart with our two names on it, Alfred. Almost faded away, and grown apart. And the tree's grown. The trunk and branches have thickened. The way we have ourselves.

(*Claire Zachanassian crosses to other trees.*)

A woodland bower. It's a long time since I last walked through these woods, in my young days, frolicking in the foliage and the purple ivy. You brutes just go and chew your gum behind the bushes, and take your sedan-chair with you; I don't want to look at your mugs all the time. And Moby, stroll away over to that stream on the right, there, and look at the fish.

(*Exit brutes, left, with sedan-chair. Exit Husband VII, right. Claire Zachanassian sits on bench.*)

Look, a doe.

(*Man Three springs off.*)

ILL. It's the close season.

(*Sits next to her.*)

CLAIRE ZACHANASSIAN. We kissed each other on this spot. More than fifty years ago. We loved each other under these boughs, under these bushes, among these toadstools on the moss. I was seventeen, and you weren't quite twenty. Then you married Matilda Blumhard with her little general store, and I married old Zachanassian with his millions from Armenia. He found me in a brothel. In Hamburg. It was my red hair took his fancy; the old, gold lecher!

ILL. Clara!

CLAIRE ZACHANASSIAN. Boby, a Henry Clay.

BLIND PAIR. A Henry Clay, a Henry Clay.

(*Butler comes out of background, passes her a cigar, lights it.*)

CLAIRE ZACHANASSIAN. I'm fond of cigars. I suppose I ought to smoke my husband's produce; but I don't trust them.

ILL. It was for your sake I married Matilda Blumhard.

CLAIRE ZACHANASSIAN. She had money.

ILL. You were young and beautiful. The future belonged to you. I wanted you to be happy. So I had to renounce being happy myself.

CLAIRE ZACHANASSIAN. And now the future's here.

ILL. If you'd stayed here, you'd have been ruined like me.

CLAIRE ZACHANASSIAN. Are you ruined?

ILL. A broken-down shopkeeper in a broken-down town.

CLAIRE ZACHANASSIAN. Now it's me who has money.

ILL. I've been living in hell since you went away from me.

CLAIRE ZACHANASSIAN. And I've grown into hell itself.

ILL. Always rowing with my family. They blame me for being poor.

CLAIRE ZACHANASSIAN. Didn't little Matilda make you happy?

ILL. Your happiness is what matters.

CLAIRE ZACHANASSIAN. Your children?

ILL. No sense of ideals.

CLAIRE ZACHANASSIAN. They'll develop one soon.

> (*He says nothing. Both gaze at the wood of childhood memory.*)

ILL. I lead a laughable life. Never once really managed to leave this township. One trip to Berlin and one to Tessin. That's all.

CLAIRE ZACHANASSIAN. Why bother, anyway. I know what the world's like.

ILL. Because you've always been able to travel.

CLAIRE ZACHANASSIAN. Because I own it.

> (*He says nothing; she smokes.*)

ILL. Everything's going to be different now.

CLAIRE ZACHANASSIAN. Sure.

ILL (*watches her*). Are you going to help us?

CLAIRE ZACHANASSIAN. I shan't leave my home-town in the lurch.

ILL. We need thousands.

CLAIRE ZACHANASSIAN. That's nothing.

ILL (*enthusiastically*). My little wildcat!

> (*Moved, he slaps her on left shoulder, then painfully withdraws hand.*)

CLAIRE ZACHANASSIAN. That hurt. You hit one of the straps for my artificial leg.

> (*Man One pulls pipe and rusty door-key from trousers-pocket, taps on pipe with key.*)

A woodpecker.

ILL. Now it's the way it used to be when we were young and bold, when we went out walking in Konrad's Village Wood, in the days of our young love. And the sun was a dazzling orb, above the pine-trees. And far away a few wisps of cloud, and somewhere in the woodland you could hear a cuckoo calling.

MAN FOUR. Cuckoo, cuckoo!

(*Ill lays hand on Man One.*)

ILL. Cool wood, and the wind in the boughs, soughing like the sea-surge.

(*The three men who are trees begin soughing and blowing and waving their arms up and down.*)

Ah, my little sorceress, if only time had really dissolved. If only life hadn't put us asunder.

CLAIRE ZACHANASSIAN. Would you wish that?

ILL. That above all, above all. I do love you!

(*Kisses her right hand.*)

The same, cool white hand.

CLAIRE ZACHANASSIAN. No, you're wrong. It's artificial too. Ivory.

(*Ill, horrified, releases her hand.*)

ILL. Clara, are you all artificial?

CLAIRE ZACHANASSIAN. Practically. My plane crashed in Afghanistan. I was the only one who crawled out of the wreckage. Even the crew died. I'm unkillable.

BLIND PAIR. She's unkillable, she's unkillable.

(*Ceremonial oom-pah music. The Hotel Apostle descends again. Guelleners bring in tables, wretched, tattered table-cloths, cutlery, crockery, food. One table, centre, one left, and one right, parallel to audience. Priest comes out of background. More Guelleners flock in, among them a Gymnast. Mayor, Schoolmaster and Policeman reappear.*
The Guelleners applaud. Mayor crosses to bench where Claire Zachanassian and Ill are sitting; the trees have metamorphosed back into citizens and moved away upstage.)

MAYOR. The storm of applause is for you, my dear lady.

CLAIRE ZACHANASSIAN. It's for the town band, Mister Mayor. It was a capital performance; and the Athletics Club did a wonderful pyramid. I love men in shorts and vests. They look so natural.

MAYOR. May I escort you to your place?
(*He escorts Claire Zachanassian to her place at table, centre, introduces her to his wife.*)
My wife.
(*Claire Zachanassian examines wife through lorgnette.*)

CLAIRE ZACHANASSIAN. Annie Dummermut, top of our class.
(*Mayor introduces her to a second woman, as worn out and embittered as his wife.*)

MAYOR. Mrs Ill.

CLAIRE ZACHANASSIAN. Matilda Blumhard. I can remember you lying in wait for Alfred behind the shop door. You've grown very thin and pale, my dear.
(*Doctor hurries in, right; a squat, thick-set fifty-year-old; moustachioed, bristly black hair, scarred face, threadbare frock-coat.*)

DOCTOR. Just managed to do it, in my old Mercedes.

MAYOR. Doctor Nuesslin, our physician.
(*Claire Zachanassian examines Doctor through lorgnette as he kisses her hand.*)

CLAIRE ZACHANASSIAN. Interesting. Do you make out Death Certificates?

DOCTOR (*taken off guard*). Death Certificates?

CLAIRE ZACHANASSIAN. If someone should die?

DOCTOR. Of course, Madam. It's my duty. As decreed by the authorities.

CLAIRE ZACHANASSIAN. Next time, diagnose heart attack.

ILL (*laughs*). Delicious, simply delicious.
(*Claire Zachanassian turns from Doctor to inspect Gymnast, clad in shorts and vest.*)

CLAIRE ZACHANASSIAN. Do another exercise.
(*Gymnast bends knees, flexes arms.*)
Marvellous muscles. Ever used your strength for strangling?

GYMNAST (*stiffens in consternation at knees-bend position*). For strangling?

CLAIRE ZACHANASSIAN. Now just bend your arms back again, Mister Gymnast, then forward into a press-up.

ILL (*laughs*). Clara has such a golden sense of humour! I could die laughing at one of her jokes!

DOCTOR (*still disconcerted*). I wonder. They chill me to the marrow.

ILL (*stage whisper*). She's promised us hundreds of thousands.

MAYOR (*gasps*). Hundreds of thousands?

ILL. Hundreds of thousands.

DOCTOR. God Almighty.

(*The millionairess turns away from Gymnast.*)

CLAIRE ZACHANASSIAN. And now, Mister Mayor, I'm hungry.

MAYOR. We were just waiting for your husband, my dear lady.

CLAIRE ZACHANASSIAN. You needn't. He's fishing. And I'm getting a divorce.

MAYOR. A divorce?

CLAIRE ZACHANASSIAN. Moby'll be surprised too. I'm marrying a German film star.

MAYOR. But you told us it was a very happy marriage.

CLAIRE ZACHANASSIAN. All my marriages are happy. But when I was a child I used to dream of a wedding in Guellen Cathedral. You should always fulfil your childhood dreams. It'll be a grand ceremony.

(*All sit. Claire Zachanassian takes her place between Mayor and Ill. Ill's wife beside Ill, Mayor's wife beside Mayor. Schoolmaster, Priest and Policeman at separate table, right. The four citizens, left. In background, more guests of honour, with wives. Above, the banner: 'Welcome Claire'. Mayor stands, beaming with joy, serviette already in position, and taps on his glass.*)

MAYOR. My dear lady, fellow-citizens. Forty-five years have

flowed by since you left our little town, our town founded by Crown Prince Hasso the Noble, our town so pleasantly nestling between Konrad's Village Wood and Pückenried Valley. Forty-five years, more than four decades, it's a long time. Many things have happened since then, many bitter things. It has gone sadly with the world, gone sadly with us. And yet we have never, my dear lady — our Claire (*applause*) — never forgotten you. Neither you, nor your family. Your mother, that magnificent and robustly healthy creature (*Ill whispers something to him*) tragically and prematurely torn from our midst by tuberculosis, and your father, that popular figure, who built the building by the station which experts and laymen still visit so often (*Ill whispers something to him*) — still admire so much, they both live on in our thoughts, for they were of our best, our worthiest. And you too, my dear lady: who, as you gambolled through our streets — our streets, alas, so sadly decrepit nowadays — you, a curly-headed, blonde (*Ill whispers something to him*) — redheaded madcap, who did not know you? Even then, everyone could sense the magic in your personality, foresee your approaching rise to humanity's dizzy heights. (*Takes out his notebook.*) You were never forgotten. Literally never. Even now, the staff at school hold up your achievements as an example to others, and in nature studies — the most essential ones — they were astonishing, a revelation of your sympathy for every living creature, indeed for all things in need of protection. And even then, people far and wide were moved to wonder at your love of justice, at your sense of generosity. (*Huge applause.*) For did not our Claire obtain food for an old widow, buying potatoes with that pocket-money so hardly earned from neighbours, and thereby save the old lady from dying of hunger, to mention but one of her deeds of charity. (*Huge applause.*) My dear lady my dear Guelleners, that happy temperament has now developed from those tender seeds to an impressive flowering, and our redheaded madcap has become a lady whose generosity stirs the world; we need only think of her social work, of her maternity homes and her soup kitchens, of her art foundations and her children's nurseries, and now, therefore, I ask you to give three cheers for the prodigal returned: Hip, Hip, Hip, Hurrah! (*Applause.*)

(*Claire Zachanassian gets to her feet.*)

CLAIRE ZACHANASSIAN. Mister Mayor, Guelleners. I am moved by your unselfish joy in my visit. As a matter of fact I was somewhat different from the child I seem to be in the Mayor's speech. When I went to school, I was thrashed. And I stole the potatoes for Widow Boll, aided by Ill; not to save the old bawd from dying of hunger, but just for once to sleep with Ill in a more comfortable bed than Konrad's Village Wood or Petersens' Barn. None the less, as my contribution to this joy of yours, I want to tell you I'm ready to give Guellen one million. Five hundred thousand for the town and five hundred thousand to be shared among each family.

(*Deathly silence.*)

MAYOR (*stammers*). One million.

(*Everyone still dumbstruck.*)

CLAIRE ZACHANASSIAN. On one condition.

(*Everyone bursts into indescribable jubilation, dancing round, standing on chairs, Gymnast performing acrobatics, etc. Ill pounds his chest enthusiastically.*)

ILL. There's Clara for you! What a jewel! She takes your breath away! Just like her, O my little sorceress!

(*Kisses her.*)

MAYOR. Madam: you said, on one condition. May I ask, on what condition?

CLAIRE ZACHANASSIAN. I'll tell you on what condition. I'm giving you a million, and I'm buying myself justice.
(*Deathly silence.*)

MAYOR. My dear lady, what do you mean by that?

CLAIRE ZACHANASSIAN. What I said.

MAYOR. Justice can't be bought.

CLAIRE ZACHANASSIAN. Everything can be bought.

MAYOR. I still don't understand.

CLAIRE ZACHANASSIAN. Boby. Step forward.
(*Butler steps forward, from right to centre, between the three tables. Takes off his dark glasses.*)

BUTLER. I don't know if any of you here still recognize me.

SCHOOLMASTER. Chief Justice Courtly.

BUTLER. Right. Chief Justice Courtly. Forty-five years ago, I was Lord Chief Justice in Guellen. I was later called to the Kaffigen Court of Appeal until, twenty-five years ago it is now, Madam Zachanassian offered me the post of Butler in her service. A somewhat unusual career, indeed, I grant you, for an academic man, however, the salary involved was really quite fantastic ...

CLAIRE ZACHANASSIAN. Get to the point, Boby.

BUTLER. As you may have gathered, Madam Claire Zachanassian is offering you the sum of one million pounds, in return for which she insists that justice be done. In other words, Madam Zachanassian will give you all a million if you right the wrong she was done in Guellen. Mr Ill, if you please.
(*Ill stands. He is pale, startled, wondering.*)

ILL. What do you want of me?

BUTLER. Step forward, Mr Ill.

ILL. Sure.
(*Steps forward, to front of table, right. Laughs uneasily. Shrugs.*)

BUTLER. The year was nineteen ten. I was Lord Chief Justice in

Guellen. I had a paternity claim to arbitrate. Claire Zachanassian, at the time Clara Wascher, claimed that you, Mr Ill, were her child's father.

(*Ill keeps quiet.*)

At that time, Mr Ill, you denied paternity. You called two witnesses.

ILL. Oh, it's an old story. I was young, thoughtless.

CLAIRE ZACHANASSIAN. Toby and Roby, bring in Koby and Loby.

(*The two gum-chewing giants lead pair of blind eunuchs on to centre of stage, blind pair gaily holding hands.*)

BLIND PAIR. We're on the spot, we're on the spot!

BUTLER. Do you recognize these two, Mr Ill?

(*Ill keeps quiet.*)

BLIND PAIR. We're Koby and Loby, we're Koby and Loby.

ILL. I don't know them.

BLIND PAIR. We've changed a lot, we've changed a lot!

BUTLER. Say your names.

FIRST BLIND MAN. Jacob Chicken, Jacob Chicken.

SECOND BLIND MAN. Louis Perch, Louis Perch.

BUTLER. Now, Mr Ill.

ILL. I know nothing about them.

BUTLER. Jacob Chicken and Louis Perch, do you know Mr Ill?

BLIND PAIR. We're blind, we're blind.

BUTLER. Do you know him by his voice?

BLIND PAIR. By his voice, by his voice.

BUTLER. In nineteen ten, I was Judge and you the witnesses. Louis Perch and Jacob Chicken, what did you swear on oath to the Court of Guellen?

BLIND PAIR. We'd slept with Clara, we'd slept with Clara.

BUTLER. You swore it on oath, before me. Before the Court. Before God. Was it the truth?

BLIND PAIR. We swore a false oath, we swore a false oath.

BUTLER. Why, Jacob Chicken and Louis Perch?

BLIND PAIR. Ill bribed us, Ill bribed us.

BUTLER. With what did he bribe you?

BLIND PAIR. With a pint of brandy, with a pint of brandy.

CLAIRE ZACHANASSIAN. And now tell them what I did with you, Koby and Loby.

BUTLER. Tell them.

BLIND PAIR. The lady tracked us down, the lady tracked us down.

BUTLER. Correct. Claira Zachanassian tracked you down. To the ends of the earth. Jacob Chicken had emigrated to Canada and Louis Perch to Australia. But she tracked you down. And then what did she do with you?

BLIND PAIR. She gave us to Toby and Roby, she gave us to Toby and Roby.

BUTLER. And what did Toby and Roby do to you?

BLIND PAIR. Castrated and blinded us, castrated and blinded us.

BUTLER. And there you have the full story. One Judge, one accused, two false witnesses: a miscarriage of justice in the year nineteen ten. Isn't that so, plaintiff?

CLAIRE ZACHANASSIAN (*stands*). That is so.

ILL (*stamping on floor*). It's over and done with, dead and buried! It's an old, crazy story.

BUTLER. What happened to the child, plaintiff?

CLAIRE ZACHANASSIAN (*gently*). It lived one year.

BUTLER. What happened to you?

CLAIRE ZACHANASSIAN. I became a prostitute.

BUTLER. What made you one?

CLAIRE ZACHANASSIAN. The judgment of that court made me one.

BUTLER. And now you desire justice, Claire Zachanassian?

CLAIRE ZACHANASSIAN. I can afford it. A million for Guellen if someone kills Alfred Ill.

(*Deathly silence. Mrs Ill rushes to Ill, flings her arms round him.*)

MRS ILL. Freddy!

ILL. My little sorceress! You can't ask that! It was long ago. Life went on.

CLAIRE ZACHANASSIAN. Life went on, and I've forgotten nothing, Ill. Neither Konrad's Village Wood, nor Petersens' Barn; neither Widow Boll's bedroom, nor your treachery. And now we're old, the pair of us. You decrepit, and me cut to bits by the surgeons' knives. And now I want accounts between us settled. You chose your life, but you forced me into mine. A moment ago you wanted time turned back, in that wood so full of the past, where we spent our young years. Well I'm turning it back now, and I want justice. Justice for a million.

(Mayor stands, pale, dignified.)

MAYOR. Madam Zachanassian: you forget, this is Europe. You forget, we are not savages. In the name of all citizens of Guellen, I reject your offer; and I reject it in the name of humanity. We would rather have poverty than blood on our hands.

(Huge applause.)

CLAIRE ZACHANASSIAN. I'll wait.

ACT TWO

The little town. (Only in outline.) In background, the Golden Apostle Hotel, exterior view. Faded 'art nouveau' architecture. Balcony. Right, a sign, 'Alfred Ill: General Store', above a grimy shop-counter backed by shelves displaying old stock. Whenever anyone enters the imaginary door, a bell rings, tinnily. Left, a sign, 'Police', above a wooden table, on it a telephone. Two chairs. It is morning. Roby and Toby, chewing gum, enter, left, bearing wreaths and flowers as at a funeral, cross stage and enter, back, the hotel. Ill at a window, watching them. His daughter on her knees scrubbing floor. His son puts a cigarette in his mouth.

ILL. Wreaths.

SON. They bring them in from the station every morning.

ILL. For the empty coffin in the Golden Apostle.

SON. It doesn't scare anyone.

ILL. The town's on my side.

    (Son lights cigarette.)

    Mother coming down for breakfast?

DAUGHTER. She's staying upstairs. Says she's tired.

ILL. You've a good mother, children. That's a fact. I just want you to know. A good mother. Let her stay upstairs, rest, save her energy. In that case, *we'll* have breakfast together. It's a long time since we've done that. I suggest eggs and a tin of American Ham. We'll do ourselves proud. Like in the good old days, when the Sunshine Foundry was still booming.

SON. You'll have to excuse me.

    (Stubs out cigarette.)

ILL. Aren't you going to eat with us, Karl?

SON. I'm going to the station. There's a railwayman off sick. Maybe they want a temporary.

ILL. Railroad work in the blazing sun is no job for my boy.

SON. It's better than no job.

230

(*Exit Son. Daughter stands.*)

DAUGHTER. I'm going too, father.

ILL. You too? I see. May one ask my lady where?

DAUGHTER. To the Labour Exchange. They may have a vacancy.

(*Exit Daughter. Ill, upset, takes out handkerchief, blows nose.*)

ILL. Good kids, fine kids.

(*A few bars of guitar-music twang down from balcony.*)

VOICE OF CLAIRE ZACHANASSIAN. Boby, pass me my left leg.

VOICE OF BUTLER. I can't find it, Madam.

VOICE OF CLAIRE ZACHANASSIAN. On the chest of drawers behind the wedding flowers.

(*Enter Man One, as first customer; he goes through imaginary door into Ill's shop.*)

ILL. 'Morning, Hofbauer.

MAN ONE. Cigarettes.

ILL. Same as usual?

MAN ONE. Not those, I want the green ones.

ILL. They cost more.

MAN ONE. On account.

ILL. Since it's you, Hofbauer, and we should all stick together.

MAN ONE. That's a guitar playing.

ILL. One of those Sing Sing gangsters.

(*Blind pair walk out of hotel carrying rods and other appurtenances proper to fishing.*)

BLIND PAIR. Lovely morning, Alfred, lovely morning.

ILL. Go to hell.

BLIND PAIR. We're going fishing, we're going fishing.

(*Exit blind pair, left.*)

MAN ONE. Gone to Guellen Pond.

ILL. With her seventh husband's fishing tackle.

MAN ONE. They say he's lost his tobacco plantations.

ILL. They belong to the millionairess.

MAN ONE. The eighth wedding will be gigantic. She announced their engagement yesterday.

(*Claire Zachanassian appears on balcony in background, dressed for the morning. Moves her right hand, her left leg. Sporadic notes plucked on the guitar accompany the balcony scene which follows, after the fashion of opera-recitative, pointing the text now with a waltz, now with snatches of national or traditional songs, anthems, etc.*)

CLAIRE ZACHANASSIAN. I'm assembled again. Roby, the Armenian folk-song!

(*Guitar music.*)

Zachanassian's favourite tune. He used to love listening to it. Every morning. An exemplary man, that old tycoon. With a veritable navy of oil tankers. And racing-stables. And millions more in cash. It was worth a marriage. A great teacher, and a great dancer; a real devil. I've copied him completely.

(*Two women come in, hand Ill milk-cans.*)

FIRST WOMAN. Milk, Mr Ill.

SECOND WOMAN. My can, Mr Ill.

ILL. A very good morning to you. A quart of milk for the ladies.

(*Opens a milk-drum, prepares to ladle milk.*)

FIRST WOMAN. Jersey milk, Mr Ill.

SECOND WOMAN. Two quarts of Jersey, Mr Ill.

ILL. Jersey.

(*Opens another drum, ladles milk.*)

(*Claire Zachanassian assesses morning critically through lorgnette.*)

CLAIRE ZACHANASSIAN. A fine autumn morning. Light mist in the streets, a silvery haze, and the sky above precisely the shade of violet-blue Count Holk used to paint. My third husband. The Foreign Minister. He used to spend his holidays painting. They were hideous paintings.
(*She sits, with elaborate ceremony.*)
The Count was a hideous person.

FIRST WOMAN. And butter. Half a pound.
SECOND WOMAN. And super-bread. Four large loaves.
ILL. I see we've had a legacy, ladies.
THE TWO WOMEN. On account.
ILL. Share the rough and share the smooth.
FIRST WOMAN. And a bar of chocolate.
SECOND WOMAN. Two bars.
ILL. On account?
FIRST WOMAN. On account.
SECOND WOMAN. We'll eat those here, Mr Ill.
FIRST WOMAN. It's much nicer here, Mr Ill.
(*They sit at back of shop eating chocolate.*)

CLAIRE ZACHANASSIAN. A Winston. I will try that brand my seventh husband made, just once, now I've divorced him; poor Moby, with his fishing passion. He must be so sad sitting in the Portugal Express.
(*Butler hands her a cigar, gives her a light.*)

MAN ONE. Look, sitting on the balcony, puffing at her cigar.
ILL. Always some wickedly expensive brand.
MAN ONE. Sheer extravagance. She ought to be ashamed, in front of the poor.

CLAIRE ZACHANASSIAN (*smoking*). Curious. Quite smokeable.

ILL. Her plan's misfired. I'm an old sinner, Hofbauer — who isn't. It was a mean trick I played on her when I was a kid, but the way they all rejected the offer, all the Guelleners in the Golden Apostle unanimously, that was the finest moment of my life.

CLAIR ZACHANASSIAN. Boby. Whisky. Neat.

(*Enter Man Two, as second customer, poor and tattered and torn, like everyone else.*)

MAN TWO. 'Morning. It'll be a hot day.

MAN ONE. Very fine and warm for the time of the year.

ILL. Extraordinary custom this morning. Not a soul for as long as you like and suddenly these past few days they're flocking in.

MAN ONE. We'll stick by you. We'll stick by *our* Ill. Come what may.

THE TWO WOMEN (*munching chocolate*). Come what may, Mr Ill, come what may.

MAN TWO. Remember, you're the town's most popular personality.

MAN ONE. Our most important personality.

MAN TWO. You'll be elected Mayor in spring.

MAN ONE. It's dead certain.

THE TWO WOMEN (*munching chocolate*). Dead certain, Mr Ill, dead certain.

MAN TWO. Brandy.

(*Ill reaches to shelf.*)

(*Butler serves whisky.*)

CLAIRE ZACHANASSIAN. Wake the new guy. Can't bear my husbands sleeping all the time.

ILL. Five and three.

MAN TWO. Not that.

ILL. It's what you always drink.

MAN TWO. Cognac.

ILL. It costs thirty-seven and nine. No one can afford that.

MAN TWO. Got to give yourself a treat sometimes.

> (*A half-naked girl rushes headlong over stage, pursued by Toby.*)

FIRST WOMAN (*munching chocolate*). It's a scandal, the way Louisa behaves.

SECOND WOMAN (*munching chocolate*). And to make matters worse she's engaged to that blond musician in Gunpowder Street.

> (*Ill takes down Cognac.*)

ILL. Cognac.

MAN TWO. And tobacco. For my pipe.

ILL. Tobacco.

MAN TWO. The Export.

> (*Ill totals account.*)

> (*Husband VIII appears on balcony — the film star, tall, slender, red moustache, bath-robe. May be played by same actor as Husband VII.*)

HUSBAND VIII. Isn't it divine, Hopsi. Our first engagement breakfast. Really a dream. A little balcony, the lime-tree rustling, the Town Hall fountain softly plashing, a few hens scampering right across the sidewalk, housewives' voices chattering away over their little daily cares and there, beyond the roof-tops, the Cathedral spires!

CLAIRE ZACHANASSIAN. Sit down, Hoby. Stop babbling. I can see the landscape. And thoughts aren't your strong point.

MAN TWO. She's sitting up there with her husband now.

FIRST WOMAN (*munching chocolate*). Her eighth.

SECOND WOMAN (*munching chocolate*). Handsome gentleman. Acts in films. My daughter saw him as the poacher in a country-life feature.

FIRST WOMAN. I saw him when he was the priest in a Graham Greene.

(Claire Zachanassian is kissed by Husband VIII. Guitar twangs chords.)

MAN TWO. You can get anything you want with money. *(Spits.)*

MAN ONE. Not from us. *(Bangs fist on table.)*

ILL. One pound three shillings and threepence.

MAN TWO. On account.

ILL. I'll make an exception this week; only you make sure you pay on the first, when the dole's due.

(Man Two crosses to door.)

ILL. Helmesberger!

(Man Two halts. Ill goes after him.)

You're wearing new shoes. New yellow shoes.

MAN TWO. So what?

(Ill stares at Man One's feet.)

ILL. You too, Hofbauer. You're wearing new shoes too.

(His gaze alights on the women; he walks slowly towards them, terror-stricken.)

You too. New shoes. New yellow shoes.

MAN ONE. What's so extraordinary about new shoes?

MAN TWO. You can't go around in the same old shoes for ever.

ILL. New shoes. How did you all get new shoes?

THE TWO WOMEN. We got them on account, Mr Ill, we got them on account.

ILL. You got them on account. You got things on account from me too. Better tobacco, better milk, Cognac. Why are all the shops suddenly giving you credit?

MAN TWO. You're giving us credit too.

ILL. How are you going to pay?

(Silence. He begins throwing his wares at the customers. They all run away.)

How are you going to pay? How are you going to pay? How? How?

(*He rushes off, back.*)

HUSBAND VIII. Township's getting rowdy.

CLAIRE ZACHANASSIAN. Village life.

HUSBAND VIII. Seems to be trouble in the shop down there.

CLAIRE ZACHANASSIAN. Haggling over the price of meat.
(*Chords on guitar, fortissimo. Husband VIII leaps up, horrified.*)

HUSBAND VIII. Hopsi, for heaven's sake! Did you hear that?

CLAIRE ZACHANASSIAN. The Black Panther. Spitting a little.

HUSBAND VIII (*awestruck*). A Black Panther?

CLAIRE ZACHANASSIAN. From the Pasha of Marakeesh. A present. He's loping around in the hall. A great wicked cat with flashing eyes. I'm very fond of him.

(*Policeman sits down at table, left. Drinks beer. Slow, portentous manner of speech. Ill arrives from back of stage.*)

CLAIRE ZACHANASSIAN. You may serve, Boby.

POLICEMAN. Ill. What can I do for you? Take a seat.
(*Ill remains standing.*)
You're trembling.

ILL. I demand the arrest of Claire Zachanassian.
(*Policeman thumbs tobacco into his pipe, lights it, comfortably.*)

POLICEMAN. Peculiar. Highly peculiar.

(*Butler serves breakfast, brings mail.*)

ILL. I demand it as future Mayor.

POLICEMAN (*puffing clouds of smoke*). We have not yet held the elections.

ILL. Arrest that woman on the spot.

POLICEMAN. What you mean is, you wish to charge this lady. It is then for the police to decide whether or not to arrest her. Has she infringed the law?

ILL. She's inciting the people of our town to kill me.

POLICEMAN. So now you want me to walk up to the lady and arrest her.

(*Pours himself beer.*)

CLAIRE ZACHANASSIAN. The mail. One from Ike. Nehru. They send congratulations.

ILL. It's your duty.

POLICEMAN. Peculiar. Highly peculiar.

(*Drinks beer.*)

ILL. It's only natural. Perfectly natural.

POLICEMAN. My dear Ill, it's not as natural as all that. Now let's examine the matter soberly. The lady makes an offer of one million to the town of Guellen in exchange for your — you know what I'm talking about, of course. True, true, I was there. All this notwithstanding, no sufficient grounds are thereby constituted for the police taking action against Mrs Claire Zachanassian. We must abide by the law.

ILL. Incitement to murder.

POLICEMAN. Now listen here, Ill. We would only have a case of incitement to murder if the proposal to murder you were meant seriously. So much is obvious.

ILL. That's what I'm saying.

POLICEMAN. Exactly. Now, this proposal cannot be meant seriously, because one million is an exorbitant price, you have to admit that yourself. People offer a hundred, or maybe two hundred, for a job like that, not a penny more, you can bet your life on it. Which again proves the proposal wasn't meant seriously, and even if it had been the police couldn't take the lady seriously, because in that case she'd be mad. Get it?

ILL. Inspector. This proposal threatens *me*, whether the woman happens to be mad or not. That's only logical.

POLICEMAN. Illogical. You can't be threatened by a proposal, only by the execution of a proposal. Show me one genuine attempt to execute that proposal, for example one man who's been pointing a gun at you, and I'll be on the spot in a flash. But no one, in point of fact, has any wish to execute the proposal; quite the contrary. That demonstration in the Golden Apostle was extremely impressive. It was a while ago now, but allow me to congratulate you.

(*Drinks beer.*)

ILL. I'm not quite so sure, Inspector.

POLICEMAN. Not quite so sure?

ILL. My customers are buying better milk, better bread, better cigarettes.

POLICEMAN. But you ought to be overjoyed! Business is better!

(*Drinks beer.*)

CLAIRE ZACHANASSIAN. Boby, buy up Dupont Shares.

ILL. Helmesberger's been in buying Cognac. A man who hasn't earned a cent for years and lives on Poor Relief soup.

POLICEMAN. I'll have a tot of that Cognac this evening. Helmesberger's invited me over.

(*Drinks beer.*)

ILL. Everyone's wearing new shoes. New yellow shoes.

POLICEMAN. Whatever can you have against new shoes? I've got a new pair on myself.

(*Displays feet.*)

ILL. You too.

POLICEMAN. Look.

ILL. Yellow as well. And you're drinking Pilsener Beer.

POLICEMAN. Tastes good.

ILL. You always used to drink local beer.

POLICEMAN. Filthy stuff.

(*Radio music.*)

ILL. Listen.

POLICEMAN. What?

ILL. Music.

POLICEMAN. *The Merry Widow.*

ILL. A radio.

POLICEMAN. It's Hagholzer next door. He ought to keep his window shut.

(*Makes note in little notebook.*)

ILL. How did Hagholzer get a radio?

POLICEMAN. That's his business.

ILL. And you, Inspector, how are you going to pay for your Pilsener Beer and your new shoes?

POLICEMAN. That's my business.

(*Telephone on table rings. Policeman picks up receiver.*)

POLICEMAN. Guellen Police Station.

CLAIRE ZACHANASSIAN. Boby, telephone the Russians and tell them I accept their offer.

POLICEMAN. O.K., we'll see to it.

ILL. And how are my customers going to pay?

POLICEMAN. That doesn't concern the police.

(*Stands, takes rifle from back of chair.*)

ILL. But it does concern me. Because it's me they're going to pay with.

POLICEMAN. Nobody's threatening you.

(*Begins loading rifle.*)

ILL. The town's getting into debt. The greater the debt, the higher the standard of living. The higher the standard of living, the greater the need to kill me. And all that woman has to do is sit on her balcony, drink coffee, smoke cigars and wait. That's all. Just wait.

POLICEMAN. You're imagining things.

ILL. You're all just waiting.

(*Bangs on table.*)

POLICEMAN. You've been drinking too much brandy.

(*Checks rifle.*)

There. Now it's loaded. Set your mind at rest. The police are here to enforce respect for the law, to maintain order and protect the individual. They know their duty. If the faintest suspicion of a threat to you arises, wheresoever it arises, from whatsoever source, the police will step in, Mr Ill, you can rely upon it.

ILL (*softly*). Then how do you explain that gold tooth in your mouth, Inspector?

POLICEMAN. What?

ILL. A gleaming new gold tooth.

POLICEMAN. Are you crazy?

(*At this point Ill perceives the gun-barrel is now directed at himself, and his hands go slowly up.*)

I've no time to argue over your ravings, man. I've got to go. That screwy millionairess has lost her little lap-dog. The black panther. Now I have to hunt it down.

(*Goes towards back of stage and off.*)

ILL. It's me you're hunting down, me.

(*Claire Zachanassian is reading a letter.*)

CLAIRE ZACHANASSIAN. He's coming, my dress-designer's coming. My fifth husband, my best-looking man. He still creates all my wedding-gowns. Roby, a minuet.

(*Guitar plays a minuet.*)

HUSBAND VIII. But your fifth was a surgeon.

CLAIRE ZACHANASSIAN. My sixth.

(*Opens another letter.*)

From the Boss of Western Railways.

HUSBAND VIII (*astonished*). I've not heard of that one at all.

CLAIRE ZACHANASSIAN. My fourth. Impoverished. His shares belong to me. I seduced him in Buckingham Palace.

HUSBAND VIII. But that was Lord Ishmael.

CLAIRE ZACHANASSIAN. So it was. You're right, Hoby. I forgot all about him and his castle in Yorkshire. Then this letter must be from my second. Met him in Cairo. We kissed beneath the Sphinx. A most impressive evening.

(*Scene-change, right. The legend 'Town Hall' descends. Man Three enters, carries off shop-till and shifts counter into position as desk. Mayor enters. Puts revolver on table, sits. Ill enters, left. A construction-plan is affixed to wall.*)

ILL. I want to talk to you, Mister Mayor.

MAYOR. Take a seat.

ILL. As man to man. As your successor.

MAYOR. By all means.

(*Ill stays standing, watches revolver.*)

Mrs Zachanassian's panther has escaped. It's climbing around in the Cathedral. So it's best to be armed.

ILL. Sure.

MAYOR. I've called up all men owning weapons. We're not letting the children go to school.

ILL (*suspiciously*). Somewhat drastic measures.

MAYOR. It's big game hunting.

(*Enter Butler.*)

BUTLER. The World Bank President, Madam. Just flown in from New York.

CLAIRE ZACHANASSIAN. I'm not at home. Tell him to fly away again.

MAYOR. What's on your mind? Go on, feel free, unburden yourself.

ILL (*suspiciously*). That's a fine brand you're smoking there.

MAYOR. A Pegasus. Virginia.

ILL. Pretty expensive.

MAYOR. Well worth the money.

ILL. Your Worship used to smoke another brand.

MAYOR. Sailor's Mates.

ILL. Cheaper.

MAYOR. Far too strong.

ILL. New tie?

MAYOR. Silk.

ILL. And I suppose you bought a pair of shoes?

MAYOR. I had some made in Kalberstadt. That's funny, how did you know?

ILL. That's why I've come to see you.

MAYOR. Whatever's the matter with you? You look pale. Are you sick?

ILL. I'm scared.

MAYOR. Scared?

ILL. Living standards are going up.

MAYOR. That's real news to me. I'd be glad if they were.

ILL. I demand official protection.

MAYOR. Eh! Whatever for?

ILL. Your Worship knows very well what for.

MAYOR. Don't you trust us?

ILL. There's a million on my head.

MAYOR. Apply to the police.

ILL. I've been to the police.

MAYOR. And that reassured you.

ILL. When the Police Inspector opened his mouth, I saw a gleaming new gold tooth.

MAYOR. You're forgetting you're in Guellen. A city of Humanist traditions. Goethe spent a night here. Brahms composed a quartet here. We owe allegiance to our lofty heritage.

(*Man Three enters, left, carrying typewriter.*)

MAN. The new typewriter, Mister Mayor. A Remington.

MAYOR. It's to go in the office.

(*Man exits, right.*)

We've not deserved your ingratitude. If you're unable to place any trust in our community, I regret it for your sake. I didn't expect such a nihilistic attitude from you. After all, we live under the rule of law.

ILL. Then arrest that woman.

MAYOR. Peculiar. Highly peculiar.

ILL. The Police Inspector said that too.

MAYOR. God knows, the lady isn't acting so unreasonably. You did bribe two kids to commit perjury and fling a young girl into the lower depths.

ILL. None the less there were quite a few millions down in those lower depths, Mister Mayor.

(*Silence.*)

MAYOR. Let me say a few frank words to you.

ILL. I wish you would.

MAYOR. As man to man, the way you wanted. You haven't any moral right to demand the arrest of that lady, and furthermore there's no question of your becoming Mayor. I'm extremely sorry to have to tell you.

ILL. Officially?

MAYOR. It's an all-party directive.

ILL. I understand.

(*Crosses slowly to window, left, turns back on Mayor and stares out.*)

MAYOR. The fact that we condemn the lady's proposal does not mean we condone the crime which led to that proposal. The post of Mayor requires certain guarantees of good moral character which you can no longer furnish. You must realize that. We shall continue of course to show you the same friendship and regard as ever. That goes without saying.

(*Roby and Toby enter, left, with more wreaths and flowers.*

cross the stage and disappear into the Golden Apostle.)
The best thing is to pass over the whole affair in silence.
I've also requested the local paper not to let any of it get
into print.

(*Ill turns.*)

ILL. They've already begun adorning my coffin, Mister Mayor.
For me, silence is too dangerous.

MAYOR. But my dear Ill, what makes you think that? You
ought to be thankful we're spreading a cloak of forgetfulness over the whole nasty business.

ILL. You've already condemned me to death.

MAYOR. Mr Ill!

ILL. That plan proves it! It proves you have!

CLAIRE ZACHANASSIAN. Onassis will be coming. The Prince
and the Princess. Aga.

HUSBAND VIII. Ali?

CLAIRE ZACHANASSIAN. All the Riviera crowd.

HUSBAND VIII. Reporters?

CLAIRE ZACHANASSIAN. From all over the world. The Press
always attend when I get married. They need me, and I
need them.

(*Opens another letter.*)

From Count Holk.

HUSBAND VIII. Hopsi, this is our first breakfast together. Must
you really spend it reading letters from your former
husbands?

CLAIRE ZACHANASSIAN. I have to keep them under observation.

HUSBAND VIII. I have problems too.

(*Rises to his feet, stares down into town.*)

CLAIRE ZACHANASSIAN. Something wrong with your Porsche?

HUSBAND VIII. Small towns like this get me down. I know the
lime-tree's rustling, the birds are singing, the fountain's

plashing, but they were all doing all that half an hour ago. And nothing else is happening at all, either to the landscape or to the people, it's all a picture of deep, carefree peace and contentment and cosy comfort. No grandeur, no tragedy. Not a trace of the spiritual dedication of a great age.

(*Enter Priest, left, with a rifle slung round his shoulder. Over the table formerly occupied by Policeman he spreads a white cloth marked with a black cross. Leans rifle against wall of hotel. Sexton helps him on with soutane. Darkness.*)

PRIEST. Come in, Ill, come into the sacristy.

(*Ill comes in, left.*)

It's dark in here, dark but cool.

ILL. I don't want to bother you, Father.

PRIEST. The doors of the Church are open to all.

(*Perceives that Ill's gaze has settled on the rifle.*)

Don't be surprised at this weapon. Mrs Zachanassian's black panther is on the prowl. It's just been up in the choir-loft. Now it's in Petersens' Barn.

ILL. I need help.

PRIEST. What kind of help?

ILL. I'm scared.

PRIEST. Scared? Of whom?

ILL. People.

PRIEST. That the people will kill you, Ill?

ILL. They're hunting me as if I were a wild animal.

PRIEST. You should fear not people, but God; not death in the body, but in the soul. Sexton, button the back of my soutane.

(*The citizens of Guellen materialize round the entire periphery of the stage; Policeman first, then Mayor, the four men, Painter, Schoolmaster, on patrol, rifles at the ready, stalking round.*)

ILL. My life's at stake.

PRIEST. Your eternal life.

ILL. There's a rise in the standard of living.

PRIEST. It's the spectre of your conscience rising.

ILL. The people are happy. The young girls are decking themselves out. The boys have put on bright shirts. The town's getting ready to celebrate my murder, and I'm dying of terror.

PRIEST. All they're doing is affirming life, that's all they're doing, affirming life.

ILL. It's Hell.

PRIEST. You are your own Hell. You are older than I am, and you think you know people, but in the end one only knows oneself. Because you once betrayed a young girl for money, many years ago, do you believe the people will betray you now for money? You impute your own nature to others. All too naturally. The cause of our fear and our sin lies in our own hearts. Once you have acknowledged that, you will have conquered your torment and acquired a weapon whereby to master it.

ILL. The Siemethofers have acquired a washing-machine.

PRIEST. Don't let that trouble you.

ILL. On credit.

PRIEST. You should rather be troubled by your soul's immortality.

ILL. And the Stockers, a television set.

PRIEST. Pray to God. Sexton, my bands.

(*Sexton positions bands round Priest.*)

Examine your conscience. Go the way of repentance, or the world will relight the fires of your terror again and again. It is the only way. No other way is open to us.

(*Silence. Men and rifles disappear. Shadows round rim of stage. Fire bell begins clanging.*)

Now I must discharge my office, Ill, I have a baptism.

The Bible, Sexton, the Liturgy, the Book of Psalms.
When little children begin to cry they must be led to
safety, into the only ray of light which illumines the
world.

(*A second bell begins to sound.*)

ILL. A second bell?

PRIEST. Hear it? Splendid tone. Rich and powerful. Just
affirming life.

ILL (*cries out*). You too, Father! You too!

(*Priest flings himself on Ill, clings to him.*)

PRIEST. Flee! We are all weak, believers and unbelievers.
Flee! The Guellen bells are tolling, tolling for treachery.
Flee! Lead us not into temptation with your presence.

(*Two shots are fired. Ill sinks to ground, Priest kneels
beside him.*)

Flee! Flee!

CLAIRE ZACHANASSIAN. Boby. They're shooting.

BUTLER. Yes, Madam, they are.

CLAIRE ZACHANASSIAN. What at?

BUTLER. The black panther escaped, Madam.

CLAIRE ZACHANASSIAN. Did they hit him?

BUTLER. He's dead, Madam, stretched out in front of Ill's
shop.

CLAIRE ZACHANASSIAN. Poor little animal. Roby, play a
funeral march.

(*Funeral march on guitar. Balcony disappears. Bell rings.
Stage set as for opening of Act One. The station. On wall,
however, is a new, untorn time-table and, stuck almost
anywhere, a great poster depicting brilliant yellow sun, with
the legend 'Travel South'. Further along same wall, another,
with the legend 'Visit the Passion Plays in Oberammergau'.
Amidst buildings in background, a few cranes and a few new
roof-tops. Thunderous pounding din of express train rushing*

through. Station-master standing on station salutes. Ill emerges from background, one hand clutching little, old suitcase, and looks around. As if by chance, citizens of Guellen come gradually closing in on him from all sides. Ill moves hesitantly, stops.)

MAYOR. Hallo, Ill.

ALL. Hallo! Hallo!

ILL *(hesitant)*. Hallo.

SCHOOLMASTER. Where are you off to with that suitcase?

ALL. Where are you off to?

ILL. To the station.

MAYOR. We'll take you there.

ALL. We'll take you there! We'll take you there!

(More Guelleners keep arriving.)

ILL. You don't need to, you really don't. It's not worth the trouble.

MAYOR. Going away, Ill?

ILL. I'm going away.

POLICEMAN. Where are you going?

ILL. I don't know. First to Kalberstadt, then a bit further to —

SCHOOLMASTER. Ah! Then a bit further?

ILL. To Australia, preferably. I'll get the money somehow or other.

(Walks on towards station.)

ALL. To Australia! To Australia!

MAYOR. But why?

ILL *(uneasily)*. You can't live in the same place for ever — year in, year out.

(Begins running, reaches station. The others amble over in his wake, surround him.)

MAYOR. Emigrating to Australia. But that's ridiculous.

DOCTOR. The most dangerous thing you could do.

SCHOOLMASTER. One of those two little eunuchs emigrated to Australia.

POLICEMAN. This is the safest place for you.

ALL. The safest place, the safest place.

(*Ill peers fearfully round like a cornered animal.*)

ILL. I wrote to the Chief Constable in Kaffigen.

POLICEMAN. And?

ILL. No answer.

SCHOOLMASTER. Why are you so suspicious? It's incomprehensible.

MAYOR. No one wants to kill you.

ALL. No one, no one.

ILL. The Post Office didn't send the letter.

PAINTER. Impossible.

MAYOR. The Postmaster is a member of the Town Council.

SCHOOLMASTER. An honourable man.

ALL. An honourable man! An honourable man!

ILL. Look at this poster: 'Travel South'.

DOCTOR. What about it?

ILL. 'Visit the Passion Plays in Oberammergau'.

SCHOOLMASTER. What about it?

ILL. They're building!

MAYOR. What about it?

ILL. And you're all wearing new trousers.

MAN ONE. What about it?

ILL. You're all getting richer, you all own more!

ALL. What about it?

(*Bell rings.*)

SCHOOLMASTER. But you must see how fond we are of you.

MAYOR. The whole town's brought you to the station.

ALL. The whole town! The whole town!

ILL. I didn't ask you to come.

MAN TWO. We're surely allowed to come and say goodbye to you.

MAYOR. As old friends.

ALL. As old friends! As old friends!

(*Noise of train. Station-master takes up flag. Guard appears, left, as after jumping down from train.*)

GUARD (*with long-drawn wail*). Guellen!

MAYOR. Here's your train.

ALL. Your train! Your train!

MAYOR. Well, have an enjoyable trip, Ill.

ALL. An enjoyable trip, an enjoyable trip!

DOCTOR. And long life and prosperity to you!

ALL. Long life and prosperity!

(*The citizens of Guellen flock round Ill.*)

MAYOR. It's time. Get on the Kalberstadt train, and God be with you.

POLICEMAN. And good luck in Australia!

ALL. Good luck, good luck!

(*Ill stands motionless staring at his compatriots.*)

ILL (*softly*). Why are you all here?

POLICEMAN. Now what do you want?

STATION-MASTER. Take your seats please!

ILL. Why are you all crowding me?

MAYOR. We're not crowding you at all.

ILL. Let me pass.

SCHOOLMASTER. But we're letting you pass.

ALL. We're letting you pass, we're letting you pass.

ILL. Someone'll stop me.

POLICEMAN. Nonsense. All you need do is get on the train, and you'll see it's nonsense.

ILL. Get out of the way.

(*No one moves. Several stand where they are, hands in pockets, and stare at him.*)

MAYOR. I don't know what you're trying to do. It's up to you to go. Just get on the train.

ILL. Get out of the way!

SCHOOLMASTER. It's simply ridiculous of you to be afraid.

(*Ill falls on knees.*)

ILL. Why have you all come so close to me!

POLICEMAN. The man's gone mad.

ILL. You want to stop me going.

MAYOR. Go on! Get on the train!

ALL. Get on the train! Get on the train!

(*Silence.*)

ILL (*softly*). If I get on the train one of you will hold me back.

ALL (*emphatically*). No we won't! No we won't!

ILL. I know you will.

POLICEMAN. It's nearly time.

SCHOOLMASTER. My dear man, will you please get on the train.

ILL. I know, I know. Someone will hold me back, someone will hold me back.

STATION-MASTER. Stand clear!

(*Waves green flag, blows whistle. Guard assumes position to jump on train as Ill, surrounded by the citizens of Guellen, his head in his hands, collapses.*)

POLICEMAN. Look! He's collapsed!

(*Leaving Ill crumpled in collapse, all walk slowly towards back of stage and disappear.*)

ILL. I am lost!

ACT THREE

Petersens' Barn. Claire Zachanassian seated, left, immobile in sedan-chair, clad in white wedding-gown, veil, etc. Further left, a ladder. Further back, a hay-cart, an old hansom-cab, straw. Centre, small cask. Rags and mouldering sacks hang from beams. Enormous outspun spiders' webs. Enter Butler from back.

BUTLER. The Doctor and the Schoolmaster.

CLAIRE ZACHANASSIAN. Show them in.

> (*Enter Doctor and Schoolmaster, groping through the gloom. When at last they locate the millionairess, they bow. Both are clad in good, solid, very nearly fashionable bourgeois clothes.*)

DOCTOR/SCHOOLMASTER. Madam.

> (*Claire Zachanassian raises lorgnette, inspects them.*)

CLAIRE ZACHANASSIAN. You appear to be covered in dust, gentlemen.

> (*Both rub away dust with hands.*)

SCHOOLMASTER. Excuse us. We had to climb in over an old hansom-cab.

CLAIRE ZACHANASSIAN. I've retired to Petersens' Barn. I need peace and quiet. I found the wedding in Guellen Cathedral a strain. I'm not a dewy young maiden any more. You can sit on that cask.

SCHOOLMASTER. Thank you.

> (*He sits on it. Doctor remains standing.*)

CLAIRE ZACHANASSIAN. Pretty hot here. Suffocating, I'd say. Still, I love this barn, and the smell of hay and straw and axle-grease. Memories. The dung-fork. The hansom-cab. That busted hay-cart, and all the other implements. They were here when I was a child.

SCHOOLMASTER. A suggestive spot.

> (*Mops away sweat.*)

CLAIRE ZACHANASSIAN. An uplifting sermon by the Priest.

253

SCHOOLMASTER. First Corinthians, thirteen.

CLAIRE ZACHANASSIAN. And a very stout performance on your part, Professor, with the mixed choir. It sounded grand.

SCHOOLMASTER. Bach. From the Saint Matthew Passion. My head is still spinning with it all. The place was packed with High Society, Financiers, Film Stars ...

CLAIRE ZACHANASSIAN. Society went whizzing back to the Capital in its Cadillacs. For the wedding breakfast.

SCHOOLMASTER. My dear lady: we don't wish to take up more of your precious time than necessary. Your husband will be growing impatient.

CLAIRE ZACHANASSIAN. Hoby? I've sent him back to Geiselgasteig in his Porsche.

DOCTOR (*staggered*). To Geiselgasteig?

CLAIRE ZACHANASSIAN. My lawyers have already filed the divorce.

SCHOOLMASTER. But Madam, the wedding guests!

CLAIRE ZACHANASSIAN. They're used to it. It's my second-shortest marriage. Only the one with Lord Ishmael was a trifle quicker. What brings you here?

SCHOOLMASTER. We've come to discuss the Ill affair.

CLAIRE ZACHANASSIAN. O, has he died?

SCHOOLMASTER. Madam! We're still loyal to our Western principles.

CLAIRE ZACHANASSIAN. Then what do you want?

SCHOOLMASTER. The Guelleners have most, most regrettably acquired a number of new possessions.

DOCTOR. A considerable number.

(*Both mop off sweat.*)

CLAIRE ZACHANASSIAN. In debt?

SCHOOLMASTER. Hopelessly.

CLAIRE ZACHANASSIAN. In spite of your principles?

SCHOOLMASTER. We're only human.

DOCTOR. And now we must pay our debts.

CLAIRE ZACHANASSIAN. You know what you have to do.

SCHOOLMASTER (*bravely*). Madam Zachanassian. Let's be frank with each other. Put yourself in our melancholy position. For two decades, I have been sowing the Humanities' tender seeds in this poverty-stricken population, and our doctor too for two decades has been trundling around curing its rickets and consumption in his antediluvian Mercedes. Why such agony of sacrifice? For the money? Hardly. Our fee is minimal. Furthermore I received and flatly rejected an offer from Kalberstadt College, just as the doctor here turned down a chair in Erlangen University. Out of pure love for our fellow-beings? No, no, that would also be saying too much. No. We, and this entire little township with us, have hung on all these endless years because of a single hope: the hope that Guellen would rise again, in all its ancient grandeur, and the untold wealth in our native soil be once again exploited. Oil is waiting under Pückenried Valley, and under Konrad's Village Wood there are minerals for the mining. Madam, we are not poor; we are merely forgotten. We need credit, confidence, contracts, then our economy and culture will boom. Guellen has much to offer: the Foundry on Sunshine Square.

DOCTOR. Bockmann's.

SCHOOLMASTER. The Wagner Factory. Buy them. Revive them. And Guellen will boom. Invest a few hundred thousand, carefully, systematically. They'll produce a good return. Don't simply squander a million!

CLAIRE ZACHANASSIAN. I've two others.

SCHOOLMASTER. Don't condemn us to a lifelong struggle in vain. We haven't come begging for alms. We've come to make a business proposition.

CLAIRE ZACHANASSIAN. Really. As business goes, it wouldn't be bad.

SCHOOLMASTER. My dear lady! I knew you wouldn't leave us in the lurch.

CLAIRE ZACHANASSIAN. Only it can't be done. I can't buy Sunshine Square, because I own it already.

SCHOOLMASTER. *You* own it?

DOCTOR. And Bockmann's?

SCHOOLMASTER. The Wagner Factory?

CLAIRE ZACHANASSIAN. I own those too. And all the factories, Pückenried Valley, Petersens' Barn, the entire township; street by street and house by house. I had my agents buy the whole ramshackle lot and shut every business down. Your hopes were lunacy, your perseverance pointless, and your self-sacrifice foolish; your lives have been a useless waste.

(*Silence.*)

DOCTOR. What a monstrous thing.

CLAIRE ZACHANASSIAN. It was winter, long ago, when I left this little town, in a schoolgirl sailor suit and long red plaits, pregnant with only a short while to go, and the townsfolk sniggering at me. I sat in the Hamburg Express and shivered; but as I watched the silhouette of Petersens' Barn sinking away on the other side of the frost-flowers, I swore a vow to myself, I would come back again, one day. I've come back now. Now it's me imposing the conditions. Me driving the bargain. (*Calls —*) Roby and Toby, to the Golden Apostle. Husband number nine's on the way with his books and manuscripts.

(*The two giants emerge from background, lift sedan-chair.*)

SCHOOLMASTER. Madam Zachanassian! You're a woman whose love has been wounded. You make me think of a heroine from antiquity: of Medea. We feel for you, deeply; we understand; but because we do, we are inspired to prove you further: cast away those evil thoughts of revenge, don't try us till we break.

Help these poor, weak yet worthy people lead a slightly more dignified life. Let your feeling for humanity prevail!

CLAIRE ZACHANASSIAN. Feeling for humanity, gentlemen, is cut for the purse of an ordinary millionaire; with financial resources like mine you can afford a new world order. The world turned me into a whore. I shall turn the world into a brothel. If you can't fork out when you want to dance, you have to put off dancing. You want to dance. They alone are eligible who pay. And I'm paying. Guellen for a murder, a boom for a body. Come on, the pair of you, off we go!

(*She is borne away into background.*)

DOCTOR. My God. What shall we do?

SCHOOLMASTER. The dictates of our conscience, Doctor Nuesslin.

(*Ill's shop appears in foreground, right. New sign. Glittering new shop-counter, new till, costlier stock. Whenever anyone enters the imaginary door, a bell rings, magnificently. Behind shop-counter, Mrs Ill. Enter, left, Man One — a thriving butcher. Scattered bloodstains on his new apron.*)

MAN ONE. That was a ceremony. The whole of Guellen was on Cathedral Square watching it.

MRS ILL. Clarie deserves a little happiness, after all she's been through.

MAN ONE. Every bridesmaid was a film starlet. With breasts like this.

MRS ILL. They're in fashion today.

MAN ONE. And newspapermen. They'll be coming here too.

MRS ILL. We're simple people, Mr Hofbauer. They won't want anything from us.

MAN ONE. They pump everybody. Cigarettes.

MRS ILL. Green?

MAN ONE. Camels. And a bottle of aspirins. Went to a party at Stocker's last night.

MRS ILL. On account?

MAN ONE. On account.

MRS ILL. How's business?

MAN ONE. Keeps me going.

MRS ILL. Me too. Can't grumble.

MAN ONE. I've got more staff.

MRS ILL. I'm getting someone on the first.

(*Miss Louisa walks across stage in stylish clothes.*)

MAN ONE. She's got her head full of dreams dressing up like that. She must imagine we'd murder Ill.

MRS ILL. Shameless.

MAN ONE. Where is he, by the way? Haven't seen him for quite a while.

MRS ILL. Upstairs.

(*Man One lights cigarette, cocks ear towards ceiling.*)

MAN ONE. Footsteps.

MRS ILL. Always walking around in his room. Has been for days.

MAN ONE. It's his bad conscience. Nasty trick he played on poor Madam Zachanassian.

MRS ILL. It's upset me terribly too.

MAN ONE. Getting a young girl in trouble. Rotten bastard. (*Speaks with decision.*) Mrs Ill, I hope your husband won't blabber when the journalists come.

MRS ILL. Not really.

MAN ONE. What with his character.

MRS ILL. I have a hard time of it, Mr Hofbauer.

MAN ONE. If he tries showing up Clara, and telling lies, claiming she offered something for his death, or some such story, when it was only a figure of speech for unspeakable suffering, then we'll *have* to step in. Not because of the million. (*He spits.*) But because of public indignation. God knows he's already put that sweet Madam Zachanassian through enough. (*He looks round.*) Is that a way up to the apartment?

MRS ILL. It's the only way up. Most inconvenient. But we're having another one built in the spring.

MAN ONE. I'd better just plant myself here. You can't be too sure.

(*Man One plants himself there, very upright stance, arms folded, quietly, like a warder. Enter Schoolmaster.*)

SCHOOLMASTER. Ill?

MAN ONE. Upstairs.

SCHOOLMASTER. It really isn't like me, but I need some kind of strong, alcoholic beverage.

MRS ILL. How nice of you to come and see us, Professor. We've a new Steinhäger in. Would you like to try it?

SCHOOLMASTER. A small glass.

MRS ILL. You too, Mr Hofbauer?

MAN ONE. No thanks. Still have to drive my Volkswagen into Kaffigen. There's pork to buy.

(*Mrs Ill pours a glassful. Schoolmaster drinks.*)

MRS ILL. But you're trembling, Professor.

SCHOOLMASTER. I've been over-drinking lately.

MRS ILL. One more won't harm.

SCHOOLMASTER. Is that him walking about?

(*Cocks ear towards ceiling.*)

MRS ILL. Up and down, all the time.

MAN ONE. God will punish him.

(*Enter, left, Painter with picture under arm. New corduroys, colourful neckerchief, black beret.*)

PAINTER. Watch out. Two reporters asked me about this shop.

MAN ONE. Suspicious.

PAINTER. I acted ignorant.

MAN ONE. Clever.

PAINTER. For you, Mrs Ill. Fresh off the easel. It's still damp.

(*Exhibits picture. Schoolmaster pours himself another drink.*)

MRS ILL. It's my husband.

PAINTER. Art's beginning to boom in Guellen. How's that for painting, eh?

MRS ILL. A real likeness.

PAINTER. Oils. Last for ever.

MRS ILL. We could hang it in the bedroom. Over the bed. Alfred'll be old one day. And you never know what might happen, it's a comfort to have a souvenir.

(*The two women from Act Two, passing by outside, stop and examine wares in imaginary shop-window. Both elegantly dressed.*)

MAN ONE. Look at those women. Going to the films in broad daylight. The way they behave, you'd think we were sheer murderers!

MRS ILL. Expensive?

PAINTER. Thirty pounds.

MRS ILL. I can't pay now.

PAINTER. Doesn't matter. I'll wait, Mrs Ill, I'll be happy to wait.

SCHOOLMASTER. Those footsteps, those footsteps all the time.

(*Enter Man Two, left.*)

MAN TWO. The Press.

MAN ONE. All stick together. It's life or death.

PAINTER. Watch out he doesn't come down.

MAN ONE. That's taken care of.

(*The Guelleners gather to right. Schoolmaster having now drunk half the bottle remains standing at counter. Enter two Reporters carrying cameras.*)

FIRST REPORTER. 'Evening, folks.

GUELLENERS. How do you do.

FIRST REPORTER. Question one: How do you all feel, on the whole?

MAN ONE (*uneasily*). We're very happy of course about Madam Zachanassian's visit.

PAINTER. Moved.

MAN TWO. Proud.

FIRST REPORTER. Proud.

SECOND REPORTER. Question two for the lady behind the counter: the story goes, you were the lucky woman instead of Madam Zachanassian.

(*Silence. Guelleners manifestly shocked.*)

MRS ILL. Where did you get that story?

(*Silence. Both Reporters write impassively in notebooks.*)

FIRST REPORTER. Madam Zachanassian's two fat blind little mannikins.

(*Silence.*)

MRS ILL (*hesitant*). What did the mannikins tell you?

SECOND REPORTER. Everything.

PAINTER. Goddam.

(*Silence.*)

SECOND REPORTER. Forty years ago Claire Zachanassian and the proprietor of this shop nearly married. Right?

MRS ILL. That's right.

SECOND REPORTER. Is Mr Ill here?

MRS ILL. He's in Kalberstadt.

ALL. He's in Kalberstadt.

FIRST REPORTER. We can imagine the Ro-mance. Mr Ill and Claire Zachanassian grow up together, maybe they're next-door kids, they go to school together, go for walks in the wood, share the first kisses, they're like brother and sister, and so it goes on till Mr Ill meets you, lady, and you're the new woman, his mystery, his passion.

MRS ILL. Passion. Yes, that's how it happened, just the way you said.

FIRST REPORTER. Foxy, foxy, Mrs Ill. Claire Zachanassian grasps the situation, in her quiet, noble fashion she renounces her claims, and you marry ...

MRS ILL. For love.

GUELLENERS (*on whom light dawns*). For love.

FIRST REPORTER. For love.

(*Enter, right, Roby leading the pair of eunuchs by their ears.*)

THE PAIR (*wailing*). We won't tell any more stories, we won't tell any more stories.

(*They are dragged towards back of stage, where Toby awaits them with whip.*)

SECOND REPORTER. About your husband, Mrs Ill, doesn't he now and then, I mean, it'd be only human for him, now and then, to feel a few regrets.

MRS ILL. Money alone makes no one happy.

SECOND REPORTER (*writing*). No one happy.

FIRST REPORTER. That's a truth we in this modern world ought to write up in the sky of our hearts.

(*Enter Son, left, wearing suede jacket.*)

MRS ILL. Our son Karl.

FIRST REPORTER. Splendid youngster.

SECOND REPORTER. Is he in the know about the relationship ?..

MRS ILL. There are no secrets in our family. What we always say is, anything God knows our children ought to know.

SECOND REPORTER (*writing*). Children ought to know.

(*Daughter walks into shop, wearing tennis-outfit, carrying tennis-racket.*)

MRS ILL. Our daughter Ottilie.

SECOND REPORTER. Charming.

(*Schoolmaster now calls up courage.*)

SCHOOLMASTER. Guelleners. I am your old schoolmaster. I've been quietly drinking my Steinhäger and keeping my thoughts to myself. But now I want to make a speech. I want to talk about the old lady's visit to Guellen.

(*Scrambles on to the little cask left over from the scene in Petersens' Barn.*)

MAN ONE. Have you gone mad?

MAN TWO. Stop him!

SCHOOLMASTER. Guelleners! I want to reveal the truth, even if our poverty endures for ever!

MRS ILL. You're drunk, Professor, you ought to be ashamed of yourself!

SCHOOLMASTER. Ashamed? You're the one to be ashamed, woman! You're paving your way to betray your own husband!

SON. Shut your trap!

MAN ONE. Drag him down!

MAN TWO. Kick him out!

SCHOOLMASTER. You've nearly contrived your doom!

DAUGHTER (*supplicating*). Please, Professor!

SCHOOLMASTER. Child, you disappoint me. It was up to you to speak out, and now your old schoolmaster must unleash the voice of thunder!

(*Painter breaks painting over his head.*)

PAINTER. There! You'll sabotage all my commissions!

SCHOOLMASTER. I protest! I wish to make a public appeal to world opinion! Guellen is planning a monstrous deed!

(*The Guelleners launch themselves at him as, simultaneously, in an old tatterdemalion suit, Ill enters, right.*)

ILL. Just what is going on here, in my shop!

(*The Guelleners fall back from Schoolmaster to stare at Ill, shocked. Deathly silence.*)

Professor! What are you up to on that cask!

(*Schoolmaster beams at Ill in happy relief.*)

SCHOOLMASTER. The truth, Ill. I'm telling the gentlemen of the Press the truth. Like an archangel I'm telling them, in forceful ringing tones. (*Wavers.*) Because I'm a humanist, a lover of the ancient Greeks, an admirer of Plato.

ILL. Hold your peace.

SCHOOLMASTER. Eh?

ILL. Get down.

SCHOOLMASTER. But humanitarianism —

ILL. Sit down.

(*Silence.*)

SCHOOLMASTER (*sobered*). Humanitarianism has to sit down. By all means — if you're going to betray truth as well.

(*Steps down from cask, sits on it, picture still round his neck.*)

ILL. Excuse this. The man's drunk.

FIRST REPORTER. Mr Ill?

ILL. What is it?

FIRST REPORTER. We're very glad we finally got to meet you. We need a few pictures. May we? (*Glances round.*) Groceries, household wares, ironmongery — I've got it: we'll take you selling an axe.

ILL (*hesitant*). An axe?

FIRST REPORTER. To the butcher. You gotta have Realism for a punch. Give me that homicidal weapon here. Your client takes the axe, weighs it in his hand, he puts an appraising expression on his face, while you lean across the counter, you're discussing it with him. O.K., let's go.

(*He arranges the shot.*)

More natural, folks, more relaxed.

(*Reporters click their cameras.*)

That's fine, just fine.

SECOND REPORTER. Now if you don't mind please, one arm round your good wife's shoulders. Son on the left, daughter on the right. That's fine. O.K., now, you're radiant with happiness, please, just brimming over with it, radiant, radiant and contented deep down inside, quietly, happily radiant.

FIRST REPORTER. Great, great, that sure was radiant.

(*Several Photographers come running in, downstage left, cross the boards and go running out, upstage left. One photographer bawls into shop —*)

PHOTOGRAPHER. Zachanassian's got a new one. They're taking a walk in Konrad's Village Wood, right now.

SECOND REPORTER. A new one!

FIRST REPORTER. That's good for a cover on *Life* magazine.

(*The two Reporters race out of shop. Silence. Man One is left still gripping axe.*)

MAN ONE (*relieved*). That was a bit of luck.

PAINTER. Forgive us, Professor. If we still hope to settle this affair amicably, we've got to exclude the Press. Agreed?

(*Exit, followed by Man Two. But passing Ill, Man Two pauses.*)

MAN TWO. Smart. Very smart you didn't shoot your mouth. No one would believe a word a bastard like you said anyway.

(*Exit Man Two.*)

MAN ONE. We'll be in the illustrateds, Ill.

ILL. Yes.

MAN ONE. We'll be famous.

ILL. In a manner of speaking.

MAN ONE. A Corona.

ILL. Certainly.

MAN ONE. On account.

ILL. Of course.

MAN ONE. Let's face it: what you did to little Clara was a real worm's trick.

(*Begins to go.*)

ILL. Hofbauer. The axe.

(*Man One hesitates, then returns axe to Ill. Silence in shop. Schoolmaster is still sitting on his cask.*)

SCHOOLMASTER. I apologize. I've been trying the Steinhäger. Must have had two or three.

ILL. It's all right.

(*The family cross to right, and exit.*)

SCHOOLMASTER. I wanted to help you. But they shouted me down, and you didn't want my help either. (*Disengages himself from picture.*) Ah, Ill. What kind of people are we. That infamous million is burning up our hearts. Pull yourself together, fight for your life. Enlist the sympathy of the Press. You haven't any more time to lose.

ILL. I'm not fighting any more.

SCHOOLMASTER (*amazed*). Tell me, has fear driven you completely out of your senses?

ILL. I've realized I haven't the least right on my side.

SCHOOLMASTER. No right? No right compared to that damned old woman, that brazen arch-whore changing husbands while we watch, and making a collection of our souls?

ILL. That's all my fault, really.

SCHOOLMASTER. Your fault?

ILL. I made Clara what she is, and I made myself what I am, a failing shopkeeper with a bad name. What shall I do, Schoolmaster? Play innocent? It's all my own work, the Eunuchs, the Butler, the coffin, the million. I can't help myself and I can't help any of you, any more.

(*Takes up torn painting and examines it.*)

My portrait.

SCHOOLMASTER. Your wife wanted to hang it in your bedroom. Over the bed.

ILL. Kuhn will paint another.

(*Lays picture down on counter. Schoolmaster stands with an effort, sways.*)

SCHOOLMASTER. I'm sober. All at once.

(*He reels across to Ill.*)

You are right. Absolutely. It's all your fault. And now I want to tell you something, Alfred Ill, something fundamental.

(*Stands facing Ill, stiff as a ramrod and hardly swaying at all.*)

They will kill you. I've known it from the beginning, and you've known it too for a long time, even if no one else in Guellen wants to admit it. The temptation is too great and our poverty is too wretched. But I know something else. I shall take part in it. I can feel myself slowly becoming a murderer. My faith in humanity is powerless to stop it. And because I know all this, I have also become a sot. I too am scared, Ill, just as you have been scared. And finally I know that one day an old lady will come for us too, and then what happened to you will also happen to us, but soon, perhaps in a few hours, I shall have lost that knowledge. (*Silence.*) Another bottle of Steinhäger.

(*Ill gets him a bottle, Schoolmaster hesitates, then firmly takes and clutches bottle.*)

Put it on my account.

(*Walks slowly out.*

The family return. Ill looks round at his shop as if dreaming.)

ILL. It's all new. Our place looks so modern nowadays. Clean. Inviting. I've always dreamed of having a shop like this.

(*Takes Daughter's tennis-racket from her hand.*)

D'you play tennis?

DAUGHTER. I've had a couple of lessons.

ILL. Early mornings, eh? Instead of going to the Labour Exchange?

DAUGHTER. All my friends play tennis.

(*Silence.*)

ILL. I was looking out of my bedroom window, Karl, and I saw you in an automobile.

SON. It's only an Opel, they aren't so expensive.

ILL. When did you learn to drive?

(*Silence.*)

Instead of looking for work on the railroad in the blazing sun, eh?

SON. Sometimes.

(*Son, embarrassed, crosses to cask on which the drunk has been sitting, shoves it to right and out.*)

ILL. I was looking for my Sunday suit. I found a fur coat hanging beside it.

MRS ILL. It's on approval.

(*Silence.*)

Everyone's making debts, Freddy. You're the only one throwing fits of hysterics. It's simply ridiculous of you to be scared. It's so obvious the thing's going to be settled peacefully, without anyone harming a hair of your head. Clarie won't go the whole way, I know her, she's too good-hearted.

DAUGHTER. Of course, father.

SON. Surely you realize that.

(*Silence.*)

ILL (*slowly*). It's Saturday. Karl, I'd like to go for a drive in your automobile, just once. In *our* automobile.

SON (*uncertainly*). You'd like that?

ILL. Put on your best clothes. We'll all go for a drive together.

MRS ILL (*uncertainly*). Am I to go with you? But surely that wouldn't do.

ILL. And why wouldn't it do? Go and put on your fur coat, this'll be an opportunity to christen it. I'll be seeing to the till in the meantime.

(*Exit Mother and Daughter, right. Exit Son, left. Ill busies himself at till. Enter, left, Mayor carrying rifle.*)

MAYOR. Good evening, Ill. Don't let me trouble you. I'll just have a quick look round.

ILL. By all means.

(*Silence.*)

MAYOR. Brought you a gun.

ILL. Thanks.

MAYOR. It's loaded.

ILL. I don't need it.

(*Mayor leans gun against counter.*)

MAYOR. There's a public meeting this evening. In the Golden Apostle. In the auditorium.

ILL. I'll be there.

MAYOR. Everyone'll be there. We're dealing with your case. We're under a certain amount of pressure.

ILL. That's what I feel.

MAYOR. The motion will be rejected,

ILL. Possibly.

MAYOR. People make mistakes, of course.

ILL. Of course.

(*Silence.*)

MAYOR (*cautiously*). In such a case, Ill, would you then submit to the judgment? Since the Press will be present.

ILL. The Press?

MAYOR. And the Radio. And the Television and News-reel cameras. Very ticklish situation. Not only for you. For us too, believe you me. We're famous as the old lady's native town, and also because of her marriage in the Cathedral here. So now they're going to run a commentary on our ancient democratic institutions.

(*Ill busies himself at till.*)

ILL. Are you making public knowledge of the lady's offer?

MAYOR. Not directly. Only the initiated will grasp the full meaning of the procedure.

ILL. The fact that my life is at stake.

(*Silence.*)

MAYOR. I've let a few hints leak out to the Press that Madam Zachanassian may — there's just a possibility she may make an endowment and that you, Ill, as her childhood friend, will have negotiated that endowment. Of course, it's well known by now that you in fact were her childhood friend. This means that so far as appearances go, you'll have an absolutely clean record.

ILL. That's kind of you.

MAYOR. To be quite frank, I didn't do it for your sake. I was really thinking of your fine, upright, honest family.

ILL. I see.

MAYOR. You've got to admit we're playing fair with you. Up to now, you've kept quiet. Good. But will you go on keeping quiet? If you intend to talk, we'll have to settle the whole business without a public meeting.

ILL. I understand.

MAYOR. Well?

ILL. I'm glad to hear an open threat.

MAYOR. I'm not threatening you, Ill, you're threatening us. If you talk, we'll have to act accordingly. First.

ILL. I'll keep quiet.

MAYOR. However the decision turns out at the meeting?

ILL. I'll accept it.

MAYOR. Good.

(*Silence.*)

I'm glad you'll abide by the ruling of our community court, Ill. You still have a certain glimmer of honour in you. But wouldn't it be better if we didn't even have to call on that community court to assemble?

ILL. What are you trying to say?

MAYOR. When I came in, you said you didn't need the gun. But now, perhaps, you do need it.

(*Silence.*)

We might then tell the lady we had brought you to justice and that way, just the same, receive the money. You can imagine the sleepless nights I've spent on that suggestion. But isn't it your duty, as a man of honour, to draw your own conclusions and make an end of your life? If only out of public spirit, and your love for your native town. You're well aware of our wretched privations, the misery here, and the hungry children ...

ILL. You're all doing very well.

MAYOR. Ill!

ILL. Mister Mayor! I have been through a Hell. I've watched you all getting into debt, and I've felt death creeping towards me, nearer and nearer with every sign of prosperity. If you had spared me that anguish, that gruesome terror, it might all have been different, this discussion might have been different, and I might have taken the gun. For all your sakes. Instead, I shut myself in. I conquered my fear. Alone. It was hard, and now it's done. There is no turning back. You *must* judge me, now. I shall accept your judgment, whatever it may be. For me, it will be justice; what it will be for you, I do not know. God grant you find your judgment justified. You may kill me, I will not complain and I will not protest, nor will I defend myself. But I cannot spare you the task of the trial.

(*Mayor takes back gun.*)

MAYOR. Pity. You're missing a chance to redeem yourself and be a more or less decent human being. I might have known it was too much to ask you.

ILL. Match, Mister Mayor.

(*Lights cigarette for Mayor. Exit Mayor.*
Enter Mrs Ill in fur coat, Daughter in red dress.)

You look very distinguished, Matilda.

MRS ILL. Persian lamb.

ILL. Like a real lady.

MRS ILL. Quite expensive.

ILL. Pretty dress, Ottilie. But isn't it a little bold?

DAUGHTER. O silly Daddy. You should just take a peek at my evening dress.

(*Shop disappears. Son drives up in motor-car.*)

ILL. Fine automobile. You know, I toiled a lifetime to get a little property, a mite of comfort, say for example an automobile like this, and now, my time's up, but still, I'd like to know how it feels to be inside one of these. Matilda, get in the back with me, you in the front, Ottilie, next to Karl.

(*They get into motor-car.*)

SON. It'll do eighty.

ILL. Not so fast. I want to see a bit of the scenery, a bit of the town, I've lived here nearly seventy years. They've cleaned up the old streets. Lot of reconstruction, already. Grey smoke, coming out of those chimneys. Geraniums there in the window-boxes. Sunflowers. The Goethe Arch, they've planted roses in the gardens. Don't the children look happy; and sweethearts, all over the place. Brahms Square, that's a new apartment block.

MRS ILL. They're re-doing the Café Hodel.

DAUGHTER. There goes the Doctor, in his Mercedes 300.

ILL. Look at the plain, and the light on the hills beyond, all golden, today. Impressive, when you go into the shadows and then out again into the light. Those cranes on the horizon by the Wagner Factory look like giants; and the Bockmann chimneys too.

SON. They're starting up again.

ILL. What's that?

SON (*louder*). They're starting up again.

(*Hoots horn.*)

MRS ILL. Funny little car.

SON. Bubble-car: Messerschmidt. Every kid in the Technical College has one.

DAUGHTER. C'est terrible.

MRS ILL. Ottilie's taking her Advanced in French and German.

ILL. Useful. Sunshine Square. The Foundry. Long time since I've been out here.

SON. They're going to build a bigger one.

ILL. You'll have to talk louder at this speed.

SON (*louder*). They're going to build a bigger one. Stocker again, who else. Passing everybody in his Buick.

DAUGHTER. Un nouveau riche.

ILL. Now drive through Pückenried Valley. Go past the Moor and down Poplar Boulevard, round Prince Hasso's Hunting Lodge. Colossal clouds in the sky, banks of them, real summer-time castles. It's a beautiful country in a soft twilight. I feel I'm seeing it today the first time.

DAUGHTER. Atmosphere like Tennyson.

ILL. Like what?

MRS ILL. Ottilie's studying literature too.

ILL. It'll give her advantages.

SON. Hofbauer in his Volkswagen. Coming back from Kaffigen.

DAUGHTER. With the pork.

MRS ILL. Karl drives well. Very smart, the way he cut that corner. You don't feel frightened with him.

SON. First gear. The road's getting steep.

ILL. I always used to get out of breath walking up here.

MRS ILL. I'm so glad I brought my fur coat. It's getting quite chilly.

ILL. You've come the wrong way. This road goes to Beisenbach. You'll have to go back and then left, into Konrad's Village Wood.

(*Motor-car reverses into background. Enter, carrying wooden bench, and wearing dress-suits now, the four citizens who designate trees.*)

MAN ONE.
We're standing in for trees again,
A spruce, a fir, a beech, a pine,

MAN TWO.
We're bird and beast, we're timid deer,
We're woodpeckers;
MAN THREE.
The cuckoos here
Sing songs of bygone nights and dawns,
MAN FOUR.
Outraged today by motor horns.

SON (*hoots horn*). Another deer. That animal just won't get
off the road.
(*Man Three jumps off the road.*)
DAUGHTER. They're so trusting. The poaching's stopped.
ILL. Stop under these trees.
SON. Sure.
MRS ILL. What do you want to do?
ILL. Walk through the woods. (*He gets out.*) The Guellen bells
are ringing. They sound so good from here. Time to
stop work.
SON. Four of them. First time they sound like real bells.
ILL. Everything's yellow. The autumn's really here. The
leaves on the ground are like layers of gold.
(*He tramples amongst leaves on the ground.*)
SON. We'll wait for you down by Guellen Bridge.
ILL. You needn't wait. I shall walk through the wood into
town. To the public meeting.
MRS ILL. In that case we'll drive into Kalberstadt, Freddy, and
see a film.
SON. 'Bye, father.
DAUGHTER. Au revoir, papa.
MRS ILL. See you soon! See you soon!
(*Motor-car with family in it disappears, returns in reverse,
the family waving; Ill watches them out of sight. Sits on
wooden bench, left.*

Rush of wind. Enter Roby and Toby, right, bearing sedan-chair in which Claire Zachanassian, seated, wearing her customary clothes. Roby carries guitar slung at his back. Husband IX comes striding in beside her — the Nobel Prize-winner, tall, slender, hair peppered grey, moustache. (May also be played by same actor as earlier husbands.) Butler brings up rear.)

CLAIRE ZACHANASSIAN. It's the Konrad's Village Wood. Roby and Toby, stop a moment.

(Claire Zachanassian descends from sedan-chair, inspects wood through lorgnette, and strokes back of Man One.)

Bark-beetle. This tree's withering away. *(Notices Ill.)* Alfred! How nice to see you! I'm visiting my Wood.

ILL. Does Konrad's Village Wood belong to you as well?

CLAIRE ZACHANASSIAN. Yes, it does. May I sit down beside you?

ILL. By all means. I've just said goodbye to my family. They've gone to the cinema. Karl's got himself an automobile.

CLAIRE ZACHANASSIAN. Progress.

(Sits down beside Ill, right.)

ILL. Ottilie's taking a course in literature. French and German as well.

CLAIRE ZACHANASSIAN. You see, they have developed a sense of ideals after all. Zoby, come and make your bow. My ninth husband. Nobel Prize-winner.

ILL. Very glad to meet you.

CLAIRE ZACHANASSIAN. He's particularly interesting when he stops thinking. Stop thinking a moment, Zoby.

HUSBAND IX. But Precious ...

CLAIRE ZACHANASSIAN. No showing off.

HUSBAND IX. Oh all right.

(Stops thinking.)

CLAIRE ZACHANASSIAN. See? Now he looks like a diplomat. Reminds me of Count Holk, except that he couldn't write books. He wants to go into retirement, publish his memoirs and manage my property.

ILL. Congratulations.

CLAIRE ZACHANASSIAN. I feel uneasy about it. You only have husbands for display purposes, they shouldn't be useful. Zoby, go away and do some research. You'll find the historical ruins on the left.

(*Husband* IX *goes away to do some research. Ill glances round.*)

ILL. What's happened to the two Eunuchs?

CLAIRE ZACHANASSIAN. They were getting garrulous. I had them shipped off to Hong Kong. Put in one of my opium dens. They can smoke and they can dream. The Butler will follow them soon. I shan't be needing him either, any more. Boby, a Romeo and Juliet.

(*Butler emerges from background, passes her a cigarette case.*)

Would you like one, Alfred?

ILL. Thank you.

CLAIRE ZACHANASSIAN. Here, then. Give us a light, Boby.

(*They smoke.*)

ILL. Smells good.

CLAIRE ZACHANASSIAN. We often smoked together in this wood; do you remember? You used to buy the cigarettes from little Matil'da. Or steal them.

(*Man One taps key on pipe.*)

That woodpecker again.

MAN FOUR. Cuckoo! Cuckoo!

CLAIRE ZACHANASSIAN. Would you like Roby to play for you on his guitar?

ILL. Please.

CLAIRE ZACHANASSIAN. My amnestied killer plays well. I need

him for meditative moments. I hate gramophones. And
radios.

ILL. There's an army marching in an African valley.

CLAIRE ZACHANASSIAN. Your favourite song. I taught it to
him.

(*Silence. They smoke. Cuckoo call, forest sounds, etc. Roby
plays ballad.*)

ILL. You had — I mean, we had a child.

CLAIRE ZACHANASSIAN. True.

ILL. Was it a boy or a girl?

CLAIRE ZACHANASSIAN. A girl.

ILL. And what name did you give it?

CLAIRE ZACHANASSIAN. Genevieve.

ILL. Pretty name.

CLAIRE ZACHANASSIAN. I only saw the thing once. At birth.
Then they took it away. The Salvation Army.

ILL. Eyes?

CLAIRE ZACHANASSIAN. Not yet open.

ILL. Hair?

CLAIRE ZACHANASSIAN. I think it had black hair. But then
new-born babies often have black hair.

ILL. Yes, they often do.

(*Silence. They smoke. Guitar plays.*)
Where did it die?

CLAIRE ZACHANASSIAN. With some people. I've forgotten
their name.

ILL. What of?

CLAIRE ZACHANASSIAN. Meningitis. Perhaps it was something
else. I did receive a card from the authorities.

ILL. In cases of death you can rely on them.

(*Silence.*)

CLAIRE ZACHANASSIAN. I've talked about our little girl. Now
you talk about me.

ILL. About you?

CLAIRE ZACHANASSIAN. The way I was, when I was seventeen, when you loved me.

ILL. I had to look for you a long while once in Petersens' Barn; I found you in the old carriage with nothing on but a blouse and a long straw between your lips.

CLAIRE ZACHANASSIAN. You were strong and brave. You fought that railwayman when he tried to paw me. I wiped the blood off your face with my red petticoat.

(*Guitar stops playing.*)

The ballad has ended.

ILL. One more: 'Home Sweet Home'.

CLAIRE ZACHANASSIAN. Yes, Roby can play that.

(*Guitar resumes play.*)

ILL. Thank you for the wreaths, and for the chrysanthemums and roses. They'll look fine on the coffin in the Golden Apostle. Distinguished. They fill two rooms already. Now the time has come. It is the last time we shall sit in our old wood and hear the cuckoo calling and the sound of the wind. They are meeting this evening. They will sentence me to death, and one of them will kill me. I don't know who it will be, and I don't know where it will happen, I only know that my meaningless life will end.

CLAIRE ZACHANASSIAN. I shall take you in your coffin to Capri. I have had a mausoleum built, in my Palace Park. It is surrounded by cypress-trees. Overlooking the Mediterranean.

ILL. I only know it from pictures.

CLAIRE ZACHANASSIAN. Deep blue. A grandiose panorama. You will remain there. A dead man beside a stone idol. Your love died many years ago. But my love could not die. Neither could it live. It grew into an evil thing, like me, like the pallid mushrooms in this wood, and the blind, twisted features of the roots, all overgrown by my golden millions. Their tentacles sought you out, to take

your life, because your life belonged to me, for ever. You
are in their toils now, and you are lost. You will soon be
no more than a dead love in my memory, a gentle ghost
haunting the wreckage of a house.

ILL. 'Home Sweet Home' has ended now as well.

(*Husband IX returns.*)

CLAIRE ZACHANASSIAN. Here's the Nobel Prize-winner. Back
from his ruins. Well, Zoby?

HUSBAND IX. Early Christian. Sacked by the Huns.

CLAIRE ZACHANASSIAN. What a pity. Give me your arm. Roby,
Toby, the sedan.

(*Gets into sedan-chair.*)

Goodbye, Alfred.

ILL. Goodbye, Clara.

(*The sedan-chair is borne away to background. Ill remains
seated on bench. The trees put away their twigs. Portal
descends, with usual curtains and draperies, also inscription:*
LIFE IS SERIOUS, ART SERENE. *Policeman emerges from background, in swashbuckling new uniform, sits beside Ill.
A Radio Commentator enters, begins talking into microphone
while the Guelleners assemble. Everyone in new evening
gowns and dress-suits. Hordes of Press Photographers,
Reporters, Cameramen.*)

RADIO COMMENTATOR. Ladies and gentlemen: Radio News-
reel has been bringing you a Scene from the Birthplace
and a Conversation with the Priest, and now it's time to
go over to the Public Meeting. We're nearing the climax
of this visit which Madam Claire Zachanassian has kindly
accorded to her charming, friendly little home-town. Of
course it's unfortunate the famous lady won't be putting
in a personal appearance, on the other hand we will be
hearing the Mayor, because he's slated to make an important announcement in her name. Right now we're coming

to you from the auditorium of the Golden Apostle, an hotel which can boast of a bed where Goethe once spent the night. And now the townsmen are assembling on the stage, in less exciting days the scene of local club gatherings and guest shows by the Kalberstadt Repertory Players. The Mayor's just informed me this is an old custom. The women are all down in the auditorium — it seems this is an old custom too. I can't tell you what a solemn atmosphere it is, the tension's really extraordinary. All the newsreel cameras are here, I can see my colleagues from T.V., there are reporters from all over the world, and now here comes the Mayor and he's going to begin his speech, we're crossing over to him now!

(*Radio Commentator crosses over to Mayor, who is standing in centre of stage, round him in a semi-circle the men of Guellen.*)

MAYOR. Ladies and gentlemen, Citizens of Guellen. I'm very happy to welcome you all here this evening. I declare this meeting open. We have one, single item on our agenda. It is my privilege to announce that Madam Claire Zachanassian, daughter of our worthy fellow-citizen Godfrey Wascher — the architect — intends to make us a donation of one million pounds.

(*Whispers among the Press.*)

Five hundred thousand for the town and five hundred thousand to be shared among all citizens.

(*Silence.*)

RADIO COMMENTATOR (*subdued*). What a sensation, listeners, what a colossal sensation. One endowment, and every inhabitant of this little town has suddenly become a well-to-do citizen. It must constitute one of the greatest social experiments of the age. The public here are gasping for breath, there's a deathly silence, O, they're awestruck, you can see it on every face.

MAYOR. I leave the floor to the Headmaster of our College.

(*Radio Commentator crosses with microphone to School-master.*)

SCHOOLMASTER. Guelleners: I want to raise one point we must all clearly understand — namely, in making her donation, Madam Claire Zachanassian has a definite aim. What is her aim? Is it her aim to make us happy with money? Is it merely her aim to heap gold on our heads? To revive the Wagner Factory and Bockmann's and the Foundry on Sunshine Square? You know very well it is not. Madam Claire Zachanassian has a more important aim. Her aim is to have the spirit of this community transformed — transformed to the spirit of justice. We, staggered by this demand, ask: have we not always been a just community?

VOICE ONE. Never!

VOICE TWO. We fostered a crime!

VOICE THREE. A false judgment!

VOICE FOUR. A perjury!

WOMAN'S VOICE. A villain!

OTHER VOICES. Hear! Hear!

SCHOOLMASTER. O people of Guellen! Such is the bitter truth! We have connived at injustice! I am of course fully aware of the material possibilities inherent for all of us in a million. Nor am I blind to the fact that poverty is the root of much evil, nay, of great hardship. And yet, and yet: we are not moved by the money (*huge applause*): we are not moved by ambitious thoughts of prosperity and good living, and luxury: we are moved by this matter of justice, and the problem of how to apply it. Nor yet by justice alone, but also by all those ideals, for which our forebears lived and fought, and for which they died; and which constitute the values of our Western World. (*Huge applause.*) When individual persons slight the ideal of brotherly love, disobey the commandment to succour the weak, spurn the marriage vow, deceive the courts and plunge young mothers into misery, then Freedom is at stake. (*Catcalls.*) Now, in God's name, we must take our ideals seriously, even unto death. (*Huge applause.*) For what would be the sense of wealth, which created not a wealth of grace? Yet grace can only be accorded those who hunger after grace. People of Guellen, do you have that hunger? Or is all your hunger common hunger, physical and profane? That is the question. As Head of your College, I put it to you all. Only if you refuse to abide any evil, refuse to live any longer under any circumstances in a world which connives at injustice, can you accept a million from Madam Zachanassian, and thereby fulfil the conditions attaching to her endowment.

(*Thunderous applause.*)

RADIO COMMENTATOR. Just listen to it, ladies and gentlemen, just listen to that applause. We're all overwhelmed. That speech by the Head evinced a moral grandeur we don't find everywhere these days. And a very brave denunciation it was too, aimed at all the little misdemeanours and injustices we find in every community, alas, all over the world.

MAYOR. Alfred Ill ...

RADIO COMMENTATOR. It's the Mayor, I think he's going to take the floor again.

MAYOR. Alfred Ill, I would like to ask you one question.

(*Policeman gives Ill a shove. Ill stands. Radio Commentator crosses with microphone to Ill.*)

RADIO COMMENTATOR. Ah. Now we're going to hear the voice of the man responsible for the Zachanassian endowment: it's the voice of Alfred Ill, our prodigal lady's childhood friend. Alfred Ill — a vigorous man around seventy, an upright Guellener of the old school, and of course he's deeply moved, full of gratitude, full of quiet satisfaction.

MAYOR. Alfred Ill: it is owing to you we have been offered this endowment. Are you aware of that?

(*Ill says something in an undertone.*)

RADIO COMMENTATOR. My dear sir, would you kindly speak a shade louder, our listeners are so eager to hear you.

ILL. All right.

MAYOR. Will you respect our decision as to acceptance or refusal of the Claire Zachanassian Endowment?

ILL. I shall respect it.

MAYOR. Are there any questions to Alfred Ill?

(*Silence.*)

The Church?

(*Priest says nothing.*)

The Medical Profession?

(*Doctor says nothing.*)

The Police?

(*Policeman says nothing.*)

The Opposition Party?

(*No one says anything.*)

I shall now put the issue to vote.

(*Silence. Hum of movie-cameras, flash of flash-lights.*)

All those pure in heart who want justice done, raise their hands.

(*All except Ill raise their hands.*)

RADIO COMMENTATOR. There's a devout silence in the auditorium. Nothing but a single sea of hands, all raised, as if making one, mighty pledge for a better, juster world. Only the old man has remained seated, absolutely motionless, he's overcome with joy. His ambition has been fulfilled, and thanks to the generosity of his childhood friend the endowment's finally assured.

MAYOR. The Claire Zachanassian Endowment is accepted. Unanimously. Not for the sake of the money,

CITIZENS. Not for the sake of the money,

MAYOR. But for justice

CITIZENS. But for justice

MAYOR. And for conscience' sake.

CITIZENS. And for conscience' sake.

MAYOR. For we cannot connive at a crime:

CITIZENS. For we cannot connive at a crime:

MAYOR. Let us then root out the wrongdoer,

CITIZENS. Let us then root out the wrongdoer,

MAYOR. And deliver our souls from evil

CITIZENS. And deliver our souls from evil

MAYOR. And all our most sacred possessions.

CITIZENS. And all our most sacred possessions.

ILL (*screams*). My God!

> (*Everyone remains standing solemnly with raised hands, but at this point, however, the news-reel camera jams.*)

CAMERAMAN. What a shame, Mister Mayor. There's a short in the light-cable. Would you just do that last vote again, please?

MAYOR. Do it again?

CAMERAMAN. For the news-reel.

MAYOR. O yes, certainly.

CAMERAMAN. O.K., spots?

A VOICE. O.K.

CAMERAMAN. O.K., shoot!

> (*Mayor assumes pose.*)

MAYOR. The Claire Zachanassian Endowment is accepted. Unanimously. Not for the sake of the money,

CITIZENS. Not for the sake of the money,

MAYOR. But for justice

CITIZENS. But for justice

MAYOR. And for conscience' sake.

CITIZENS. And for conscience' sake.

MAYOR. For we cannot connive at a crime:

CITIZENS. For we cannot connive at a crime:

MAYOR. Let us then root out the wrongdoer,

CITIZENS. Let us then root out the wrongdoer,

MAYOR. And deliver our souls from evil

CITIZENS. And deliver our souls from evil

MAYOR. And all our most sacred possessions.

CITIZENS. And all our most sacred possessions.

(*Silence.*)

CAMERAMAN (*stage whisper*). Hey! Ill! Come on!

(*Silence.*)

(*Disappointed*) O.K., so he won't. Pity we didn't get his cry of joy the first time. That 'My God' was most impressive.

MAYOR. And now we invite the gentlemen of the Press, Cinema and Radio to a little Refreshment. In the Restaurant. The easiest way out of the auditorium is through the stage-door. Tea is being served for the ladies on the Golden Apostle lawn.

(*Those of the Press, Cinema and Radio cross to background, right, and go off. Men of Guellen remain on stage, immobile. Ill stands, moves to go.*)

POLICEMAN. You stay here!

(*He pushes Ill down on to bench.*)

ILL. Were you going to do it today?

POLICEMAN. Of course.

ILL. I'd have thought it would be better at my place.

POLICEMAN. It'll be done here.

MAYOR. No one left in the stalls?

(*Man Three and Man Four peer down into stalls.*)

MAN THREE. No one.

MAYOR. What about the gallery?

MAN FOUR. Empty.

MAYOR. Lock the doors. Don't let anyone else into the auditorium.

(*Man Three and Man Four step down into stalls.*)

MAN THREE. Locked.

MAN FOUR. Locked.

MAYOR. Put out the lights. The moon is shining through the gallery window. It's enough.

(*The stage dims. In the pale moonlight, people are only dimly visible.*)

Form a lane.

(*Men of Guellen form a lane: it ends at Gymnast, clad now in elegant white slacks and vest, round which a red scarf.*)

Father. If you please.

(*Priest crosses slowly to Ill, sits beside him.*)

PRIEST. Now, Ill, your hardest hour is at hand.

ILL. Give me a cigarette.

PRIEST. Mister Mayor, a cigarette.

MAYOR (*warmly*). But of course. A good one.

(*Passes packet to Priest, who offers it to Ill, who takes a cigarette; Policeman proffers light, Priest returns packet to Mayor.*)

PRIEST. As the prophet Amos said —

ILL. Please don't.

(*Ill smokes.*)

PRIEST. Are you not afraid?

ILL. Not much, any more.

(*Ill smokes.*)

PRIEST (*helpless*). I'll pray for you.

ILL. Pray for Guellen.

(*Ill smokes. Priest gets slowly to his feet.*)

PRIEST. God have mercy upon us.

(*Priest slowly rejoins the Guelleners' ranks.*)

MAYOR. Alfred Ill. Stand up.

(*Ill hesitates.*)

POLICEMAN. Get up, you bastard.

(*Drags Ill to his feet.*)

MAYOR. Inspector, control yourself.

POLICEMAN. Sorry. It just slipped out.

MAYOR. Alfred Ill. Come here.

(*Ill drops cigarette, treads it out. Then walks slowly to centre of stage, turns his back to audience.*)

Walk down that lane.

(*Ill hesitates.*)

POLICEMAN. Get moving.

(*Ill walks slowly into lane of silent men. When he gets to the end, he comes up against Gymnast planted facing him. Ill stops, turns round, and seeing lane close mercilessly in on him, sinks to his knees. The lane becomes a silent knot of men, swelling up, then slowly crouching down. Silence. Enter Reporters, downstage, left. Lights up.*)

FIRST REPORTER. What's going on here?

(*The knot of men opens, loosed. The men assemble quietly in background. Only Doctor remains, kneeling beside a corpse over which is spread, as if in an hotel, a chequered table-cloth. Doctor stands, puts away stethoscope.*)

DOCTOR. Heart attack.

(*Silence.*)

MAYOR. Died of joy.

FIRST REPORTER. Died of joy.

SECOND REPORTER. Life writes the most beautiful stories.

FIRST REPORTER. Better get to work.

(*Reporters hurry off to background, right. Enter, left, Claire Zachanassian, followed by Butler. She sees corpse, stops, then walks slowly to centre of stage, turns to face audience.*)

CLAIRE ZACHANASSIAN. Bring him here.

(*Enter Roby and Toby with stretcher, on which they lay Ill, then bring him to Claire Zachanassian's feet.*)

(*unmoving*) Uncover him, Boby.

(*Butler uncovers Ill's face. She examines it at length, does not move.*)

Now he looks the way he was, a long while ago: the
black panther. Cover him.
(*Butler covers face.*)
Carry him to the coffin.
(*Roby and Toby carry out body, left.*)
Take me to my room, Boby. Get the bags packed. We
are going to Capri.
(*Butler offers her his arm, she walks slowly out to left, then
stops.*)
Mayor.
(*Mayor emerges from ranks of silent men in background,
comes slowly forward.*)
The cheque.
(*She passes him a piece of paper; and exit, with Butler.*)

(*As the clothing, that outward visible form of a mounting
standard of living, improves by degrees discreet and unobtrusive yet less and less to be ignored, and as the stage grows
more inviting, while rung by rung it scales the social ladder
and metamorphoses into wealth, like a gradual change of
house from a slum to a well-to-do neighbourhood, so the
epitome of that ascent occurs in the concluding tableau. The
erstwhile grey and dreary world has been transformed; it has
grown rich and dazzling new, a flashy incarnation of
up-to-the-minute technics, as if the world and all were
ending happily. Flags and streamers, posters, neon-lights now
surround the renovated railway station, and the men and
women of Guellen clad in evening gowns and dress-suits
form two choruses, resembling those of Greek tragedy, nor is
this an accident but rather to orientate the close, as if some
stricken ship, borne far, far away, were sending out its last
signals.*)

CHORUS ONE.
Many, many the monstrous things on earth,
The volcano spewing and spitting its fire,
The shattering earthquake and the tidal wave,
And wars:
      Across the corn the clatter of tanks
      While the radiant mushroom grows
      From the spoor of the atom bomb.

CHORUS TWO.
These monstrous things
      do not exceed
The monstrous plight
      of poverty
Which excites
      no tragic deed
Is not heroic
      but condemns
Our human race
      to barren days
After hopeless
      yesterdays.

THE WOMEN.
The mothers are helpless, they watch
      Their loved ones pining away;

THE MEN.
But the men rumour rebellion.
      The men think treachery.

MAN ONE.
In worn-out shoes they pace the town.

MAN THREE.
A filthy fag-end in their mouths.

CHORUS ONE.
For the jobs, the jobs that earned them bread,
      The jobs are gone.

CHORUS TWO.
And the station scorned by the screaming trains.

ALL.
Now God be praised

MRS ILL.
For kindly fate

ALL.
Has changed all that.

THE WOMEN.
Our tender forms are clad in fitting frocks,

SON.
Young guys with any future drive a Sports,

THE MEN.
The business-men relax in limousines,

DAUGHTER.
All tennis-girls play tennis on hard courts.

DOCTOR.
Our operating-theatres are the best:
The instruments are new, the tiles green;
Medical morale will stand the test.

ALL.
Our suppers now are simmering at home
And Everyman, contented and well-shod,
Buys cigarettes of quality at last.

SCHOOLMASTER.
Assiduous students study their studies,

MAN TWO.
Dynamic tycoons amass fortunes,

ALL.
Rembrandts after Rubens,

PAINTER.
And the painters of today
Get an excellent living in Art.

PRIEST.

At Christmas and at Easter and at Whitsun
The Cathedral is packed to the portals
With Flocks of the Christian religion.

ALL.

And the trains, the trains come haughtily roaring
In on the iron
        Railway to Guellen
Hurrying people from town to town,
      Commuting,
           Stopping.

(*Enter Guard, left.*)

GUARD.

Guellen!

STATION-MASTER.

Guellen-Rome Express! All seats please!
      Diner up front!
(*Enter from background Claire Zachanassian seated immobile
in sedan-chair, like an old stone idol, and moves down-stage
with retinue, between the two Choruses.*)

MAYOR.

Our lady and her noble retinue,

ALL.

Her wealth endowed on Guellen town,

DAUGHTER.

The benefactrice of us all

MAYOR.

Is leaving now!
(*Exit Claire Zachanassian, right, followed last and very
slowly by servants bearing coffin.*)

MAYOR.

Long may she live.

ALL.

      She bears a precious charge.

STATION-MASTER.

(Whistles, waves green flag.)
Stand clear!

PRIEST.

Now let us pray to God

ALL.

To protect us all

MAYOR.

In these hustling, booming, prosperous times:

ALL.

Protect all our sacred possessions,
Protect our peace and our freedom,
Ward off the night, nevermore
Let it darken our glorious town
Grown out of the ashes anew.
Let us go and enjoy our good fortune.

The Balcony

by
Jean Genet

Translated by Bernard Frechtman

The first American performance of THE BALCONY was presented at Circle In The Square, New York City, March, 3, 1960. It was directed by José Quintero, scenery and lights by David Hays, costumes by Patricia Zipprodt, and with the following cast:

THE BISHOP	F. M. Kimball
IRMA	Nancy Marchand
THE WOMAN PENITENT	Grayson Hall
THE THIEF	Sylvia Miles
THE JUDGE	Arthur Malet
THE EXECUTIONER	John Perkins
THE GENERAL	John S. Dodson
THE GIRL	Salome Jens
CARMEN	Betty Miller
THE CHIEF OF POLICE	Roy Poole
THE ENVOY	Jock Livingston
ROGER	Joseph Daubenas
THE SLAVE	William Goodwin

THE MAN, ARTHUR, GEORGETTE, CHANTAL, THE WOUNDED MAN, ARMAND, LUKE, LOUIS, MARK, ROSINE, THE BEGGAR, FIRST PHOTOGRAPHER, SECOND PHOTOGRAPHER, THIRD PHOTOGRAPHER, THE QUEEN

The play is in nine scenes

SCENE ONE

On the ceiling, a chandelier, which will remain the same in each scene. The set represents a sacristy, formed by three blood-red, cloth folding-screens. The one at the rear has a built-in door. Above, a huge Spanish crucifix. On the right wall, a mirror, with a carved gilt frame, reflects an unmade bed which, if the room were arranged logically, would be in the first rows of the orchestra. A table with a large jug. A yellow arm-chair. On the chair, a pair of black trousers, a shirt and a jacket. THE BISHOP, *in miter and gilded cope, is sitting in the chair. He is obviously larger than life. The role is played by an actor wearing tragedian's cothurni about twenty inches high. His shoulders, on which the cope lies, are inordinately broadened so that when the curtain rises he looks huge. He wears garish make-up. At the side, a* WOMAN, *rather young, highly made up and wearing a lace dressing-gown, is drying her hands with a towel. Standing by is another woman,* IRMA. *She is about forty, dark, severe-looking, and is wearing a black tailored suit.*

THE BISHOP (*sitting in the chair, middle of the stage; in a low but fervent voice*): In truth, the mark of a prelate is not mildness or unction, but rather the most rigorous intelligence. Our heart is our undoing. We think we are master of our kindness; we are the slave of a serene laxity. In fact, it is something quite other than intelligence that is involved . . . (*He hesitates.*) It may be cruelty. And beyond that cruelty—and through it—a skilful, vigorous heading towards Absence. Towards Death. God? (*Smiling.*) I can read your mind! (*To his miter.*) Miter, bishop's bonnet, when my eyes close for the last time, it is you that I shall see behind my eyelids, you, my beautiful gilded hat . . . you, my handsome ornaments, copes, laces. . . .

IRMA (*bluntly; throughout the scene she will hardly move. She is standing very near the door*): An agreement's an agreement. When a deal's been made. . . .

THE BISHOP (*very gently, waving her aside with a gesture*): And when the die is cast. . . .

IRMA: No. Twenty. Twenty, and no nonsense. Or I'll lose my temper. And that's not like me. . . . Now, if you have any difficulties. . . .

295

THE BISHOP (*curtly, and tossing away the miter*): Thank you.

IRMA: And don't break anything. We need that. (*To* THE WOMAN.) Put it away. (*She lays the miter on the table, near the jug.*)

THE BISHOP (*after a deep sigh*): I've been told that this house is going to be besieged? The rebels have already crossed the river.

IRMA: You can slip around behind the Archbishop's Palace. Then, down Fishmarket Street. . . .

Suddenly a scream of pain, uttered by a woman off-stage.

IRMA (*annoyed*): But I instructed them to be quiet. Good thing I took care to cover the windows with padded curtains. (*Suddenly amiable, insidious.*) Well, and what was it this evening? A blessing? A prayer? A mass? A perpetual adoration?

THE BISHOP (*gravely*): Let's not talk about that now. It's over. I'm concerned only about getting home. . . .

THE WOMAN: There was a blessing, Madame. Then, my confession. . . .

IRMA: And after that?

THE BISHOP: That'll do!

THE WOMAN: That was all. At the end, my absolution.

IRMA: Won't anyone be able to witness it? Just once?

THE BISHOP (*frightened*): No, no. Those things must remain secret, and they shall. It's indecent enough to talk about them while I'm being undressed. Nobody. And all the doors must be closed. Oh, firmly closed, shut, buttoned, laced, hooked, sewn. . . .

IRMA: I merely asked. . . .

THE BISHOP: Sewn, Madame.

IRMA (*annoyed*): You'll allow me at least, won't you, to feel a little uneasy . . . professionally? I said twenty.

THE BISHOP (*his voice suddenly grows clear and sharp, as if he were awakening; he displays a little annoyance*): We didn't tire ourselves. Barely six sins, and far from my favorite ones.

THE WOMAN: Six, but deadly ones! And it was a job finding *those*.

THE BISHOP (*uneasy*): What? You mean they were false?

THE WOMAN: They were real, all right! I mean it was a job committing them. If only you realized what it takes, what a person has to go through, in order to reach the point of disobedience.

THE BISHOP: I can imagine, my child. The order of the world is so lax that you can do as you please there—or almost. But if your sins were false, you may say so now.

IRMA: Oh no! I can already hear you complaining the next time you come. No. They were real. (*To* THE WOMAN.) Untie his laces. Take off his shoes. And when you dress him, be careful he doesn't catch cold. (*To* THE BISHOP.) Would you like a toddy, a hot drink?

THE BISHOP: Thank you. I haven't time. I must be going. (*Dreamily.*) Yes, six, but deadly ones!

IRMA: Come here, we'll undress you!

THE BISHOP (*pleading, almost on his knees*): No, no, not yet.

IRMA: It's time. Come on! Quick! Make it snappy!

> *While they talk, the women undress him. Or rather they merely remove pins and untie cords that seem to secure the cope, stole and surplice.*

THE BISHOP (*to* THE WOMAN): About the sins, you really did commit them?

THE WOMAN: I did.

THE BISHOP: You really made the gestures? All the gestures?

THE WOMAN: I did.

THE BISHOP: When you moved towards me with your face forward, was it really aglow with the light of the flames?

THE WOMAN: It was.

THE BISHOP: And when my ringed hand came down on your forehead, forgiving it. . . .

THE WOMAN: It was.

THE BISHOP: And when my gaze pierced your lovely eyes?

THE WOMAN: It was.

IRMA: Was there at least a glimmer of repentance in her lovely eyes, your Lordship?

THE BISHOP (*standing up*): A fleeting glimmer. But was I seeking repentance in them? I saw there the greedy longing for transgression. In flooding it, evil all at once baptized it. Her big eyes opened on the abyss . . . a deathly pallor lit up—yes, Madame —lit up her face. But our holiness lies only in our being able to forgive you your sins. Even if they're only make-believe.

THE WOMAN (*suddenly coy*): And what if my sins were real?

THE BISHOP (*in a different, less theatrical tone*): You're mad! I hope you really didn't do all that!

IRMA (*to* THE BISHOP): Don't listen to her. As for her sins, don't worry. Here there's no. . .

THE BISHOP (*interrupting her*): I'm quite aware of that. Here there's no possibility of doing evil. You live in evil. In the absence of remorse. How could you do evil? The Devil makes believe. That's how one recognizes him. He's the great Actor. And that's why the Church has anathematized actors.

THE WOMAN: Reality frightens you, doesn't it?

THE BISHOP: If your sins were real, they would be crimes, and I'd be in a fine mess.

THE WOMAN: Would you go to the police?

> IRMA *continues to undress him. However, he still has the cope on his shoulders.*

IRMA: Stop plaguing her with all those questions.

> *The same terrible scream is heard again.*

IRMA: They're at it again! I'll go shut them up.

THE BISHOP: That wasn't a make-believe scream.

IRMA: How do we know? And what does it matter?

THE BISHOP (*going slowly to the mirror. He stands in front of it*): Now answer, mirror, answer me. Do I come here to discover evil and innocence? (*To* IRMA, *very gently*.) Leave the room! I want to be by myself.

IRMA: It's late. And the later it gets, the more dangerous it'll be. . . .

THE BISHOP (*pleading*): Just one more minute.

IRMA: You've been here two hours and twenty minutes. In other words, twenty minutes too long. . . .

THE BISHOP (*suddenly incensed*): I want to be by myself. Eavesdrop, if you want to—I know you do, anyway—and don't come back till I've finished.

> *The two women leave with a sigh, looking as if they were out of patience.* THE BISHOP *remains alone.*

THE BISHOP (*after making a visible effort to calm himself, in front of the mirror and holding his surplice*): Now answer, mirror, answer me. Do I come here to discover evil and innocence? And in your gilt-edged glass, what was I? Never—I affirm it before God Who sees me—I never desired the episcopal throne. To become bishop, to work my way up—by means of virtues or vices —would have been to turn away from the ultimate dignity of bishop. I shall explain: (THE BISHOP *speaks in a tone of great precision, as if pursuing a line of logical reasoning.*) in order to become a bishop, I would have had to make a zealous effort not to be one, but to do what would have resulted in my being one. Having become a bishop, in order to be one I would have had— in order to be one for myself, of course!—I would have had to be constantly aware of being one so as to perform my function. (*He seizes the flap of his surplice and kisses it.*) Oh laces, laces, fashioned by a thousand little hands to veil ever so many panting bosoms, buxom bosoms, and faces, and hair, you illustrate me with branches and flowers! Let us continue. But—there's the crux! (*He laughs.*) So I speak Latin!—a function is a function! It's not a mode of being. But a bishop—that's a mode of being. It's a trust. A burden. Miters, lace, gold-cloth and glass trinkets, genuflexions. . . . F . . k the function!

Crackling of machine-gun fire.

IRMA (*putting her head through the door*): Have you finished?
THE BISHOP: For Christ's sake, leave me alone. Get the hell out! I'm questioning myself.

IRMA *shuts the door.*

THE BISHOP (*to the mirror*): The majesty, the dignity, that light up my person, do not emanate from the attributions of my function. —No more, good heavens! than from my personal merits.—The majesty, the dignity that light me up come from a more mysterious brilliance: the fact that the bishop precedes me. Do I make myself clear, mirror, gilded image, ornate as a box of Mexican cigars? And I wish to be bishop in solitude, for appearance alone. . . . And in order to destroy all function, I want to cause a scandal and feel you up, you slut, you bitch, you trollop, you tramp. . . .
IRMA (*entering*): That'll do now. You've got to leave.
THE BISHOP: You're crazy! I haven't finished.

Both women have entered.

IRMA: I'm not trying to pick an argument, and you know it, but you've no time to waste. . . .

THE BISHOP (*ironically*): What you mean is that you need the room for someone else and you've got to arrange the mirrors and jugs.

IRMA (*very irritated*): That's no business of yours. I've given you every attention while you've been here. And I repeat that it's dangerous for anyone to loiter in the streets.

Sound of gunfire, in the distance.

THE BISHOP (*bitterly*): That's not true! You don't give a damn about my safety. When the job's finished, you don't give a damn about anyone!

IRMA (*to* THE GIRL): Stop listening to him and undress him.

IRMA (*to* THE BISHOP, *who has stepped down from his cothurni and has now assumed the normal size of an actor, of the most ordinary of actors*): Lend a hand. You're stiff.

THE BISHOP (*with a foolish look*): Stiff? I'm stiff? A solemn stiffness! Final immobility. . . .

IRMA (*to* THE GIRL): Hand him his jacket. . . .

THE BISHOP (*looking at his clothes, which are heaped on the floor*): Ornaments, laces, through you I re-enter myself. I reconquer a domain. I beleaguer a very ancient place from which I was driven. I install myself in a clearing where suicide at last becomes possible. The judgment depends on me, and here I stand, face to face with my death.

IRMA: That's all very fine, but you've got to go. You left your car at the front door, near the power-station.

THE BISHOP (*to* IRMA): Because our Chief of Police, that wretched incompetent, is letting us be slaughtered by the rabble! (*Turning to the mirror and declaiming.*) Ornaments! Miters! Laces! You, above all, oh gilded cope, you protect me from the world. Where are my legs, where are my arms? Under your wavy, lustrous flaps, what have my hands been doing? Fit only for fluttering gestures, they've become mere stumps of wings—not of angels, but of partridges!—rigid cope, you make it possible for the most tender and luminous sweetness to ripen in warmth and darkness. My charity, a charity that will flood the world—it was under this carapace that I distilled it. . . . Would my hand emerge at times, knifelike, to bless? Or cut, mow down? My hand, the head of a turtle, would push aside the flaps. A turtle or a cautious snake? And go back into the rock. Underneath, my hand would dream. . . . Ornaments, gilded copes. . . .

The stage moves from left to right, as if it were plunging into the wings. The following set then appears.

SCENE TWO

Same chandelier. Three brown folding-screens. Bare walls. At right, same mirror, in which is reflected the same unmade bed as in the first scene. A woman, young and beautiful, seems to be chained, with her wrists bound. Her muslin dress is torn. Her breasts are visible. Standing in front of her is THE EXECUTIONER. *He is a giant, stripped to the waist. Very muscular. His whip has been slipped through the loop of his belt, in back, so that he seems to have a tail. A* JUDGE, *who, when he stands up, will seem larger than life (he, too, is mounted on cothurni, which are invisible beneath his robe, and his face is made up), is crawling towards the woman, who shrinks as he approaches.*

THE THIEF (*holding out her foot*): Not yet! Lick it! Lick it first. . . .

> THE JUDGE *makes an effort to continue crawling. Then he stands up and, slowly and painfully, though apparently happy, goes and sits down on a stool.* THE THIEF (*the woman described above*) *drops her domineering attitude and becomes humble.*

THE JUDGE (*severely*): For you're a thief! You were caught. . . . Who? The police. . . . Have you forgotten that your movements are constricted by a strong and subtle network, my brawny cops? They're watchful, swivel-eyed insects that lie in wait for you. All of you! And they bring you captive, all of you, to the Bench. . . . What have you to say for yourself? You were caught. . . . Under your skirt . . . (*To* THE EXECUTIONER.) Put your hand under her skirt. You'll find the pocket, the notorious Kangaroo Pocket . . . (*To* THE THIEF.) that you fill with any old junk you pick up. Because you're an idiot to boot. . . . (*To* THE EXECUTIONER.) What was there in that notorious Kangaroo Pocket? In that enormous paunch?

THE EXECUTIONER: Perfumes, Your Honor, a flashlight, a bottle of Fly-tox, some oranges, several pairs of socks, bear-skins, a Turkish towel, a scarf. (*To* THE JUDGE.) Do you hear me? I said: a scarf.

THE JUDGE (*with a start*): A scarf? Ah ha, so that's it? Why the scarf? Eh? What were you going to do with it? Whom were you planning to strangle? Answer. Who? . . . Are you a thief or a strangler?

302

(*Very gently, imploringly.*) Tell me, my child, I beg of you, tell
me you're a thief.

THE THIEF: Yes, your Honor.

THE EXECUTIONER: No!

THE THIEF (*looking at him in surprise*): No?

THE EXECUTIONER: That's for later.

THE THIEF: Eh?

THE EXECUTIONER: I mean the confession is supposed to come later.
Plead not guilty.

THE THIEF: What, and get beaten again!

THE JUDGE (*mealy-mouthed*): Exactly, my child: and get beaten. You
must first deny, then admit and repent. I want to see hot tears
gush from your lovely eyes. Oh! I want you to be drenched in
them. The power of tears! Where's my statute-book? (*He fishes
under his robe and pulls out a book.*)

THE THIEF: I've already cried. . . .

THE JUDGE (*he seems to be reading*): Under the blows. I want tears
of repentance. When I see you wet as a meadow I'll be utterly
satisfied!

THE THIEF: It's not easy. I tried to cry before. . . .

THE JUDGE (*no longer reading; in a half-theatrical, almost familiar
tone*): You're quite young. Are you new here? At least you're
not a minor?

THE THIEF: Oh no, sir.

THE JUDGE: Call me Your Honor. How long have you been here?

THE EXECUTIONER: Since the day before yesterday, Your Honor.

THE JUDGE (*reassuming the theatrical tone and resuming the reading*):
Let her speak. I like that puling voice of hers, that voice without
resonance. . . . Look here: you've got to be a model thief if I'm
to be a model judge. If you're a fake thief, I become a fake judge.
Is that clear?

THE THIEF: Oh yes, Your Honor.

THE JUDGE (*he continues reading*): Good. Thus far everything has
gone off well. My executioner has hit hard . . . for he too has his
function. We are bound together, you, he and I. For example, if
he didn't hit, how could I stop him from hitting? Therefore, he
must strike so that I can intervene and demonstrate my authority.
And you must deny your guilt so that he can beat you. (*A noise
is heard, as of something having fallen in the next room. In a*

natural tone.) What's that? Are all the doors firmly shut? Can anyone see us, or hear us?

THE EXECUTIONER: No, no, you needn't worry. I bolted the door. (*He goes to examine a huge bolt on the rear door.*) And the corridor's out of bounds.

THE JUDGE (*in a natural tone*): Are you sure?

THE EXECUTIONER: You can take my word for it. (*He puts his hand into his pocket.*) Can I have a smoke?

THE JUDGE (*in a natural tone*): The smell of tobacco inspires me. Smoke away. (*Same noise as before.*) Oh, what *is* that? What *is* it? Can't they leave me in peace? (*He gets up.*) What's going on?

THE EXECUTIONER (*curtly*): Nothing at all. Someone must have dropped something. You're getting nervous.

THE JUDGE (*in a natural tone*): That may be, but my nervousness makes me aware of things. It keeps me on my toes. (*He gets up and moves towards the wall.*) May I have a look?

THE EXECUTIONER: Just a quick one, because it's getting late. (THE EXECUTIONER *shrugs his shoulders and exchanges a wink with* THE THIEF.)

THE JUDGE (*after looking*): It's lit up. Brightly lit, but empty.

THE EXECUTIONER (*shrugging his shoulders*): Empty!

THE JUDGE (*in an even more familiar tone*): You seem anxious. Has anything new happened?

THE EXECUTIONER: This afternoon, just before you arrived, the rebels took three key-positions. They set fire to several places. Not a single fireman came out. Everything went up in flames. The Palace. . . .

THE JUDGE: What about the Chief of Police? Twiddling his thumbs, as usual?

THE THIEF: There's been no news of him for four hours. If he can get away, he's sure to come here. He's expected at any moment.

THE JUDGE (*to* THE THIEF, *and sitting down*): In any case, he'd better not plan to come by way of Queen's Bridge. It was blown up last night.

THE THIEF: We know that. We heard the explosion from here.

THE JUDGE (*resuming his theatrical tone; he reads the statute-book*): All right. Let's get on with it. Thus, taking advantage of the sleep of the just, taking advantage of a moment's inattention, you rob them, you ransack, you pilfer and purloin. . . .

THE THIEF: No, Your Honor, never. . . .

THE EXECUTIONER: Shall I tan her hide?

THE THIEF (*crying out*): Arthur!

THE EXECUTIONER: What's eating you? Don't address me. Answer His Honor. And call me Mr. Executioner.

THE THIEF: Yes, Mr. Executioner.

THE JUDGE (*reading*): I continue: did you steal?

THE THIEF: I did. I did, Your Honor.

THE JUDGE (*reading*): Good. Now answer quickly, and to the point: what else did you steal?

THE THIEF: Bread, because I was hungry.

THE JUDGE (*he draws himself up and lays down the book*): Sublime! Sublime function! I'll have all that to judge. Oh, child, you reconcile me with the world. A judge! I'm going to be judge of your acts! On me depends the weighing, the balance. The world is an apple. I cut it in two: the good, the bad. And you agree, thank you, you agree to be the bad! (*Facing the audience.*) Right before your eyes: nothing in my hands, nothing up my sleeve, remove the rot and cast it off. But it's a painful occupation. If every judgment were delivered seriously, each one would cost me my life. That's why I'm dead. I inhabit that region of exact freedom. I, King of Hell, weigh those who are dead, like me. She's a dead person, like myself.

THE THIEF: You frighten me, sir.

THE JUDGE (*very bombastically*): Be still. In the depths of Hell I sort out the humans who venture there. Some to the flames, the others to the boredom of the fields of asphodel. You, thief, spy, she-dog, Minos is speaking to you, Minos weighs you. (*To* THE EXECUTIONER.) Cerberus?

THE EXECUTIONER (*imitating the dog*): Bow-wow, bow-wow!

THE JUDGE: You're handsome! And the sight of a fresh victim makes you even handsomer. (*He curls up* THE EXECUTIONER'S *lips.*) Show your fangs. Dreadful. White. (*Suddenly he seems anxious. To* THE THIEF.) But at least you're not lying about those thefts—you did commit them, didn't you?

THE EXECUTIONER: Don't worry. She committed them, all right. She wouldn't have dared not to. I'd have made her.

THE JUDGE: I'm almost happy. Continue. What did you steal? (*Suddenly, machine-gun fire.*)

THE JUDGE: There's simply no end to it. Not a moment's rest.

THE THIEF: I told you: the rebellion has spread all over the north of the city. . . .

THE EXECUTIONER: Shut up!

THE JUDGE (*irritated*): Are you going to answer, yes or no? What else have you stolen? Where? When? How? How much? Why? For whom?

THE THIEF: I very often entered houses when the maids were off. I used the service entrance. . . . I stole from drawers, I broke into children's piggy-banks. (*She is visibly trying to find words.*) Once I dressed up as a lady. I put on a dark brown suit, a black straw hat with cherries, a veil and a pair of black shoes—with Cuban heels—then I went in. . . .

THE JUDGE (*in a rush*): Where? Where? Where? Where—where—where? Where did you go in?

THE THIEF: I can't remember. Forgive me.

THE EXECUTIONER: Shall I let her have it?

THE JUDGE: Not yet. (*To* THE THIEF.) Where did you go in? Tell me where?

THE THIEF (*in a panic*): But I swear to you, I don't remember.

THE EXECUTIONER: Shall I let her have it? Shall I, Your Honor?

THE JUDGE (*to* THE EXECUTIONER, *and going up to him*): Ah! ah! your pleasure depends on me. You like to thrash, eh? I'm pleased with you, Executioner! Masterly mountain of meat, hunk of beef that's set in motion at a word from me! (*He pretends to look at himself in* THE EXECUTIONER.) Mirror that glorifies me! Image that I can touch, I love you. Never would I have the strength or skill to leave streaks of fire on her back. Besides, what could I do with such strength and skill? (*He touches him.*) Are you there? You're all there, my huge arm, too heavy for me, too big, too fat for my shoulder, walking at my side all by itself! Arm, hundred-weight of meat, without you I'd be nothing. . . . (*To* THE THIEF.) And without you too, my child. You're my two perfect complements. . . . Ah, what a fine trio we make! (*To* THE THIEF.) But you, you have a privilege that he hasn't, nor I either, that of priority. My being a judge is an emanation of your being a thief. You need only refuse—but you'd better not!—need only refuse to be who you are—what you are, therefore who you are—for me to cease to be . . . to vanish, evaporated. Burst. Volatized. Denied. Hence: good born of . . . What then? What then? But you won't refuse, will you? You won't refuse to be a thief? That would be wicked.

It would be criminal. You'd deprive me of being! (*Imploringly.*) Say it, my child, my love, you won't refuse?

THE THIEF (*coyly*): I might.

THE JUDGE: What's that? What's that you say? You'd refuse? Tell me where. And tell me again what you've stolen.

THE THIEF (*curtly, and getting up*): I won't.

THE JUDGE: Tell me where. Don't be cruel. . . .

THE THIEF: Your tone is getting too familiar. I won't have it!

THE JUDGE: Miss. . . . Madame. I beg of you. (*He falls to his knees.*) Look, I beseech you. Don't leave me in this position, waiting to be a judge. If there were no judges, what would become of us, but what if there were no thieves?

THE THIEF (*ironically*): And what if there weren't?

THE JUDGE: It would be awful. But you won't do that to me, will you? Please understand me: I don't mind your hiding, for as long as you can and as long as my nerves can bear it, behind the refusal to confess—it's all right to be mean and make me yearn, even prance, make me dance, drool, sweat, whinny with impatience, crawl . . . do you want me to crawl?

THE EXECUTIONER (*to* THE JUDGE): Crawl.

THE JUDGE: I'm proud!

THE EXECUTIONER (*threateningly*): Crawl! (THE JUDGE, *who was on his knees, lies flat on his stomach and crawls slowly towards* THE THIEF. *As he crawls forward,* THE THIEF *moves back.*)

THE EXECUTIONER: Good. Continue.

THE JUDGE (*to* THE THIEF): You're quite right, you rascal, to make me crawl after my judgeship, but if you were to refuse for good, you hussy, it would be criminal. . . .

THE THIEF: Call me Madame, and ask politely.

THE JUDGE: Will I get what l want?

THE THIEF (*coyly*): It costs a lot—stealing does.

THE JUDGE: I'll pay! I'll pay whatever I have to, Madame. But if I no longer had to divide the Good from the Evil, of what use would I be? I ask you?

THE THIEF: I ask myself.

THE JUDGE (*infinitely sad*): A while ago I was going to be Minos. My Cerberus was barking. (*To* THE EXECUTIONER.) Do you remember? (THE EXECUTIONER *interrupts* THE JUDGE *by cracking his whip.*) You were so cruel, so mean! So good! And me, I was pitiless. I was going to fill Hell with the souls of the damned, to fill prisons.

Prisons! Prisons! Prisons, dungeons, blessed place where evil is impossible since they are the crossroads of all the malediction in the world. One cannot commit evil in evil. Now, what I desire above all is not to condemn, but to judge. . . . (*He tries to get up.*)

THE EXECUTIONER: Crawl! And hurry up, I've got to go and get dressed.

THE JUDGE (*to* THE THIEF): Madame! Madame, please, I beg of you. I'm willing to lick your shoes, but tell me you're a thief. . . .

THE THIEF (*in a cry*): Not yet! Lick! Lick! Lick first!

The stage moves from left to right, as at the end of the preceding scene, and plunges into the right wing. In the distance, machine-gun fire.

SCENE THREE

Three dark green folding-screens, arranged as in the preceding scenes. The same chandelier. The same mirror reflecting the unmade bed. On an armchair, a horse of the kind used by folk-dancers, with a little kilted skirt. In the room, a timid-looking gentleman: THE GENERAL. *He removes his jacket, then his bowler hat and his gloves.* IRMA *is near him.*

THE GENERAL (*pointing to the hat, jacket and gloves*): Have that cleared out.

IRMA: It'll be folded and wrapped.

THE GENERAL: Have it removed from sight.

IRMA: It'll be put away. Even burned.

THE GENERAL: Yes, yes, of course, I'd like it to burn! Like cities at twilight.

IRMA: Did you notice anything on the way?

THE GENERAL: I ran very serious risks. The populace has blown up dams. Whole areas are flooded. The arsenal in particular. So that all the powder kegs are wet. And the weapons rusty. I had to make some rather wide detours—though I didn't trip over a single drowned body.

IRMA: I wouldn't take the liberty of asking you your opinions. Everyone is free, and I'm not concerned with politics.

THE GENERAL: Then let's talk of something else. The important thing is how I'm going to get out of this place. It'll be late by the time I leave. . . .

IRMA: About it's being late. . . .

THE GENERAL: That does it. (*He reaches into his pocket, takes out some banknotes, counts them and gives some to* IRMA. *She keeps them in her hand.*)

THE GENERAL: I'm not keen about being shot down in the dark when I leave. For, of course, there won't be anyone to escort me?

IRMA: I'm afraid not, unfortunately. Arthur's not free. (*A long pause.*)

THE GENERAL (*suddenly impatient*): But . . . isn't she coming?

IRMA: I can't imagine what she's doing. I gave instructions that everything was to be ready by the time you arrived. The horse is already here. . . . I'll ring.

309

THE GENERAL: Don't, I'll attend to that. (*He rings.*) I like to ring! Ringing's authoritative. Ah, to ring out commands.

IRMA: In a little while, General. Oh, I'm so sorry, here am I giving you your rank. . . . In a little while you'll. . . .

THE GENERAL: Sh! Don't say it.

IRMA: You have such force, such youth! such dash!

THE GENERAL: And spurs. Will I have spurs? I said they were to be fixed to my boots. Oxblood boots, right?

IRMA: Yes, General. Oxblood. And patent-leather.

THE GENERAL: Patent-leather very well, but with mud?

IRMA: With mud and perhaps a little blood. I've had the decorations prepared.

THE GENERAL: Authentic ones?

IRMA. Authentic ones.

Suddenly a woman's long scream.

THE GENERAL: What's that? (*He starts going to the right wall and is already bending down to look, as if there were a small crack, but* IRMA *steps in front of him.*)

IRMA: Nothing. There's always some carelessness, on both sides.

THE GENERAL: But that cry? A woman's cry. A call for help perhaps? My pounding heart skips a beat. . . . I spring forward. . . .

IRMA: What on earth can she be doing?

She goes to ring, but by the rear door enters a very beautiful young woman, red-headed, hair undone, disheveled. Her bosom is almost bare. She is wearing a black corset, black stockings and very high-heeled shoes. She is holding a general's uniform, complete with sword, cocked hat and boots.

THE GENERAL (*severely*): So you finally got here? Half an hour late. That's more than's needed to lose a battle.

IRMA: She'll redeem herself, General, I know her.

THE GENERAL (*looking at the boots*): What about the blood? I don't see any blood.

IRMA: It dried. Don't forget that it's the blood of your past battles. Well, then, I'll leave you. Do you have everything you need?

THE GENERAL (*looking to the right and left*): You're forgetting. . . .

IRMA: Good God! Yes, I was forgetting.

She lays on the chair the towels she has been carrying on her arm. Then she leaves by the rear. THE GENERAL *goes to the door, then locks it. But no sooner is the door closed than someone knocks.* THE GIRL *goes to open it. Behind, and standing slightly back,* THE EXECUTIONER, *sweating, wiping himself with a towel.*

THE EXECUTIONER: Is Mme. Irma here?

THE GIRL (*curtly*): In the Rose-garden. (*Correcting herself.*) I'm sorry, in the Funeral Chapel. (*She closes the door.*)

THE GENERAL (*irritated*): I'll be left in peace, I hope. And you're late. Where the hell were you? Didn't they give you your feed-bag? You're smiling, are you? Smiling at your rider? You recognize his hand, gentle but firm? (*He strokes her.*) My proud steed! My handsome mare, we've had many a spirited gallop together!

THE GIRL: And that's not all! I want to trip through the world with my nervous legs and well-shod hooves. Take off your pants and shoes so I can dress you.

THE GENERAL (*he has taken the cane*): All right, but first down on your knees! Come on, come on, bend your knees, bend them. . . .

The girl rears, utters a whinny of pleasure and kneels like a circus horse before THE GENERAL.

THE GENERAL: Bravo! Bravo, Dove! You haven't forgotten a thing. And now, you're going to help me and answer my questions. It's fitting and proper for a nice filly to help her master unbutton himself and take off his gloves, and to be at his beck and call. Now start by untying my laces.

During the entire scene that follows, THE GIRL *helps* THE GENERAL *remove his clothes and then dress up as a general. When he is completely dressed, he will be seen to have taken on gigantic proportions, by means of trick effects: invisible foot-gear, broadened shoulders, excessive make-up.*

THE GIRL: Left foot still swollen?

THE GENERAL: Yes. It's my leading-foot. The one that prances. Like your hoof when you toss your head.

THE GIRL: What am I doing? Unbutton yourself.

THE GENERAL: Are you a horse or an illiterate? If you're a horse, you toss your head. Help me. Pull. Don't pull so hard. See here, you're not a plough-horse.

THE GIRL: I do what I have to do.

THE GENERAL: Are you rebelling? Already? Wait till I'm ready. When I put the bit into your mouth. . . .

THE GIRL: Oh no, not that.

THE GENERAL: A general reprimanded by his horse! You'll have the bit, the bridle, the harness, the saddlegirth, and I, in boots and helmet, will whip and plunge!

THE GIRL: The bit is awful. It makes the gums and the corners of the lips bleed. I'll drool blood.

THE GENERAL: Foam pink and spit fire! But what a gallop! Along the ryefields, through the alfalfa, over the meadows and dusty roads, over hill and dale, awake or asleep, from dawn to twilight and from twilight. . . .

THE GIRL: Tuck in your shirt. Pull up your suspenders. It's quite a job dressing a victorious general who's to be buried. Do you want the sabre?

THE GENERAL: Let it lie on the table, like Lafayette's. Conspicuously, but hide the clothes. Where? How should *I* know? Surely there's a hiding-place somewhere. (THE GIRL *bundles up his clothes and hides them behind the armchair.*)

THE GENERAL: The tunic? Good. Got all the medals? Count 'em.

THE GIRL (*after counting them, very quickly*): They're all here, sir.

THE GENERAL: What about the war? Where's the war?

THE GIRL (*very softly*): It's approaching, sir. It's evening in an apple-orchard. The sky is calm and pink. The earth is bathed in a sudden peace—the moan of doves—the peace that precedes battles. The air is very still. An apple has fallen to the grass. A yellow apple. Things are holding their breath. War is declared. The evening is very mild. . . .

THE GENERAL: But suddenly?

THE GIRL: We're at the edge of the meadow. I keep myself from flinging out, from whinnying. Your thighs are warm and you're pressing my flanks. Death. . . .

THE GENERAL: But suddenly?

THE GIRL: Death has pricked up her ears. She puts a finger to her lips, asking for silence. Things are lit up with an ultimate goodness. You yourself no longer heed my presence. . . .

THE GENERAL: But suddenly?

THE GIRL: Button up by yourself, sir. The water lay motionless in the pools. The wind itself was awaiting an order to unfurl the flags. . . .

THE GENERAL: But suddenly?

THE GIRL: Suddenly? Eh? Suddenly? (*She seems to be trying to find the right words.*) Ah, yes, suddenly all was fire and sword! Widows! Miles of crape had to be woven to put on the standards. The mothers and wives remained dry-eyed behind their veils. The bells came clattering down the bombed towers. As I rounded a corner I was frightened by a blue cloth. I reared, but, steadied by your gentle and masterful hand, I ceased to quiver. I started forward again. How I loved you, my hero!

THE GENERAL: But . . . the dead? Weren't there any dead?

THE GIRL: The soldiers died kissing the standard. You were all victory and kindness. One evening, remember. . . .

THE GENERAL: I was so mild that I began to snow. To snow on my men, to shroud them in the softest of winding-sheets. To snow. Moskova!

THE GIRL: Splinters of shell had gashed the lemons. Now death was in action. She moved nimbly from one to the other, deepening a wound, dimming an eye, tearing off an arm, opening an artery, discoloring a face, cutting short a cry, a song. Death was ready to drop. Finally, exhausted, herself dead with fatigue, she grew drowsy and rested lightly on your shoulder, where she fell asleep.

THE GENERAL (*drunk with joy*): Stop, stop, it's not time for that yet, but I feel it'll be magnificent. The cross-belt? Good. (*He looks at himself in the mirror.*) Austerlitz! General! Man of war and in full regalia, behold me in my pure appearance. Nothing, no contingent trails behind me. I appear, purely and simply. If I went through wars without dying, went through sufferings, without dying, it was for this minute close to death. (*Suddenly he stops; he seems troubled by an idea.*) Tell me, Dove?

THE GIRL: What is it, sir?

THE GENERAL: What's the Chief of Police been doing? (THE GIRL *shakes her head.*) Nothing? Still nothing? In short, everything slips through his fingers. And what about us, are we wasting our time?

THE GIRL (*imperiously*): Not at all. And, in any case, it's no business of ours. Continue. You were saying: for this minute close to death . . . and then?

THE GENERAL (*hesitating*): . . . close to death . . . where I shall be nothing, though reflected *ad infinitum* in these mirrors, nothing but my image. . . . Quite right, comb your mane. Curry yourself. I require a well-groomed filly. So, in a little while, to the blare of trumpets, we shall descend—I on your back—to death and glory, for I am about to die. It is indeed a descent to the grave. . . .

THE GIRL: But, sir, you've been dead since yesterday.

THE GENERAL: I know . . . but a formal and picturesque descent, by unexpected stairways. . . .

THE GIRL: You are a dead general, but an eloquent one.

THE GENERAL: Because I'm dead, prating horse. What is now speaking, and so beautifully, is Example. I am now only the image of my former self. Your turn, now. Lower your head and hide your eyes, for I want to be a general in solitude. Not even for myself, but for my image, and my image for its image, and so on. In short, we'll be among equals. Dove, are you ready? (THE GIRL *nods.*) Come now. Put on your bay dress, horse, my fine Arab steed. (THE GENERAL *slips the mock-horse over her head. Then he cracks his whip.*) We're off! (*He bows to his image in the mirror.*) Farewell, general! (*Then he stretches out in the armchair with his feet on another chair and bows to the audience, holding himself rigid as a corpse.* THE GIRL *places herself in front of the chair and, on the spot, makes the movements of a horse in motion.*)

THE GIRL: The procession has begun. . . . We're passing through the City. . . . We're going along the river. I'm sad. . . . The sky is overcast. The nation weeps for that splendid hero who died in battle. . . .

THE GENERAL (*starting*): Dove!

THE GIRL (*turning around, in tears*): Sir?

THE GENERAL: Add that I died with my boots on! (*He then resumes his pose.*)

THE GIRL: My hero died with his boots on! The procession continues. Your aides-de-camp precede me. . . . Then come I, Dove, your war-horse. . . . The military band plays a funeral march. . . . (*Marching in place,* THE GIRL *sings Chopin's* Funeral March, *which is continued by an invisible orchestra [with brasses]. Far off, machine-gun fire.*)

SCENE FOUR

A room, the three visible panels of which are three mirrors in which is reflected a little old MAN, *dressed as a tramp though neatly combed. He is standing motionless in the middle of the room. Near him, looking very indifferent, a very beautiful red-haired* GIRL. *Leather corselet, leather boots. Naked and beautiful thighs. Fur jacket. She is waiting. So is the man. He is impatient, nervous. The girl is motionless.*

The man removes his torn gloves tremblingly. He takes from his pocket a handkerchief and mops his face. He takes off his glasses, folds them and puts them into a case, which he slips into his pocket. He wipes his hands with his handkerchief.

All the gestures of the little old man are reflected in the three mirrors. (Three actors are needed to play the roles of the reflections.)

At length, there are three raps at the rear door. The red-haired girl goes to the door. She says: "Yes." The door opens a little, and through the opening appear IRMA's *hand and arm holding a whip and a very dirty and shaggy wig. The girl takes them. The door closes.*

The man's face lights up. The red-haired girl has an exaggeratedly lofty and cruel air. She puts the wig on his head roughly.

The man takes a bouquet of artificial flowers from his pocket. He holds it as if he were going to offer it to the girl, who whips him and lashes it from his hand. The man's face is lit up with tenderness.

Very nearby, machine-gun fire.

The man touches his wig.

THE MAN: What about the lice?
THE GIRL (*very coarsely*): They're there.

315

IRMA's *room. Very elegant. It is the same room that was reflected in the mirrors in the first three scenes. The same chandelier. Large lace hangings suspended from the flies. Three arm-chairs. Large window at left; door at right.* IRMA *is sitting at her dressing-table, going over her accounts. Near her, a girl:* CARMEN. *Machine-gun fire.*

CARMEN (*counting*): The bishop, twenty . . . the judge, twenty. . . . (*She raises her head.*) No, Madame, nothing yet. No Chief of Police.

IRMA (*irritated*): And yet!

CARMEN: Yes, I know: it takes all kinds to make a world. But no Chief of Police. (*She counts again.*) The general, twenty . . . the sailor, thirty . . . the baby . . .

IRMA: I've told you, Carmen, I don't like that.

CARMEN (*sharply*): A person can make a mistake.

IRMA: And no back-talk either. And I demand respect for the visitors. Vi-si-tors! I don't allow myself—my own self (*she stresses the word "own"*)—even to refer to them as clients. And yet! . . . (*She flashily snaps the sheaf of fresh banknotes that she has in her hand.*)

CARMEN (*severely; she has turned around and is glaring at* IRMA): For you, yes: cash and refinement.

IRMA (*trying to be conciliatory*): Those eyes! Don't be unjust. You've been irritable for some time now. I know that everyone's upset by what's going on, but things will quiet down. The sun will come out again. George. . . .

CARMEN: Ah, him!

IRMA: Don't sneer at the Chief of Police. If not for him we'd be in a fine mess. Yes, we, because you're tied up with me. And with him. (*A long pause.*) What disturbs me most is your sadness. (*Wisely.*) You've changed, Carmen.

CARMEN: There's nothing much left for me to do at your place, Mme. Irma.

IRMA (*disconcerted*): But . . . I've put you in charge of my bookkeeping. You sit down at my desk, and all at once my entire life opens out before you. I haven't a secret left, and you're not happy?

316

CARMEN: Of course, I'm grateful to you for your confidence, but . . . it's not the same thing.

IRMA: Do you miss "that," Carmen? (CARMEN *is silent.*) Come, come, Carmen, when you mounted the snow-covered rock with the yellow paper rosebush—by the way, I'm going to have to store that in the cellar—and when the miraculously-healed leper swooned at the sight of you, you didn't take yourself seriously, did you, Carmen? (*Brief silence.*)

CARMEN: When our sessions are over, Madame, you never allow anyone to talk about them. So you have no idea of how we really feel. You observe it all from a distance. But if ever you once put on the dress and the blue veil, or if you were the unbuttoned penitent, or the general's mare, or the country girl tumbled in the hay. . . .

IRMA (*shocked*): Me!

CARMEN: Yes, you, Mme. Irma. Or the maid in a pink apron, or the archduchess deflowered by the policeman, or . . . but I'm not going to run through the whole list . . . you'd know what that does to a girl's soul, and that she's got to use a little irony in self-defense. But no, you don't even want us to talk about it among ourselves. You're afraid of a smile, of a joke.

IRMA (*very severely*): True, I don't allow any joking. A giggle, or even a smile, spoils everything. A smile means doubt. The clients want sober ceremonies. My house is a severe place. You're allowed to play cards.

CARMEN: Then don't be surprised that we're sad. But I'm thinking of my daughter.

IRMA (*she stands—for a bell has buzzed—and goes to a curious piece of furniture at the left, a kind of switchboard with a view-finder and earphone. While talking, she looks into the view-finder, after pushing down a switch*): Every time I ask you a slightly intimate question, you shut up like a clam, and you throw your daughter up to me. Are you still set on going to see her? Don't be a fool. Between this place and the nursery in the country there's fire and water, rebellion and bullets. I even wonder whether . . . (*The bell buzzes again.* MME. IRMA *pulls up the switch and pushes down another.*) . . . whether they didn't get George on the way. Though a Chief of Police knows how to take care of himself. (*She looks at a watch that she takes from her bosom.*) He's late.

CARMEN: In order to get to your studios, those gentlemen of yours go through gunfire without fear, whereas I, in order to see my daughter. . . .

IRMA: Without fear? In a state of jitters that excites them. Their gaping nostrils can sniff the orgy behind the wall of flame and steel. As for you, the orgies of your heart. . . .

CARMEN: . . . they don't help matters, Madame. My daughter loves me.

IRMA: You're the fairy godmother who comes to see her with toys and perfumes. She pictures you in Heaven. (*Bursting out laughing.*) Ah, that's the limit—to think there's someone for whom my brothel—which is Hell—is Heaven! It's Heaven for your brat! (*She laughs.*) Are you going to make a whore of her later on?

CARMEN: Mme. Irma!

IRMA: That's right! I ought to leave you to your secret brothel, your precious pink cat-house, your soulful whorehouse. . . . You think I'm cruel? This rebellion is getting me down, too. Yet I've tried everything, even prayer. (*She smiles.*) Like your miraculously-healed leper. Have I wounded you?

CARMEN (*with decision*): Twice a week, on Tuesdays and Fridays, I had to be the Immaculate Conception of Lourdes and appear to a bankclerk of the National City. For you it meant money in the bank and justified your brothel, whereas for me, a believer, it was. . . .

IRMA (*astonished*): You agreed to it. You didn't seem to mind it.

CARMEN: Mind it! I was happy.

IRMA: Well? Where's the harm?

CARMEN: I saw the effect I had on him. I saw his state of terror, how he'd break out in a sweat, I heard the rattle in his throat. . . .

IRMA: That'll do. He doesn't come any more. I wonder why. Maybe his wife found out.

CARMEN: Who cares! But you can understand, Madame, that this world of illusion oppresses me and that everything inside me yearns for my daughter. She's in a real garden. . . .

IRMA: You'll have a hard time getting to her, and before long the garden will be in your heart.

CARMEN: Be still!

IRMA (*inexorably*): The city is full of corpses. All the roads are cut off. The peasants are also going over to the rebels. I wonder why? Contagion? The rebellion is an epidemic. It has the same fatal and sacred character. In any case, we're going to find ourselves more and more isolated. The rebels have it in for the Clergy, for

the Army, for the Magistracy, for me, Irma, a bawd and madame
of a whorehouse. As for you, you'll be killed, disemboweled, and
your daughter will be adopted by some virtuous rebel.

Suddenly a buzz. IRMA *runs to the apparatus and looks and
listens as before.*

IRMA: Studio 24, Chamber of the Sands. What's going on?

She watches very attentively. A long pause.

CARMEN (*she has sat down at* IRMA's *table and gone back to the accounts. Without raising her head*): The Foreign Legion?
IRMA (*with her eye still glued to the apparatus*): Yes. It's the heroic
Legionnaire falling to the sand. And that idiot Rachel has
thrown a dart at his ear. He might have been disfigured. What
an idea, having himself shot at as if by an Arab, and dying—if
you want to call it that!—at attention, on a sand pile! (*A silence.
She watches attentively.*) Ah, Rachel's doctoring him. She's preparing a dressing for him, and he has a happy look. (*Very much
interested.*) My, my, he seems to like it. I have a feeling he wants
to alter his scenario and that starting today he's going to die in
the military hospital, tucked in by his nurse. . . . Another uniform
to buy. Always expenses. (*Suddenly anxious.*) Say, I don't like
that. Not one bit. I'm getting more and more worried about
Rachel. She'd better not double-cross me the way Chantal did.
(*Turning around, to* CARMEN:) By the way, no news of Chantal?
CARMEN: No, none.
IRMA (*picks up the apparatus again*): And the machine's not work-
ing right! What's he saying to her? He's explaining . . . she's
listening . . . she understands. I'm afraid he understands too.
(*Buzzing again. She pushes down another switch and looks.*)
False alarm. It's the plumber leaving.
CARMEN: Which one?
IRMA: The real one.
CARMEN: Which is the real one?
IRMA: The one who repairs the taps.
CARMEN: Is the other one fake?
IRMA (*shrugs her shoulders and pushes down the first switch*): Ah, I
told you so: the three or four drops of blood from his ear have

inspired him. Now he's having her pamper him. Tomorrow morning he'll be in fine fettle for going to his Embassy.

CARMEN: He's married, isn't he?

IRMA: As a rule, I don't like to talk about the private life of my visitors. The Grand Balcony has a world-wide reputation. It's the most artful, yet the most decent house of illusions. . . .

CARMEN: Decent?

IRMA: Discreet. But I might as well be frank with you, you inquisitive girl. Most of them are married.

CARMEN: When they're with their wives, whom they love, do they keep a tiny, small-scale version of their revels in a brothel. . . .

IRMA: Bitch!

CARMEN: Excuse me, Madame . . . in a house of illusions. I was saying: do they keep their revels in a house of illusions tucked away in the back of their heads in miniature form, far off? But present?

IRMA: It's possible, child. No doubt they do. Like a Chinese lantern left over from a carnival, and waiting for the next one, or, if you prefer, like an imperceptible light in the imperceptible window of an imperceptible castle that they can enlarge instantly whenever they feel like going there to relax.

CARMEN: All the same, it must be nice in a real house.

IRMA: Who knows! But Carmen, if my girls start bothering their heads about such things, it'll be the ruin of the brothel. I really think you miss your apparition. Look, I can do something for you. I did promise it to Regina, but I promise it to you. If you want to, of course. Someone rang me up yesterday and asked for a Saint Theresa. . . . (*A pause.*) Ah, obviously, it's a come-down from the Immaculate Conception to Saint Theresa, but it's not bad either. . . . (*A pause.*) Well, what do you say? It's for a banker. Very clean, you know. Not demanding.

CARMEN: I liked my dress and veil and rosebush.

IRMA: There's a rosebush in the "Saint Theresa" too. Think it over.

A pause.

CARMEN: And what'll the authentic detail be?

IRMA: The ring. He's got it all worked out. The wedding ring. You know that every nun wears a wedding ring, as a bride of God. (CARMEN *makes a gesture of astonishment.*) That's so. That's how he'll know he's dealing with a real nun.

CARMEN: What about the fake detail?

IRMA: It's almost always the same: black lace under the homespun skirt. Well, how about it? You have the kind of gentleness he likes. He'll be pleased.

CARMEN: It's really very kind of you, to think of him.

IRMA: I'm thinking of you.

CARMEN: You're so kind, Madame—I wasn't being ironic. The thing to be said for your house is that it brings consolation. You set up and prepare their secret theatres. . . . You've got your feet on the ground. The proof is that you rake in money. Whereas they . . . their awakening must be brutal. No sooner is it finished than it starts all over again.

IRMA: Luckily for me.

CARMEN: . . . starts all over again, and always the same adventure. They'd like it never to end.

IRMA: You miss the entire point. When it's over, their minds are clear. I can tell from their eyes. Suddenly they understand mathematics. They love their children and their country. Like you.

CARMEN (*puffing herself up*): I'm the daughter of a high-ranking officer. . . .

IRMA: I know. There always has to be one in a brothel. But bear in mind that General, Bishop and Judge are, in real life. . . .

CARMEN: Which are you talking about?

IRMA: Real ones.

CARMEN: Which are real? The ones here?

IRMA: The others. In real life they're the props of a display that they have to drag in the mud of the real and commonplace. Here, Comedy and Appearance remain pure, and the Revels intact.

CARMEN: The revels that I indulge in. . . .

IRMA (*interrupting her*): I know what they are: to forget theirs.

CARMEN: Do you blame me for that?

IRMA: And theirs are to forget yours. They, too, love their chil'ren. Afterwards.

> *Buzzing again, as before.* IRMA, *who has been sitting all the while near the apparatus, turns about, looks into the view-finder and puts the receiver to her ear.* CARMEN *goes back to her accounts.*

CARMEN (*without raising her head*): The Chief of Police?

IRMA: No. The waiter who just arrived. He's going to start complaining again . . . there he goes, he's flaring up because Elyane is handing him a white apron.

CARMEN: I warned you. He wants a pink one.

IRMA: Go to the Five-and-Ten tomorrow, if it's open. And buy a duster for the railwayman. A green one.

CARMEN: If only Elyane doesn't forget to drop the tip on the floor. He demands a true revolt. And dirty glasses.

IRMA: They all want everything to be as true as possible. . . . Minus something indefinable, so that it won't be true. (*Changing her tone.*) Carmen, it was I who decided to call my establishment a house of illusions, but I'm only the manager. Each individual, when he rings the bell and enters, brings his own scenario, perfectly thought out. My job is merely to rent the hall and furnish the props, actors and actresses. My dear, I've succeeded in lifting it from the ground—do you see what I mean? I unloosed it long ago and it's flying. I cut the moorings. It's flying. Or, if you like, it's sailing in the sky, and I with it. Well, my darling . . . may I say something tender—every madame always, traditionally, has a slight partiality for one of her young ladies. . . .

CARMEN: I had noticed it, Madame, and I too, at times. . . . (*She looks at* IRMA *languidly.*)

IRMA (*standing up and looking at her*): I have a strange feeling, Carmen. (*A long pause.*) But let's continue. Darling, the house really does take off, leaves the earth, sails in the sky when, in the secrecy of my heart, I call myself, but with great precision, a keeper of a bawdy-house. Darling, when secretly, in silence, I repeat to myself silently, "You're a bawd, boss of a whorehouse," darling, everything (*Suddenly lyrical.*), everything flies off—chandeliers, mirrors, carpets, pianos, caryatids and my studios, my famous studios: the studio known as the Hay Studio, hung with rustic scenes, the Studio of the Hangings, spattered with blood and tears, the Throne Room Studio, draped in velvet with a fleur-de-lys pattern, the Studio of Mirrors, the Studio of State, the Studio of the Perfumed Fountains, the Urinal Studio, the Amphitrite Studio, the Funeral Studio, adorned with marble urns, the Moonlight Studio, everything flies off: studios—Oh! I was forgetting the studio of the beggars, of the tramps, where filth and poverty are magnified. To continue: studios, girls, crystals, laces, balconies, everything takes it on the lam, rises up and carries me off!

A long pause. The two women are standing motionless, facing each other.

CARMEN: How well you speak.

IRMA (*modestly*): I went through elementary school.

CARMEN: So I assumed. My father, the artillery colonel. . . .

IRMA (*correcting her sharply*): You mean cavalry, my dear.

CARMEN: Excuse me. That's right. The cavalry colonel wanted me to have an education. Alas. . . . As for you, you've been successful. You've been able to surround your loveliness with a sumptuous theatre, a gala, the splendors of which envelop you and hide you from the world. Your whoredom required such pomp. But what about me, am I to have only myself and be only myself? No, Madame. Thanks to vice and men's heartache, I too have had my moment of glory! With the receiver at your ear, you could see me through the view-finder, standing erect, sovereign and kind, maternal yet feminine, with my heel on the cardboard snake and the pink paper-roses. You could also see the bankclerk from the National City kneeling before me and swooning when I appeared to him. Unfortunately he had his back to you and so you weren't aware of the ecstasy on his face and the wild pounding of my heart. My blue veil, my blue robe, my blue apron, my blue eyes. . . .

IRMA: They're hazel.

CARMEN: They were blue that day. For him I was Heaven in person descending on his brow. I was a Madonna to whom a Spaniard might have prayed and sworn an oath. He hymned me, fusing me with his beloved color, and when he carried me to bed, it was into the blue that he penetrated. Unhappily, I won't ever appear to him again.

IRMA: I've offered you Saint Theresa.

CARMEN: I'm not prepared, Mme. Irma. One has to know what the client's going to require. Has everything been worked out?

IRMA: Every whore should be able—I hope you'll excuse me, but since we've gone so far, let's talk man to man—should be able to handle any situation.

CARMEN: I'm one of your whores, Mme. Irma, and one of your best. I boast of it. In the course of an evening, I can . . .

IRMA: I'm aware of your feats. But when you start glorifying yourself as soon as you hear the word whore, which you keep repeating to yourself and which you flaunt as if it were a title, it's not quite the same as when I use the word to designate a function. But you're right, darling, to extol your profession and to glory in it. Make it shine. Let it illuminate you, if that's the only thing you have. (*Tenderly.*) I'll do all I can to help you. . . . You're not only the purest jewel of all my girls, you're the one on whom I bestow all my tenderness. You realize I can do that only in secret, because of Arthur. . . .

A knock at the door. IRMA *starts.*

IRMA (*lowering her voice*): Speak of the devil. . . . (*To* CARMEN.) Quick, make up your mind. Are you staying? (CARMEN *is silent.*) Say yes. A grey homespun dress, Carmen, a bouquet of roses. . . .

Knocking at the door again.

CARMEN: But, Madame, I believe in her. . . .

Knocking again, more imperious.

IRMA: You're a fool! . . . Come in!

The door opens. Enter THE EXECUTIONER, *whom hereafter we shall call* ARTHUR. *Classical pimp's outfit: light grey suit, white felt hat, etc. He finishes knotting his tie.*)

IRMA: Is the session over? He went through it fast.

ARTHUR: Yes, the little geezer's buttoning up. He's pooped. Two sessions in half an hour.

IRMA: You went easy, I hope? Last time, the poor girl was laid up for two days.

ARTHUR: Don't pull that kind-hearted-whore stuff on me. Both last time and tonight she got what was coming to her: in dough and in wallops. Right on the line. The banker wants to see stripes on her back. So I stripe it.

IRMA: At least you don't get any pleasure out of it?

ARTHUR: Not with her. You're my only love. And a job's a job. I'm conscientious about my work.

IRMA (*sternly*): I'm not jealous of the girl, but I wouldn't want you to disable the personnel. It's getting harder and harder to replace.

ARTHUR: I tried a couple of times to draw marks on her back with purple paint, but it didn't work. The old guy inspects her when he arrives and insists I deliver her in good shape.

IRMA: Paint? Who gave you permission?

ARTHUR (*shrugging his shoulders*): What's one illusion more or less! I thought I was doing the right thing. But don't worry. Now I whip, I flagellate, she screams, and he crawls.

IRMA: In any case, be careful. The house is being watched.

ARTHUR: I know. All the north part of town was taken last night. Too bad the Judge wants screaming.

IRMA: The Bishop's less dangerous. He's satisfied with pardoning sins.

CARMEN: Though he gets pleasure out of pardoning, he expects you to commit them. No, the best of the lot is the one you tie up, spank, whip and soothe, and then he snores.

ARTHUR: Who cuddles him? (*To* CARMEN.) You? Do you give him your breast?

CARMEN (*curtly*): I do my job right, too.

ARTHUR: Would the young lady like to give me a lesson?

IRMA: Let Carmen alone. She's suffering. (*To* CARMEN.) Well, what about Saint Theresa? Will you?

CARMEN (*plaintively*): Let me think it over a little longer.

ARTHUR (*bowing to* CARMEN *ironically*): Her cashier? No, I beg your pardon, her bookkeeper? (*To* IRMA.) How much did you take in today?

IRMA (*on the defensive*): Carmen and I haven't finished the accounts.

ARTHUR: But I have. According to my calculations, it runs to a good two hundred.

IRMA: That's possible. In any case, don't worry. I don't cheat.

ARTHUR: I believe you, my love, but I can't help it: the figures arrange themselves in my head. Two hundred! War, rebellion, shooting, frost, hail, rain, showers of shit, nothing stops them! On the contrary. People are killing each other in the streets, the joint's being watched, but all the same, they come charging in. As for me, I've got you right at home, sweetie-pie, otherwise. . . .

IRMA (*bluntly*): You'd be cowering in a cellar, paralyzed with fear.

ARTHUR (*ambiguously*): I'd do as the others do, my love. You're not forgetting my little percentage?

IRMA: I give you what you need.

ARTHUR: My love! I've ordered the silk shirts. And do you know what kind of silk? And what color?

IRMA (*tenderly*): All right, cut it. Not in front of Carmen.

ARTHUR: On the contrary. Do you know what kind of silk?

IRMA: Darling! The thought that Carmen will know that your chest—in the silk of my blouses. . . . Oh, darling . . . be still. . . .

ARTHUR: Then it's O.K.?

IRMA: Our accounts aren't done.

ARTHUR: And do you know what else? You should have seen the shirt-maker's face. I insisted that they button on the left. As if they were for you!

IRMA: My love!

ARTHUR: Then it's O.K.?

IRMA: Yes.

ARTHUR: How much?

IRMA (*regaining her self-possession*): We'll see. I have to go over the accounts with Carmen.

ARTHUR: You'll tell me when I get back. I trust you. I've got to deliver the rest of the stuff—I've got my orders. You might have asked the Bishop to remember me in his prayers. . . . It's true I don't interest him. I wonder whether I'll bring your Arthur back all in one piece. No, I'm not keen about it. If I could. . . .

IRMA (*severely*): You've no right. You've no right to hesitate. You were entrusted with a mission, and you accepted it. You'll carry it out. And me ready to tremble for your life.

ARTHUR: Don't work yourself up. I'm going. But at the risk of my life, whereas you're under cover in a nice warm place, waiting for George to arrive.

IRMA: If I belonged entirely to you and only you, we'd be in clover. Get going. And be back fairly soon. You have a session this evening. Did you know?

ARTHUR (*on his way to the door*): This evening? Another one? What is it?

IRMA: I thought I told you: a corpse.

ARTHUR: How delightful! And what am I supposed to do?

IRMA: Nothing. You're to remain motionless, and you'll be buried. You'll be able to rest.

ARTHUR: Ah, because I'm the one who . . . ? All right. Who's the client? Someone new?

IRMA (*mysteriously*): A very important person, and stop asking questions.

ARTHUR (*starting to leave, then hesitating*): You bitch! (*He turns round and smiles.*) You adorable bitch! (*He exits.*)

IRMA (*to* CARMEN, *after a pause*): Let's get back to the accounts, shall we?

CARMEN: In all, counting the sailor and the simple jobs, it comes to three hundred twenty.

IRMA: Splendid. The more killing there is in the working-class districts, the more the men roll into my studios.

CARMEN: The men?

IRMA (*after a pause*): Some men. Drawn by my mirrors and chandeliers, always the same ones. As for the others, heroism takes the place of women.

CARMEN (*bitterly*): Women?

IRMA: What shall I call you, my big, long, sterile girls? Their seed never ripens in you, and yet . . . if you weren't there?

CARMEN: You have your revels, Mme. Irma.

IRMA: Be still. It's this chilling game that makes me sad and melancholy. Fortunately I have my jewels. Which, as it happens, are in great danger. I may lose them at any moment.

Machine-gun fire.

You hear?

CARMEN: The Army is fighting bravely.

IRMA: And the Rebels even more bravely. And we're in the shadow of the cathedral, a few feet from the Archbishop's Palace. There's no price on my head. No, that would be too much to expect, but it's known that I serve supper to prominent people. So they're out to get me. And there are no men in the house.

CARMEN: Arthur will be back.

IRMA: Are you trying to be funny? He's no man, he's my stage-prop.

CARMEN: Assuming the worst. . . .

IRMA: If the Rebels win? I'm a goner. They're workers. Without imagination. Prudish and maybe chaste.

CARMEN: It won't take them long to get used to debauchery. Just wait till they get a little bored. . . .

IRMA: You're wrong. Or else they won't let themselves get bored. But I'm the one who's most exposed. For you it's different. In every revolution there's the glorified whore who sings an anthem and is virginified. That'll be you. The others'll piously bring water for the dying to drink. Afterwards . . . they'll marry you off. Would you like to get married?

CARMEN: Orange blossoms, tulle. . . .

IRMA: Wonderful! To you, getting married means masquerading. Darling, you certainly are one of us. No, I can't imagine you married either. Besides, what they're really dreaming of doing is murdering us. We'll have a lovely death, Carmen. It will be terrible and sumptuous. They may break into my studios, shatter the crystals, tear the brocades and slit our throats. . . .

CARMEN: They'll take pity. . . .

IRMA: They won't. They'll thrill at the thought that their fury is sacrilegious. All bedraggled, with caps on their heads, or in helmets and boots, they'll destroy us by fire and sword. It'll be very beautiful. We oughtn't to wish for any other kind of end, and you, you're thinking of leaving. . . .

CARMEN: But Mme. Irma. . . .

IRMA: Yes, yes. When the house is about to go up in flames, when the rose is about to be stabbed, all you think of, Carmen, is fleeing.

CARMEN: If I wanted to be elsewhere, you know very well why.

IRMA: Your daughter? But your daughter is dead. . . .

CARMEN: Madame!

IRMA: Whether dead or alive, your daughter is dead. Think of the charming grave, adorned with daisies and artificial wreaths, at the far end of the garden . . . and that garden in your heart, where you'll be able to look after it. . . .

CARMEN: I'd have loved to see her again. . . .

IRMA: You'll keep her image in the image of the garden and the garden in your heart under the flaming robe of Saint Theresa. And you hesitate? I offer you the very finest of deaths, and you hesitate? Are you a coward?

CARMEN: You know very well I'm devoted to you.

IRMA: Well? Will you stay? I'll teach you figures! The wonderful figures that we'll spend nights together calligraphing.

CARMEN (softly): The war is raging. As you said, it's the horde.

IRMA (triumphantly): The horde, but we have our cohorts, our armies, our hosts, legions, batallions, vessels, heralds, clarions, trumpets, our colors, streamers, standards, banners. . . . And yet you tremble? But darling, all's not lost. They'll be crushed. George is still all-powerful. In any case, I hope he'll get through. A Chief of Police always finds a way. Now come and dress me. But first I want to see how Rachel's getting on.

> *Same buzzing as before.* IRMA *glues her eyes to the view-finder. A pause. She peers.*

Christ is leaving with his paraphernalia. I've never been able to understand why he has himself tied to the cross with ropes that he brings in a valise. Maybe they're ropes that have been blessed. Where does he put them when he gets home? Who the hell cares! Let's take a look at Rachel. (*She pushes down another switch.*) Ah, they've finished. They're talking. They're putting away the little arrows, the bow, the gauze bandages, the white officer's cap. . . . No, I don't at all like the way they're looking at each other: it's too candid and straightforward. (*She turns to* CARMEN.) There you have the dangers of regularity. It would be a catastrophe if my clients and girls smiled at each other affectionately. It would be an even greater catastrophe than if it were a question of love. (*She presses the switch mechanically and lays down the receiver. Pensively.*) Dress me.

CARMEN: What are you wearing?

IRMA: The cream-colored negligee.

> CARMEN *opens the door of a closet and takes out the negligee, while* IRMA *unhooks her suit.*

Tell me, Carmen, what about Chantal? . . .

CARMEN: Madame?

> *A pause.*

IRMA: Yes. About Chantal, tell me, what do you know about her?

CARMEN: I've questioned all the girls: Rosine, Elyane, Florence, Marlyse. They've each prepared a little report. I'll let you have them. But I didn't get much out of them. It's possible to spy beforehand. During the fighting, it's harder. For one thing, the camps are more sharply defined. You can choose. When there's peace, it's too vague. You don't quite know whom you're betraying. Nor even whether you're betraying. There's no news about Chantal. They don't even know whether she's still alive.

IRMA: But, tell me, wouldn't you have any scruples about it?

CARMEN: No. Entering a brothel means rejecting the world. Here I am and here I stay. Your laws and orders and the passions are my reality. What jewels are you wearing?

IRMA: The pearls. My jewels. They're the only things I have that are real. I feel everything else is sham. I have my jewels as others have little girls in gardens.—Who's double-crossing? You're hesitating.

CARMEN: The girls all mistrust me. I collect their little report. I pass it on to you. You pass it on to the police. The police check on it. . . . Me, I know nothing.

IRMA: You're cautious. Give me a handkerchief.

CARMEN: No. Viewed from here, where, in any case, men show their naked selves, life seems to me so remote, so profound, that it has all the unreality of a film or of the birth of Christ in the manger. When I'm in a room with a man and he forgets himself so far as to say to me: "The arsenal will be taken tomorrow night," I feel as if I were reading an obscene scrawl. His act becomes as mad, as . . . voluminous as those described in a certain way on certain walls. . . .

A knocking. IRMA *rushes to her apparatus and, by means of a mechanism, conceals it in the wall. Then she cries out.*

IRMA: Yes. Come in. (*To* CARMEN.) You, leave the room.

CARMEN *starts leaving, but, from the rear, enters* THE CHIEF OF POLICE. *Heavy fur-lined coat, hat, cigar.*

THE CHIEF OF POLICE: No, no, stay, Carmen. I like having you around.

He keeps his hat and coat on. Does not remove his cigar from his mouth, but bows to IRMA.

Pleasant warmth, light fragrance. . . . (*Kissing* IRMA's *hand.*) Beautiful lady!

IRMA (*breathlessly*): Put your hand here. (*On her breast.*) I'm all tense. I'm still wrought up. I knew you were on your way, which meant you were in danger. I waited for you all a-tremble.

THE CHIEF OF POLICE: Easy, easy, let me take it all in. You were saying?

IRMA: You rat.

THE CHIEF OF POLICE: All right, that'll do. Let's cut the comedy. The situation's getting more and more serious—it's not desperate, but it will be before long—hap-pi-ly! The Royal Palace is surrounded. The Queen's in hiding. The city—it's a miracle that I got through —the city's being ravaged by fire and sword. Out there the rebellion is tragic and joyous, whereas in this house everything's dying a slow death. So, today's my day. By tonight I'll be in the grave or on a pedestal. So whether I love you or desire you is unimportant. How are things going at the moment?

IRMA: Marvelously. I had some great performances.

THE CHIEF OF POLICE (impatiently): What kind?

IRMA: Carmen has a talent for description. Ask her.

THE CHIEF OF POLICE (to CARMEN): Tell me, still. . . ?

CARMEN: Yes, sir, still. Still the pillars of the Empire: the Judge . . .

THE CHIEF OF POLICE (ironically): Our allegories, our talking weapons. And is there also. . . ?

CARMEN: As every week, a new theme.

THE CHIEF OF POLICE makes a gesture of curiosity.

This time it's the baby who gets slapped, spanked, tucked in, then cries and is cuddled.

THE CHIEF OF POLICE (impatiently): Fine. But. . . .

CARMEN: He's charming, Sir. And so sad!

THE CHIEF OF POLICE (exploding): Well, yes or no, is there a simulation. . . .

CARMEN (bewildered): Simulation?

THE CHIEF OF POLICE: You idiot! Yes! An impersonation of the Chief of Police?

Very heavy silence.

IRMA: The time's not ripe. My dear, your function isn't noble enough to offer dreamers an image that would enshrine them. Perhaps because it lacks illustrious ancestors? No, my dear fellow. . . .

You have to resign yourself to the fact that your image does not yet conform to the liturgies of the brothel.

THE CHIEF OF POLICE: Who's represented in them?

IRMA: You know who. You have your index-cards. (*She enumerates on her fingers.*) There are two kings of France with coronation ceremonies and different rituals, an admiral at the stern of his sinking destroyer, a bishop during the perpetual adoration, a judge performing his functions, a general on horseback, a dey of Algiers surrendering, a fireman putting out a fire, a goat attached to a stake, a housewife returning from market, a pickpocket, a robbed man who's bound and beaten up, a Saint Sebastian, a farmer in his barn . . . but no chief of police . . . nor colonial administrator, though there *is* a missionary dying on the cross, and Christ in person.

THE CHIEF OF POLICE (*after a pause*): You're forgetting the mechanic.

IRMA: He doesn't come any more. What with tightening screws, he'd have ended by constructing a machine. And it might have worked. Back to the factory!

THE CHIEF OF POLICE: So not a single one of your clients has had the idea . . . the remotest idea, the barest suggestion. . . .

IRMA: No. I know you do what you can. You try hatred and love. But glory gives you the cold shoulder.

THE CHIEF OF POLICE (*forcefully*): My image is growing bigger and bigger. It's becoming colossal. Everything around me repeats and reflects it. And you've never seen it represented in this place?

IRMA: In any case, even if it were celebrated here, I wouldn't see anything. The ceremonies are secret.

THE CHIEF OF POLICE: You liar. You've got secret peep-holes in every wall. Every partition, every mirror, is rigged. In one place, you can hear the sighs, in another the echo of the moans. You don't need me to tell you that brothel tricks are mainly mirror tricks. . . . (*Very sadly.*) Nobody yet! But I'll make my image detach itself from me. I'll make it penetrate into your studios, force its way in, reflect and multiply itself. Irma, my function weighs me down. Here, it will appear to me in the blazing light of pleasure and death.

IRMA: You must keep killing, my dear George.

THE CHIEF OF POLICE: I do what I can, I assure you. People fear me more and more.

IRMA: Not enough. You must plunge into darkness, into shit and blood.

THE CHIEF OF POLICE (*very irritated*): I repeat: I do what I can to prove to the nation that I'm a leader, a lawgiver, a builder. . . .

IRMA (*uneasily*): You're raving. Or else you really do expect to build an empire. In which case you're raving.

THE CHIEF OF POLICE (*with conviction*): When the rebellion's been put down, and put down by me, when I've been appealed to by the Queen and have the nation behind me, nothing can stop me. Then, and only then, will you see who I now am! (*Musingly.*) Yes, my dear, I want to build an empire . . . so that the empire will, in exchange, build *me*. . . .

IRMA: . . . a tomb.

THE CHIEF OF POLICE (*somewhat taken aback*): But, after all, why not? Doesn't every conqueror have one? So? (*Exalted.*) Alexandria! I'll have my tomb, Irma. And when the cornerstone is laid, you'll be guest of honor.

IRMA: Thank you. (*To* CARMEN.) Carmen, my dress.

THE CHIEF OF POLICE (*to* CARMEN, *who is about to leave*): Just a minute, Carmen. What do you think of the idea?

CARMEN: That you want to merge your life with one long funeral, Sir.

THE CHIEF OF POLICE (*aggressively*): Is life anything else? You seem to know everything—so tell me: in this sumptuous theatre where every moment a drama is performed—in the sense that the outside world says a mass is celebrated—what have you observed?

CARMEN (*after a hesitation*): As for anything serious, anything worth reporting, only one thing: that without the thighs it contained, a pair of pants on a chair is beautiful, Sir. Emptied of our little old men, our ornaments are deathly sad. They're the ones that are placed on the catafalques of high dignitaries. They cover only corpses that never stop dying. And yet, . . .

IRMA (*to* CARMEN): That's not what the Chief of Police is asking.

THE CHIEF OF POLICE: Let her alone, my dear. I'm used to Carmen's speeches. (*To* CARMEN.) You were saying: and yet . . . ?

CARMEN: And yet, I'm sure that the sudden joy in their eyes when they see the cheap finery is really the gleam of innocence. . . .

THE CHIEF OF POLICE: People claim that our house sends them to Death.

Suddenly a ringing. IRMA *starts. A pause.*

IRMA: Someone's opened the door. Who can it be at this hour? (*To* CARMEN.) Carmen, go down and shut the door.

> CARMEN *exits. A rather long silence between* IRMA *and* THE CHIEF OF POLICE, *who remain alone.*

IRMA: It was I who rang. I wanted to be alone with you for a moment. (*A pause, during which they look into each other's eyes seriously.*) Tell me, George.... (*She hesitates.*)

THE CHIEF OF POLICE (*a little annoyed*): Say it.

IRMA: Do you still insist on keeping up the game? No, no, don't be impatient. Aren't you tired of it?

THE CHIEF OF POLICE: But. . . . What do you mean? In a little while I'll be going home.

IRMA: If you can. If the rebellion leaves you free to go.

THE CHIEF OF POLICE: Irma, you're mad. Or you're acting as if you were. The rebellion itself is a game. From here you can't see anything of the outside, but every rebel is playing a game. And he loves his game.

IRMA: But supposing they let themselves be carried beyond the game? I mean if they get so involved in it that they destroy and replace everything. Yes, yes, I know, there's always the false detail that reminds them that at a certain moment, at a certain point in the drama, they have to stop, and even withdraw. . . . But what if they're so carried away by passion that they no longer recognize anything and leap, without realizing it, into . . .

THE CHIEF OF POLICE: You mean into reality? What of it? Let them try. I do as they do, I penetrate right into the reality that the game offers us, and since I have the upper hand, it's I who score.

IRMA: They'll be stronger than you.

THE CHIEF OF POLICE: Why do you say "they'll be"? Don't I have treasures invested, a thousand resources? All right, enough of that. Are you or aren't you the mistress of a house of illusions? You are. Good. If I come to your place, it's to find satisfaction in your mirrors and their trickery. (*Tenderly.*) Don't worry. Everything will be just as it's always been.

IRMA: I don't know why, but today I feel uneasy. Carmen seems strange to me. The rebels—how shall I put it?—have a kind of gravity. . . .

THE CHIEF OF POLICE: Their role requires it.

IRMA: No, no, a kind of determination. They walk by the windows threateningly, but they don't sing. The threat is in their eyes.

THE CHIEF OF POLICE: What of it? Supposing it is, do you take me for a coward? Do you think I should give up and go home?

IRMA (*pensively*): No. Besides, I think it's too late.

THE CHIEF OF POLICE: Do you have any news?

IRMA: From Chantal, before she lit out. The power-house will be occupied around 3 A.M.

THE CHIEF OF POLICE: Are you sure? Who told her?

IRMA: The partisans of the Fourth Sector. The "Andromeda Sector."

THE CHIEF OF POLICE: That's plausible. How did she find out?

IRMA: It's through her that there were leaks, and through her alone. So don't belittle my house. . . .

THE CHIEF OF POLICE: Your cat-house, my love.

IRMA: Cat-house, whorehouse, bawdyhouse. Brothel. F . . kery. Call it anything you like. So Chantal's the only one who's on the other side. . . . She lit out. But before she did, she confided in Carmen, and Carmen's no fool.

THE CHIEF OF POLICE: Who tipped her off?

IRMA: Roger. The plumber. An idiotic affair. It's not easy for men to get into this place: it's a convent. By "men" you know whom I mean . . . ?

THE CHIEF OF POLICE: The ones with cool heads.

IRMA: Very neatly put. Well, I allowed him to come to repair the plumbing. Wear and tear's pretty heavy here: piping costs me a hundred a month. . . . Does that interest you?

THE CHIEF OF POLICE: Your plumbing? I'll send around the head of my works department.

IRMA: To continue: I let the plumber come. How do you imagine him? Young and handsome? No. He's forty. Thick-set. Serious, with ironic eyes. Chantal spoke to him. I put him out: too late. He belongs to the Andromeda network.

THE CHIEF OF POLICE: Andromeda? Splendid. The rebellion's riding high, it's moving out of this world. If it gives its sectors the names of constellations, it'll evaporate in no time and be metamorphosed into song. Let's hope the songs are beautiful.

IRMA: And what if their songs give the rebels courage? What if they're willing to die for them?

THE CHIEF OF POLICE: The beauty of their songs will make them soft. Unfortunately, they haven't yet reached the point of either beauty or softness. In any case, Chantal's tender passions were providential.

IRMA: Don't bring God into....

THE CHIEF OF POLICE: I'm a freemason. Therefore....

IRMA: You? You never told me.

THE CHIEF OF POLICE (*solemnly*): Sublime Prince of the Royal Secret.

IRMA (*ironically*): You, a brother in a little apron! With a hood and taper and a little mallet! That's odd. (*A pause.*) You too?

THE CHIEF OF POLICE: Why? You too?

IRMA (*with mock solemnity*): I'm a guardian of far more solemn rites. (*Suddenly sad.*) Since that's all I am now.

THE CHIEF OF POLICE: As usual, you're going to bring up our grand passion.

IRMA (*gently*): Not our passion, but the time when we loved each other.

THE CHIEF OF POLICE (*ironically*): Well, would you like to give a historical account of it and deliver a eulogy? You think my visits would have less zest if you didn't flavor them with the memory of a pretended innocence?

IRMA: It's a question of tenderness. Neither the wildest concoctions of my clients nor my own fancies nor my constant endeavor to enrich my studios with new themes nor the passing of time nor the gilding and crystals nor bitter cold can dispel the moments when you cuddled in my arms or keep me from remembering them.

THE CHIEF OF POLICE: Do you really miss them?

IRMA (*tenderly*): I'd give my kingdom to relive a single one of them! And you know which one. I need just one word of truth—as when one looks at one's wrinkles at night, or rinses one's mouth....

THE CHIEF OF POLICE: It's too late. (*A pause.*) Besides, we couldn't cuddle each other eternally. You don't know what I was already secretly moving towards when I was in your arms.

IRMA: I know that I loved you....

THE CHIEF OF POLICE: Could you give up Arthur?

IRMA: It was you who forced him on me. You insisted on there being a man here—against my better judgment—in a domain that should have remained virgin. . . . You fool, don't laugh. Virgin, that is, sterile. But you wanted a pillar, a shaft, a phallus present —an upright bulk. Well, it's here. You saddled me with that hunk of congested meat, that milksop with wrestler's arms. He may look like a strong man at a fair, but you don't realize how fragile he is. You stupidly forced him on me because you felt yourself aging.

THE CHIEF OF POLICE: Be still.

IRMA (*with rising vehemence*): No. I feel like talking. Catastrophe is at my door. . . .

THE CHIEF OF POLICE: You've nothing to fear. The house is guarded by the police.

IRMA (*shrugging her shoulders*): Who's guarding the police? But I feel like talking because in this tense situation it's the only thing I can do to share your emotion. I repeat, you felt yourself aging. You were concerned with power, but without fulfilling yourself. And you relaxed here through Arthur.

THE CHIEF OF POLICE: The danger of the situation has banished boredom and the taste for pleasure by proxy. In acting I've become active again and I want to have you. Kick Arthur out.

IRMA: I need him. I have no illusions. I'm his man and he relies on me, but I need that rugged storewindow dummy hanging onto my skirts. He's my body, as it were, but set beside me.

THE CHIEF OF POLICE: I'm jealous!

IRMA: Of that big doll made up as an executioner in order to satisfy a phony judge? Look, darling, the spectacle of me under the spectacle of that magnificent body never used to bother you. . . . Let me repeat. . . .

THE CHIEF OF POLICE (*he slaps* IRMA, *who falls on the sofa*): And don't blubber or I'll break your jaw. If ever I hear that you've told anyone what happened, I'll send your joint up in smoke. I'll set fire to your hair and bush and I'll turn you loose. I'll light up the town with blazing whores. (*Very gently.*) Do you think I'm capable of it?

IRMA (*in a panting whisper*): Yes, darling.

THE CHIEF OF POLICE: All right, add up the accounts for me. If you like, you can deduct Apollo's crepe de Chine. And hurry up. I've got to get back to my post. For the time being, I have to act.

Afterwards. . . . Afterwards, things'll run themselves. My name will act in my place. Well, what about Arthur?

IRMA: He'll be dead this evening.

THE CHIEF OF POLICE: Dead? You mean . . . really . . . really dead?

IRMA (*with resignation*): Come, come, George, the way one dies here.

THE CHIEF OF POLICE: Indeed? Meaning. . . .

IRMA: The Minister . . . (*She is interrupted by the voice of* CARMEN.)

CARMEN (*in the wings*): Lock Studio 17! Elyane, hurry up! And lower the studio . . . no, no, wait. . . . (*Enter* CARMEN.) Madame, the Queen's Envoy is in the drawing-room. . . .

IRMA: Nonsense! There's no one there. It was I . . . (*She breaks off.*) I'll go and receive him.

> *The door opens, left, and* ARTHUR *appears, trembling and with his clothes torn.*

ARTHUR: Oh, I'm sorry, I thought you were alone. My respects, sir.

IRMA: Well, what's new? You may speak. Carmen's on our side.

ARTHUR (*panting*): Well, I delivered the stuff, as agreed. The whole city's lit up with fires. The Rebels are in control practically everywhere. I doubt if you can get home, sir. I was able to reach the Royal Palace, and I saw the Grand Chamberlain. He said he'd try to come. I might add that he shook my hand. And then I left. The women are the most excited. They're urging the men to loot and kill. But what was most awful was a girl who was singing. . .

> *A shot is heard. A windowpane is shivered. Also a mirror near the bed.* ARTHUR *falls down, hit in the forehead by a bullet coming from outside.* CARMEN *bends over him, then rises to her feet again.* IRMA *goes to the window, then comes back.*

THE CHIEF OF POLICE: In short, I'm stuck here?

CARMEN (*softly*): If the house is to be blown up. . . . Is Saint Theresa's costume in the closet, Mme. Irma?

IRMA (*anxiously*): Yes, at the left. But first have Arthur removed. I'm going to receive the Envoy.

SCENE SIX

The interior of an old-fashioned café. Mirrors. Bottles on the shelves. Bar.

ROGER, *aged 40, model of the proletarian leader, is writing at a small table, rear, without raising his head.*

ARMAND, *aged 25, is sitting silently on a wall-bench.*

MARK, *who is standing, is holding a map on which he places little flags according to instructions he receives by telephone.*

In the foreground, CHANTAL *finishes bandaging the arm of a wounded rebel. She hesitates to insert the pin.*

GEORGETTE, *aged about 30, nervously snatches it from her and pins the bandage herself.*

GEORGETTE: Your eyes fondle everything you do.

CHANTAL: I've got to look and see where to put the pin.

GEORGETTE: You don't look. You contemplate. You stand back and observe. (*To* THE WOUNDED MAN.) Go to the back room. The comrades'll get you out of here. You'll be evacuated in a little while.

THE WOUNDED MAN: Any good news? Except for the things we're directly involved in, we have no idea what's happening.

GEORGETTE (*putting away the compresses*): We don't get much news in this place either. But I've heard that almost all the contacts have been made.

THE WOUNDED MAN (*anxiously*): Is there any hope?

GEORGETTE (*curtly*): No. A man who hopes is already dreaming. Stop hoping. We'll win.

THE WOUNDED MAN: But what about the Archbishop? And the General? And the Judge? What's being done about them?

GEORGETTE: No one bothers about them any more. We're fighting against men. When men start losing, the Great Figures crumble.

339

(*She leads* THE WOUNDED MAN *to the door at the left.*) When you get to the window, hug the wall and walk on all fours. They're shooting from the roofs.

THE WOUNDED MAN *exits.* GEORGETTE *returns to* CHANTAL.

I'm sorry, Chantal. I was a little rough with you just before.
CHANTAL: Forget it. The main thing is that I learn to dress wounds right. (*She smiles.*) To do a good job as a nurse.

ARMAND, *who has been seated, stands up, stretches and looks at himself complacently in a mirror.*

ROGER (*without raising his head*): How long are you going to stand there primping.
ARMAND: I'm arranging my hardware for the ball.
ROGER (*severely*): Not the ball, the fight. . . .

A pause.

Do you admire yourself in your role? You want it to last?
ARMAND (*gaily*): It has its charm. And it's better than being at the shop. (*He laughs as he looks at himself in the mirror; then, spreading his legs, he plants himself in the middle of the stage.*) Like on the enlistment posters for the Marines: the tanks roll between my legs! (*He strikes another pose.*) Taras Bulba! (*He laughs, takes out his revolver and aims at the bottles.*) Big Chief Buffalo! *We* don't have the right to play. The other side would have painted the town red long ago. They'd have smashed the crockery and shivered the mirrors!
ROGER: You itching to do it?
ARMAND: It's a little dismal on our side. All week long we operate machines, and on a red-letter day like this, instead of raising hell, we fuss around with a mechanism that may run away with us.
ROGER: If ever we had the misfortune of taking pleasure in shooting at men and bottles, it would be good-bye to the revolutionary spirit! As for a red-letter day, this is it! The Law Court's been burned to the ground. The churches have been looted. There are

men who are going out to fight in judges' robes and surplices. It's a regular carnival. That ought to please you.

ARMAND: Our red-letter days are always a mockery of theirs!

ROGER: Later on, we'll organize leisure activities. . . .

ARMAND (*taking a stance like a movie character, he pretends to machine-gun the entire café*): Bangbangbangbangbang! (*He laughs and looks at himself in the mirror. Then, by the street-door enters a wounded man supported by another man who leaves almost at once.*)

THE MAN (*to* GEORGETTE, *who rushes up*): Been shot in the right thigh. I don't think it's serious, but better attend to him right away.

ARMAND (*jokingly*): Or finish him off. The wounded get in our way.

ROGER (*to* ARMAND): This is no time for kidding a comrade.

GEORGETTE (*to* THE WOUNDED MAN): He's young. (*To* CHANTAL.) Attend to him. Here, take the scissors . . . cut it. . . .

> CHANTAL *cuts and tears the man's trousers. Then she takes the cotton and alcohol that* GEORGETTE *hands her. She cleans the wound.*

SECOND WOUNDED MAN: Take it easy! You're not washing a corpse! For Christ's sake, take it easy!

CHANTAL (*aggressively*): Does a drop of alcohol make you keel over?

GEORGETTE (*curtly*): Being rough is also a game.

CHANTAL (*hurrying to dress the wound*): The main thing is that the wounded be attended to.

GEORGETTE: The main thing, as Roger says, is that the rebellion start off by despising make-believe. (*A pause.*) And complacency.

CHANTAL (*to* ROGER): If I don't feel I have a talent for dressing wounds. . . .

ROGER: Georgette's right, Chantal. What we . . .

GEORGETTE (*to* THE WOUNDED MAN, *and interrupting* ROGER): Come over here. (*She takes him to the door by which* THE FIRST WOUNDED MAN *went out.*) Turn left, and be careful they don't spot you.

ROGER (*pedantically*): I repeat, Georgette's right. What we're engaged in is too serious to be undertaken lightly. If we behave like those on the other side, then we *are* the other side. Instead of changing the world, all we'll achieve is a reflection of the one we want to destroy.

GEORGETTE (*same tone*): Everything must be aimed at utility.

ROGER: If we use charm, we're in danger of being taken in by that of the others. It's better to remain silent and motionless than make a remark or gesture that can't be utilized. . . .

GEORGETTE (*in the same tone*): . . . for purposes of the revolution.

ARMAND (*to* ROGER): In two minutes I'm going out for a leak. You mean I really don't have the right to amuse myself by squirting it up along the wall?

ROGER (*shocked*): You mean you usually fool around like that, you, who've been involved in the revolution from the very beginning?

ARMAND (*acting as if he were hurt*): If not that, then what *am* I allowed?

ROGER (*beginning a lecture*): At the basis . . .

LUKE (*interrupting him*): I'm not impressed by your speeches. I still maintain that in certain cases you've got to use the enemy's weapons. That it's indispensable. Enthusiasm for freedom? It's a fine thing, I don't deny it, but it would be even finer if freedom were a pretty girl with a warm voice. After all, what does it matter to you if we storm the barricades by following a female like a pack of males in heat? And what of it if the groans of the dying are groans of love?

ROGER: Men don't revolt in order to go chasing after a female.

LUKE (*stubbornly*): Even if the chase leads them to victory?

ROGER: Then their victory is already sick. Their victory has a dose of clap, to talk like you. . . .

LOUIS *enters. Aged about 40. Gay and good-humored.*

LOUIS: Well, boys, it looks pretty good. All our forces, or almost all, are in contact. The Palace is expected to surrender tonight, or tomorrow morning at the latest. Lots of soldiers and a large part of the police force are already fighting on our side. We don't have everything in hand yet, but we've got reason for more than just hoping. . . .

GEORGETTE: Before, too, we did better than just hope. We were sure of winning.

LOUIS: Luck is with us tonight. Unless those fine gentlemen, those gentlemen who smoke and fart in silk, are planning to pull a fast one on us. (*Noticing* ARMAND.) That worked out all right. I've already heard about it. But you had a pretty close shave!

ARMAND (*laughing*): Are you telling me! I went out to plant the bomb. When I got half-way up the street, some son of a bitch started firing away, but he missed me. I saw the machine gun almost in front of me. The guy was reloading. I just stood and stared at him, cool as a cucumber. He looked as if he were posing, with the light beaming on him. The guy took aim. And then, he toppled over. One of our boys had picked him off. I continued on my way, calm as could be. I planted my bomb, and here I am. I wasn't scared for a second. Didn't even bat an eyelash.

LOUIS: Even so, go take a rest in the back room. We'll be needing you in a little while.

ARMAND: Don't be shy, if you want me. (ARMAND *exits left.*)

ROGER (*as if to himself*): Too much youth, too hot-blooded.

LOUIS: You sound as if you were put out because he wasn't scared.

ROGER: I know him and a thousand like him. He wasn't scared because the danger and the foiling of the danger didn't depend on him. But if ever once in his life he warded off death by his intelligence, you'd see him tremble. He'd realize that he had to accomplish things by intelligence and will-power! He'd be less sure of himself. For the time being, he thinks he's the darling of fate.

LOUIS (*ironically*): You don't dare say "of the gods."

ROGER (*glumly*): I don't mean of the gods. If the heavens are studded with such constellations as that of the Archbishop and the Hero, then we've got to tear heaven down. Not invoke it, nor even ever name it, but strip it, and make it dance naked on the cathedral squares.

LOUIS (*to* MARK): Any news from the Central Committee?

MARK (*still planting flags*): They're electing a president tonight.

LOUIS: Where'll the government be set up?

ROGER: That's a secret.

MARK: At the Royal Palace, if it's taken tonight.

LOUIS: What if things don't work out?

MARK: The fight'll continue, but in shit and darkness. Incognito. Let me get on with my work.

Silence.

ROGER (*to* LOUIS): We were waiting for you. (*He points to* LUKE.) He claims they need someone to spur on the section.

LUKE (*to* LOUIS): It's not that they lack courage. It's not that. But they've got to be keyed up. Just a little.

LOUIS (*to* LUKE): So? Can't you work them up? Can't you give them a pep-talk? You need a bugle?

LUKE (*to* LOUIS): Words aren't enough, and you know it. We came to ask you to lend us Chantal. . . .

ROGER: No. Chantal was useful—I won't deny it—at the beginning of the revolution. She's played her part. Now it's over.

LOUIS: Chantal was taking on too much importance. That's true. On the other hand, if they're really inarticulate. . . . (*To* ROGER.) Did you ask for the bazookas?

ROGER: Again? Bazookas, bazookas! That's the magic word, it's a regular fetish. Bazookas for everyone!

LOUIS: We've got to take advantage of youthful enthusiasm. And youngsters can't fight unless they adorn themselves with war cries. They try to get wounded so as to show their scars. They want bazookas.

ROGER (*bluntly*): No bazookas.

LOUIS (*irritably*): Then according to you we ought to be fighting hand-to-hand?

ROGER: As the word implies, hand-to-hand fighting eliminates distance.

LOUIS: Do you distrust enthusiasm?

ROGER: I distrust nervousness. The rebellion's riding high, and the people are having a carnival. They're shooting for the fun of it.

LUKE: They're right. Damn it, let them have their fling. I've never seen such excitement: one hand on the trigger, the other on the fly. They shoot and screw.

ROGER: Must you use such language! (*With sudden anger.*) What exactly is it you're after? If I yanked Chantal from the brothel, it wasn't to plant her in another—or in the same one—that's a mockery of the old one. Carnival! Carnival! You know well enough we ought to beware of it like the plague, since its logical conclusion is death. You know well enough that a carnival that goes to the limit is a suicide!

LOUIS: Without the people's anger there'd be no revolt. And anger is a carnival.

GEORGETTE: Then we must fight without anger. Reason should be enough.

ROGER: The enemy's losses are high; ours are incalculable. We've got to win at any cost. Those gentlemen on the other side are as happy as can be about our war. Because of it, they'll be able to attain, as they put it, even greater renown. The people mustn't enjoy themselves. And they mustn't play. Starting now, they've got to be in dead earnest.

Enter a WOUNDED MAN.

LOUIS (*to* THE WOUNDED MAN): Is it serious?

THE WOUNDED MAN: No. In the shoulder. But I think the bullet's still there.

CHANTAL (*to* GEORGETTE): Take care of him.

GEORGETTE: Right away. (*To* THE WOUNDED MAN.) Sit down. (*To* CHANTAL.) But what about you?

CHANTAL: I've had enough.

THE WOUNDED MAN: I know how you feel. It's no fun patching up the wounded. All the same, that's a woman's job. . . . My own wife's always busy with that kind of thing: plastering up a kid who gets hurt, mending a broken broomstick. . . .

ROGER (*going up to* CHANTAL): Are you giving up already?

CHANTAL: Forgive me, Roger, but I don't feel I'm cut out for that. I know you despise me. I'm just about ready to drop out. Yet I can't be on the other side either. And I want to sing.

ROGER (*gravely*): I told you, that's over. And you promised.

CHANTAL: I want to sing! To sing the excitement of the brawl, that and nothing else! For the sake of justice, if you like, I agree, but above all for the fighters for justice.

ROGER: You know where that can lead you?

CHANTAL: To the vaudeville stage. Is that what you're thinking?

ROGER (*ardently*): I've placed all my hope in you, Chantal. It was on you that I worked first. I wanted to disenchant you. Singer or whore, it comes to the same thing. You've got to stop charming and serve.

THE WOUNDED MAN (*turning his head in the direction of* CHANTAL): Is that you, Chantal? I didn't recognize you! What the hell are you doing here instead of leading the men forward the way you did yesterday, on the parapet? (*A silence.*) It takes women like you to loosen us up. It's your voice that tears out the cobblestones. It's your voice that stretches the barbed wire. It's your voice. . . .

GEORGETTE (*to* THE WOUNDED MAN): That does it. Keep your arm folded. Now come along. You've got to lie down and rest.

She accompanies him to the door, left. Exit THE WOUNDED MAN.

LUKE (*to* ROGER, *pointing to* CHANTAL): We're asking you to let us have her for two hours. . . .

ROGER: Chantal belongs . . .

CHANTAL: To nobody!

ROGER: To my section . . . and to me.

LUKE: To the insurrection.

ROGER: If you want a woman to lead men forward, then create one.

LUKE (*seriously*): We tried to. We looked for one. We tried to build one up: nice voice, nice bosom, with the right kind of free and easy manner, but . . . her eyes lacked fire, and you know that without fire . . . we asked the north quarter and the port quarter to let us have theirs; they weren't free.

CHANTAL: A woman like me? Another one? You really mean another one? All I have is the face of an inspired owl and my hoarse voice. I give them or lend them for hatred's sake. All I am is my face, my voice, and inside me a sweet and deadly kindness. You mean I have two popular rivals, two other poor devils? Let them come. I'll walk all over them. I have no rival.

LUKE (*to* LOUIS): She'll have hardly anything to do. As you know, we're attacking the bridge at dawn. Under our protection, she'll enter a house overlooking the dock. And she'll sing from the balcony. . . .

LOUIS: If we lend her to you . . .

LUKE: That's not what we're asking. If we take her, we'll hire her.

CHANTAL (*banteringly*): How much?

ROGER (*to* CHANTAL): You think that's funny?

LOUIS (*to* LUKE): What if we let you have her to sing and spur on your district and if she got bumped off? We'd lose everything. She's irreplaceable.

LUKE: It's for her to decide.

LOUIS: She's no longer her own master. She belongs to us. All that your women are good for is tearing up and carrying cobblestones or reloading your guns. I know that's useful, but . . .

LUKE: How many women do you want in exchange?

ROGER (*dumfounded*): Is a singer on the barricades as precious as all that?

LUKE: How many? Ten women for Chantal? (*Silence.*) Twenty?

Silence.

ROGER: Twenty women? Would you be ready to lend us twenty measly women, twenty oxen, twenty head of cattle? So Chantal's something special?

CHANTAL: Chantal? Here's the picture: every morning I go back—because at night I'm ablaze—I go back to a hovel to sleep and knock myself out with red wine. And I, with my raspy voice, my sham anger, my glassy eyes, my painted illumination, my Andalusian hair, I comfort and enchant the rabble. They'll win out, and my victory'll be a queer sort of thing. Maybe I get my talent from the brothel, but I'll never know how to swab a wound.

Suddenly the telephone rings. MARK *answers.*

MARK (*into the telephone*): Hello . . . this is Mark . . . B. 880. . . . Yes . . . yes . . . she's here. . . . (*A long silence.*) Is it serious? . .

A silence. Everyone is still and attentive.

O.K. . . . no, no . . . there's no objection. . . . But . . . is there any possible danger? No? . . . You don't know? . . . In any case, I'll send her. When the time comes, you'll have both sections. . . . (*A silence.*) So long. (*He hangs up.*)

LOUIS: The Central Committee?

MARK: Yes. Everything's working out right. The Palace is surrounded. The enemy has collapsed. It's the end. The bodies of several high dignitaries have been identified. (*A pause.*) Since there's no longer any central authority, we'll have to set up something at once to prevent anarchy. But there's a plot afoot. We've got to work fast.

ROGER: Are they asking you to be a member of the provisional government?

MARK: I've been appointed.

ROGER (*to* MARK): What's to be done?

MARK: Give orders to design posters showing Chantal on the barricades and on the balcony of the Palace. See to it that they're pasted on every wall and billboard. (ROGER *makes a gesture.*) Do as I tell you. According to information, the Grand Chamberlain has gone to The Balcony, which is where the Chief of Police is said to be. They've gone there to work out the usual kind of operation. They know very well that as far as they're concerned the revolt must have only one purpose: to heighten their glory by putting down the insurrection. We're going to cramp their carnival by countering with our own.

ROGER: A carnival?

MARK (*forcefully*): We're going to use Chantal. Her job is to embody the revolution. The job of the mothers and widows is to mourn the dead. The job of the dead is to cry for revenge. The job of our heroes is to die with a smile. . . . The Palace will be occupied this evening. From the balcony of the Palace Chantal will rouse the people, and sing. The time for reasoning is past; now's the time to get steamed up and fight like mad. Chantal embodies the struggle; the people are waiting for her to represent victory.

ROGER: And when we're the victors, what'll we have gained?

MARK: There'll be time enough to think of that. For the moment, there's not a minute to waste. We're racing against the clock. If they succeed in working out their scheme, we're up the creek . . . The royal carriage has managed to get through the lines. It's parked near The Balcony. . . . Was the Queen in it? . . . Does anyone know? (*To* LUKE.) You'll escort Chantal. To get to the Palace you'll have to go along the river. . . . (*He goes back to pinning his flags.*)

LUKE: I know. I'm used to it.

ROGER (*to* CHANTAL, *in a hurt voice*): But it was I who . . . if Chantal . . . (*Humbly, but with resolution.*) I love you, Chantal.

CHANTAL (*to* ROGER): You're the first, the only one, the only one there'll ever be, but let me leave.

ROGER: The minutes without you will be unbearable.

GEORGETTE: Is that why you wanted her to learn to dress wounds?

ROGER: That was why, and also that she be born again.

CHANTAL: We won't be separated. I'll speak to them in an icy voice, and at the same time I'll murmur words of love for you. You'll hear them from here, and I'll listen to those you say to me.

ROGER: They may keep you, Chantal. They're strong—strong as death.

CHANTAL: Don't be afraid, I know their power. Your sweetness and tenderness are stronger. I'll speak to them in a tone of severity. They'll listen to me, and they'll be afraid. All *they* can do is fight, and all *you* can do is talk. That's the role you've learned to play. The brothel has at least been of some use to me, for it has taught me the art of shamming and acting. I've had to play so many roles that I know almost all of them. And I've had so many partners. . . .

ROGER: Be still.

CHANTAL: . . . And such artful ones, such crafty ones, that my skill and guile are incomparable.

GEORGETTE: You'll never forget the brothel. . . .

CHANTAL: Never completely. You and your kind who are pure and just, you resent never having had the experience.

GEORGETTE: Personally, I didn't have a calling for it.

ROGER (*vehemently*): But I dragged you—dragged you!—from the grave! And you're already escaping me and mounting to the sky. . . . Your name's on the lips of people who've never seen or heard you. Before long, they'll think it's for you they're fighting. You're already a kind of saint. Women try to imitate you. . . . (*In a fury.*) I didn't carry you off, I didn't steal you, for you to become a unicorn or two-headed eagle. . . .

GEORGETTE (*contemptuously*): Don't you like unicorns?

CHANTAL (*to* ROGER): I'll come back, and everything will be the same. We love each other. . . .

ROGER: Nothing will be the same, and you know it. You'll be what you've always dreamt of being: an emblem forever escaping from her womanliness.

LOUIS: You're forgetting that it's for the revolution and that she may remain there.

ROGER: That's the only thing that could save her.

MARK (*still planting his flags*): It's time to go.

CHANTAL (*to* ROGER): Shall I kiss you?

ROGER *hugs her; then she leaves, preceded by* LUKE. *A silence.*

GEORGETTE (*to the men*): Excuse me, but I've got medicines to prepare.

GEORGETTE *exits. A silence.*

LOUIS (*to* ROGER): You love her, and she's escaping you. I can understand your anger.

ROGER (*sadly*): She's flying into the other camp!

LOUIS: You're dreaming!

ROGER: Me?

LOUIS: You're dreaming. Dreaming of an impossible revolution that's carried out reasonably and cold-bloodedly. You're fascinated by it, the way those in the other camp are by other games. But you've got to realize that the most reasonable man always manages, when he pulls the trigger, to become a dispenser of justice.

ROGER: In the eyes of whom?

LOUIS: I wonder. (*A pause. Musingly.*) Chantal! But . . . it's Georgette that you ought to love.

ROGER (*surprised*): Georgette?

LOUIS: Because she loves you. . . . But what you love in Chantal is the very thing you're bent on destroying, the thing that made it possible for her to enter the brothel, the thing that's still part of her. . . .

> Suddenly a terrible explosion. The windowpanes tremble. The three men pull themselves together. They look at each other anxiously.

Ring up the Central Committee.

> MARK *removes the receiver. He waits a few seconds.*

MARK: Is that you, Robert? This is Mark, B. 880. . . . Did you hear that? . . . Eh? . . . The Palace? . . . Who? . . . The North Section? . . . Good! So long. (*He hangs up.*) Did you get that? (*He smiles.*) The Royal Palace has been blown up.

ROGER: Chantal is saved!

MARK: This time it seems pretty sure that we've got the upper hand. The streets around the cathedral are occupied. So are the bridges. . . . The revolutionary tribunal is in permanent session. . . .

LOUIS: Have there been any executions?

MARK: Quite a number. Execution follows immediately upon condemnation. No standing on ceremony.

ROGER: Chantal's coming back. She'll help Georgette. . . .

LOUIS (*to* MARK): If the Royal Palace has been blown up, the Queen must be under the rubble?

MARK: Let's hope so. But the Grand Chamberlain managed to get to The Balcony. He's still there, and the royal carriage. . . .

ARMAND *enters in a state of wild excitement.*

ARMAND: The Palace has been blown up! You can see it blazing from the windows! The opposition has completely collapsed. Everything's giving way. . . . It's all over. And The Balcony's on fire!

MARK: Is that why you're pale?

ARMAND: Me? Pale?

MARK: I didn't say you're scared. I said you're pale.

ARMAND: I didn't think we'd make it as soon as that. Who's going to take over the controls. And what's to be done with the Queen, and the Archbishop, and the others?

ROGER: First undress them.

ARMAND: What if they don't give in? They've good reason for knowing they're sacred. I personally don't believe in their masquerade, not one bit. But is there any stronger force to replace them?

ROGER: You, and everybody.

LOUIS: The Central Committee's already been set up.

ARMAND: The Central Committee—they're pals. . . .

MARK (*roughly*): Go get your gun. You're coming with me.

ARMAND (*after a very brief hesitation*): O.K. And The Balcony's on fire? No more Balcony, no more whores. . . .

MARK: I was appointed an hour ago. You're to obey me. Get going. (ARMAND *exits. To* ROGER, *in a hurried tone.*) Invent a Chantal who becomes more and more fabulous! She's the only one who'll be able to electrify the people, precisely because she comes from the brothel. Get going. Encourage them. Loudspeakers everywhere. Her voice on all the barricades. Photos. Her face on all the billboards. Have tracts printed, by the thousands, and see that they're distributed. Brightly colored. With a picture of her and a declaration. Invent a historic statement signed Chantal. Write a poem to the glory of wrath, rebellion and war.

ROGER: Yes, a poem hailing freedom, the people and their virtue. . . .

MARK (*weightily*): Hell, no! None of that. That kind of thing would shoot them up into a heaven of abstractions, where they'd hang permanently. If you magnify freedom and the people and virtue, if you make them untouchable, how can you approach them, how can you love them? You've got to leave them in their living reality. Let there be .poems and pictures, but they mustn't give pleasure, they've got to sting. And do what I say—Committee orders.

SCENE SEVEN

The Funeral Studio mentioned in MME. IRMA's *listing of the studios. The studio is in ruins. The lace and velvet are torn. The artificial wreaths are tattered. An impression of desolation.* IRMA's *dress is in rags. So is the suit of the* CHIEF OF POLICE. ARTHUR's *corpse is lying on a kind of fake tomb of fake black marble. Nearby, a new character: the Court* ENVOY. *Embassy uniform. He is the only one unscathed.* CARMEN *is dressed as at the beginning; she is carrying the Saint Theresa outfit.*

IRMA (*touching the corpse with her foot*): He didn't think he'd be acting his role of corpse this evening in earnest.

THE ENVOY (*smiling*): Our dear Minister of the Interior would have been delighted had not he himself met the same fate. It is unfortunately I who have had to replace him in his mission here, and I have no taste for pleasures of this kind. (*He pinches* CARMEN's *chin.*) We prefer this modest rose! I'm pleased with her. Everything has gone off splendidly, to our great joy. (*Suddenly embarrassed.*) And despite the Fair One's apparent irritation.

CARMEN (*curtly*): I did my job.

IRMA (*to* CARMEN): Be still. (*To* THE ENVOY.) Forgive her, your Excellency, she feels humiliated, because with you she's only a saint. With one of these gentlemen she had higher ranking. But she knows her duty.

THE ENVOY: It's therefore for me to apologize. I know only too well how hard it is to assume the appearance of our abyss. (*He touches* ARTHUR's *corpse with his foot.*) Yes, this body would have sent our dear Minister into raptures.

IRMA: Not at all, your Excellency. It's make-believe that these gentlemen want. The Minister desired a fake corpse. But this one is real. Look at it: it's truer than life. His entire being was speeding towards immobility.

THE ENVOY: He was therefore meant for grandeur.

THE CHIEF OF POLICE: Him? He was a spineless dummy.

THE ENVOY: He was, like us, haunted by a quest of immobility. By what we call the hieratic. And, in passing, allow me to pay tribute to the imagination responsible for there being a funeral parlor in this house. Whose idea was it?

IRMA: The Wisdom of Nations, your Excellency.

THE ENVOY: It does things well. But we were talking about the Queen, to protect whom is my mission.

THE CHIEF OF POLICE: You're going about it in a curious way. The Palace, according to what you say. . . .

THE ENVOY (*smiling*): For the time being, Her Majesty is in safety. But time is pressing. The prelate is said to have been beheaded. The Archbishop's Palace has been ransacked. The Law Court and Military Headquarters have been routed. . . .

THE CHIEF OF POLICE: But what about the Queen?

THE ENVOY (*in a very light tone*): She's embroidering. For a moment she thought of nursing the wounded. But it was pointed out to her that, as the throne was threatened, she had to carry to an extreme the Royal prerogatives.

IRMA: Which are?

THE ENVOY: Absence. Her Majesty has retired to a chamber, in solitude. The disobedience of her people saddens her. She is embroidering a handkerchief. The design of it is as follows: the four corners will be adorned with poppy heads. In the middle of the handkerchief, embroidered in pale blue silk, will be a swan, resting on the water of a lake. That's the only point about which Her Majesty is troubled: will it be the water of a lake, a pond or a pool? Or simply of a tank or a cup? It is a grave problem. We have chosen it because it is insoluble, and the Queen can engross herself in an infinite meditation.

IRMA: Is the Queen amused?

THE ENVOY: Her Majesty is occupying herself in becoming entirely what she must be: the Queen. (*He looks at the corpse.*) She, too, is moving rapidly towards immobility.

IRMA: And she's embroidering?

THE ENVOY: No, Madame, I say the Queen is embroidering a handkerchief, for though it is my duty to describe her, it is also my duty to conceal her.

IRMA: Do you mean she's not embroidering?

THE ENVOY: I mean that the Queen is embroidering and that she is not embroidering. She picks her nose, examines the pickings and lies down again. Then, she dries the dishes.

IRMA: The Queen?

THE ENVOY: She is not nursing the wounded. She is embroidering an invisible handkerchief. . . .

THE CHIEF OF POLICE: By God! What have you done with Her Majesty? I want a straight answer. I'm not amused. . . .

THE ENVOY: She is in a chest. She is sleeping. Wrapped in the folds of Royalty, she is snoring. . . .

THE CHIEF OF POLICE (*threateningly*): Is the Queen dead?

THE ENVOY (*unperturbed*): She is snoring and she is not snoring. Her head, which is tiny, supports, without wavering, a crown of metal and stones.

THE CHIEF OF POLICE (*more and more threateningly*): Enough of that. You said the Palace was in danger. . . . What's to be done? I still have almost the entire police force behind me. Those who are still with me are ready to die for me. . . . They know who I am and what I'll do for them. . . . How far has the rebellion gone? I want a clear answer.

THE ENVOY: You can judge from the state of this house. And from your own. . . . All seems lost.

IRMA: You belong to the Court, your Excellency. Before coming here, I was with the troops. That's where I won my first spurs. I can assure you I've known worse situations. The populace—from which I broke away with a kick of my heels—the populace is howling beneath my windows, which have been multiplied by the bombs: my house stands its ground. My rooms aren't intact, but they've held up. My whores, except for one lunatic, are on the job. If the center of the Palace is a woman like me . . .

THE ENVOY (*imperturbably*): The Queen is standing on one foot in the middle of an empty room, and she . . .

THE CHIEF OF POLICE: That'll do! I've had enough of your riddles. For me, the Queen has to be someone. And the situation has to be concrete. Describe it to me exactly. I've no time to waste.

THE ENVOY: Whom do you want to save?

THE CHIEF OF POLICE: The Queen!

IRMA: My hide!

THE ENVOY (*to* THE CHIEF OF POLICE): If you're eager to save the Queen—and, beyond her, our flag, and all its gold fringe, and its eagle, cords and pole, would you describe them to me?

THE CHIEF OF POLICE: Until now I've served the things you mention, and served them with distinction, and without bothering to know any more about them than what I saw. And I'll continue. What's happening about the rebellion?

THE ENVOY (*resignedly*): The garden gates will, for a moment longer, hold back the crowd. The guards are devoted, like us, with an obscure devotion. They'll die for their sovereign. They'll give their blood. Unhappily there won't be enough of it to drown the rebellion. Sandbags have been piled up in front of the doors. In order to confuse even reason, Her Majesty removes herself from one secret chamber to another, from the servants' hall to the Throne Room, from the latrines to the chicken-coop, the chapel, the guard-room. . . . She makes herself unfindable and thus attains a threatened invisibility. So much for the inside of the Palace. Outside—and from here you cannot be aware of it— the insurrection has attained such proportions that the very nation is in peril.

THE CHIEF OF POLICE: I've been getting reports from my agents. . . .

THE ENVOY (*interrupting him*): I don't doubt their courage or cleverness, but my spies are in the thick of the revolution, and in some cases they're rebels themselves. Now, the populace, which is intoxicated with its first victories, has reached the point of exaltation at which one light-heartedly forsakes actual combat for useless sacrifice. It will be easy to take the leap. The people are not engaging in battle. They're indulging in revelry.

IRMA: When a person's on a spree, he no longer knows what he's doing. While roaring with laughter, one can grab hold of a live wire. . . .

THE ENVOY: Exactly. And you're not the only one who knows it. A revolutionary committee has been set up. You don't quite realize it, but we, who have eyes everywhere, can tell you that the situation is increasingly dangerous for you. It's composed of grim technicians. Dressed in black. . . .

IRMA: As in Studio 28 . . .

THE ENVOY (*interrupting her*): Not at all. That's precisely the difference. Those gentlemen—and this seems a new phenomenon— aren't playing, or rather, don't realize what they're playing. They calculate. Their faces are pale and sad, their gestures sharp and precise, their speech always exact. They don't cheat. They have tremendous power over the people. They want to save them. . . .

IRMA: What if I let loose my army among them—though it *has* suffered from the course of events—and if they were lured into my studios?

THE ENVOY: They've anticipated that. They're taking no risks. Now, for the time being, though they haven't triumphed, they're gaining ground. . . .

THE CHIEF OF POLICE: What about the Generalissimo?

THE ENVOY: Gone mad. He wanders among the crowd, where nobody will harm him, protected by his madness.

THE CHIEF OF POLICE: What about the Attorney General?

THE ENVOY: Died of fright.

THE CHIEF OF POLICE: And the Bishop?

THE ENVOY: His case is more difficult. The Church is secretive. Nothing is known about him. Nothing definite. His decapitated head was said to have been seen on the handlebars of a bicycle. Of course, the rumor was false. We're therefore relying entirely on you. But your orders aren't getting through.

IRMA: We want to win, and not in death.

THE ENVOY: To save whom?

A pause.

Won't you answer? Would it perturb you to see things as they are? To gaze at the world tranquilly and accept responsibility for your gaze, whatever it might see?

THE CHIEF OF POLICE: But, after all, in coming to see me, you did have something definite in mind, didn't you? You had a plan? Let's hear it.

Suddenly a terrific blast. Both men, but not IRMA, *fall flat on the floor, then stand up again and dust each other off.*

THE ENVOY: That may have been the Royal Palace. Long live the Royal Palace!

THE CHIEF OF POLICE (*aghast*): But the Queen. . . . Then the Queen's under the rubble?

THE ENVOY (*smiling mysteriously*): You need not worry. Her Majesty is in a safe place. And that phoenix, when dead, can rise up from the ashes of a Royal Palace. I can understand your impatience to prove your valor, your devotion . . . but the Queen will wait for you as long as necessary. (*To* IRMA.) I must pay tribute, Madame, to your coolness. And to your courage. They are worthy of the highest respect. . . . (*Musingly.*) Of the highest. . . .

IRMA: You're forgetting to whom you're speaking. I may run a brothel, but I wasn't born of the marriage of the moon and a crocodile. I've lived among the people. . . . All the same, it was a heavy blow. And the people . . .

THE ENVOY (*severely*): That's behind you. When life departs, the hands cling to a sheet. What significance has that rag when you're about to penetrate into the providential fixity?

IRMA: Sir? Do you mean I'm at my last gasp?

THE ENVOY (*examining her, part by part*): Splendid head! Sturdy thighs! Solid shoulders!

IRMA (*laughing*): So I've been told, and it didn't make me lose my head. In short, I'll make a presentable corpse if the rebels act fast and if they leave me intact. But if the Queen is dead . . .

THE ENVOY (*bowing*): Long live the Queen, Madame.

IRMA (*anxiously*): What? You wouldn't dare . . .

THE ENVOY (*spiritedly*): I've described the situation. The populace, in its joy and fury, is at the brink of ecstasy. It's for us to press it forward. The Queen was less beautiful than you.

IRMA: Her lineage was more ancient . . . she was older. . . . And, after all, maybe she was just as frightened as I.

THE CHIEF OF POLICE: It is in order to approach her, to be worthy of her, that one makes such a mighty effort. But what if one is Herself?

IRMA: And I don't know how to talk. I'm always hemming and hawing.

THE ENVOY: All must unfold in a silence that etiquette allows no one to break.

THE CHIEF OF POLICE: I'm going to have the rubble of the Palace cleared away. If, as you said, the Queen was in a chest, it may be possible to save her.

THE ENVOY (*shrugging his shoulders*): It was made of rosewood! And it was so old, so worn. . . . (*To* IRMA, *running his hand over the back of her neck.*) Yes, it requires solid vertebrae . . . they've got to carry several pounds. . . .

THE CHIEF OF POLICE: . . . and resist the axe, don't they? Irma, don't listen to him!

IRMA (*to* THE ENVOY): But, your Excellency, I'm really very weak, and very frail. Though a while ago I was boasting . . .

THE ENVOY: Around this delicate and precious kernel we'll forge a shell of gold and iron. But you must make up your mind quickly. If it's noticed . . .

IRMA: Allow me just a little more respite. . . .

THE ENVOY: A few seconds, for time is pressing.

THE CHIEF OF POLICE: If only there were some way of knowing what the late sovereign would have thought of it. We can't decide just like that. To appropriate a heritage . . .

THE ENVOY (*scornfully*): You're knuckling under already. Do you tremble if there's no authority above you to decide? But it's for Mme. Irma to declare. . . .

IRMA (*in a highfalutin tone*): In the records of our family, which goes a long way back, there was some question of . . .

THE ENVOY (*severely*): Nonsense, Mme. Irma. In our vaults,. genealogists are working day and night. History is submitted to them. I said we hadn't a minute to waste in conquering our people, but beware! Although the populace may worship you, its high-flown pride is capable of sacrificing you. It sees you as red, either crimson or blood-red. If it kills its idols and thrusts them into the sewers, it will sweep us up with them. . . .

THE CHIEF OF POLICE: And you say that without trembling, you who survive all revolutions?

IRMA (*to* THE CHIEF OF POLICE): Let the Grand Chamberlain finish what he has to say. It concerns me. If necessary, I'll take you all under my protection.

THE ENVOY (*to* THE CHIEF OF POLICE): Sir, in the northern part of the country lies a vast plain. Nearby is a mountain. Laborers were already at work when the revolt broke out, but we'll be able to bring them back. In addition to that mountain, and a few others, the country is rich in marble quarries. . . .

THE CHIEF OF POLICE (*marveling*): Marble? And granite? Is there pink granite?

THE ENVOY: And even porphyry, sir. I refer to a project for a tomb. The plan of it is in my possession.

THE CHIEF OF POLICE (*eagerly*): Let me see it.

THE ENVOY: Later. The architect who conceived it was a poet, philosopher and man of science. Imagine a splendid structure. Five or six law-courts piled one on top of the other, a dozen opera houses, twenty large stations, thirty pagodas, a hundred memorial monuments, and you'll have a slight idea of what it will be.

Upon one mountain will be placed another, and on that other still another, and in the middle of the first a tiny diamond sentry-box.

THE CHIEF OF POLICE (*greedily*): Will I be able to stand there—or sit—and keep vigil over my entire death?

THE ENVOY (*banteringly*): Who said anything about designating it for you? But he who gets it will be there—dead—for eternity. The world will center about it. About it will rotate the planets. It will no doubt be the most imposing funeral-pile in the universe. From a secret point of the third mountain will run a road that will lead, after many and many a complication, to a room where mirrors will reflect to infinity—I say to infinity!—the image of the dead man. To infinity—and for eternity—in the depths of a vault ... His image. ...

THE CHIEF OF POLICE: It's an enormous risk. ...

THE ENVOY: That is for Mme. Irma to decide.

IRMA (*to* THE ENVOY): Are you quite sure of what you're saying? Do you really know what's going on? What about your spies?

THE ENVOY: They inform us as accurately as the peep-holes that peer into your studios. (*Smiling.*) And I may add that we consult them with the same pleasurable thrill.

IRMA: Too bad I can't peep into the rebellion as I can into Studio 23. ...

THE ENVOY: You would see faces wrought with anger and hatred and the lust of murder. The populace has ceased to be the submissive animal that tamely licks our feet, or rather our patent-leather pumps. It has become a kind of wild beast that drools blood at the corners of its mouth. ...

THE CHIEF OF POLICE: Don't you worry. I'll tame it all right! When it comes to action, I'm all there.

IRMA (*to* THE CHIEF OF POLICE): Well, then, you accept?

THE ENVOY: . . . Nothing is ever wholly lost. Our latest information is a few hours old. We know that those gentlemen, who are a tough-minded lot, think they have us. What they want is that each individual be both himself and a shining specimen of himself. More nonsense! They're unaware that our resources are inexhaustible, that we need only choose from the storehouse of mummery. But we must act fast. We're engaged in a race against the clock. It's we or they. Mme. Irma, think speedily.

IRMA (*holding her head in her hands*): I'm hurrying, sir. I'm approaching my destiny as fast as I can. (*To* CARMEN.) Are our Great Figures there?

CARMEN: The gentlemen tried to return home, Madame, but the house is surrounded. They all had to come back and take refuge here.

IRMA: Go see what they're doing. Hurry. . . .

THE ENVOY (*to* CARMEN): What about you, what's to be done with you?

CARMEN: I'll stick to my post, sir. (CARMEN *exits.*)

THE ENVOY: One other matter, a more delicate one. I mentioned an image that for some days now has been mounting in the sky of the revolution.

IRMA: The revolution has its sky too?

THE ENVOY: Don't envy it. Chantal's image is circulating in the streets. A stylized image that resembles her and does not resemble her. She towers above the battles. At first, people were fighting against illustrious and illusory tyrants, then for freedom. To-morrow they'll be ready to die for Chantal alone.

IRMA: The ungrateful wretch! She who was in such demand as Lucrezia Borgia.

THE CHIEF OF POLICE: She won't last. She's like me: she has neither father nor mother. And if she becomes an image, we'll make use of it.

Suddenly a bell rings. IRMA *is about to dart forward, but stops.*

IRMA (*to* THE CHIEF OF POLICE): It's Carmen. What's she saying? What are they doing?

THE CHIEF OF POLICE *lifts one of the earphones.*

THE-CHIEF OF POLICE (*transmitting the message*): While waiting to go home, they're standing around looking at themselves in the mirrors.

IRMA: Tell her to smash the mirrors or veil them.

A silence. Then a burst of machine-gun fire.

Good. My mind's made up. I presume I've been summoned from

all eternity and that God will bless me. I'm going to prepare myself by prayer.

THE ENVOY (*gravely*): Do you have the outfits?

IRMA: My closets are as famous as my studios. (*Suddenly worried.*) But everything must be in an awful state! The bombs, the plaster, the dust. Tell Carmen to brush the costumes! (*To* THE CHIEF OF POLICE.) George . . . this is our last minute together! From now on, we'll no longer be us. . . .

> THE ENVOY *discreetly moves off and goes to the window.*

THE CHIEF OF POLICE: Are you sure that something of us won't subsist?

IRMA: We'll have to strive to reduce it until it disappears. And when we die, what will seem to die will be only a gilded corpse. In a few minutes the metamorphosis will begin. We'll be strangers to each other, for good and all. Do you consent, George?

THE CHIEF OF POLICE: I've got to. If I didn't, what would become of me?

> IRMA *and* THE CHIEF OF POLICE *draw apart from each other.*

IRMA (*to* THE ENVOY): So I'll be real? My robe will be real? My lace, my jewels will be real? The rest of the world will be a copy of what I'll be?

> *Machine-gun fire.*

THE ENVOY (*after a last glance through the shutters*): Yes, Madame, but make haste. As I've told you, the people is awaiting its idol in order to grovel before it. . . . It will be you . . . or the other. Go to your apartments. Embroider an interminable handker-chief. . . . (*To* THE CHIEF OF POLICE.) You, give your last orders to your last men.

> IRMA *and* THE CHIEF OF POLICE *exit.* THE ENVOY *remains alone for a few seconds. He goes to a mirror, takes from his pocket a whole collection of decorations and fastens them to his tunic.*

VOICE OF THE BISHOP (*from the wings*): But you yourself, Carmen, you know perfectly well it's sheer madness! It was stupid of me to come back here to hide. . . .

THE BISHOP *enters in civilian clothes, followed by* CARMEN. *On seeing* THE ENVOY *and the unfamiliar studio, he is taken aback. He looks about him.*

THE ENVOY (*to* THE BISHOP, *after bowing to him*): I myself am here—though I've been here longer than you—for a reason not unlike your own. Before Carmen went to get you, she succeeded in convincing me. (*To* CARMEN.) As I have nothing further to do here, I shall return to Her Majesty.

He bows and leaves.

CARMEN: Do you love the Queen?

THE BISHOP: What a question!

CARMEN: I'm not so sure. Last night you managed to get home. It was dangerous in the streets, but you were smart enough to find your way, your house, your wife and your son. Then . . . you fought against us . . . I mean . . .

THE BISHOP: The rebels were blocking the streets. There was shooting from the roofs, from the cellars. . . . Bullets were whizzing high and low. . . . (*Pointing to* THE ENVOY *as he leaves.*) Who's that?

CARMEN: And you preferred to come and take refuge at Irma's place, knowing that they were going to attack the house and that you'd die there. If I understood correctly, you wanted to go up in flames in the midst of what you cherish?

THE BISHOP: I forbid you. . . .

CARMEN: Let's not joke. And above all, let's not put on an act, not even one of delicacy. No one knows better than I the charming drama of which you're the hero. No, no, don't protest. I'm playing in another one myself. . . . But you won't know which. Let's get back to ourselves. Orders have been issued from very high. . . .

THE BISHOP: I'm only a gas-man.

CARMEN: How could you still be a gas-man if nobody recognizes you as the gas-man? Because you know how to do sums? So does a bishop. But you won't be doing that any more. You'll start by knowing nothing. You'll make your appearance—but first, you'll bow to the Queen. . . .

THE BISHOP: Is she here?

CARMEN: You'll bow to your sovereign. The Judge, the General and you will pay homage to her. She'll accept it. Then the Hero will appear. The Queen and he, with the three of you about them, will appear on the Grand Balcony of this house. The acclamation of the crowd will ring out. The Queen will bow. The Hero will bow. Then . . . (*She hesitates.*)

THE BISHOP: Then?

CARMEN: You will go in a carriage to . . . amidst the spellbound or raging crowd, to the cathedral . . . or to the scaffold.

THE BISHOP (*horror-stricken*): What death have you in store for me?

CARMEN: You'll ride in a carriage through a city which has been pacified by your gesture, or you'll be trampled by the horses.

THE BISHOP: But I'll never be able to. . . . I'll be recognized. . . . My acne . . . my mannerisms . . . my voice. . . .

CARMEN: They'll become either your personal, endearing idiosyncrasies—or the permanent stamp of the Bishop.

THE BISHOP: But I won't be alone, will I?

CARMEN: Several of the gentlemen—regular clients, of course—have already complied, and very eagerly.

THE BISHOP: But then, they'll see me, they'll recognize me?

CARMEN: You'll see them, you'll recognize them. You'll see and recognize each other . . . faintly—and withdraw into the most secret chamber of your dignity.

Enter THE ENVOY.

THE ENVOY (*in a vulgar tone*): Make it snappy. I don't have time to listen to your crap. (*To* CARMEN.) If the gentleman doesn't fill the bill, then get a dummy, but get a move on.

SCENE EIGHT

THE BALCONY

The scene is the balcony itself, which projects beyond the façade of the brothel. The shutters, which face the audience, are closed. Suddenly, all the shutters open by themselves. The edge of the balcony is at the very edge of the footlights. Through the windows can be seen THE BISHOP, THE GENERAL *and* THE JUDGE, *who are getting ready. Finally the French windows are flung wide open. The three men come out on the balcony. First* THE BISHOP, *then* THE GENERAL, *then* THE JUDGE. *They are followed by* THE HERO. *Then comes* THE QUEEN: MME. IRMA, *wearing a diadem on her brow and an ermine cloak. All the characters step forward and take their positions with great timidity. They are silent. They simply show themselves. All are of huge proportions, gigantic—except* THE HERO, *that is,* THE CHIEF OF POLICE—*and are wearing their ceremonial garments, which are torn and dusty. Then, near them, but not on the balcony, appears* THE BEGGAR. *In a gentle voice, he cries out:*

THE BEGGAR: Long live the Queen! (*He goes off timidly, as he came.*)

Finally, a strong wind stirs the curtains: CHANTAL *appears.* THE QUEEN *bows to her. A shot.* CHANTAL *falls.* THE GENERAL *and* THE QUEEN *carry her away dead.*

SCENE NINE

IRMA'S *room, which looks as if it had been hit by a hurricane. Rear, a large two-panelled mirror which forms the wall. Right, a door; left, another. Three cameras on tripods. The stage is empty. Enter, in turn, very timidly, right,* THE BISHOP *and, left,* THE JUDGE *and* THE GENERAL. *On seeing each other, they bow deeply. Then,* THE GENERAL *salutes and* THE BISHOP *blesses* THE GENERAL.

THE JUDGE (*with a sigh of relief*): What we've been through!

THE GENERAL: And it's not over! We have to invent an entire life.... That's hard....

THE BISHOP: Hard or not, we've got to go through with it. We can no longer back out. Before entering the carriage ...

THE GENERAL: The slowness of the carriage!

THE BISHOP: .... entering the carriage, it was still possible to chuck the whole business. But now....

THE JUDGE: Do you think we were recognized? I was in the middle, hidden by your profiles. Opposite me, Irma. . . . (*The name astonishes him.*) Irma? The Queen. . . . The Queen hid my face.... Do you think we were?

THE BISHOP: No danger of that. You know whom I saw . . . at the right (*Unable to keep from laughing.*) with his fat, good-natured mug and pink cheeks, though the town was in smithereens? (*The other two smile.*) With his pimples and decayed teeth? and who threw himself on my hand . . . I thought to bite me, and I was about to pull away my fingers . . . to kiss my ring? Who? My fruit-and-vegetable man.

    THE JUDGE *laughs.*

THE GENERAL (*grimly*): The slowness of the carriage. The carriage wheels on the people's feet and hands! The dust!

THE JUDGE (*uneasily*): I was opposite the Queen. Through the back window, a woman ...

THE BISHOP (*continuing his account*): I saw her too, at the left-hand door, she was running along and throwing kisses at us!

THE GENERAL (*more and more grimly*): The slowness of the carriage!

We moved forward so slowly amidst the sweaty mob! Their roars were like threats, but they were only cheering. Someone could have hamstrung the horses, fired a shot, could have unhitched the traces and harnessed *us*, attached us to the shaft or the horses, could have drawn and quartered us or turned us into draft-horses. But no. Just flowers tossed from a window, and a people hailing its Queen, who stood upright beneath her golden crown. (*A pause.*) And the horses going at a walking pace . . . and the Envoy standing on the footboard!

A silence.

THE BISHOP: No one could have recognized us. We were in the gold and glitter. They were blinded. It hit them in the eye. . . .

THE JUDGE: It wouldn't have taken much. . . .

THE BISHOP: Exhausted by the fighting, choked by the dust, the people stood waiting for the procession. The procession was all they saw. In any case, we can no longer back out. We've been chosen.

THE GENERAL: By whom?

THE BISHOP: By glory in person.

THE GENERAL: This masquerade?

THE BISHOP: It lies with us for this masquerade to change meaning. First, we must use words that magnify. We must act fast, and with precision. No errors allowed. (*With authority.*) As for me, instead of being merely the symbolic head of the country's church, I've decided to become its actual head. Instead of blessing and blessing and blessing until I've had my fill. I'm going to sign decrees and appoint priests. The clergy is being organized. A basilica is under construction. It's all in there. (*He points to a folder under his arm.*) Full of plans and projects. (*To* THE JUDGE.) What about you?

THE JUDGE (*looking at his wristwatch*): I have an appointment with a number of magistrates. We're drafting bills, we're revising the legal code. (*To* THE GENERAL.) What about you?

THE GENERAL: Oh, me, your ideas drift through my poor head like smoke through a log shanty. The art of war's not something you can master just like that. The general-staffs . . .

THE BISHOP (*interrupting*): Like everything else, the fate of arms can be read in your stars. Read your stars, damn it!

THE GENERAL: That's easy to say. But when the Hero comes back, planted firmly on his rump, as if on a horse . . . For, of course, nothing's happened yet?

THE BISHOP: Nothing. But let's not crow too soon. Though his image hasn't yet been consecrated by the brothel, it still may. If it does, we're done for. Unless we make a positive effort to seize power.

Suddenly, he breaks off. With a slamming of doors enter, right, three photographers. They are dressed like newspaper reporters. Their voices are loud, their speech brash. Their gestures contrast sharply with the delicate manners of THE THREE FIGURES, *to whom they toss a rather familiar sign of greeting.*

FIRST PHOTOGRAPHER: Evening, gentlemen.

A pause. THE THREE FIGURES *look bewildered.* THE BISHOP *is the first to pull himself together.*

THE BISHOP (*aloof*): Good evening, my friends. We've been expecting you.

SECOND PHOTOGRAPHER (*looking at the lights*): Well, we made it, as you can see.

THE BISHOP (*severely*): Indeed, you have come. Please do your job quickly, and in silence, if possible. You're to take each of our profiles, one smiling, the other rather stern.

FIRST PHOTOGRAPHER: We'll do our job, don't worry. (*To* THE BISHOP.) Get set for prayer, because the world ought to be bombarded with the picture of a pious man.

THE BISHOP (*without moving*): In fervent meditation.

FIRST PHOTOGRAPHER: Right, fervent. Get set.

THE BISHOP (*ill at ease*): But . . . how?

FIRST PHOTOGRAPHER: Don't you know how to compose yourself for prayer? Okay, facing both God and the camera. Hands together. Head up. Eyes down. That's the classical pose. A return to order, a return to classicism.

THE BISHOP (*kneeling*): Like this?

FIRST PHOTOGRAPHER (*looking at him with curiosity*): That's it. . . . (*He looks at the camera.*) No. you're not in the frame. . . .

(*Shuffling on his knees,* THE BISHOP *places himself in front of the camera.*) Okay.

SECOND PHOTOGRAPHER (*to* THE JUDGE): Would you mind pulling a longer face? You don't quite look like a judge. A little longer.

THE JUDGE: Horselike? Sullen?

SECOND PHOTOGRAPHER: Horselike and sullen, Mr. Attorney General. And both hands in front, on your brief. What I want is a shot of *the* Judge. A good photographer is one who gives a definitive image. Perfect.

FIRST PHOTOGRAPHER (*to* THE BISHOP): Turn your head . . . just a little. . . . (*He turns* THE BISHOP's *head.*)

THE BISHOP (*angrily*): You're unscrewing the neck of a prelate!

FIRST PHOTOGRAPHER: I want a three-quarter view of you praying, Monsignor.

SECOND PHOTOGRAPHER (*to* THE JUDGE): Mr. Attorney General, if you possibly can, a little more severity . . . with a pendulous lip. (*Crying out.*) That's it! Perfect! Stay that way! (*He rushes behind his camera, but there is a flash before he gets there.* THE FIRST PHOTOGRAPHER *has just taken his shot.* THE SECOND PHOTOGRAPHER *puts his head under the black hood of his camera.*)

THE GENERAL (*to* THE THIRD PHOTOGRAPHER): The finest pose is Poniatovsky's.

THIRD PHOTOGRAPHER (*striking a pose*): With the sword?

THE GENERAL: No, no. That's Lafayette. No, with the arm extended and the marshal's baton. . . .

THIRD PHOTOGRAPHER: Ah, you mean Wellington?

THE GENERAL: Unfortunately, I don't have a baton. . . .

Meanwhile, THE FIRST PHOTOGRAPHER *has gone back to* THE BISHOP, *who has not moved, and looks him over silently.*

THIRD PHOTOGRAPHER (*to* THE GENERAL): We've got just what we need. Here, now strike the pose. (*Rolls up a sheet of paper in the form of a marshal's baton. He hands it to* THE GENERAL, *who strikes a pose, and then dashes to his camera. A flash:* THE SECOND PHOTOGRAPHER *has just taken his shot.*)

THE BISHOP (*to* THE FIRST PHOTOGRAPHER): I hope the negative comes out well. Now we'll have to flood the world with a picture of me receiving the Eucharist. Unfortunately, we don't have a Host on hand. . . .

FIRST PHOTOGRAPHER: Leave it to us, Monsignor. Newspapermen are a resourceful bunch. (*Calls out.*) Mr. Attorney General!

THE JUDGE *approaches.*

I'm going to try a stunt. Lend me a hand a minute. (*Without further ado, he takes him by the hand and sets him in place.*) But I want only your hand to show . . . there . . . roll up your sleeve a little . . . above Monsignor's tongue. More. Okay. (*Still fumbling in his pocket. To* THE BISHOP.) Stick out your tongue. More. Okay. (*Still fumbling in his pocket. A flash:* THE GENERAL *has just been photographed; he resumes his natural pose.*) Damn it! I don't have a thing! (*He looks about. To* THE GENERAL.) That's perfect. May I? (*Without waiting for an answer, he takes* THE GENERAL'S *monocle from his eye and goes back to the group formed by* THE BISHOP *and* THE JUDGE. *He makes* THE JUDGE *hold the monocle above* THE BISHOP'S *tongue as if it were a Host, and he rushes to his camera. A flash.*)

THE QUEEN (*who has entered with* THE ENVOY, *has been watching these proceedings for some moments*): Curious. Curious method. (*To* THE PHOTOGRAPHERS.) You're presenting the people with a false image? I won't tolerate . . .

THE ENVOY: It's a true image, born of a false spectacle.

FIRST PHOTOGRAPHER (*cynically*): That's common practice, your Majesty. When some rebels were captured, we paid a militiaman to bump off a chap I'd just sent to buy me a pack of cigarettes. The photo shows a rebel shot down while trying to escape.

THE QUEEN: Monstrous!

THE ENVOY: But have things ever happened otherwise? History was lived so that a glorious page might be written, and then read. It's reading that counts. (*To* THE PHOTOGRAPHERS.) Gentlemen, the Queen informs me that she congratulates you. She asks that you return to your posts.

THE THREE PHOTOGRAPHERS *put their heads under the black hoods of their cameras.*

A silence.

THE QUEEN (*looking about her*): Isn't he here?

THE ENVOY (*with irony, but elegantly*): Invisible, in any case. One encounters him occasionally wandering through the corridors, looking very pensive and taciturn. Most of the time, he has appointments with specialists and tailors. He tries on uniforms.

THE QUEEN (*to* THE ENVOY): It's no laughing matter. In his effort to win renown, he has chosen a more difficult path than ours. (*She reads to* THE THREE FIGURES *from a paper she holds in her hand.*) I wished to thank you, gentlemen, for your devotion to my cause, to my people's cause, and for your gallant conduct. Thanks to you and the Chief of Police, the rebellion has been bathed in blood. There is nothing more to fear. . . . (*She returns the paper to* THE ENVOY, *who keeps it in his hand.*) I hope so.

THE BISHOP: Madame, if it has to be done all over again, we're ready. (*To the others.*) Aren't we, gentlemen?

THE QUEEN (*with a wan, sad smile*): I observe in passing that it is you, Monsignor, who are gaining the ascendancy. No, no, don't defend yourself. It's well that it emanates from the highest spirituality. . . . (*A pause.*) Well, gentlemen . . .

THE THREE FIGURES *hesitate to speak.*

THE ENVOY: The Queen would like to know what you're doing, what you plan to do.

THE BISHOP: We've been recovering as many dead bodies as possible. We were planning to embalm them and lodge them in our heaven. Your grandeur requires your having slaughtered the rebels wholesale. We shall keep for ourselves only a few of our fallen martyrs, to whom we shall pay honor that will honor us.

THE QUEEN (*to* THE ENVOY): That will serve my glory, will it not?

THE ENVOY (*smiling*): The massacres, too, are revels wherein the people indulge to their heart's content in the pleasure of hating us. I am speaking, to be sure, of "our" people. They can at last set up a statue to us in their hearts so as to shower it with blows. At least, I hope so.

THE QUEEN: Does that mean that leniency and kindness are of no avail?

THE ENVOY (*smiling*): A St. Vincent de Paul Studio?

THE QUEEN: You're right. It's hard to imagine. (*Evasively.*) Yet, I've seen old men . . .

THE ENVOY: Old men, perhaps. But to experience the thrill of brushing against galley-slaves. However, our hero is still young.

THE QUEEN (*to* THE ENVOY): Isn't anyone going to tell me about the Mausoleum? How far along is the construction?

THE ENVOY: The work's going on, Madame.

THE QUEEN (*testily*): But not fast enough. You, Your Honor, what's being done? I'd ordered fewer death penalties and more sentences to forced labor. I hope the underground galleries are finished? (*To* THE ENVOY.) It's the word galley-slaves that made me think of the galleries of the Mausoleum. Are they finished?

THE JUDGE: Completely. And open to the public on Sundays. Some of the arches are completely adorned with the skeletons of prisoners who died during the digging.

THE QUEEN (*in the direction of* THE BISHOP): Very good. What about the Church? I suppose that anyone who hasn't done at least a week's work on this extraordinary chapel is in a state of mortal sin?

THE BISHOP *bows.*

(*To* THE GENERAL.) As for you, I'm aware of your severity. Your soldiers are watching over the workers, and they thoroughly deserve the fine name of builders. (*Smiling gently, with feigned fatigue.*) For, as you know, gentlemen, I plan to present this tomb to the Hero. You know how downcast he feels, don't you, and how he suffers at not yet having been impersonated?

THE GENERAL (*plucking up courage*): He'll have a hard time attaining glory. The places have been filled for ages. Every niche has its statue. (*Fatuously.*) We, at least . . .

THE JUDGE: That's how it always is when one wants to start from the bottom. And particularly by rejecting or neglecting the traditional. The established order of things, as it were.

THE QUEEN (*suddenly vibrant*): Yet it was he who saved everything. He wants glory. He insists on breaking open the gates of legend, but he has allowed you to carry on with your ceremonies.

THE BISHOP (*arrogantly*): To be frank, Madame, we're no longer concerned with that. As for me, my skirt hampers me, and my hands get caught in the lace. We're going to have to act.

THE QUEEN (*indignantly*): Act? You? You mean to say you're going to strip us of our power?

THE JUDGE: We have to fulfill our functions, don't we?

THE QUEEN: Functions! You're planning to overthrow him, to lower him, to take his place! That's right, isn't it? And you think I'm going to let you? I, too, have my fanatics. If I've decorated and ennobled him, I've done so to heighten his prestige.

THE BISHOP: Somewhere in time—in time or in space!—perhaps there exist high dignitaries invested with absolute dignity and attired with veritable ornaments. . . .

THE QUEEN (*very angrily*): Veritable! And what about those? You mean that those you're wrapped and swathed in—my whole paraphernalia!—which come from my closets, aren't veritable?

THE BISHOP (*pointing to* THE JUDGE's *ermine, the silk of his robe, etc.*): Rabbit, sateen, machine-made lace . . . you think we're going to be satisfied with make-believe to the end of our days?

THE QUEEN (*outraged*): But this morning . . .

She breaks off. Enter THE CHIEF OF POLICE, *quietly, humbly.*

George, beware of them.

THE CHIEF OF POLICE (*trying to smile*): I think that . . . victory . . . we've won the day. May I sit down?

He sits down. Then he looks about, as if questioning everyone.

THE ENVOY (*ironically*): No, nobody's come yet. Nobody has yet felt the need to abolish himself in your fascinating image.

THE CHIEF OF POLICE: That means the projects you submitted to me aren't very effective. (*To* THE QUEEN.) Nothing? Nobody?

THE QUEEN (*very gently*): Nobody. And yet, the blinds have been drawn again. The men ought to be coming in. Besides, the apparatus has been set up; so we'll be informed by a full peal of bells.

THE ENVOY (*to* THE CHIEF OF POLICE): You didn't care for the project I submitted to you this morning. Yet that's the image that haunts you and that ought to haunt others.

THE CHIEF OF POLICE: Ineffectual.

THE ENVOY (*showing a photographic negative*): The executioner's red coat and his axe. I suggested amarinth red and the steel axe.

THE QUEEN (*testily*): Studio 14, known as the Studio of Executions. Already been done.

THE CHIEF OF POLICE (*to* THE ENVOY): You see. These masquerades prove how unimaginative you are. Maybe you're exhausted? As a matter of fact, you look anemic to me. No. I want my image to be both legendary and human. It should, of course, accord with eternal principles, but my face should be recognizable in it.

THE JUDGE (*making himself agreeable*): Yet you're feared. You're dreaded. You're envied. The people's hymns of love are proof of it.

THE CHIEF OF POLICE: I'm afraid that they fear and envy a man, but . . . (*Groping for words.*) . . . but not a wrinkle, for example, or a curl . . . or a cigar . . . or a whip. The latest image that was proposed to me . . . I hardly dare mention it to you.

THE JUDGE: Was it . . . very audacious?

THE CHIEF OF POLICE: Very. Too audacious. I'd never dare tell you what it was. (*Suddenly, he seems to make up his mind.*) Gentlemen, I have sufficient confidence in your judgment and devotion. After all, I want to carry on the fight by boldness of ideas as well. But the fact is—I don't know where to turn first. It was this: I've been advised to appear in the form of a gigantic phallus. A prick of great stature. . . .

THE THREE FIGURES *and* THE QUEEN *are dumfounded.*

THE QUEEN: George! You?

THE CHIEF OF POLICE: What do you expect? If I'm to symbolize the nation, your joint. . . .

THE ENVOY (*to* THE QUEEN): Allow him, Madame. It's the tone of the age.

THE JUDGE: A phallus? Of great stature? You mean—enormous?

THE CHIEF OF POLICE: Of my stature.

THE JUDGE: That'll be very difficult to bring off.

THE ENVOY: Not so very. What with new techniques and our rubber industry, remarkable things can be worked out. No, I'm not worried about that, but rather . . . (*Turning the* THE BISHOP.) . . . what the Church will think of it?

THE BISHOP (*after reflection, shrugging his shoulders*): No definite pronouncement can be made this evening. To be sure, the idea is a bold one. (*To* THE CHIEF OF POLICE.) But if your case is desperate, we shall have to examine the matter. For . . . it would be a formidable figure-head, and if you were to transmit yourself in that guise from generation to generation . . .

THE QUEEN (*alarmed*): No room's been provided for it. No studio is equipped. . . . After all, though my house is reputed for its imaginativeness, it's known for its decency, and for a certain tone as well.

THE CHIEF OF POLICE (*gently*): Would you like to see the model?

THE GENERAL (*briskly*): No, no. Even if one did imagine you with that rigor, your appearance would scare off your most fanatical followers!

THE JUDGE (*to* THE CHIEF OF POLICE): It's wrong of you to be impatient. *We* waited two thousand years to perfect our roles. Keep hoping . . .

THE GENERAL (*interrupting him*): Glory is achieved in combat. You haven't enough illustrious Waterloos to your credit. Keep fighting, or sit down and wait out the regulation two thousand years.

Everyone laughs.

THE QUEEN (*violently*): You don't care a damn about his suffering. And it was I who singled you out! I who fished you out of the rooms of my brothel and hired you for his glory. And you agreed to serve him.

A pause.

THE BISHOP (*firmly*): It is at this point that a question, and a very serious one, arises: are you going to use what we represent, or are we (*He points to the other two* FIGURES.) going to use you to serve what we represent?

THE QUEEN (*flaring up*): Your conditions, you? Puppets who without their rabbit, as you put it, would be nothing, you, a man who was made to dance naked—in other words, skinned!—on the public square of Seville and Toledo! To the click of castenets! Your conditions, Monsignor?

THE BISHOP: That day I *had* to dance. As for the rabbit, it's what it *must* be—the sacred image of ermine—it has the same power.

THE QUEEN: George! Go on, defend yourself. It's God Himself Who has chosen us. . . .

THE ENVOY (*admiringly*): Sublime! Continue. . . .

THE QUEEN (*to* THE CHIEF OF POLICE): Help yourself. Help us. Keep the power. Outdo yourself. . . . Real blood flows in my veins, real sweat in my armpits. I'm all afever, and I want power.

THE CHIEF OF POLICE: I'm weak, I'm inept. . . .

THE QUEEN (*imploring him*): Pull yourself together, I beg of you . . . they'll devour us!

THE BISHOP: You can see that his failure is preying on him. Our power . . .

THE CHIEF OF POLICE (*with sudden violence*): I have force, intelligence and passion on my side!

THE BISHOP: With your intelligence and its clear notions, the people can engage in a two-sided discussion—as the weekly magazines would say. They can argue. Our power is obscure and beyond argument.

THE BISHOP (*beside himself*): Exactly. So long as we were in a room in a brothel, we belonged to our own fantasies. But once having exposed them, having named them, having proclaimed them, we're now tied up with human beings, tied to you, and forced to go on with this adventure according to the laws of visibility.

THE CHIEF OF POLICE: You have no power.

THE BISHOP: No one has power. But you want us to have power over the people. In order for us to have power over them, you must first recognize that we have power over you.

THE CHIEF OF POLICE: Never!

THE BISHOP: Very well. Then we shall go back to our rooms and there continue the quest of an absolute dignity. We ought never to have left them. For we were content there, and it was you who came and dragged us away. For ours was a happy state. And absolutely safe. In peace, in comfort, behind shutters, behind padded curtains, protected by a police force that protects brothels, we were able to be a general, judge and bishop to the point of perfection and to the point of rapture! You tore us brutally from that delicious, enviable, untroubled state, but we have since tasted· other delights, the bitter delights of action and responsibility. We were judge, general and bishop in order to be bishop, judge and general beneath a perfect, total, solitary and sterile appearance. You wanted us to be these dignitaries this evening in order to conspire in a revolution, or rather in an order, and to round it off, to ground it, as it were. Our public appearance was already a participation in the adventure.

THE GENERAL (*interrupting* THE BISHOP): My breeches! What joy when I pulled on my breeches! I now sleep in my general's breeches, I eat in my breeches, I waltz—*when* I waltz—in my breeches, I live in my general's breeches. I'm a general the way one is a priest.

THE BISHOP: As for my lace, I no longer look forward to it—it's myself.

THE JUDGE: I'm just a dignity represented by a robe.

THE GENERAL (*to* THE BISHOP:) At no moment can I prepare myself— I used to start a month in advance!—prepare myself for pulling on my general's boots and breeches. I'm rigged in them for all eternity. By Jove, I no longer dream.

THE BISHOP (*to* THE CHIEF OF POLICE): You see, he no longer dreams. Our ornamental purity, our luxurious and barren—and sublime— appearance has been eaten away. It's gone forever. Well and good. But the taste of that bitter delight of responsibility of which I've spoken has remained with us, and we find it to our liking. Our rooms are no longer secret. You hurt us by dragging us into the light. But as for dancing? You spoke of dancing? You referred to that notorious afternoon when, stripped—or skinned, whichever word amuses you—stripped of our priestly ornaments, we had to dance naked on the cathedral square. I danced, I admit it, with people laughing at me, but at least I danced. Whereas now, if ever I have an itch for that kind of thing, I'll have to go on the sly to the Balcony, where there probably is a room prepared for prelates who like to be ballerinas a few hours a week. No, no. . . . We're going to live in the light, but with all that that implies. We—magistrate, soldier, prelate—we're now going to act in such a way as to impoverish these ornaments and dignities unceasingly! We're going to render them useful! But in order that they be of use, and of use to you—since it's your order that we've chosen to defend (I mean that it's the only one our dignity could defend)—you must recognize their power and pay homage to them.

THE QUEEN: Careful, George! Watch out for their saliva!

THE CHIEF OF POLICE (*calmly*): I shall be not the hundred-thousandth-reflection-within-a-reflection in a mirror, but the One and Only, into whom a hundred thousand want to merge. If not for me, you'd have all been done for. The expression "beaten hollow" would have had meaning.

THE BISHOP: If you didn't have our age-old glory—which has demonstrated its worth—to back up your success, what would you be? A rebel, faced with the insipid problems of freedom.

THE QUEEN (*to* THE BISHOP, *insinuatingly*): You happen to be wearing that robe this evening simply because you were unable to clear out of the studios in time. You just couldn't tear yourself away from one of your hundred thousand reflections, but the clients are beginning to come back. . . . There's no rush yet, but Carmen has recorded several entries. . . . (*To* THE CHIEF OF POLICE.) Don't let them intimidate you. Before the revolt, there were lots of them. . . . (*To* THE BISHOP.) If you hadn't had the abominable idea of having Chantal assassinated. . . .

THE BISHOP (*frightened*): A stray bullet!

THE QUEEN: Who can say? Whether the bullet was stray or not, Chantal was assassinated on *my* balcony! When she came back here to see me, to visit her boss . . .

THE BISHOP: I had the presence of mind to make her one of our saints.

THE CHIEF OF POLICE: A traditional attitude. A churchman's reflex. But there's no need to congratulate yourself. The image of her on our flag has hardly any power. Or rather . . . I've had reports from all quarters that owing to the possibility that she was playing a double game, Chantal has been condemned by those she was supposed to save.

THE QUEEN: But then the whole business is starting all over again?

THE CHIEF OF POLICE: No doubt about it. Another revolt—that has nothing to do with the one I put down—is beginning to brew. . . .

THE GENERAL: Are we going to have to . . . to get into the carriage again? The slowness of the carriage!

THE CHIEF OF POLICE: And that's why I'm sure of you. At least, as long as I've not been impersonated, because after that I'll just sit back and take it easy. (*Inspired.*) Besides, I'll know by a sudden weakness of my muscles that my image is escaping from me to go and haunt men's minds. When that happens, my visible end will be near. For the time being, and before long, we'll have to act. (*To* THE BISHOP.) Who will assume real responsibilities?

THE BISHOP (*hesitantly*): We can, all the same . . . express, as it were . . . a glimmer of a desire . . . perform an act. . . .

THE QUEEN (*sharply*): Be careful! Don't grant anything!

THE CHIEF OF POLICE: You! (*Shrugs his shoulders.*) Be logical: if you are what you are, judge, general, bishop, it's because you wanted to become that and wanted it known that you had become it.

You therefore did what was necessary to achieve your purpose and to be a focus of attention. Is that right?

THE JUDGE: Pretty much.

THE CHIEF OF POLICE: Very well. That means you've never performed an act for its own sake, but always so that, when linked with other acts, it would make a bishop, a judge, a general. . . .

THE BISHOP: That's both true and false. For each act contained within itself its leaven of novelty.

THE CHIEF OF POLICE (*correcting him*): Forgive me, Monsignor, but this leaven of novelty was immediately nullified by the fact that the act turned in on itself.

THE JUDGE: We acquired greater dignity thereby.

THE CHIEF OF POLICE: No doubt, Your Honor, but this dignity, which has become as inhuman as a crystal, makes you unfit for governing men. No, no, gentlemen, above you, more sublime than you, is the Queen. It's from her, for the time being, that you derive your power and your rights. Above her—that to which she refers —is our standard, on which I've blazoned the image of Chantal Victorious, our saint.

THE BISHOP (*aggressively*): Above Her Majesty, whom we venerate, and above her flag, is God, Who speaks through my voice. As for Chantal, who's painted on the flag . . .

THE CHIEF OF POLICE: Stop talking nonsense!

THE BISHOP: Listen to me . . .

THE CHIEF OF POLICE (*irritably*): And above God?

A silence.

THE BISHOP *moves off, looking extremely troubled until his next speech.*

THE CHIEF OF POLICE: Well, gentlemen, above God are you, without whom God would be nothing. And above you shall be I, without whom . . .

THE JUDGE: What about the people? The photographers?

THE CHIEF OF POLICE: On their knees before the people who are on their knees before God. Therefore . . .

They all burst out laughing.

That's why I want you to serve me. But a while ago you were holding forth quite volubly. I should therefore like to pay homage to your eloquence, your facility of elocution, the limpidity of your timbre. As for me, I'm a mere man of action who gets tangled up in words and ideas when they're not immediately applied. That's why I was wondering whether to send you back to your kennel. I won't do it. In any case, not right away, since you're already there.

THE GENERAL: Sir!

THE CHIEF OF POLICE: Lie down! Lie down, General! You're stuck. And it's not I who forbid you to act, but your dignities themselves.

THE JUDGE: My skirt can be tucked up. . . .

THE CHIEF OF POLICE: Lie down! Since you want to be recognized as a judge, do you want to hold on to your dignity according to my idea of it? And according to the general meaning attached to such a dignity? Very well. Must I therefore grant you increasing recognition along these lines? Yes or no?

No one answers.

Well gentlemen, yes or no?

THE QUEEN (*very blandly*): Excuse him, if he gets carried away. I'm quite aware of what you used to come here for: you, Monsignor, to seek by devious ways a manifest saintliness. No, no, I'm not being ironic. The gold of my chasubles had little to do with it, I'm sure. It wasn't mere gross ambition that brought you behind my closed shutters. Love of God was hidden there. I realize that. You, Mr. Attorney General, you were indeed guided by a concern for justice, since it was the image of a magistrate that you wished to see reflected a thousand times in my mirrors. And you, General, it was bravery and military glory and the heroic deed that haunted you. So let yourselves go, relax, without too many scruples. . . .

THE JUDGE (*timidly*): We can try, carefully of course, to make a slight shift along a different line. . . .

THE GENERAL: Are you mad? If we think, people may start following us in our thinking, and then where'll we stop?

THE CHIEF OF POLICE: Well spoken, General. And now, back to the kennel! Well, gentlemen, if I—and through me, the entire people—recognize your dignity, and increasingly so, and in its strictest sense, well, gentlemen, but . . . you're still in the brothel!

THE QUEEN (*thrilled*): My hero—how well he speaks!

One after the other, the three men heave a deep sigh.

THE CHIEF OF POLICE (*continuing*): That's a relief to you, isn't it? You never really wanted to get out of yourselves and communicate, if only by acts of meanness, with the world. I understand you. (*Amiably.*) You see, I too, when I'm too tired of inventing for people, when I'm too harassed by the burden of power and responsibility, I, too, occasionally have the desire to flee into an image of myself. Unfortunately, my role is still a fighting one. It's still effective in carrying out an action. It's not impersonated. It keeps inciting to further progress. And if I try to crawl into my role, I find no rest in it. My role, unfortunately, is in motion. In short, as you probably know, it's not in the nomenclature of the brothels. . . .

THE QUEEN: In the pink handbook. . . .

THE CHIEF OF POLICE: Yes, in the pink handbook. (*To* THE THREE FIGURES.) Come now, gentlemen, don't you feel sorry for a poor fellow like me? (*He looks at them one after the other.*) Come, come, gentlemen, you're not hardhearted are you? It's for you that these Studios and Illustrious Rites were perfected, by means of exquisite experimentation. They required long labor, infinite patience. You have the good fortune to benefit from them, and you want to go back to the light of day? (*To* THE BISHOP.) You, Monsignor, you're silent. . . .

THE BISHOP: There's still the matter of Chantal. . . . I'm thinking of your glory.

THE CHIEF OF POLICE: Let's forget about that. . . .

THE BISHOP (*very gravely*): On the contrary, I ask that you listen to me. If I had her shot, and then canonized, if I had her image blazoned on our flag, it was for a reason. . . .

THE QUEEN: It's *my* image that ought to be there. . . .

THE ENVOY (*to* THE QUEEN): You're on the postage stamps, on the banknotes, on the seals in the government offices . . . and even that's too much. Your Majesty can be represented only by an abstraction.

THE CHIEF OF POLICE (*to* THE BISHOP): You were saying . . . that for my glory . . .

THE BISHOP (*after a brief hesitation*): The rebels, and perhaps the entire populace as well, must have had high hopes for this rebellion. The fighting—and you realize it more than anyone else—has been murderous. They've been fighting in desperation.

THE QUEEN: The people love their Queen. . . .

THE ENVOY *motions her to be still.*

THE BISHOP: No doubt they do, Madame. But their wrath proves their longing to be rid of us. You, sir, have been seeking the glory accorded by the nomenclature of the brothels. You have crushed the rebellion. You have, as the saying goes, bathed it in blood, but you've done so in a curious way! Without quite knowing whether you have or not, the populace has a right to assume you've triumphed—doubtless because you were the stronger—but also because Chantal's image wanted to return to the brothel that was its starting point. . . .

THE CHIEF OF POLICE: You mean . . . ?

THE BISHOP: That, in a very strange and delightfully equivocal way, your image may merge with Chantal's. The people must be in a state of frightful despair, but they must have a way out, a way that is ghastly, horrendous. Every beaten and humiliated rebel is perhaps haunted by Chantal's image, which is likewise defiled—forgive me, but that's your chance for salvation!—defiled by yours. If my expectations are correct. . . .

THE QUEEN (*to* THE CHIEF OF POLICE): That woman again! Clinging to you even in her death! And I, doomed to be represented formally, merely by four blue bands and three red ones! I don't want to lose you! Or lose myself!

THE ENVOY: Silly jealousy! We've reached the point at which we can no longer be actuated by human feelings. Our function will be to support, establish and justify metaphors.

THE QUEEN: But *I* haven't yet decided to go along with you in this adventure. I love love and I love power and I want to experience them with my body.

THE ENVOY (*sternly*): Then you should have sided with the rebels. Among them one can, if need be, dominate through personal qualities.

THE QUEEN: Will I therefore never be who I am?

THE ENVOY: Never again.

THE QUEEN (*as if frightened*): Never again? Nothing will ever again relate to my person alone? Nothing concerning me will ever again be able to happen to others?

THE ENVOY (*curtly*): Quite.

THE QUEEN: Every event of my life—my blood that trickles if I scratch myself . . .

THE ENVOY: Quite, Madame. Each event will be written with a capital. And now . . .

THE QUEEN: But that's Death?

THE ENVOY: It is indeed. Here's Carmen.

Enter CARMEN *from the door at the left.*

CARMEN: Madame? (*She stands there without moving.*)

THE QUEEN (*crossly*): I gave orders that we were not to be disturbed. And you enter without warning. Come here. What do you want?

CARMEN *goes to her.*

CARMEN: I tried to ring, but the apparatus is out of order. I beg your pardon. I'd like to speak with you.

THE QUEEN: Well, what is it? Speak up!

CARMEN (*hesitantly*): It's . . . I don't know . . .

THE QUEEN (*resignedly*): Well, when at Court do as the Court does. Let's speak in an undertone. (*She conspicuously lends ear to* CARMEN, *who leans forward and murmurs a few words.* THE QUEEN *seems very upset.*)

THE QUEEN: Are you sure?

CARMEN: Quite, Madame.

THE QUEEN *bolts from the room, followed by* CARMEN. THE CHIEF OF POLICE *starts to follow them, but* THE ENVOY *intervenes.*

THE ENVOY: One does not follow Her Majesty.

THE CHIEF OF POLICE: What's going on? Where's she going?

THE ENVOY (*ironically*): To embroider. The Queen is embroidering, and she is not embroidering . . . you know the refrain? The

Queen attains her reality when she withdraws, absents herself, or dies.

THE CHIEF OF POLICE: What's happening outside? (*To* THE JUDGE.) Do you have any news?

THE JUDGE: What you call outside is as mysterious to us as we are to it. His Lordship described it quite well.

THE BISHOP: I shall try to depict the grief of this people which thought it had liberated itself by rebelling. Alas—or rather, thank Heaven! —there will never be a movement powerful enough to destroy our imagery.

THE CHIEF OF POLICE: So you think I have a chance?

THE BISHOP: You're in the best possible position. There's consternation everywhere, in all families, in all institutions. People have trembled so violently that your image is beginning to make them doubt themselves.

THE CHIEF OF POLICE: Am I their only hope?

THE BISHOP: Their only hope lies in utter collapse. Since they've lost everything: a hypothetical but intoxicating freedom, their guides —a criminal lot, I might add—and Chantal who was the very illustration of their efforts, you're all that's left.

THE CHIEF OF POLICE: In short, I'm like a pool in which they behold themselves?

THE GENERAL (*delighted, with a burst of laughter*): And if they lean over too far, they fall in and drown. Before long, you'll be full of drowned bodies! (*No one seems to share his merriment.*) Oh well . . . they're not yet at the brink! (*Embarrassed.*) Let's wait.

A silence.

THE CHIEF OF POLICE: Well, gentlemen, so you really think the people had a wild hope? And that in losing all hope they lose everything? And that in losing everything they'll come and lose themselves in me?

THE BISHOP: That may very well happen. But, believe me, not if we can help it.

THE CHIEF OF POLICE: When I am offered that final consecration. . . .

THE ENVOY (*ironically*): For you, but for you alone, for a second the Earth will stop rotating. . . .

Suddenly the door at the left opens and THE QUEEN *appears, beaming.*

THE QUEEN: George! (*She falls into the arms of* THE CHIEF OF POLICE.)

THE CHIEF OF POLICE (*incredulous*): It's not true. (THE QUEEN *nods yes.*) But where? . . . When?

THE QUEEN (*deeply moved*): There! . . . Now! The studio. . . .

THE CHIEF OF POLICE: You're pulling my leg. I didn't hear anything.

Suddenly a tremendous ringing, a kind of peal of bells.

So it's true? It's for me? (*He pushes* THE QUEEN *away. Solemnly.*) Gentlemen, I belong to the Nomenclature! (*To* THE QUEEN.) But are you really sure?

THE QUEEN: It was I who received him and ushered him into the Mausoleum Studio. The one that's being built in your honor. I left Carmen behind to attend to the preparations and I ran to let you know. I'm trembling like a leaf. . . .

THE BISHOP (*gloomily*) : We're up the creek.

THE CHIEF OF POLICE: The apparatus is working. You can see. . . . (*He goes to the left, followed by* THE QUEEN.)

THE ENVOY: That is not the practice. Matters of that kind are secret.

THE CHIEF OF POLICE (*shrugging his shoulders*): Where's the mechanism? (*To* THE QUEEN.) Let's watch together.

She stands at the left, facing a small porthole. After a brief hesitation, THE JUDGE, GENERAL *and* BISHOP *place themselves at the right, at another porthole symmetrical with the first. Then, the two panels of the double mirror forming the back of the stage silently draw apart, revealing the interior of the Special Studio.* THE ENVOY, *with resignation, joins* THE CHIEF OF POLICE.

Description of the Mausoleum Studio: The stones of the wall, which is circular, are visible. At the rear, a stairway that descends. In the center of this well there seems to be another, in which the steps of a stairway are visible. On the walls, four laurel wreaths, adorned with crape. When the panels separate, ROGER *is at the middle of the stairway, which he is descending.* CARMEN *seems to be guiding him.* ROGER *is dressed like* THE CHIEF OF POLICE, *though, mounted on the same cothurni as* THE THREE FIGURES, *he looks taller. His shoulders have also been broadened. He descends the stairs to the rhythm of a drum.*

CARMEN (*approaching, and handing him a cigar*): It's on the house.

ROGER (*putting the cigar into his mouth*): Thanks.

CARMEN (*taking the cigar from him*): That end's for the light. This one's for the mouth. (*She turns the cigar around.*) Is this your first cigar?

ROGER: Yes. . . . (*A pause.*) I'm not asking for your advice. You're here to serve me. I've paid. . . .

CARMEN: I beg your pardon, sir.

ROGER: The slave?

CARMEN: He's being untied.

ROGER: He knows what it's about?

CARMEN: Completely. You're the first. You're inaugurating this Studio, but, you know, the scenarios are all reducible to a major theme. . . .

ROGER: Which is . . . ?

CARMEN: Death.

ROGER (*touching the walls*): And so this is my tomb?

CARMEN (*correcting him*): Mausoleum.

ROGER: How many slaves are working on it?

CARMEN: The entire people, sir. Half of the population during the day and the other half at night. As you have requested, the whole mountain will be burrowed and tunnelled. The interior will have the complexity of a termite nest or of the Basilica of Lourdes —we don't know yet. No one will be able to see anything from the outside. All they'll know is that the mountain is sacred, but, inside, the tombs are already being enshrined in tombs, the cenotaphs in cenotaphs, the coffins in coffins, the urns . . .

ROGER: What about here, where I am now?

CARMEN (*with a gesture of disdain*): An antechamber. An antechamber called the Valley of the Fallen. (*She mounts the underground stairway.*) In a little while, you'll go farther down.

ROGER: I'm not to hope to see the light of day again?

CARMEN: But . . . do you still want to?

A silence.

ROGER: It's really true that no one's ever been here before me?

CARMEN: In this . . . tomb, or in this . . . Studio?

A silence.

ROGER: Is everything really on right? My outfit? My toupee?

THE CHIEF OF POLICE *turns to* THE QUEEN.

THE CHIEF OF POLICE: He knew I wear a toupee?

THE BISHOP (*snickering, to* THE JUDGE *and* THE GENERAL): He's the only one who doesn't know that everyone knows it.

CARMEN (*to* ROGER): Everything was carefully planned long ago. It's all been worked out. The rest is up to you.

ROGER (*anxiously*): You realize I'm feeling my way too. I've got to imagine what the Hero's like, and he's never shown himself much.

CARMEN: That's why we've taken you to the Mausoleum Studio. It's not possible to make many errors here, nor indulge your imagination.

A pause.

ROGER: Will I be alone?

CARMEN: Everything is padded. The doors are lined. So are the walls.

ROGER (*hesitantly*): What about . . . the Mausoleum?

CARMEN (*forcefully*): Built into the rock. The proof is that there's water oozing from the walls. Deathly silent. As for light, the darkness is so thick that your eyes have developed astounding qualities. The cold? Yes, the coldness of death. It's been a gigantic job drilling through the mountain. Men are still groaning in order to hollow out a granite niche for you. Everything proves that you're loved and that you're a conqueror.

ROGER: Groaning? Could . . . could I hear the groaning?

CARMEN *turns toward a hole dug out at the foot of the wall, from which emerges the head of* THE BEGGAR.

CARMEN: Come here!

THE BEGGAR *crawls in.*

ROGER (*looking* THE SLAVE *over*): Is that it?

CARMEN: A fine specimen, isn't he? Skinny. With lice and sores. He dreams of dying for you. I'll leave you alone now.

ROGER: With him? No, no. (*A pause.*) Stay. Everything always takes place in the presence of a woman. It's in order for a woman's face to be a witness that, usually . . .

Suddenly, the sound of a hammer striking an anvil. Then a cock crows.

Is life so near?

CARMEN (*in a normal voice, not acting*): As I've told you, everything's padded, but some sounds always manage to filter through. Does it bother you? Life's starting up again little by little . . . as before. . . .

ROGER (*he seems anxious*): Yes, as before. . . .

CARMEN (*gently*): You were . . .

ROGER: Yes. Everything's washed up. . . . And what's saddest of all is people's saying: "the rebellion was wonderful!"

CARMEN: You mustn't think about it any more. And you must stop listening to the sounds from outside. Besides, it's raining. The whole mountain has been swept by a tornado. (*Stage voice.*) You are at home here. (*Pointing to* THE SLAVE.) Make him talk.

ROGER (*playing his role*): For you can talk? And what else can you do?

THE SLAVE (*lying on his belly*): First, bow; then, shrink into myself a little more (*He takes* ROGER's *foot and places it on his own back.*) like this! . . . and even . . .

ROGER (*impatiently*): Yes . . . and even?

THE SLAVE: Sink into the earth, if it's possible.

ROGER (*drawing on his cigar*): Sink in, really? But there's no mud?

THE QUEEN (*to the others*): He's right. We should have provided mud. In a well-run house. . . . But it's opening day, and he's the first client to use the Studio. . . .

THE SLAVE (*to* ROGER): I feel it all over my body, sir. It's all over me, except in my mouth, which is open so that I can sing your praises and utter the groans that made me famous.

ROGER: Famous? You're famous, you?

THE SLAVE: Famous for my chants, sir, which are hymns to your glory.

ROGER: So your glory accompanies mine? (*To* CARMEN.) Does he mean that my reputation will be kept going by his words? And . . . if he says nothing, I'll cease to exist . . . ?

CARMEN (*curtly*): I'd like very much to satisfy you, but you ask questions that aren't in the scenario.

ROGER (*to* THE SLAVE): But what about you, who sings to you?

THE SLAVE: Nobody. I'm dying.

ROGER: But without me, without my sweat, without my tears and blood, what would you be?

THE SLAVE: Nothing.

ROGER (*to* THE SLAVE): You sing? But what else do you do?

THE SLAVE: We do all we possibly can to be more and more unworthy of you.

ROGER: What, for example?

THE SLAVE: We try hard just to stand and rot. And, believe me, it's not always easy. Life tries to prevail. . . . But we stand our ground. We keep shrinking more and more every . . .

ROGER: Day?

THE SLAVE: Week.

THE CHIEF OF POLICE (*to the others*): That's not much. With a little effort. . . .

THE ENVOY (*to* THE CHIEF OF POLICE): Be still. Let them play out their roles.

ROGER: That's not much. With a little effort. . . .

THE SLAVE (*with exaltation*): With joy, Your Excellency! You're so splendid! So splendid that I wonder whether you're aglow or whether you're all the darkness of all the nights?

ROGER: What does it matter, since I'm no longer to have any reality except in the reality of your phrases.

THE SLAVE (*crawling in the direction of the upper stairway*): You have not mouth nor ears nor eyes, but all of you is a thundering mouth and at the same time a dazzling and watchful eye. . . .

ROGER: *You* see it, but do the others know it? Does the night know it? Does death? Do the stones? What do the stones say?

THE SLAVE (*still dragging on his belly and beginning to crawl up the stairs*): The stones say . . .

ROGER: Well, I'm listening.

THE SLAVE (*he stops crawling, and facing the audience*): The cement that holds us together to form your tomb . . .

THE CHIEF OF POLICE (*facing the audience and joyfully beating his breast*): The stones venerate me!

THE SLAVE (*continuing*): . . . the cement is molded of tears, spit and blood. The workers' eyes and hands that rested upon us have matted us with grief. We are yours, and only yours.

THE SLAVE *starts crawling up the stairs again.*

ROGER (*with rising exaltation*): Everything proclaims me! Everything breathes me and everything worships me! My history was lived so that a glorious page might be written and then read. It's reading that counts. (*He suddenly notices that* THE SLAVE *has disappeared. To* CARMEN.) But . . . where's he going? . . . Where is he? . . .

CARMEN: He's gone off to sing. He's going up into the light of day. He'll tell . . . that he carried your footsteps . . . and that . . .

ROGER (*anxiously*): Yes, and that? What else will he tell?

CARMEN: The truth: that you're dead, or rather that you don't stop dying and that your image, like your name, reverberates to infinity.

ROGER: He knows that my image is everywhere?

CARMEN: Yes, everywhere, inscribed and engraved and imposed by fear.

ROGER: In the palms of stevedores? In the games of children? On the teeth of soldiers? In war?

CARMEN: Everywhere.

THE CHIEF OF POLICE (*to the others*): So I've made it?

THE QUEEN (*fondly*): Are you happy?

THE CHIEF OF POLICE: You've done a good job. That puts the finishing touch to your house.

ROGER (*to* CARMEN): Is it in prisons? In the wrinkles of old people?

CARMEN: It is.

ROGER: In the curves of roads?

CARMEN: You mustn't ask the impossible.

Same sounds as earlier: the cock and the anvil.

It's time to go, sir. The session's over. Turn left, and when you reach the corridor . . .

The sound of the anvil again, a little louder.

You hear? You've got to go home. . . . What are you doing?

ROGER: Life is nearby . . . and far away. Here all the women are beautiful. Their purpose is purely ornamental. . . . One can lose oneself in them. . . .

CARMEN (*curtly*): That's right. In ordinary language, we're called whores. But you've got to leave. . . .

ROGER: And go where? Into life? To carry on, as they say, with my activities. . . .

CARMEN (*a little anxiously*): I don't know what you're doing, and I haven't the right to inquire. But you've got to leave. Your time's up.

The sound of the anvil and other sounds indicate an activity: cracking of a whip, humming of a motor, etc.

ROGER: They give you the rush in this place! Why do you want me to go back where I came from?

CARMEN: You've nothing further to do. . . .

ROGER: There? No. Nothing further. Nor here either. And outside, in what you call life, everything has crashed. No truth was possible. . . . Did you know Chantal?

CARMEN (*suddenly frightened*): Get going! Clear out of here!

THE QUEEN: I won't allow him to create a rumpus in my Studios! Who was it who sent me that individual? Whenever there are disturbances, the riff-raff always crop up. I hope that Carmen . . .

CARMEN (*to* ROGER): Get out! You've no right to ask questions either. You know that brothels are very strictly regulated and that we're protected by the police.

ROGER: No! Since I'm playing the Chief of Police and since you allow me to be here. . . .

CARMEN (*pulling him away*): You're crazy! You wouldn't be the first who thought he'd risen to power. . . . Come along!

ROGER (*disengaging himself*): If the brothel exists and if I've a right to go there, then I've a right to lead the character I've chosen to the very limit of his destiny . . . no, of mine . . . of merging his destiny with mine. . . .

CARMEN: Stop shouting, sir. All the studios are occupied. Come along. . . .

CARMEN tries to make him leave. She opens a door, then another, then a third, unable to find the right one. ROGER takes out a knife and, with his back to the audience, makes the gesture of castrating himself.

THE QUEEN: On my rugs! On the new carpet! He's a lunatic!

CARMEN (*crying out*): Doing that here! (*She yells.*) Madame! Mme. Irma! (CARMEN *finally manages to drag* ROGER *out.*)

> THE QUEEN *rushes from the room. All the characters—*THE CHIEF OF POLICE, THE ENVOY, THE JUDGE, THE GENERAL, THE BISHOP— *turn and leave the portholes.* THE CHIEF OF POLICE *moves forward to the middle of the stage.*

THE CHIEF OF POLICE: Well played. He thought he had me. (*He places his hand on his fly, very·visibly feels his balls and, reassured, heaves a sigh.*) Mine are here. So which of us is washed up? He or I? Though my image be castrated in every brothel in the world, I remain intact. Intact, gentlemen. (*A pause.*) That plumber didn't know how to handle his role, that was all. (*He calls out, joyfully:*) Irma! Irma! . . . Where is she? It's not her job to dress wounds.

THE QUEEN (*entering*) : George! The vestibule . . . the rugs are covered with blood . . . the vestibule's full of clients. . . . We're wiping up as best we can. . . . Carmen doesn't know where to put them. . . .

THE ENVOY (*bowing to* THE CHIEF OF POLICE): Nice work.

THE CHIEF OF POLICE: An image of me will be perpetuated in secret. Mutilated? (*He shrugs his shoulders.*) Yet a low mass will be said to my glory. Notify the kitchens! Have them send me enough grub for two thousand years.

THE QUEEN: What about me? George, *I'm* alive!

THE CHIEF OF POLICE (*without hearing her*): So . . . I'm. . . . Where? Here, or . . . a thousand times there? (*He points to the tomb.*) Now I can be kind . . . and pious . . . and just. . . . Did you see? Did you see me? There, just before, larger than large, stronger than strong, deader than dead? So I've nothing more to do with you.

THE QUEEN: George! But I still love you!

THE CHIEF OF POLICE (*moving towards the tomb*) : I've won the right to go and sit and wait for two thousand years. (*To* THE PHOTOGRAPHERS.) You! Watch me live, and die. For posterity: shoot! (*Three almost simultaneous flashes.*) I've won! (*He walks backwards into the tomb, very slowly.*)

THE QUEEN: But it was I who did everything, who organized everything. . . . Stay. . . . What will. . . .

Suddenly a burst of machine-gun fire.

You hear!
THE CHIEF OF POLICE (*with a burst of laughter*): Think of me!

THE JUDGE *and* THE GENERAL *rush forward to stop him, but the
doors start closing as* THE CHIEF OF POLICE *descends the first
steps. A second burst of machine-gun fire.*

THE JUDGE (*clinging to the door*): Don't leave us alone!
THE GENERAL (*gloomily*): That carriage again!
THE ENVOY (*to* THE JUDGE): Be careful, you'll get your fingers caught.

*The door has definitely closed. The characters remain bewild-
ered for a moment. A third burst of machine-gun fire.*

THE QUEEN: Gentlemen, you are free. . . .
THE BISHOP: But . . . in the middle of the night?
THE QUEEN (*interrupting him*): You'll leave by the narrow door that
leads into the alley. There's a car waiting for you.

She nods courteously. THE THREE FIGURES *exit right. A fourth
burst of machine-gun fire.*

Who is it? . . . Our side? . . . Or rebels? . . . Or? . . .
THE ENVOY: Someone dreaming, Madame. . . .

THE QUEEN *goes to various parts of the room and presses buttons. Each time, a light goes out.*

THE QUEEN (*continuing to extinguish lights*) : . . . Irma. . . .
Call me Mme. Irma, and go home. Good night, sir.
THE ENVOY: Good night, Mme. Irma.

THE ENVOY *exits.*

IRMA (*alone, and continuing to extinguish lights*): It took so much light . . . five dollars worth of electricity a day! Thirty-eight studios! Every one of them gilded, and all of them rigged with machinery so as to be able to fit into and combine with each other. . . . And all these performances so that I can remain alone, mistress and assistant mistress of this house and of myself. (*She pushes in a button, then pushes it out again.*) Oh no, that's the tomb. He needs light, for two thousand years! . . . and food for two thousand years. . . . (*She shrugs her shoulders.*) Oh well, everything's in working order, and dishes have been prepared. Glory means descending into the grave with tons of victuals! . . . (*She calls out, facing the wings.*) Carmen? Carmen? . . . Bolt the doors, my dear, and put the furniture-covers on. . . . (*She continues extinguishing.*) In a little while, I'll have to start all over again . . . put all the lights on again . . . dress up. . . . (*A cock crows.*) Dress up . . . ah, the disguises! Distribute roles again . . . assume my own. . . . (*She stops in the middle of the stage, facing the audience.*) . . . Prepare yours . . . judges, generals, bishops, chamberlains, rebels who allow the revolt to congeal, I'm going to prepare my costumes and studios for tomorrow. . . . You must now go home, where everything—you can be quite sure—will be even falser than here. . . . You must go now. You'll leave by the right, through the alley. . . . (*She extinguishes the last light.*) It's morning already.

A burst of machine-gun fire.

THE END

The Birthday Party

by
Harold Pinter

THE BIRTHDAY PARTY was first presented by Michael Codron and David Hall at the Arts Theatre, Cambridge, April 28, 1958, and subsequently at the Lyric Opera House, Hammersmith; directed by Peter Wood and with the following cast:

PETEY, *a man in his sixties* . . . . Willoughby Gray

MEG, *a woman in her sixties* . . . . Beatrix Lehmann

STANLEY, *a man in his late thirties* . . . . . . Richard Pearson

LULU, *a girl in her twenties* . . . . Wendy Hutchinson

GOLDBERG, *a man in his fifties* . . . . John Slater

MCCANN, *a man of thirty* . . . . John Stratton

Act I, *A morning in summer*

Act II, *Evening of the same day*

Act III, *The next morning*

To Vivien

ACT ONE

The living-room of a house in a seaside town. A door leading to the hall down left. Back door and small window up left. Kitchen hatch, centre back. Kitchen door up right. Table and chairs, centre.

PETEY enters from the door on the left with a paper and sits at the table. He begins to read. MEG's voice comes through the kitchen hatch.

MEG: Is that you, Petey? (*Pause.*) Petey, is that you? (*Pause.*) Petey?
PETEY: What?
MEG: Is that you?
PETEY: Yes, it's me.
MEG: What? (*Her face appears at the hatch.*) Are you back?
PETEY: Yes.
MEG: I've got your cornflakes ready. (*She disappears and reappears.*) Here's your cornflakes.

He rises and takes the plate from her, sits at the table, props up the paper and begins to eat. MEG enters by the kitchen door.

Are they nice?
PETEY: Very nice.
MEG: I thought they'd be nice. (*She sits at the table.*) You got your paper?
PETEY: Yes.
MEG: Is it good?
PETEY: Not bad.
MEG: What does it say?
PETEY: Nothing much.
MEG: You read me out some nice bits yesterday.
PETEY: Yes, well, I haven't finished this one yet.
MEG: Will you tell me when you come to something good?
PETEY: Yes.

Pause.

MEG: Have you been working hard this morning?

PETEY: No. Just stacked a few of the old chairs. Cleaned up a bit.
MEG: Is it nice out?
PETEY: Very nice.

Pause.

MEG: Is Stanley up yet?
PETEY: I don't know. Is he?
MEG: I don't know. I haven't seen him down yet.
PETEY: Well then, he can't be up.
MEG: Haven't you seen him down?
PETEY: I've only just come in.
MEG: He must be still asleep.

She looks round the room, stands, goes to the sideboard and takes a pair of socks from a drawer, collects wool and a needle and goes back to the table.

What time did you go out this morning, Petey?
PETEY: Same time as usual.
MEG: Was it dark?
PETEY: No, it was light.
MEG (*beginning to darn*): But sometimes you go out in the morning and it's dark.
PETEY: That's in the winter.
MEG: Oh, in winter.
PETEY: Yes, it gets light later in winter.
MEG: Oh. (*Pause.*) What are you reading?
PETEY: Someone's just had a baby.
MEG: Oh, they haven't! Who?
PETEY: Some girl.
MEG: Who, Petey, who?
PETEY: I don't think you'd know her.
MEG: What's her name?
PETEY: Lady Mary Splatt.
MEG: I don't know her.
PETEY: No.
MEG: What is it?
PETEY (*studying the paper*): Er—a girl.
MEG: Not a boy?

PETEY: No.

MEG: Oh, what a shame. I'd be sorry. I'd much rather have a little boy.

PETEY: A little girl's all right.

MEG: I'd much rather have a little boy. (*Pause. Vaguely.*) Is it nice out?

PETEY: Yes, it's a nice day.

MEG: Is the sun shining?

PETEY: Yes.

MEG: I wish Stanley would take me for a walk along the front one day. When was I last along the front? Why don't you ask him to take me for a walk one day, Petey?

PETEY: Why don't you ask him yourself?

MEG: No. You ask him. (*Pause.*) He goes through his socks terrible.

PETEY: Why? He's in bed half the week.

MEG: That boy should be up. Why isn't he up? What's the time?

PETEY: About half past ten.

MEG: He should be down. He's late for his breakfast.

PETEY: I've finished my cornflakes.

MEG: Were they nice?

PETEY: Very nice.

MEG: I've got something else for you.

PETEY: Good.

She rises, takes his plate and exits into the kitchen. She then appears at the hatch with two pieces of fried bread on a plate.

MEG: Here you are, Petey.

He rises, collects the plate, looks at it, sits at the table. MEG *re-enters.*

Is it nice?

PETEY: I haven't tasted it yet.

MEG: I bet you don't know what it is.

PETEY: Yes, I do.

MEG: What is it, then?

PETEY: Fried bread.

MEG: That's right.

He begins to eat.

PETEY: No bacon?

MEG: I've run out.

PETEY: Ah.

MEG: I'm going out soon, to do some shopping.

She watches him eat.

PETEY: Very nice.

MEG: I knew it was.

PETEY (*turning to her*): Oh, Meg, two men came up to me on the beach last night.

MEG: Two men?

PETEY: Yes. They wanted to know if we could put them up for a couple of nights.

MEG: Put them up? Here?

PETEY: Yes.

MEG: How many men?

PETEY: Two.

MEG: What did you say?

PETEY: Well, I said I didn't know. So they said they'd come round to find out.

MEG: Are they coming?

PETEY: Well, they said they would.

MEG: Had they heard about us, Petey?

PETEY: They must have done.

MEG: Yes, they must have done. They must have heard this was a very good boarding house. It is. This house is on the list.

PETEY: It is.

MEG: I know it is.

PETEY: They might turn up today. Can you do it?

MEG: Oh, I've got that lovely room they can have.

PETEY: You've got a room ready?

MEG: I've got the room with the armchair all ready for visitors.

PETEY: You're sure?

MEG: Yes, that'll be all right then, if they come today.

PETEY: Good.

She takes the socks etc. back to the sideboard drawer.

MEG: I'm going to wake that boy.

PETEY: There's a new show coming to the Palace.

MEG: On the pier?

PETEY: No. The Palace, in the town.

MEG: Stanley could have been in it, if it was on the pier.

PETEY: This is a straight show.

MEG: What do you mean?

PETEY: No dancing or singing.

MEG: What do they do then?

PETEY: They just talk.

Pause.

MEG: Oh.

PETEY: You like a song, eh, Meg?

MEG: I like listening to the piano. I used to like watching Stanley play the piano. Of course, he didn't sing. (*Looking at the door.*) I'm going to call that boy.

PETEY: Didn't you take him up his cup of tea?

MEG: I always take him up his cup of tea. But that was a long time ago.

PETEY: Did he drink it?

MEG: I made him. I stood there till he did. I tried to get him up then. But he wouldn't, the little monkey. I'm going to call him. (*She goes to the door.*) Stan! Stanny! (*She listens.*) Stan! I'm coming up to fetch you if you don't come down! I'm coming up! I'm going to count three! One! Two! Three! I'm coming to get you! (*She exits and goes upstairs. In a moment, shouts from* STANLEY, *wild laughter from* MEG. PETEY *takes his plate to the hatch. Shouts. Laughter.* PETEY *sits at the table. Silence. She returns.*) He's coming down. (*She is panting and arranges her hair.*) I told him if he didn't hurry up he'd get no breakfast.

PETEY: That did it, eh?

MEG: I'll get his cornflakes.

MEG *exits to the kitchen.* PETEY *reads the paper.* STANLEY *enters. He is unshaven, in his pyjama jacket and wears glasses. He sits at the table.*

PETEY: Morning, Stanley.

STANLEY: Morning.

Silence. MEG *enters with the bowl of cornflakes, which she sets on the table.*

MEG: So he's come down at last, has he? He's come down at last for his breakfast. But he doesn't deserve any, does he, Petey? (STANLEY *stares at the cornflakes.*) Did you sleep well?

STANLEY: I didn't sleep at all.

MEG: You didn't sleep at all? Did you hear that, Petey? Too tired to eat your breakfast, I suppose? Now you eat up those cornflakes like a good boy. Go on.

He begins to eat.

STANLEY: What's it like out today?

PETEY: Very nice.

STANLEY: Warm?

PETEY: Well, there's a good breeze blowing.

STANLEY: Cold?

PETEY: No, no, I wouldn't say it was cold.

MEG: What are the cornflakes like, Stan?

STANLEY: Horrible.

MEG: Those flakes? Those lovely flakes? You're a liar, a little liar. They're refreshing. It says so. For people when they get up late.

STANLEY: The milk's off.

MEG: It's not. Petey ate his, didn't you, Petey?

PETEY: That's right.

MEG: There you are then.

STANLEY: All right, I'll go on to the second course.

MEG: He hasn't finished the first course and he wants to go on to the second course!

STANLEY: I feel like something cooked.

MEG: Well, I'm not going to give it to you.

PETEY: Give it to him.

MEG (*sitting at the table, right*): I'm not going to.

Pause.

STANLEY: No breakfast. (*Pause.*) All night long I've been dreaming about this breakfast.

MEG: I thought you said you didn't sleep.

STANLEY: Day-dreaming. All night long. And now she won't give me any. Not even a crust of bread on the table. (*Pause.*) Well, I can see I'll have to go down to one of those smart hotels on the front.

MEG (*rising quickly*): You won't get a better breakfast there than here.

> She exits to the kitchen. STANLEY *yawns broadly.* MEG *appears at the hatch with a plate.*

Here you are. You'll like this.

> PETEY *rises, collects the plate, brings it to the table, puts it in front of* STANLEY, *and sits.*

STANLEY: What's this?

PETEY: Fried bread.

MEG (*entering*): Well, I bet you don't know what it is.

STANLEY: Oh yes I do.

MEG: What?

STANLEY: Fried bread.

MEG: He knew.

STANLEY: What a wonderful surprise.

MEG: You didn't expect that, did you?

STANLEY: I bloody well didn't.

PETEY (*rising*): Well, I'm off.

MEG: You going back to work?

PETEY: Yes.

MEG: Your tea! You haven't had your tea!

PETEY: That's all right. No time now.

MEG: I've got it made inside.

PETEY: No, never mind. See you later. Ta-ta, Stan.

STANLEY: Ta-ta.

> PETEY *exits, left.*

Tch, tch, tch, tch.

MEG (*defensively*): What do you mean?

STANLEY: You're a bad wife.

MEG: I'm not. Who said I am?

STANLEY: Not to make your husband a cup of tea. Terrible.

MEG: He knows I'm not a bad wife.

STANLEY: Giving him sour milk instead.

MEG: It wasn't sour.

STANLEY: Disgraceful.

MEG: You mind your own business, anyway. (STANLEY *eats*.) You won't find many better wives than me, I can tell you. I keep a very nice house and I keep it clean.

STANLEY: Whoo!

MEG: Yes! And this house is very well known, for a very good boarding house for visitors.

STANLEY: Visitors? Do you know how many visitors you've had since I've been here?

MEG: How many?

STANLEY: One.

MEG: Who?

STANLEY: Me! I'm your visitor.

MEG: You're a liar. This house is on the list.

STANLEY: I bet it is.

MEG: I know it is.

He pushes his plate away and picks up the paper.

Was it nice?

STANLEY: What?

MEG: The fried bread.

STANLEY: Succulent.

MEG: You shouldn't say that word.

STANLEY: What word?

MEG: That word you said.

STANLEY: What, succulent—?

MEG: Don't say it!

STANLEY: What's the matter with it?

MEG: You shouldn't say that word to a married woman.

STANLEY: Is that a fact?

MEG: Yes.

STANLEY: Well, I never knew that.

MEG: Well, it's true.

STANLEY: Who told you that?

MEG: Never you mind.

STANLEY: Well, if I can't say it to a married woman who can I say it to?

MEG: You're bad.

STANLEY: What about some tea?

MEG: Do you want some tea? (STANLEY *reads the paper.*) Say please.

STANLEY: Please.

MEG: Say sorry first.

STANLEY: Sorry first.

MEG: No. Just sorry.

STANLEY: Just sorry!

MEG: You deserve the strap.

> *She takes his plate and ruffles his hair as she passes.* STANLEY *exclaims and throws her arm away. She goes into the kitchen. He rubs his eyes under his glasses and picks up the paper. She enters.*

I brought the pot in.

STANLEY (*absently*): I don't know what I'd do without you.

MEG: You don't deserve it though.

STANLEY: Why not?

MEG (*pouring the tea, coyly*): Go on. Calling me that.

STANLEY: How long has that tea been in the pot?

MEG: It's good tea. Good strong tea.

STANLEY: This isn't tea. It's gravy!

MEG: It's not.

STANLEY: Get out of it. You succulent old washing bag.

MEG: I am not! And it isn't your place to tell me if I am!

STANLEY: And it isn't your place to come into a man's bedroom and—wake him up.

MEG: Stanny! Don't you like your cup of tea of a morning—the one I bring you?

STANLEY: I can't drink this muck. Didn't anyone ever tell you to warm the pot, at least?

MEG: My father wouldn't let you insult me the way you do.

STANLEY: Your father? Who was he when he was at home?

MEG: He would report you.

STANLEY (*sleepily*): Now would I insult you, Meg? Would I do a terrible thing like that?

MEG: You did.

STANLEY (*putting his head in his hands*): Oh God, I'm tired.

Silence. MEG *goes to the sideboard, collects a duster, and vaguely dusts the room, watching him. She comes to the table and dusts it.*

Not the bloody table!

Pause.

MEG: Stan?

STANLEY: What?

MEG (*shyly*): Am I really succulent?

STANLEY: Oh, you are. I'd rather have you than a cold in the nose any day.

MEG: You're just saying that.

STANLEY (*violently*): Look, why don't you get this place cleared up! It's a pigsty. And another thing, what about my room? It needs sweeping. It needs papering. I need a new room!

MEG (*sensual, stroking his arm*): Oh, Stan, that's a lovely room. I've had some lovely afternoons in that room.

He recoils from her hand in disgust, stands and exits quickly by the door on the left. She collects his cup and the teapot and takes them to the hatch shelf. The street door slams. STANLEY *returns.*

MEG: Is the sun shining? (*He crosses to the window, takes a cigarette and matches from his pyjama jacket, and lights his cigarette.*) What are you smoking, Stan?

STANLEY: A cigarette.

MEG: Are you going to give me one?

STANLEY: No.

MEG: I like cigarettes. (*He stands at the window, smoking. She crosses behind him and tickles the back of his neck.*) Tickle, tickle.

STANLEY (*pushing her*): Get away from me.

MEG: Are you going out?

STANLEY: Not with you.

MEG: But I'm going shopping in a minute.

STANLEY: Go.

MEG: You'll be lonely, all by yourself.

STANLEY: Will I?

MEG: Without your old Meg. I've got to get things in for the two gentlemen.

A pause. STANLEY *slowly raises his head. He speaks without turning.*

STANLEY: What two gentlemen?

MEG: I'm expecting visitors.

He turns.

STANLEY: What?

MEG: You didn't know that, did you?

STANLEY: What are you talking about?

MEG: Two gentlemen asked Petey if they could come and stay for a couple of nights. I'm expecting them. (*She picks up the duster and begins to wipe the cloth on the table.*)

STANLEY: I don't believe it.

MEG: It's true.

STANLEY (*moving to her*): You're saying it on purpose.

MEG: Petey told me this morning.

STANLEY (*grinding his cigarette*): When was this? When did he see them?

MEG: Last night.

STANLEY: Who are they?

MEG: I don't know.

STANLEY: Didn't he tell you their names?

MEG: No.

STANLEY (*pacing the room*): Here? They wanted to come here?

MEG: Yes, they did. (*She takes the curlers out of her hair.*)

STANLEY: Why?

MEG: This house is on the list.

STANLEY: But who are they? I mean, why. . . . ?

MEG: You'll see when they come.

STANLEY (*decisively*): They won't come.

MEG: Why not?

STANLEY (*quickly*): I tell you they won't come. Why didn't they come last night, if they were coming?

MEG: Perhaps they couldn't find the place in the dark. It's not easy to find in the dark.

STANLEY: They won't come. Someone's taking the Michael. Forget all about it. It's a false alarm A false alarm. (*He sits at the table.*) Where's my tea?

MEG: I took it away. You didn't want it.

STANLEY: What do you mean, you took it away?

MEG: I took it away.

STANLEY: What did you take it away for?

MEG: You didn't want it!

STANLEY: Who said I didn't want it?

MEG: You did!

STANLEY: Who gave you the right to take away my tea?

MEG: You wouldn't drink it.

> STANLEY *stares at her.*

STANLEY (*quietly*): Who do you think you're talking to?

MEG (*uncertainly*): What?

STANLEY: Come here.

MEG: What do you mean?

STANLEY: Come over here.

MEG: No.

STANLEY: I want to ask you something. (MEG *fidgets nervously. She does not go to him.*) Come on. (*Pause.*) All right. I can ask it from here just as well. (*Deliberately.*) Tell me, Mrs. Boles, when you address yourself to me, do you ever ask yourself who exactly you are talking to? Eh?

> Silence. He groans, his trunk falls forward, his head falls into his hands.

MEG (*in a small voice*): Didn't you enjoy your breakfast, Stan? (*She approaches the table.*) Stan? When are you going to play the piano again? (STANLEY *grunts.*) Like you used to? (STANLEY *grunts.*) I used to like watching you play the piano. When are you going to play it again?

STANLEY: I can't, can I?

MEG: Why not?

STANLEY. I haven't got a piano, have I?

MEG: No, I meant like when you were working. That piano.

STANLEY: Go and do your shopping.

MEG: But you wouldn't have to go away if you got a job, would you? You could play the piano on the pier.

He looks at her, then speaks airily.

STANLEY: I've . . . er . . . I've been offered a job, as a matter of fact.

MEG: What?

STANLEY: Yes. I'm considering a job at the moment.

MEG: You're not.

STANLEY: A good one, too. A night club. In Berlin.

MEG: Berlin?

STANLEY: Berlin. A night club. Playing the piano. A fabulous salary. And all found.

MEG: How long for?

STANLEY: We don't stay in Berlin. Then we go to Athens.

MEG: How long for?

STANLEY: Yes. Then we pay a flying visit to . . . er . . . whatsisname. . . .

MEG: Where?

STANLEY: Constantinople. Zagreb. Vladivostock. It's a round the world tour.

MEG (*sitting at the table*): Have you played the piano in those places before?

STANLEY: Played the piano? I've played the piano all over the world. All over the country. (*Pause.*) I once gave a concert.

MEG: A concert?

STANLEY (*reflectively*): Yes. It was a good one, too. They were all there that night. Every single one of them. It was a great success. Yes. A concert. At Lower Edmonton.

MEG: What did you wear?

STANLEY (*to himself*): I had a unique touch. Absolutely unioue. They came up to me. They came up to me and said they were grateful. Champagne we had that night, the lot. (*Pause.*) My father nearly came down to hear me. Well, I dropped him a card anyway. But I don't think he could make it. No, I—I lost the address, that was it. (*Pause.*) Yes. Lower Edmonton. Then after that, you know what they did? They carved me up. Carved me up. It was all arranged, it was all worked out. My next concert. Somewhere else it was. In winter. I went down there to play.

Then, when I got there, the hall was closed, the place was shuttered up, not even a caretaker. They'd locked it up. (*Takes off his glasses and wipes them on his pyjama jacket.*) A fast one. They pulled a fast one. I'd like to know who was responsible for that. (*Bitterly.*) All right, Jack, I can take a tip. They want me to crawl down on my bended knees. Well I can take a tip . . . any day of the week. (*He replaces his glasses, then looks at* MEG.) Look at her. You're just an old piece of rock cake, aren't you? (*He rises and leans across the table to her.*) That's what you are, aren't you?

MEG: Don't you go away again, Stan. You stay here. You'll be better off. You stay with your old Meg. (*He groans and lies across the table.*) Aren't you feeling well this morning, Stan? Did you pay a visit this morning?

He stiffens, then lifts himself slowly, turns to face her and speaks low and meaningfully.

STANLEY: Meg. Do you know what?

MEG: What?

STANLEY: Have you heard the latest?

MEG: No.

STANLEY: I'll bet you have.

MEG: I haven't.

STANLEY: Shall I tell you?

MEG: What latest?

STANLEY: You haven't heard it?

MEG: No.

STANLEY (*advancing*): They're coming today.

MEG: Who?

STANLEY: They're coming in a van.

MEG: Who?

STANLEY: And do you know what they've got in that van?

MEG: What?

STANLEY: They've got a wheelbarrow in that van.

MEG (*breathlessly*): They haven't.

STANLEY: Oh yes they have.

MEG: You're a liar.

STANLEY (*advancing upon her*): A big wheelbarrow. And when the van stops they wheel it out, and they wheel it up the garden path, and then they knock at the front door.

MEG: They don't.

STANLEY: They're looking for someone.

MEG: They're not.

STANLEY: They're looking for someone. A certain person.

MEG (*hoarsely*): No, they're not!

STANLEY: Shall I tell you who they're looking for?

MEG: No!

STANLEY: You don't want me to tell you?

MEG: You're a liar!

> *A sudden knock on the front door.* MEG *edges past* STANLEY *and collects her shopping bag. Another knock on the door* MEG *goes out.* STANLEY *sidles to the door and listens.*

VOICE: Hullo Mrs. Boles. It's come.

MEG: Oh, has it come?

VOICE: Yes, it's just come.

MEG: What, is that it?

VOICE: Yes. I thought I'd bring it round.

MEG: Is it nice?

VOICE: Very nice. What shall I do with it?

MEG: Well, I don't . . . (*Whispers.*)

VOICE: No, of course not . . . (*Whispers.*)

MEG: All right, but . . . (*Whispers.*)

VOICE: I won't . . . (*Whispers.*) Ta-ta, Mrs. Boles.

> STANLEY *quickly sits at the table. Enter* LULU.

LULU: Oh, hullo.

STANLEY: Ay-ay.

LULU: I just want to leave this in here.

STANLEY: Do. (LULU *crosses to the sideboard and puts a solid, round parcel upon it.*) That's a bulky object.

LULU: You're not to touch it.

STANLEY: Why would I want to touch it?

LULU: Well, you're not to, anyway.

STANLEY: Sit down a minute.

LULU *walks upstage.*

LULU: Why don't you open the door? It's all stuffy in here.

She opens the back door.

STANLEY *(rising)*: What are you talking about? I disinfected the place this morning.

LULU *(at the door)*: Oh, that's better.

STANLEY: Don't you believe me, then?

LULU: What?

STANLEY: Don't you believe I scrubbed the place out with Dettol this morning?

LULU: You didn't scrub yourself, I suppose?

STANLEY: I was in the sea at half past six.

LULU: Were you?

STANLEY: Sit down.

LULU: A minute.

She sits, takes out a compact and powders her nose.

STANLEY: So you're not going to tell me what's in that parcel?

LULU: Who said I knew?

STANLEY: Don't you?

LULU: I never said so.

STANLEY *(triumphantly)*: Well, how can you tell me what's in it if you don't know what's in it?

LULU: I'm not going to tell you.

STANLEY: I think it's going to rain today, what do you think?

LULU: Why don't you have a shave?

STANLEY: Don't you believe me then, when I tell you I was in the sea at half past six this morning?

LULU: I'd rather not discuss it.

STANLEY: You think I'm a liar then?

LULU *(offering him the compact)*: Do you want to have a look at your face? (STANLEY *withdraws from the table.*) You could do with a shave, do you know that? (STANLEY *sits, right, at the table.*) Don't you ever go out? (*He does not answer.*) I mean, what do you do, just sit around the house like this all day long? (*Pause.*) Hasn't

Mrs. Boles got enough to do without having you under her feet all day long?

STANLEY: I always stand on the table when she sweeps the floor.

LULU: Why don't you ever go out?

STANLEY: I was out—this morning—before breakfast—

LULU: I've never seen you out, not once.

STANLEY: Well, perhaps you're never out when I'm out.

LULU: I'm always out.

STANLEY: We've just never met, that's all.

LULU: Why don't you have a wash? You look terrible.

STANLEY: A wash wouldn't make any difference.

LULU (*rising*): Come out and get a bit of air. You depress me, looking like that.

STANLEY: Air? Oh, I don't know about that.

LULU: It's lovely out. And I've got a few sandwiches.

STANLEY: What sort of sandwiches?

LULU: Cheese.

STANLEY: I'm a big eater, you know.

LULU: That's all right. I'm not hungry.

STANLEY (*abruptly*): How would you like to go away with me?

LULU: Where.

STANLEY: Nowhere. Still, we could go.

LULU: But where could we go?

STANLEY: Nowhere. There's nowhere to go. So we could just go. It wouldn't matter.

LULU: We might as well stay here.

STANLEY: No. It's no good here.

LULU: Well, where else is there?

STANLEY: Nowhere.

LULU: Well, that's a charming proposal. (*He gets up.*) Are you going to wash?

STANLEY (*going round to her*): Listen. I want to ask you something.

LULU: You've just asked me.

STANLEY: No. Listen. (*Urgently.*) Has Meg had many guests staying in this house, besides me, I mean before me?

LULU: Besides you?

STANLEY (*impatiently*): Was she very busy, in the old days?

LULU: Why should she be?

STANLEY: What do you mean? This used to be a boarding house, didn't it?

LULU: Did it?

STANLEY: Didn't it?

LULU: Did it?

STANLEY: Didn't . . . oh, skip it.

LULU: Why do you want to know?

STANLEY: She's expecting two guests, for the first time since I've been here.

LULU: Oh. Do you have to wear those glasses?

STANLEY: Yes.

LULU: So you're not coming out for a walk?

STANLEY: I can't at the moment.

LULU: You're a bit of a washout, aren't you?

> *She exits, left.* STANLEY *stands. He then goes to the mirror and looks in it. He goes into the kitchen, takes off his glasses and begins to wash his face. A pause. Enter, by the back door,* GOLDBERG *and* MCCANN. MCCANN *carries two suitcases,* GOLDBERG *a briefcase. They halt inside the door, then walk downstage.* STANLEY, *wiping his face, glimpses their backs through the hatch.* GOLDBERG *and* MCCANN *look round the room.* STANLEY *slips on his glasses, sidles through the kitchen door and out of the back door.*

MCCANN: Is this it?

GOLDBERG: This is it.

MCCANN: Are you sure?

GOLDBERG: Sure I'm sure.

> *Pause.*

MCCANN: What now?

GOLDBERG: Don't worry yourself, McCann. Take a seat.

MCCANN: What about you?

GOLDBERG: What about me?

MCCANN: Are you going to take a seat?

GOLDBERG: We'll both take a seat. (MCCANN *puts down the suitcases and sits at the table, left.*) Sit back, McCann. Relax. What's the matter with you? I bring you down for a few days to the sea-side. Take a holiday. Do yourself a favour. Learn to relax, Mc-Cann, or you'll never get anywhere.

MCCANN: Ah sure, I do try, Nat.

GOLDBERG (*sitting at the table, right*): The secret is breathing. Take my tip. It's a well-known fact. Breathe in, breathe out, take a chance, let yourself go, what can you lose? Look at me. When I was an apprentice yet, McCann, every second Friday of the month my Uncle Barney used to take me to the seaside, regular as clockwork. Brighton, Canvey Island, Rottingdean—Uncle Barney wasn't particular. After lunch on Shabbuss we'd go and sit in a couple of deck chairs—you know, the ones with canopies—we'd have a little paddle, we'd watch the tide coming in, going out, the sun coming down—golden days, believe me, McCann. (*Reminiscent.*) Uncle Barney. Of course, he was an impeccable dresser. One of the old school. He had a house just outside Basingstoke at the time. Respected by the whole community. Culture? Don't talk to me about culture. He was an all-round man, what do you mean? He was a cosmopolitan.

MCCANN: Hey, Nat. . . .

GOLDBERG (*reflectively*): Yes. One of the old school.

MCCANN: Nat. How do we know this is the right house?

GOLDBERG: What?

MCCANN: How do we know this is the right house?

GOLDBERG: What makes you think it's the wrong house?

MCCANN: I didn't see a number on the gate.

GOLDBERG: I wasn't looking for a number.

MCCANN: No?

GOLDBERG (*settling in the armchair*): You know one thing Uncle Barney taught me? Uncle Barney taught me that the word of a gentleman is enough. That's why, when I had to go away on business I never carried any money. One of my sons used to come with me. He used to carry a few coppers. For a paper, perhaps, to see how the M.C.C. was getting on overseas. Otherwise my name was good. Besides, I was a very busy man.

MCCANN: I didn't know you had any sons.

GOLDBERG: But of course. I've been a family man.

MCCANN: How many did you have?

GOLDBERG: I lost my last two—in an accident. But the first, the first grew up to be a fine boy.

MCCANN: What's he doing now?

GOLDBERG: I often wonder that myself. Yes. Emanuel. A quiet fellow. He never said much. Timmy I used to call him.

MCCANN: Emanuel?

GOLDBERG: That's right. Manny.

MCCANN: Manny?

GOLDBERG: Sure. It's short for Emanuel.

MCCANN: I thought you called him Timmy.

GOLDBERG: I did.

MCCANN: What about this, Nat? Isn't it about time someone came in?

GOLDBERG: McCann, what are you so nervous about? Pull yourself together. Everywhere you go these days it's like a funeral.

MCCANN: That's true.

GOLDBERG: True? Of course it's true. It's more than true. It's a fact.

MCCANN: You may be right.

GOLDBERG: What is it, McCann? You don't trust me like you did in the old days?

MCCANN: Sure I trust you, Nat.

GOLDBERG: I'm glad. But why is it that before you do a job you're all over the place, and when you're doing the job you're as cool as a whistle?

MCCANN: I don't know, Nat. I'm just all right once I know what I'm doing. When I know what I'm doing, I'm all right.

GOLDBERG: Well, you do it very well.

MCCANN: Thank you, Nat.

GOLDBERG: As a matter of fact I was talking about you only the other day. I gave you a very good name.

MCCANN: That was kind of you, Nat.

GOLDBERG: And then this job came up out of the blue. Naturally they approached me to take care of it. And you know who I asked for?

MCCANN: Who?

GOLDBERG: You.

MCCANN: That was very good of you, Nat.

GOLDBERG: No, it was nothing. You're a capable man, McCann.

MCCANN: That's a great compliment, Nat, coming from a man in your position.

GOLDBERG: Well, I've got a position, I won't deny it.

MCCANN: You certainly have.

GOLDBERG: I would never deny that I had a position.

MCCANN: And what a position!

GOLDBERG: It's not a thing I would deny.

MCCANN: Yes, it's true, you've done a lot for me. I appreciate it.

GOLDBERG: Say no more.

MCCANN: You've always been a true Christian.

GOLDBERG: In a way.

MCCANN: No, I just thought I'd tell you that I appreciate it.

GOLDBERG: It's unnecessary to recapitulate.

MCCANN: You're right there.

GOLDBERG: Quite unnecessary.

Pause. MCCANN *leans forward.*

MCCANN: Hey Nat, just one thing. . . .

GOLDBERG: What now?

MCCANN: This job—no, listen—this job, is it going to be like anything we've ever done before?

GOLDBERG: Tch, tch, tch.

MCCANN: No, just tell me that. Just that, and I won't ask any more.

GOLDBERG *sighs, stands, goes behind the table, ponders, looks at* MCCANN, *and then speaks in a quiet, fluent, official tone.*

GOLDBERG: The main issue is a singular issue and quite distinct from your previous work. Certain elements, however, might well approximate in points of procedure to some of your other activities. All is dependent on the attitude of our subject. At all events, McCann, I can assure you that the assignment will be carried out and the mission accomplished with no excessive aggravation to you or myself. Satisfied?

MCCANN: Sure. Thank you, Nat.

MEG *enters, left.*

GOLDBERG: Ah, Mrs. Boles?

MEG: Yes?

GOLDBERG: We spoke to your husband last night. Perhaps he mentioned us? We heard that you kindly let rooms for gentlemen. So I brought my friend along with me. We were after a nice place, you understand. So we came to you. I'm Mr. Goldberg and this is Mr. McCann.

MEG: Very pleased to meet you.

They shake hands.

GOLDBERG: We're pleased to meet you, too.

MEG: That's very nice.

GOLDBERG: You're right. How often do you meet someone it's a pleasure to meet?

MCCANN: Never.

GOLDBERG: But today it's different. How are you keeping, Mrs. Boles?

MEG: Oh, very well, thank you.

GOLDBERG: Yes? Really?

MEG: Oh yes, really.

GOLDBERG: I'm glad. What do you say, McCann? Oh, Mrs. Boles, would you mind if my friend went into your kitchen and had a little gargle?

MEG (*to* MCCANN): Why, have you got a sore throat?

MCCANN: Er—yes.

MEG: Do you want some salt?

MCCANN: Salt?

MEG: Salt's good.

GOLDBERG: Good? It's wonderful. Go on, off you go, McCann.

MCCANN: Where is the kitchen?

MEG: Over there. (MCCANN *goes to the kitchen.*) There's some salt on the shelf.

MCCANN *exits.* GOLDBERG *sits at the table, right.*

GOLDBERG: So you can manage to put us up, eh, Mrs. Boles?

MEG: Well, it would have been easier last week.

GOLDBERG: Last week.

MEG: Or next week.

GOLDBERG: Next week.

MEG: Yes.

GOLDBERG: How many have you got here at the moment?

MEG: Just one at the moment.

GOLDBERG: Just one?

MEG: Yes. Just one. Until you came.

GOLDBERG: And your husband, of course?

MEG: Yes, but he sleeps with me.

GOLDBERG: What does he do, your husband?

MEG: He's a deck-chair attendant.

GOLDBERG: Oh, very nice.

MEG: Yes, he's out in all weathers.

She begins to take her purchases from her bag.

GOLDBERG: Of course. And your guest? Is he a man?

MEG: A man?

GOLDBERG: Or a woman?

MEG: No. A man.

GOLDBERG: Been here long?

MEG: He's been here about a year now.

GOLDBERG: Oh yes. A resident. What's his name?

MEG: Stanley Webber.

GOLDBERG: Oh yes? Does he work here?

MEG: He used to work. He used to be a pianist. In a concert party on the pier.

GOLDBERG: Oh yes? On the pier, eh? Does he play a nice piano?

MEG: Oh, lovely. (*She sits at the table.*) He once gave a concert.

GOLDBERG: Oh? Where?

MEG (*falteringly*): In . . . a big hall. His father gave him champagne. But then they locked the place up and he couldn't get out. The caretaker had gone home. So he had to wait until the morning before he could get out. (*With confidence.*) They were very grateful. (*Pause.*) And then they all wanted to give him a tip. And so he took the tip. And then he got a fast train and he came down here.

GOLDBERG: Really?

MEG: Oh yes. Straight down.

Pause.

MEG: I wish he could have played tonight.

GOLDBERG: Why tonight?

MEG: It's his birthday today.

GOLDBERG: His birthday?

MEG: Yes. Today. But I'm not going to tell him until tonight.

GOLDBERG: Doesn't he know it's his birthday?

MEG: He hasn't mentioned it.

GOLDBERG (*thoughtfully*): Well, well, well. Tell me. Are you going to have a party?

MEG: A party?

GOLDBERG: Weren't you going to have one?

MEG (*her eyes wide*): No

GOLDBERG: Well, of course, you must have one. (*He stands.*) We'll have a party, eh? What do you say?

MEG: Oh yes!

GOLDBERG: Sure. We'll give him a party. Leave it to me.

MEG: Oh, that's wonderful, Mr. Gold—

GOLDBERG: Berg.

MEG: Berg.

GOLDBERG: You like the idea?

MEG: Oh, I'm so glad you came today.

GOLDBERG: If we hadn't come today we'd have come tomorrow Still, I'm glad we came today. Just in time for his birthday.

MEG: I wanted to have a party. But you must have people for a party.

GOLDBERG: And now you've got McCann and me. McCann's the life and soul of any party.

MCCANN *enters from the kitchen.*

MEG: I'll invite Lulu this afternoon. (*To* MCCANN.) We're going to have a party tonight.

MCCANN: What?

GOLDBERG: There's a gentleman living here, McCann, who's got a birthday today, and he's forgotten all about it. So we're going to remind him. We're going to give him a party.

MCCANN: Oh, is that a fact?

MEG: Tonight.

GOLDBERG: Tonight. Did you have a good gargle?

MCCANN: Yes, thanks.

MEG: I'll put on my party dress.

GOLDBERG: And I'll get some bottles.

MEG: Oh, this is going to cheer Stanley up. It will. He's been down in the dumps lately.

GOLDBERG: We'll bring him out of himself.

MEG: I hope I look nice in my dress.

GOLDBERG: Madam, you'll look like a tulip.

MEG: What colour?

GOLDBERG: Er—well, I'll have to see the dress first.

MCCANN: Could I go up to my room?

MEG: Oh, I've put you both together. Do you mind being both together?

GOLDBERG: I don't mind. Do you mind, McCann?

MCCANN: No.

MEG: What time shall we have the party?

GOLDBERG: Nine o'clock.

MCCANN (*at the door*): Is this the way?

MEG (*rising*): I'll show you. If you don't mind coming upstairs.

GOLDBERG: With a tulip? It's a pleasure.

> MEG and GOLDBERG *exit laughing, followed by* MCCANN. STANLEY *appears at the window. He enters by the back door. He goes to the door on the left, opens it and listens. Silence. He walks to the table. He stands. He sits, as* MEG *enters. She crosses and hangs her shopping bag on a hook. He lights a match and watches it burn.*

STANLEY: Who is it?

MEG: The two gentlemen.

STANLEY: What two gentlemen?

MEG: The ones that were coming. I just took them to their room. They were thrilled with their room.

STANLEY: They've come?

MEG: They're very nice, Stan.

STANLEY: Why didn't they come last night?

MEG: They said the beds were wonderful.

STANLEY: Who are they?

MEG (*sitting*): They're very nice, Stanley.

STANLEY: I said, who are they?

MEG: I've told you, the two gentlemen.

STANLEY: I didn't think they'd come.

> *He rises and walks to the window.*

MEG: They have. They were here when I came in.

STANLEY: What do they want here?

MEG: They want to stay.

STANLEY: How long for?

MEG: They didn't say.

STANLEY (*turning*): But why here? Why not somewhere else?

MEG: This house is on the list.

STANLEY (*coming down*): What are they called? What are their names?

MEG: Oh, Stanley, I can't remember.

STANLEY: They told you, didn't they? Or didn't they tell you?

MEG: Yes, they. . . .

STANLEY: Then what are they? Come on. Try to remember.

MEG: Why, Stan? Do you know them?

STANLEY: How do I know if I know them until I know their names?

MEG: Well . . . he told me, I remember.

STANLEY: Well?

She thinks.

MEG: Gold—something.

STANLEY: Goldsomething?

MEG: Yes. Gold. . . .

STANLEY: Yes?

MEG: Goldberg.

STANLEY: Goldberg?

MEG: That's right. That was one of them.

STANLEY *slowly sits at the table, left.*

Do you know them?

STANLEY *does not answer.*

Stan, they won't wake you up, I promise. I'll tell them they must be quiet.

STANLEY *sits still.*

They won't be here long, Stan. I'll still bring you up your early morning tea.

STANLEY *sits still.*

You mustn't be sad today. It's your birthday.

A pause.

STANLEY (*dumbly*): Uh?

MEG: It's your birthday, Stan. I was going to keep it a secret until tonight.

STANLEY: No.

MEG: It is. I've brought you a present. (*She goes to the sideboard, picks up the parcel, and places it on the table in front of him.*) Here. Go on. Open it.

STANLEY: What's this?

MEG: It's your present.

STANLEY: This isn't my birthday, Meg.

MEG: Of course it is. Open your present.

He stares at the parcel, slowly stands, and opens it. He takes out a boy's drum.

STANLEY (*flatly*): It's a drum. A boy's drum.

MEG (*tenderly*): It's because you haven't got a piano. (*He stares at her, then turns and walks towards the door, left.*) Aren't you going to give me a kiss? (*He turns sharply, and stops. He walks back towards her slowly. He stops at her chair, looking down upon her. Pause. His shoulders sag, he bends and kisses her on the cheek.*) There are some sticks in there. (STANLEY *looks into the parcel. He takes out two drumsticks. He taps them together. He looks at her.*)

STANLEY: Shall I put it round my neck?

She watches him, uncertainly. He hangs the drum around his neck, taps it gently with the sticks, then marches round the table, beating it regularly. MEG, *pleased, watches him. Still beating it regularly, he begins to go round the table a second time. Halfway round the beat becomes erratic, uncontrolled.* MEG *expresses dismay. He arrives at her chair, banging the drum, his face and the drumbeat now savage and possessed.*

Curtain.

ACT TWO

MCCANN *is sitting at the table tearing a sheet of newspaper into five equal strips. It is evening. After a few moments* STANLEY *enters from the left. He stops upon seeing* MCCANN, *and watches him. He then walks towards the kitchen, stops, and speaks.*

STANLEY: Evening.
MCCANN: Evening.

Chuckles are heard from outside the back door, which is open.

STANLEY: Very warm tonight. (*He turns towards the back door, and back.*) Someone out there?

MCCANN *tears another length of paper.* STANLEY *goes into the kitchen and pours a glass of water. He drinks it looking through the hatch. He puts the glass down, comes out of the kitchen and walks quickly towards the door, left.* MCCANN *rises and intercepts him.*

MCCANN: I don't think we've met.
STANLEY: No, we haven't.
MCCANN: My name's McCann.
STANLEY: Staying here long?
MCCANN: Not long. What's your name?
STANLEY: Webber.
MCCANN: I'm glad to meet you, sir. (*He offers his hand.* STANLEY *takes it, and* MCCANN *holds the grip.*) Many happy returns of the day. (STANLEY *withdraws his hand. They face each other.*) Were you going out?
STANLEY: Yes.
MCCANN: On your birthday?
STANLEY: Yes. Why not?
MCCANN: But they're holding a party here for you tonight.
STANLEY: Oh really? That's unfortunate.
MCCANN: Ah no. It's very nice.

425

Voices from outside the back door.

STANLEY: I'm sorry. I'm not in the mood for a party tonight.
MCCANN: Oh, is that so? I'm sorry.
STANLEY: Yes, I'm going out to celebrate quietly, on my own.
MCCANN: That's a shame.

They stand.

STANLEY: Well, if you'd move out of my way—
MCCANN: But everything's laid on. The guests are expected.
STANLEY: Guests? What guests?
MCCANN: Myself for one. I had the honour of an invitation.

MCCANN *begins to whistle "The Mountains of Morne."*

STANLEY (*moving away*): I wouldn't call it an honour, would you?
It'll just be another booze-up.

STANLEY *joins* MCCANN *in whistling "The Mountains of Morne." During the next five lines the whistling is continuous, one whistling while the other speaks, and both whistling together.*

MCCANN: But it is an honour.
STANLEY: I'd say you were exaggerating.
MCCANN: Oh no. I'd say it was an honour.
STANLEY: I'd say that was plain stupid.
MCCANN: Oh no.

They stare at each other.

STANLEY: Who are the other guests?
MCCANN: A young lady.
STANLEY: Oh yes? And. . . . ?
MCCANN: My friend.
STANLEY: Your friend?
MCCANN: That's right. It's all laid on.

STANLEY *walks round the table towards the door.* MCCANN *meets him.*

STANLEY: Excuse me.

MCCANN: Where are you going?

STANLEY: I want to go out.

MCCANN: Why don't you stay here?

STANLEY *moves away, to the right of the table.*

STANLEY: So you're down here on holiday?

MCCANN: A short one. (STANLEY *picks up a strip of paper.* MCCANN *moves in.*) Mind that.

STANLEY: What is it?

MCCANN: Mind it. Leave it.

STANLEY: I've got a feeling we've met before.

MCCANN: No we haven't.

STANLEY: Ever been anywhere near Maidenhead?

MCCANN: No.

STANLEY: There's a Fuller's teashop. I used to have my tea there.

MCCANN: I don't know it.

STANLEY: And a Boots Library. I seem to connect you with the High Street.

MCCANN: Yes?

STANLEY: A charming town, don't you think?

MCCANN: I don't know it.

STANLEY: Oh no. A quiet, thriving community. I was born and brought up there. I lived well away from the main road.

MCCANN: Yes?

Pause.

STANLEY: You're here on a short stay?

MCCANN: That's right.

STANLEY: You'll find it very bracing.

MCCANN: Do you find it bracing?

STANLEY: Me? No. But you will. (*He sits at the table.*) I like it here, but I'll be moving soon. Back home. I'll stay there too, this time. No place like home. (*He laughs.*) I wouldn't have left, but business calls. Business called, and I had to leave for a bit. You know how it is.

MCCANN (*sitting at the table, left*): You in business?

STANLEY: No. I think I'll give it up. I've got a small private income,

you see. I think I'll give it up. Don't like being away from home.
I used to live very quietly—played records, that's about all. Everything delivered to the door. Then I started a little private business, in a small way, and it compelled me to come down here
—kept me longer than I expected. You never get used to living in
someone else's house. Don't you agree? I lived so quietly. You
can only appreciate what you've had when things change. That's
what they say, isn't it? Cigarette?

MCCANN: I don't smoke.

STANLEY *lights a cigarette. Voices from the back.*

STANLEY: Who's out there?

MCCANN: My friend and the man of the house.

STANLEY: You know what? To look at me, I bet you wouldn't think
I'd led such a quiet life. The lines on my face, eh? It's the drink.
Been drinking a bit down here. But what I mean is . . . you
know how it is . . . away from your own . . . all wrong, of course
. . . I'll be all right when I get back . . . but what I mean is, the
way some people look at me you'd think I was a different person.
I suppose I have changed, but I'm still the same man that I
always was. I mean, you wouldn't think, to look at me, really . . .
I mean, not really, that I was the sort of bloke to—to cause any
trouble, would you? (MCCANN *looks at him.*) Do you know what
I mean?

MCCANN: No. (*As* STANLEY *picks up a strip of paper.*) Mind that.

STANLEY (*quickly*): Why are you down here?

MCCANN: A short holiday.

STANLEY: This is a ridiculous house to pick on. (*He rises.*)

MCCANN: Why?

STANLEY: Because it's not a boarding house. It never was.

MCCANN: Sure it is.

STANLEY: Why did you choose this house?

MCCANN: You know, sir, you're a bit depressed for a man on his
birthday.

STANLEY (*sharply*): Why do you call me sir?

MCCANN: You don't like it?

STANLEY (*to the table*): Listen. Don't call me sir.

MCCANN: I won't, if you don't like it.

STANLEY (*moving away*): No. Anyway, this isn't my birthday.

MCCANN: No?

STANLEY: No. It's not till next month.

MCCANN: Not according to the lady.

STANLEY: Her? She's crazy. Round the bend.

MCCANN: That's a terrible thing to say.

STANLEY (*to the table*): Haven't you found that out yet? There's a lot you don't know. I think someone's leading you up the garden path.

MCCANN: Who would do that?

STANLEY (*leaning across the table*): That woman is mad!

MCCANN: That's slander.

STANLEY: And you don't know what you're doing.

MCCANN: Your cigarette is near that paper.

Voices from the back.

STANLEY: Where the hell are they? (*Stubbing his cigarette.*) Why don't they come in? What are they doing out there?

MCCANN: You want to steady yourself.

STANLEY *crosses to him and grips his arm.*

STANLEY (*urgently*): Look—

MCCANN: Don't touch me.

STANLEY: Look. Listen a minute.

MCCANN: Let go my arm.

STANLEY: Look. Sit down a minute.

MCCANN (*savagely, hitting his arm*): Don't do that!

STANLEY *backs across the stage, holding his arm.*

STANLEY: Listen. You knew what I was talking about before, didn't you?

MCCANN: I don't know what you're at at all.

STANLEY: It's a mistake! Do you understand?

MCCANN: You're in a bad state, man.

STANLEY (*whispering, advancing*): Has he told you anything? Do you know what you're here for? Tell me. You needn't be frightened of me. Or hasn't he told you?

MCCANN: Told me what?

STANLEY (*hissing*): I've explained to you, damn you, that all those years I lived in Basingstoke I never stepped outside the door.

MCCANN: You know, I'm flabbergasted with you.

STANLEY (*reasonably*): Look. You look an honest man. You're being made a fool of, that's all. You understand? Where do you come from?

MCCANN: Where do you think?

STANLEY: I know Ireland very well. I've many friends there. I love that country and I admire and trust its people. I trust them. They respect the truth and they have a sense of humour. I think their policemen are wonderful. I've been there. I've never seen such sunsets. What about coming out to have a drink with me? There's a pub down the road serves draught Guinness. Very difficult to get in these parts— (*He breaks off.*)

The voices draw nearer. GOLDBERG *and* PETEY *enter from the back door.*

GOLDBERG (*as he enters*): A mother in a million. (*He sees* STANLEY.) Ah.

PETEY: Oh hullo, Stan. You haven't met Stanley, have you, Mr. Goldberg?

GOLDBERG: I haven't had the pleasure.

PETEY: Oh well, this is Mr. Goldberg, this is Mr. Webber.

GOLDBERG: Pleased to meet you.

PETEY: We were just getting a bit of air in the garden.

GOLDBERG: I was telling Mr. Boles about my old mum. What days. (*He sits at the table, right.*) Yes. When I was a youngster, of a Friday, I used to go for a walk down the canal with a girl who lived down my road. A beautiful girl. What a voice that bird had! A nightingale, my word of honour. Good? Pure? She wasn't a Sunday school teacher for nothing. Anyway, I'd leave her with a little kiss on the cheek—I never took liberties—we weren't like the young men these days in those days. We knew the meaning of respect. So I'd give her a peck and I'd bowl back home. Humming away I'd be, past the children's playground. I'd tip my hat to the toddlers, I'd give a helping hand to a couple of stray dogs, everything came natural. I can see it like yesterday. The sun falling behind the dog stadium. Ah! (*He leans back contentedly.*)

MCCANN: Like behind the town hall.

GOLDBERG: What town hall?

MCCANN: In Carrikmacross.

GOLDBERG: There's no comparison. Up the street, into my gate, inside the door, home. "Simey!" my old mum used to shout, "quick before it gets cold." And there on the table what would I see? The nicest piece of gefilte fish you could wish to find on a plate.

MCCANN: I thought your name was Nat.

GOLDBERG: She called me Simey.

PETEY: Yes, we all remember our childhood.

GOLDBERG: Too true. Eh, Mr. Webber, what do you say? Childhood. Hot water bottles. Hot milk. Pancakes. Soap suds. What a life.

Pause.

PETEY (*rising from the table*): Well, I'll have to be off.

GOLDBERG: Off?

PETEY: It's my chess night.

GOLDBERG: You're not staying for the party?

PETEY: No, I'm sorry, Stan. I didn't know about it till just now. And we've got a game on. I'll try and get back early.

GOLDBERG: We'll save some drink for you, all right? Oh, that reminds me. You'd better go and collect the bottles.

MCCANN: Now?

GOLDBERG: Of course, now. Time's getting on. Round the corner, remember? Mention my name.

PETEY: I'm coming your way.

GOLDBERG: Beat him quick and come back, Mr. Boles.

PETEY: Do my best. See you later, Stan.

PETEY *and* MCCANN *go out, left.* STANLEY *moves to the centre.*

GOLDBERG: A warm night.

STANLEY (*turning*): Don't mess me about!

GOLDBERG: I beg your pardon?

STANLEY (*moving downstage*): I'm afraid there's been a mistake. We're booked out. Your room is taken. Mrs. Boles forgot to tell you. You'll have to find somewhere else.

GOLDBERG: Are you the manager here?

STANLEY: That's right.

GOLDBERG: Is it a good game?

STANLEY: I run the house. I'm afraid you and your friend will have to find other accommodation.

GOLDBERG (*rising*): Oh, I forgot, I must congratulate you on your birthday. (*Offering his hand.*) Congratulations.

STANLEY (*ignoring hand*): Perhaps you're deaf.

GOLDBERG: No, what makes you think that? As a matter of fact, every single one of my senses is at its peak. Not bad going, eh? For a man past fifty. But a birthday, I always feel, is a great occasion, taken too much for granted these days. What a thing to celebrate —birth! Like getting up in the morning. Marvellous! Some people don't like the idea of getting up in the morning. I've heard them. Getting up in the morning, they say, what is it? Your skin's crabby, you need a shave, your eyes are full of muck, your mouth is like a boghouse, the palms of your hands are full of sweat, your nose is clogged up, your feet stink, what are you but a corpse waiting to be washed? Whenever I hear that point of view I feel cheerful. Because I know what it is to wake up with the sun shining, to the sound of the lawnmower, all the little birds, the smell of the grass, church bells, tomato juice—

STANLEY: Get out.

Enter MCCANN, *with bottles.*

Get that drink out. These are unlicensed premises.

GOLDBERG: You're in a terrible humour today, Mr. Webber. And on your birthday too, with the good lady getting her strength up to give you a party.

MCCANN *puts the bottles on the sideboard.*

STANLEY: I told you to get those bottles out.

GOLDBERG: Mr. Webber, sit down a minute.

STANLEY: Let me—just make this clear. You don't bother me. To me, you're nothing but a dirty joke. But I have a responsibility towards the people in this house. They've been down here too long. They've lost their sense of smell. I haven't. And nobody's going to take advantage of them while I'm here. (*A little less forceful.*) Anyway, this house isn't your cup of tea. There's nothing here for you, from any angle. So why don't you just go, without any more fuss?

GOLDBERG: Mr. Webber, sit down.

STANLEY: It's no good starting any kind of trouble.

GOLDBERG: Sit down.

STANLEY: Why should I?

GOLDBERG: If you want to know the truth, Webber, you're beginning to get on my breasts.

STANLEY: Really? Well, that's—

GOLDBERG: Sit down.

STANLEY: No.

GOLDBERG *sighs, and sits at the table, right.*

GOLDBERG: McCann.

MCCANN: Nat?

GOLDBERG: Ask him to sit down.

MCCANN: Yes, Nat. (MCCANN *moves to* STANLEY.) Do you mind sitting down?

STANLEY: Yes, I do mind.

MCCANN: Yes now, but—it'd be better if you did.

STANLEY: Why don't you sit down?

MCCANN: No, not me—you.

STANLEY: No thanks.

Pause.

MCCANN: Nat.

GOLDBERG: What?

MCCANN: He won't sit down.

GOLDBERG: Well, ask him.

MCCANN: I've asked him.

GOLDBERG: Ask him again.

MCCANN (*to* STANLEY): Sit down.

STANLEY: Why?

MCCANN: You'd be more comfortable.

STANLEY: So would you.

Pause.

MCCANN: All right. If you will I will.

STANLEY: You first.

MCCANN *slowly sits at the table, left.*

MCCANN: Well?

STANLEY: Right. Now you've both had a rest you can get out!

MCCANN (*rising*): That's a dirty trick! I'll kick the shite out of him!

GOLDBERG (*rising*): No! I have stood up.

MCCANN: Sit down again!

GOLDBERG: Once I'm up I'm up.

STANLEY: Same here.

MCCANN (*moving to* STANLEY): You've made Mr. Goldberg stand up.

STANLEY (*his voice rising*): It'll do him good!

MCCANN: Get in that seat.

GOLDBERG: McCann.

MCCANN: Get down in that seat!

GOLDBERG (*crossing to him*): Webber. (*Quietly.*) SIT DOWN.

> *Silence.* STANLEY *begins to whistle "The Mountains of Morne."
> He strolls casually to the chair at the table. They watch him.
> He stops whistling. Silence. He sits.*

STANLEY: You'd better be careful.

GOLDBERG: Webber, what were you doing yesterday?

STANLEY: Yesterday?

GOLDBERG: And the day before. What did you do the day before that?

STANLEY: What do you mean?

GOLDBERG: Why are you wasting everybody's time, Webber? Why are you getting in everybody's way?

STANLEY: Me? What are you—

GOLDBERG: I'm telling you, Webber. You're a washout. Why are you getting on everybody's wick? Why are you driving that old lady off her conk?

MCCANN: He likes to do it!

GOLDBERG: Why do you behave so badly, Webber? Why do you force that old man out to play chess?

STANLEY: Me?

GOLDBERG: Why do you treat that young lady like a leper? She's not the leper, Webber!

STANLEY: What the—

GOLDBERG: What did you wear last week, Webber? Where do you keep your suits?

MCCANN: Why did you leave the organization?

GOLDBERG: What would your old mum say, Webber?

MCCANN: Why did you betray us?

GOLDBERG: You hurt me, Webber. You're playing a dirty game.

MCCANN: That's a Black and Tan fact.

GOLDBERG: Who does he think he is?

MCCANN: Who do you think you are?

STANLEY: You're on the wrong horse.

GOLDBERG: When did you come to this place?

STANLEY: Last year.

GOLDBERG: Where did you come from?

STANLEY: Somewhere else.

GOLDBERG: Why did you come here?

STANLEY: My feet hurt!

GOLDBERG: Why did you stay?

STANLEY: I had a headache!

GOLDBERG: Did you take anything for it?

STANLEY: Yes.

GOLDBERG: What?

STANLEY: Fruit salts!

GOLDBERG: Enos or Andrews?

STANLEY: En—An—

GOLDBERG: Did you stir properly? Did they fizz?

STANLEY: Now, now, wait, you—

GOLDBERG: Did they fizz? Did they fizz or didn't they fizz?

MCCANN: He doesn't know!

GOLDBERG: You don't know. What's happened to your memory, Webber? When did you last have a bath?

STANLEY: I have one every—

GOLDBERG: Don't lie.

MCCANN: You betrayed the organization. I know him!

STANLEY: You don't!

GOLDBERG: What can you see without your glasses?

STANLEY: Anything.

GOLDBERG: Take off his glasses.

MCCANN *snatches his glasses and as* STANLEY *rises, reaching for them, takes his chair downstage centre, below the table,* STANLEY *stumbling as he follows.* STANLEY *clutches the chair and stays bent over it.*

Webber, you're a fake.

They stand on each side of the chair.

When did you last wash up a cup?
STANLEY: The Christmas before last.
GOLDBERG: Where?
STANLEY: Lyons Corner House.
GOLDBERG: Which one?
STANLEY: Marble Arch.
GOLDBERG: Where was your wife?
STANLEY: In—
GOLDBERG: Answer.
STANLEY (*turning, crouched*): What wife?
GOLDBERG: What have you done with your wife?
MCCANN: He's killed his wife!
GOLDBERG: Why did you kill your wife?
STANLEY (*sitting, his back to the audience*): What wife?
MCCANN: How did he kill her?
GOLDBERG: How did you kill her?
MCCANN: You throttled her.
GOLDBERG: With arsenic.
MCCANN: There's your man!
GOLDBERG: Where's your old mum?
STANLEY: In the sanatorium.
MCCANN: Yes!
GOLDBERG: Why did you never get married?
MCCANN: She was waiting at the porch.
GOLDBERG: You skedaddled from the wedding.
MCCANN: He left her in the lurch.
GOLDBERG: You left her in the pudding club.
MCCANN: She was waiting at the church.
GOLDBERG: Webber! Why did you change your name?
STANLEY: I forgot the other one.
GOLDBERG: What's your name now?
STANLEY: Joe Soap.
GOLDBERG: You stink of sin.
MCCANN: I can smell it.
GOLDBERG: Do you recognise an external force?
STANLEY: What?

GOLDBERG: Do you recognise an external force?

MCCANN: That's the question!

GOLDBERG: Do you recognise an external force, responsible for you, suffering for you?

STANLEY: It's late.

GOLDBERG: Late! Late enough! When did you last pray?

MCCANN: He's sweating!

GOLDBERG: When did you last pray?

MCCANN: He's sweating!

GOLDBERG: Is the number 846 possible or necessary?

STANLEY: Neither.

GOLDBERG: Wrong! Is the number 846 possible or necessary?

STANLEY: Both.

GOLDBERG: Wrong! It's necessary but not possible.

STANLEY: Both.

GOLDBERG: Wrong! Why do you think the number 846 is necessarily possible?

STANLEY: Must be.

GOLDBERG: Wrong! It's only necessarily necessary! We admit possibility only after we grant necessity. It is possible because necessary but by no means necessary through possibility. The possibility can only be assumed after the proof of necessity.

MCCANN: Right!

GOLDBERG: Right? Of course right! We're right and you're wrong, Webber, all along the line.

MCCANN: All along the line!

GOLDBERG: Where is your lechery leading you?

MCCANN: You'll pay for this.

GOLDBERG: You stuff yourself with dry toast.

MCCANN: You contaminate womankind.

GOLDBERG: Why don't you pay the rent?

MCCANN: Mother defiler!

GOLDBERG: Why do you pick your nose?

MCCANN: I demand justice!

GOLDBERG: What's your trade?

MCCANN: What about Ireland?

GOLDBERG: What's your trade?

STANLEY: I play the piano.

GOLDBERG: How many fingers do you use?

STANLEY: No hands!

GOLDBERG: No society would touch you. Not even a building society.

MCCANN: You're a traitor to the cloth.

GOLDBERG: What do you use for pyjamas?

STANLEY: Nothing.

GOLDBERG: You verminate the sheet of your birth.

MCCANN: What about the Albigensenist heresy?

GOLDBERG: Who watered the wicket in Melbourne?

MCCANN: What about the blessed Oliver Plunkett?

GOLDBERG: Speak up Webber. Why did the chicken cross the road?

STANLEY: He wanted to—he wanted to—he wanted to. . . .

MCCANN: He doesn't know!

GOLDBERG: Why did the chicken cross the road?

STANLEY: He wanted to—he wanted to. . . .

GOLDBERG: Why did the chicken cross the road?

STANLEY: He wanted. . . .

MCCANN: He doesn't know. He doesn't know which came first!

GOLDBERG: Which came first?

MCCANN: Chicken? Egg? Which came first?

GOLDBERG and MCCANN: Which came first? Which came first? Which came first?

STANLEY *screams.*

GOLDBERG: He doesn't know. Do you know your own face?

MCCANN: Wake him up. Stick a needle in his eye.

GOLDBERG: You're a plague, Webber. You're an overthrow.

MCCANN: You're what's left!

GOLDBERG: But we've got the answer to you. We can sterilise you.

MCCANN: What about Drogheda?

GOLDBERG: Your bite is dead. Only your pong is left.

MCCANN: You betrayed our land.

GOLDBERG: You betray our breed.

MCCANN: Who are you, Webber?

GOLDBERG: What makes you think you exist?

MCCANN: You're dead.

GOLDBERG: You're dead. You can't live, you can't think, you can't love. You're dead. You're a plague gone bad. There's no juice in you. You're nothing but an odour!

Silence. They stand over him. He is crouched in the chair. He

looks up slowly and kicks GOLDBERG *in the stomach.* GOLDBERG
falls. STANLEY *stands.* MCCANN *seizes a chair and lifts it above
his head.* STANLEY *seizes a chair and covers his head with it.*
MCCANN *and* STANLEY *circle.*

GOLDBERG: Steady, McCann.
STANLEY (*circling*): Uuuuuhhhhh!
MCCANN: Right, Judas.
GOLDBERG (*rising*): Steady, McCann.
MCCANN: Come on!
STANLEY: Uuuuuuuhhhhh!
MCCANN: He's sweating.
GOLDBERG: Easy, McCann.
MCCANN: The bastard sweatpig is sweating.

A loud drumbeat off left, descending the stairs. GOLDBERG *takes
the chair from* STANLEY. *They put the chairs down. They stop
still. Enter* MEG, *in evening dress, holding sticks and drum.*

MEG: I brought the drum down. I'm dressed for the party.
GOLDBERG: Wonderful.
MEG: You like my dress?
GOLDBERG: Wonderful. Out of this world.
MEG: I know. My father gave it to me. (*Placing drum on table.*)
    Doesn't it make a beautiful noise?
GOLDBERG: It's a fine piece of work. Maybe Stan'll play us a little tune
    afterwards.
MEG: Oh yes. Will you, Stan?
STANLEY: Could I have my glasses?
GOLDBERG: Ah yes. (*He holds his hand out to* MCCANN. MCCANN *passes
    him his glasses.*) Here they are. (*He holds them out for* STANLEY,
    who reaches for them.) Here they are. (STANLEY *takes them.*) Now.
    What have we got here? Enough to scuttle a liner. We've got
    four bottles of Scotch and one bottle of Irish.
MEG: Oh, Mr. Goldberg, what should I drink?
GOLDBERG: Glasses, glasses first. Open the Scotch, McCann.
MEG (*at the sideboard*): Here's my very best glasses in here.
MCCANN: I don't drink Scotch.
GOLDBERG: You drink that one.
MEG (*bringing the glasses*): Here they are.

GOLDBERG: Good. Mrs. Boles, I think Stanley should pour the toast, don't you?

MEG: Oh yes. Come on, Stanley. (STANLEY *walks slowly to the table.*) Do you like my dress, Mr. Goldberg?

GOLDBERG: It's out on its own. Turn yourself round a minute. I used to be in the business. Go on, walk up there.

MEG: Oh no.

GOLDBERG: Don't be shy. (*He slaps her bottom.*)

MEG: Oooh!

GOLDBERG: Walk up the boulevard. Let's have a look at you. What carriage. What's your opinion, McCann? Like a Countess, nothing less. Madam, now turn about and promenade to the kitchen. What a deportment!

MCCANN (*to* STANLEY): You can pour my Irish too.

GOLDBERG: You look like a gladiola.

MEG: Stan, what about my dress?

GOLDBERG: One for the lady, one for the lady. Now madam—your glass.

MEG: Thank you.

GOLDBERG: Lift your glasses, ladies and gentlemen. We'll drink a toast.

MEG: Lulu isn't here.

GOLDBERG: It's past the hour. Now—who's going to propose the toast? Mrs. Boles, it can only be you.

MEG: Me?

GOLDBERG: Who else?

MEG: But what do I say?

GOLDBERG: Say what you feel. What you honestly feel. (MEG *looks uncertain.*) It's Stanley's birthday. Your Stanley. Look at him. Look at him and it'll come. Wait a minute, the light's too strong. Let's have proper lighting. McCann, have you got your torch?

MCCANN (*bringing a small torch from his pocket*): Here.

GOLDBERG: Switch out the light and put on your torch. (MCCANN *goes to the door, switches off the light, comes back, shines the torch on* MEG. *Outside the window there is still a faint light.*) Not on the lady, on the gentleman! You must shine it on the birthday boy. (MCCANN *shines the torch in* STANLEY's *face.*) Now, Mrs. Boles, it's all yours.

Pause.

MEG: I don't know what to say.

GOLDBERG: Look at him. Just look at him.

MEG: Isn't the light in his eyes?

GOLDBERG: No, no. Go on.

MEG: Well—it's very, very nice to be here tonight, in my house, and I want to propose a toast to Stanley, because it's his birthday, and he's lived here for a long while now, and he's my Stanley now. And I think he's a good boy, although sometimes he's bad. (*An appreciative laugh from* GOLDBERG.) And he's the only Stanley I know, and I know him better than all the world, although he doesn't think so. ("*Hear—hear*" *from* GOLDBERG.) Well, I could cry because I'm so happy, having him here and not gone away, on his birthday, and there isn't anything I wouldn't do for him, and all you good people here tonight. . . . (*She sobs.*)

GOLDBERG. Beautiful! A beautiful speech. Put the light on, McCann. (MCCANN *goes to the door.* STANLEY *remains still.*) That was a lovely toast. (*The light goes on.* LULU *enters from the door, left.* GOLDBERG *comforts* MEG.) Buck up now. Come on, smile at the birdy. That's better. We've got to drink yet. Ah, look who's here.

MEG: Lulu.

GOLDBERG: How do you do, Lulu? I'm Nat Goldberg. Stanley, a drink for your guest. You just missed the toast, my dear, and what a toast.

LULU: Did I?

GOLDBERG: Stanley, a drink for your guest. Stanley. (STANLEY *hands a glass to* LULU.) Right. Now raise your glasses. Everyone standing up? No, not you, Stanley. You must sit down.

MCCANN: Yes, that's right. He must sit down.

GOLDBERG: You don't mind sitting down a minute? We're going to drink to you.

MEG: Come on!

STANLEY *sits in a chair at the table.*

GOLDBERG: Right. Now Stanley's sat down. (*Taking the stage.*) Well, I want to say first that I've never been so touched to the heart as by the toast we've just heard. How often, in this day and age, do you come across real, true warmth? Once in a lifetime. Until a few minutes ago, ladies and gentlemen, I, like all of you, was asking the same question. What's happened to the love, the bonhomie, the unashamed expression of affection of the day before yesterday, that our mums taught us in the nursery?

MCCANN: Gone with the wind.

GOLDBERG: That's what I thought, until today. I believe in a good laugh, a day's fishing, a bit of gardening. I was very proud of my old greenhouse, made out of my own spit and faith. That's the sort of man I am. Not size but quality. A little Austin, tea in Fullers, a library book from Boots, and I'm satisfied. But just now, I say just now, the lady of the house said her piece and I for one am knocked over by the sentiments she expressed. Lucky is the man who's at the receiving end, that's what I say. (*Pause.*) How can I put it to you? We all wander on our tod through this world. It's a lonely pillow to kip on. Right!

LULU (*admiringly*): Right!

GOLDBERG: Agreed. But tonight, Lulu, McCann, we've known a great fortune. We've heard a lady extend the sum total of her devotion, in all its pride, plume and peacock, to a member of her own living race. Stanley, my heartfelt congratulations. I wish you, on behalf of us all, a happy birthday. I'm sure you've never been a prouder man than you are today. Mazoltov! And may we only meet at Simchahs! (LULU *and* MEG *applaud.*) Turn out the light, McCann, while we drink the toast.

LULU: That was a wonderful speech.

> MCCANN *switches out the light, comes back, and shines the torch in* STANLEY'S *face. The light outside the window is fainter.*

GOLDBERG: Lift your glasses. Stanley—happy birthday.

MCCANN: Happy birthday.

LULU: Happy birthday.

MEG: Many happy returns of the day, Stan.

GOLDBERG: And well over the fast.

> *They all drink.*

MEG (*kissing him*): Oh, Stanny. . . .

GOLDBERG: Lights!

MCCANN: Right! (*He switches on the lights.*)

MEG: Clink my glass, Stan.

LULU: Mr. Goldberg—

GOLDBERG: Call me Nat.

MEG (*to* MCCANN): You clink my glass.

LULU (*to* GOLDBERG): You're empty. Let me fill you up.

GOLDBERG: It's a pleasure.

LULU: You're a marvellous speaker, Nat, you know that? Where did
you learn to speak like that?

GOLDBERG: You liked it, eh?

LULU: Oh yes!

GOLDBERG: Well, my first chance to stand up and give a lecture was
at the Ethical Hall, Bayswater. A wonderful opportunity. I'll
never forget it. They were all there that night. Charlotte Street
was empty. Of course, that's a good while ago.

LULU: What did you speak about?

GOLDBERG: The Necessary and the Possible. It went like a bomb. Since
then I always speak at weddings.

> STANLEY *is still.* GOLDBERG *sits left of the table.* MEG *joins*
> MCCANN *downstage, right,* LULU *is downstage, left.* MCCANN
> *pours more Irish from the bottle, which he carries, into his
> glass.*

MEG: Let's have some of yours.

MCCANN: In that?

MEG: Yes.

MCCANN: Are you used to mixing them?

MEG: No.

MCCANN: Sit down. Give me your glass.

> MEG *sits on a shoe-box, downstage, right.* LULU, *at the table,
> pours more drink for* GOLDBERG *and herself, and gives* GOLD-
> BERG *his glass.*

GOLDBERG: Thank you.

MEG (*to* MCCANN): Do you think I should?

GOLDBERG: Lulu, you're a big bouncy girl. **Come** and sit on my lap.

MCCANN: Why not?

LULU: Do you think I should?

GOLDBERG: Try it.

MEG (*sipping*): Very nice.

LULU: I'll bounce up to the ceiling.

MCCANN: I don't know how you can mix that stuff.

GOLDBERG: Take a chance.

MEG (*to* MCCANN): Sit down on this stool.

> LULU *sits on* GOLDBERG'S *lap.*

MCCANN: This?

GOLDBERG: Comfortable?

LULU: Yes, thanks.

MCCANN (*sitting*): It's comfortable.

GOLDBERG: You know, there's a lot in your eyes.

LULU: And in yours, too.

GOLDBERG: Do you think so?

LULU (*giggling*): Go on!

MCCANN (*to* MEG): Where'd you get it?

MEG: My father gave it to me.

LULU: I didn't know I was going to meet you here tonight.

MCCANN (*to* MEG): Ever been to Carrikmacross?

MEG (*drinking*): I've been to King's Cross.

LULU: You came right out of the blue, you know that?

GOLDBERG (*as she moves*): Mind how you go. You're cracking a rib.

MEG (*standing*): I want to dance! (LULU *and* GOLDBERG *look into each other's eyes.* MCCANN *drinks.* MEG *crosses to* STANLEY.) Stanley. Dance. (STANLEY *sits still.* MEG *dances round the room alone, then comes back to* MCCANN, *who fills her glass. She sits.*)

LULU (*to* GOLDBERG): Shall I tell you something?

GOLDBERG: What?

LULU: I trust you.

GOLDBERG (*lifting his glass*): Gesundheit.

LULU: Have you got a wife?

GOLDBERG: I had a wife. What a wife. Listen to this. Friday, of an afternoon, I'd take myself for a little constitutional, down over the park. Eh, do me a favour, just sit on the table a minute, will you? (LULU *sits on the table. He stretches and continues.*) A little constitutional. I'd say hullo to the little boys, the little girls—I never made distinctions—and then back I'd go, back to my bungalow with the flat roof. "Simey," my wife used to shout, "quick, before it gets cold!" And there on the table what would I see? The nicest piece of rollmop and pickled cucumber you could wish to find on a plate.

LULU: I thought your name was Nat.

GOLDBERG: She called me Simey.

LULU: I bet you were a good husband.

GOLDBERG: You should have seen her funeral.

LULU: Why?

GOLDBERG (*draws in his breath and wags head*): What a funeral.

MEG (*to* MCCANN): My father was going to take me to Ireland once. But then he went away by himself.

LULU (*to* GOLDBERG): Do you think you knew me when I was a little girl?

GOLDBERG: Were you a nice little girl?

LULU: I was.

MEG: I don't know if he went to Ireland.

GOLDBERG: Maybe I played piggy-back with you.

LULU: Maybe you did.

MEG: He didn't take me.

GOLDBERG: Or pop goes the weasel.

LULU: Is that a game?

GOLDBERG: Sure it's a game!

MCCANN: Why didn't he take you to Ireland?

LULU: You're tickling me!

GOLDBERG: You should worry.

LULU: I've always liked older men. They can soothe you.

They embrace.

MCCANN: I know a place. Roscrea. Mother Nolan's.

MEG: There was a night-light in my room, when I was a little girl.

MCCANN: One time I stayed there all night with the boys. Singing and drinking all night.

MEG: And my Nanny used to sit up with me, and sing songs to me.

MCCANN: And a plate of fry in the morning. Now where am I?

MEG: My little room was pink. I had a pink carpet and pink curtains, and I had musical boxes all over the room. And they played me to sleep. And my father was a very big doctor. That's why I never had any complaints. I was cared for, and I had little sisters and brothers in other rooms, all different colours.

MCCANN: Tullamore, where are you?

MEG (*to* MCCANN): Give us a drop more.

MCCANN (*filling her glass and singing*): Glorio, Glorio, to the bold Fenian men!

MEG: Oh, what a lovely voice.

GOLDBERG: Give us a song, McCann.

LULU: A love song!

MCCANN (*reciting*): The night that poor Paddy was stretched, the boys they all paid him a visit.

GOLDBERG: A love song!

MCCANN (*in a full voice, sings*):

> Oh, the Garden of Eden has vanished, they say,
> But I know the lie of it still.
> Just turn to the left at the foot of Ben Clay
> And stop when halfway to Coote Hill.
> It's there you will find it, I know sure enough,
> And it's whispering over to me:
> Come back, Paddy Reilly, to Bally-James-Duff,
> Come home, Paddy Reilly, to me!

LULU (*to* GOLDBERG): You're the dead image of the first man I ever loved.

GOLDBERG: It goes without saying.

MEG (*rising*): I want to play a game!

GOLDBERG: A game?

LULU: What game?

MEG: Any game.

LULU (*jumping up*): Yes, let's play a game.

GOLDBERG: What game?

MCCANN: Hide and seek.

LULU: Blind man's buff.

MEG: Yes!

GOLDBERG: You want to play blind man's buff?

LULU and MEG: Yes!

GOLDBERG: All right. Blind man's buff. Come on! Everyone up! (*Rising.*) McCann. Stanley—Stanley!

MEG: Stanley. Up.

GOLDBERG: What's the matter with him?

MEG (*bending over him*): Stanley, we're going to play a game. Oh, come on, don't be sulky, Stan.

STANLEY *rises.* MCCANN *rises.*

GOLDBERG: Right! Now—who's going to be blind first?

LULU: Mrs. Boles.

MEG: Not me.

GOLDBERG: Of course you.

MEG: Who, me?

LULU (*taking her scarf from her neck*): Here you are.

MCCANN: How do you play this game?

LULU (*tying her scarf round* MEG's *eyes*): Haven't you ever played blind man's buff? Keep still, Mrs. Boles. You mustn't be touched. But you can't move after she's blind. You must stay where you are after she's blind. And if she touches you then you become blind. Turn round. How many fingers am I holding up?

MEG: I can't see.

LULU: Right.

GOLDBERG: Right! Everyone move about. McCann. Stanley. Now stop. Now still. Off you go!

> STANLEY *is downstage, right,* MEG *moves about the room.* GOLD-BERG *fondles* LULU *at arm's length.* MEG *touches* MCCANN.

MEG: Caught you!

LULU: Take off your scarf.

MEG: What lovely hair!

LULU (*untying the scarf*): There.

MEG: It's you!

GOLDBERG: Put it on, McCann.

LULU (*tying it on* MCCANN): There. Turn round. How many fingers am I holding up?

MCCANN: I don't know.

GOLDBERG: Right! Everyone move about. Right. Stop! Still!

> MCCANN *begins to move.*

MEG: Oh, this is lovely!

GOLDBERG: Quiet! Tch, tch, tch. Now—all move again. Stop! Still!

> MCCANN *moves about.* GOLDBERG *fondles* LULU *at arm's length.* MCCANN *draws near* STANLEY. *He stretches his arm and touches* STANLEY's *glasses.*

MEG: It's Stanley!
GOLDBERG (*to* LULU): Enjoying the game?
MEG: It's your turn, Stan.

MCCANN *takes off the scarf.*

MCCANN (*to* STANLEY): I'll take your glasses.

MCCANN *takes* STANLEY'S *glasses.*

MEG: Give me the scarf.
GOLDBERG (*holding* LULU): Tie his scarf, Mrs. Boles.
MEG: That's what I'm doing.
LULU (*to* GOLDBERG): Kiss me. (*They kiss.*)
MEG (*to* STANLEY): Can you see my nose?
GOLDBERG: He can't. Ready? Right! Everyone move. Stop! And still!

> STANLEY *stands blindfold.* MCCANN *backs slowly across the stage to the left. He breaks* STANLEY'S *glasses, snapping the frames.* MEG *is downstage, left,* LULU *and* GOLDBERG *upstage centre, close together.* STANLEY *begins to move, very slowly, across the stage to the left.* MCCANN *picks up the drum and places it sideways in* STANLEY'S *path.* STANLEY *walks into the drum and falls over with his foot caught in it.*

MEG: Ooh!
GOLDBERG: Sssh!

> STANLEY *rises. He begins to move towards* MEG, *dragging the drum on his foot. He reaches her and stops. His hands move towards her and they reach her throat. He begins to strangle her.* MCCANN *and* GOLDBERG *rush forward and throw him off.*

Blackout

> *There is now no light at all through the window. The stage is in darkness.*

LULU: The lights!
GOLDBERG: What's happened?

LULU: The lights!

MCCANN: Wait a minute.

GOLDBERG: Where is he?

MCCANN: Let go of me!

LULU: Someone's touching me!

GOLDBERG: Who's this?

MEG: It's me!

MCCANN: Where is he?

MEG: Why has the light gone out?

GOLDBERG: Where's your torch? (MCCANN *shines the torch in* GOLD-BERG's *face.*) Not on me! (MCCANN *shifts the torch. It is knockea from his hand and falls. It goes out.*)

MCCANN: My torch!

LULU: Oh God!

GOLDBERG: Where's your torch? Pick up your torch!

MCCANN: I can't find it.

LULU: Hold me. Hold me.

GOLDBERG: Get down on your knees. Help him find the torch.

LULU: I can't.

MCCANN: It's gone.

MEG: Why has the light gone out?

GOLDBERG: Everyone quiet! Help him find the torch.

> *Silence. Grunts from* MCCANN *and* GOLDBERG *on their knees Suddenly there is a sharp, sustained rat-a-tat with a stick on the side of the drum from the back of the room. Silence. Whimpers from* LULU.

GOLDBERG: Over here. McCann!

MCCANN: Here.

GOLDBERG: Come to me, come to me. Easy. Over there.

> GOLDBERG *and* MCCANN *move up left of the table.* STANLEY *moves down right of the table.* LULU *suddenly perceives him moving towards her, screams and faints.* GOLDBERG *and* MCCANN *turn and stumble against each other.*

GOLDBERG: What is it?

MCCANN: Who's that?

GOLDBERG: What is it?

In the darkness STANLEY *picks up* LULU *and places her on the table.*

MEG: It's Lulu!

GOLDBERG *and* MCCANN *move downstage, right.*

GOLDBERG: Where is she?
MCCANN: She fell.
GOLDBERG: Where?
MCCANN: About here.
GOLDBERG: Help me pick her up.
MCCANN (*moving downstage, left*): I can't find her.
GOLDBERG: She must be somewhere.
MCCANN: She's not here.
GOLDBERG (*moving downstage, left*): She must be.
MCCANN: She's gone.

MCCANN *finds the torch on the floor, shines it on the table and* STANLEY. LULU *is lying spread-eagled on the table,* STANLEY *bent over her.* STANLEY, *as soon as the torchlight hits him, begins to giggle.* GOLDBERG *and* MCCANN *move towards him. He backs, giggling, the torch on his face. They follow him upstage, left. He backs against the hatch, giggling. The torch draws closer. His giggle rises and grows as he flattens himself against the wall. Their figures converge upon him.*

Curtain.

The next morning. PETEY *enters, left, with a newspaper and sits at the table. He begins to read.* MEG's *voice comes through the kitchen hatch.*

MEG: Is that you, Stan? (*Pause.*) Stanny?
PETEY: Yes?
MEG: Is that you?
PETEY: It's me.
MEG (*appearing at the hatch*): Oh, it's you. I've run out of cornflakes.
PETEY: Well, what else have you got?
MEG: Nothing.
PETEY: Nothing?
MEG: Just a minute. (*She leaves the hatch and enters by the kitchen door.*) You got your paper?
PETEY: Yes.
MEG: Is it good?
PETEY: Not bad.
MEG: The two gentlemen had the last of the fry this morning.
PETEY: Oh, did they?
MEG: There's some tea in the pot though. (*She pours tea for him.*) I'm going out shopping in a minute. Get you something nice.
PETEY: Good.
MEG: Oh, I must sit down a minute. (*Sits at the table, right.*)
PETEY: How are you then, this morning?
MEG: I've got a splitting headache.
PETEY (*reading*): You slept like a log last night.
MEG: Did I?
PETEY: Why don't you have a walk down to the shops? It's fresh out. It'll clear your head.
MEG: Will it?
PETEY: Bound to.
MEG: I will then. Did I sleep like a log?
PETEY: Dead out.
MEG: I must have been tired. (*She looks about the room and sees the broken drum in the fireplace.*) Oh, look. (*She rises and picks it up.*) The drum's broken. (PETEY *looks up.*) Why is it broken?
PETEY: I don't know.

451

She hits it with her hand.

MEG: It still makes a noise.

PETEY: You can always get another one.

MEG (*sadly*): It was probably broken in the party. I don't remember it being broken though, in the party. (*She puts it down.*) What a shame.

PETEY: You can always get another one, Meg.

MEG: Well, at least he did have it on his birthday, didn't he? Like I wanted him to.

PETEY (*reading*): Yes.

MEG: Have you seen him down yet? (PETEY *does not answer.*) Petey.

PETEY: What?

MEG: Have you seen him down?

PETEY: Who?

MEG: Stanley.

PETEY: No.

MEG: Nor have I. That boy should be up. He's late for his breakfast.

PETEY: There isn't any breakfast.

MEG: Yes, but he doesn't know that. I'm going to call him.

PETEY (*quickly*): No, don't do that, Meg. Let him sleep.

MEG: But you say he stays in bed too much.

PETEY: Let him sleep . . . this morning. Leave him.

MEG: I've been up once, with his cup of tea. But Mr. McCann opened the door. He said they were talking. He said he'd made him one. He must have been up early. I don't know what they were talking about. I was surprised. Because Stanley's usually fast asleep when I wake him. But he wasn't this morning. I heard him talking. (*Pause.*) Do you think they know each other? I think they're old friends. Stanley had a lot of friends. I know he did. (*Pause.*) I didn't give him his tea. He'd already had one. I came down again and went on with my work. Then, after a bit, they came down to breakfast. Stanley must have gone to sleep again.

Pause.

PETEY: When are you going to do your shopping, Meg?

MEG: Yes, I must. (*Collecting the bag.*) I've got a rotten headache. (*She goes to the back door, stops suddenly and turns.*) Did you see what's outside this morning?

PETEY: What?

MEG: That big car.

PETEY: Yes.

MEG: It wasn't there yesterday. Did you . . . did you have a look inside it?

PETEY: I had a peep.

MEG (*coming down tensely, and whispering*): Is there anything in it?

PETEY: In it?

MEG: Yes.

PETEY: What do you mean, in it?

MEG: Inside it.

PETEY: What sort of thing?

MEG: Well . . . I mean . . . is there . . . is there a wheelbarrow in it?

PETEY: A wheelbarrow?

MEG: Yes.

PETEY: I didn't see one.

MEG: You didn't? Are you sure?

PETEY: What would Mr. Goldberg want with a wheelbarrow?

MEG: Mr. Goldberg?

PETEY: It's his car.

MEG (*relieved*): His car? Oh, I didn't know it was his car.

PETEY: Of course it's his car.

MEG: Oh, I feel better.

PETEY: What are you on about?

MEG: Oh, I do feel better.

PETEY: You go and get a bit of air.

MEG: Yes, I will. I will. I'll go and get the shopping. (*She goes towards the back door. A door slams upstairs. She turns.*) It's Stanley! He's coming down—what am I going to do about his breakfast? (*She rushes into the kitchen.*) Petey, what shall I give him? (*She looks through the hatch.*) There's no cornflakes. (*They both gaze at the door. Enter* GOLDBERG. *He halts at the door, as he meets their gaze, then smiles.*)

GOLDBERG: A reception committee!

MEG: Oh, I thought it was Stanley.

GOLDBERG: You find a resemblance?

MEG: Oh no. You look quite different.

GOLDBERG (*coming into the room*): Different build, of course.

MEG (*entering from the kitchen*): I thought he was coming down for his breakfast. He hasn't had his breakfast yet.

GOLDBERG: Your wife makes a very nice cup of tea, Mr. Boles, you know that?

PETEY: Yes, she does sometimes. Sometimes she forgets.

MEG: Is he coming down?

GOLDBERG: Down? Of course he's coming down. On a lovely sunny day like this he shouldn't come down? He'll be up and about in next to no time. (*He sits at the table.*) And what a breakfast he's going to get.

MEG: Mr. Goldberg.

GOLDBERG: Yes?

MEG: I didn't know that was your car outside.

GOLDBERG: You like it?

MEG: Are you going to go for a ride?

GOLDBERG (*to* PETEY): A smart car, eh?

PETEY: Nice shine on it all right.

GOLDBERG: What is old is good, take my tip. There's room there. Room in the front, and room in the back. (*He strokes the teapot.*) The pot's hot. More tea, Mr. Boles?

PETEY: No thanks.

GOLDBERG (*pouring tea*): That car? That car's never let me down.

MEG: Are you going to go for a ride?

GOLDBERG (*ruminatively*): And the boot. A beautiful boot. There's just room . . . for the right amount.

MEG: Well, I'd better be off now. (*She moves to the back door, and turns.*) Petey, when Stanley comes down. . . .

PETEY: Yes?

MEG: Tell him I won't be long.

PETEY: I'll tell him.

MEG (*vaguely*): I won't be long. (*She exits.*)

GOLDBERG (*sipping his tea*): A good woman. A charming woman. My mother was the same. My wife was identical.

PETEY: How is he this morning?

GOLDBERG: Who?

PETEY: Stanley. Is he any better?

GOLDBERG (*a little uncertainly*): Oh . . . a little better, I think, a little better. Of course, I'm not really qualified to say, Mr. Boles. I mean, I haven't got the . . . the qualifications. The best thing would be if someone with the proper . . . mnn . . . qualifications . . . was to have a look at him. Someone with a few letters after his name. It makes all the difference.

PETEY: Yes.

GOLDBERG: Anyway, Dermot's with him at the moment. He's . . . keeping him company.

PETEY: Dermot?

GOLDBERG: Yes.

PETEY: It's a terrible thing.

GOLDBERG (*sighs*): Yes. The birthday celebration was too much for him.

PETEY: What came over him?

GOLDBERG (*sharply*): What came over him? Breakdown, Mr. Boles. Pure and simple. Nervous breakdown.

PETEY: But what brought it on so suddenly?

GOLDBERG (*rising, and moving upstage*): Well, Mr. Boles, it can happen in all sorts of ways. A friend of mine was telling me about it only the other day. We'd both been concerned with another case—not entirely similar, of course, but . . . quite alike, quite alike. (*He pauses.*) Anyway, he was telling me, you see, this friend of mine, that sometimes it happens gradual—day by day it grows and grows and grows . . . day by day. And then other times it happens all at once. Poof! Like that! The nerves break. There's no guarantee how it's going to happen, but with certain people . . . it's a foregone conclusion.

PETEY: Really?

GOLDBERG: Yes. This friend of mine—he was telling me about it—only the other day. (*He stands uneasily for a moment, then brings out a cigarette case and takes a cigarette.*) Have an Abdullah.

PETEY: No, no, I don't take them.

GOLDBERG: Once in a while I treat myself to a cigarette. An Abdullah, perhaps, or a . . . (*He snaps his fingers.*)

PETEY: What a night. (GOLDBERG *lights his cigarette with a lighter.*) Came in the front door and all the lights were out. Put a shilling in the slot, came in here and the party was over.

GOLDBERG (*coming downstage*): You put a shilling in the slot?

PETEY: Yes.

GOLDBERG: And the lights came on.

PETEY: Yes, then I came in here.

GOLDBERG (*with a short laugh*): I could have sworn it was a fuse.

PETEY (*continuing*): There was dead silence. Couldn't hear a thing. So I went upstairs and your friend—Dermot—met me on the landing. And he told me.

GOLDBERG (*sharply*): Who?

PETEY: Your friend—Dermot.

GOLDBERG (*heavily*): Dermot. Yes. (*He sits.*)

PETEY: They get over it sometimes though, don't they? I mean, they can recover from it, can't they?

GOLDBERG: Recover? Yes, sometimes they recover, in one way or another.

PETEY: I mean, he might have recovered by now, mightn't he?

GOLDBERG: It's conceivable. Conceivable.

PETEY *rises and picks up the teapot and cup.*

PETEY: Well, if he's no better by lunchtime I'll go and get hold of a doctor.

GOLDBERG (*briskly*): It's all taken care of, Mr. Boles. Don't worry yourself.

PETEY (*dubiously*): What do you mean? (*A door slams upstairs. They look towards the door. Enter* MCCANN *with two suitcases.*) Oh, it's you. All packed up?

PETEY *takes the teapot and cups into the kitchen.* MCCANN *crosses left and puts down the suitcases. He goes up to the window and looks out.*

GOLDBERG: Well? (MCCANN *does not answer.*) McCann. I asked you well.

MCCANN (*without turning*): Well what?

GOLDBERG: What's what? (MCCANN *does not answer.*) What is what?

MCCANN (*turning to look at* GOLDBERG, *grimly*): I'm not going up there again.

GOLDBERG: Why not?

MCCANN: I'm not going up there again.

GOLDBERG: What's going on now?

MCCANN (*moving down*): He's quiet now. He stopped all that . . . talking a while ago.

PETEY *appears at the kitchen hatch, unnoticed.*

GOLDBERG: When will he be ready?

MCCANN (*sullenly*): You can go up yourself next time.

GOLDBERG: What's the matter with you?

MCCANN (*quietly*): I gave him. . . .

GOLDBERG: What?

MCCANN: I gave him his glasses.

GOLDBERG: Wasn't he glad to get them back?

MCCANN: The frames are bust.

GOLDBERG: How did that happen?

MCCANN: He tried to fit the eyeholes into his eyes. I left him doing it.

PETEY (*at the kitchen door*): There's some Sellotape somewhere. We can stick them together.

GOLDBERG *and* MCCANN *turn to see him. Pause.*

GOLDBERG: Sellotape? No, no, that's all right, Mr. Boles. It'll keep him quiet for the time being, keep his mind off other things.

PETEY (*moving downstage*): What about a doctor?

GOLDBERG: It's all taken care of.

MCCANN *moves over right to the shoe-box, and takes out a brush and brushes his shoes.*

PETEY (*moves to the table*): I think he needs one.

GOLDBERG: I agree with you. It's all taken care of. We'll give him bit of time to settle down, and then I'll take him to Monty.

PETEY: You're going to take him to a doctor?

GOLDBERG (*staring at him*): Sure. Monty.

Pause. MCCANN *brushes his shoes.* PETEY *sits, left, at the table.*

So Mrs. Boles has gone out to get us something nice for lunch?

PETEY: That's right.

GOLDBERG: Unfortunately we may be gone by then.

PETEY: Will you?

GOLDBERG: By then we may be gone.

MCCANN (*breaking in*): You know that girl?

GOLDBERG: What girl?

MCCANN: That girl had nightmares in the night.

GOLDBERG: Those weren't nightmares.

MCCANN: No?

GOLDBERG (*irritably*): I said no.

MCCANN: How do you know?

GOLDBERG: I got up. I went to see what was the matter.

MCCANN: I didn't know that.

GOLDBERG (*sharply*): It may be that you didn't know that. Nevertheless, that's what happened.

MCCANN: Well, what was the matter?

GOLDBERG: Nothing. Nothing at all. She was just having a bit of a sing-song.

MCCANN: A sing-song?

GOLDBERG (*to* PETEY): Sure. You know how young girls sing. She was singing.

MCCANN: So what happened then?

GOLDBERG: I joined in. We had a few songs. Yes. We sang a few of the old ballads and then she went to bye-byes.

> PETEY *rises.*

PETEY: Well, I think I'll see how my peas are getting on, in the meantime.

GOLDBERG: The meantime?

PETEY: While we're waiting.

GOLDBERG: Waiting for what? (PETEY *walks towards the back door.*) Aren't you going back to the beach?

PETEY: No, not yet. Give me a call when he comes down, will you, Mr. Goldberg?

GOLDBERG (*earnestly*): You'll have a crowded beach today . . . on a day like this. They'll be lying on their backs, swimming out to sea. My life. What about the deck-chairs? Are the deck-chairs ready?

PETEY: I put them all out this morning.

GOLDBERG: But what about the tickets? Who's going to take the tickets?

PETEY: That's all right. That'll be all right, Mr. Goldberg. Don't you worry about that. I'll be back.

> *He exits.* GOLDBERG *rises, goes to the window and looks after him.* MCCANN *crosses to the table, left, sits, picks up the paper and begins to tear it into strips.*

GOLDBERG: Is everything ready?

MCCANN: Sure.

GOLDBERG *walks heavily, brooding, to the table. He sits right of it noticing what* MCCANN *is doing.*

GOLDBERG: Stop doing that!

MCCANN: What?

GOLDBERG: Why do you do that all the time? It's childish, it's pointless. It's without a solitary point.

MCCANN: What's the matter with you today?

GOLDBERG: Questions, questions. Stop asking me so many questions. What do you think I am?

MCCANN *studies him. He then folds the paper, leaving the strips inside.*

MCCANN: Well?

Pause. GOLDBERG *leans back in the chair, his eyes closed.*

MCCANN: Well?

GOLDBERG (*with fatigue*): Well what?

MCCANN: What's what?

GOLDBERG: Yes, what is what. . . .

MCCANN: Do we wait or do we go and get him?

GOLDBERG (*slowly*): You want to go and get him?

MCCANN: I want to get it over.

GOLDBERG: That's understandable.

MCCANN: So do we wait or do we—?

GOLDBERG (*interrupting*): I don't know why, but I feel knocked out. I feel a bit . . . It's uncommon for me.

MCCANN: Is that so?

GOLDBERG: It's unusual.

MCCANN (*rising swiftly and going behind* GOLDBERG's *chair. Hissing*): Let's finish and go. Let's get it over and go. Get the thing done. Let's finish the bloody thing. Let's get the thing done and go! (*Pause.*) Will I go up? (*Pause.*) Nat!

GOLDBERG *sits humped.* MCCANN *slips to his side.*

Simey!

GOLDBERG (*opening his eyes, regarding* MCCANN): What—did—you—call—me?

MCCANN: Who?

GOLDBERG (*murderously*): Don't call me that! (*He seizes* MCCANN *by the throat.*) NEVER CALL ME THAT!

MCCANN (*writhing*): Nat, Nat, Nat, NAT! I called you Nat. I was asking you, Nat. Honest to God. Just a question, that's all, just a question, do you see, do you follow me?

GOLDBERG (*jerking him away*): What question?

MCCANN: Will I go up?

GOLDBERG (*violently*): Up? I thought you weren't going to go up there again?

MCCANN: What do you mean? Why not?

GOLDBERG: You said so!

MCCANN: I never said that!

GOLDBERG: No?

MCCANN (*from the floor, to the room at large*): Who said that? I never said that! I'll go up now!

He jumps up and rushes to the door, left.

GOLDBERG: Wait!

He stretches his arms to the arms of the chair.

Come here.

MCCANN *approaches him very slowly*

I want your op n on. Have a look in my mouth.

He opens his mouth wide.

Take a good look

MCCANN *looks.*

You know what I mean?

MCCANN *peers.*

You know what? I've never lost a tooth. Not since the day I

was born. Nothing's changed. (*He gets up.*) That's why I've reached my position, McCann. Because I've always been as fit as a fiddle. All my life I've said the same. Play up, play up, and play the game. Honour thy father and thy mother. All along the line. Follow the line, the line, McCann, and you can't go wrong. What do you think, I'm a self-made man? No! I sat where I was told to sit. I kept my eye on the ball. School? Don't talk to me about school. Top in all subjects. And for why? Because I'm telling you, I'm telling you, follow my line? Follow my mental? Learn by heart. Never write down a thing. No. And don't go too near the water. And you'll find—that what I say is true.
Because I believe that the world ... (*Vacant.*).   .
Because I believe that the world ... (*Desperate.*). . . .
BECAUSE I BELIEVE THAT THE WORLD ... (*Lost.*). . . .

He sits in chair.

Sit down, McCann, sit here where I can look at you.

MCCANN *kneels in front of the table.*

(*Intensely, with growing certainty.*) My father said to me, Benny, Benny, he said, come here. He was dying. I knelt down. By him day and night. Who else was there? Forgive, Benny, he said, and let live. Yes, Dad. Go home to your wife. I will, Dad. Keep an eye open for low-lives, for schnorrers and for layabouts. He didn't mention names. I lost my life in the service of others, he said, I'm not ashamed. Do your duty and keep your observations. Always bid good morning to the neighbours. Never, never forget your family, for they are the rock, the constitution and the core! If you're ever in any difficulties Uncle Barney will see you in the clear. I knelt down. (*He kneels, facing* MCCANN.) I swore on the good book. And I knew the word I had to remember —Respect! Because McCann— (*Gently.*) Seamus—who came before your father? His father. And who came before him? Before him?
(*Vacant—triumphant.*) Who came before your father's father but your father's father's mother! Your great-gran-granny

Silence. He slowly rises.

And that's why I've reached my position, McCann. Because I've always been as fit as a fiddle. My motto. Work hard and play hard. Not a day's illness. (*He emits a high-pitched wheeze-whine. He looks round.*) What was that?

MCCANN: What?

GOLDBERG: I heard something.

MCCANN: What was it?

GOLDBERG: A noise. A funny noise.

MCCANN: That was you.

GOLDBERG: Me?

MCCANN: Sure.

GOLDBERG (*interested*): What, you heard it too?

MCCANN: I did.

GOLDBERG: It was me, eh? (*A slight chuckle.*) Huh. What did I do?

MCCANN: You gave . . . you let out a class of a wheeze, like.

GOLDBERG: Go on! (*He laughs. They both laugh. Then suddenly, quickly, anxiously.*) Where's your spoon? You got your spoon?

MCCANN (*producing it*): Here.

GOLDBERG: Test me. (*He opens his mouth and sticks out his tongue.*) Here. (MCCANN *places the spoon on* GOLDBERG's *tongue.*) Aaaahhh! Aaaaahhhh!

MCCANN: Perfect condition.

GOLDBERG: You really mean that?

MCCANN: My word of honour.

GOLDBERG: So now you can understand why I occupy such a position, eh?

MCCANN: I can, of course.

GOLDBERG *laughs. They both laugh.*

GOLDBERG (*stopping*): All the same, give me a blow. (*Pause.*) Blow in my mouth.

MCCANN *stands, puts his hands on his knees, bends, and blows in* GOLDBERG's *mouth.*

One for the road.

MCCANN *blows again in his mouth.* GOLDBERG *breathes deeply, shakes his head, and bounds from the chair.*

Right. We're here. Wait a minute, just a minute. You got everything packed?

MCCANN: I have.

GOLDBERG: The expander?

MCCANN: Yes.

GOLDBERG: Fetch it to me.

MCCANN: Now?

GOLDBERG: At once.

> MCCANN *goes to the suitcase and takes out a chest expander. He gives it to* GOLDBERG, *who pulls it playfully, masterfully, bearing down on* MCCANN. *They both chuckle.* GOLDBERG *pulls it to full stretch. It breaks. He smiles.*

What did I tell you?

> *He throws it at* MCCANN. *Enter* LULU, *left.*

Well, look who's here.

> MCCANN *looks at them, and goes to the door.*

MCCANN (*at the door*): I'll give you five minutes. (*He exits with the expander.*)

GOLDBERG: Come over here.

LULU: What's going to happen?

GOLDBERG: Come over here.

LULU: No, thank you.

GOLDBERG: What's the matter? You got the needle to Uncle Natey?

LULU: I'm going.

GOLDBERG: Have a game of pontoon first, for old time's sake.

LULU: I've had enough games.

GOLDBERG: A girl like you, at your age, at your time of health, and you don't take to games?

LULU: You're very smart.

GOLDBERG: Anyway, who says you don't take to them?

LULU: Do you think I'm like all the other girls?

GOLDBERG: Are all the other girls like that, too?

LULU: I don't know about any other girls.

GOLDBERG: Nor me. I've never touched another woman.

LULU (*distressed*): What would my father say, if he knew? And what would Eddie say?

GOLDBERG: Eddie?

LULU: He was my first love, Eddie was. And whatever happened, it was pure. With him! He didn't come into my room at night with a briefcase!

GOLDBERG: Who opened the briefcase, me or you?

LULU: You got around me. It was only because I was so upset by last night.

GOLDBERG: Lulu, schmulu, let bygones be bygones, do me a turn. Kiss and make up.

LULU: I wouldn't touch you.

GOLDBERG: And today I'm leaving.

LULU: You're leaving?

GOLDBERG: Today.

LULU (*with growing anger*): You used me for a night. A passing fancy.

GOLDBERG: Who used who?

LULU: You made use of me by cunning when my defences were down.

GOLDBERG: Who took them down?

LULU: That's what you did. You quenched your ugly thirst. You took advantage of me when I was overwrought. I wouldn't do those things again, not even for a Sultan!

GOLDBERG: One night doesn't make a harem.

LULU: You taught me things a girl shouldn't know before she's been married at least three times!

GOLDBERG: Now you're a jump ahead! What are you complaining about?

Enter MCCANN *quickly.*

LULU: You didn't appreciate me for myself. You took all those liberties only to satisfy your appetite.

GOLDBERG: Now you're giving me indigestion.

LULU: And after all that had happened. An old woman nearly killed and a man gone mad—How can I go back behind that counter now? Oh Nat, why did you do it?

GOLDBERG: You wanted me to do it, Lulula, so I did it.

MCCANN: That's fair enough.

LULU (*turning*): Oh!

MCCANN (*advancing*): You had a long sleep, Miss.

LULU (*backing upstage left*): Me?

MCCANN: Your sort, you spend too much time in bed.

LULU: What do you mean?

MCCANN: Have you got anything to confess?

LULU: What?

MCCANN (*savagely*): Confess!

LULU: Confess what?

MCCANN: Down on your knees and confess!

LULU: What does he mean?

GOLDBERG: Confess. What can you lose?

LULU: What, to him?

GOLDBERG: He's only been unfrocked six months.

MCCANN: Kneel down, woman, and tell me the latest!

LULU (*retreating to the back door*): I've seen everything that's happened. I know what's going on. I've got a pretty shrewd idea.

MCCANN (*advancing*): I've seen you hanging about the Rock of Cashel, profaning the soil with your goings-on. Out of my sight!

LULU: I'm going.

> *She exits.* MCCANN *goes to the door, left, and goes out. He ushers in* STANLEY, *who is dressed in striped trousers, black jacket, and white collar. He carries a bowler hat in one hand and his broken glasses in the other. He is clean-shaven.* MCCANN *follows and closes the door.* GOLDBERG *meets* STANLEY, *seats him in a chair, right, and puts his hat on the table.*

GOLDBERG: How are you, Stan? (*Pause.*) Are you feeling any better? (*Pause.*) What's the matter with your glasses? (GOLDBERG *bends to look.*) They're broken. A pity.

> STANLEY *stares blankly at the floor.*

MCCANN (*at the table*): He looks better, doesn't he?

GOLDBERG: Much better.

MCCANN: A new man.

GOLDBERG: You know what we'll do?

MCCANN: What?

GOLDBERG: We'll buy him another pair.

> *They begin to woo him gently and with relish. During the*

following sequence STANLEY *shows no reaction. He remains, with no movement, where he sits.*

MCCANN: Out of our own pockets.

GOLDBERG: It goes without saying. Between you and me, Stan, it's about time you had a new pair of glasses.

MCCANN: You can't see straight.

GOLDBERG: It's true. You've been cockeyed for years.

MCCANN: Now you're even more cockeyed.

GOLDBERG: He's right. You've gone from bad to worse.

MCCANN: Worse than worse.

GOLDBERG: You need a long convalescence.

MCCANN: A change of air.

GOLDBERG: Somewhere over the rainbow.

MCCANN: Where angels fear to tread.

GOLDBERG: Exactly.

MCCANN: You're in a rut.

GOLDBERG: You look anaemic.

MCCANN: Rheumatic.

GOLDBERG: Myopic.

MCCANN: Epileptic.

GOLDBERG: You're on the verge.

MCCANN: You're a dead duck.

GOLDBERG: But we can save you.

MCCANN: From a worse fate.

GOLDBERG: True.

MCCANN: Undeniable.

GOLDBERG: From now on, we'll be the hub of your wheel.

MCCANN: We'll renew your season ticket.

GOLDBERG: We'll take tuppence off your morning tea.

MCCANN: We'll give you a discount on all inflammable goods.

GOLDBERG: We'll watch over you.

MCCANN: Advise you.

GOLDBERG: Give you proper care and treatment.

MCCANN: Let you use the club bar.

GOLDBERG: Keep a table reserved.

MCCANN: Help you acknowledge the fast days.

GOLDBERG: Bake you cakes.

MCCANN: Help you kneel on kneeling days.

GOLDBERG: Give you a free pass.

MCCANN: Take you for constitutionals.

GOLDBERG: Give you hot tips.

MCCANN: We'll provide the skipping rope.

GOLDBERG: The vest and pants.

MCCANN: The ointment.

GOLDBERG: The hot poultice.

MCCANN: The fingerstall.

GOLDBERG: The abdomen belt.

MCCANN: The ear plugs.

GOLDBERG: The baby powder.

MCCANN: The back scratcher.

GOLDBERG: The spare tyre.

MCCANN: The stomach pump.

GOLDBERG: The oxygen tent.

MCCANN: The prayer wheel.

GOLDBERG: The plaster of Paris.

MCCANN: The crash helmet.

GOLDBERG: The crutches.

MCCANN: A day and night service.

GOLDBERG: All on the house.

MCCANN: That's it.

GOLDBERG: We'll make a man of you.

MCCANN: And a woman.

GOLDBERG: You'll be re-orientated.

MCCANN: You'll be rich.

GOLDBERG: You'll be adjusted.

MCCANN: You'll be our pride and joy.

GOLDBERG: You'll be a mensch.

MCCANN: You'll be a success.

GOLDBERG: You'll be integrated.

MCCANN: You'll give orders.

GOLDBERG: You'll make decisions.

MCCANN: You'll be a magnate.

GOLDBERG: A statesman.

MCCANN: You'll own yachts.

GOLDBERG: Animals.

MCCANN: Animals.

GOLDBERG *looks at* MCCANN.

GOLDBERG: I said animals. (*He turns back to* STANLEY.) You'll be able to make or break, Stan. By my life. (*Silence.* STANLEY *is still.*) Well? What do you say?

> STANLEY's *head lifts very slowly and turns in* GOLDBERG's *direction.*

GOLDBERG: What do you think? Eh, boy?

> STANLEY *begins to clench and unclench his eyes.*

MCCANN: What's your opinion, sir? Of this prospect, sir?
GOLDBERG: Prospect. Sure. Sure it's a prospect.

> STANLEY's *hands clutching his glasses begin to tremble.*

What's your opinion of such a prospect? Eh, Stanley?

> STANLEY *concentrates, his mouth opens, he attempts to speak, fails and emits sounds from his throat.*

STANLEY: Uh-gug . . . uh-gug . . . eeehhh-gag . . . (*On the breath.*) Caahh . . . caahh. . . .

> *They watch him. He draws a long breath which shudders down his body. He concentrates.*

GOLDBERG: Well, Stanny boy, what do you say, eh?

> *They watch. He concentrates. His head lowers, his chin draws into his chest, he crouches.*

STANLEY: Uh-gughh . . . uh-gughhh. . . .
MCCANN: What's your opinion, sir?
STANLEY: Caaahhh . . . caaahhh. . . .
MCCANN: Mr. Webber! What's your opinion?
GOLDBERG: What do you say, Stan? What do you think of the prospect?
MCCANN: What's your opinion of the prospect?

> STANLEY's *body shudders, relaxes, his head drops, he becomes still again, stooped.* PETEY *enters from door, downstage, left.*

GOLDBERG: Still the same old Stan. Come with us. Come on, boy.
MCCANN: Come along with us.
PETEY: Where are you taking him?

They turn. Silence.

GOLDBERG: We're taking him to Monty.
PETEY: He can stay here.
GOLDBERG: Don't be silly.
PETEY: We can look after him here.
GOLDBERG: Why do you want to look after him?
PETEY: He's my guest.
GOLDBERG: He needs special treatment.
PETEY: We'll find someone.
GOLDBERG: No. Monty's the best there is. Bring him, McCann.

They help STANLEY *out of the chair.* GOLDBERG *puts the bowler hat on* STANLEY's *head. They all three move towards the door, left.*

PETEY: Leave him alone!

They stop. GOLDBERG *studies him.*

GOLDBERG (*insidiously*): Why don't you come with us, Mr. Boles?
MCCANN: Yes, why don't you come with us?
GOLDBERG: Come with us to Monty. There's plenty of room in the car.

PETEY *makes no move. They pass him and reach the door.* MCCANN *opens the door and picks up the suitcases.*

PETEY (*broken*): Stan, don't let them tell you what to do!

They exit.

Silence. PETEY *stands. The front door slams. Sound of a car starting. Sound of a car going away. Silence.* PETEY *slowly goes to the table. He sits on a chair, left. He picks up the paper and opens it. The strips fall to the floor. He looks down at them.* MEG *comes past the window and enters by the back door.* PETEY *studies the front page of the paper.*

MEG (*coming downstage*): The car's gone.

PETEY: Yes.

MEG: Have they gone?

PETEY: Yes.

MEG: Won't they be in for lunch?

PETEY: No.

MEG: Oh, what a shame. (*She puts her bag on the table.*) It's hot out. (*She hangs her coat on a hook.*) What are you doing?

PETEY: Reading.

MEG: Is it good?

PETEY: All right.

She sits by the table.

MEG: Where's Stan? (*Pause.*) Is Stan down yet, Petey?

PETEY: No . . . he's. . . .

MEG: Is he still in bed?

PETEY: Yes, he's . . . still asleep.

MEG: Still? He'll be late for his breakfast.

PETEY: Let him . . . sleep.

Pause.

MEG: Wasn't it a lovely party last night?

PETEY: I wasn't there.

MEG: Weren't you?

PETEY: I came in afterwards.

MEG: Oh. (*Pause.*) It was a lovely party. I haven't laughed so much for years. We had dancing and singing. And games. You should have been there.

PETEY: It was good, eh?

Pause.

MEG: I was the belle of the ball.

PETEY: Were you?

MEG: Oh yes. They all said I was.

PETEY: I bet you were, too.

MEG: Oh, it's true. I was. (*Pause.*) I know I was.

Curtain.

Rhinoceros

by
Eugène Ionesco

Translated by Derek Prouse

RHINOCEROS was first produced in Paris by Jean-Louis Barrault at the Odéon, January 25, 1960, with the following cast:

BERENGER	Jean-Louis Barrault
JEAN	William Sabatier
DAISY	Simone Valère
DUDARD	Gabriel Cattand
THE LOGICIAN	Jean Parédès
THE WAITRESS	Jane Martel
THE HOUSEWIFE	Marie-Hélène Dasté
THE OLD GENTLEMAN	Robert Lombard
MRS. BOEUF	Simone Paris
MR. PAPILLON	Michel Bertay

THE GROCER, THE GROCER'S WIFE, THE CAFE PROPRIETOR, BOTARD, A FIRE-MAN, THE LITTLE OLD MAN, THE LITTLE OLD MAN'S WIFE, AND A LOT OF RHINOCEROS HEADS.

The play is in three acts and four scenes

ACT ONE

The scene is a square in a small provincial town. Up-stage a house composed of a ground floor and one storey. The ground floor is the window of a grocer's shop. The entrance is up two or three steps through a glass-paned door. The word EPICERIE is written in bold letters above the shop window. The two windows on the first floor are the living quarters of the grocer and his wife. The shop is up-stage, but slightly to the left, not far from the wings. In the distance a church steeple is visible above the grocer's house. Between the shop and the left of the stage there is a little street in perspective. To the right, slightly at an angle, is the front of a café. Above the café, one floor with a window; in front, the café terrace; several chairs and tables reach almost to centre stage. A dusty tree stands near the terrace chairs. Blue sky; harsh light; very white walls. The time is almost mid-day on a Sunday in summertime. JEAN *and* BERENGER *will sit at one of the terrace tables.*

The sound of church bells is heard, which stop a few moments before the curtain rises. When the curtain rises, a woman carrying a basket of provisions under one arm and a cat under the other crosses the stage in silence from right to left. As she does so, the GROCER'S WIFE *opens her shop door and watches her pass.*

GROCER'S WIFE: Oh that woman gets on my nerves! (*To her husband who is in the shop.*) Too stuck-up to buy from us nowadays.

The GROCER'S WIFE *leaves; the stage is empty for a few moments.*

JEAN *enters right, at the same time as* BERENGER *enters left.* JEAN *is very fastidiously dressed: brown suit, red tie, stiff collar, brown hat. He has a reddish face. His shoes are yellow and well-polished.* BERENGER *is unshaven and hatless, with unkempt hair and creased clothes; everything about him indicates negligence. He seems weary, half-asleep; from time to time he yawns.*

JEAN (*advancing from right*): Oh, so you managed to get here at last, Berenger!

BERENGER (*advancing from left*): Morning, Jean!

JEAN: Late as usual, of course. (*He looks at his wrist watch.*) Our appointment was for 11:30. And now it's practically mid-day.

BERENGER: I'm sorry. Have you been waiting long?

JEAN: No, I've only just arrived myself, as you saw.

They go and sit at one of the tables on the café terrace.

BERENGER: In that case I don't feel so bad, if you've only just . . .

JEAN: It's different with me. I don't like waiting; I've no time to waste. And as you're never on time, I come late on purpose—at a time when I presume you'll be there.

BERENGER: You're right . . . quite right, but . . .

JEAN: Now don't try to pretend you're ever on time!

BERENGER: No, of course not . . . I wouldn't say that.

JEAN *and* BERENGER *have sat down.*

JEAN: There you are, you see!

BERENGER: What are you drinking?

JEAN: You mean to say you've got a thirst even at this time in the morning?

BERENGER: It's so hot and dry.

JEAN: The more you drink the thirstier you get, popular science tells us that . . .

BERENGER: It would be less dry, and we'd be less thirsty, if they'd invent us some scientific clouds in the sky.

JEAN (*studying* BERENGER *closely*): That wouldn't help you any. You're not thirsty for water, Berenger . . .

BERENGER: I don't understand what you mean.

JEAN: You know perfectly well what I mean. I'm talking about your parched throat. That's a territory that can't get enough!

BERENGER: To compare my throat to a piece of land seems . . .

JEAN (*interrupting him*): You're in a bad way, my friend.

BERENGER: In a bad way? You think so?

JEAN: I'm not blind, you know. You're dropping with fatigue. You've gone without your sleep again, you yawn all the time, you're dead-tired . . .

BERENGER: There is something the matter with my hair . . .

JEAN: You reek of alcohol.

BERENGER: I have got a bit of a hang-over, it's true!

JEAN: It's the same every Sunday morning—not to mention the other days of the week.

BERENGER: Oh no, it's less frequent during the week, because of the office . . .

JEAN: And what's happened to your tie? Lost it during your orgy, I suppose!

BERENGER (*putting his hand to his neck*) : You're right. That's funny! Whatever could I have done with it?

JEAN (*taking a tie out of his coat pocket*) : Here, put this one on.

BERENGER: Oh thank you, that is kind. (*He puts on the tie.*)

JEAN (*while* BERENGER *is unskilfully tying his tie*) : Your hair's all over the place.

BERENGER *runs his fingers through his hair.*

Here, here's a comb! (*He takes a comb from his other pocket.*)

BERENGER (*taking the comb*) : Thank you. (*He vaguely combs his hair.*)

JEAN: You haven't even shaved! Just take a look at yourself!

He takes a mirror from his inside pocket, hands it to BERENGER, *who looks at himself; as he does so, he examines his tongue.*

BERENGER: My tongue's all coated.

JEAN (*taking the mirror and putting it back in his pocket*) : I'm not surprised! (*He takes back the comb as well, which* BERENGER *offers to him, and puts it in his pocket.*) You're heading for cirrhosis, my friend.

BERENGER (*worried*) : Do you think so?

JEAN (*to* BERENGER, *who wants to give him back his tie*) : Keep the tie, I've got plenty more.

BERENGER (*admiringly*) : You always look so immaculate.

JEAN (*continuing his inspection of* BERENGER) : Your clothes are all crumpled, they're a disgrace! Your shirt is downright filthy, and your shoes . . . (BERENGER *tries to hide his feet under the table.*) Your shoes haven't been touched. What a mess you're in! And look at your shoulders . . .

BERENGER: What's the matter with my shoulders?

JEAN: Turn round! Come on, turn round! You've been leaning against some wall. (BERENGER *holds his hand out docilely to*

JEAN.) No, I haven't got a brush with me; it would make my pockets bulge. (*Still docile,* BERENGER *flicks his shoulders to get rid of the white dust;* JEAN *averts his head.*) Heavens! Where did you get all that from?

BERENGER: I don't remember.

JEAN: It's a positive disgrace! I feel ashamed to be your friend.

BERENGER: You're very hard on me . . .

JEAN: I've every reason to be.

BERENGER: Listen, Jean. There are so few distractions in this town— I get so bored. I'm not made for the work I'm doing . . . every day at the office, eight hours a day—and only three weeks' holiday a year! When Saturday night comes round I feel exhausted and so—you know how it is—just to relax . . .

JEAN: My dear man, everybody has to work. I spend eight hours a day in the office the same as everyone else. And I only get three weeks off a year, but even so you don't catch me . . . Will-power, my good man!

BERENGER: But everybody hasn't got as much will-power as you have. I can't get used to it. I just can't get used to life.

JEAN: Everybody has to get used to it. Or do you consider yourself some superior being?

BERENGER: I don't pretend to be . . .

JEAN (*interrupting him*): I'm just as good as you are; I think with all due modesty I may say I'm better. The superior man is the man who fulfils his duty.

BERENGER: What duty?

JEAN: His duty . . . His duty as an employee, for example.

BERENGER: Oh yes, his duty as an employee . . .

JEAN: Where did your debauch take place last night? If you can remember!

BERENGER: We were celebrating Auguste's birthday, our friend Auguste . . .

JEAN: Our friend Auguste? Nobody invited me to our friend Auguste's birthday . . .

At this moment a noise is heard, far off, but swiftly approaching, of a beast panting in its headlong course, and of a long trumpeting.

BERENGER: I couldn't refuse. It wouldn't have been nice . . .

JEAN: Did I go there?

BERENGER: Well, perhaps it was because you weren't invited.

WAITRESS (*coming out of café*): Good morning, gentlemen. Can I get you something to drink?

The noise becomes very loud.

JEAN (*to* BERENGER, *almost shouting to make himself heard above the noise which he has not become conscious of*): True, I was not invited. That honour was denied me. But in any case, I can assure you, that even if I had been invited, I would not have gone, because...

The noise has become intense.

What's going on?

The noise of a powerful, heavy animal, galloping at great speed is heard very close; the sound of panting.

Whatever is it?

WAITRESS: Whatever is it?

> BERENGER, *still listless without appearing to hear anything at all, replies tranquilly to* JEAN *about the invitation; his lips move but one doesn't hear what he says;* JEAN *bounds to his feet, knocking his chair over as he does so, looks off left pointing, whilst* BERENGER, *still a little dopey, remains seated.*

JEAN: Oh, a rhinoceros!

The noise made by the animal dies away swiftly and one can already hear the following words. The whole of this scene must be played very fast, each repeating in swift succession: 'Oh, a rhinoceros!'

WAITRESS: Oh, a rhinoceros!

GROCER'S WIFE (*sticks her head out of her shop doorway*): Oh, a rhinoceros! (*To her husband still inside the shop.*) Quick, come and look; it's a rhinoceros!

They are all looking off left after the animal.

JEAN: It's rushing straight ahead, brushing up against the shop windows.
GROCER (*in his shop*) : Whereabouts?
WAITRESS (*putting her hands on her hips*) : Well!
GROCER'S WIFE (*to her husband who is still in shop*) : Come and look!

At this moment the GROCER puts his head out.

GROCER: Oh, a rhinoceros!
LOGICIAN (*entering quickly left*) : A rhinoceros going full-tilt on the opposite pavement!

> *All these speeches from the time when JEAN says 'Oh, a rhinoceros' are practically simultaneous. A woman is heard crying 'Ah!' She appears. She runs to the centre-stage; it is a HOUSEWIFE with a basket on her arm; once arrived centre-stage she drops her basket; the contents scatter all over the stage, a bottle breaks, but she does not drop her cat.*

HOUSEWIFE: Ah! Oh!

> *An elegant OLD GENTLEMAN comes from left stage, after the HOUSEWIFE, rushes into the GROCER's shop, knocks into the GROCER and his WIFE, whilst the LOGICIAN installs himself against the back wall on the left of the grocery entrance. JEAN and the WAITRESS, standing, and BERENGER, still apathetically seated, together form another group. At the same time, coming from the left, cries of 'Oh' and 'Ah' and the noise of people running have been heard. The dust raised by the animal spreads over the stage.*

CAFÉ PROPRIETOR (*sticking his head out of the first-floor window*) : What's going on?
OLD GENTLEMAN (*disappearing behind the GROCER and his WIFE*) : Excuse me, please!

> *The OLD GENTLEMAN is elegantly dressed, with white spats, a soft hat and an ivory-handled cane; the LOGICIAN, propped up*

*against the wall has a little grey moustache, an eyeglass, and is
wearing a straw hat.*

GROCER'S WIFE (*jostled and jostling her husband; to the* OLD GENTLE-
MAN) : Watch out with that stick!

GROCER: Look where you're going, can't you!

The head of the OLD GENTLEMAN *is seen behind the* GROCER
and his WIFE.

WAITRESS (*to the* PROPRIETOR) : A rhinoceros!

PROPRIETOR (*to the* WAITRESS *from his window*) : You're seeing things.
(*He sees the rhinoceros.*) Well, I'll be . . . !

HOUSEWIFE: Ah!

*The 'Ohs' and 'Ahs' from off-stage form a background accom-
paniment to her 'Ah.' She has dropped her basket, her provisions and the bottle, but has nevertheless kept tight hold of
her cat which she carries under her other arm.*

There, they frightened the poor pussy!

PROPRIETOR (*still looking off left, following the distant course of the
animal as the noises fade; hooves, trumpetings, etc.*):

BERENGER *sleepily averts his head a little on account of the
dust, but says nothing; he simply makes a grimace.*

Well, of all things!

JEAN (*also averting his head a little, but very much awake*) : Well, of
all things! (*He sneezes.*)

HOUSEWIFE (*she is centre-stage but turned towards left; her provisions
scattered on the ground round her*): Well of all things! (*She
sneezes.*)

The OLD GENTLEMAN, GROCER'S WIFE *and* GROCER *up-stage re-
opening the glass door of the* GROCER'S *shop that the* OLD GEN-
TLEMAN *has closed behind him.*

ALL THREE: Well, of all things!

JEAN: Well, of all things! (*To* BERENGER.) Did you see that?

The noise of the rhinoceros and its trumpeting are now far away; the people are still staring after the animal, all except for BERENGER *who is still apathetically seated.*

ALL (*except* BERENGER) : Well, of all things!

BERENGER (*to* JEAN) : It certainly looked as if it was a rhinoceros. It made plenty of dust. (*He takes out a handkerchief and blows his nose.*)

HOUSEWIFE: Well, of all things! Gave me such a scare.

GROCER (*to the* HOUSEWIFE) : Your basket . . . and all your things . . .

OLD GENTLEMAN *approaching the lady and bending to pick up her things scattered about the stage. He greets her gallantly, raising his hat.*

PROPRIETOR: Really, these days, you never know . . .

WAITRESS: Fancy that!

OLD GENTLEMAN (*to the* HOUSEWIFE) : May I help you pick up your things?

HOUSEWIFE (*to the* OLD GENTLEMAN) : Thank you, how very kind! Do put on your hat. Oh, it gave me such a scare!

LOGICIAN: Fear is an irrational thing. It must yield to reason.

WAITRESS: It's already out of sight.

OLD GENTLEMAN (*to the* HOUSEWIFE *and indicating the* LOGICIAN) : My friend is a logician.

JEAN (*to* BERENGER) : Well, what did you think of that?

WAITRESS: Those animals can certainly travel!

HOUSEWIFE (*to the* LOGICIAN): Very happy to meet you!

GROCER'S WIFE (*to the* GROCER) : That'll teach her to buy her things from somebody else!

JEAN (*to the* PROPRIETOR *and the* WAITRESS): What did you think of that?

HOUSEWIFE: I still didn't let my cat go.

PROPRIETOR (*shrugging his shoulders, at window*) : You don't often see that!

HOUSEWIFE (*to the* LOGICIAN *and the* OLD GENTLEMAN *who is picking up her provisions*): Would you hold him a moment!

WAITRESS (*to* JEAN) : First time I've seen that!

LOGICIAN (*to the* HOUSEWIFE, *taking the cat in his arms*) : It's not spiteful, is it?

PROPRIETOR (*to* JEAN) : Went past like a comet!

HOUSEWIFE (*to the* LOGICIAN) : He wouldn't hurt a fly. (*To the others.*) What happened to my wine?

GROCER (*to the* HOUSEWIFE) : I've got plenty more.

JEAN (*to* BERENGER) : Well, what did you think of that?

GROCER (*to the* HOUSEWIFE) : And good stuff, too!

PROPRIETOR (*to the* WAITRESS): Don't hang about! Look after these gentlemen! (*He indicates* BERENGER *and* JEAN. *He withdraws.*)

BERENGER (*to* JEAN) : What did I think of what?

GROCER'S WIFE (*to the* GROCER) : Go and get her another bottle!

JEAN (*to* BERENGER) : Of the rhinoceros, of course! What did you think I meant?

GROCER (*to the* HOUSEWIFE) : I've got some first-class wine, in unbreakable bottles! (*He disappears into his shop.*)

LOGICIAN (*stroking the cat in his arms*) : Puss, puss, puss.

WAITRESS (*to* BERENGER *and* JEAN) : What are you drinking?

BERENGER: Two pastis.

WAITRESS: Two pastis—right! (*She walks to the café entrance.*)

HOUSEWIFE (*picking up her things with the help of the* OLD GENTLEMAN) : Very kind of you, I'm sure.

WAITRESS: Two pastis! (*She goes into café.*)

OLD GENTLEMAN (*to the* HOUSEWIFE) : Oh, please don't mention it, it's a pleasure.

The GROCER'S WIFE *goes into shop.*

LOGICIAN (*to the* OLD GENTLEMAN *and the* HOUSEWIFE *picking up the provisions*) : Replace them in an orderly fashion.

JEAN (*to* BERENGER) : Well, what did you think about it?

BERENGER (*to* JEAN, *not knowing what to say*) : Well...nothing...it made a lot of dust...

GROCER (*coming out of shop with a bottle of wine; to the* HOUSEWIFE) : I've some good leeks as well.

LOGICIAN (*still stroking the cat*): Puss, puss, puss.

GROCER (*to the* HOUSEWIFE) : It's a hundred francs a litre.

HOUSEWIFE (*paying the* GROCER, *then to the* OLD GENTLEMAN *who has managed to put everything back in the basket*): Oh, you are kind! Such a pleasure to come across the old French courtesy. Not like the young people today!

GROCER (*taking money*): You should buy from me. You wouldn't even have to cross the street, and you wouldn't run the risk of these accidents. (*He goes back into his shop.*)

JEAN (*who has sat down and is still thinking of the rhinoceros*) : But you must admit it's extraordinary.

OLD GENTLEMAN (*taking off his hat, and kissing the* HOUSEWIFE'S *hand*) : It was a great pleasure to meet you!

HOUSEWIFE (*to the* LOGICIAN) : Thank you very much for holding my cat.

> The LOGICIAN *gives the* HOUSEWIFE *back her cat. The* WAITRESS *comes back with drinks.*

WAITRESS: Two pastis!

JEAN (*to* BERENGER) : You're incorrigible!

OLD GENTLEMAN (*to the* HOUSEWIFE) : May I accompany you part of the way?

BERENGER (*to* JEAN, *and pointing to the* WAITRESS *who goes back into the café*) : I asked for mineral water. She's made a mistake.

> JEAN, *scornful and disbelieving, shrugs his shoulders.*

HOUSEWIFE (*to the* OLD GENTLEMAN): My husband's waiting for me, thank you. Perhaps some other time . . .

OLD GENTLEMAN (*to the* HOUSEWIFE) : I sincerely hope so, Madame.

HOUSEWIFE (*to the* OLD GENTLEMAN): So do I! (*She gives him a sweet look as she leaves left.*)

BERENGER: The dust's settled . . .

> JEAN *shrugs his shoulders again.*

OLD GENTLEMAN (*to the* LOGICIAN, *and looking after the* HOUSEWIFE) : Delightful creature!

JEAN (*to* BERENGER) : A rhinoceros! I can't get over it!

> The OLD GENTLEMAN *and the* LOGICIAN *move slowly right and off. They chat amiably.*

OLD GENTLEMAN (*to the* LOGICIAN, *after casting a last fond look after the* HOUSEWIFE) : Charming, isn't she?

LOGICIAN (*to the* OLD GENTLEMAN) : I'm going to explain to you what a syllogism is.

OLD GENTLEMAN: Ah yes, a syllogism.

JEAN (*to* BERENGER): I can't get over it! It's unthinkable!

BERENGER *yawns.*

LOGICIAN: A syllogism consists of a main proposition, a secondary one, and a conclusion.

OLD GENTLEMAN: What conclusion?

The LOGICIAN *and the* OLD GENTLEMAN *go out.*

JEAN: I just can't get over it.

BERENGER: Yes, I can see you can't. Well, it was a rhinoceros—all right, so it was a rhinoceros! It's miles away by now ... miles away ...

JEAN: But you must see it's fantastic! A rhinoceros loose in the town, and you don't bat an eyelid! It shouldn't be allowed!

BERENGER *yawns.*

Put your hand in front of your mouth!

BERENGER: Yais ... yais ... It shouldn't be allowed. It's dangerous. I hadn't realized. But don't worry about it, it won't get us here.

JEAN: We ought to protest to the Town Council! What's the Council there for?

BERENGER (*yawning, then quickly putting his hand to his mouth*): Oh excuse me ... perhaps the rhinoceros escaped from the zoo.

JEAN: You're day-dreaming.

BERENGER: But I'm wide awake.

JEAN: Awake or asleep, it's the same thing.

BERENGER: But there is some difference.

JEAN: That's not the point.

BERENGER: But you just said being awake and being asleep were the same thing ...

JEAN: You didn't understand. There's no difference between dreaming awake and dreaming asleep.

BERENGER: I do dream. Life is a dream.

JEAN: You're certainly dreaming when you say the rhinoceros escaped from the zoo ...

BERENGER: I only said: perhaps.

JEAN: ... because there's been no zoo in our town since the animals were destroyed in the plague ... ages ago ...

BERENGER (*with the same indifference*): Then perhaps it came from a circus.

JEAN: What circus are you talking about?

BERENGER: I don't know ... some travelling circus.

JEAN: You know perfectly well that the Council banned all travelling performers from the district ... There haven't been any since we were children.

BERENGER (*trying unsuccessfully to stop yawning*): In that case, maybe it's been hiding ever since in the surrounding swamps?

JEAN: The surrounding swamps! The surrounding swamps! My poor friend, you live in a thick haze of alcohol.

BERENGER (*naïvely*): That's very true ... it seems to mount from my stomach ...

JEAN: It's clouding your brain! Where do you know of any surrounding swamps? Our district is known as 'little Castille' because the land is so arid.

BERENGER (*surfeited and pretty weary*): How do I know, then? Perhaps it's been hiding under a stone? ... Or maybe it's been nesting on some withered branch?

JEAN: If you think you're being witty, you're very much mistaken! You're just being a bore with ... with your stupid paradoxes. You're incapable of talking seriously!

BERENGER: Today, yes, only today ... because of ... because of ... (*He indicates his head with a vague gesture.*)

JEAN: Today the same as any other day!

BERENGER: Oh, not quite as much.

JEAN: Your witticisms are not very inspired.

BERENGER: I wasn't trying to be ...

JEAN (*interrupting him*): I can't bear people to try and make fun of me!

BERENGER (*hand on his heart*): But my dear Jean, I'd never allow myself to ...

JEAN (*interrupting him*): My dear Berenger, you are allowing yourself ...

BERENGER: Oh no, never. I'd never allow myself to.

JEAN: Yes, you would; you've just done so.

BERENGER: But how could you possibly think ...

JEAN (*interrupting him*): I think what is true!

BERENGER: But I assure you ...

JEAN (*interrupting him*): ... that you were making fun of me!

BERENGER: You really can be obstinate, sometimes.

JEAN: And now you're calling me a mule into the bargain. Even you must see how insulting you're being.

BERENGER: It would never have entered my mind.

JEAN: You have no mind!

BERENGER: All the more reason why it would never enter it.

JEAN: There are certain things which enter the minds of even people without one.

BERENGER: That's impossible.

JEAN: And why, pray, is it impossible?

BERENGER: Because it's impossible.

JEAN: Then kindly explain to me why it's impossible, as you seem to imagine you can explain everything.

BERENGER: I don't imagine anything of the kind.

JEAN: Then why do you act as if you do? And, I repeat, why are you being so insulting to me?

BERENGER: I'm not insulting you. Far from it. You know what tremendous respect I have for you.

JEAN: In that case, why do you contradict me, making out that it's not dangerous to let a rhinoceros go racing about in the middle of the town—particularly on a Sunday morning when the streets are full of children . . . and adults, too . . .

BERENGER: A lot of them are in church. They don't run any risk . . .

JEAN (*interrupting him*): If you will allow me to finish . . . and at market time, too.

BERENGER: I never said it wasn't dangerous to let a rhinoceros go racing about the town. I simply said I'd personally never considered the danger. It had never crossed my mind.

JEAN: You never consider anything.

BERENGER: All right, I agree. A rhinoceros roaming about is not a good thing.

JEAN: It shouldn't be allowed.

BERENGER: I agree. It shouldn't be allowed. It's a ridiculous thing all right! But it's no reason for you and me to quarrel. Why go on at me just because some wretched perissodactyle happens to pass by. A stupid quadruped not worth talking about. And ferocious into the bargain. And which has already disappeared, which doesn't exist any longer. We're not going to bother about some animal that doesn't exist. Let's talk about something else, Jean, please; (*He yawns.*) there are plenty of other subjects for conversation. (*He takes his glass.*) To you!

At this moment the LOGICIAN *and the* OLD GENTLEMAN *come back on stage from left; they walk over, talking as they go, to one of the tables on the café terrace, some distance from* BERENGER *and* JEAN, *behind and to the right of them.*

JEAN: Put that glass back on the table! You're not to drink it.

JEAN takes a large swallow from his own pastis and puts back the glass, half-empty, on the table. BERENGER *continues to hold his glass, without putting it down, and without daring to drink from it either.*

BERENGER (*timidly*): There's no point in leaving it for the proprietor. (*He makes as if to drink.*)
JEAN: Put it down, I tell you!
BERENGER: Very well.

He is putting the glass back on the table when DAISY *passes. She is a young blonde typist and she crosses the stage from right to left. When he sees her,* BERENGER *rises abruptly, and in doing so makes an awkward movement; the glass falls and splashes* JEAN's *trousers.*

Oh, there's Daisy!
JEAN: Look out! How clumsy you are!
BERENGER: That's Daisy ... I'm so sorry ... (*He hides himself out of sight of* DAISY.) I don't want her to see me in this state.
JEAN: Your behaviour's unforgivable, absolutely unforgivable! (*He looks in the direction of* DAISY, *who is just disappearing.*) Why are you afraid of that young girl?
BERENGER: Oh, be quiet, please be quiet!
JEAN: She doesn't look an unpleasant person!
BERENGER (*coming back to* JEAN, *now that* DAISY *has gone*): I must apologize once more for ...
JEAN: You see what comes of drinking, you can no longer control your movements, you've no strength left in your hands, you're

besotted and fagged out. You're digging your own grave, my friend, you're destroying yourself.

BERENGER: I don't like the taste of alcohol much. And yet if I don't drink, I'm done for; it's as if I'm frightened, and so I drink not to be frightened any longer.

JEAN: Frightened of what?

BERENGER: I don't know exactly. It's a sort of anguish difficult to describe. I feel out of place in life, among people, and so I take to drink. That calms me down and relaxes me so I can forget.

JEAN: You try to escape from yourself!

BERENGER: I'm so tired, I've been tired for years. It's exhausting to drag the weight of my own body about . . .

JEAN: That's alcoholic neurasthenia, drinker's gloom . . .

BERENGER (*continuing*): I'm conscious of my body all the time, as if it were made of lead, or as if I were carrying another man around on my back. I can't seem to get used to myself. I don't even know if I *am* me. Then as soon as I take a drink, the lead slips away and I recognize myself, I become me again.

JEAN: That's just being fanciful. Look at me, Berenger, I weigh more than you do. And yet I feel light, light as a feather! (*He flaps his arms as if about to fly. The* OLD GENTLEMAN *and the* LOGICIAN *have come back and have taken a few steps on stage deep in talk. At this moment they are passing by* JEAN *and* BERENGER. JEAN'S *arm deals the* OLD GENTLEMAN *a sharp knock which precipitates him into the arms of the* LOGICIAN.)

LOGICIAN: An example of a syllogism . . . (*He is knocked.*) Oh!

OLD GENTLEMAN (*to* JEAN): Look out! (*To the* LOGICIAN.) I'm so sorry.

JEAN (*to the* OLD GENTLEMAN): I'm so sorry.

LOGICIAN (*to the* OLD GENTLEMAN): No harm done.

OLD GENTLEMAN (*to* JEAN): No harm done.

> *The* OLD GENTLEMAN *and the* LOGICIAN *go and sit at one of the terrace tables a little to the right and behind* JEAN *and* BERENGER.

BERENGER (*to* JEAN): You certainly are strong.

JEAN: Yes, I'm strong. I'm strong for several reasons. In the first place I'm strong because I'm naturally strong, and secondly I'm strong because I have moral strength. I'm also strong because I'm not riddled with alcohol. I don't wish to offend you, my dear Berenger, but I feel I must tell you that it's alcohol which weighs so heavy on you.

LOGICIAN (*to the* OLD GENTLEMAN) : Here is an example of a syllogism. The cat has four paws. Isidore and Fricot both have four paws. Therefore Isidore and Fricot are cats.

OLD GENTLEMAN (*to the* LOGICIAN) : My dog has got four paws.

LOGICIAN (*to the* OLD GENTLEMAN) : Then it's a cat.

BERENGER (*to* JEAN) : I've barely got the strength to go on living. Maybe I don't even want to.

OLD GENTLEMAN (*to the* LOGICIAN, *after deep reflection*) : So then logically speaking, my dog must be a cat?

LOGICIAN (*to the* OLD GENTLEMAN) : Logically, yes. But the contrary is also true.

BERENGER (*to* JEAN) : Solitude seems to oppress me. And so does the company of other people.

JEAN (*to* BERENGER) : You contradict yourself. What oppresses you— solitude, or the company of others? You consider yourself a thinker, yet you're devoid of logic.

OLD GENTLEMAN (*to the* LOGICIAN) : Logic is a very beautiful thing.

LOGICIAN (*to the* OLD GENTLEMAN) : As long as it is not abused.

BERENGER (*to* JEAN) : Life is an abnormal business.

JEAN: On the contrary. Nothing could be more natural, and the proof is that people go on living.

BERENGER: There are more dead people than living. And their numbers are increasing. The living are getting rarer.

JEAN: The dead don't exist, there's no getting away from that!... Ah! Ah...! (*He gives a huge laugh.*) Yet you're oppressed by them, too? How can you be oppressed by something that doesn't exist?

BERENGER: I sometimes wonder if I exist myself.

JEAN: You don't exist, my dear Berenger, because you don't think. Start thinking, then you will.

LOGICIAN (*to the* OLD GENTLEMAN) : Another syllogism. All cats die. Socrates is dead. Therefore Socrates is a cat.

OLD GENTLEMAN: And he's got four paws. That's true. I've got a cat named Socrates.

LOGICIAN: There you are, you see ...

JEAN (*to* BERENGER) : Fundamentally you're just a bluffer. And a liar.

You say that life doesn't interest you. And yet there's somebody who does.

BERENGER: Who?

JEAN: Your little friend from the office who just went past. You're very fond of her!

OLD GENTLEMAN (*to the* LOGICIAN) : So Socrates was a cat, was he?

LOGICIAN: Logic has just revealed the fact to us.

JEAN (*to* BERENGER) : You didn't want her to see you in your present state. (BERENGER *makes a gesture.*) That proves you're not indifferent to everything. But how can you expect Daisy to be attracted to a drunkard?

LOGICIAN (*to the* OLD GENTLEMAN) : Let's get back to our cats.

OLD GENTLEMAN (*to the* LOGICIAN) : I'm all ears.

BERENGER (*to* JEAN) : In any case, I think she's already got her eye on someone.

JEAN: Oh, who?

BERENGER: Dudard. An office colleague, qualified in law, with a big future in the firm—and in Daisy's affections. I can't hope to compete with him.

LOGICIAN (*to the* OLD GENTLEMAN) : The cat Isidore has four paws.

OLD GENTLEMAN: How do you know?

LOGICIAN: It's stated in the hypothesis.

BERENGER (*to* JEAN) : The Chief thinks a lot of him. Whereas I've no future, I've no qualifications. I don't stand a chance.

OLD GENTLEMAN (*to the* LOGICIAN) : Ah! In the hypothesis.

JEAN (*to* BERENGER): So you're giving up, just like that . . . ?

BERENGER: What else can I do?

LOGICIAN (*to the* OLD GENTLEMAN) : Fricot also has four paws. So how many paws have Fricot and Isidore?

OLD GENTLEMAN: Separately or together?

JEAN (*to* BERENGER) : Life is a struggle, it's cowardly not to put up a fight!

LOGICIAN (*to the* OLD GENTLEMAN) : Separately or together, it all depends.

BERENGER (*to* JEAN) : What can I do? I've nothing to put up a fight with.

JEAN: Then find yourself some weapons, my friend.

OLD GENTLEMAN (*to the* LOGICIAN, *after painful reflection*) : Eight, eight paws.

LOGICIAN: Logic involves mental arithmetic, you see.

OLD GENTLEMAN: It certainly has many aspects!

BERENGER (*to* JEAN) : Where can I find the weapons?

LOGICIAN (*to the* OLD GENTLEMAN) : There are no limits to logic.

JEAN: Within yourself. Through your own will.

BERENGER: What weapons?

LOGICIAN (*to the* OLD GENTLEMAN): I'm going to show you . . .

JEAN (*to* BERENGER) : The weapons of patience and culture, the weapons of the mind. (BERENGER *yawns.*) Turn yourself into a keen and brilliant intellect. Get yourself up to the mark!

BERENGER: How do I get myself up to the mark?

LOGICIAN (*to the* OLD GENTLEMAN) : If I take two paws away from these cats—how many does each have left?

OLD GENTLEMAN: That's not so easy.

BERENGER (*to* JEAN) : That's not so easy.

LOGICIAN (*to the* OLD GENTLEMAN) : On the contrary, it's simple.

OLD GENTLEMAN (*to the* LOGICIAN) : It may be simple for you, but not for me.

BERENGER (*to* JEAN) : It may be simple for you, but not for me.

LOGICIAN (*to the* OLD GENTLEMAN) : Come on, exercise your mind. Concentrate!

JEAN (*to* BERENGER) : Come on, exercise your will. Concentrate!

OLD GENTLEMAN (*to the* LOGICIAN) : I don't see how.

BERENGER (*to* JEAN) : I really don't see how.

LOGICIAN (*to the* OLD GENTLEMAN) : You have to be told everything.

JEAN (*to* BERENGER) : You have to be told everything.

LOGICIAN (*to the* OLD GENTLEMAN) : Take a sheet of paper and calculate. If you take six paws from the two cats, how many paws are left to each cat?

OLD GENTLEMAN: Just a moment . . . (*He calculates on a sheet of paper which he takes from his pocket.*)

JEAN: This is what you must do: dress yourself properly, shave every day, put on a clean shirt.

BERENGER: The laundry's so expensive . . .

JEAN: Cut down on your drinking. This is the way to come out: wear a hat, a tie like this, a well-cut suit, shoes well polished. (*As he mentions the various items of clothing he points self-contentedly to his own hat, tie and shoes.*)

OLD GENTLEMAN (*to the* LOGICIAN) : There are several possible solutions.

LOGICIAN (*to the* OLD GENTLEMAN) : Tell me.

BERENGER (*to* JEAN): Then what do I do? Tell me . . .

LOGICIAN (*to the* OLD GENTLEMAN) : I'm listening.

BERENGER (*to* JEAN) : I'm listening.

JEAN: You're a timid creature, but not without talent.

BERENGER: I've got talent, me?

JEAN: So use it. Put yourself in the picture. Keep abreast of the cultural and literary events of the times.

OLD GENTLEMAN (*to the* LOGICIAN) : One possibility is: one cat could have four paws and the other two.

BERENGER (*to* JEAN) : I get so little spare time!

LOGICIAN (*to the* OLD GENTLEMAN) : You're not without talent. You just needed to exercise it.

JEAN: Take advantage of what free time you *do* have. Don't just let yourself drift.

OLD GENTLEMAN: I've never had the time. I was an official, you know.

LOGICIAN: One can always find time to learn.

JEAN (*to* BERENGER) : One can always find time.

BERENGER (*to* JEAN) : It's too late now.

OLD GENTLEMAN (*to the* LOGICIAN) : It's a bit late in the day for me.

JEAN (*to* BERENGER) : It's never too late.

LOGICIAN (*to the* OLD GENTLEMAN) : It's never too late.

JEAN (*to* BERENGER) : You work eight hours a day, like me and everybody else, but not on Sundays, nor in the evening, nor for three weeks in the summer. That's quite sufficient, with a little method.

LOGICIAN (*to the* OLD GENTLEMAN) : Well, what about the other solutions? Use a little method, a little method!

The OLD GENTLEMAN *starts to calculate anew.*

JEAN (*to* BERENGER) : Look, instead of drinking and feeling sick, isn't it better to be fresh and eager, even at work? And you can spend your free time constructively.

BERENGER: How do you mean?

JEAN: By visiting museums, reading literary periodicals, going to lectures. That'll solve your troubles, it will develop your mind. In four weeks you'll be a cultured man.

BERENGER: You're right!

OLD GENTLEMAN (*to the* LOGICIAN): There could be one cat with five paws . . .

JEAN (*to* BERENGER) : You see, you even think so yourself!

OLD GENTLEMAN (*to the* LOGICIAN): And one cat with one paw. But would they still be cats, then?

LOGICIAN (*to the* OLD GENTLEMAN): Why not?

JEAN (*to* BERENGER): Instead of squandering all your spare money on drink, isn't it better to buy a ticket for an interesting play? Do you know anything about the avant-garde theatre there's so much talk about? Have you seen Ionesco's plays?

BERENGER (*to* JEAN): Unfortunately, no. I've only heard people talk about them.

OLD GENTLEMAN (*to the* LOGICIAN): By taking two of the eight paws away from the two cats . . .

JEAN (*to* BERENGER): There's one playing now. Take advantage of it.

OLD GENTLEMAN (*to the* LOGICIAN): . . . we could have one cat with six paws . . .

BERENGER: It would be an excellent initiation into the artistic life of our times.

OLD GENTLEMAN (*to the* LOGICIAN): We could have one cat with no paws at all.

BERENGER: You're right, perfectly right. I'm going to put myself into the picture, like you said.

LOGICIAN (*to the* OLD GENTLEMAN): In that case, one cat would be specially privileged.

BERENGER (*to* JEAN): I will, I promise you.

JEAN: You promise yourself, that's the main thing.

OLD GENTLEMAN: And one under-privileged cat deprived of all paws.

BERENGER: I make myself a solemn promise, I'll keep my word to myself.

LOGICIAN: That would be unjust, and therefore not logical.

BERENGER: Instead of drinking, I'll develop my mind. I feel better already. My head already feels clearer.

JEAN: You see!

OLD GENTLEMAN (*to the* LOGICIAN): Not logical?

BERENGER: This afternoon I'll go to the museum. And I'll book two seats for the theatre this evening. Will you come with me?

LOGICIAN (*to the* OLD GENTLEMAN): Because Logic means Justice.

JEAN (*to* BERENGER): You must persevere. Keep up your good resolutions.

OLD GENTLEMAN (*to the* LOGICIAN): I get it. Justice . . .

BERENGER (*to* JEAN): I promise you, and I promise myself. Will you come to the museum with me this afternoon?

JEAN (*to* BERENGER) : I have to take a rest this afternoon; it's in my programme for the day.

OLD GENTLEMAN: Justice is one more aspect of Logic.

BERENGER (*to* JEAN) : But you will come with me to the theatre this evening?

JEAN: No, not this evening.

LOGICIAN (*to the* OLD GENTLEMAN) : Your mind is getting clearer!

JEAN (*to* BERENGER) : I sincerely hope you'll keep up your good resolutions. But this evening I have to meet some friends for a drink.

BERENGER: For a drink?

OLD GENTLEMAN (*to the* LOGICIAN) : What's more, a cat with no paws at all . . .

JEAN (*to* BERENGER) : I've promised to go. I always keep my word.

OLD GENTLEMAN (*to the* LOGICIAN): . . . wouldn't be able to run fast enough to catch mice.

BERENGER (*to* JEAN) : Ah, now it's you that's setting me a bad example! You're going out drinking.

LOGICIAN (*to the* OLD GENTLEMAN) : You're already making progress in logic.

A sound of rapid galloping is heard approaching again, trumpeting and the sound of rhinoceros hooves and pantings; this time the sound comes from the opposite direction approaching from backstage to front, in the left wings.

JEAN (*furiously to* BERENGER) : It's not a habit with me, you know. It's not the same as with you. With you . . . you're . . . it's not the same thing at all . . .

BERENGER: Why isn't it the same thing?

JEAN (*shouting over the noise coming from the café*) : I'm no drunkard, not me!

LOGICIAN (*shouting to the* OLD GENTLEMAN) : Even with no paws a cat must catch mice. That's in it's nature.

BERENGER (*shouting very loudly*) : I didn't mean you were a drunkard. But why would it make me one any more than you, in a case like that?

OLD GENTLEMAN (*shouting to the* LOGICIAN) : What's in the cat's nature?

JEAN (*to* BERENGER) : Because there's moderation in all things. I'm a moderate person, not like you!

LOGICIAN (*to the* OLD GENTLEMAN, *cupping his hands to his ears*) : What did you say?

Deafening sounds drown the words of the four characters.

BERENGER (*to* JEAN, *cupping his hands to his ears*) : What about me, what? What did you say?

JEAN (*roaring*): I said that . . .

OLD GENTLEMAN (*roaring*): I said that . . .

JEAN (*suddenly aware of the noises which are now very near*) : Whatever's happening?

LOGICIAN: What is going on?

JEAN (*rises, knocking his chair over as he does so; looks towards left wings where the noises of the passing rhinoceros are coming from*): Oh, a rhinoceros!

LOGICIAN (*rising, knocking over his chair*) : Oh, a rhinoceros!

OLD GENTLEMAN (*doing the same*) : Oh, a rhinoceros!

BERENGER (*still seated, but this time, taking more notice*) : Rhinoceros! In the opposite direction!

WAITRESS (*emerging with a tray and glasses*) : What is it? Oh, a rhinoceros! (*She drops the tray, breaking the glasses.*)

PROPRIETOR (*coming out of the café*): What's going on?

WAITRESS (*to the* PROPRIETOR): A rhinoceros!

LOGICIAN: A rhinoceros, going full-tilt on the opposite pavement!

GROCER (*coming out of his shop*): Oh, a rhinoceros!

JEAN: Oh, a rhinoceros!

GROCER'S WIFE (*sticking her head through the upstairs window of shop*): Oh, a rhinoceros!

PROPRIETOR: It's no reason to break the glasses.

JEAN: It's rushing straight ahead, brushing up against the shop windows.

DAISY (*entering left*): Oh, a rhinoceros!

BERENGER (*noticing* DAISY): Oh, Daisy!

Noise of people fleeing, the same 'Ohs' and 'Ahs' as before.

WAITRESS: Well, of all things!

PROPRIETOR (*to the* WAITRESS): You'll be charged up for those!

BERENGER *tries to make himself scarce, not to be seen by* DAISY.

The OLD GENTLEMAN, *the* LOGICIAN, *the* GROCER *and his* WIFE *move to centre-stage and say together:*

ALL: Well, of all things!
JEAN *and*
BERENGER: Well, of all things!

> *A piteous mewing is heard, then an equally piteous cry of a woman.*

ALL: Oh!

> *Almost at the same time, and as the noises are rapidly dying away the* HOUSEWIFE *appears without her basket but holding the blood-stained corpse of her cat in her arms.*

HOUSEWIFE (*wailing*): It ran over my cat, it ran over my cat!
WAITRESS: It ran over her cat!

> *The* GROCER, *his* WIFE (*at the window*), *the* OLD GENTLEMAN, DAISY *and the* LOGICIAN *crowd round the* HOUSEWIFE, *saying:*

ALL: What a tragedy, poor little thing!
OLD GENTLEMAN: Poor little thing!
DAISY *and*
WAITRESS: Poor little thing!
GROCER'S WIFE (*at the window*): ⎫
OLD GENTLEMAN: ⎬ Poor little thing!
LOGICIAN: ⎭
PROPRIETOR (*to the* WAITRESS, *pointing to the broken glasses and the upturned chairs*): Don't just stand there! Clear up the mess!

> JEAN *and* BERENGER *also rush over to the* HOUSEWIFE *who continues to lament, her dead cat in her arms.*

WAITRESS (*moving to the café terrace to pick up the broken glasses and the chairs, and looking over her shoulder at the* HOUSEWIFE): Oh, poor little thing!
PROPRIETOR (*pointing, for the* WAITRESS's *benefit, to the debris*): Over there, over there!

OLD GENTLEMAN *(to the* GROCER): Well, what do you think of that?

BERENGER *(to the* HOUSEWIFE): You mustn't cry like that, it's too heart-breaking!

DAISY *(to* BERENGER): Were you there, Mr. Berenger? Did you see it?

BERENGER *(to* DAISY): Good morning, Miss Daisy, you must excuse me, I haven't had a chance to shave . . .

PROPRIETOR *(supervising the clearing up of the debris, then glancing towards the* HOUSEWIFE): Poor little thing!

WAITRESS *(clearing up the mess, her back to the* HOUSEWIFE): Poor little thing!

> *These remarks must obviously be made very rapidly, almost simultaneously.*

GROCER'S WIFE *(at window)*: That's going too far!

JEAN: That's going too far!

HOUSEWIFE *(lamenting, and cradling the dead cat in her arms)*: My poor little pussy, my poor little cat.

OLD GENTLEMAN *(to the* HOUSEWIFE): What can you do, dear lady, cats are only mortal.

LOGICIAN: What do you expect, Madame? All cats are mortal! One must accept that.

HOUSEWIFE *(lamenting)*: My little cat, my poor little cat.

PROPRIETOR *(to the* WAITRESS *whose apron is full of broken glass)*: Throw that in the dustbin! *(He has picked up the chairs.)* You owe me a thousand francs.

WAITRESS *(moving into the café)*: All you think of is money!

GROCER'S WIFE *(to the* HOUSEWIFE *from window)*: Don't upset yourself!

OLD GENTLEMAN *(to the* HOUSEWIFE): Don't upset yourself, dear lady!

GROCER'S WIFE *(from window)*: It's very upsetting a thing like that!

HOUSEWIFE: My little cat, my little cat!

DAISY: Yes, it's very upsetting a thing like that.

OLD GENTLEMAN *(supporting the* HOUSEWIFE, *and guiding her to a table on the terrace followed by the others)*: Sit down here, dear lady.

JEAN *(to the* OLD GENTLEMAN): Well, what do you think of that?

GROCER *(to the* LOGICIAN): Well, what do you think of that?

GROCER'S WIFE *(to* DAISY, *from window)*: Well, what do you think of that?

PROPRIETOR *(to the* WAITRESS, *who comes back while they are installing the weeping* HOUSEWIFE *at one of the terrace tables, still cradling her dead cat*): A glass of water for the lady.

OLD GENTLEMAN (*to the* HOUSEWIFE): Sit down, dear lady!

JEAN: Poor woman!

GROCER'S WIFE (*from window*): Poor cat!

BERENGER (*to the* WAITRESS): Better give her a brandy.

PROPRIETOR (*to the* WAITRESS): A brandy! (*Pointing to* BERENGER.) This gentleman is paying!

WAITRESS (*going into the café*): One brandy, right away!

HOUSEWIFE (*sobbing*): I don't want any, I don't want any!

GROCER: It went past my shop a little while ago.

JEAN (*to the* GROCER): It wasn't the same one!

GROCER (*to* JEAN): But I could have . . .

GROCER'S WIFE: Yes it was, it was the same one.

DAISY: Did it go past twice, then?

PROPRIETOR: I think it was the same one.

JEAN: No, it was not the same rhinoceros. The one that went by first had two horns on its nose, it was an Asiatic rhinoceros; this only had one, it was an African rhinoceros!

> *The* WAITRESS *appears with a glass of brandy and takes it to the* HOUSEWIFE.

OLD GENTLEMAN: Here's a drop of brandy to pull you together.

HOUSEWIFE (*in tears*): No . . . o . . . o . . .

BERENGER (*suddenly unnerved, to* JEAN): You're talking nonsense . . . How could you possibly tell about the horns? The animal flashed past at such speed, we hardly even saw it . . .

DAISY (*to the* HOUSEWIFE): Go on, it will do you good!

OLD GENTLEMAN (*to* BERENGER): Very true. It did go fast.

PROPRIETOR (*to the* HOUSEWIFE): Just have a taste, it's good.

BERENGER (*to* JEAN): You had no time to count its horns . . .

GROCER'S WIFE (*to the* WAITRESS, *from window*): Make her drink it.

BERENGER (*to* JEAN): What's more, it was travelling in a cloud of dust.

DAISY (*to the* HOUSEWIFE): Drink it up.

OLD GENTLEMAN (*to the* HOUSEWIFE): Just a sip, dear little lady . . . be brave . . .

> *The* WAITRESS *forces her to drink it by putting the glass to her lips; the* HOUSEWIFE *feigns refusal, but drinks all the same.*

WAITRESS: There, you see!

GROCER'S WIFE (*from her window*)

and DAISY: There, you see!

JEAN (*to* BERENGER): I don't have to grope my way through a fog. I can calculate quickly, my mind is clear!

OLD GENTLEMAN (*to the* HOUSEWIFE): Better now?

BERENGER (*to* JEAN): But it had its head thrust down.

PROPRIETOR (*to the* HOUSEWIFE): Now wasn't that good?

JEAN (*to* BERENGER): Precisely, one could see all the better.

HOUSEWIFE (*after having drunk*): My little cat!

BERENGER (*irritated*): Utter nonsense!

GROCER'S WIFE (*to the* HOUSEWIFE, *from window*): I've got another cat you can have.

JEAN (*to* BERENGER): What me? You dare to accuse me of talking nonsense?

HOUSEWIFE (*to the* GROCER'S WIFE): I'll never have another! (*She weeps, cradling her cat.*)

BERENGER (*to* JEAN): Yes, absolute, blithering nonsense!

PROPRIETER (*to the* HOUSEWIFE): You have to accept these things!

JEAN (*to* BERENGER): I've never talked nonsense in my life!

OLD GENTLEMAN (*to the* HOUSEWIFE): Try and be philosophic about it!

BERENGER (*to* JEAN): You're just a pretentious show-off— (*Raising his voice.*) a pedant!

PROPRIETOR (*to* JEAN *and* BERENGER): Now, gentlemen!

BERENGER (*to* JEAN, *continuing*): . . . and what's more, a pedant who's not certain of his facts because in the first place it's the Asiatic rhinoceros with only one horn on its nose, and it's the African with two . . .

> *The other characters leave the* HOUSEWIFE *and crowd round* JEAN *and* BERENGER *who argue at the top of their voices.*

JEAN (*to* BERENGER): You're wrong, it's the other way about!

HOUSEWIFE (*left alone*): He was so sweet!

BERENGER: Do you want to bet?

WAITRESS: They want to make a bet!

DAISY (*to* BERENGER): Don't excite yourself, Mr. Berenger.

JEAN (*to* BERENGER): I'm not betting with you. If anybody's got two horns, it's you! You Asiatic Mongol!

WAITRESS: Oh!

GROCER'S WIFE (*from window to her husband*): They're going to have a fight!

GROCER (*to his wife*): Nonsense, it's just a bet!

PROPRIETOR (*to* JEAN *and* BERENGER): We don't want any scenes here!

OLD GENTLEMAN: Now look . . . What kind of rhinoceros has one horn on its nose? (*To the* GROCER.) You're a tradesman, you should know.

GROCER'S WIFE (*to her husband*): Yes, you should know!

BERENGER (*to* JEAN): I've got no horns. And I never will have.

GROCER (*to the* OLD GENTLEMAN): Tradesmen can't be expected to know everything.

JEAN (*to* BERENGER): Oh yes, you have!

BERENGER (*to* JEAN): I'm not Asiatic either. And in any case, Asiatics are people the same as everyone else . . .

WAITRESS: Yes, Asiatics are people the same as we are . . .

OLD GENTLEMAN (*to the* PROPRIETOR): That's true!

PROPRIETOR (*to the* WAITRESS): Nobody's asking for your opinion!

DAISY (*to the* PROPRIETOR): She's right. They're people the same as we are.

The HOUSEWIFE *continues to lament throughout this discussion.*

HOUSEWIFE: He was so gentle, just like one of us.

JEAN (*beside himself*): They're yellow!

The LOGICIAN, *a little to one side between the* HOUSEWIFE *and the group which has formed round* JEAN *and* BERENGER, *follows the controversy attentively, without taking part.*

Good-bye gentlemen! (*To* BERENGER.) You, I will not deign to include!

HOUSEWIFE: He was devoted to us! (*She sobs.*)

DAISY: Now listen a moment, Mr. Berenger, and you, too, Mr. Jean . . .

OLD GENTLEMAN: I once had some friends who were Asiatics! But perhaps they weren't real ones . . .

PROPRIETOR: I've known some real ones.

WAITRESS (*to the* GROCER'S WIFE): I had an Asiatic friend once.

HOUSEWIFE (*still sobbing*): I had him when he was a little kitten.

JEAN (*still quite beside himself*): They're yellow, I tell you, bright yellow!

BERENGER (*to* JEAN): Whatever they are, you're bright red!

GROCER'S WIFE (*from window*)

and WAITRESS: Oh!

PROPRIETOR: This is getting serious!

HOUSEWIFE: He was so clean. He always used his tray.

JEAN (*to* BERENGER): If that's how you feel, it's the last time you'll see me. I'm not wasting my time with a fool like you.

HOUSEWIFE: He always made himself understood.

> JEAN *goes off right, very fast and furious . . . but doubles back before making his final exit.*

OLD GENTLEMAN (*to the* GROCER): There are white Asiatics as well, and black and blue, and even some like us.

JEAN (*to* BERENGER): You drunkard!

> *Everybody looks at him in consternation.*

BERENGER (*to* JEAN): I'm not going to stand for that!

ALL (*looking in* JEAN's *direction*): Oh!

HOUSEWIFE: He could almost talk—in fact he did.

DAISY (*to* BERENGER): You shouldn't have made him angry.

BERENGER (*to* DAISY): It wasn't my fault.

PROPRIETOR (*to the* WAITRESS): Go and get a little coffin for the poor thing . . .

OLD GENTLEMAN (*to* BERENGER): I think you're right. It's the Asiatic rhinoceros with two horns and the African with one . . .

GROCER: But he was saying the opposite.

DAISY (*to* BERENGER): You were both wrong!

OLD GENTLEMAN (*to* BERENGER): Even so, you were right.

WAITRESS (*to the* HOUSEWIFE): Come with me, we're going to put him in a little box.

HOUSEWIFE (*sobbing desperately*): No, never!

GROCER: If you don't mind my saying so, I think Mr. Jean was right.

DAISY (*turning to the* HOUSEWIFE): Now, you must be reasonable!

> DAISY *and the* WAITRESS *lead the* HOUSEWIFE, *with her dead cat, towards the café entrance.*

OLD GENTLEMAN (*to* DAISY *and the* WAITRESS): Would you like me to come with you?

GROCER: The Asiatic rhinoceros has one horn and the African rhinoceros has two. And vice versa.

DAISY (*to the* OLD GENTLEMAN): No, don't you bother.

DAISY *and the* WAITRESS *enter the café leading the inconsolable* HOUSEWIFE.

GROCER'S WIFE (*to the* GROCER, *from window*): Oh you always have to be different from everybody else!

BERENGER (*aside, whilst the others continue to discuss the horns of the rhinoceros*): Daisy was right, I should never have contradicted him.

PROPRIETOR (*to the* GROCER'S WIFE): Your husband's right, the Asiatic rhinoceros has two horns and the African one must have two, and vice versa.

BERENGER (*aside*): He can't stand being contradicted. The slightest disagreement makes him fume.

OLD GENTLEMAN (*to the* PROPRIETOR): You're mistaken, my friend.

PROPRIETOR (*to the* OLD GENTLEMAN): I'm very sorry, I'm sure.

BERENGER (*aside*): His temper's his only fault.

GROCER'S WIFE (*from window, to the* OLD GENTLEMAN, *the* PROPRIETOR *and the* GROCER): Maybe they're both the same.

BERENGER (*aside*): Deep down, he's got a heart of gold; he's done me many a good turn.

PROPRIETOR (*to the* GROCER'S WIFE): If the one has two horns, then the other must have one.

OLD GENTLEMAN: Perhaps it's the other with two and the one with one.

BERENGER (*aside*): I'm sorry I wasn't more accommodating. But why is he so obstinate? I didn't want to exasperate him. (*To the others.*) He's always making fantastic statements! Always trying to dazzle people with his knowledge. He never will admit he's wrong.

OLD GENTLEMAN (*to* BERENGER): Have you any proof?

BERENGER: Proof of what?

OLD GENTLEMAN: Of the statement you made just now which started the unfortunate row with your friend.

GROCER (*to* BERENGER): Yes, have you any proof?

OLD GENTLEMAN (*to* BERENGER): How do you know that one of the two rhinoceroses has one horn and the other two? And which is which?

GROCER'S WIFE: He doesn't know any more than we do.

BERENGER: In the first place we don't know that there were two. I myself believe there was only one.

PROPRIETOR: Well, let's say there were two. Does the single-horned one come from Asia?

OLD GENTLEMAN: No. It's the one from Africa with two, I think.

PROPRIETOR: Which is two-horned?

GROCER: It's not the one from Africa.

GROCER'S WIFE: It's not easy to agree on this.

OLD GENTLEMAN: But the problem must be cleared up.

LOGICIAN (*emerging from his isolation*): Excuse me gentlemen for interrupting. But that is not the question. Allow me to introduce myself . . .

HOUSEWIFE (*coming out of the café in tears*): He's a logician.

PROPRIETOR: Oh! A logician, is he?

OLD GENTLEMAN (*introducing the* LOGICIAN *to* BERENGER): My friend, the Logician.

BERENGER: Very happy to meet you.

LOGICIAN (*continuing*): Professional Logician; my card. (*He shows his card.*)

BERENGER: It's a great honour.

GROCER: A great honour for all of us.

PROPRIETOR: Would you mind telling us then, sir, if the African rhinoceros is single-horned . . .

OLD GENTLEMAN: Or bicorned . . .

GROCER'S WIFE: And is the Asiatic rhinoceros bicorned . . .

GROCER: Or unicorned.

LOGICIAN: Exactly, that is not the question. Let me make myself clear.

GROCER: But it's still what we want to find out.

LOGICIAN: Kindly allow me to speak, gentlemen.

OLD GENTLEMAN: Let him speak!

GROCER'S WIFE (*to the* GROCER, *from window*): Give him a chance to speak.

PROPRIETOR: We're listening, sir.

LOGICIAN (*to* BERENGER): I'm addressing you in particular. And all the others present as well.

GROCER: Us as well . . .

LOGICIAN: You see, you have got away from the problem which instigated the debate. In the first place you were deliberating whether or not the rhinoceros which passed by just now was the same one that passed by earlier, or whether it was another. That is the question to decide.

BERENGER: Yes, but how?

LOGICIAN: Thus: you may have seen on two occasions a single rhinoceros bearing a single horn . . .

GROCER (*repeating the words, as if to understand better*): On two occasions a single rhinoceros . . .

PROPRIETOR (*doing the same*): Bearing a single horn . . .

LOGICIAN: . . . or you may have seen on two occasions a single rhinoceros with two horns.

OLD GENTLEMAN (*repeating the words*): A single rhinoceros with two horns on two occasions . . .

LOGICIAN: Exactly. Or again, you may have seen one rhinoceros with one horn, and then another also with a single horn.

GROCER'S WIFE (*from window*): Ha, ha . . .

LOGICIAN: Or again, an initial rhinoceros with two horns, followed by a second with two horns . . .

PROPRIETOR: That's true.

LOGICIAN: Now, if you had seen . . .

GROCER: If we'd seen . . .

OLD GENTLEMAN: Yes, if we'd seen . . .

LOGICIAN: If on the first occasion you had seen a rhinoceros with two horns . . .

PROPRIETOR: With two horns . . .

LOGICIAN: And on the second occasion, a rhinoceros with one horn . . .

GROCER: With one horn . . .

LOGICIAN: That wouldn't be conclusive either.

OLD GENTLEMAN: Even that wouldn't be conclusive.

PROPRIETOR: Why not?

GROCER'S WIFE: Oh, I don't get it at all.

GROCER: Shoo! Shoo!

> The GROCER'S WIFE *shrugs her shoulders and withdraws from her window.*

LOGICIAN: For it is possible that since its first appearance, the rhinoceros may have lost one of its horns, and that the first and second transit were still made by a single beast.

BERENGER: I see, but . . .

OLD GENTLEMAN (*interrupting* BERENGER): Don't interrupt!

LOGICIAN: It may also be that two rhinoceroses both with two horns may each have lost a horn.

OLD GENTLEMAN: That is possible.

PROPRIETOR: Yes, that's possible.

GROCER: Why not?

BERENGER: Yes, but in any case . . .

OLD GENTLEMAN (*to* BERENGER): Don't interrupt.

LOGICIAN: If you could prove that on the first occasion you saw a rhinoceros with one horn, either Asiatic or African . . .

OLD GENTLEMAN: Asiatic or African . . .

LOGICIAN: And on the second occasion a rhinoceros with two horns . . .

GROCER: One with two . . .

LOGICIAN: No matter whether African or Asiatic . . .

OLD GENTLEMAN: African or Asiatic . . .

LOGICIAN: . . . we could then conclude that we were dealing with two different rhinoceroses, for it is hardly likely that a second horn could grow sufficiently in a space of a few minutes to be visible on the nose of a rhinoceros.

OLD GENTLEMAN: It's hardly likely.

LOGICIAN (*enchanted with his discourse*): That would imply one rhinoceros either Asiatic or African . . .

OLD GENTLEMAN: Asiatic or African . . .

LOGICIAN: . . . and one rhinoceros either African or Asiatic.

PROPRIETOR: African or Asiatic.

GROCER: Er . . . yais.

LOGICIAN: For good logic cannot entertain the possibility that the same creature be born in two places at the same time . . .

OLD GENTLEMAN: Or even successively.

LOGICIAN (*to* OLD GENTLEMAN): Which was to be proved.

BERENGER (*to* LOGICIAN): That seems clear enough, but it doesn't answer the question.

LOGICIAN (*to* BERENGER, *with a knowledgeable smile*): Obviously, my dear sir, but now the problem is correctly posed.

OLD GENTLEMAN: It's quite logical. Quite logical.

LOGICIAN (*raising his hat*): Good-bye, gentlemen.

He retires, going out left, followed by the OLD GENTLEMAN.

OLD GENTLEMAN: Good-bye, gentlemen. (*He raises his hat and follows the* LOGICIAN *out.*)

GROCER: Well, it may be logical . . .

At this moment the HOUSEWIFE *comes out of the café in deep mourning, and carrying a box; she is followed by* DAISY *and the* WAITRESS *as if for a funeral. The* cortège *moves towards the right exit.*

. . . it may be logical, but are we going to stand for our cats being run down under our very eyes by one-horned rhinoceroses or two, whether they're Asiatic *or* African? (*He indicates with a theatrical gesture the* cortège *which is just leaving.*)

PROPRIETOR: He's absolutely right! We're not standing for our cats being run down by rhinoceroses or anything else!

GROCER: We're not going to stand for it!

GROCER'S WIFE (*sticking her head round the shop door, to her husband*): Are you coming in? The customers will be here any minute.

GROCER (*moving to the shop*): No, we're not standing for it.

BERENGER: I should never have quarrelled with Jean! (*To the* PROPRIETOR.) Get me a brandy! A double!

PROPRIETOR: Coming up! (*He goes into the café for the brandy.*)

BERENGER (*alone*): I never should have quarrelled with Jean. I shouldn't have got into such a rage!

The PROPRIETOR *comes out carrying a large glass of brandy.*

I feel too upset to go to the museum. I'll cultivate my mind some other time. (*He takes the glass of brandy and drinks it.*)

Curtain.

ACT TWO

SCENE ONE

A government office, or the office of a private concern—such as a large firm of law publications. Up-stage centre, a large double door, above which a notice reads: 'Chef du Service.' Up-stage left, near to the Head of the Department's door, stands DAISY's *little table with a typewriter. By the left wall, between a door which leads to the staircase and* DAISY's *table, stands another table on which the time sheets are placed, which the employees sign on arrival. The door leading to the staircase is down-stage left. The top steps of the staircase can be seen, the top of a stair-rail and a small landing. In the foreground, a table with two chairs. On the table: printing proofs, an inkwell, pens; this is the table where* BOTARD *and* BERENGER *work;* BERENGER *will sit on the left chair,* BOTARD *on the right. Near to the right wall, another bigger, rectangular table, also covered with papers, proofs, etc.*

Two more chairs stand at each end of this table—more elegant and imposing chairs. This is the table of DUDARD *and* MR. BOEUF. DUDARD *will sit on the chair next to the wall, the other employees facing him. He acts as Deputy-Head. Between the up-stage door and the right wall, there is a window. If the theatre has an orchestra pit it would be preferable to have simply a window frame in front of the stage, facing the auditorium. In the rigt-hand corner, up-stage, a coat-stand, on which grey blouses or old coats are hung. The coat-stand could also be placed down-stage, near to the right wall.*

On the walls are rows of books and dusty documents. On the back wall, left, above the shelves, there are signs: 'Jurisprudence,' 'Codes'; on the right-hand wall which can be slightly on an angle, the signs read: 'Le Journal Officiel,' 'Lois fiscales.' Above the Head of the Department's door a clock registers three minutes past nine.

When the curtain rises, DUDARD *is standing near his chair, his right profile to the auditorium; on the other side of the desk, left profile to the auditorium, is* BOTARD; *between them, also near to the desk, facing*

506

the auditorium, stands the Head of the Department; DAISY *is near to
the Chief, a little up-stage of him. She holds some sheets of typing
paper. On the table round which the three characters stand, a large
open newspaper lies on the printing proofs.*

*When the curtain rises the characters remain fixed for a few seconds
in position for the first line of dialogue. They make a* tableau vivant.
The same effect marks the beginning of the first act.

*The Head of the Department is about forty, very correctly dressed:
dark blue suit, a rosette of the Legion of Honour, starched collar,
black tie, large brown moustache. He is* MR. PAPILLON.

DUDARD, *thirty-five years old; grey suit; he wears black lustrine sleeves
to protect his coat. He may wear spectacles. He is a quite tall, young
employee with a future. If the Department Head became the Assistant
Director he would take his place:* BOTARD *does not like him.* BOTARD:
*former schoolteacher; short, he has a proud air, and wears a little
white moustache; a brisk sixty year-old: (he knows everything, understands everything, judges everything). He wears a Basque beret, and
wears a long grey blouse during working hours; spectacles on a longish
nose; a pencil behind his ear; he also wears protective sleeves at work.*
DAISY: *young blonde.*

Later, MRS. BOEUF; *a large woman of some forty to fifty years old,
tearful, and breathless.*

> *As the curtain rises, the characters therefore are standing mo-
> tionless around the table, right; the Chief with index finger
> pointing to the newspaper;* DUDARD, *with his hand extended in*
> BOTARD's *direction, seems to be saying: 'so you see!'* BOTARD,
> *hands in the pocket of his blouse, wears an incredulous smile
> and seems to say: 'You won't take me in.'* DAISY, *with her typing
> paper in her hand seems, from her look, to be supporting*
> DUDARD. *After a few brief seconds,* BOTARD *starts the attack.*

BOTARD: It's all a lot of made-up nonsense.
DAISY: But I saw it, I saw the rhinoceros!
DUDARD: It's in the paper, in black and white, you can't deny that.
BOTARD (*with an air of the greatest scorn*): Pfff!

DUDARD: It's all here; it's down here in the dead cats column! Read it for yourself, Chief.

PAPILLON: 'Yesterday, just before lunch time, in the church square of our town, a cat was trampled to death by a pachyderm.'

DAISY: It wasn't exactly in the church square.

PAPILLON: That's all it says. No other details.

BOTARD: Pfff!

DUDARD: Well, that's clear enough.

BOTARD: I never believe journalists. They're all liars. I don't need them to tell me what to think; I believe what I see with my own eyes. Speaking as a former teacher, I like things to be precise, scientifically valid; I've got a methodical mind.

DUDARD: What's a methodical mind got to do with it?

DAISY (*to* BOTARD): I think it's stated very precisely, Mr. Botard.

BOTARD: You call that precise? And what, pray, does it mean by a pachyderm? What does the editor of a dead cats column understand by a pachyderm? He doesn't say. And what does he mean by a cat?

DUDARD: Everybody knows what a cat is.

BOTARD: Does it concern a male cat or a female? What breed was it? And what colour? The colour bar is something I feel strongly about. I hate it.

PAPILLON: What has the colour bar to do with it, Mr. Botard? It's quite beside the point.

BOTARD: Please forgive me, Mr. Papillon. But you can't deny that the colour problem is one of the great stumbling blocks of our time.

DUDARD: I know that, we all know that, but it has nothing to do with . . .

BOTARD: It's not an issue to be dismissed lightly, Mr. Dudard. The course of history has shown that racial prejudice . . .

DUDARD: I tell you it doesn't enter into it.

BOTARD: I'm not so sure.

PAPILLON: The colour bar is not the issue at stake.

BOTARD: One should never miss an occasion to denounce it.

DAISY: But we told you that none of us is in favour of the colour bar. You're obscuring the issue; it's simply a question of a cat being run over by a pachyderm—in this case, a rhinoceros.

BOTARD: I'm a Northerner myself. Southerners have got too much imagination. Perhaps it was merely a flea run over by a mouse. People make mountains out of molehills.

PAPILLON (*to* DUDARD): Let us try and get things clear. Did you yourself, with your own eyes, see a rhinoceros strolling through the streets of the town?

DAISY: It didn't stroll, it ran.

DUDARD: No, I didn't see it personally. But a lot of very reliable people...!

BOTARD (*interrupting him*): It's obvious they were just making it up. You put too much trust in these journalists; they don't care what they invent to sell their wretched newspapers and please the bosses they serve! And you mean to tell me they've taken you in—you, a qualified man of law! Forgive me for laughing! Ha! Ha! Ha!

DAISY: But I saw it, I saw the rhinoceros. I'd take my oath on it.

BOTARD: Get away with you! And I thought you were a sensible girl!

DAISY: Mr. Botard, I can see straight! And I wasn't the only one; there were plenty of other people watching.

BOTARD: Pfff! They were probably watching something else! A few idlers with nothing to do, work-shy loafers!

DUDARD: It happened yesterday, Sunday.

BOTARD: I work on Sundays as well. I've no time for priests who do their utmost to get you to church, just to prevent you from working, and earning your daily bread by the sweat of your brow.

PAPILLON (*indignant*): Oh!

BOTARD: I'm sorry, I didn't mean to offend you. The fact that I despise religion doesn't mean I don't esteem it highly. (*To* DAISY.) In any case, do you know what a rhinoceros looks like?

DAISY: It's a... it's a very big, ugly animal.

BOTARD: And you pride yourself on your precise thinking! The rhinoceros, my dear young lady...

PAPILLON: There's no need to start a lecture on the rhinoceros here. We're not in school.

BOTARD: That's a pity.

> *During these last speeches* BERENGER *is seen climbing the last steps of the staircase; he opens the office door cautiously; as he does so one can read the notice on it: 'Editions de Droit.'*

PAPILLON: Well! It's gone nine, Miss Daisy; put the time sheets away. Too bad about the later-comers.

DAISY *goes to the little table, left, on which the time sheets are placed, at the same moment as* BERENGER *enters.*

BERENGER (*entering, whilst the others continue their discussion, to* DAISY): Good morning, Miss Daisy. I'm not late, am I?

BOTARD (*to* DUDARD *and* PAPILLON): I campaign against ignorance wherever I find it . . . !

DAISY (*to* BERENGER): Hurry up, Mr. Berenger.

BOTARD: . . . in palace or humble hut!

DAISY (*to* BERENGER): Quick! Sign the time sheet!

BERENGER: Oh thank you! Has the Boss arrived?

DAISY (*a finger on her lips*): Shh! Yes, he's here.

BERENGER: Here already? (*He hurries to sign the time sheet.*)

BOTARD (*continuing*): No matter where! Even in printing offices.

PAPILLON (*to* BOTARD): Mr. Botard, I consider . . .

BERENGER (*signing the sheet, to* DAISY): But it's not ten past . . .

PAPILLON (*to* BOTARD): I consider you have gone too far.

DUDARD (*to* PAPILLON): I think so too, sir.

PAPILLON (*to* BOTARD): Are you suggesting that Mr. Dudard, my colleague and yours, a law graduate and a first-class employee, is ignorant?

BOTARD: I wouldn't go so far as to say that, but the teaching you get at the university isn't up to what you get at the ordinary schools.

PAPILLON (*to* DAISY): What about that time sheet?

DAISY (*to* PAPILLON): Here it is, sir. (*She hands it to him.*)

BOTARD (*to* DUDARD): There's no clear thinking at the universities, no encouragement for practical observation.

DUDARD (*to* BOTARD): Oh come now!

BERENGER (*to* PAPILLON): Good morning, Mr. Papillon. (*He has been making his way to the coat-rack behind the Chief's back and around the group formed by the three characters; there he takes down his working overall or his well-worn coat, and hangs up his street coat in its place; he changes his coat by the coat-rack, then makes his way to his desk, from the drawer of which he takes out his black protective sleeves, etc.*) Morning, Mr. Papillon! Sorry I was almost late. Morning, Dudard! Morning, Mr. Botard.

PAPILLON: Well Berenger, did you see the rhinoceros by any chance?

BOTARD (*to* DUDARD): All you get at the universities are effete intellectuals with no practical knowledge of life.

DUDARD (*to* BOTARD): Rubbish!

BERENGER (*continuing to arrange his working equipment with excessive zeal as if to make up for his late arrival; in a natural tone to* PAPILLON): Oh yes, I saw it all right.

BOTARD (*turning round*): Pfff!

DAISY: So you see, I'm not mad after all.

BOTARD (*ironic*): Oh, Mr. Berenger says that out of chivalry—he's a very chivalrous man even if he doesn't look it.

DUDARD: What's chivalrous about saying you've seen a rhinoceros?

BOTARD: A lot—when it's said to bolster up a fantastic statement by Miss Daisy. Everybody is chivalrous to Miss Daisy, it's very understandable.

PAPILLON: Don't twist the facts, Mr. Botard. Mr. Berenger took no part in the argument. He's only just arrived.

BERENGER (*to* DAISY): But you did see it, didn't you? We both did.

BOTARD: Pfff! It's possible that Mr. Berenger thought he saw a rhinoceros. (*He makes a sign behind* BERENGER's *back to indicate he drinks.*) He's got such a vivid imagination! Anything's possible with him!

BERENGER: I wasn't alone when I saw the rhinoceros! Or perhaps there were two rhinoceroses.

BOTARD: He doesn't even know how many he saw.

BERENGER: I was with my friend Jean! And other people were there, too.

BOTARD (*to* BERENGER): I don't think you know what you're talking about.

DAISY: It was a unicorned rhinoceros.

BOTARD: Pff! They're in league, the two of them, to have us on.

DUDARD (*to* DAISY): I rather think it had two horns, from what I've heard!

BOTARD: You'd better make up your minds.

PAPILLON (*looking at the time*): That will do, gentlemen, time's getting on.

BOTARD: Did you see one rhinoceros, Mr. Berenger, or two rhinoceroses?

BERENGER: Well, it's hard to say!

BOTARD: You don't know. Miss Daisy saw one unicorned rhinoceros.

What about your rhinoceros, Mr. Berenger, if indeed there was one, did it have one horn or two?

BERENGER: Exactly, that's the whole problem.

BOTARD: And it's all very dubious.

DAISY: Oh!

BOTARD: I don't mean to be offensive. But I don't believe a word of it. No rhinoceros has ever been seen in this country!

DAISY: There's a first time for everything.

BOTARD: It has never been seen! Except in school-book illustrations. Your rhinoceroses are a flower of some washerwoman's imagination.

BERENGER: The word 'flower' applied to a rhinoceros seems a bit out of place.

DUDARD: Very true.

BOTARD (*continuing*): Your rhinoceros is a myth!

DAISY: A myth?

PAPILLON: Gentlemen I think it is high time we started to work.

BOTARD (*to* DAISY): A myth—like flying saucers.

DUDARD: But nevertheless a cat was trampled to death—that you can't deny.

BERENGER: I was a witness to that.

DUDARD (*pointing to* BERENGER): In front of witnesses.

BOTARD: Yes, and what a witness!

PAPILLON: Gentlemen, gentlemen!

BOTARD (*to* DUDARD): An example of collective psychosis, Mr. Dudard. Just like religion—the opiate of the people!

DAISY: Well I believe flying saucers exist!

BOTARD: Pfff!

PAPILLON (*firmly*): That's quite enough. There's been enough gossip! Rhinoceros or no rhinoceros, saucers or no saucers, work must go on! You're not paid to waste your time arguing about real or imaginary animals.

BOTARD: Imaginary!

DUDARD: Real!

DAISY: Very real!

PAPILLON: Gentlemen, I remind you once again that we are in working hours. I am putting an end to this futile discussion.

BOTARD (*wounded and ironic*): Very well, Mr. Papillon. You are the Chief. Your wishes are our commands.

PAPILLON: Get on, gentlemen. I don't want to be forced to make a deduction from your salaries! Mr. Dudard, how is your report on the alcoholic repression law coming along?

DUDARD: I'm just finishing it off, sir.

PAPILLON: Then do so. It's very urgent. Mr. Berenger and Mr. Botard, have you finished correcting the proofs for the wine trade control regulations?

BERENGER: Not yet, Mr. Papillon. But they're well on the way.

PAPILLON: Then finish off the corrections together. The printers are waiting. And Miss Daisy, you bring the letters to my office for signature. Hurry up and get them typed.

DAISY: Very good, Mr. Papillon.

> DAISY *goes and types at her little desk.* DUDARD *sits at his desk and starts to work.* BERENGER *and* BOTARD *sit at their little tables in profile to the auditorium.* BOTARD, *his back to the staircase, seems in a bad temper.* BERENGER *is passive and limp; he spreads the proofs on the table, passes the manuscript to* BOTARD; BOTARD *sits down grumbling, whilst* PAPILLON *exits banging the door loudly.*

PAPILLON: I shall see you shortly, gentlemen. (*Goes out.*)

BERENGER (*reading and correcting whilst* BOTARD *checks the manuscript with a pencil*): Laws relating to the control of proprietary wine produce . . . (*He corrects.*) control with one L . . . (*He corrects.*) proprietary . . . one P, proprietary . . . The controlled wines of the Bordeaux region, the lower sections of the upper slopes . . .

BOTARD: I haven't got that! You've skipped a line.

BERENGER: I'll start again. The Wine Control!

DUDARD (*to* BERENGER *and* BOTARD): Please don't read so loud. I can't concentrate with you shouting at the tops of your voices.

BOTARD (*to* DUDARD, *over* BERENGER'S *head, resuming the recent discussion, whilst* BERENGER *continues the corrections on his own for a few moments; he moves his lips noiselessly as he reads*): It's all a hoax.

DUDARD: What's all a hoax?

BOTARD: Your rhinoceros business, of course. You've been making all this propaganda to get these rumours started!

DUDARD (*interrupting his work*): What propaganda?

BERENGER (*breaking in*): No question of any propaganda.

DAISY (*interrupting her typing*): Do I have to tell you again, I saw it ... I actually saw it, and others did, too.

DUDARD (*to* BOTARD): You make me laugh! Propaganda! Propaganda for what?

BOTARD (*to* DUDARD): Oh you know more about that than I do. Don't make out you're so innocent.

DUDARD (*getting angry*): At any rate, Mr. Botard, I'm not in the pay of any furtive underground organization.

BOTARD: That's an insult, I'm not standing for that ... (*Rises.*)

BERENGER (*pleading*): Now, now, Mr. Botard ...

DAISY (*to* DUDARD, *who has also risen*): Now, now, Mr. Dudard ...

BOTARD: I tell you it's an insult.

> MR. PAPILLON's *door suddenly opens.* BOTARD *and* DUDARD *sit down again quickly;* MR. PAPILLON *is holding the time sheet in his hand; there is silence at his appearance.*

PAPILLON: Is Mr. Boeuf not in today?

BERENGER (*looking around*): No, he isn't. He must be absent.

PAPILLON: Just when I needed him. (*To* DAISY.) Did he let anyone know he was ill or couldn't come in?

DAISY: He didn't say anything to me.

PAPILLON (*opening his door wide, and coming in*): If this goes on I shall fire him. It's not the first time he's played me this trick. Up to now I haven't said anything, but it's not going on like this. Has anyone got the key to his desk?

> At this moment MRS. BOEUF *enters. She has been seen during the last speech coming up the stairs. She bursts through the door, out of breath, apprehensive.*

BERENGER: Oh here's Mrs. Boeuf.

DAISY: Morning, Mrs. Boeuf.

MRS. BOEUF: Morning, Mr. Papillon. Good morning everyone.

PAPILLON: Well, where's your husband? What's happened to him? Is it too much trouble for him to come any more?

MRS. BOEUF (*breathless*): Please excuse him, my husband I mean ... he went to visit his family for the week-end. He's got a touch of flu.

PAPILLON: So he's got a touch of flu, has he?

MRS. BOEUF (*handing a paper to* PAPILLON): He says so in the telegram. He hopes to be back on Wednesday . . . (*Almost fainting.*) Could I have a glass of water . . . and sit down a moment . . .

BERENGER *takes his own chair centre-stage, on which she flops.*

PAPILLON (*to* DAISY): Give her a glass of water.

DAISY: Yes, straightaway! (*She goes to get her a glass of water, and gives it to her during the following speeches.*)

DUDARD (*to* PAPILLON): She must have a weak heart.

PAPILLON: It's a great nuisance that Mr. Boeuf can't come. But that's no reason for you to go to pieces.

MRS. BOEUF (*with difficulty*): It's not . . . it's . . . well I was chased here all the way from the house by a rhinoceros . . .

BERENGER: How many horns did it have?

BOTARD (*guffawing*): Don't make me laugh!

DUDARD (*indignant*): Give her a chance to speak!

MRS. BOEUF (*making a great effort to be exact, and pointing in the direction of the staircase*): It's down there, by the entrance. It seemed to want to come upstairs.

At this moment a noise is heard. The staircase steps are seen to crumble under an obviously formidable weight. From below an anguished trumpeting is heard. As the dust clears after the collapse of the staircase, the staircase landing is seen to be hanging in space.

DAISY: My God!

MRS. BOEUF (*seated, her hand on her heart*): Oh! Ah!

BERENGER *runs to administer to* MRS. BOEUF, *patting her cheeks and making her drink.*

BERENGER: Keep calm!

Meanwhile PAPILLON, DUDARD *and* BOTARD *rush left, jostling each other in their efforts to open the door, and stand covered in dust on the landing; the trumpetings continue to be heard*

DAISY (*to* MRS. BOEUF): Are you feeling better now, Mrs. Boeuf?

PAPILLON (*on the landing*): There it is! Down there! It is one!

BOTARD: I can't see a thing. It's an illusion.

DUDARD: Of course it's one, down there, turning round and round.

DUDARD: It can't get up here. There's no staircase any longer.

BOTARD: It's most strange. What can it mean?

DUDARD (*turning towards* BERENGER): Come and look. Come and have a look at your rhinoceros.

BERENGER: I'm coming.

> BERENGER *rushes to the landing, followed by* DAISY *who abandons* MRS. BOEUF.

PAPILLON (*to* BERENGER): You're the rhinoceros expert—take a good look.

BERENGER: I'm no rhinoceros expert . . .

DAISY: Oh look at the way it's going round and round. It looks as if it was in pain . . . what can it want?

DUDARD: It seems to be looking for someone. (*To* BOTARD.) Can you see it now?

BOTARD (*vexed*): Yes, yes, I can see it.

DAISY (*to* PAPILLON): Perhaps we're all seeing things. You as well . . .

BOTARD: I never see things. Something is definitely down there.

DUDARD (*to* BOTARD): What do you mean, something?

PAPILLON (*to* BERENGER): It's obviously a rhinoceros. That's what you saw before, isn't it? (*To* DAISY.) And you, too?

DAISY: Definitely.

BERENGER: It's got two horns. It's an African rhinoceros, or Asiatic rather. Oh! I don't know whether the African rhinoceros has one horn or two.

PAPILLON: It's demolished the staircase—and a good thing, too! When you think how long I've been asking the management to install stone steps in place of that worm-eaten old staircase.

DUDARD: I sent a report a week ago, Chief.

PAPILLON: It was bound to happen, I knew that. I could see it coming, and I was right.

DAISY (*to* PAPILLON, *ironically*): As always.

BERENGER (*to* DUDARD *and* PAPILLON): Now look, are two horns a characteristic of the Asiatic rhinoceros or the African? And is one horn a characteristic of the African or the Asiatic one. . . ?

DAISY: Poor thing, it keeps on trumpeting and going round and round.

What does it want? Oh, it's looking at us! (*To the rhinoceros.*) Puss, puss, puss . . .

DUDARD: I shouldn't try to stroke it, it's probably not tame . . .

PAPILLON: In any case, it's out of reach.

The rhinoceros gives a horrible trumpeting.

DAISY: Poor thing!

BERENGER (*to* BOTARD, *still insisting*): You're very well informed, don't you think that the ones with two horns are . . .

PAPILLON: What are you rambling on about, Berenger? You're still a bit under the weather, Mr. Botard was right.

BOTARD: How can it be possible in a civilized country. . . ?

DAISY (*to* BOTARD): All right. But does it exist or not?

BOTARD: It's all an infamous plot! (*With a political orator's gesture he points to* DUDARD, *quelling him with a look.*) It's all your fault!

DUDARD: Why mine, rather than yours?

BOTARD (*furious*): Mine? It's always the little people who get the blame. If I had my way . . .

PAPILLON: We're in a fine mess with no staircase.

DAISY (*to* BOTARD *and* DUDARD): Calm down, this is no time to quarrel!

PAPILLON: It's all the management's fault.

DAISY: Maybe. But how are we going to get down?

PAPILLON (*joking amorously and caressing* DAISY's *cheek*): I'll take you in my arms and we'll float down together.

DAISY (*rejecting* PAPILLON's *advances*): You keep your horny hands off my face, you old pachyderm!

PAPILLON: I was only joking!

Meanwhile the rhinoceros has continued its trumpeting. MRS. BOEUF *has risen and joined the group. For a few moments she stares fixedly at the rhinoceros turning round and round below; suddenly she lets out a terribly cry.*

MRS. BOEUF: My God! It can't be true!

BERENGER (*to* MRS. BOEUF): What's the matter?

MRS. BOEUF: It's my husband. Oh Boeuf, my poor Boeuf, what's happened to you?

DAISY (*to* MRS. BOEUF): Are you positive?

MRS. BOEUF: I recognize him, I recognize him!

The rhinoceros replies with a violent but tender trumpeting.

PAPILLON: Well! That's the last straw. This time he's fired for good!
DUDARD: Is he insured?
BOTARD (*aside*): I understand it all now . . .
DAISY: How can you collect insurance in a case like this?
MRS. BOEUF (*fainting into* BERENGER's *arms*): Oh! My God!
BERENGER: Oh!
DAISY: Carry her over here!

> BERENGER, *helped by* DUDARD *and* DAISY, *install* MRS. BOEUF *in a chair.*

DUDARD (*while they are carrying her*): Don't upset yourself, Mrs. Boeuf.
MRS. BOEUF: Ah! Oh!
DAISY: Maybe it can all be put right . . .
PAPILLON (*to* DUDARD): Legally, what can be done?
DUDARD: You need to get a solicitor's advice.
BOTARD (*following the procession, raising his hands to heaven*): It's the sheerest madness! What a society!

> *They crowd round* MRS. BOEUF, *pinching her cheeks; she opens her eyes, emits an 'Ah' and closes them again; they continue to pinch her cheeks as* BOTARD *speaks.*

You can be certain of one thing: I shall report this to my union. I don't desert a colleague in the hour of need. It won't be hushed up.
MRS. BOEUF (*coming to*): My poor darling, I can't leave him like that, my poor darling. (*A trumpeting is heard.*) He's calling me. (*Tenderly.*) He's calling me.
DAISY: Feeling better now, Mrs. Boeuf?
DUDARD: She's picking up a bit.
BOTARD (*to* MRS. BOEUF): You can count on the union's support. Would you like to become a member of the committee?
PAPILLON: Work's going to be delayed again. What about the post, Miss Daisy?
DAISY: I want to know first how we're going to get out of here.
PAPILLON: It is a problem. Through the window.

They all go to the window with the exception of MRS. BOEUF *slumped in her chair and* BOTARD *who stays centre-stage.*

BOTARD: I know where it came from.

DAISY (*at window*): It's too high.

BERENGER: Perhaps we ought to call the firemen, and get them to bring ladders!

PAPILLON: Miss Daisy, go to my office and telephone the Fire Brigade. (*He makes as if to follow her.*)

> DAISY *goes out up-stage and one hears her voice on the telephone say: 'Hello, hello, is that the Fire Brigade?' followed by a vague sound of telephone conversation.*

MRS. BOEUF (*rising suddenly*): I can't desert him, I can't desert him now!

PAPILLON: If you want to divorce him . . . you'd be perfectly justified.

DUDARD: You'd be the injured party.

MRS. BOEUF: No! Poor thing! This is not the moment for that. I won't abandon my husband in such a state.

BOTARD: You're a good woman.

DUDARD (*to* MRS. BOEUF): But what are you going to do?

> *She runs left towards the landing.*

BERENGER: Watch out!

MRS. BOEUF: I can't leave him, I can't leave him now!

DUDARD: Hold her back!

MRS. BOEUF: I'm taking him home!

PAPILLON: What's she trying to do?

MRS. BOEUF (*preparing to jump; on the edge of the landing*): I'm coming my darling, I'm coming!

BERENGER: She's going to jump.

BOTARD: It's no more than her duty.

DUDARD: She can't do that.

> *Everyone with the exception of* DAISY, *who is still telephoning, is near to* MRS. BOEUF *on the landing; she jumps;* BERENGER *who tries to restrain her, is left with her skirt in his hand.*

BERENGER: I couldn't hold her back.

The rhinoceros is heard from below, tenderly trumpeting.

VOICE OF MRS. BOEUF: Here I am, my sweet, I'm here now.
DUDARD: She landed on his back in the saddle.
BOTARD: She's a good rider.
VOICE OF MRS. BOEUF: Home now, dear, let's go home.
DUDARD: They're off at a gallop.

> DUDARD, BOTARD, BERENGER, PAPILLON *come back on-stage and go to the window.*

BERENGER: They're moving fast.
DUDARD (*to* PAPILLON): Ever done any riding?
PAPILLON: A bit . . . a long time ago . . . (*Turning to the up-stage door, to* DUDARD.) Is she still on the telephone?
BERENGER (*following the course of the rhinoceros*): They're already a long way off. They're out of sight.
DAISY (*coming on-stage*): I had trouble getting the firemen.
BOTARD (*as if concluding an interior monologue*): A fine state of affairs!
DAISY: . . . I had trouble getting the firemen!
PAPILLON: Are there fires all over the place, then?
BERENGER: I agree with Mr. Botard. Mrs. Boeuf's attitude is very moving; she's a woman of feeling.
PAPILLON: It means one employee less, who has to be replaced.
BERENGER: Do you really think he's no use to us any more?
DAISY: No, there aren't any fires, the firemen have been called out for other rhinoceroses.
BERENGER: For other rhinoceroses?
DAISY: Yes, other rhinoceroses. They've been reported all over the town. This morning there were seven, now there are seventeen.
BOTARD: What did I tell you?
DAISY: As many as thirty-two have been reported. They're not official yet, but they're bound to be confirmed soon.
BOTARD (*less certain*): Pff!! They always exaggerate.
PAPILLON: Are they coming to get us out of here?
BERENGER: I'm hungry . . . !
DAISY: Yes, they're coming; the firemen are on the way.

PAPILLON: What about the work?

DUDARD: It looks as if it's out of our hands.

PAPILLON: We'll have to make up the lost time.

DUDARD: Well, Mr. Botard, do you still deny all rhinocerotic evidence?

BOTARD: Our union is against your dismissing Mr. Boeuf without notice.

PAPILLON: It's not up to me; we shall see what conclusions they reach at the enquiry.

BOTARD (*to* DUDARD): No, Mr. Dudard, I do not deny the rhinocerotic evidence. I never have.

DUDARD: That's not true.

DAISY: Oh no, that's not true.

BOTARD: I repeat I have never denied it. I just wanted to find out exactly where it was all leading. Because I know my own mind. I'm not content to simply state that a phenomenon exists. I make it my business to understand and explain it. At least I could explain it if . . .

DUDARD: Then explain it to us.

DAISY: Yes, explain it, Mr. Botard.

PAPILLON: Explain it, when your colleagues ask you.

BOTARD: I will explain it . . .

DUDARD: We're all listening.

DAISY: I'm most curious.

BOTARD: I will explain it . . . one day . . .

DUDARD: Why not now?

BOTARD (*menacingly; to* MR. PAPILLON): We'll go into the explanation later, in private. (*To everyone.*) I know the whys and the wherefores of this whole business . . .

DAISY: What whys?

BERENGER: What wherefores?

DUDARD: I'd give a lot to know these whys and wherefores . . .

BOTARD (*continuing; with a terrible air*): And I also know the names of those responsible. The names of the traitors. You can't fool me. I'll let you know the purpose and the meaning of this whole plot! I'll unmask the perpetrators!

BERENGER: But who'd want to . . .

DUDARD (*to* BOTARD): You're evading the question, Mr. Botard.

PAPILLON: Let's have no evasions.

BOTARD: Evading? What, me?

DAISY: Just now you accused us of suffering from hallucinations.

BOTARD: Just now, yes. Now the hallucination has become a provocation.

DUDARD: And how do you consider this change came about?

BOTARD: It's an open secret, gentlemen. Even the man in the street knows about it. Only hypocrites pretend not to understand.

The noise and hooting of a fire-engine is heard. The brakes are abruptly applied just under the window.

DAISY: That's the firemen!

BOTARD: There're going to be some big changes made; they won't get away with it as easily as that.

DUDARD: That doesn't mean anything, Mr. Botard. The rhinoceroses exist, and that's that. That's all there is to it.

DAISY (*at the window, looking down*): Up here, firemen!

A bustling is heard below, commotion, engine noises.

VOICE OF FIREMAN: Put up the ladder!

BOTARD (*to* DUDARD): I hold the key to all these happenings, an infallible system of interpretation.

PAPILLON: I want you all back in the office this afternoon.

The firemen's ladder is placed against the window.

BOTARD: Too bad about the office, Mr. Papillon.

PAPILLON: I don't know what the management will say!

DUDARD: These are exceptional circumstances.

BOTARD (*pointing to the window*): They can't force us to come back this way. We'll have to wait till the staircase is repaired.

DUDARD: If anyone breaks a leg, it'll be the management's responsibility.

PAPILLON: That's true.

A fireman's helmet is seen, followed by the FIREMAN.

BERENGER (*to* DAISY, *pointing to the window*): After you Miss Daisy.

FIREMAN: Come on, Miss.

The FIREMAN *takes* DAISY *in his arms; she steps astride the window and disappears with him.*

DUDARD: Good-bye Miss Daisy. See you soon.

DAISY (*disappearing*): See you soon, good-bye!

PAPILLON (*at window*): Telephone me tomorrow morning, Miss Daisy. You can come and type the letters at my house. (*To* BERENGER.) Mr. Berenger, I draw your attention to the fact that we are not on holiday, and that work will resume as soon as possible. (*To the other two.*) You hear what I say, gentlemen?

DUDARD: Of course, Mr. Papillon.

BOTARD: They'll go on exploiting us till we drop, of course.

FIREMAN (*reappearing at window*): Who's next?

PAPILLON (*to all three of them*): Go on!

DUDARD: After you, Mr. Papillon.

BERENGER: After you, Chief.

BOTARD: You first, of course.

PAPILLON (*to* BERENGER): Bring me Miss Daisy's letters. There, on the table.

BERENGER *goes and gets the letters, brings them to* PAPILLON.

FIREMAN: Come on, hurry up. We've not got all day. We've got other calls to make.

BOTARD: What did I tell you?

PAPILLON, *the letters under his arm, steps astride the window.*

PAPILLON (*to the* FIREMAN): Careful of the documents! (*Turning to the others.*) Good-bye, gentlemen.

DUDARD: Good-bye, Mr. Papillon.

BERENGER: Good-bye, Mr. Papillon.

PAPILLON (*he has disappeared; one hears him say*): Careful of my papers. Dudard! Lock up the offices!

DUDARD (*shouting*): Don't you worry, Mr. Papillon. (*To* BOTARD.) After you, Mr. Botard.

BOTARD: I am about to descend, gentlemen. And I am going to take this matter up immediately with the proper authorities. I'll get to the bottom of this so-called mystery. (*He moves to window.*)

DUDARD (*to* BOTARD): I thought it was all perfectly clear to you!

BOTARD (*astride the window*): Your irony doesn't affect me. What I'm after are the proofs and the documents—yes, proof positive of your treason.

DUDARD: That's absurd . . .

BOTARD: Your insults . . .

DUDARD (*interrupting him*): It's you who are insulting me . . .

BOTARD (*disappearing*): I don't insult. I merely prove.

VOICE OF FIREMAN: Come on there!

DUDARD (*to* BERENGER): What are you doing this afternoon? Shall we meet for a drink?

BERENGER: Sorry, I can't. I'm taking advantage of this afternoon off to go and see my friend Jean. I do want to make it up with him, after all. We got carried away. It was all my fault.

The FIREMAN's *head reappears at the window.*

FIREMAN: Come along there!

BERENGER (*pointing to the window*): After you.

DUDARD: After you.

BERENGER: Oh no, after you.

DUDARD: No, I insist, after you.

BERENGER: No, please, after you, after you.

FIREMAN: Hurry up!

DUDARD: After you, after you.

BERENGER: No, after you, after you.

They climb through the window together. The FIREMAN *helps them down, as the curtain falls.*

ACT TWO

JEAN's *house. The layout is roughly the same as Act Two, Scene One. That is to say, the stage is divided into two. To the right, occupying three-quarters or four-fifths of the stage, according to size, is* JEAN's *bedroom. Up-stage, a chair or an armchair, on which* BERENGER *will sit. Right centre, a door leading to* JEAN's *bathroom. When* JEAN *goes in to wash, the noise of a tap is heard, and that of the shower. To the left of the room, a partition divides the stage in two. Centre-stage, the door leading to the stairs. If a less realistic, more stylized décor is preferred, the door may be placed without a partition. To the left is the staircase; the top steps are visible, leading to* JEAN's *flat, the banister and the landing. At the back, on the landing level, is the door to the neighbour's flat. Lower down, at the back, there is a glass door, over which is written: 'Concierge.'*

When the curtain rises, JEAN *is in bed, lying under the blanket, his back to the audience. One hears him cough.*

After a few moments BERENGER *is seen, climbing the top steps of the staircase. He knocks at the door;* JEAN *does not answer.* BERENGER *knocks again.*

BERENGER: Jean! (*He knocks again.*) Jean!

> *The door at the end of the landing opens slightly, and a little old man with a white goatee appears.*

OLD MAN: What is it?
BERENGER: I want to see Jean. I am a friend of his.
OLD MAN: I thought it was me you wanted. My name's Jean as well, but it's the other one you want.
VOICE OF OLD MAN'S WIFE (*from within the room*): Is it for us?
OLD MAN (*turning to his wife who is not seen*): No, for the other one.
BERENGER (*knocking*): Jean!

OLD MAN: I didn't see him go out. But I saw him last night. He looked in a bad temper.

BERENGER: Yes, I know why; it was my fault.

OLD MAN: Perhaps he doesn't feel like opening the door to you. Try again.

VOICE OF OLD MAN'S WIFE: Jean, don't stand gossiping, Jean!

BERENGER (*knocking*): Jean!

OLD MAN (*to his wife*): Just a moment. Oh dear, dear . . . (*He close the door and disappears.*)

JEAN (*still lying down, his back to the audience, in a hoarse voice*) What is it?

BERENGER: I've dropped by to see you, Jean.

JEAN: Who is it?

BERENGER: It's me, Berenger. I hope I'm not disturbing you.

JEAN: Oh it's you, is it? Come in!

BERENGER (*trying to open the door*): The door's locked.

JEAN: Just a moment. Oh dear, dear . . . (JEAN *gets up in a pretty bad temper. He is wearing green pyjamas, his hair is tousled.*) Just a moment. (*He unlocks the door.*) Just a moment. (*He goes back to bed, gets under the blanket.*) Come in!

BERENGER (*coming in*): Hello Jean!

JEAN (*in bed*): What time is it? Aren't you at the office?

BERENGER: You're still in bed; you're not at the office, then? Sorry if I'm disturbing you.

JEAN (*still with his back turned*): Funny, I didn't recognize your voice.

BERENGER: I didn't recognize yours either.

JEAN (*still with his back turned*): Sit down!

BERENGER: Aren't you feeling well?

JEAN *replies with a grunt.*

You know, Jean, it was stupid of me to get so upset yesterday over a thing like that.

JEAN: A thing like what?

BERENGER: Yesterday . . .

JEAN: When yesterday? Where yesterday?

BERENGER: Don't you remember? It was about that wretched rhinoceros.

JEAN: What rhinoceros?

BERENGER: The rhinoceros, or rather, the two wretched rhinoceroses we saw.

JEAN: Oh, yes, I remember . . . How do you know they were wretched?

BERENGER: Oh I just said that.

JEAN: Oh. Well let's not talk any more about it.

BERENGER: That's very nice of you.

JEAN: Then that's that.

BERENGER: But I would like to say how sorry I am for being so insistent . . . and so obstinate . . . and getting so angry . . . in fact . . . I acted stupidly.

JEAN: That's not surprising with you.

BERENGER: I'm very sorry.

JEAN: I don't feel very well. (*He coughs.*)

BERENGER: That's probably why you're in bed. (*With a change of tone.*) You know, Jean, as it turned out, we were both right.

JEAN: What about?

BERENGER: About . . . well, you know, the same thing. Sorry to bring it up again, but I'll only mention it briefly. I just wanted you to know that in our different ways we were both right. It's been proved now. There are some rhinoceroses in the town with two horns and some with one.

JEAN: That's what I told you! Well, that's just too bad.

BERENGER: Yes, too bad.

JEAN: Or maybe it's all to the good; it depends.

BERENGER (*continuing*): In the final analysis it doesn't much matter which comes from where. The important thing, as I see it, is the fact that they're there at all, because . . .

JEAN (*turning and sitting on his unmade bed, facing* BERENGER): I don't feel well, I don't feel well at all!

BERENGER: Oh I am sorry! What do you think it is?

JEAN: I don't know exactly, there's something wrong somewhere . .

BERENGER: Do you feel weak?

JEAN: Not at all. On the contrary, I feel full of beans.

BERENGER: I meant just a passing weakness. It happens to everybody.

JEAN: It never happens to me.

BERENGER: Perhaps you're too healthy then. Too much energy can be a bad thing. It unsettles the nervous system.

JEAN: My nervous system is in perfect order. (*His voice has become more and more hoarse.*) I'm sound in mind and limb. I come from a long line of . .

BERENGER: I know you do. Perhaps you've just caught a chill. Have you got a temperature?

JEAN: I don't know. Yes, probably I have a touch of fever. My head aches.

BERENGER: Just a slight migraine. Would you like me to leave you alone?

JEAN: No, stay. You don't worry me.

BERENGER: Your voice is hoarse, too.

JEAN: Hoarse?

BERENGER: A bit hoarse, yes. That's why I didn't recognize it.

JEAN: Why should I be hoarse? My voice hasn't changed; it's yours that's changed!

BERENGER: Mine?

JEAN: Why not?

BERENGER: It's possible. I hadn't noticed.

JEAN: I sometimes wonder if you're capable of noticing anything. (*Putting his hand to his forehead.*) Actually it's my forehead that hurts. I must have given it a knock. (*His voice is even hoarser.*)

BERENGER: When did you do that?

JEAN: I don't know. I don't remember it happening.

BERENGER: But it must have hurt you.

JEAN: I must have done it while I was asleep.

BERENGER: The shock would have wakened you up. You must have just dreamed you knocked yourself.

JEAN: I never dream . . .

BERENGER (*continuing*): Your headache must have come on while you were asleep. You've forgotten you dreamed, or rather you only remember subconsciously.

JEAN: Subconsciously, me? I'm master of my own thoughts, my mind doesn't wander. I think straight, I always think straight.

BERENGER: I know that. I haven't made myself clear.

JEAN: Then make yourself clearer. And you needn't bother to make any of your unpleasant observations to me.

BERENGER: One often has the impression that one has knocked oneself when one has a headache. (*Coming closer to* JEAN.) If you'd really knocked yourself, you'd have a bump. (*Looking at* JEAN.) Oh, you've got one, you do have a bump, in fact.

JEAN: A bump?

BERENGER: Just a tiny one.

JEAN: Where?

BERENGER (*pointing to* JEAN's *forehead*): There, it starts just above your nose.

JEAN: I've no bump. We've never had bumps in my family.

BERENGER: Have you got a mirror?

JEAN: That's the limit! (*Touching his forehead.*) I can feel something. I'm going to have a look, in the bathroom. (*He gets up abruptly and goes to the bathroom.* BERENGER *watches him as he goes. Then, from the bathroom.*) It's true, I have got a bump. (*He comes back; his skin has become greener.*) So you see I did knock myself.

BERENGER: You don't look well, your skin is quite green.

JEAN: You seem to delight in saying disagreeable things to me. Have you taken a look at yourself lately?

BERENGER: Forgive me. I didn't mean to upset you.

JEAN (*very hoarse*): That's hard to believe.

BERENGER: Your breathing's very heavy. Does your throat hurt?

JEAN *goes and sits on his bed again.*

If your throat hurts, perhaps it's a touch of quinsy.

JEAN: Why should I have a touch of quinsy?

BERENGER: It's nothing to be ashamed of—I sometimes get it. Let me feel your pulse. (*He rises and takes* JEAN's *pulse.*)

JEAN (*in an even hoarser voice*): Oh, it'll pass.

BERENGER: Your pulse is normal. You needn't get alarmed.

JEAN: I'm not alarmed in the slightest—why should I be?

BERENGER: You're right. A few days' rest will put you right.

JEAN: I've no time to rest. I must go and buy some food.

BERENGER: There's not much the matter with you, if you're hungry. But even so, you ought to take a few days' rest. It's wise to take care. Has the doctor been to see you?

JEAN: I don't need a doctor.

BERENGER: Oh but you ought to get the doctor.

JEAN: You're not going to get the doctor because I don't want the doctor. I can look after myself.

BERENGER: You shouldn't reject medical advice.

JEAN: Doctors invent illnesses that don't exist.

BERENGER: They do it in good faith—just for the pleasure of looking after people.

JEAN: They invent illnesses, they invent them, I tell you.

BERENGER: Perhaps they do—but after they invent them they cure them.

JEAN: I only have confidence in veterinary surgeons. There!

BERENGER (*who has released* JEAN's *wrist, now takes it up again*): Your veins look swollen. They're jutting out.

JEAN: It's a sign of virility.

BERENGER: Of course it's a sign of health and strength. But . . . (*He examines* JEAN's *forearm more closely, until* JEAN *violently withdraws it.*)

JEAN: What do you think you're doing—scrutinizing me as if I were some strange animal?

BERENGER: It's your skin . . .

JEAN: What's my skin got to do with you? I don't go on about your skin, do I?

BERENGER: It's just that . . . it seems to be changing colour all the time. It's going green. (*He tries to take* JEAN's *hand.*) It's hardening as well.

JEAN (*withdrawing his hand again*): Stop mauling me about! What's the matter with you? You're getting on my nerves.

BERENGER (*to himself*): Perhaps it's more serious than I thought. (*To* JEAN.) We must get the doctor. (*He goes to the telephone.*)

JEAN: Leave that thing alone. (*He darts over to* BERENGER *and pushes him.* BERENGER *staggers.*) You mind your own business.

BERENGER: All right. It was for your own good.

JEAN (*coughing and breathing noisily*): I know better than you what's good for me.

BERENGER: You're breathing very hard.

JEAN: One breathes as best one can. You don't like the way I breathe, and I don't like the way you breathe. Your breathing's too feeble, you can't even hear it; it's as if you were going to drop dead any moment.

BERENGER: I know I'm not as strong as you.

JEAN: I don't keep trying to get you to the doctor, do I? Leave people to do as they please.

BERENGER: Don't get angry with me. You know very well I'm your friend.

JEAN: There's no such thing as friendship. I don't believe in your friendship.

BERENGER: That's a very hurtful thing to say.

JEAN: There's nothing for you to get hurt about.

BERENGER: My dear Jean . . .

JEAN: I'm not your dear Jean.

BERENGER: You're certainly in a very misanthropic mood today.

JEAN: Yes, I am misanthropic, very misanthropic indeed. I like being misanthropic.

BERENGER: You're probably still angry with me over our silly quarrel yesterday. I admit it was my fault. That's why I came to say I was sorry . . .

JEAN: What quarrel are you talking about?

BERENGER: I told you just now. You know, about the rhinoceros.

JEAN (*not listening to* BERENGER): It's not that I hate people. I'm just indifferent to them—or rather, they disgust me; and they'd better keep out of my way, or I'll run them down.

BERENGER: You know very well that I shall never stand in your way.

JEAN: I've got one aim in life. And I'm making straight for it.

BERENGER: I'm sure you're right. But I feel you're passing through a moral crisis.

> JEAN *has been pacing the room like a wild beast in a cage, from one wall to the other.* BERENGER *watches him, occasionally step ping aside to avoid him.* JEAN's *voice has become more and more hoarse.*

You mustn't excite yourself, it's bad for you.

JEAN: I felt uncomfortable in my clothes; now my pyjamas irritate me as well. (*He undoes his pyjama jacket and does it up again.*)

BERENGER: But whatever's the matter with your skin?

JEAN: Can't you leave my skin alone? I certainly wouldn't want to change it for yours.

BERENGER: It's gone like leather.

JEAN: That makes it more solid. It's weatherproof.

BERENGER: You're getting greener and greener.

JEAN: You've got colour mania today. You're seeing things, you've been drinking again.

BERENGER: I did yesterday, but not today.

JEAN: It's the result of all your past debauches.

BERENGER: I promised you to turn over a new leaf. I take notice when friends like you give me advice. And I never feel humiliated— on the contrary!

JEAN: I don't care what you feel. Brrr .

BERENGER: What did you say?

JEAN: I didn't say anything. I just went Brrr . . . because I felt like it.

BERENGER (*looking fixedly at* JEAN): Do you know what's happened to Boeuf? He's turned into a rhinoceros.

JEAN: What happened to Boeuf?

BERENGER: He's turned into a rhinoceros.

JEAN (*fanning himself with the flaps of his jacket*): Brrr . . .

BERENGER: Come on now, stop joking.

JEAN: I can puff if I want to, can't I? I've every right . . . I'm in my own house.

BERENGER: I didn't say you couldn't.

JEAN: And I shouldn't if I were you. I feel hot, I feel hot. Brrr . . . Just a moment. I must cool myself down.

BERENGER (*whilst* JEAN *darts to the bathroom*): He must have a fever.

> JEAN *is in the bathroom, one hears him puffing, and also the sound of a running tap.*

JEAN (*off*): Brrr . . .

BERENGER: He's got the shivers. I'm jolly well going to 'phone the doctor. (*He goes to the telephone again then comes back quickly when he hears* JEAN's *voice*.)

JEAN (*off*): So old Boeuf turned into a rhinoceros, did he? Ah, ah, ah . . . ! He was just having you on, he'd disguised himself. (*He pokes his head round the bathroom door. He is very green. The bump over his nose is slightly larger.*) He was just disguised.

BERENGER (*walking about the room, without seeing* JEAN): He looked very serious about it, I assure you.

JEAN: Oh well, that's his business.

BERENGER (*turning to* JEAN *who disappears again into the bathroom*): I'm sure he didn't do it on purpose. He didn't want to change.

JEAN (*off*): How do you know?

BERENGER: Well, everything led one to suppose so.

JEAN: And what if he did do it on purpose? Eh? What if he did it on purpose?

BERENGER: I'd be very surprised. At any rate, Mrs. Boeuf didn't seem to know about it . . .

JEAN (*in a very hoarse voice*): Ah, ah, ah! Fat old Mrs. Boeuf. She's just a fool!

BERENGER: Well fool or no fool . . .

JEAN (*he enters swiftly, takes off his jacket, and throws it on the bed.* BERENGER *discreetly averts his gaze.* JEAN, *whose back and chest are now green, goes back into the bathroom. As he walks in and out.*) Boeuf never let his wife know what he was up to . . .

BERENGER: You're wrong there, Jean—it was a very united family.

JEAN: Very united, was it? Are you sure? Hum, hum, Brr . . .

BERENGER (*moving to the bathroom, where* JEAN *slams the door in his face*): Very united. And the proof is that . . .

JEAN (*from within*): Boeuf led his own private life. He had a secret side to him deep down which he kept to himself.

BERENGER: I shouldn't make you talk, it seems to upset you.

JEAN: On the contrary, it relaxes me.

BERENGER: Even so, let me call the doctor, I beg you.

JEAN: I absolutely forbid it. I can't stand obstinate people.

> JEAN *comes back into the bedroom.* BERENGER *backs away a little scared, for* JEAN *is greener than ever and speaks only with difficulty. His voice is unrecognizable.*)

Well, whether he changes into a rhinoceros on purpose or against his will, he's probably all the better for it.

BERENGER: How can you say a thing like that? Surely you don't think . . .

JEAN: You always see the black side of everything. It obviously gave him great pleasure to turn into a rhinoceros. There's nothing extraordinary in that.

BERENGER: There's nothing extraordinary in it, but I doubt if it gave him much pleasure.

JEAN: And why not, pray?

BERENGER: It's hard to say exactly why; it's just something you feel.

JEAN: I tell you it's not as bad as all that. After all, rhinoceroses are living creatures the same as us; they've got as much right to life as we have!

BERENGER: As long as they don't destroy ours in the process. You must admit the difference in mentality.

JEAN (*pacing up and down the room, and in and out of the bathroom*): Are you under the impression that our way of life is superior?

BERENGER: Well at any rate, we have our own moral standards which I consider incompatible with the standards of these animals.

JEAN: Moral standards! I'm sick of moral standards! We need to go beyond moral standards!

BERENGER: What would you put in their place?

JEAN (*still pacing*): Nature!

BERENGER: Nature?

JEAN: Nature has its own laws. Morality's against Nature.

BERENGER: Are you suggesting we replace our moral laws by the law of the jungle?

JEAN: It would suit me, suit me fine.

BERENGER: You say that. But deep down, no one . . .

JEAN (*interrupting him, pacing up and down*): We've got to build our life on new foundations. We must get back to primeval integrity.

BERENGER: I don't agree with you at all.

JEAN (*breathing noisily*): I can't breathe.

BERENGER: Just think a moment. You must admit that we have a philosophy that animals don't share, and an irreplaceable set of values, which it's taken centuries of human civilization to build up . . .

JEAN (*in the bathroom*): When we've demolished all that, we'll be better off!

BERENGER: I know you don't mean that seriously. You're joking! It's just a poetic fancy.

JEAN: Brrr. (*He almost trumpets.*)

BERENGER: I'd never realized you were a poet.

JEAN (*comes out of the bathroom*): Brrr. (*He trumpets again.*)

BERENGER: That's not what you believe fundamentally—I know you too well. You know as well as I do that mankind . . .

JEAN (*interrupting him*): Don't talk to me about mankind!

BERENGER: I mean the human individual, humanism . . .

JEAN: Humanism is all washed up! You're a ridiculous old sentimentalist. (*He goes into the bathroom.*)

BERENGER: But you must admit that the mind . . .

JEAN (*from the bathroom*): Just clichés! You're talking rubbish!

BERENGER: Rubbish!

JEAN (*from the bathroom in a very hoarse voice, difficult to understand*): Utter rubbish!

BERENGER: I'm amazed to hear you say that, Jean, really! You must be out of your mind. You wouldn't like to be a rhinoceros yourself, now would you?

JEAN: Why not? I'm not a victim of prejudice like you.

BERENGER: Can you speak more clearly? I didn't catch what you said. You swallowed the words.

JEAN (*still in the bathroom*): Then keep your ears open.

BERENGER: What?

JEAN: Keep your ears open. I said what's wrong with being a rhinoceros? I'm all for change.

BERENGER: It's not like you to say a thing like that . . .

> BERENGER *stops short, for* JEAN's *appearance is truly alarming.* JEAN *has become, in fact, completely green. The bump on his forehead is practically a rhinoceros horn.*

Oh! You really must be out of your mind!

> JEAN *dashes to his bed, throws the covers on the floor, talking in a fast and furious gabble, and making very weird sounds.*

You mustn't get into such a state—calm down! I hardly recognize you any more.

JEAN (*hardly distinguishable*): Hot . . . far too hot! Demolish the lot, clothes itch, they itch! (*He drops his pyjama trousers.*)

BERENGER: What are you doing? You're not yourself! You're generally so modest!

JEAN: The swamps! The swamps!

BERENGER: Look at me! Can't you see me any longer? Can't you hear me?

JEAN: I can hear you perfectly well! I can see you perfectly well! (*He lunges towards* BERENGER, *head down.* BERENGER *gets out of the way.*)

BERENGER: Watch out!

JEAN (*puffing noisily*): Sorry! (*He darts at great speed into the bathroom.*)

BERENGER (*makes as if to escape by the door left, then comes back and goes into the bathroom after* JEAN, *saying*): I really can't leave him like that—after all he is a friend. (*From the bathroom.*) I'm going to get the doctor! It's absolutely necessary, believe me!

JEAN (*from the bathroom*): No!

BERENGER (*from the bathroom*): Calm down, Jean, you're being ridic-

ulous! Oh, your horn's getting longer and longer—you're a rhinoceros!

JEAN (*from the bathroom*): I'll trample you, I'll trample you down!

*A lot of noise comes from the bathroom, trumpetings, objects
falling, the sound of a shattered mirror; then* BERENGER *reappears, very frightened; he closes the bathroom door with difficulty against the resistance that is being made from inside.*

BERENGER (*pushing against the door*): He's a rhinoceros, he's a rhinoceros!

BERENGER *manages to close the door. As he does so, his coat is
pierced by a rhinoceros horn. The door shakes under the animal's constant pressure and the din continues in the bathroom;
trumpetings are heard, interspersed with indistinct phrases
such as: 'I'm furious! The swine!' etc.* BERENGER *rushes to the
door right.*

I never would have thought it of him—never!

*He opens the staircase door and goes and knocks at the landing
door; he bangs repeatedly on it with his fist.*

There's a rhinoceros in the building! Get the police!

OLD MAN (*poking his head out*): What's the matter?

BERENGER: Get the police! There's a rhinoceros in the house!

VOICE OF OLD MAN'S WIFE: What are you up to, Jean? Why are you
making all that noise?

OLD MAN (*to his wife*): I don't know what he's talking about. He's
seen a rhinoceros.

BERENGER: Yes, here in the house. Get the police!

OLD MAN: What do you think you're up to, disturbing peopl like
that. What a way to behave! (*He shuts the door in his face.*)

BERENGER (*rushing to the stairs*): Porter, porter, there's a rhinoceros
in the house, get the police! Porter!

*The upper part of the porter's lodge is seen to open; the head
of a rhinoceros appears.*

Another!

BERENGER rushes upstairs again. He wants to go back into JEAN's room, hesitates, then makes for the door of the OLD MAN again. At this moment the door of the room opens to reveal two rhinoceros heads.

Oh, my God!

BERENGER goes back into JEAN's room where the bathroom door is still shaking. He goes to the window which is represented simply by the frame, facing the audience. He is exhausted, almost fainting; he murmurs.

My God! Oh my God!

He makes a gigantic effort, and manages to get astride the window (that is, towards the audience) but gets back again quickly, for at the same time, crossing the orchestra pit at great speed, move a large number of rhinoceros heads in line. BERENGER gets back with all speed, looks out of the window for a moment.

There's a whole herd of them in the street now! An army of rhinoceroses, surging up the avenue . . . ! (*He looks all around.*) Where can I get out? Where can I get out? If only they'd keep to the middle of the road! They're all over the pavement as well. Where can I get out? Where can I get out?

Distracted, he goes from door to door and to the window, whilst the bathroom door continues to shake and JEAN continues to trumpet and hurl incomprehensible insults. This continues for some moments; whenever BERENGER in his disordered attempts to escape reaches the door of the Old People's flat or the stairway, he is greeted by rhinoceros heads which trumpet and cause him to beat a hasty retreat. He goes to the window for the last time and looks out.

A whole herd of them! And they always said the rhinoceros was a solitary animal! That's not true, that's a conception they'll have to revise! They've smashed up all the public benches. (*He wrings his hands.*) What's to be done?

He goes once more to the various exits, but the spectacle of the rhinoceros halts him. When he gets back to the bathroom door it seems about to give way. BERENGER *throws himself against the back wall, which yields; the street is visible in the background; he flees, shouting:*

Rhinoceros! Rhinoceros!

Noises. The bathroom door is on the point of yielding.

Curtain.

ACT THREE

The arrangement is roughly the same as in the previous scene.

It is BERENGER'S *room, which bears a striking resemblance to that of* JEAN. *Only certain details, one or two extra pieces of furniture, reveal that it is a different room. Staircase to the left, and landing. Door at the end of the landing. There is no porter's lodge. Up-stage is a divan. An armchair, and a little table with a telephone. Perhaps an extra telephone, and a chair. Window up-stage, open. A window frame in the foreground.*

BERENGER *is lying on his divan, his back to the audience.* BERENGER *is lying fully dressed. His head is bandaged. He seems to be having a bad dream, and writhes in his sleep.*

BERENGER: No. (*Pause.*) Watch out for the horns! (*Pause.*)

> *The noise of a considerable number of rhinoceroses is heard passing under the up-stage window.*

No! (*He falls to the floor still fighting with what he has seen in his dream, and wakes up. He puts his hand to his head with an apprehensive air, then moves to the mirror and lifts his bandage, as the noises fade away. He heaves a sigh of relief when he sees he has no bump.*

He hesitates, goes to the divan, lies down, and instantly gets up again. He goes to the table where he takes up a bottle of brandy and a glass, and is about to pour himself a drink. Then after a short internal struggle he replaces the bottle and glass.) Now, now, where's your will-power! (*He wants to go back to his divan, but the rhinoceroses are heard again under the up-stage window. The noises stop; he goes to the little table, hesitates a moment, then with a gesture of 'Oh what's it matter!' he pours himself a glass of brandy which he downs at one go. He puts the bottle and glass back in place. He coughs. His cough seems to worry him; he coughs again and listens hard to the sound. He looks at him-*

539

self again in the mirror, coughing, then opens the window; the panting of the animals becomes louder; he coughs again.) No, it's not the same! *(He calms down, shuts the window, feels his bandaged forehead, goes to his divan, and seems to fall asleep.)*

DUDARD *is seen mounting the top stairs; he gets to the landing and knocks on* BERENGER's *door.*

BERENGER *(starting up)*: What is it?

DUDARD: I've dropped by to see you, Berenger.

BERENGER: Who is it?

DUDARD: It's me.

BERENGER: Who's me?

DUDARD: Me, Dudard.

BERENGER: Ah, it's you, come in!

DUDARD: I hope I'm not disturbing you. *(He tries to open the door.)* The door's locked.

BERENGER: Just a moment. Oh dear, dear! *(He opens the door. DUD-ARD enters.)*

DUDARD: Hello Berenger.

BERENGER: Hello Dudard, what time is it?

DUDARD: So, you're still barricaded in your room! Feeling any better, old man?

BERENGER: Forgive me, I didn't recognize your voice. *(Goes to open the window.)* Yes, yes, I think I'm a bit better.

DUDARD: My voice hasn't changed. I recognized yours easily enough.

BERENGER: I'm sorry, I thought that... you're right, your voice is quite normal. Mine hasn't changed either, has it?

DUDARD: Why should it have changed?

BERENGER: I'm not a bit... a bit hoarse, am I?

DUDARD: Not that I notice.

BERENGER: That's good. That's very reassuring.

DUDARD: Why, what's the matter with you?

BERENGER: I don't know—does one ever know? Voices can suddenly change—they do change, alas!

DUDARD: Have you caught cold, as well?

BERENGER: I hope not... I sincerely hope not. But do sit down, Dudard, take a seat. Sit in the armchair.

DUDARD *(sitting in the armchair)*: Are you still feeling a bit off colour? Is your head still bad? *(He points to* BERENGER's *bandage.)*

BERENGER: Oh yes, I've still got a headache. But there's no bump, I haven't knocked myself ... have I? (*He lifts the bandage, shows his forehead to* DUDARD.)

DUDARD: No, there's no bump as far as I can see.

BERENGER: I hope there never will be. Never.

DUDARD: If you don't knock yourself, why should there be?

BERENGER: If you really don't want to knock yourself, you don't.

DUDARD: Obviously. One just has to take care. But what's the matter with you? You're all nervous and agitated. It must be your migraine. You just stay quiet and you'll feel better.

BERENGER: Migraine! Don't talk to me about migraines! Don't talk about them!

DUDARD: It's understandable that you've got a migraine after all that emotion.

BERENGER: I can't seem to get over it!

DUDARD: Then it's not surprising you've got a headache.

BERENGER (*darting to the mirror, lifting the bandage*): Nothing there ... You know, it can all start from something like that.

DUDARD: What can all start?

BERENGER: I'm frightened of becoming someone else.

DUDARD: Calm yourself, now, and sit down. Dashing up and down the room like that can only make you more nervous.

BERENGER: You're right, I must keep calm. (*He goes and sits down.*) I just can't get over it, you know.

DUDARD: About Jean you mean?—I know.

BERENGER: Yes, Jean, of course—and the others, too.

DUDARD: I realize it must have been a shock to you.

BERENGER: Well, that's not surprising, you must admit.

DUDARD: I suppose so, but you mustn't dramatize the situation; it's no reason for you to ...

BERENGER: I wonder how you'd have felt. Jean was my best friend. Then to watch him change before my eyes, and the way he got so furious!

DUDARD: I know. You felt let down; I understand. Try and not think about it.

BERENGER: How can I help thinking about it? He was such a warm-hearted person, always so human! Who'd have thought it of him! We'd known each other for ... for donkey's years. He was the last person I'd have expected to change like that. I felt more sure of him than of myself! And then to do that to me!

DUDARD: I'm sure he didn't do it specially to annoy you!

BERENGER: It seemed as if he did. If you'd seen the state he was in . . . the expression on his face . . .

DUDARD: It's just that you happened to be with him at the time. It would have been the same no matter who was there.

BERENGER: But after all our years together he might have controlled himself in front of me.

DUDARD: You think everything revolves round you, you think that everything that happens concerns you personally; you're not the centre of the universe, you know.

BERENGER: Perhaps you're right. I must try to re-adjust myself, but the phenomenon in itself is so disturbing. To tell the truth, it absolutely shatters me. What can be the explanation?

DUDARD: For the moment I haven't found a satisfactory explanation. I observe the facts, and I take them in. They exist, so they must have an explanation. A freak of Nature, perhaps, some bizarre caprice, an extravagant joke, a game—who knows?

BERENGER: Jean was very proud, of course. I'm not ambitious at all. I'm content to be what I am.

DUDARD: Perhaps he felt an urge for some fresh air, the country, the wide-open spaces . . . perhaps he felt a need to relax. I'm not saying that's any excuse . . .

BERENGER: I understand what you mean, at least I'm trying to. But you know—if someone accused me of being a bad sport, or hopelessly middle class, or completely out of touch with life, I'd still want to stay as I am.

DUDARD: We'll all stay as we are, don't worry. So why get upset over a few cases of rhinoceritis. Perhaps it's just another disease.

BERENGER: Exactly! And I'm frightened of catching it.

DUDARD: Oh stop thinking about it. Really, you attach too much importance to the whole business. Jean's case isn't symptomatic, he's not a typical case—you said yourself he was proud. In my opinion—if you'll excuse me saying this about your friend—he was far too excitable, a bit wild, an eccentric. You mustn't base your judgments on exceptions. It's the average case you must consider.

BERENGER: I'm beginning to see daylight. You see, you couldn't explain this phenomenon to me. And yet you just provided me with a plausible explanation. Yes, of course, he must have been in a critical condition to have got himself into that state. He must have been temporarily unbalanced. And yet he gave his reasons for it, he'd obviously given it a lot of thought, and weighed the pros and cons... And what about Boeuf then, was he mad, too...? and what about all the others...?

DUDARD: There's still the epidemic theory. It's like influenza. It's not the first time there's been an epidemic.

BERENGER: There's never been one like this. And what if it's come from the colonies?

DUDARD: In any case you can be sure that Boeuf and the others didn't do what they did—become what they became—just to annoy you. They wouldn't have gone to all that trouble.

BERENGER: That's true, that makes sense, it's a reassuring thought ...or on the other hand, perhaps that makes it worse? (*Rhinoceroses are heard, galloping under the up-stage window.*) There, you hear that? (*He darts to the window.*)

DUDARD: Oh, why can't you leave them alone!

BERENGER *closes the window again.*

They're not doing you any harm. Really, you're obsessed by them! It's not good for you. You're wearing yourself out. You've had one shock, why look for more? You just concentrate on getting back to normal.

BERENGER: I wonder if I really am immune?

DUDARD: In any case it's not fatal. Certain illnesses are good for you. I'm convinced this is something you can cure if you want to. They'll get over it, you'll see.

BERENGER: But it's bound to have certain after-effects! An organic upheaval like that can't help but leave..

DUDARD: It's only temporary, don't you worry.

BERENGER: Are you absolutely certain?

DUDARD: I think so, yes, I suppose so.

BERENGER: But if one really doesn't want to, really doesn't want to catch this thing, which after all is a nervous disease—then you don't catch it, you simply don't catch it! Do you feel like a brandy? (*He goes to the table where the bottle stands.*)

DUDARD: Not for me, thank you, I never touch it. But don't mind me if you want some—you go ahead, don't worry about me. But watch out it doesn't make your headache worse.

BERENGER: Alcohol is good for epidemics. It immunizes you. It kills influenza microbes, for instance.

DUDARD: Perhaps it doesn't kill all microbes. They don't know about rhinoceritis yet.

BERENGER: Jean never touched alcohol. He just pretended to. Maybe that's why he ... perhaps that explains his attitude. (*He offers a full glass to* DUDARD.) You're sure you won't?

DUDARD: No, no, never before lunch, thank you.

> BERENGER *empties his glass, continues to hold it, together with the bottle, in his hands; he coughs.*

You see, you can't take it. It makes you cough.

BERENGER (*worried*): Yes, it did make me cough. How did I cough?

DUDARD: Like everyone coughs when they drink something a bit strong.

BERENGER (*moving to put the glass and bottle back on the table*): There wasn't anything odd about it, was there? It *was* a real human cough?

DUDARD: What are you getting at? It was an ordinary human cough. What other sort of cough could it have been?

BERENGER: I don't know ... Perhaps an animal's cough ... Do rhinoceroses cough?

DUDARD: Look, Berenger, you're being ridiculous, you invent difficulties for yourself, you ask yourself the weirdest questions ... I remember you said yourself that the best protection against the thing was will-power.

BERENGER: Yes, I did.

DUDARD: Well then, prove you've got some.

BERENGER: I have, I assure you ...

DUDARD: Prove it to yourself—now, don't drink any more brandy. You'll feel more sure of yourself then.

BERENGER: You deliberately misunderstand me. I told you the only reason I take it is because it keeps the worst at bay; I'm doing it quite deliberately. When the epidemic's over, then I shall stop drinking. I'd already decided that before the whole business began. I'm just putting it off for the time being!

DUDARD: You're inventing excuses for yourself.

BERENGER: Do you think I am ... ? In any case, that's got nothing to do with what's happening now.

DUDARD: How do we know?

BERENGER (*alarmed*): Do you really think so? You think that's how the rot sets in? I'm not an alcoholic. (*He goes to the mirror and examines himself.*) Do you think, by any chance ... (*He touches his face, pats his bandaged forehead.*) Nothing's changed; it hasn't done any harm so it must have done good ... or it's harmless at any rate.

DUDARD: I was only joking. I was just teasing you. You see the black side of everything—watch out, or you'll become a neurotic. When you've got over your shock completely and you can get out for a breath of fresh air, you'll feel better--you'll see! All these morbid ideas will vanish.

BERENGER: Go out? I suppose I'll have to. I'm dreading the moment. I'll be bound to meet some of them ...

DUDARD: What if you do? You only have to keep out of their way. And there aren't as many as all that.

BERENGER: I see them all over the place. You'll probably say that's being morbid, too.

DUDARD: They don't attack you. If you leave them alone, they just ignore you. You can't say they're spiteful. They've even got a certain natural innocence, a sort of frankness. Besides I walked right along the avenue to get to you today. I got here safe and sound, didn't I? No trouble at all.

BERENGER: Just the sight of them upsets me. It's a nervous thing. I don't get angry—no, it doesn't pay to get angry, you never know where it'll lead to, I watch out for that. But it does something to me, here! (*He points to his heart.*) I get a tight feeling inside.

DUDARD: I think you're right to a certain extent to have some reaction. But you go too far. You've no sense of humour, that's your trouble, none at all. You must learn to be more detached, and try and see the funny side of things.

BERENGER: I feel responsible for everything that happens. I feel involved, I just can't be indifferent.

DUDARD: Judge not lest ye be judged. If you start worrying about everything that happens you'd never be able to go on living.

BERENGER: If only it had happened somewhere else, in some other country, and we'd just read about it in the papers, one could discuss it quietly, examine the question from all points of view and come to an objective conclusion. We could organize debates with professors and writers and lawyers, and blue-stockings and artists and people. And the ordinary man in the street, as well— it would be very interesting and instructive. But when you're involved yourself, when you suddenly find yourself up against the brutal facts you can't help feeling directly concerned—the shock is too violent for you to stay cool and detached. I'm frankly surprised, I'm very very surprised. I can't get over it.

DUDARD: Well I'm surprised, too. Or rather I was. Now I'm starting to get used to it.

BERENGER: Your nervous system is better balanced than mine. You're lucky. But don't you agree it's all very unfortunate...

DUDARD (*interrupting him*): I don't say it's a good thing. And don't get the idea that I'm on the rhinoceroses' side...

More sounds of rhinoceroses passing, this time under the downstage window-frame.

BERENGER (*with a start*): There they are, there they are again! Oh, it's no use, I just can't get used to them. Maybe it's wrong of me, but they obsess me so much in spite of myself, I just can't sleep at night. I get insomnia. I doze a bit in the daytime out of sheer exhaustion.

DUDARD: Take some sleeping tablets.

BERENGER: That's not the answer. If I sleep, it's worse. I dream about them, I get nightmares.

DUDARD: That's what comes of taking things too seriously. You get a kick out of torturing yourself—admit it!

BERENGER: I'm no masochist, I assure you.

DUDARD: Then face the facts and get over it. This is the situation and there's nothing you can do about it.

BERENGER: That's fatalism.

DUDARD: It's common sense. When a thing like this happens there's bound to be a reason for it. That's what we must find out.

BERENGER (*getting up*): Well, I don't want to accept the situation.

DUDARD: What else can you do? What are your plans?

BERENGER: I don't know for the moment. I must think it over. I shall write to the papers; I'll draw up manifestos; I shall apply for an audience with the mayor—or his deputy, if the mayor's too busy.

DUDARD: You leave the authorities to act as they think best! I'm not sure if morally you have the right to butt in. In any case, I still think it's not all that serious. I consider it's silly to get worked up because a few people decide to change their skins. They just didn't feel happy in the ones they had. They're free to do as they like.

BERENGER: We must attack the evil at the roots.

DUDARD: The evil! That's just a phrase! Who knows what is evil and what is good? It's just a question of personal preferences. You're worried about your own skin—that's the truth of the matter. But you'll never become a rhinoceros, really you won't . . . you haven't got the vocation!

BERENGER: There you are, you see! If our leaders and fellow citizens all think like you, they'll never take any action.

DUDARD: You wouldn't want to ask for help from abroad, surely? This is an internal affair, it only concerns our country.

BERENGER: I believe in international solidarity . . .

DUDARD: You're a Don Quixote. Oh, I don't mean that nastily, don't be offended! I'm only saying it for your own good, because you really need to calm down.

BERENGER: You're right, I know—forgive me. I get too worked up. But I'll change, I will change. I'm sorry to keep you all this time listening to my ramblings. You must have work to do. Did you get my application for sick leave?

DUDARD: Don't worry about that. It's all in order. In any case, the office hasn't resumed work.

BERENGER: Haven't they repaired the staircase yet? What negligence! That's why everything goes so badly.

DUDARD: They're repairing it now. But it's slow work. It's not easy to find the workmen. They sign on and work for a couple of days, then don't turn up any more. You never see them again. Then you have to look for others.

BERENGER: And they talk about unemployment! At least I hope we're getting a stone staircase.

DUDARD: No, it's wood again, but new wood this time.

BERENGER: Oh! The way these organizations stick to the old routine. They chuck money down the drain but when it's needed for something really useful they pretend they can't afford it. I bet Mr. Papillon's none too pleased. He was dead set on having a stone staircase. What's he say about it?

DUDARD: We haven't got a Chief any more. Mr. Papillon's resigned.

BERENGER: It's not possible!

DUDARD: It's true, I assure you.

BERENGER: Well, I'm amazed . . . Was it on account of the staircase?

DUDARD: I don't think so. Anyway that wasn't the reason he gave.

BERENGER: Why was it then? What got into him?

DUDARD: He's retiring to the country.

BERENGER: Retiring? He's not the age. He might still have become the Director.

DUDARD: He's given it all up! Said he needed a rest.

BERENGER: I bet the management's pretty upset to see him go; they'll have to replace him. All your diplomas should come in useful— you stand a good chance.

DUDARD: I suppose I might as well tell you ... it's really rather funny— the fact is, he turned into a rhinoceros.

Distant rhinoceros noises.

BERENGER: A rhinoceros!!!! Mr. Papillon a rhinoceros! I can't believe it! I don't think it's funny at all! Why didn't you tell me before?

DUDARD: Well you know you've no sense of humour. I didn't want to tell you ... I didn't want to tell you because I knew very well you wouldn't see the funny side, and it would upset you. You know how impressionable you are!

BERENGER (*raising his arms to heaven*): Oh that's awful ... Mr. Papillon! And he had such a good job.

DUDARD: That proves his metamorphosis was sincere.

BERENGER: He couldn't have done it on purpose. I'm certain it must have been involuntary.

DUDARD: How can we tell? It's hard to know the real reasons for people's decisions.

BERENGER: He must have made a mistake. He'd got some hidden complexes. He should have been psychoanalysed.

DUDARD: Even if it's a case of dissociation it's still very revealing. It was his way of sublimating himself.

BERENGER: He let himself be talked into it, I feel sure.

DUDARD: That could happen to anybody!

BERENGER (*alarmed*): To anybody? Oh no, not to you it couldn't— could it? And not to me!

DUDARD: We must hope not.

BERENGER: Because we don't want to ... that's so, isn't it? Tell me, that *is* so, isn't it?

DUDARD: Yes, yes, of course ...

BERENGER (*a little calmer*): I still would have thought Mr. Papillon would have had the strength to resist. I thought he had a bit more character! Particularly as I fail to see where his interest lay—what possible material or moral interest...

DUDARD: It was obviously a disinterested gesture on his part.

BERENGER: Obviously. There were extenuating circumstances...or were they aggravating? Aggravating, I should think, because if he did it from choice...You know, I feel sure that Botard must have taken a very poor view of it—what did he think of his Chief's behaviour?

DUDARD: Oh poor old Botard was quite indignant, absolutely outraged. I've rarely seen anyone so incensed.

BERENGER: Well for once I'm on his side. He's a good man after all. A man of sound common sense. And to think I misjudged him.

DUDARD: He misjudged you, too.

BERENGER: That proves how objective I'm being now. Besides, you had a pretty bad opinion of him yourself.

DUDARD: I wouldn't say I had a bad opinion. I admit I didn't often agree with him. I never liked his scepticism, the way he was always so incredulous and suspicious. Even in this instance I didn't approve of him entirely.

BERENGER: This time for the opposite reasons.

DUDARD: No, not exactly—my own reasoning and my judgment are a bit more complex than you seem to think. It was because there was nothing precise or objective about the way Botard argued. I don't approve of the rhinoceroses myself, as you know—not at all, don't go thinking that! But Botard's attitude was too passionate, as usual, and therefore over-simplified. His stand seems to me entirely dictated by hatred of his superiors. That's where he gets his inferiority complex and his resentment. What's more he talks in clichés, and commonplace arguments leave me cold.

BERENGER: Well forgive me, but this time I'm in complete agreement with Botard. He's somebody worthwhile.

DUDARD: I don't deny it, but that doesn't mean anything.

BERENGER: He's a very worthwhile person—and they're not easy to find these days. He's down-to-earth, with four feet planted firmly on the ground—I mean, both feet. I'm in complete agreement with him, and I'm proud of it. I shall congratulate him when I see him. I deplore Mr. Papillon's action; it was his duty not to succumb.

DUDARD: How intolerant you are! Maybe Papillon felt the need for a bit of relaxation after all these years of office life.

BERENGER (*ironically*): And you're too tolerant, far too broadminded!

DUDARD: My dear Berenger, one must always make an effort to understand. And in order to understand a phenomenon and its effects you need to work back to the initial causes, by honest intellectual effort. We must try to do this because, after all, we are thinking beings. I haven't yet succeeded, as I told you, and I don't know if I shall succeed. But in any case one has to start out favourably disposed—or at least, impartial; one has to keep an open mind— that's essential to a scientific mentality. Everything is logical. To understand is to justify.

BERENGER: You'll be siding with the rhinoceroses before long.

DUDARD: No, no, not at all. I wouldn't go that far. I'm simply trying to look the facts unemotionally in the face. I'm trying to be realistic. I also contend that there is no real evil in what occurs naturally. I don't believe in seeing evil in everything. I leave that to the inquisitors.

BERENGER: And you consider all this natural?

DUDARD: What could be more natural than a rhinoceros?

BERENGER: Yes, but for a man to turn into a rhinoceros is abnormal beyond question.

DUDARD: Well, of course, that's a matter of opinion . . .

BERENGER: It is beyond question, absolutely beyond question!

DUDARD: You seem very sure of yourself. Who can say where the normal stops and the abnormal begins? Can you personally define these conceptions of normality and abnormality? Nobody has solved this problem yet, either medically or philosophically. You ought to know that.

BERENGER: The problem may not be resolved philosophically—but in practice it's simple. They may prove there's no such thing as movement . . . and then you start walking . . . (*He starts walking up and down the room.*) . . . and you go on walking, and you say to yourself, like Galileo, 'E pur si muove' . . .

DUDARD: You're getting things all mixed up! Don't confuse the issue. In Galileo's case it was the opposite; theoretic and scientific thought proving itself superior to mass opinion and dogmatism.

BERENGER (*quite lost*): What does all that mean? Mass opinion, dogmatism—they're just words! I may be mixing everything up in my head but you're losing yours. You don't know what's nor-

mal and what isn't any more. I couldn't care less about Galileo
... I don't give a damn about Galileo.

DUDARD: You brought him up in the first place and raised the whole
question, saying that practice always had the last word. Maybe
it does, but only when it proceeds from theory! The history of
thought and science proves that.

BERENGER (*more and more furious*): It doesn't prove anything of the
sort! It's all gibberish, utter lunacy!

DUDARD: There again we need to define exactly what we mean by
lunacy ...

BERENGER: Lunacy is lunacy and that's all there is to it! Everybody
knows what lunacy is. And what about the rhinoceroses—are they
practice or are they theory?

DUDARD: Both!

BERENGER: How do you mean—both?

DUDARD: Both the one and the other, or one or the other. It's a de-
batable point!

BERENGER: Well in that case ... I refuse to think about it!

DUDARD: You're getting all het up. Our opinions may not exactly coincide but we can still discuss the matter peaceably. These things
should be discussed.

BERENGER (*distracted*): You think I'm getting all het up, do you? I
might be Jean. Oh no, no, I don't want to become like him. I
mustn't be like him. (*He calms down.*) I'm not very well up in
philosophy. I've never studied; you've got all sorts of diplomas.
That's why you're so at ease in discussion, whereas I never know
what to answer—I'm so clumsy. (*Louder rhinoceros noises passing
first under the up-stage window and then the downstage.*) But I
do feel you're in the wrong ... I feel it instinctively—no, that's
not what I mean, it's the rhinoceros which has instinct—I feel it
intuitively, yes, that's the word, intuitively.

DUDARD: What do you understand by 'intuitive'?

BERENGER: Intuitively means ... well, just like that! I feel it, just
like that. I think your excessive tolerance, and your generous
indulgence ... believe me, they're really only weakness ... just
blind spots ...

DUDARD: You're innocent enough to think that.

BERENGER: You'll always be able to dance rings round me. But, you
know what? I'm going to try and get hold of the Logician ...

DUDARD: What logician?

BERENGER: The Logician, the philosopher, a logician, you know ... you know better than I do what a logician is. A logician I met, who explained to me ...

DUDARD: What did he explain to you?

BERENGER: He explained that the Asiatic rhinoceroses were African and the African ones Asiatic.

DUDARD: I don't follow you.

BERENGER: No ... no ... he proved the contrary—that the African ones were Asiatic and the Asiatic ones ... I know what I mean. That's not what I wanted to say. But you'll get on very well with him. He's your sort of person, a very good man, a very subtle mind, brilliant.

> *Increasing noises from the rhinoceroses. The words of the two men are drowned by the animals passing under the windows; for a few moments the lips of* DUDARD *and* BERENGER *are seen to move without any words being heard.*

There they go again! Will they never stop! (*He runs to the up-stage window.*) Stop it! Stop it! You devils!

> *The rhinoceroses move away.* BERENGER *shakes his fist after them.*

DUDARD (*seated*): I'd be happy to meet your Logician. If he can enlighten me on these obscure and delicate points, I'd be only too delighted.

BERENGER (*as he runs to the down-stage window*): Yes, I'll bring him along, he'll talk to you. He's a very distinguished person, you'll see. (*To the rhinoceroses, from the window.*) You devils! (*Shakes his fist as before.*)

DUDARD: Let them alone. And be more polite. You shouldn't talk to people like that ...

BERENGER (*still at the window*): There they go again!

> *A boater pierced by a rhinoceros horn emerges from the orchestra pit under the window and passes swiftly from left to right.*

There's a boater impaled on a rhinoceros horn. Oh, it's the

Logician's hat! It's the Logician's! That's the bloody limit! The Logician's turned into a rhinoceros!

DUDARD: That's no reason to be coarse!

BERENGER: Dear Lord, who can you turn to—who? I ask you! The Logician a rhinoceros!

DUDARD (*going to the window*): Where is he?

BERENGER (*pointing*): There, that one there, you see!

DUDARD: He's the only rhinoceros in a boater! That makes you think. You're sure it's your Logician?

BERENGER: The Logician . . . a rhinoceros!!!

DUDARD: He's still retained a vestige of his old individuality.

BERENGER (*shakes his fist again at the straw-hatted rhinoceros, which has disappeared*): I'll never join up with you! Not me!

DUDARD: If he was a genuine thinker, as you say, he couldn't have got carried away. He must have weighed all the pros and cons before deciding.

BERENGER (*still shouting after the ex-Logician and the other rhinoceroses who have moved away*): I'll never join up with you!

DUDARD (*settling into the armchair*): Yes, that certainly makes you think!

> BERENGER *closes the down-stage window; goes to the up-stage window where other rhinoceroses are passing, presumably making a tour of the house. He opens the window and shouts.*

BERENGER: No, I'll never join up with you!

DUDARD (*aside, in his armchair*): They're going round and round the house. They're playing! Just big babies!

> DAISY *has been seen mounting the top stairs. She knocks on* BERENGER'S *door. She is carrying a basket.*

There's somebody at the door, Berenger!

> *He takes* BERENGER, *who is still at the window, by the sleeve.*

BERENGER (*shouting after the rhinoceroses*): It's a disgrace, masquerading like this, a disgrace!

DUDARD: There's someone knocking, Berenger, can't you hear?

BERENGER: Open, then, if you want to! (*He continues to watch the rhinoceroses whose noise is fading away.*)

DUDARD *goes to open the door.*

DAISY (*coming in*): Morning, Mr. Dudard.
DUDARD: Oh, it's you, Miss Daisy.
DAISY: Is Berenger here, is he any better?
DUDARD: How nice to see you, my dear. Do you often visit Berenger?
DAISY: Where is he?
DUDARD (*pointing*): There.
DAISY: He's all on his own, poor thing. And he's not very well at the moment, somebody has to give him a hand.
DUDARD: You're a good friend, Miss Daisy.
DAISY: That's just what I am, a good friend.
DUDARD: You've got a warm heart.
DAISY: I'm a good friend, that's all.
BERENGER (*turning, leaving the window open*): Oh Miss Daisy! How kind of you to come, how very kind!
DUDARD: It certainly is.
BERENGER: Did you know, Miss Daisy, that the Logician is a rhinoceros?
DAISY: Yes, I did. I caught sight of him in the street as I arrived. He was running very fast for someone his age! Are you feeling any better, Mr. Berenger?
BERENGER: My head's still bad! Still got a headache! Isn't it frightful? What do you think about it?
DAISY: I think you ought to be resting ... you should take things quietly for a few more days.
DUDARD (*to* BERENGER *and* DAISY): I hope I'm not disturbing you!
BERENGER (*to* DAISY): I meant about the Logician ...
DAISY (*to* DUDARD): Why should you be? (*To* BERENGER.) Oh, about the Logician? I don't think anything at all!
DUDARD (*to* DAISY): I thought I might be in the way!
DAISY (*to* BERENGER): What do you expect me to think? (*To both.*) I've got some news for you: Botard's a rhinoceros!
DUDARD: Well, well!
BERENGER: I don't believe it. He was against it. You must be mistaken. He protested. Dudard has just been telling me. Isn't that so, Dudard?

DUDARD: That is so.

DAISY: I know he was against it. But it didn't stop him turning, twenty-four hours after Mr. Papillon.

DUDARD: Well, he must have changed his mind! Everybody has the right to do that.

BERENGER: Then obviously anything can happen!

DUDARD (*to* BERENGER): He was a very good man according to you just now.

BERENGER (*to* DAISY): I just can't believe you. They must have lied to you.

DAISY: I saw him do it.

BERENGER: Then he must have been lying; he was just pretending.

DAISY: He seemed very sincere; sincerity itself.

BERENGER: Did he give any reasons?

DAISY: What he said was: we must move with the times! Those were his last human words.

DUDARD (*to* DAISY): I was almost certain I'd meet you here, Miss Daisy.

BERENGER: . . . Move with the times! What a mentality! (*He makes a wide gesture.*)

DUDARD (*to* DAISY): Impossible to find you anywhere else, since the office closed.

BERENGER (*continuing, aside*): What childishness! (*He repeats the same gesture.*)

DAISY (*to* DUDARD): If you wanted to see me, you only had to telephone.

DUDARD (*to* DAISY): Oh you know me, Miss Daisy, I'm discretion itself.

BERENGER: But now I come to think it over, Botard's behaviour doesn't surprise me. His firmness was only a pose. Which doesn't stop him from being a good man, of course. Good men make good rhinoceroses, unfortunately. It's because they are so good that they get taken in.

DAISY: Do you mind if I put this basket on the table? (*She does so.*)

BERENGER: But he was a good man with a lot of resentment . . .

DUDARD (*to* DAISY, *and hastening to help her with the basket*): Excuse me, excuse us both, we should have given you a hand before.

BERENGER (*continues*): . . . He was riddled with hatred for his superiors, and he'd got an inferiority complex . . .

DUDARD (*to* BERENGER): Your argument doesn't hold water, because the example he followed was the Chief's, the very instrument of the people who exploited him, as he used to say. No, it seems to me that with him it was a case of community spirit triumphing over his anarchic impulses.

BERENGER: It's the rhinoceroses which are anarchic, because they're in the minority.

DUDARD: They are, it's true—for the moment.

DAISY: They're a pretty big minority, and getting bigger all the time. My cousin's a rhinoceros now, and his wife. Not to mention leading personalities like the Cardinal de Retz...

DUDARD: A prelate!

DAISY: Mazarin.

DUDARD: This is going to spread to other countries, you'll see.

BERENGER: And to think it all started with us!

DAISY: ... and some of the aristocracy. The Duke of St. Simon.

BERENGER (*with uplifted arms*): All our great names!

DAISY: And others, too. Lots of others. Maybe a quarter of the whole town.

BERENGER: We're still in the majority. We must take advantage of that. We must do something before we're inundated.

DUDARD: They're very potent, very.

DAISY: Well for the moment, let's eat. I've brought some food.

BERENGER: You're very kind, Miss Daisy.

DUDARD (*aside*): Very kind indeed.

BERENGER: I don't know how to thank you.

DAISY (*to* DUDARD): Would you care to stay with us?

DUDARD: I don't want to be a nuisance.

DAISY: Whatever do you mean, Mr. Dudard? You know very well we'd love you to stay.

DUDARD: Well, you know, I'd hate to be in the way...

BERENGER: Of course, stay, Dudard. It's always a pleasure to talk to you.

DUDARD: As a matter of fact I'm in a bit of a hurry. I have an appointment.

BERENGER: Just now you said you had nothing to do.

DAISY (*unpacking her basket*): You know, I had a lot of trouble finding food. The shops have been plundered; they just devour everything. And a lot of the shops are closed. It's written up outside: 'Closed on account of transformation.'

BERENGER: They should be all rounded up in a big enclosure, and kept under strict supervision.

DUDARD: That's easier said than done. The animals' protection league would be the first to object.

DAISY: And besides everyone has a close relative or a friend among them, and that would make it even more difficult.

BERENGER: So everybody's mixed up in it!

DUDARD: Everybody's in the same boat!

BERENGER: But how can people be rhinoceroses? It doesn't bear thinking about! (*To* DAISY.) Shall I help you lay the table?

DAISY: No, don't bother. I know where the plates are. (*She goes to a cupboard and takes out the plates.*)

DUDARD (*aside*): She's obviously very familiar with the place...

DAISY (*to* DUDARD): I'm laying for three—all right? You are staying with us?

BERENGER (*to* DUDARD): Yes, of course you're staying.

DAISY (*to* BERENGER): You get used to it, you know. Nobody seems surprised any more to see herds of rhinoceroses galloping through the streets. They just stand aside, and then carry on as if nothing had happened.

DUDARD: It's the wisest course to take.

BERENGER: Well I can't get used to it.

DUDARD (*reflectively*): I wonder if one oughtn't to give it a try?

DAISY: Well right now, let's have lunch.

BERENGER: I don't see how a legal man like yourself can...

A great noise of rhinoceroses travelling very fast is heard outside. Trumpets and drums are also heard.

What's going on?

They rush to the down-stage window.

What is it?

The sound of a wall crumbling is heard. Dust covers part of the stage, enveloping, if possible, the characters. They are heard speaking through it.

BERENGER: You can't see a thing! What's happening?

DUDARD: You can't see, but you can hear all right.

BERENGER: That's no good!

DAISY: The plates will be all covered in dust.

BERENGER: How unhygienic!

DAISY: Let's hurry up and eat. We won't pay any attention to them.

The dust disperses.

BERENGER (*pointing into the auditorium*): They've demolished the walls of the Fire Station.

DUDARD: That's true, they've demolished them!

DAISY (*who after moving from the window to near the table holding the plate which she is endeavouring to clean, rushes to join the other two*): They're coming out.

BERENGER: All the firemen, a whole regiment of rhinoceroses, led by drums.

DAISY: They're pouring up the streets!

BERENGER: It's gone too far, much too far!

DAISY: More rhinoceroses are streaming out of the courtyard.

BERENGER: And out of the houses ...

DUDARD: And the windows as well!

DAISY: They're joining up with the others.

A man comes out of the landing door left and dashes downstairs at top speed; then another with a large horn on his nose; then a woman wearing an entire rhinoceros head.

DUDARD: There aren't enough of us left any more.

BERENGER: How many with one horn, and how many with two?

DUDARD: The statisticians are bound to be compiling statistics now. There'll be plenty of erudite controversy you can be sure!

BERENGER: They can only calculate approximately. It's all happening so fast. It leaves them no time. No time to calculate.

DAISY: The best thing is to let the statisticians get on with it. Come and eat, my dear. That'll calm you down. You'll feel better afterwards. (*To* DUDARD.) And you, too.

They move away from the window. DAISY *takes* BERENGER'S *arm; he allows himself to be led docilely.* DUDARD *suddenly halts.*

DUDARD: I don't feel very hungry—or rather, to be frank, I don't like tinned food very much. I feel like eating outside on the grass.

BERENGER: You mustn't do that. Think of the risk!

DUDARD: But really I don't want to put you to the trouble.

BERENGER: But we've already told you ...

DUDARD (*interrupting* BERENGER): I really mean it.

DAISY (*to* DUDARD): Of course if you really don't want to stay, we can't force you ...

DUDARD: I didn't mean to offend you.

BERENGER (*to* DAISY): Don't let him go, he mustn't go.

DAISY: I'd like him to stay ... but people must do as they please.

BERENGER (*to* DUDARD): Man is superior to the rhinoceros.

DUDARD: I didn't say he wasn't. But I'm not with you absolutely either. I don't know; only experience can tell.

BERENGER (*to* DUDARD): You're weakening too, Dudard. It's just a passing phase which you'll regret.

DAISY: If it's just a passing phase then there's no great danger.

DUDARD: I feel certain scruples! I feel it's my duty to stick by my employers and my friends, through thick and thin.

BERENGER: It's not as if you were married to them.

DUDARD: I've renounced marriage. I prefer the great universal family to the little domestic one.

DAISY (*softly*): We shall miss you a lot, Dudard, but we can't do anything about it.

DUDARD: It's my duty to stick by them; I have to do my duty.

BERENGER: No you're wrong, your duty is to ... you don't see where your real duty lies ... your duty is to oppose them, with a firm, clear mind.

DUDARD: I shall keep my mind clear. (*He starts to move round the stage in circles.*) As clear as ever it was. But if you're going to criticize, it's better to do so from the inside. I'm not going to abandon them. I won't abandon them.

DAISY: He's very good-hearted.

BERENGER: He's too good-hearted. (*To* DUDARD, *then dashing to the door.*) You're too good-hearted, you're human. (*To* DAISY.) Don't let him go. He's making a mistake. He's human.

DAISY: What can I do?

> DUDARD *opens the door and runs off; he goes down the stairs at top speed followed by* BERENGER *who shouts after him from the landing.*

BERENGER: Come back, Dudard! We're fond of you, don't go! It's too late! (*He comes back.*) Too late!

DAISY: We couldn't do anything. (*She closes the door behind* BERENGER, *who darts to the down-stage window.*)

BERENGER: He's joined up with them. Where is he now?

DAISY (*moving to the window*): With them.

BERENGER: Which one is he?

DAISY: You can't tell. You can't recognize him any more.

BERENGER: They all look alike, all alike. (*To* DAISY.) He *did* hesitate. You should have held him back by force.

DAISY: I didn't dare to.

BERENGER: You should have been firmer with him, you should have insisted; he was in love with you, wasn't he?

DAISY: He never made me any official declaration.

BERENGER: Everybody knew he was. He's done this out of thwarted love. He was a shy man. He wanted to make a big gesture to impress you. Don't you feel like going after him?

DAISY: Not at all. Or I wouldn't be here!

BERENGER (*looking out of the window*): You can see nothing but them in the street. (*He darts to the up-stage window.*) Nothing but them! You were wrong, Daisy. (*He looks through the down-stage window again.*) Not a single human being as far as the eye can see. They're all over the street. Half with one horn and half with two, and that's the only distinction!

> *Powerful noises of moving rhinoceroses are heard, but somehow it is a musical sound. On the up-stage wall stylized heads appear and disappear; they become more and more numerous from now on until the end of the play. Towards the end they stay fixed for longer and longer, until eventually they fill the entire back wall, remaining static. The heads, in spite of their monstrous appearance, seem to become more and more beautiful.*

You don't feel let down, do you, Daisy? There's nothing you regret?

DAISY: No, no.

BERENGER: I want so much to be a comfort to you. I love you, Daisy; don't ever leave me.

DAISY: Shut the window, darling. They're making such a noise. And the dust is rising even up to here. Everything will get filthy.

BERENGER: Yes, you're right. (*He closes the down-stage window and* DAISY *closes the up-stage one. They meet centre-stage.*) I'm not afraid of anything as long as we're together. I don't care what happens. You know, Daisy, I thought I'd never be able to fall in love again. (*He takes her hands, strokes her arms.*)

DAISY: Well you see, everything is possible.

BERENGER: I want so much to make you happy. Do you think you can be happy with me.

DAISY: Why not? If you're happy, then I'll be happy, too. You say nothing scares you, but you're really frightened of everything. What can possibly happen to us?

BERENGER (*stammering*): My love, my dear love . . . let me kiss your lips. I never dreamed I could still feel such tremendous emotion!

DAISY: You must be more calm and more sure of yourself, now.

BERENGER: I am; let me kiss you.

DAISY: I'm very tired, dear. Stay quiet and rest yourself. Sit in the armchair.

BERENGER, *led by* DAISY, *sits in the armchair.*

BERENGER: There was no point in Dudard quarrelling with Botard, as things turned out.

DAISY: Don't think about Dudard any more. I'm here with you. We've no right to interfere in other people's lives.

BERENGER: But you're interfering in mine. You know how to be firm with me.

DAISY: That's not the same thing; I never loved Dudard.

BERENGER: I see what you mean. If he'd stayed he'd always have been an obstacle between us. Ah, happiness is such an egotistical thing!

DAISY: You have to fight for happiness, don't you agree?

BERENGER: I adore you, Daisy; I admire you as well.

DAISY: Maybe you won't say that when you get to know me better.

BERENGER: The more I know you the better you seem; and you're so beautiful, so very beautiful. (*More rhinoceroses are heard passing.*) Particularly compared to them . . . (*He points to the window.*) You probably think that's no compliment, but they make you seem more beautiful than ever . . .

DAISY: Have you been good today? You haven't had any brandy?

BERENGER: Oh yes, I've been good.

DAISY: Is that the truth?

BERENGER: Yes, it's the truth I assure you.

DAISY: Can I believe you, I wonder?

BERENGER (*a little flustered*): Oh yes, you must believe me.

DAISY: Well all right then, you can have a little glass. It'll buck you up.

> BERENGER *is about to leap up.*

You stay where you are, dear. Where's the bottle?

BERENGER (*pointing to it*): There, on the little table.

DAISY (*going to the table and getting the bottle and glass*): You've hidden it well away.

BERENGER: It's out of the way of temptation.

DAISY (*pours a small glass and gives it to* BERENGER): You've been a good boy. You're making progress.

BERENGER: I'll make a lot more now I'm with you.

DAISY (*handing him the glass*): Here you are. That's your reward.

BERENGER (*downing it at one go*): Thank you. (*He holds up his empty glass to* DAISY).

DAISY: Oh no, dear. That's enough for this morning. (*She takes his glass, puts it back on the table with the bottle.*) I don't want it to make you ill. (*She comes back to him.*) How's your head feel now?

BERENGER: Much better, darling.

DAISY: Then we'll take off the bandage. It doesn't suit you at all.

BERENGER: Oh no, don't touch it.

DAISY: Nonsense, we'll take it off now.

BERENGER: I'm frightened there might be something underneath.

DAISY (*removing the bandage in spite of his protests*): Always frightened, aren't you, always imagining the worst! There's nothing there, you see. Your forehead's as smooth as a baby's.

BERENGER (*feeling his brow*): You're right; you're getting rid of my complexes. (DAISY *kisses him on the brow.*) What should I do without you?

DAISY: I'll never leave you alone again.

BERENGER: I won't have any more fears now I'm with you.

DAISY: I'll keep them all at bay.

BERENGER: We'll read books together. I'll become clever.

DAISY: And when there aren't so many people about we'll go for long walks.

BERENGER: Yes, along the Seine, and in the Luxembourg Gardens...

DAISY: And to the Zoo.

BERENGER: I'll be brave and strong. I'll keep you safe from harm.

DAISY: You won't need to defend me, silly! We don't wish anyone any harm. And no one wishes us any, my dear.

BERENGER: Sometimes one does harm without meaning to, or rather one allows it to go unchecked. I know you didn't like poor old Mr. Papillon very much—but perhaps you shouldn't have spoken to him so harshly that day when Boeuf turned into a rhinoceros. You needn't have told him he had such horny hands.

DAISY: But it was true—he had!

BERENGER: I know he had, my dear. But you could have said so less bluntly and not hurt his feelings so much. It had a big effect on him.

DAISY: Do you think so?

BERENGER: He didn't show it—he was too proud for that—but the remark certainly went home. It must have influenced his decision. Perhaps you might have been the means of saving him.

DAISY: I couldn't possibly foresee what was going to happen to him ... besides he was so ill-mannered.

BERENGER: For my own part, I shall never forgive myself for not being nicer to Jean. I never managed to give him a really solid proof of the friendship I felt for him. I wasn't sufficiently understanding with him.

DAISY: Don't worry about it. You did all you could. Nobody can do the impossible. There's no point in reproaching yourself now. Stop thinking about all those people. Forget about them. You must forget all those bad memories.

BERENGER: But they keep coming back to me. They're very real memories.

DAISY: I never knew you were such a realist—I thought you were more poetic. Where's your imagination? There are many sides to reality. Choose the one that's best for you. Escape into the world of the imagination.

BERENGER: It's easy to say that!

DAISY: Aren't I enough for you?

BERENGER: Oh yes, more than enough!

DAISY: You'll spoil everything if you go on having a bad conscience.

Everybody has their faults, but you and I have got less than a lot of people.

BERENGER: Do you really think so?

DAISY: We're comparatively better than most. We're good, both of us.

BERENGER: That's true, you're good and I'm good. That's true.

DAISY: Well then we have the right to live. We even owe ourselves a duty to be happy in spite of everything. Guilt is a dangerous symptom. It shows a lack of purity.

BERENGER: You're right, it can lead· to that ... (*He points to the window under which the rhinoceroses are passing and to the up-stage wall where another rhinoceros head appears.*) ... a lot of them started like that!

DAISY: We must try and not feel guilty any more.

BERENGER: How right you are, my wonderful love ... You're all my happiness; the light of my life ... We are together, aren't we? No one can separate us. Our love is the only thing that's real. Nobody has the right to stop us from being happy—in fact, nobody could, could they?

The telephone rings.

Who could that be?

DAISY (*fearful*): Don't answer.

BERENGER: Why not?

DAISY: I don't know. I just feel it's better not to.

BERENGER: It might be Mr. Papillon, or Botard, or Jean or Dudard ringing to say they've had second thoughts. You did say it was probably only a passing phase.

DAISY: I don't think so. They wouldn't thave changed their minds so quickly. They've not had time to think it over. They're bound to give it a fair trial.

BERENGER: Perhaps the authorities have decided to take action at last; maybe they're ringing to ask our help in whatever measures they've decided to adopt.

DAISY: I'd be surprised if it was them.

The telephone rings again.

BERENGER: It is the authorities, I tell you, I recognize the ring—a long drawn-out ring, I can't ignore an appeal from them. It can't be anyone else. (*He picks up the receiver.*) Hallo? (*Trumpetings are heard coming from the receiver.*) You hear that? Trumpeting! Listen!

DAISY *puts the telephone to her ear, is shocked by the sound, quickly replaces the receiver.*

DAISY (*frightened*): What's going on?
BERENGER: They're playing jokes now.
DAISY: Jokes in bad taste!
BERENGER: You see! What did I tell you?
DAISY: You didn't tell me anything.
BERENGER: I was expecting that; it was just what I'd predicted.
DAISY: You didn't predict anything. You never do. You can only predict things after they've happened.
BERENGER: Oh yes, I can; I can predict things all right.
DAISY: That's not nice of them—in fact it's very nasty. I don't like being made fun of.
BERENGER: They wouldn't dare make fun of you. It's me they're making fun of.
DAISY: And naturally I come in for it as well because I'm with you. They're taking their revenge. But what have we done to them?

The telephone rings again.

Pull the plug out.
BERENGER: The telephone authorities say you mustn't.
DAISY: Oh you never dare to do anything—and you say you could defend me!
BERENGER (*darting to the radio*): Let's turn on the radio for the news!
DAISY: Yes, we must find out how things stand!

The sound of trumpeting comes from the radio. BERENGER *peremptorily switches it off. But in the distance other trumpetings, like echoes, can be heard.*

Things are getting really serious! I tell you frankly, I don't like it! (*She is trembling.*)
BERENGER (*very agitated*): Keep calm! Keep calm!

DAISY: They've taken over the radio stations!

BERENGER (*agitated and trembling*): Keep calm, keep calm!

> DAISY *runs to the up-stage window, then to the down-stage window and looks out;* BERENGER *does the same in the opposite order, then the two come and face each other centre-stage.*

DAISY: It's no joke any longer. They mean business!

BERENGER: There's only them left now; nobody but them. Even the authorities have joined them.

> *They cross to the windows as before, and meet again centre-stage.*

DAISY: Not a soul left anywhere.

BERENGER: We're all alone, we're left all alone.

DAISY: That's what you wanted.

BERENGER: You mean that's what you wanted!

DAISY: It was you!

BERENGER: You!

> *Noises come from everywhere at once. Rhinoceros heads fill the up-stage wall. From left and right in the house, the noise of rushing feet and the panting breath of the animals. But all these disquieting sounds are nevertheless somehow rhythmical, making a kind of music. The loudest noises of all come from above; a noise of stamping. Plaster falls from the ceiling. The house shakes violently.*

DAISY: The earth's trembling! (*She doesn't know where to run.*)

BERENGER: No, that's our neighbours, the Perissodactyles! (*He shakes his fist to left and right and above.*) Stop it! You're preventing us from working! Noise is forbidden in these flats! Noise is forbidden!

DAISY: They'll never listen to you!

> *However the noise does diminish, merely forming a sort of musical background.*

BERENGER (*he, too, is afraid*): Don't be frightened, my dear. We're together—you're happy with me, aren't you? It's enough that I'm with you, isn't it? I'll chase all your fears away.

DAISY: Perhaps it's all our own fault.

BERENGER: Don't think about it any longer. We mustn't start feeling remorse. It's dangerous to start feeling guilty. We must just live our lives, and be happy. We have the right to be happy. They're not spiteful, and we're not doing them any harm. They'll leave us in peace. You just keep calm and rest. Sit in the armchair. (*He leads her to the armchair.*) Just keep calm! (DAISY *sits in the armchair.*) Would you like a drop of brandy to pull you together?

DAISY: I've got a headache.

BERENGER (*taking up his bandage and binding* DAISY's *head*): I love you, my darling. Don't you worry, they'll get over it. It's just a passing phase.

DAISY: They won't get over it. It's for good.

BERENGER: I love you. I love you madly.

DAISY (*taking off the bandage*): Let things just take their course. What can we do about it?

BERENGER: They've all gone mad. The world is sick. They're all sick.

DAISY: We shan't be the ones to cure them.

BERENGER: How can we live in the same house with them?

DAISY (*calming down*): We must be sensible. We must adapt ourselves and try and get on with them.

BERENGER: They can't understand us.

DAISY: They must. There's no other way.

BERENGER: Do you understand them?

DAISY: Not yet. But we must try to understand the way their minds work, and learn their language.

BERENGER: They haven't got a language! Listen ... do you call that a language?

DAISY: How do you know? You're no polyglot!

BERENGER: We'll talk about it later. We must have lunch first.

DAISY: I'm not hungry any more. It's all too much. I can't take any more.

BERENGER: But you're the strong one. You're not going to let it get you down. It's precisely for your courage that I admire you so.

DAISY: You said that before.

BERENGER: Do you feel sure of my love?

DAISY: Yes, of course.

BERENGER: I love you so.

DAISY: You keep saying the same thing, my dear.

BERENGER: Listen, Daisy, there *is* something we can do. We'll have children, and our children will have children—it'll take time, but together we can regenerate the human race.

DAISY: Regenerate the human race?

BERENGER: It happened once before.

DAISY: Ages ago. Adam and Eve . . . They had a lot of courage.

BERENGER: And we, too, can have courage. We don't need all that much. It happens automatically with time and patience.

DAISY: What's the use?

BERENGER: Of course we can—with a little bit of courage.

DAISY: I don't want to have children—it's a bore.

BERENGER: How can we save the world, if you don't?

DAISY: Why bother to save it?

BERENGER: What a thing to say! Do it for me, Daisy. Let's save the world.

DAISY: After all, perhaps it's we who need saving. Perhaps we're the abnormal ones.

BERENGER: You're not yourself, Daisy, you've got a touch of fever.

DAISY: There aren't any more of our kind about anywhere, are there?

BERENGER: Daisy, you're not to talk like that!

> DAISY *looks all around at the rhinoceros heads on the walls, on the landing door, and now starting to appear along the footlights.*

DAISY: Those are the real people. They look happy. They're content to be what they are. They don't look insane. They look very natural. They were right to do what they did.

BERENGER (*clasping his hands and looking despairingly at* DAISY): We're the ones who are doing right, Daisy, I assure you.

DAISY: That's very presumptuous of you!

BERENGER: You know perfectly well I'm right.

DAISY: There's no such thing as absolute right. It's the world that's right—not you and me.

BERENGER: I *am* right, Daisy. And the proof is that you understand me when I speak to you.

DAISY: What does that prove?

BERENGER: The proof is that I love you as much as it's possible for a man to love a woman.

DAISY: Funny sort of argument!

BERENGER: I don't understand you any longer, Daisy. You don't know what you're saying, darling. Think of our love! Our love . . .

DAISY: I feel a bit ashamed of what you call love—this morbid feeling, this male weakness. And female, too. It just doesn't compare with the ardour and the tremendous energy emanating from all these creatures around us.

BERENGER: Energy! You want some energy, do you? I can let you have some energy! (*He slaps her face.*)

DAISY: Oh! I never would have believed it possible . . . (*She sinks into the armchair.*)

BERENGER: Oh forgive me, my darling, please forgive me! (*He tries to embrace her, she evades him.*) Forgive me, my darling. I didn't mean it. I don't know what came over me, losing control like that!

DAISY: It's because you've run out of arguments, that's why.

BERENGER: Oh dear! In the space of a few minutes we've gone through twenty-five years of married life.

DAISY: I pity you. I understand you all too well . . .

BERENGER (*as* DAISY *weeps*): You're probably right that I've run out of arguments. You think they're stronger than me, stronger than us. Maybe they are.

DAISY: Indeed they are.

BERENGER: Well, in spite of everything, I swear to you I'll never give in, never!

DAISY (*she rises, goes to* BERENGER, *puts her arms round his neck*): My poor darling, I'll help you to resist—to the very end.

BERENGER: Will you be capable of it?

DAISY: I give you my word. You can trust me.

The rhinoceros noises have become melodious.

Listen, they're singing!

BERENGER: They're not singing, they're roaring.

DAISY: They're singing.

BERENGER: They're roaring, I tell you.

DAISY: You're mad, they're singing.

BERENGER: You can't have a very musical ear, then.

DAISY: You don't know the first thing about music, poor dear—and look, they're playing as well, and dancing.

BERENGER: You call that dancing?

DAISY: It's their way of dancing. They're beautiful.

BERENGER: They're disgusting!

DAISY: You're not to say unpleasant thing about them. It upsets me.

BERENGER: I'm sorry. We're not going to quarrel on their account.

DAISY: They're like gods.

BERENGER: You go too far, Daisy; take a good look at them.

DAISY: You mustn't be jealous, my dear.

She goes to BERENGER *again and tries to embrace him. This time it is* BERENGER *who frees himself.*

BERENGER: I can see our opinions are directly opposed. It's better not to discuss the matter.

DAISY: Now you mustn't be nasty.

BERENGER: Then don't you be stupid!

DAISY (*to* BERENGER, *who turns his back on her. He looks at himself closely in the mirror*): It's no longer possible for us to live together.

As BERENGER *continues to examine himself in the mirror she goes quietly to the door, saying:*

He isn't very nice, really, he isn't very nice. (*She goes out, and is seen slowly descending the stairs.*)

BERENGER (*still looking at himself in the mirror*): Men aren't so bad-looking, you know. And I'm not a particularly handsome specimen! Believe me, Daisy! (*He turns round.*) Daisy! Daisy! Where are you, Daisy? You can't do that to me! (*He darts to the door.*) Daisy! (*He gets to the landing and leans over the banister.*) Daisy! Come back! Come back, my dear! You haven't even had your lunch. Daisy, don't leave me alone! Remember your promise! Daisy! Daisy! (*He stops calling, makes a despairing gesture, and comes back into the room.*) Well, it was obvious we weren't getting along together. The home was broken up. It just wasn't working out. But she shouldn't have left like that with no explanation. (*He looks all around.*) She didn't even leave a message. That's no way to behave. Now I'm all on my own. (*He locks the door carefully, but angrily.*) But they won't get me. (*He carefully closes the windows.*) You won't get me! (*He addresses all the rhinoceros heads.*) I'm not joining you; I don't understand you! I'm staying as I am. I'm a human being. A human being. (*He sits in the armchair.*) It's an impossible situation. It's my fault she's gone. I meant everything to her. What'll become of her? That's one more person on my conscience. I can easily picture the worst, because the worst can easily happen. Poor little thing left all alone in this world of monsters! Nobody can help me find her, nobody, because there's nobody left.

Fresh trumpetings, hectic racings, clouds of dust.

I can't bear the sound of them any longer, I'm going to put cotton wool in my ears. (*He does so, and talks to himself in the mirror.*) The only solution is to convince them—but convince them of what? Are the changes reversible, that's the point? Are they reversible? It would be a labour of Hercules, far beyond me. In any case, to convince them you'd have to talk to them. And to talk to them I'd have to learn their language. Or they'd have to learn mine. But what language do I speak? What is my language? Am I talking French? Yes, it must be French. But what is French? I can call it French if I want, and nobody can say it isn't—I'm the only one who speaks it. What am I saying? Do I understand what I'm saying? Do I? (*He crosses to the middle of the room.*) And what if it's true what Daisy said, and they're the ones in the right? (*He turns back to the mirror.*) A man's not ugly to look at, not ugly at all! (*He examines himself, passing his hand over his face.*) What a funny-looking thing! What do I look like? What? (*He darts to a cupboard, takes out some photographs which he examines.*) Photographs! Who are all these people? Is it Mr. Papillon—or is it Daisy? And is that Botard or Dudard or Jean? Or it is me? (*He rushes to the cupboard again and takes out two or three pictures.*) Now I recognize me: that's me, that's me! (*He hangs the pictures on the back wall, beside the rhinoceros heads.*) That's me, that's me!

When he hangs the pictures one sees that they are of an old man, a huge woman, and another man. The ugliness of these

*pictures is in contrast to the rhinoceros heads which have be-
come very beautiful,* BERENGER *steps back to contemplate the
pictures.*

I'm not good-looking, I'm not good-looking. (*He takes down
the pictures, throws them furiously to the ground, and goes over
to the mirror.*) They're the good-looking ones. I was wrong! Oh,
how I wish I was like them! I haven't got any horns, more's the
pity! A smooth brow looks so ugly. I need one or two horns to
give my sagging face a lift. Perhaps one will grow and I needn't
be ashamed any more—then I could go and join them. But it will
never grow! (*He looks at the palms of his hands.*) My hands are
so limp—oh, why won't they get rough! (*He takes his coat off,
undoes his shirt to look at his chest in the mirror.*) My skin is so
slack. I can't stand this white, hairy body. Oh I'd love to have a
hard skin in that wonderful dull green colour—a skin that looks
decent naked without any hair on it, like theirs! (*He listens to
the trumpetings.*) Their song is charming—a bit raucous perhaps,
but it does have charm! I wish I could do it! (*He tries to imitate
them.*) Ahh, Ahh, Brr! No, that's not it! Try again, louder! Ahh,
Ahh, Brr! No, that's not it, it's too feeble, it's got no drive behind
it. I'm not trumpeting at all; I'm just howling. Ahh, Ahh, Brr.
There's a big difference between howling and trumpeting. I've
only myself to blame; I should have gone with them while there
was still time. Now it's too late! Now I'm a monster, just a monster. Now I'll never become a rhinoceros, never, never! I've gone
past changing. I want to, I really do, but I can't, I just can't. I
can't stand the sight of me. I'm too ashamed! (*He turns his back
on the mirror.*) I'm so ugly! People who try to hang on to their
individuality always come to a bad end! (*He suddenly snaps out
of it.*) Oh well, too bad! I'll take on the whole of them! I'll put
up a fight against the lot of them, the whole lot of them! I'm the
last man left, and I'm staying that way until the end. I'm not
capitulating!

Curtain.

Tango

by
Slawomir Mrozek

*Translated by Ralph Manheim
and Teresa Dzieduscycka*

Tango was first performed at the Jugoslovensko Dramsko Pozoriske in Belgrade, Yugoslavia on April 21, 1965. The first Polish performance took place in Warsaw on July 7, 1965 at the Teatr Wspòłozesny, directed by Erwin Axer. The first performance of *Tango* in New York took place at the Pocket Theater on January 20, 1969. The production was staged by Heinz Engels and based on the original staging by Erwin Axer, with setting by Jason Phillips, costumes by John E. Hirsch, lighting by Paul Holland, and dance arranged by Jon Devlin. The cast was as follows:

EUGENIA	Muriel Kirkland
EDDIE	Clifford A. Pellow
EUGENE	Arthur Ed Forman
ARTHUR	David Margulies
ELEANOR	Lilyan Wilder
STOMIL	Stefan Schnabel
ALA	Elizabeth Swain

ACT ONE

A large, high room. The wall on the right ("right" and "left" are always taken from the point of view of the audience) is not visible. This gives the impression that the room extends beyond the edge of the stage. The wall on the left does not reach to the front of the stage but forms a right angle a few steps behind it and continues leftward along the proscenium. Between this corner of the wall and the left edge of the stage there is a door leading into a second room. This produces a kind of corridor leading off-stage to the left and into the main room on the right. At the left and right of the rear wall, two more doors. The doors all look the same: double doors, high, painted a dark color, and ornamented in a style befitting old, solidly middle-class houses. Between the two doors in the rear wall, an alcove covered by a curtain. In the room: a table with eight chairs, armchairs, a couch, small tables, a large mirror on the left-hand wall. The furniture is arranged haphazardly as though the family had just moved in or were about to move out. Great confusion. In addition, the whole stage is full of draperies, hanging, lying or rolled, adding to the impression of confusion and blurring the outlines of the room. The room seems to be covered with spots. At one point on the floor draperies are thrown into a heap, forming a kind of bed. An old-fashioned black baby carriage on high, thin wheels. A dusty wedding dress. A derby hat. The velvet tablecloth is shoved half-aside. Three persons are seated at the uncovered part of the table. The first, who will be called

575

GRANDMA *for the present, is an elderly but well-preserved and lively lady, who suffers only occasionally from senile absentmindedness. Her dress, in a garish-colored flower pattern, has a train attached; she wears a jockey cap and sneakers. She seems to be near-sighted. A gray-haired, extremely polite old man. He is wearing glasses with thin gold rims, but his dress is disordered, and he seems dusty and intimidated. Swallow-tail coat, dirty stiff collar, a wide tie with a pearl stickpin, but khaki-colored shorts, scotch-plaid knee socks, torn patent-leather shoes, bare knees. The third individual, who gives the impression of being crude and shady, wears baggy, light-gray, rumpled pants and an ugly checked shirt, open at the chest. His shirtsleeves are rolled up. He habitually scratches his fat behind. Long greasy hair, which he frequently combs with a comb which he takes from his back pocket. Small, square mustache. Unshaven. A watch with a shiny gold wristband. All three are deep in their card game. On the velvet tablecloth: dishes, cups, carafes, artificial flowers, scraps of food. But also a few incongruous objects: a large, empty, bottomless bird cage; a lady's shoe; a pair of riding breeches. Even more than the rest of the furnishings, this table gives an impression of haphazardness, eccentricity and disorder. Each plate comes from a different set, each object is of a different period and style. From the right enters a young man of twenty-five at the most: imposing and pleasant appearance. Neat, freshly pressed, ready-made suit that fits him perfectly, white shirt, tie. Under his arm he is carrying books and papers. He stands still and observes the scene. The three card players do not notice him. The table is quite far to the left. The person temporarily known as* GRANDMA *is sitting with her back to the young man, her profile to the audience. The elderly gentleman is facing her. At the head of*

*the table the third player, with his back to the audience.
The young man who has just come in is to one side of him.*

PERSON TEMPORARILY KNOWN AS GRANDMA (*throwing a card
on the table with exaggerated gusto*): Three of spades.
Razor blades.

PLAYER WITH MUSTACHE (*throwing down a card*): Down
on the table goes old Aunt Mabel. (*He drinks beer
from a bottle standing beside his chair.*)

OLD GENTLEMAN (*timidly clearing his throat; speaks with a
visible effort*): Indeed, yes. I mean. . . . Well, plunk!
(*He throws down a card.*)

PERSON TEMPORARILY KNOWN AS GRANDMA (*waits for a moment, then with disapproval*): Plunk! Oh come on,
Eugene! Plunk what?

OLD GENTLEMAN *or* EUGENE (*stuttering helplessly*): Plunk
. . . plunk. . . .

PLAYER WITH MUSTACHE: The old gentleman's not in form
today.

He takes a swig from the bottle.

PERSON TEMPORARILY KNOWN AS GRANDMA: Eugene! If
you're going to play with us, you've got to do it right.
Plunk's all right, but then what?

EUGENE: Well, just plain plunk!

PERSON TEMPORARILY KNOWN AS GRANDMA: Good Lord,
you're blushing again!

EUGENE: Well then, plunk—trunk. Will that do?

PERSON TEMPORARILY KNOWN AS GRANDMA: Certainly not.
Why don't you help him out, Eddie?

PLAYER WITH MUSTACHE *or* EDDIE: With plunk? That's a
tough word to work with. How about: Scram, Sam.
We're on the lam.

EUGENE: Splendid! Splendid. But if you'll excuse my asking, what does it mean? Who's on the lam?

EDDIE: It's what they say, that's all.

PERSON TEMPORARILY KNOWN AS GRANDMA: Eugene. Eddie knows best.

EUGENE (*throwing the same card on the table again*): Scram, Sam. We're on the lam.

PERSON TEMPORARILY KNOWN AS GRANDMA: See, with a little effort you can do it too.

EDDIE: The old gentleman is a bit bashful.

PERSON TEMPORARILY KNOWN AS GRANDMA: Thank you, Eddie dear. I don't know what we would do without you.

EDDIE: Don't mention it. (*He sees the* YOUNG MAN *and quickly hides the bottle under the table.*) I'd better be leaving.

PERSON TEMPORARILY KNOWN AS GRANDMA: What? Why? What's got into you? Right in the middle of our game?

YOUNG MAN: Good morning!

PERSON TEMPORARILY KNOWN AS GRANDMA (*turns around, annoyed*): Oh, it's you.

YOUNG MAN: Yes, me. What's going on here anyway?

PERSON TEMPORARILY KNOWN AS GRANDMA: What do you mean? We're just having our little game.

YOUNG MAN: I can see that. But with whom?

PERSON TEMPORARILY KNOWN AS GRANDMA: With whom? Don't you recognize your Uncle Eugene any more?

YOUNG MAN: I wasn't asking about Uncle Eugene. I'll settle with him later. Who is this individual? (*He indicates* EDDIE.)

EDDIE (*stands up*): I'll just be running along now: Madam, the pleasure was mine.

PERSON TEMPORARILY KNOWN AS GRANDMA: Edward! Stay!

YOUNG MAN: Out! Out!

EDDIE (*reproachfully to* GRANDMA): Dear lady, didn't I tell you we shouldn't have played today?

EUGENE (*pointing to* GRANDMA): It's her fault. Entirely her fault. I didn't even want to play.

YOUNG MAN (*stepping up to the table*): I said Out!

EDDIE: Easy, Aces. I'm going!

> On his way out he comes close to the YOUNG MAN. He takes one of the books from under his arm and opens it.

YOUNG MAN (*rushing toward the table*): How often have I told you never to let this happen again?

> He runs around the table in pursuit of GRANDMA, who tries to evade him.

PERSON TEMPORARILY KNOWN AS GRANDMA: No! No!

YOUNG MAN: Oh yes, oh yes! And right now too!

EDDIE (*leafing through the book*): Fabulous!

PERSON TEMPORARILY KNOWN AS GRANDMA: What do you want of me anyway?

YOUNG MAN (*running after her*): You know very well what I want.

EUGENE: Arthur, have you no pity for your own grandmother?

YOUNG MAN, *or* ARTHUR: Oh, so you're talking back again are you, Uncle?

EUGENE: Not at all. I simply wanted to say that even if Eugenia may have forgotten herself a bit . . .

ARTHUR: Then I'll just have to remind her. And you too, Uncle. Pity! How can you talk about pity? Do any of you have any pity for me? Does she ever try to understand me? Oh, but this time, Uncle, you're going to get what's coming to you. Why aren't you working? Why aren't you writing your memoirs?

EUGENE: I did write a bit this morning, but then they came barging into my room, and . . .

PERSON HITHERTO KNOWN AS GRANDMA, *or* EUGENIA: Eugene! Traitor!

EUGENE (*hysterically*): Why can't you all just leave me in peace?

ARTHUR: Oh, we will. But you've got to be punished too. (*He puts the bottomless bird cage over Eugene's head.*) Now sit there until I let you out.

EUGENIA: Serves him right.

ARTHUR: Don't think you're going to get off free. (*He pulls back the curtain over the alcove, revealing a catafalque covered with a discolored black cloth and surmounted by several candelabra.*) Hup! Up you go!

EDDIE (*looking through the book with increasing interest*): Terrific! (*He sits down off to one side.*)

EUGENIA: Again? I don't want to!

ARTHUR: Not another word!

EUGENIA *humbly approaches the catafalque,* EUGENE *attentively offers her his arm.*

Up you go.

EUGENIA (*icily*): Thank you, Judas!

EUGENE: Your cards were no good anyway.

EUGENIA: Fool!

ARTHUR: This ought to cure you of your disgusting frivolity. (*Tapping his pockets.*) Matches! Who's got a match?

EUGENIA (*lying down on the catafalque*): At least spare me the candles, Arthur.

ARTHUR: Quiet, or I'll think up something really grim.

EDDIE (*without taking his eyes off the book, produces a box of matches*): Here!

> ARTHUR *takes the matches, lights the candles.* EUGENE *takes the artificial flowers from the table, places them beside* EUGENIA, *takes a few steps back to examine the effect, adjusts the flowers again.*

Great pictures! (*He giggles.*)

EUGENIA (*raising her head*): What's he looking at?

ARTHUR: Lie down!

EUGENE (*steps up to* EDDIE *and looks over his shoulder*): *Handbook of Anatomy.*

EUGENIA: Just what he needs!

EDDIE: Is Mr. Arthur studying medicine?

EUGENE: He's studying for three different degrees. One in philosophy.

EDDIE: Is there something like this for philosophy?

EUGENE: Don't be ridiculous! They don't illustrate philosophy.

EDDIE: Too bad. It might be good.

EUGENIA (*sitting up*): Let me see!

ARTHUR: Lie down!

EUGENIA: To think that you're the youngest one of us all! Why don't you enter a monastery?

ARTHUR: Why do you simply refuse to understand me, Grandmother?

EUGENE: Yes, I've been wondering about that myself. Why do you refuse to understand him, Eugenia?

ARTHUR: I just can't live in a world like this!

> ELEANOR *enters from the door on the extreme left. She has definitely crossed the threshold of middle age. She is wearing slacks with suspenders in the style of the 1930's.*

ELEANOR: What kind of world? What *are* you people doing?

ARTHUR: Good morning, Mother.

ELEANOR: Mama! On the catafalque again?

EUGENIA: A good thing you've come, Eleanor. Now you can see for yourself how he treats me.

ARTHUR: How *I* treat *you*? She had to be disciplined.

EUGENIA: He's trying to educate me.

ARTHUR: She really goes too far.

ELEANOR: What did she do?

ARTHUR: She knows.

ELEANOR: But why the catafalque?

ARTHUR: To remind her of eternity. Let her lie there and look within.

ELEANOR (*seeing* EDDIE): Ah, Eddie.

EDDIE: Hi!

ARTHUR: You mean you know each other?

EUGENE (*to himself*): Here we go.

ELEANOR: Everybody knows Eddie. Why not?

ARTHUR: I'm going mad. I come home and what do I find? Laxity, chaos, shady characters, ambiguous relationships. And on top of all that, it turns out that even you . . . No! No! Why does all this have to happen? Where is it all going to end?

ELEANOR: Perhaps you'd like something to eat?

ARTHUR: Eat? No. All I want is to get the situation under control.

ELEANOR: Oh Lord. I sleep with Eddie from time to time. Don't I, Eddie?

EDDIE (*absently*): What? Oh yes. Of course. (*He unfolds some color plates inserted in the book.*) Look at that! And all in color!

ARTHUR: What's that? What did you say, Mother?

ELEANOR: I'll get you something to eat. I won't be long.

She goes out through the door right rear. ARTHUR *sits down distraught.*

EUGENE (*to himself*): She did put that a bit bluntly. I must say. (*To* ARTHUR.) May I take this off now? (*Silence.*) Arthur? (*Silence.*) Arthur! (*Silence.*) Arthur, I say, may I take this thing off now?

ARTHUR: Take it off. (*To himself.*) Nothing matters now.

EUGENE (*taking the bird cage off his head*): Thank you! (*He sits down next to* ARTHUR.) What's wrong, Arthur?

EUGENIA: Christ, this thing is hard!

EUGENE: I can understand that this business about your mother must be rather upsetting. I can well understand that. I'm an old-timer. (*Pause.*) Eddie's not a bad sort. He has a good heart even if he doesn't look very bright. (*More softly.*) Between you and me, he's not quite all there. . . . (*Louder.*) But what can you expect, my dear boy? Life must be taken as it is . . . (*more softly*) . . . or must it? (*Louder.*) Now, now, Arthur. Chin up! Eddie has his good points, and after all, my goodness . . . we've got to face up to it: your mother isn't quite what she used to be. (*More softly.*) You should have seen her when she was young, before you were born, of course. Even before Stomil came along . . . (*Ponders, moves his chair closer to* ARTHUR; *very softly.*) What are you planning to do about Eddie anyway? Frankly, he's a thoroughly bad sort. His fingernails are always so dirty. A sleazy type, wouldn't you say? And I'm convinced that he cheats at cards. He smacks his lips when he eats and he goes around here as if he owned the place. I wouldn't even shake hands with him if I weren't afraid of offending Eugenia. You know what he did yesterday? I go to Eugenia and I say: "Look here, it's fine with me if Eddie doesn't brush his teeth, but if he has to borrow my toothbrush, I wish he'd brush his teeth with it instead of his shoes." And what does he say? "There's nothing wrong with my teeth. They're white. They're sharp. But sometimes my shoes get dirty." That's what he says and then throws me out. I wouldn't want to influence you one way or another, but if I were you, I'd get rid of him. How about throwing him down the stairs? Hm?

ARTHUR: Oh, that wouldn't really solve anything.

EUGENE: Or maybe a left hook right in the face?

ARTHUR: That, too, would leave the basic situation unchanged.

EUGENE: Just a small one right in the face? It couldn't do any harm. If it's all right with you, I'll tell him to get ready for one.

> EUGENIA *has meanwhile sat up and is listening. As soon as* EUGENE *notices this, he moves away from* ARTHUR. *Louder.*

Eddie is simple, yes, simple and very decent. I have never in all my years met a simpler man.

EUGENIA: What's wrong with him?

EUGENE: I don't know. He just doesn't react anymore.

EUGENIA: What are you whispering in his ear?

EUGENE: Me? Nothing. I've just been telling him about the life of the bees.

ELEANOR (*brings in a tray with a cup and cookies*): Breakfast is ready, Arthur!

ARTHUR (*waking out of his thoughts; automatically*): Thank you, Mother.

He sits down at the table. ELEANOR *sets the tray down in front of him, roughly shoving other objects aside.* ARTHUR *stirs his coffee. The tray is tilted up. He pulls a woman's shoe out from under it and heaves it angrily into the corner.*

EDDIE: Could you let me have this until Tuesday?

ARTHUR: I'm afraid not. I've got an exam on Monday.

EDDIE: Too bad. Some terrific pictures in here.

ELEANOR: Mother, get down off that thing, will you? You look like a character out of Edgar Allen Poe.

EUGENIA: A who, out of what?

ELEANOR: Oh, just like somebody on a catafalque. It's all so terribly old-fashioned.

EUGENIA (*motioning toward* ARTHUR): But what will he say?

ELEANOR: He's eating now. He won't say anything.

EUGENIA: Arthur, may I get down?

ARTHUR: It's all the same to me. (*He drinks.*) This coffee's bitter.

ELEANOR: We're all out of sugar. Eugene ate it.

EUGENE: I beg your pardon. All I ate was the jam. It was Eddie who ate up the sugar.

EUGENIA *comes down from the catafalque.*

ELEANOR: And blow those candles out, will you? We've got to economize. (*Looking at the cards.*) Who's winning?

EUGENIA: Eddie.

EUGENE: There is something positively unnatural about Edward's good luck.

ELEANOR: Eddie, have you been cheating?

EDDIE: Me? Never.

ELEANOR: You haven't? But you promised you'd lose today, remember? I need the money for groceries.

EDDIE (*throwing up his arms*): I must be a born winner. Tough luck!

Enter STOMIL, *Arthur's father. In pajamas, sleepy. Yawning and scratching himself. He is a large, corpulent man with gray hair like a lion's mane.*

STOMIL: I smelled coffee. (*Catching sight of* EDDIE.) Hello, Eddie.

ARTHUR *thrusts the tray aside and observes the scene with tense interest.*

ELEANOR: I thought this was your day to sleep until noon. The bed will be occupied after lunch.

STOMIL: I can't sleep. A whole new idea suddenly came to me. Who's drinking coffee anyway? Oh, it's you, Arthur . . . (*He steps up to the table.*)

ARTHUR (*disgustedly*): Good God, Father, can't you at least button up your pajamas?

STOMIL: What for?

ARTHUR: What for? What do you mean, what for?

STOMIL: I mean: What for? Such a simple question and you can't find an answer.

ARTHUR: Because . . . because one just doesn't appear like that.

STOMIL (*drinking Arthur's coffee*): You see? Your answer is meaningless. It's pure convention. It won't stand up under the scrutiny of the intellect.

ARTHUR: Isn't that enough?

STOMIL: Not at all. Not for me. I'm the kind of man who goes deeper. If we're going to discuss this, we've got to take the imponderables into account.

ARTHUR: Oh Lord, Father, can't you button your fly first and then talk it over?

STOMIL: That would be a complete reversal of the logical thought process. The effect would precede the cause. Man should never act without thinking, never act like an automaton.

ARTHUR: I take it then that you will not button your pajamas.

STOMIL: No, son. Anyway, I can't. No buttons.

He takes a swallow of coffee. He sets the cup down on the table. Unnoticed, EDDIE *has crept up behind* ARTHUR.

ARTHUR: I might have expected as much.

STOMIL: Not at all. In this case at least, matter springs from the mind.

EDDIE *reaches over Arthur's shoulder for the cup and drinks.*

ARTHUR: That's precisely what I wanted to talk to you about, Father.

STOMIL: Later, boy. Later. (*Takes a swallow out of the cup which is now in front of* EDDIE. *Looks toward the catafalque.*) Isn't anybody ever going to remove that thing?

ELEANOR: Why?

STOMIL: Well, I have nothing against it on purely formal grounds. Actually it enriches reality, stimulates the imagination. But I could use the space for my experiments.

ELEANOR: But you've got the whole house.

EUGENIA: I'd be glad, too, if you got rid of it. Then Arthur couldn't torture me.

ARTHUR (*pounding the table with his fist*): You see? What's going on in this house? Chaos, anarchy, entropy! How long has it been since Grandfather died? Ten years!

And all that time nobody's ever thought of ridding the
house of that catafalque. Incredible! We should be
grateful, though, that you at least took Grandfather
out of the house.

EUGENE: We couldn't keep Grandfather any longer.

ARTHUR: I'm not interested in the details. It's the principle
of the thing.

STOMIL (*drinking coffee, bored*): Really?

ARTHUR (*jumps up and runs across the stage*): But it's not
only Grandfather. I was born twenty-five years, ago
and my baby carriage is still standing here. (*He kicks
the baby carriage.*) Why isn't it up in the attic? And
what's this thing? Mother's wedding dress. (*He pulls
the dusty veil from under a pile of rubbish.*) Why
isn't it put away in a closet? And Uncle Eugene's riding
breeches. What are they lying around here for when
the last horse he ever rode died forty years ago? No
order, no sense of reality, no decency, no initiative.
You can't move in this place, you can't breathe, you
can't live!

Taking advantage of the confusion, EDDIE *empties the
cup at one gulp.*

ELEANOR (*aside to* EDDIE): How beautifully you drink,
Eddie!

STOMIL: My boy, tradition doesn't interest me in the
slightest. Your indignation is absurd. You know very
well we attach no importance to these monuments of
the past, these relics of family tradition. That's why
everything's lying around like this. We live in freedom.
(*He looks into the cup.*) Where's my coffee?

ARTHUR: No, no, Father, you just don't understand me.
That's not what bothers me. No, that's not it.

STOMIL: Then kindly explain yourself more clearly, will you, boy? (*To* ELEANOR.) Isn't there any more coffee?

ELEANOR: No, there won't be any until the day after tomorrow.

STOMIL: Why the day after tomorrow?

ELEANOR: How should I know?

STOMIL: All right. Never mind.

ARTHUR: Listen to me! It's not this particular tradition that bothers me. It's a fact that in this family there's no frame of reference at all. All that's left is bits and pieces, fragments, rubbish. You've destroyed everything but you go on destroying; you've gone on so long you've finally forgotten why you began in the first place.

ELEANOR: He's right. Stomil, do you still remember how we shattered tradition? How, in protest against tradition, I gave myself to you with Mummy and Daddy looking on? In the first row of the orchestra at the opening night of *Tannhäuser*. What a gorgeous scandal that was! Where are the days when people were still shocked by such things? And then you proposed to me.

STOMIL: As I recall it was at the National Museum's first avant-garde exhibition. The critics gave us rave reviews.

ELEANOR: No. It was at the opera. At the exhibition it wasn't you, or maybe it wasn't me. You're getting everything mixed up.

STOMIL: Possibly. (*With enthusiasm.*) The days of revolt, the time of the great leap forward. Liberation from the fetters of the old art and the old way of life. Man coming into his own, man overthrowing the old gods and putting himself on the pedestal. The seed burst open, the chains snapped. Revolution and release. That was our slogan then. Away with outmoded forms, down with convention! Long live the dynamic! Life as creation, an incessant striving toward new frontiers! Movement and struggle! All form transcended!

ELEANOR: Stomil! You've been drinking at the fountain of youth! I hardly recognize you.

STOMIL: Yes, we were young once.

ELEANOR: What do you mean? We haven't grown any older. We've never betrayed our ideals. Why, even now our motto is still: Forward! Ever forward!

STOMIL (*without enthusiasm*): Yes. Yes. That's right.

ELEANOR: Do we have any prejudices? Do conventions mean anything to us? Aren't we still fighting against the old? Aren't we free?

STOMIL: The old what?

ELEANOR: Well, the old times. Don't you remember? Don't tell me you've forgotten what we were just talking about? All those fetters, those rusty chains of religion, morality, society, art. Especially art, Stomil. Art!

STOMIL: Yes, of course. But when was all that actually?

ELEANOR: Just a minute. Let me figure it out. We were married in 1900 . . . no, just let me think . . . Arthur was born in 1930, or . . . oh, be quiet, will you? Or was it 1940?

STOMIL: Oh, *then*. I see. (*He stops in front of the mirror, passes his hand over his face.*)

ELEANOR: Don't interrupt me. You're getting me all mixed up . . . (*Figures in an undertone, thoroughly absorbed.*) 1914 . . . 1918 . . . 1921 . . .

STOMIL (*at the mirror*): We're young. Eternally young . . .

ARTHUR: Father's right.

STOMIL: What do you mean?

ARTHUR: It's all dead and gone now. All in the past.

ELEANOR *runs across the stage, whispering dates, becoming more and more entangled in her calculations.*

STOMIL: What's gone?

ARTHUR: All those fetters and chains! They're all gone now, unfortunately.

STOMIL: Unfortunately? You don't know what you're saying. If you'd lived in those days, you'd know how much we've done for you. You have no idea what the world was like then. Can you imagine how much courage it took to dance the tango? Do you realize that in those days there were hardly any fallen women? That the only recognized style of painting was naturalism? That the theater was utterly bourgeois? Stifling. Insufferable. You couldn't even put your elbows down on the dinner table! I can still remember a youth demonstration on that very issue. Why, it wasn't until after 1900 that the boldest, the most advanced spirits stopped giving up their seats to elderly people. No, we didn't spare ourselves in our struggle for these rights and if you today can push your grandmother around, its to us your thanks are due. You simply can't imagine how much you owe us. To think how we struggled to give you this freedom which you now despise!

ARTHUR: And what did you do with it? What did you produce? This bawdyhouse where nothing works because everyone can do what he pleases, where there are no laws and no violations?

STOMIL: I know only one law: Don't hesitate, do what you feel like. Every man is entitled to his own kind of happiness.

ELEANOR: Stomil, I've got it! I've figured it out! It was 1928.

STOMIL: What was?

ELEANOR (*in consternation*): I've forgotten.

ARTHUR: You've poisoned the generations before you and after you with your freedom. Look at Grandmother! She's completely addled. Haven't you noticed?

EUGENIA: I just knew he'd drag me into it.

STOMIL: There's nothing wrong with Mama. What do you mean?

ARTHUR: Naturally you're not shocked by her senile demoralization. Once she was a dignified, self-respecting grandmother. And now? Now she plays poker with Eddie!

EDDIE: I beg your pardon. We also play bridge, you know.

ARTHUR: I wasn't talking to you.

STOMIL: Each has the right to do what he wants and with whomever he chooses. Old people too.

ARTHUR: That's not a right. It's a moral obligation to be immoral.

STOMIL: You astonish me. Your opinions are so terribly outdated. When we were your age, we considered every kind of conformity disgraceful. Rebellion! Rebellion alone had any value for us.

ARTHUR: What value?

STOMIL: A dynamic and therefore positive value, though sometimes in a negative way. I trust you don't think we were merely blind anarchists? Certainly not. We were a column marching off to the future, a movement, a historical process. History is indebted to us. What is rebellion? The rock on which progress builds its temple and the greater the scope of the rebellion the grander the temple will be. Believe me: the scope of our rebellion was prodigious.

ARTHUR: But if that's the case . . . why these misunderstandings? If you too are trying to do something constructive, why can't we build together?

STOMIL: Impossible. What I said just now was purely objective. I described our historical role, but said nothing of our intentions. Well then, what were our intentions? Why, to do what we wanted, go our own ways, each for himself. We have always pursued our own inclinations. But by opposing everything, we paved the way for the future.

ARTHUR: What future?

STOMIL: That's not my affair. My job was to shatter existing forms.

ARTHUR: In other words, we're still enemies?

STOMIL: Why take it so tragically? All you need to do is stop worrying about principles.

ELEANOR: Yes. What I still can't understand is why you, the youngest of us all, should be the one to harp on principles. It used to be the other way around.

ARTHUR: Because I'm starting out in the world. But what a world! If I want a world, I've got to make one.

STOMIL: But you're young, Arthur. Don't you want to be modern? At your age?

ARTHUR: That's just the point. These modern times of yours. Even Grandmother has grown old in this world that has lost its standards. That's how modern your era is. What's more, you've grown old in it.

EUGENE: If you'll allow me to put in a word, I should like to call your attention to certain achievements, for instance, the right to wear short pants . . . ah, the fresh feel of the breeze . . .

ARTHUR: Oh, keep quiet, Uncle. Don't you realize that, precisely because everything is possible, nothing is possible anymore? If you were at least bucking convention with your short pants. But all convention was broken ages ago. By the time you came along it was all taken care of. The whole thing is absurd.

STOMIL: Well, what *do* you want then? Tradition?

ARTHUR: An orderly world!

STOMIL: That's all?

ARTHUR: . . . and the right to rebel.

STOMIL: That's it. That's what I've been telling you all along: *rebel!*

ARTHUR: Don't you see that you've deprived me of every last chance to revolt? You've been nonconformists so long that there aren't any conventions left to rebel against. You've left nothing for me . . . nothing! Your only norm is the absence of all norms. The only thing left for me to rebel against is you . . . you and your immorality.

STOMIL: Go right ahead. Did I ever tell you not to?

EUGENE: That's the stuff, Arthur. You'll show them.

ELEANOR: Maybe it would calm you down. You've been so jittery lately. . . .

EUGENIA *makes signs to* EDDIE; *they come to an understanding behind Arthur's back and pick up the cards.*

ARTHUR (*falls into an armchair with resignation*): Impossible!

ELEANOR: Why?

EUGENE: We're all in favor of it.

ARTHUR: Rebel against you? What are you anyway? A formless mass, an amorphous blob, an atomized world, a mob without shape or structure. Your world can't even be blown up; it's disintegrated all by itself.

STOMIL: You mean we're no good for anything?

ARTHUR: Exactly.

ELEANOR: But couldn't you just try?

ARTHUR: There's nothing to try. It's hopeless. You're all so disgustingly tolerant.

STOMIL: Yes, that could be irritating, I suppose. Still, I don't like to see you feeling so left out.

ELEANOR (*stands behind him and strokes his hair*): Poor little Arthur. You mustn't think your mother's heart is made of stone.

EUGENE: We all love you, Arthur. We want to help you.

EUGENIA (*to* EDDIE): I pass.

ARTHUR: It's hopeless. This nonconformism you're pushing me into is only a new kind of conformism. But I can't be a conformist forever. I'm twenty-five. My friends are all laughing at me.

STOMIL: But what about art, Arthur? What about art?

ELEANOR: Exactly. You've taken the words out of my mouth.

ARTHUR: What art?

STOMIL: Well, art in general. I've devoted my whole life to art. Art is eternal rebellion. Why don't you give it a try?

EDDIE: Bring your bedding. Skip the wedding.

EUGENIA: Crash, smash, I'm out of cash.

ARTHUR: Father, you bore me. I want to be a doctor.

ELEANOR: A disgrace to the whole family! I've always dreamed of his becoming an artist. When I was carrying him in my womb, I ran through the woods stark naked, singing Bach. All for nothing!

ARTHUR: Maybe you sang out of tune.

STOMIL: All the same, don't give up hope. You still don't understand the value of art. I've just had an idea for a new experiment. You'll see.

ELEANOR (*clapping her hands*): Eugenia, Eddie. Stomil has come up with something new.

EUGENIA: Again?

STOMIL: Yes. It came to me this morning. It's absolutely original.

ELEANOR: You'll put it on right away, won't you, Stomil?

STOMIL: I'm ready.

EUGENE: Heaven help us!

ELEANOR: Eugene, move the table. Make room.

EUGENE *shoves the table aside with a good deal of crashing and thumping.* EUGENIA *and* EDDIE *pick up the cards and step to one side. Under the mound of draperies suggesting a bed, something starts to move. Finally Cousin Ala's head comes to light.*

ALA (*a girl of eighteen with a good figure and long hair. She blinks in the light and yawns*): Where am I? First all that shouting and now they're moving furniture . . . What time is it anyway?

ARTHUR: Ala!

ELEANOR: I forgot to tell you, Ala has been here since six o'clock this morning.

STOMIL: This is marvelous, Ala. You're just in time for the show. (*To* EUGENE.) That's fine. Now the catafalque.

ARTHUR: But why didn't you tell me? If I'd known, I'd have kept them quiet.

He notices that EDDIE *is approaching* ALA *with interest.*

Back Eddie. Face to the wall.

EDDIE *steps back obediently and stands with his face to the wall.*

Did you sleep well?

ALA: So so.

ARTHUR: How long can you stay?

ALA: I don't know. I told Mother I might never go back.

ARTHUR: And what did she say?

ALA: Nothing. She wasn't there.

ARTHUR: Then how could you tell her?

ALA: Maybe I didn't. I don't remember.

ARTHUR: You've forgotten?

ALA: It was so long ago.

ARTHUR: How about some breakfast? Oh! We're out of coffee. May I sit beside you?

ALA: Why not?

ARTHUR *gets a chair and sits down beside the pile of draperies.*

ARTHUR: You're very lovely.

ALA *laughs loudly.*

What are you laughing about?

ALA (*suddenly stops laughing. Gloomily*): Me? Laughing? I'm not laughing.

ARTHUR: But you *were.*

ALA: Are you trying to pick a fight?

ARTHUR: I've been thinking about you a lot, Ala.

ALA (*loud and coarse*): Go on.

ARTHUR: I thought about meeting you!

ALA: Go on.

ARTHUR: And sitting down beside you . . .

ALA: Go on.

ARTHUR: . . . and talking with you . . .

ALA (*gradually growing excited as though watching a boxing match*): Go on.

ARTHUR: . . . about one thing and another . . .

ALA: Go on.
ARTHUR (*louder*): About different kinds of things.
ALA: Go on! Go on!

> ARTHUR *picks up the book that* EDDIE *has left on the chair and throws it at* ALA. *She dodges and hides under the covers.*

ARTHUR: Come out!
ALA (*sticking her head out*): What's wrong with you?

> ARTHUR *says nothing.*

Why did you do that?

> ARTHUR *says nothing.*

What do you want anyway?
ARTHUR: That's what they all keep asking me.
ALA: Never mind. I don't need to know.
STOMIL: Kindly take your seats. Kindly take your seats.

> *The stage is set for Stomil's experiment. To one side, the table. Nearer the proscenium, four chairs are lined up with their backs to the audience.* EUGENIA, ELEANOR *and* EUGENE *sit down from left to right.* EDDIE *picks up his bottle of beer, still half-full, and tries to tiptoe away.* EUGENE *sees him and points him out to* ELEANOR.

ELEANOR: Eddie, where are you going?
EDDIE: Be back in a minute.
ELEANOR: You stay right here!

> EDDIE *turns around with resignation, sits down on the chair to the right of* EUGENE, *intentionally stepping on his foot.* STOMIL *goes into the room opening into the corridor on the left-hand side of the stage.*

Arthur, Ala, what are you doing? We're waiting for you.

ALA: What's going on?

ARTHUR: Experimental drama. You know my father.

He gives her his hand. ALA jumps up. She has on a long nightgown that reaches the floor. It should not be transparent—this is called expressly to the attention of directors who like to make things easy for themselves. The cut and ruching make it look almost like a dress. They stand beside the chair on the extreme right. EDDIE stretches out his arm and takes ALA by the waist. ARTHUR changes places with her.

STOMIL (*who has meanwhile come back with a big box and gone behind the catafalque so that only his head can be seen*): Ladies and gentlemen, your attention please. Here are the principal characters of our drama. (*In the tone of a circus director introducing the next number.*) Adam and Eve in paradise! (*Over the catafalque which serves as the stage, two puppets manipulated by STOMIL are seen: Adam and Eve, with the apple in her hand.*)

EUGENE: We've had that.

STOMIL (*in consternation*): When?

EUGENE: At the beginning of the world.

STOMIL: That was the old version. This is a new one.

EDDIE: Where's the snake?

ELEANOR (*whispering*): Shhh!

STOMIL: The snake is in our imagination. We all know the story. Attention please! Here we go! (*In a deep voice.*)

So this is Paradise.
I'm Adam and before me lies

A world of possibilities.
But now it starts. From Adam's bone
Eve steps upon the earth.
To what will *she* give birth?
O Destiny, 'tis known
To you alone.

(*In a soprano.*)

Adam was first, but he
Did not exist until
I also came to be.
He walks so proudly still.
Doesn't the poor man see
For all his intellection
That there is no perfection
Except in what is not?
Where does the darkness go
When the sun comes out?
O Destiny!

A *loud report and all the lights go out.*

ELEANOR'S VOICE: Stomil, Stomil, what's happened? You're not dead, are you?
EUGENE'S VOICE: Fire! Fire!

ARTHUR *lights a match and then the candles over the catafalque.* STOMIL *appears, he is holding an enormous revolver.*

STOMIL: Well, what do you say? Not bad, eh?
ELEANOR: Stomil, you frightened us so!
STOMIL: Every experiment must shock. That's my first principle.
EUGENE: If that's what you were after, it was a success all right. My heart's still pounding.

ELEANOR: How did you do it, Stomil?

STOMIL: I unscrewed the fuse and fired the revolver.

ELEANOR: Marvelous!

EUGENE: What's so marvelous about it?

STOMIL: Don't you understand?

EUGENE: No, I don't.

ELEANOR: Don't mind him, Stomil. Eugene has always been slow.

STOMIL: How about you, Eugenia?

EUGENIA: Huh?

STOMIL (*louder*): Did you understand the experiment, Mama?

ELEANOR: The experiment has made her deaf.

EUGENE: That doesn't surprise me.

STOMIL: Let me explain. The shock method creates an immediate unity of action and perception. See?

EUGENE: Yes, but . . .

STOMIL: Yes, but what?

EUGENE: But what's that got to do with Adam and Eve?

ELEANOR: Eugene, do try to concentrate.

STOMIL: What we are dealing with here is an intrinsically theatrical phenomenon, the dynamics of sense perception. That means something to you, doesn't it?

EUGENE: Frankly, I don't think it does.

STOMIL (*throws the revolver on the catafalque*): I give up.

ELEANOR: Don't be discouraged, Stomil. Who's going to experiment if you lose heart?

All stand up and put the chairs back in their places.

EUGENE: A flop, friends.

EDDIE: Give me the movies.

ELEANOR: Well, now what should we do?

ARTHUR: Clear out! All of you. Out!

STOMIL: What's got into you?

ARTHUR: All of you! I can't bear the sight of you.

STOMIL: Is that a way to treat your own father?

ARTHUR: I used to have a father. Not anymore. I'll have to make myself a father.

STOMIL: You? *You* make *me?*

ARTHUR: You and the whole lot of you. I'm going to make you all over. And now get out. This minute!

STOMIL: That boy's going just a bit too far.

ELEANOR: Never mind, Stomil. Thank God, we're enlightened.

STOMIL: You think I should really go?

ELEANOR: Why not? After all, you're not really interested in anything but your experiments.

STOMIL: Ah yes, art! Modern art! Give me God and I'll make an experiment out of Him.

ELEANOR: There. You see!

They all go out through the door left rear.

EDDIE (*to* EUGENIA): Come on, Grandma.

EUGENIA: Don't forget the cards.

EDDIE picks up the cards and goes out with EUGENIA.

EDDIE (*turning around again, to* ARTHUR): If you need anything . . .

ARTHUR (*stamping his foot*): Get out!

EDDIE (*conciliatory*): Okay, okay!

He goes out left with EUGENIA.

EUGENE (*after making sure that the others are gone*): You're absolutely right, Arthur. Between you and me, they're a bad lot.

ARTHUR: You too. Out!

EUGENE: Certainly. Certainly, my boy. I'm going. I only wanted to tell you that you can count on me.

ARTHUR: What do you mean?

EUGENE: Never mind. Just do what you think right. But remember. I can be useful to you. I'm not as far gone as the rest of them. (*More softly.*) I'm an old-timer.

ARTHUR: Glad to hear it. But now leave us alone, will you?

EUGENE (*goes out left, turns around again and says with emphasis*): An old-timer. (*Exits.*)

ALA: Now what?

ARTHUR: Now I'll explain everything.

ACT TWO

The same scene as in Act One. The only light comes from a simple standing lamp. ARTHUR *is sitting in an armchair. Someone enters from the right.*

ARTHUR: Who's there?

FIGURE: Me.

ARTHUR: Who's me?

FIGURE: Your Uncle Eugene.

ARTHUR: Password?

EUGENE: New life. Countersign?

ARTHUR: Rebirth. (*Pause.*) All right. Come in.

> EUGENE *steps into the light. He sits down facing* ARTHUR.

EUGENE: Oof. I'm exhausted.

ARTHUR: Is everything ready?

EUGENE: I've brought everything I could down from the attic. You should see the moths! You think it will work?

ARTHUR: It's got to work.

EUGENE: I'm worried, worried. They're so demoralized . . . Think of it. A whole lifetime in this bawdy-house . . . I beg your pardon, I meant this atmosphere of moral disintegration. You see, it's contagious. Forgive me.

ARTHUR: Forget it. What's my father doing?

EUGENE: He's in his room, working on a new production. Don't you feel sorry for him sometimes? After all, he actually believes in that art of his.

ARTHUR: Then why do you discourage him?

EUGENE: For spite. To get his goat. But the fact is, those experiments of his don't mean a thing to me. What do you make of them?

ARTHUR: I've got other problems. And Mother?

EUGENE *stands up, goes to the door left rear and looks through the keyhole.*

EUGENE: Can't see a thing. Either she's turned the light out or hung something over the keyhole. (*He goes back to his former place.*)

ARTHUR: And Grandmother Eugenia?

EUGENE: Probably sitting at her mirror, putting on makeup.

ARTHUR: Good. You may go now. I have an important appointment in a few minutes.

EUGENE (*stands up*): Any further orders?

ARTHUR: Be vigilant. Eyes open, mouth shut, and ready for action.

EUGENE: Yes, sir. (*On his way out.*) God protect you, Arthur, my boy . . . Maybe we'll manage to bring the good old days back again yet.

Goes out to the right. ALA *enters by way of the corridor right. She is still wearing her nightgown.*

ALA (*yawning*): What did you want me for?

ARTHUR: Shh . . . quiet.

ALA: Why?

ARTHUR: This is private—between you and me.

ALA: You think they care what we do? We could climb up the walls and sleep on the ceiling for all they care. (*She sits down, wincing as though in pain.*)

ARTHUR: What's wrong?

ALA: Stomil pinched me twice today.

ARTHUR: The rotter!

ALA: Arthur, he's your father!

ARTHUR (*kissing her hand gallantly*): Thank you for reminding me.

ALA: It sounds so old-fashioned, nobody calls his father a rotter nowadays.

ARTHUR: What *do* you call him then?

ALA: Nothing. You just ignore him.

ARTHUR (*disappointed*): Then I was mistaken.

ALA: Well, it's your headache that he's your father. Personally, I think he's great.

ARTHUR (*contemptuously*): An artist!

ALA: What's wrong with that?

ARTHUR: Artists are a plague. They were the first to contaminate our society.

ALA (*bored*): Oh, who cares? (*Yawns.*) What did you want me for? It's cold in here. I'm practically naked. Hadn't you noticed?

ARTHUR: Well, what do you say? Have you thought it over?

ALA: You mean will I marry you? But I've already told you. I don't see the point.

ARTHUR: You mean the answer is no?

ALA: Why do you get so worked up about it? I mean—I don't care—if it means so much to you, we can get married tomorrow. We're already cousins.

ARTHUR: But I *want* you to care! I want you to realize that marriage is something very important.

ALA: Important? Why? I don't get it. If I'm going to have a baby it'll be with you, not with the minister. So what's the problem?

ARTHUR: Well, if it's not important in itself, then we've got to make it important.

ALA: What for?

ARTHUR: Nothing is important in itself. Things in themselves are meaningless. Unless we give them character, we drown in a sea of indifference. We have to create meanings, because they don't exist in nature.

ALA: But what for? What for?

ARTHUR: Well if you must have a reason, let's say: for our own pleasure and profit.

ALA: Pleasure?

ARTHUR: Yes. We derive pleasure from profit and we only profit from doing things we attach importance to— difficult things, the unusual things that seem rare and precious. And that's why we have to create a system of values.

ALA: Philosophy bores me. I think I prefer Stomil. (*She sticks her leg out from under the nightgown.*)

ARTHUR: You only think that. Kindly remove that leg.

ALA: You don't like it?

ARTHUR: That has nothing whatsoever to do with the subject.

ALA (*obstinately*): You really don't like it?

ARTHUR (*with difficulty takes his eyes off her leg*): Oh, all right, show your leg if you want to. Anyway, it only proves my point.

ALA: My leg? (*She examines her leg closely.*)

ARTHUR: Yes. Do you know why you're showing your leg? Because I don't leap all over you like my artist father and everybody else does. That worries you. You were pretty bewildered this morning when we were all alone. You thought you knew what I wanted from you.

ALA: That's not true.

ARTHUR: Not true? Ha. You think I didn't see how upset you were when I proposed marriage instead of just picking you up and throwing you down on the bed?

ALA: I had a headache.

ARTHUR: Headache? Go on. You just couldn't figure out *what* was going on. You thought I wasn't attracted, that you must be losing your charms. If I suddenly started acting like my father, it would be a relief, wouldn't it? Yes. Except you'd run away, just to get even with me.

ALA (*stands up with dignity*): I'm running all right.

ARTHUR (*takes her by the hand and pulls her down into the chair*): Sit down. I haven't finished yet. All you care about is your sex appeal. You're so primitive! You can't think about anything else. You don't know anything else!

ALA: Are you suggesting that I'm backward? (*She tries again to stand up.*)

ARTHUR (*holding her down*): You stay right here. You've confirmed my theory. My behavior was atypical; that baffled you. The unusual is a value in itself. See? I have given meaning to an encounter that would otherwise have meant nothing. I!

ALA: Well, if you're so terribly clever, what do you need me for? If you're so awfully superior, why don't you just live all by yourself?

ARTHUR: You don't have to be so touchy.

ALA: We'll see how far you get alone. Or with Uncle Eugene. (*She resolutely draws her nightgown over her knees, buttons it up to the neck, and wraps herself in a steamer rug. She puts on the bowler and draws it down deep over her forehead.*)

ARTHUR (*shyly*): Don't be angry.

ALA: What do you care?

Pause.

ARTHUR: Aren't you too warm . . . in that blanket?

ALA: No.

ARTHUR: Uncle Eugene's hat doesn't look very good on you.

ALA: I don't care.

ARTHUR: Suit yourself. Where were we anyway? Oh yes, a system of values . . . (*He moves his chair closer to* ALA.) Now, generally speaking, a system of values is indispensable to the proper functioning both of the individual and of society. (*He seizes Ala's hand.*) Without the right kind of values we can never hope to create a harmonious world or establish the necessary balance between those elements commonly termed good and evil—though of course I use these words in their larger rather than strictly ethical sense. Now in this connection our task is two-fold: We must, one, restore the practical relevance of these concepts and, two, formulate rules of conduct which . . .

He flings himself at ALA *and tries to kiss her. She struggles free; they wrestle.* EDDIE *enters with his towel around his neck and a hairnet on his head.*

EDDIE (*with the pretentious enunciation typical of the semi-literate*): Oh, do excuse me.

ARTHUR (*lets* ALA *go as if nothing had happened.* ALA *straightens her hat and rubs her shoulder demonstratively*): What are *you* doing here?

EDDIE: I was just going to the kitchen for a drink of water. I beg your pardon, I didn't know you were conversing.

ARTHUR: Water? Water? What for?

EDDIE (*with dignity*): Because I'm thirsty, sir.

ARTHUR: At this hour? In the middle of the night?

EDDIE (*offended*): If that's the way you feel about it, I can go without.

ARTHUR (*furious*): Drink and get out!

EDDIE: As you wish. (*He goes majestically to the door left rear.*)

ARTHUR: Just a minute.

EDDIE: Yes, sir?

ARTHUR: The kitchen is on the right.

EDDIE: There? Impossible.

ARTHUR: I believe I know where the kitchen is in my own house.

EDDIE: You just can't be sure of anything these days. (*He changes his direction and goes out through the door right rear.*)

ARTHUR: That idiot! I'll have to take care of him once and for all.

ALA (*icily*): Have you finished taking care of me?

ARTHUR: It's all his fault.

ALA: I suppose it was his fault you nearly twisted my arm off.

ARTHUR: Does it hurt very much?

ALA: What do you care?

She affects a cry of pain. ARTHUR, *troubled, tries to examine her shoulder.*

ARTHUR: Where does it hurt? (*He touches her shoulder, but not with his original purpose.*)

ALA (*uncovering her shoulder*): Here . . .

ARTHUR: I'm terribly sorry.

ALA (*uncovering her back*): . . . and here . . .

ARTHUR (*dismayed*): Really, I didn't mean to . . .

ALA (*thrusts her leg forward*): . . . and here . . .

ARTHUR: How can I ever make it up to you? . . .

ALA (*lays her forefinger on her rib*): . . . and here too!

ARTHUR: Forgive me. I didn't mean to . . .

ALA: Now you've shown what you really are—a brute. First a lot of talk and then the usual. (*She sinks tragically into an armchair.*) We poor women! Is it our fault we have bodies? If we could only check them somewhere like a hat or a coat. Then maybe we'd be safe from our sweet-talking cousins. Frankly, I'm surprised. You with your noble ideals.

ARTHUR (*confused*): But really, I . . .

ALA: No excuses! You don't think I like a good conversation too? But that calls for a nice restful atmosphere. How can I converse when some philosopher is clutching at my legs? But never mind. What were we talking about? It was just beginning to be interesting when you . . .

Behind the door through which EDDIE *has passed a sound of gushing water is heard. Then gargling.*

ARTHUR: This is too much. Do you seriously think I wanted to rape you?

ALA (*alarmed*): Didn't you?

ARTHUR: Certainly not. I was only teaching you a lesson.

ALA: Thanks. I know that subject.

ARTHUR: You can only think about one thing. Then why did you resist? Come on. Why?

ALA: You're vulgar.

ARTHUR: Science knows no shame. Why?

ALA: Well, why did you attack me?

ARTHUR: Attack you? I was sacrificing myself.

ALA: What?

ARTHUR: Yes, sacrificing myself in my effort to make certain things clear to you. It was a pure exercise in sexual pragmatics.

ALA: Pig! Scientific pig! Pragmatics? What is it anyway?

Some new kind of perversion?

ARTHUR: There's nothing new about it. I'm sure we'll always be friends. Yes, women will follow me.

ALA: Women? Which women?

ARTHUR: All women. Women throughout the world will be my allies. And once the women are convinced, the men will soon come around.

ALA: What women? Anybody I know? Anyway, do what you like with them. I couldn't care less.

ARTHUR: Look here. The central fact of history is the total enslavement of women, children and artists by men.

ALA: I thought you didn't approve of artists.

ARTHUR: That's beside the point. The reason men don't like artists is that artists aren't men. That's what has always brought artists and women together—unfortunately. The ideas men have dreamed up—like honor, logic, progress—have always been foreign to women and artists. It's only very recently that the male has even begun to suspect the existence of such things as ambiguity, relativity, forgetfulness—in short, the glamor and poetry of this world, the exact opposite of what he had originally invented in that thick soldier's skull of his and tried to impose on women, children and artists.

ALA: But what about you? Aren't you a male?

ARTHUR: I transcend myself; I take an objective view. That's essential if I'm to carry out my plan.

ALA: Can I trust you?

ARTHUR: It was only to make up for their lack of imagination that men invented the concept of honor. And, at the same time, of effeminacy. Why? To guarantee male solidarity. Anyone who dared question the code of manly virtues was immediately accused of being effeminate. The result was that, in self-defense, women, children and artists closed ranks to form a single community. They had no choice. . . . Just a second.

The gargling is still heard from the kitchen. ARTHUR *goes to the kitchen door.*

ALA: Maybe he's washing.

ARTHUR: Him? Not likely! (*He goes back to his place.*) Let's get back to the subject.

ALA: I just don't believe you. I see what you're getting at. You can't fool me.

ARTHUR: I have no desire to fool you. I'm simply trying to make you aware of your own interests as a woman.

ALA: What does that mean? You want me to strip?

ARTHUR: Oh, don't be tedious. Once you've finally come to see that our interests coincide, you'll be willing to work with me. What do men want? They want to abolish all conventions relating to sex. And why? To make life easier for *them,* to do away with all barriers between desire and satisfaction.

ALA: You've got something there. They jump you like a bull. Like you did just now.

ARTHUR: I can't deny that as an individual I'm subject to natural drives. But I have a higher goal. Taking advantage of the general breakdown in values, men have done everything they could to do away with the last remaining rules governing sexual behavior. I can't believe that women really like it, and that's the basis of my plan.

ALA: I like it fine.

ARTHUR: That's a lie. You *can't.*

ALA: Yes, I like it. It means I'm free, I can do as I please. For instance, if I take my clothes off right now, what can you do about it? (*She throws off the steamer rug and removes her hat.*)

ARTHUR: Stop it. This is a serious discussion.

ALA (*undoing the ribbons of her nightgown*): Why should I? Who's going to stop me? You? My mother? God? (*She bares her shoulders.*)

ARTHUR: Cover yourself this minute! Pull up that nightgown. (*He tries desperately to look away.*)

ALA: I will not. It's my nightgown.

Eddie's head is seen in the doorway.

Oh, hi, Eddie. Come on in.

ARTHUR (*pushing* EDDIE *away*): Get out or I'll kill you. Taking your clothes off in front of this . . . Have you no shame?

ALA: He may not be very cultured, but he has marvelous eyes.

ARTHUR: Eyes like a pig.

ALA: I like them.

ARTHUR: I'll kill him.

ALA (*sweetly*): You wouldn't be jealous by any chance?

ARTHUR: I am not jealous.

ALA: First he's brutal. Then he's jealous. You ought to be ashamed of yourself.

ARTHUR (*furious, face to face with* ALA): Go on then. Undress! I'm not stopping you.

ALA: I don't feel like it anymore.

ARTHUR: Suit yourself.

ALA (*retreating*): I've changed my mind.

ARTHUR (*following her*): Oh, you don't feel like it anymore? Tell me, why don't you want to anymore! Tell me why you wanted to before.

ALA: My God, what a lunatic!

ARTHUR (*seizes her by the arm*): Why?

ALA: I don't know.

ARTHUR: Tell me!

ALA: What should I say? I don't know, I just don't know. Let me go.

ARTHUR (*letting her go*): You know perfectly well. It's because you only pretend to like all this absence of rules, this debauchery, this promiscuity.

ALA: Oh, I only pretend, do I?

ARTHUR: Of course. You really hate it, because it's not to your advantage. This lack of forms and norms cuts down your freedom of choice. There's nothing left for you to do but take off your clothes and put them back on again.

ALA: That's not true.

ARTHUR: Then why this sudden modesty?

Pause.

ALA: Now you're being logical. You just said that logic was nonsense.

ARTHUR: I said that?

ALA: Yes, only a minute ago. I heard you.

ARTHUR (*disgruntled*): You must have heard wrong.

ALA: I heard you quite clearly.

ARTHUR: Well, let's not bicker. But I still don't believe you. I'm convinced that the convention of unconventionality goes against your grain. You didn't make it up.

ALA: Who did then?

ARTHUR: Men! You only pretend to like it. And now you're stuck with it, and nobody likes to admit he's just following the herd.

ALA: But if I don't like it why should I go along with it?

ARTHUR: For fear of losing your attractiveness. To keep up with the fashion. Admit it!

ALA: No.

ARTHUR: No? All right. At least you admit there's something to admit. Come on. Why all these lies? Can't you see that important issues are at stake? I simply refuse to believe that you want to go to bed with every man in the world. Wanting to attract them is something else again. You want to be able to choose for yourself. But how can a woman choose when there are no conventions? Tell me that.

ALA: I'm free. I know exactly what I want.

ARTHUR: But you're weak by nature. What chance do you have when you're all alone with a strange man who's stronger than you and there's no convention to protect you? Let's assume, for instance, that you don't care for me. If Eddie hadn't butted in, you'd have been sunk, because I'm the stronger.

ALA: I could always take up judo.

ARTHUR: You take everything so literally. Can't you women ever understand a general idea?

ALA: Lots of girls study judo. I'd have you begging for mercy.

ARTHUR: Excellent. You're getting there. You're coming around. Don't you see? Why does it have to be judo when conventions are quite effective? I'd be kneeling at your feet with a bouquet in my hand begging you to take pity on me, to grant me a ray of hope. Behind a solid wall of conventions, without any wrestling, without even getting your hair mussed, you'd have me at your mercy. Wouldn't that be better than judo?

ALA: You really mean it? Down on your knees?

ARTHUR: Certainly.

ALA: Okay. Go ahead.

ARTHUR: Go ahead and what?

ALA: Down on your knees!

ARTHUR: Impossible.

ALA (*disappointed*): Why?

ARTHUR: Because there are no conventions left. Now do you see what a fix you're in?

ALA: Isn't there anything we can do about it?

ARTHUR: Yes.

ALA: What?

ARTHUR: Establish new conventions or bring back the old ones. And that's exactly what I'm going to do—with your help. Everything's prepared. All I need is your help.

ALA: Great! And you'll really get down on your knees?

ARTHUR: I will.

ALA: All right. Now what can I do to help?

ARTHUR: Marry me. That's the first step. No more promiscuity, no more *dolce vita*. A real marriage. Not just dropping into city hall between breakfast and lunch. A genuine old-fashioned wedding with an organ playing and bridesmaids marching down the aisle. I'm especially counting on the procession. It will take them by surprise. That's the whole idea. And, from then on, they won't have time to think, to organize resistance and spread defeatism. It's the first shot that counts. Catching them off guard like that, we can force them to accept conventions they'll never break out of again. It's going to be the kind of wedding they'll have to take part in, and on my terms. I'll turn them into a bridal procession, and at long last my father will be forced to button his fly. What do you say?

ALA: And I'll get to wear a white wedding gown?

ARTHUR: White as snow. Everything strictly according to the rules. And at the same time you'll be helping all the women in the world. The rebirth of convention will set them free. What used to be the first rule of every encounter between a man and a woman? Conversation. A man couldn't get what he wanted just by making inarticulate sounds. He couldn't just grunt, he had to talk. And while he was talking, you—the woman—sat there demurely, sizing your opponent up. You let him talk and he showed his hand. Listening serenely, you drew up your own order of battle. Observing his tactics, you planned your own accordingly. Free to maneuver, you were always in command of the situation. You had time to think before coming to a decision and you could drag things out as long as you wanted. Even if he gnashed his teeth and secretly wished you in the bottom of hell, you knew he would never dare hit you. Up to the very last minute you could move freely, securely, triumphantly. Once you were engaged, you were safe, and even then traditional avenues of escape were open to you. Such were the blessings of conversation! But nowadays? Nowadays a man doesn't even have to introduce himself—and you will admit it's handy to know who a man is and what he does for a living.

EDDIE *tiptoes from the kitchen door to the door right. As he disappears in the doorway,* ARTHUR *sees him and goes after him.*

ALA: Was somebody listening?

ARTHUR (*coming back*): No.

ALA: I had the feeling there was.

ARTHUR: Let's settle this matter once and for all. Do you consent?

ALA: I don't know yet.

ARTHUR: You don't know? You mean I haven't convinced you?

ALA: Yes.

ARTHUR: Yes? Then you consent?

ALA: No . . .

ARTHUR: Yes or no?

ALA: I've got to think about it.

ARTHUR: But what is there to think about? It's as plain as day. I've got to rebuild a world, and for that I must have a wedding. It's perfectly simple. What don't you understand?

ALA: The whole thing, I guess.

ARTHUR: What do you mean?

ALA: Wait . . . Give me time.

ARTHUR: No, I can't wait. There just isn't time. I'll stay here while you go think it over. When you've made up your mind, come back and give me your answer. It's sure to be yes. I've explained everything.

ALA: And you really have nothing else to say? There's really nothing else you want to tell me?

ARTHUR: Run along now. I'll see you later.

ALA: You're throwing me out?

ARTHUR: No, I have a little private business to attend to.

ALA: Can't I stay?

ARTHUR: No. This is a family matter.

ALA: All right. Then I'll have my little secrets too. Just wait. You'll see.

ARTHUR (*impatiently*): Yes, yes, but run along now. Remember, I'll be waiting for you here.

ALA *goes out right.* ARTHUR *listens at the door left rear, and then goes to the door in the corridor. He knocks softly.*

STOMIL'S VOICE: Who's there?

ARTHUR (*rather softly*): Me. Arthur.

STOMIL: What do you want?

ARTHUR: Father, I've got to talk to you.

STOMIL: At this time of night? I'm busy. Come back tomorrow.

ARTHUR: It's urgent.

Pause.

STOMIL: But I've already told you, I'm busy. You can speak to me tomorrow.

ARTHUR *tries the door and sees that it is locked. He shoves with his shoulder.* STOMIL *opens. He is in pajamas as usual.*

Are you mad? What's going on?

ARTHUR (*in an ominous whisper*): Not so loud, Father.

STOMIL (*whispering, too, in spite of himself*): Why aren't you in bed?

ARTHUR: I can't sleep. It's time to take action.

STOMIL: In that case, good night.

He starts for his room. ARTHUR *holds him back.*

ARTHUR: I only wanted to ask you, Father, doesn't it bother you?

STOMIL: What?

ARTHUR: This thing with Eddie.

STOMIL: Eddie? Oh yes, I remember the man.

ARTHUR: What do you think of him?

STOMIL: He's amusing.

ARTHUR: Amusing? He's repulsive.

STOMIL: Oh I wouldn't say that. Eddie's an unusual type. A very modern, very authentic type.

ARTHUR: Is that all you have to say about him?

STOMIL: You see, our trouble is that we're still too conscious, too cerebral. Enslaved by centuries of culture.

Of course we've been doing our best to throw culture off, but we're still a long way from nature. But Eddie's lucky. He was born with what the rest of us can acquire only by art and effort. He interests me as an artist. I admire him the way a painter admires a landscape.

ARTHUR: Some landscape!

STOMIL: But don't you know there's been a complete revolution in aesthetics and morality. You keep making me remind you of things that ought to be self-evident. If Eddie shocks us now and then, it's because we're decadent. Sometimes I can't help feeling guilty toward Eddie. But I fight it down. We've got to get rid of these atavistic attitudes.

ARTHUR: And that's all you have to say?

STOMIL: I've been perfectly frank with you.

ARTHUR: Then I'll have to start all over again. Why do you tolerate him in your house?

STOMIL: Why not? He enriches our environment, he gives it a new tone, he adds a dash of authenticity. He even stimulates my imagination. We artists need an exotic touch now and then.

ARTHUR: Then you really don't know?

STOMIL: No, I don't know a thing.

ARTHUR: You're lying. You know perfectly well.

STOMIL: I repeat—I don't know. I don't want to know.

ARTHUR: He sleeps with Mother.

STOMIL *starts pacing.*

What do you say to that?

STOMIL: My dear boy. Let's assume what you say is true. Sexual freedom is the cornerstone of human freedom. What do *you* say to that?

ARTHUR: But it's the truth! They *do* sleep together!

STOMIL: I said we'd assume it's true. What follows? Nothing.

ARTHUR: Then you insist on treating it as an abstract hypothesis?

STOMIL: Why not? I'm a modern man. On the intellectual plane we can envisage any hypothesis, even the most ticklish. Without such hypotheses human thought would mark time. So do speak freely. I trust we can discuss this business without prudery. Now, what's your opinion?

ARTHUR: My opinion? I haven't got any opinion and I refuse to treat this matter as a theoretical exercise. This isn't a philosophical problem. It's the naked truth. Can't you see that? It's life. They've put horns on you. Long ones! And arguing isn't going to make them go away.

STOMIL: Horns! Horns! Horns are a primitive image, not an instrument of analysis. (*Nervously.*) Let's not descend to that low level.

ARTHUR: Father, you're a cuckold.

STOMIL: Hold your tongue. I forbid you to talk to me like that.

ARTHUR: You can't stop me. You're a cuckold.

STOMIL: I don't believe it.

ARTHUR: Ha! Now I've got you where I want you. Want me to prove it? Open that door. (*He points to the door left rear.*)

STOMIL: No!

ARTHUR: Are you afraid? Of course it's easier to perform theatrical experiments. When it comes to experiments you're a giant. In real life you're a midget.

STOMIL: Me?

ARTHUR: A hero in pajamas! A pint-sized Agamemnon!

STOMIL: I'll show you. You say they're in there?

ARTHUR: Look for yourself.

STOMIL: I'll show them. I'll show you. I'll show the whole lot of you! (*He runs to the door, stops.*) Or you know what I'll do? I'll take care of this whole thing tomorrow. (*He turns around.*)

ARTHUR (*barring the way*): No you won't. You're going in there right now.

STOMIL: Tomorrow! Or by mail. A letter. What do you say?

ARTHUR: Phony!

STOMIL: What did you say?

> ARTHUR *makes horns on his forehead and laughs sardonically.*

All right then. Here I go!

ARTHUR (*stops him*): Just a second.

STOMIL (*with a martial air*): Let me at them.

ARTHUR: You'd better take this.

> *He takes the revolver which* STOMIL *had left on the catafalque in Act One and gives it to his father.*

STOMIL: What's that?

ARTHUR: You can't go in there bare-handed.

> *Pause.*

STOMIL (*calmly*): Now I see through you.

ARTHUR (*pushing him toward the door*): Get in there! There's not a minute to lose.

STOMIL (*tearing himself loose*): Now I understand. You want a tragedy!

ARTHUR (*retreating*): A tragedy? What do you mean?

STOMIL: So that's what you're after, you dim little runt of a brainstorm, you . . .

ARTHUR: What are you trying . . .

STOMIL (*throwing the revolver on the table*): You want me to kill him? And then her? And then myself? Right?

ARTHUR: Of course not. I was only joking. I just thought that in case Eddie . . . he might do anything.

STOMIL: You'd love that, wouldn't you! The injured husband wiping out his shame in blood. Where do you *get* such ideas? From romantic novels?

ARTHUR: Father, you know I never . . .

STOMIL: I always knew the younger generation cared more about ideas than life, but I never expected my own son to sacrifice his father to an idea. Sit down!

ARTHUR *sits down obediently*.

That's it. Now we'll have a little talk. You want to bring back the old values. What for? Well, never mind that. That's your business. I've let you talk, I've heard you out, but now you're going just a bit too far. How fiendishly clever! So you need a tragedy! Tragedy has always been the most perfect expression of a society with established values. So you needed a tragedy and thought you'd drag me into it. Instead of the art form—which demands time and effort—you wanted the thing itself. Or, never mind if somebody's killed, never mind if your own father goes off to prison. No, all you care about is your idea. Do you want to know what I think of you? A formalist. A vulgar formalist. That's what you are. Your father and mother mean nothing to you. We can all die as long as form wins out. And the worst of it is that you don't even care about yourself. You're a fanatic!

ARTHUR: Maybe my motives aren't as formal as you think.

STOMIL: You dislike Eddie?

ARTHUR: I hate him.

STOMIL: Why? Eddie is necessity. He's the pure truth we've been searching for so long because we always thought it was somewhere else. Eddie is a fact. You can't hate facts. You've got to accept them.

ARTHUR: What do you want me to do, hug him?

STOMIL: Good Lord! You talk like a petulant child. I can only see one explanation. Maybe you've got an Oedipus.

ARTHUR: A what?

STOMIL: An Oedipus complex. Have you consulted an analyst?

ARTHUR: No. Mother's wonderful, but that's not it.

STOMIL: Too bad. Then at least we'd know where we were at. Anything is better than sheer lunacy. I guess you're just a formalist.

ARTHUR: I am not.

STOMIL: Oh yes you are. And an insufferable and dangerous one at that.

ARTHUR: It may look that way to you, but the truth is that I . . . I just can't go on like this. I can't live with you people.

STOMIL: I see. That's more like it. In other words, you're an egoist.

ARTHUR: Call it whatever you like. That's the way I am, that's all.

STOMIL: But suppose you succeeded in making me kill him, in packing me off to prison for life, what good would that do you?

ARTHUR: Something would be accomplished. Something tragic. You're right. Please forgive me. Tragedy is a form so vast and powerful that reality can never escape its grip.

STOMIL: You poor devil. You really believe that? Don't

you realize that tragedy isn't possible anymore? Reality erodes all forms and that goes for tragedy too. Suppose I actually killed him. What would be the good of it?

ARTHUR: It would be something irrevocable, masterful, classical.

STOMIL.: Not for a minute. It would be a farce. In our time only farce is possible. A corpse won't change anything. Why can't you face facts? Actually, a farce can be very nice too.

ARTHUR: Not for me.

STOMIL.: Lord, you can be stubborn!

ARTHUR: I can't help it. I've got to find a way out.

STOMIL.: Regardless of reality?

ARTHUR: Yes. At any cost.

STOMIL.: That's not so easy. I'd like to help you, but I don't see how.

ARTHUR: Couldn't we give it a try?

STOMIL.: Give what a try?

ARTHUR (*pointing to the door left rear*): With them.

STOMIL.: You still have illusions?

ARTHUR: Even if you're right about farce . . . (*Gradually he resumes his aggressiveness.*) It's only because you people are such cowards. You complain, but you're stuck in a farce because no one has the courage to rebel. Why can't you free yourself by one act of sheer violence? You're so logical, so analytical, you see everything in the abstract. Instead of changing anything, you make diagrams. You've come a long way, but what have you actually done? Sat in a chair and discussed. But this situation calls for action. If tragedy has become extinct it's only because you don't believe in it. You and your damned compromises.

STOMIL.: But why should we believe in tragedy? Come here,

son. I want to tell you something. All right. Eleanor is unfaithful to me with Eddie. What's so bad about that?

ARTHUR: But, Father, don't you know?

STOMIL: So help me, when you come right down to it, I don't. Maybe you can explain.

ARTHUR: I've never been in such a situation . . .

STOMIL: Try.

ARTHUR: It's obvious . . . Let me think . . .

STOMIL: Think away. Actually, I'd be delighted if you could convince me.

ARTHUR: Really?

STOMIL: To tell you the truth, I don't much care for this kind of thing either. In fact, I detest it. Only the more I think about it, the less I know why.

ARTHUR: So if I could convince you . . .

STOMIL: . . . I'd be very grateful.

ARTHUR: And you'd . . .

STOMIL: Go in and make a scene they'd remember as long as they lived. But I need a rational justification.

ARTHUR: Then you'd go in? Without being pushed?

STOMIL: I'd be delighted to. I've had it in for that bastard a long time. Believe it or not, nothing would please me doesn't tell me why.

more than to settle his hash. Except that my reason

ARTHUR: Father, let me hug you.

They hug each other.

To hell with reason!

STOMIL: But what can we do? It won't let go of us. You were talking about compromise. It's reason that makes us compromise.

ARTHUR: Well, then, Father, shall we give it a try? What

have we got to lose? If the worst comes to the worst, you'll shoot him.

STOMIL: Think so? If I could only be sure.

ARTHUR: Certainty comes later. The main thing now is to make up your mind.

STOMIL: Hm. Maybe you're right.

ARTHUR: I know I'm right. You'll see. We'll have our tragedy!

STOMIL: You've given me back my strength. The enthusiasm of youth untrammeled by the skepticism of the times. Ah, youth, youth!

ARTHUR: Shall we go in?

STOMIL: Yes. With you beside me, I feel better.

They stand up.

ARTHUR: Just one more thing. Give up those experiments of yours, will you? They only speed up the process of disintegration.

STOMIL: Well, but what can we do? Tragedy impossible, farce a bore—what's left but experiments?

ARTHUR: They only make things worse. Give them up, Father.

STOMIL: I don't know . . .

ARTHUR: Promise.

STOMIL: Later. Now we go in.

ARTHUR *puts the revolver back into Stomil's hand.*

ARTHUR: I'll wait here. If you need any help, just shout.

STOMIL: That won't be necessary. If anybody yells, it'll be him, not me.

ARTHUR: Father, I've always had confidence in you.

STOMIL: With good reason, my boy. I was the best shot in my regiment. Farewell! (*He goes to the door right rear.*)

ARTHUR: No, that's the kitchen.

STOMIL (*irresolute*): I could use a drink.

ARTHUR: Later. When it's all over. No time now.

STOMIL: Right! I'll kill him on the spot. (*He goes to the left-hand door, puts his hand on the knob.*) That scoundrel! Now he's going to pay!

He enters the room cautiously, closes the door behind him. ARTHUR *waits tensely. Total silence.* ARTHUR *paces nervously back and forth. Grows more and more impatient. Looks at his watch. Finally he makes a decision and flings both wings of the door open, so that the whole room can be seen. Under a bright, low-hanging lamp* ELEANOR, EDDIE, EUGENIA *and* STOMIL *are sitting at a round table, playing cards.*

ARTHUR: What's Eddie doing here? Why isn't Eddie . . . ?

STOMIL: Shhh! Take it easy, boy!

ELEANOR: Oh, it's you, Arthur? Are you still up?

EUGENIA: I told you he'd find us. He sticks his nose into everything.

ARTHUR: Father! . . . You . . . with them!

STOMIL: That's how it worked out . . . It's not *my* fault.

ELEANOR: Stomil turned up just in time. We needed a fourth.

ARTHUR: Father, how could you!

STOMIL: I told you it would end in a farce.

EDDIE: Your play, Mr. Stomil. What you got?

STOML: Here you are. (*To* ARTHUR.) A harmless pastime. You see the situation. What could I do?

ARTHUR: But, Father, you promised!

STOMIL: I promised nothing. We'll just have to wait.

ELEANOR: Instead of talking so much, would you please put your mind on the game, Stomil?

ARTHUR: For shame!

EUGENIA (*throws down her cards*): I · simply can't play under these conditions. Can't anybody throw this little twerp out of here?

EDDIE: Easy, Grandma. Take it easy.

ELEANOR: Arthur, you ought to be ashamed, upsetting your grandmother like this.

EUGENIA: I told you we · should lock the door. He's always looking for some way to pester me. You'll see. He'll put me back up on the catafalque!

ELEANOR: Oh, no he won't! We've got to finish this rubber first.

ARTHUR (*pounding the table with his fist*): Stop it!

ELEANOR: But we've just started.

EDDIE: You'd better listen to your mother. She's right. Look at the score cards, they're practically blank.

ARTHUR (*tearing the cards out of their hands*): Now you listen to me! I've got something to tell you. Now! This minute!

STOMIL: But Arthur, that was strictly between the two of us. Don't shout it from the rooftops.

ARTHUR: I pleaded with you. You wouldn't listen. Now I'm going to use force. Stop the game!

ELEANOR: What's going on?

EDDIE: What's got into you anyway? If I were your father, know what I'd do? I'd give you a good hiding.

ARTHUR: You shut up. (*Calmly but firmly.*) Father, the revolver.

EDDIE: A guy can still make a joke, can't he?

ELEANOR: A revolver? For God's sake, Stomil, don't give it to him. Talk to him. Do *something*. After all, you're his father.

STOMIL (*trying to take a severe tone*): Now see here,

Arthur, you're not a child. I'm sorry to have to speak to you like this, but . . .

ARTHUR *takes the revolver from Stomil's pajama pocket. All jump up.*

EUGENIA: He's gone mad. Stomil, why on earth did you make this child? Criminal negligence—that's what I call it.

EDDIE: Look here, Mr. Arthur . . .

ARTHUR: Silence! Into the living room, everybody.

One after another they go to the center of the stage. ARTHUR *remains standing at the door. As* STOMIL *passes him.*

I'll talk to you later.

STOMIL: What's wrong? I did my best.

ARTHUR: Your best!

EUGENIA *sits down on the sofa,* ELEANOR *in an arm-chair.* EDDIE *stands in the corner, takes a comb from his back pocket and runs it nervously through his hair.*

STOMIL (*facing* ELEANOR, *raises his arms*): I did everything I could to quiet him down. You saw me . . .

ELEANOR: Idiot. And you call yourself a father. Oh, if I were only a man!

STOMIL: That's easier said than done.

EUGENE *runs in.*

EUGENE (*to* ARTHUR): Has it started yet?

ARTHUR: Not yet. I'm still waiting for an answer.

EUGENE: I thought it had started. I heard a noise and I came running.

ARTHUR: That's all right. I'm glad you've come. Stay here and keep an eye on them. I'll be back in a second.

He gives him the revolver.

EUGENE: Yes, sir.

ELEANOR: Am I dreaming?

ARTHUR (*to* EUGENE): Don't let anybody make a move.

EUGENE: Yes, sir.

ELEANOR: Have you both gone mad?

ARTHUR: If anybody does move, shoot to kill. Understand?

EUGENE: Yes, sir.

ELEANOR: It's a plot! Mama, your brother's a gangster!

EUGENIA: Eugene, do put that thing away. People don't play cowboys at your age. (*She starts to stand up.*)

EUGENE: Stay where you are!

EUGENIA (*astonished*): Eugene, it's me—your sister Eugenia.

EUGENE: When I'm on duty, I have no sister.

EUGENIA: What duty? Don't be a fool.

EUGENE: I have enlisted in the service of an ideal!

ARTHUR: Splendid. I see I can rely on you. I'm going to leave you for a moment.

STOMIL: But, Arthur, can't you tell me, at least, what's going on? I thought we'd just become friends.

ARTHUR: I'll tell you everything in due time.

He goes out. EUGENE *sits down with his back to the wall, holding his revolver in readiness. He aims it vaguely but menacingly at each in turn.*

ELEANOR (*after a pause*): So that's it . . . Eugene, you've betrayed us.

EUGENE: Silence! (*Then justifying himself.*) That's not true I haven't betrayed anybody.

ARTHUR'S VOICE (*off*): Ala! Ala!

ELEANOR: You've betrayed your generation.

EUGENE: No, you're the traitors. You've all betrayed our good old days. I'm the only one who hasn't.

ARTHUR'S VOICE (*off*): Ala! Ala!

ELEANOR: All you are is the tool of a mad pack of young zealots. With a missionary complex. You think you're so clever. They'll use you and then kick you out like a dog.

EUGENE: We'll see who uses whom. I've been waiting a long time for someone like Arthur to come along.

ELEANOR: Now at least you've shown who you really are. All these years you've been wearing a mask, you hypocrite.

EUGENE: Yes, I have. And all these years I've suffered. I hated you for your degradation but I kept quiet because I had to, because you were the stronger. Now at last I can tell you what I think of you! What a pleasure!

ELEANOR: What are you going to do to us?

EUGENE: We're going to give you back your dignity. We're going to turn you degenerates back into human beings with decent principles—that's what we're going to do.

ELEANOR: By force?

EUGENE: If we can't do it any other way, yes.

STOMIL: This is a counter-reformation.

EUGENE: But for you it's salvation.

STOMIL: Salvation? From what?

EUGENE: From your damnable, diabolical freedom.

ARTHUR (*enters*): Uncle!

EUGENE: Sir?

ARTHUR: She's gone.

EUGENE: Look for her. She must be somewhere.

ARTHUR: Yes. She's got to be. I'm still waiting for her answer.

EUGENE: What? You mean she hasn't consented yet?

ARTHUR: She's got to. Everything else is ready now. She can't leave me in the lurch at a moment like this.

EUGENE: I don't mean to criticize you, Arthur, but haven't you rushed things a bit? I mean, shouldn't you have made sure of *her* before starting in on (*he points to the others with his pistol barrel*) these people?

ARTHUR: The time was ripe. I couldn't put it off.

EUGENE: Well, that's how it is with a *coup d'état*. Always some unforeseeable factor. Still, we can't back out now.

ARTHUR: Who could have dreamed of such a thing? I was so sure I had convinced her. (*He calls.*) Ala, Ala! (*Irritably.*) All because of some dumb cousin. Incredible! (*He calls.*) Ala, Ala.

EUGENE: Women have been the ruin of kingdoms and empires.

ALA (*enters*): Gosh, are you all still up?

ARTHUR (*reproachfully*): At last! I've been looking all over for you.

ALA: What's going on? Uncle with a gun? Is it real? Is Uncle real?

ARTHUR: That's none of your business. Where have you been?

ALA: Out for a walk. Anything wrong with that?

EUGENE: Yes! At this solemn hour, there is.

ARTHUR: Steady, Uncle. You're on duty, remember. (*To* ALA.) Well?

ALA: Well, what? It's a lovely night.

ARTHUR: I wasn't asking about the weather. Do you consent?

ALA: I think I need a little more time, Arthur.

ARTHUR: I need an answer immediately. You've had plenty of time.

Pause.

ALA: Yes.

EUGENE: Hurrah!

ARTHUR: Thank God! Now we can start!

He gives ALA *his arm and leads her to the sofa where* EUGENIA *is sitting.*

Grandmother, your blessing.

EUGENIA (*starts up from the sofa in a fright*): Oh, leave me alone. I haven't done anything to you.

ARTHUR: But Grandmother, everything's changed now. I'm going to marry Ala. Give us your blessing.

EUGENE (*to the others*): On your feet, everybody! Can't you see this is a solemn occasion?

ELEANOR: My goodness, is Arthur going to get married?

STOMIL: Is that any reason to make such a fuss?

EUGENIA: Get that boy out of here! He's going to torture me again.

ARTHUR (*menacingly*): Grandmother, your blessing.

STOMIL: A tasteless joke. It's gone on long enough now.

EUGENE (*triumphantly*): The jokes are over now. You've been having your jokes for fifty years. Stomil, button your pajamas immediately! Your son has just plighted his troth. The day of the wide-open fly is past. Bless them, Eugenia.

EUGENIA: What should I do, Eleanor?

ELEANOR: Give them your blessing if it means so much to them.

EUGENIA: Can't they do without it? It makes me feel so old.

EUGENE: A good old-fashioned engagement. Give them your blessing, or I'll shoot. I'm going to count to three. One . . .

STOMIL: This is incredible. If a man can't be comfortable in his own house . . . (*He tries to button his pajamas.*)

EUGENE: Two . . .

EUGENIA (*lays her hand on the heads of* ALA *and* ARTHUR): My blessing upon you, dear children . . . and now go to hell!

EUGENE (*moved*): Just like old times.

ARTHUR (*stands up and kisses Eugenia's hand*): We thank you, Grandmother.

EUGENE: Stomil has buttoned his fly! A whole new era has begun!

STOMIL: Eleanor! You're crying?

ELEANOR (*sobbing with emotion*): Forgive me . . . But Arthur's getting engaged . . . and after all he is our son . . . I know I'm being terribly old-fashioned, but it's so moving. Forgive me.

STOMIL: Oh, do what you want, all of you! (*He runs out of the room in a rage.*)

EDDIE: If you'll permit me, on this joyous occasion I would like to wish the young couple all the best for the days to come and especially . . .

Holds out his hand to ARTHUR.

ARTHUR (*not taking his hand*): You! To the kitchen!

He points dramatically to the kitchen door. EDDIE *saunters out.*

And stay there until you're called.

EUGENE: To the kitchen.

ELEANOR (*in tears*): When's the wedding?

ARTHUR: Tomorrow.

EUGENE: Hurray! We've won!

ACT THREE

Daylight. *The same room, but with no trace now of the former disorder: a conventional middle-class living room of about fifty years ago. None of the previous confusion and blurred contours. The draperies which had been lying about, giving the impression of an unmade bed, are now hung in orderly fashion. The catafalque is still in its old place—the curtain in front of the alcove is drawn back— but it is covered with napkins and knicknacks, so that it looks like a buffet.*

On stage ELEANOR, EUGENIA, STOMIL, *and* EUGENE. EUGENIA *is sitting on the sofa in the middle of the room. She is wearing a bonnet and a dark gray or brown dress buttoned up to the neck and adorned with lace cuffs and ruching. She has a lorgnette which she frequently raises to her eyes. To her right sits* ELEANOR *with her hair done up in a chignon; she is wearing earrings and a striped violet or burgundy-colored dress gathered at the waist. Both sit bolt upright, immobile, their hands on their knees. Beside them stands* STOMIL, *his hair combed, pomaded and parted in the middle. His stiff collar forces him to stretch his head as though looking into the distance. He is wearing a brown suit that is obviously too tight for him, and white spats. He is resting one hand on a little round table on which stands a vase with flowers; the other is braced on his hip. One foot is balanced nonchalantly on the tip of his shoe. In front of the group near the proscenium, a large camera on a tripod, covered with black velvet. Behind the camera stands*

637

EUGENE. *He is still wearing his black swallowtail coat but his khaki shorts have been replaced by long black trousers with pin stripes. A red carnation in his buttonhole. In front of him on the floor, his top hat, white gloves and a cane with a silver knob. He fusses with the camera while the others hold their pose.* EUGENIA *says* "Ah . . . ah" *several times and sneezes loudly.*

EUGENE: Don't move!

EUGENIA: I can't help it. It's the moth balls.

EUGENE: Hold it!

> STOMIL *removes his hand from his hip and scratches his chest.*

Stomil, your hand.

STOMIL: But I'm itching all over.

ELEANOR: Why should you be itching?

STOMIL: Moths.

ELEANOR: Moths! (*She jumps up and runs across the stage, chasing moths, occasionally clapping her hands.*)

EUGENE: At this rate we'll never get a picture. Sit down, Eleanor.

ELEANOR (*reproachfully*): The moths come from Mama.

EUGENIA: They do not. They come out of this old rag.

EUGENE: Let's not quarrel. They come from the attic.

EDDIE (*enters dressed as a valet, in a crimson vest with black stripes*): You called, Madame?

ELEANOR (*stops clapping her hands*): What? What is it now? Oh yes. My salts, Edward!

EDDIE: Salts, Madame?

ELEANOR: Those smelling salts . . . you know . . .

EDDIE: Certainly, Madame. (*He goes out.*)

STOMIL (*looking after him*): I must admit it's a relief to see that fellow put in his place.

EUGENE: You haven't seen anything yet. Everything's going splendidly. You won't regret a thing.

STOMIL (*tries to loosen his collar*): If only this collar weren't so damn tight!

EUGENE: That's the price you've got to pay for having Eddie wait on you. Everything has its price.

STOMIL: And my experiments? Will I have to give them up?

EUGENE: I couldn't say. Arthur hasn't announced his decision on that point yet.

STOMIL: Maybe he'll let me go on with them. He hasn't said anything?

EUGENE: There hasn't been time. He went out early this morning.

STOMIL: Perhaps you could put in a good word for me, Uncle?

EUGENE (*patronizingly*): I'll speak to him when the opportunity arises.

STOMIL: At least once a week. After all these years I can't just suddenly stop. You ought to realize that.

EUGENE: That will depend entirely on your conduct, Stomil.

STOMIL: But I'm on your side. What more do you want? I'm even putting up with this collar. (*He tries again to loosen it.*)

EUGENE: Well, I can't promise.

EDDIE *enters with a tray on which a bottle of vodka is very much in evidence.*

What is that?

EDDIE: The salts for Madame, sir.

EUGENE (*menacingly*): Eleanor, what is the meaning of this?

ELEANOR: I can't imagine. (*To* EDDIE.) I asked for my smelling salts.

EDDIE: Madame no longer drinks?

ELEANOR: Take it away immediately!

EUGENIA: Why? As long as he's brought it . . . I don't feel too well.

EDDIE: As you wish, Madame.

He goes out. On the way he takes a good swig from the bottle. Only EUGENIA, *looking after him longingly, notices.*

EUGENE: Don't let it happen again!

EUGENIA: God, am I bored!

EUGENE: Back to your places!

ELEANOR, STOMIL *and* EUGENIA *sit up and freeze as at the beginning of the act.* EUGENE *ducks under the velvet cloth, the ticking of the timer is heard.* EUGENE *reaches quickly for his stick, top hat and gloves, and takes a stance beside* EUGENIA. *The ticking stops. Relieved, they all relax.*

STOMIL: Can't I unbutton these buttons for just a second?

EUGENE: Certainly not! The wedding is at twelve!

STOMIL: I seem to have put on weight. The last time I wore these things was forty years ago.

EUGENE: You have only your experiments to blame for that. Experimental art pays so well these days.

STOMIL: That's not my fault, is it?

ELEANOR: When will that picture be ready? I think I blinked. I know I'm going to look simply awful.

EUGENE: Don't worry. The camera hasn't worked for years.

ELEANOR: What? Then why take the picture?

EUGENE: It's the principle of the thing. It's a tradition.

STOMIL: You begrudge me my innocent experiments but is an old-fashioned broken-down camera any better? You know what I think of your counterrevolution? It's a fiasco.

EUGENE: Watch your tongue.

STOMIL: I bow to superior force, but I can still say what I think.

ELEANOR (*to* EUGENIA): What do you say, Mother?

EUGENIA: I say we're in one hell of a mess and this is only the beginning.

EUGENE: It can't be helped. Our first job is to create the form. The content comes later.

STOMIL: You're making a colossal mistake, Eugene. Formalism will never free you from chaos. You'd be better off if you could just accept the spirit of the times.

EUGENE: That's enough out of you. Defeatism will not be tolerated!

STOMIL: All right, all right. I can still have an opinion, can't I?

EUGENE: Of course. As long as it agrees with ours.

ELEANOR: Listen!

Bells are heard in the distance.

STOMIL: Bells!

EUGENE: Wedding bells.

ALA *enters. She is wearing a wedding dress with a long veil.* STOMIL *kisses her hand.*

STOMIL: Ah, here comes our dear little bride!

ELEANOR: Oh, Ala, it's so becoming!

EUGENIA: My dear child!

ALA: Isn't Arthur back yet?

EUGENE: We're expecting him any minute. He had a few final formalities to attend to.

ALA: These damned formalities.

EUGENE: But the spirit of life can't run around naked. It must always be dressed with taste and care. You mean Arthur hasn't discussed that point with you yet?

ALA: For hours on end.

EUGENE: And rightly so. Someday you'll understand and be grateful to him.

ALA: Oh, stop making such an ass of yourself, Uncle.

ELEANOR: You mustn't talk like that, Ala dear. Today is your wedding day and no time for family quarrels. There'll be plenty of time for that later.

EUGENE: Don't worry. No offense. I quite understand.

ALA: So old and so stupid. I can understand it in Arthur. But you, Uncle . . .

ELEANOR: Ala!

STOMIL: He had it coming.

ELEANOR: Forgive her, Eugene. She's so excited she doesn't know what she's saying. After all, this is a big day in her life. I remember the day I was married to Stomil . . .

EUGENE: I can tell when I'm not wanted. But don't delude yourselves. You can laugh at me as much as you like but childish insults won't change a thing. Stomil, come with me. I have a proposition to make to you.

STOMIL: All right. Just don't try to brainwash me!

They go out.

ELEANOR: Mama, you might go for a stroll too.

EUGENIA: Anything you say. It's all the same to me. Either way I'll be bored to death. (*She goes out.*)

ELEANOR: There. Now we can talk. Tell me, what's happened?

ALA: Nothing.

ELEANOR: Something's bothering you. I can see that.

ALA: Nothing's bothering me. This veil doesn't fall quite right. Help me with it, will you, Mother?

ELEANOR: Of course. But you don't have to take that tone with me. With the others it's different. They're such fools.

ALA (*sits down at the mirror; the bells are still ringing*): Why do you all despise each other?

ELEANOR: I don't know. Maybe because we have no reason to respect each other.

ALA: Yourselves or each other?

ELEANOR: It comes to the same thing. Shall I fix your hair?

ALA: It's got to be done all over again.

She takes off her veil. ELEANOR *combs her hair.*

Are you happy, Mother?

ELEANOR: I beg your pardon?

ALA: I asked if you were happy. What's so funny about that?

ELEANOR: It's a very indiscreet question.

ALA: Why? Is it a disgrace to be happy?

ELEANOR: No, I wouldn't say that.

ALA: Then you're not very happy, are you? Because you're ashamed. People are always ashamed about not being happy. It's like having pimples or not doing your homework. It makes them feel guilty, almost criminal.

ELEANOR: "It is the right and duty of all to be happy, now that the new era has set us free." Stomil taught me that.

ALA: Oh. So that's why everybody's so ashamed nowadays. But how do *you* feel about it?

ELEANOR: I've always done as much as I could.

ALA: To make Stomil happy?

ELEANOR: No. Myself. That's the way he wanted it.

ALA: Then in a way it was for him?

ELEANOR: Of course it was for him. Oh, if you'd only known him when he was young . . .

ALA: It's not right yet on this side. Does he know?

ELEANOR: What?

ALA: Don't be like that. I'm not a baby. Your affair with Eddie.

ELEANOR: Of course he knows.

ALA: And what does he say?

ELEANOR: Nothing, unfortunately. He pretends not to notice.

ALA: That's bad.

EDDIE *comes in with a white tablecloth.*

EDDIE: May I set the table now?

ELEANOR: Sure, Eddie. (*She corrects herself.*) Yes, Edward, you may set the table.

EDDIE: Yes, Madame. (*He lays the cloth on the table and takes the camera out with him.*)

ALA: What do you see in him?

ELEANOR: Oh, he's just so simple . . . like life itself. He can be rough, of course, but that's the secret of his charm. A man without complexes—it's so refreshing. He just wants what he wants. Wonderful. And the way he sits —nothing unusual about it, but it's real, honest-to-goodness sitting. And when he eats, when he drinks! His stomach becomes a symphony of nature. I just love to watch him digest. It's so simple, so direct. It's like the elements. Have you ever noticed how divinely he hitches his trousers up? Stomil admires authenticity too.

ALA: I know. It doesn't fascinate me very much. I'm afraid.

ELEANOR: You're too young. You haven't had time to learn the value of genuine simplicity. You will. It takes experience.

ALA: I'll certainly try. Tell me, Mother, do you think it's a good idea for me to marry Arthur?

ELEANOR: Oh, Arthur is something else again. He has principles.

ALA: But Stomil has principles too. You said so yourself. All that stuff about the right and duty to be happy.

ELEANOR: Oh, those were only opinions. Stomil has always detested principles. Arthur, on the other hand, has cast-iron principles.

ALA: And that's all he has.

ELEANOR: Ala, how can you say a thing like that? Arthur's the first man in fifty years to have principles. Doesn't that appeal to you? It's so original! And it's so becoming to him!

ALA: You really think principles are enough for me?

ELEANOR: Well, I admit, they're rather old-fashioned. But so unusual these days . . .

ALA: I'll take Arthur with principles if I have to, Mother. But principles without Arthur—no.

ELEANOR: But didn't he propose to you? Isn't he going to marry you?

ALA: Not Arthur.

ELEANOR: Then who? What are you talking about?

ALA: His principles!

ELEANOR: Then why did you accept?

ALA: Because I still have hope.

ELEANOR: That, my dear, is fatal.

EDDIE *enters with a stack of plates.*

EDDIE: May I continue?

ALA: Clatter away, Eddie boy. (*Corrects herself.*) I mean, yes, Edward, clatter away. I mean, do continue, Edward.

ELEANOR: Tell me, Eddie, does it depress you? All these changes thought up by a bunch of fools?

EDDIE: Why should it depress me?

ELEANOR: Didn't I tell you? He's as free and natural as a butterfly. Oh, Eddie, you set the table so gracefully.

EDDIE: I'm not knocking myself out, that's for sure.

ALA: Eddie, come here.

EDDIE: At your service. What can I do for you, Miss?

Suddenly the bells fall silent.

ALA: Tell me, Eddie, have you got principles?

EDDIE: Principles? Sure.

ALA: What kind?

EDDIE: The best.

ALA: Tell me one. Please.

EDDIE: What's in it for me?

ALA: Well, can you or can't you?

EDDIE: If I have to, I guess. Just a sec. (*He puts the plates down on the floor and takes a little memo book from his pocket.*) I've got one written down here somewhere. (*He leafs through the book.*) Here it is! (*He reads.*) "I love you, and you're sound asleep."

ALA: That's all?

EDDIE: "You made your bed, now lie in it."

ALA: Oh, come on, Eddie. Read.

EDDIE: I did read. That's a principle.

ALA: Then read another!

EDDIE *giggles.*

What's so funny?

EDDIE: Well, there's one here . . .

ALA: Read it! ..

EDDIE: I can't, not in mixed company. It's too good.

ALA: And those are your principles?

EDDIE: Actually, no. I borrowed them from a friend who works for the movies.

ALA: You haven't got any of your own?

EDDIE (*proudly*): No.

ALA: Why not?

EDDIE: What do I need them for? I know my way around.

ELEANOR: Oh yes, Eddie. You certainly do.

> STOMIL *rushes in, pursued by* EUGENE *carrying a laced corset.* EDDIE *goes on setting the table.*

STOMIL: No, no! That's asking too much!

EUGENE: Take my word for it. You'll be glad once it's on.

ELEANOR: Now what's wrong?

STOMIL (*running from* EUGENE): He wants to strap me into that thing.

ELEANOR: What is it?

EUGENE: Great grandfather's corset. Indispensable. Pulls in the waist, guarantees a perfect figure for every occasion.

STOMIL: No, no, no. I'm wearing spats, I've got this collar on. What are you trying to do—kill me?

EUGENE: Now, Stomil, let's not do things by halves.

STOMIL: I've gone far enough. Let me live!

EUGENE: You're falling back into your old habits, Stomil. Come on. Stop making such a fuss. You admitted yourself you'd been putting on weight.

STOMIL: But I want to be fat! I want to live in harmony with nature!

EUGENE: You just don't want to be bothered. Come on. Don't fight it. It won't do any good.

STOMIL: Eleanor, save me!

ELEANOR: You don't think it might improve your looks?

STOMIL: My looks? What for? I'm a free fat artist.

He runs into his room. EUGENE *following. The door closes behind them.*

ELEANOR: These perpetual scenes. And you say you still have hope?

ALA: Yes.

ELEANOR: And if you're only deluding yourself?

ALA: What difference does it make?

ELEANOR (*tries to take her in her arms*): My poor Ala! . . .

ALA (*freeing herself*): You don't need to pity me. I can take care of myself.

ELEANOR: But what if things don't work out?

ALA: That's my secret.

ELEANOR: You won't tell even me?

ALA: It will be a surprise.

STOMIL'S VOICE: Help!

ELEANOR: That's Stomil.

ALA: Uncle Eugene is really overdoing it. Do you think he has any influence on Arthur?

STOMIL'S VOICE: Let me go!

ELEANOR: I doubt it. It's probably the other way around.

ALA: Too bad. I thought it was all Uncle's fault.

STOMIL'S VOICE: Get out of here!

ELEANOR: I'd better go see what they're up to. I have a feeling something awful is going to happen.

ALA: So do I.

STOMIL'S VOICE: Murderer! Let me go!

ELEANOR: Good God, how will it all end?

STOMIL'S VOICE: No, no! I'll burst! I'll explode! Help!

ELEANOR: Eugene's going too far. But you, Ala, do be careful.

ALA: Careful?

ELEANOR: Don't go too far—like Uncle Eugene. (*She goes into Stomil's room.*)

ALA: Eddie, my veil!

> EDDIE *hands her the veil and stands behind her. From Stomil's room screaming and the sound of a struggle are heard.* ARTHUR *enters.* ALA *and* EDDIE *don't notice him. Arthur's coat is open. He looks gray. His listless, unnatural movements show that he is having great difficulty keeping himself going. He carefully removes his coat and throws it down somewhere. Sits down in an armchair and sprawls out his legs.*

STOMIL'S VOICE: Damn you!

ARTHUR (*in a low, dull voice*): What's going on?

> ALA *turns around.* EDDIE *dutifully picks up* ARTHUR'S *coat and goes out.*

ALA (*as though merely making an observation*): You're late.

> ARTHUR *stands up and opens Stomil's door.*

ARTHUR: Let him go.

> STOMIL, EUGENE *and then* ELEANOR *come out of the room.*

EUGENE: Why? It would have given him that final polish.

ARTHUR: I said let him go.

STOMIL: Thank you, Arthur. I'm glad to see you're not completely devoid of human feeling.

EUGENE: I protest!

> ARTHUR *grabs him by the tie and pushes him back.*

ELEANOR: Arthur, what's happened? He's as pale as a ghost!

ARTHUR: You whited skeleton!

EUGENE: Arthur, it's me, it's your Uncle Eugene! Don't you know me? You and I together . . . the new life . . . saving the world. Don't you remember? You're choking me. You and I . . . together . . . Don't . .

ARTHUR (*pushing him back step by step*): You stuffed zero, you synthetic blob . . . you worm-eaten false bottom!

ELEANOR: Do something! He's choking him!

ARTHUR: You fake . . .

Mendelssohn's "Wedding March" resounds, loud and triumphant. ARTHUR *lets* EUGENE *go, picks up a carafe from the table and hurls it off stage where it lands with a loud crash. The march breaks off in the middle of a measure.* ARTHUR *sinks into an armchair.*

EDDIE (*enters*): Do you wish me to change the record?

ELEANOR: Who told you to put that on?

EDDIE: Mr. Eugene. His orders were to put it on as soon as Mr. Arthur entered the room.

EUGENE (*gasping for air*): My orders. Yes, that's right.

ELEANOR: We won't need any music right now.

EDDIE: As you wish, Madame. (*He goes out.*)

ARTHUR: It's a fraud . . . The whole thing . . . a fraud! (*He collapses.*)

STOMIL (*leans over him*): He's dead drunk.

EUGENE: That's a slander, an infamous slander. This young man knows his duty. He's the soul of moderation.

ELEANOR: I can't believe it either. Arthur never drinks.

STOMIL: Take it from me. I'm an expert.

ELEANOR: But why today of all days?

STOMIL: His last hours as a free man.

ALA *pours water into a glass and feeds it to* ARTHUR.

EUGENE: There must be some misunderstanding. It would be unwise to draw premature conclusions. The truth will soon be known.

STOMIL: Yes. If we wait just a minute, he'll explain. He was just getting started.

ELEANOR: Shh . . . he's coming to.

ARTHUR (*raises his head and points to* STOMIL): What on earth is that?

ELEANOR: He doesn't know his own father. Ohhh! (*She bursts into tears.*)

ARTHUR: Quiet, you females! It's not my parents I'm asking about. What's the meaning of this masquerade?

STOMIL (*looking at his legs*): These . . . these are spats.

ARTHUR: Oh . . . yes, of course. They're spats. (*He sinks into thought.*)

EUGENE: Arthur's a little tired. Conditions will return to normal in a moment. Take your places. Attention! There will be no change in the program. (*To* ARTHUR *in a very friendly tone:*) Ha ha, well, Arthur, my boy, you were just joking, weren't you? Putting us to the test, you little devil! Don't worry. We won't abandon our positions. Here we are, all buttoned up from top to toe, once and for all. Stomil was even going to put on a corset. Cheer up, my boy. A little rest, and then . . . on with the wedding!

STOMIL: Same old song and dance! Can't you see, you ghost of the past, that he's stewed to the gills? His father's son all right.

EUGENE: That's a lie! Quiet! Come on, Arthur. It's time for action now. Everything's ready. Just one last step.

ARTHUR (*goes down on his knees to* STOMIL): Father, forgive me.

STOMIL: What's this? Some new trick?

ARTHUR (*dragging himself after* STOMIL *on his knees*): 1 was insane! There's no going back, no present, no future. There's nothing.

STOMIL (*evading him*): What is he now? A nihilist?

ALA (*tearing off her veil*): What about me? Am I nothing?

ARTHUR (*changing direction and dragging himself after her*): You too . . . forgive me!

ALA: You're a ·coward, that's all you are. A child and a coward and impotent!

ARTHUR: No, please don't say that. I'm not afraid, but I can't believe anymore. I'll do anything. I'll lay down my life . . . but there's no turning back to the old forms. They can't create a reality for us. I was wrong.

ALA: What are you talking about?

ARTHUR: About creating a world.

ALA: And me? Isn't anybody going to say anything about me?

EUGENE: This is treason!

ARTHUR (*changing direction again and heading for* EUGENE): You must forgive me too. I raised your hopes and I've let you down. But believe me, it's impossible . . .

EUGENE: I refuse to listen to this kind of talk. Pull yourself together. Stand up and get married. Raise a family, brush your teeth, eat with a knife and fork, make the world sit up straight. You'll see, we'll do it yet. You're not going to throw away our last chance, are you, Arthur?

ARTHUR: There never was a chance. We were wrong. It's hopeless.

EUGENE: Stomil's right. You're drunk. You don't know what you're saying.

ARTHUR: Yes, drunk. When I was sober I let myself be deceived, so I got drunk to dispel my illusions. You'd better have a drink too, Uncle

EUGENE: Me? Certainly not. . . . Well, perhaps just a little one. (*He pours himself a shot of vodka and downs it at one gulp.*)

ARTHUR: I had cold sober reasons for getting drunk. I drank myself sane again.

STOMIL: Nonsense. You got drunk out of despair.

ARTHUR: Yes, despair too. Despair that form can never save the world.

EUGENE: Then what can?

ARTHUR (*stands up, solemnly*): An idea!

EUGENE: What idea?

ARTHUR: If I only knew. Conventions always spring from an idea. Father was right. I'm a contemptible formalist.

STOMIL: Don't take it so hard, son. You know I've always been indulgent. Frankly, though, I've suffered plenty from your ideas. Thank God, that's all over now. (*Starts taking off his morning coat.*) Where are my pajamas?

ARTHUR (*rushes over to him and prevents him from taking off his coat*): Stop! A reversion to pajamas is equally impossible.

STOMIL: Why? Are you still trying to save us? I thought you'd got over that.

ARTHUR (*aggressively, going from one extreme to the other as drunks do; triumphantly*): Did you think I was going to cave in completely just like that?

STOMIL: Just a minute ago you were acting like a human being. Don't tell me you want to be an apostle again.

ARTHUR (*releasing* STOMIL, *with emphasis*): My sin was reason . . . and abstraction, the lewd daughter of reason. Now I have drowned my reason in alcohol. I didn't get drunk the usual way. Though my aim was mystical, I drank most rationally. The fire water cleansed me. You've got to forgive me because I stand before you purified. I clothed you in vestments and tore them off again because they proved to be shrouds. But I will not abandon you, naked, to the gales of history; I'd rather have you curse me. Eddie!

EDDIE *enters.*

Shut the door.

ELEANOR: Yes, Eddie, shut the door, there's a draft.

ARTHUR: Don't let anybody leave.

EDDIE: Okay, boss.

STOMIL: This is a violation of civil rights!

ARTHUR: You want freedom? There is no freedom from life, and life is synthesis. You'd analyze yourselves to death. Luckily, however, you have me.

EUGENE: Arthur, you know I don't agree with Stomil. But aren't you going a little too far? I feel it's my duty to warn you. In spite of everything, I stand by the freedom of the individual.

ARTHUR: Good. Now what we need is to find an idea.

STOMIL (*simultaneously with* EUGENE *and* ELEANOR): Is this any way to treat your father?

EUGENE: I wash my hands of the whole business.

ELEANOR: Arthur, lie down for a while. I'll make you a nice cold compress.

ARTHUR: Until we come up with an idea, nobody leaves this room. Eddie. Guard the door!

EDDIE: Yes, sir.

Pause.

ELEANOR: Find him an idea, somebody, so he'll leave us alone. If I don't go to the kitchen, the cake will be burned to a crisp.

EUGENE: Better humor him.

ARTHUR: What do you suggest, Uncle?

EUGENE: Search me . . . God, maybe?

ARTHUR: That's been done. Lost His appeal.

EUGENE: True. Even in my time there wasn't much you could do with God. I grew up in an age of enlightenment and exact science. I only mentioned Him for the sake of form.

ARTHUR: Forget about form. What we're after now is a living idea.

EUGENE: How about sports? I used to ride horseback.

ARTHUR: Everybody goes in for sports nowadays. A lot of good it does them.

EUGENE: Sorry. Maybe Stomil has an idea.

STOMIL: Experiment. There's an idea.

ARTHUR: Please, this is serious.

STOMIL: Well, I'm serious too. Blazing trails, opening new frontiers! Man is always looking for new worlds to conquer and conquest comes from experiment. From trial and error. But always with an aim in view: the new life, radically new!

ARTHUR: A new life! I don't even know what to do with the old one.

STOMIL: Well, everything is still in the experimental stage, that's why.

EUGENE: Eleanor, have you got an idea?

ARTHUR: There's no sense asking a woman.

ELEANOR: I had an idea, but I've forgotten. I'm supposed to

look after everything. Why don't you ask Eddie? He's got a good head on his shoulders, and when he does say something, you can depend on it.

STOMIL: That's right. Eddie is the collective mind.

ARTHUR: Well, what do you say then, Eddie?

EDDIE: Well, if anybody were to ask me, I'd say progress, sir.

ARTHUR: Meaning what?

EDDIE: Well, just that, sir: progress.

ARTHUR: But what kind of progress?

EDDIE: The progressive kind, the kind that goes right ahead.

ARTHUR: You mean forward?

EDDIE: Right. With the front moving forward.

ARTHUR: And the back?

EDDIE: The back moving forward too. Right out there in front.

ARTHUR: Then the front is in back?

EDDIE: Depends on how you look at it. If you look from back to front, the front is in front, though somehow or other it's also in back.

ARTHUR: That doesn't sound very clear to me.

EDDIE: No. But it's progressive.

EUGENIA *enters, leaning on a cane.*

EUGENIA (*timidly*): There's something I must tell you . . .

ELEANOR: Not now, Mother. Can't you see the men are discussing politics?

EUGENIA: Just two words . . .

ARTHUR: No, I don't like it. I need an idea that naturally, inevitably, leads to form. Your kind of progress leads nowhere.

EUGENIA: Please listen to me, my darlings. I won't take much of your time.

STOMIL: What is it now?

ELEANOR: I don't know. Something's wrong with Mama.

STOMIL: Later. We're busy now. (*To* ARTHUR.) I still say we should get back to experiments. Then the idea will come by itself.

EUGENIA *takes the knicknacks and napkins off the catafalque.*

ELEANOR: What are you doing, Mama?

EUGENIA (*matter-of-factly*): I'm dying.

ELEANOR: Mother! That's not very funny, you know.

Silently EUGENIA *tidies up the catafalque. She wipes away the dust with her sleeve.*

Mother says she's dying.

EUGENE: What? Dying? Can't she see we're busy?

ELEANOR: Did you hear that, Mama?

EUGENIA: Help me.

Involuntarily ELEANOR *gives her her arm.* EUGENIA *climbs up on the catafalque.*

ELEANOR: But don't be silly, Mama. There's going to be a wedding today. You wouldn't want to spoil everything by dying, would you?

STOMIL: Dying? What's all this about death? I never thought about that . . .

ARTHUR (*to himself*): Death? Excellent idea! . . .

EUGENE: This is ridiculous, Eugenia. Pull yourself together. This is no way to behave.

ALA: It wouldn't be normal, Grandmother.

EUGENIA: I don't understand you people. You're all so intelligent, but if somebody wants to do something as simple as dying, you don't know what to make of it. Really, you are very strange people. (*She lies down on her back and folds her hands over her breast.*)

ELEANOR: Look at her. Do something . . . Maybe she's really . . .

EUGENE: Eugenia, this is carrying eccentricity too far. This sort of thing isn't done in our family.

STOMIL: It's sheer hypocrisy.

EUGENIA: You'll find the key to my room on the table. I won't need it anymore. I'll be able to come and go as I please. The cards are in the drawer. All marked . . .

ARTHUR: Death . . . the supreme form!

STOMIL: Not exactly viable, though, is it?

ARTHUR: Why not? When it's somebody else's death.

He seems to have had a revelation, beats his forehead.

Grandma, you're brilliant!

ELEANOR: You ought to be ashamed of yourself! You all ought to be ashamed of yourselves.

EUGENE: Eugenia, lie properly at least. You're all hunched up. Elbows at your sides. Or get up this minute. Dying is no way to behave in society. Death is irrational.

STOMIL: Death is final and therefore no good as an experiment. An experiment has to be repeatable. Of course, if you're only rehearsing, that's something else again. But even so, there's not much point in it.

ALA: Stop! Can't you see what's happening?

EUGENIA: Come closer, my children.

All except EDDIE *go over to the catafalque.*

Eddie, you too!

EDDIE *joins the others.*

Who are you?

EUGENE: We're . . . it's just us.

EUGENIA *starts giggling, first softly, then loudly.*

Now she's insulting us. Did I say something funny?

STOMIL: I'm not feeling so well myself. Must be a headache. (*He steps aside, feels his pulse, takes a mirror out of his pocket, and looks at his tongue.*)

ARTHUR: Thank you, Grandmother, I'll make use of your idea.

STOMIL (*putting the mirror away*): Nothing serious, I guess. Must be these tight clothes.

EUGENIA *dies.*

ELEANOR: Try again, Mama.

ARTHUR: She's dead. Strange. She was always so frivolous.

ALA: I can't stand it!

EUGENE: I don't understand.

STOMIL: I don't want to have anything to do with this.

ELEANOR: I never dreamed . . . Stomil, why didn't you warn me?

STOMIL: Of course, it's all my fault. Frankly I don't see that this changes anything at all. My collar's as tight as ever.

ARTHUR (*drawing the curtain in front of the catafalque*): Eddie, come here.

EDDIE *comes over and stands at attention.* ARTHUR *feels his muscle.*

You pack a good punch, don't you?

EDDIE: Not bad, sir.

ARTHUR: And if necessary, you could . . ? (*He runs his finger across his throat.*)

EDDIE (*phlegmatically after a pause*): You ask me a question, Mr. Arthur? I'm not sure I heard you right.

Pause. ARTHUR *laughs, unsure of himself, as though waiting to see.* EDDIE *laughs with a similar "ha ha."*

ARTHUR *laughs once again more loudly and with more assurance. Whereupon* EDDIE *utters a resounding laugh.* ARTHUR *slaps him on the shoulder.*

ARTHUR: Eddie, I like you. I've always liked you.

EDDIE: And I've always thought we'd understand each other someday.

ARTHUR: Then you do understand?

EDDIE: Eddie understands all right.

STOMIL: This business has rather upset me. I'm going to lie down for a while.

ARTHUR: Stay right where you are, Father.

STOMIL: Oh stop ordering me around, you little punk. I'm tired. (*He starts for his room.*)

ARTHUR: Eddie!

EDDIE *bars Stomil's way.*

STOMIL: Who do you think you are? (*Furiously pointing at* EDDIE, *to* ELEANOR:) And you've been having an affair with this flunky? ·

ELEANOR: For God's sake, not now. Not with Mama lying there.

EDDIE *pushes* STOMIL *into an armchair.*

ARTHUR: Just a bit more patience, please. It's all quite clear to me now. I shall show you the way to a better future.

EUGENE (*sitting down with resignation*): I just don't seem to care anymore . . . I must be getting old. We're just not as young as we used to be, are we, Stomil?

STOMIL: Speak for yourself. You're almost as old as Eugenia was, you old hypocrite. I feel fine. By and large. (*Pleading.*) Eleanor, where are you?

ELEANOR: Here, Stomil, right beside you.

STOMIL: Come here.

ELEANOR (*resting her hand on his forehead*): How do you feel?

STOMIL: I don't know what's wrong, but not well at all.

ARTHUR: Uncertainty and indecision are behind us now. Now the road lies before us, straight and clear. From now on there will be only one law and one herd.

STOMIL: What's he jabbering about now? . . . Oh, my head!

EUGENE: Something about a new legal code for livestock.

ARTHUR: Don't you see the logical conclusion? Ah, creatures of flesh, caught up in your glandular secretions and terrified at the thought of your death, *are you incapable of all understanding?* But I understand! Unthinking cattle, behold your redeemer! I have risen above this world, and I will draw you all up after me, because I alone have a brain freed from the snares of the bowels.

EUGENE: Instead of insulting us, my dear great-nephew, kindly express yourself more clearly.

ARTHUR: Won't you ever understand, you whose lives rot away like mushrooms? You're like blind puppies that would walk in circles forever if they had no master to lead them. Without form or ideas, you would crumble to chaos and be consumed by the void if I weren't on hand to save you. Do you know what I'm going to do with you? I'm going to create a system in which rebellion will be combined with order, nonbeing with being. I will transcend all contradictions.

EUGENE: It would perhaps be better if you'd just leave the room. You've disappointed me. It's all over between us. (*To himself.*) I'll probably return to writing my memoirs.

ARTHUR: Let me just ask you this: if nothing exists and if even rebellion is impossible, then what *can* be raised up out of this nothingness and made to exist?

EUGENE (*takes out a watch with a little chain*): It's late. We could all do with a bite to eat.

ARTHUR: Isn't anybody going to answer me?

STOMIL: Eleanor, what are we having for lunch today? I'd like something light. My stomach's a bit queasy. It's high time we took better care of it.

ELEANOR: You're right, Stomil. From now on we'll look after you. A little nap after lunch, a little stroll after napping. The morning will be for experiments.

STOMIL: And everything cooked in butter, or maybe cut out fats entirely.

ELEANOR: Yes. We'll sleep better that way too.

ARTHUR: What? Silence? All right, I'll tell you. (*He puts his chair on the set table, climbs reeling on the table and sits down in the chair.*)

ELEANOR: Careful of the dishes, Arthur.

ARTHUR: The only possible answer is power.

EUGENE: Power? What power? We're your family, remember?

STOMIL: He's raving. Don't pay any attention to him.

ARTHUR: Power alone can exist in a vacuum. Now I am up here above you, and you are beneath me.

EUGENE: Brilliant, isn't he?

ELEANOR: Arthur, come down. You're getting the tablecloth all dirty.

ARTHUR: You grovel beneath me in dust and ashes.

EUGENE: How long are we going to put up with this?

STOMIL: Let him talk. We'll take care of him after lunch. It's beyond me where he gets these tendencies. Must be his upbringing.

ARTHUR: Everything depends on being strong and decisive. I am strong. Look at me then. I am the answer to your dreams. Uncle Eugene, there will be order. Father, you have always rebelled, but your rebellion consumed itself in chaos. Now look at me. Power, too, is rebellion. A revolution in form and order, the revolt of the top against the bottom, the high against the low. The mountain needs the plain and the plain needs the mountain, otherwise each would cease to be what it is. Power resolves the paradox of opposites. Neither synthesis nor analysis, I am the act, the will and the way. I am power. I am above, within and beside all things. Give thanks to me for fulfilling the dreams of your youth. This is my gift to you. Yet I have a gift for myself as well: the form I have always longed for. For I can now create and destroy not just one but a thousand possible forms. I can incarnate and disincarnate myself. I have here within me—everything. (*He beats his breast.*)

EUGENE: Poor boy. Sad to see a thing like this happen.

STOMIL: Oh don't take it so seriously. Adolescent foolishness. Words, words, words. What power has he got over us?

EUGENE: Right! What does all his talk amount to anyway? We're united by blood, not by abstractions. He can't do a thing to us.

ARTHUR: It's very simple. I can kill you.

STOMIL (*rises from his chair and falls back again*): I absolutely forbid you . . . There are limits.

ARTHUR: Limits can be transcended. *You* taught me that. Power over life and death. What greater power can there be? A simple but profoundly important discovery!

EUGENE: Nonsense! I'll live as long as I please. That is, I mean, as long as it pleases. . . . I don't know whom, do you, Stomil?

STOMIL: Well . . . Nature?

EUGENE: Exactly. Nature or fate.

ARTHUR: No. *Me!*

EUGENE (*jumping up*): Don't make me laugh!

ARTHUR: But suppose I become your fate, Uncle?

EUGENE: Eleanor, Stomil, what does this mean? I won't stand for it. He's your son, after all.

ELEANOR: Look what you've done, Arthur. You've frightened your uncle. He's white as a sheet. Don't get up, Stomil. I'll get you a pillow.

ARTHUR: Did you really think I'd start something I couldn't finish? Each one of you has a death shut inside you like a nightingale locked in a cage. All I have to do is let it out. Well, do you still think I'm a utopian, a babbler, a dreamer?

EUGENE: Ha ha! There's no getting around it, Arthur— you've got a head on your shoulders. You've thought ·this whole thing out very nicely. Nothing like a good university education, I always say. Hopeless to argue with you; you'll always win. But while we talk, time is flying and though there's nothing I enjoy more than a philosophico-scientific discussion, especially with the younger generation, we've talked long enough. Our horizons have been expanded, but now it's time for something concrete. Enough theory. Let's have something to eat. What do you say, Eleanor?

ELEANOR: I wanted to suggest that some time ago, but I couldn't get a word in edgewise. Enough now, Arthur, come down. Or at least take your shoes off.

ARTHUR: You're right, Uncle, it's time for something concrete. Eddie, my dark angel, are you ready?

EDDIE: Ready, chief.

ARTHUR: Then grab him.

EUGENE (*trying to escape*): What are you going to do?

ARTHUR: First we're going to rub out Uncle Eugene.

ELEANOR: Rub out? Where on earth did you pick that up?

STOMIL: And now of all times, with my blood pressure sky-rocketing!

EUGENE (*still trying to reach the door*): Why me?

EDDIE *bars the way.*

ARTHUR: So I'm all just theory, am I? Eddie, show him he's mistaken. You trash! What do you take me for?

EDDIE *tries to catch* EUGENE.

EUGENE: This isn't a system. It's mob rule.

ARTHUR: Do your duty, Eddie.

EUGENE (*running from* EDDIE, *who follows him with sure, catlike movements*): What does this ape want of me? Keep your hands off me!

ARTHUR: He's not an ape. He's the right arm of my spirit, my word made flesh.

STOMIL (*tearing his collar open*): Eleanor, I feel awful. Eleanor!

ELEANOR: Look, your father's fainted.

EUGENE (*still running away*): Madman! Murderer!

ARTHUR (*stands up and stretches out his arm*): No! A man who has seen the one possibility and doesn't shrink from it. I am as pure as nature. I am free. Free!

ALA: Arthur! . . .

ARTHUR: Wait. First we've got to save the world.

ALA: I've been unfaithful to you. With Eddie.

EDDIE *and* EUGENE *suddenly stop still and look at* ARTHUR *and* ALA. ELEANOR *is busy slapping Stomil's checks, trying to rouse him from his faint.*

ARTHUR (*slowly lowering his arms, after a moment of silence*): What?

ALA: I didn't think you'd mind. After all, you only wanted to marry me out of principle.

ARTHUR (*sits down, dazed*): When?

ALA: This morning.

ARTHUR (*to himself*): I see . . .

ALA: I didn't think you'd care. I thought . . . Look, I'm ready for the wedding. (*She puts on her veil.*) How do I look?

ARTHUR (*gropes his way clumsily off the table*): Wait a second, wait . . . You? You did that to me?

ALA (*with affected nonchalance*): I forgot to tell you. You were so busy . . . We can go now. Should I wear my gloves? They're a bit tight. You like the way I've done my hair?

ARTHUR (*bellowing*): You did that to *me?*

ALA (*affecting surprise*): You still going on about that? I didn't think you'd even be interested. Let's change the subject, shall we?

ARTHUR (*in a state of collapse, gropes his way around the table; he seems to have lost control over his movements; in a plaintive monotone*): How could you . . . how could you?

ALA: But you said you only needed me to help you with your plan. Don't you remember? I didn't misunderstand you, did I? Yesterday, when we were talking and you said such clever things, I was impressed. Really. Eddie could never have spoken like that.

ARTHUR (*bellowing*): Eddie!

ALA: Eddie's something else again.

ARTHUR (*plaintively*): Why did you do that to me?

ALA: What's got into you, darling? I've told you, I didn't think you'd care. Frankly, I'm surprised at you, making such a fuss over nothing. Now I'm sorry I even told you.

ARTHUR: But why?

ALA: Oh, my stubborn darling! I had my reasons.

ARTHUR (*shouting*): What reasons?

ALA: Let's forget about it. You're just getting yourself all worked up.

ARTHUR: Tell me!

ALA: I only wanted to . . .

ARTHUR: Go on. Your reasons . . .

ALA (*frightened*): Oh, the stupidest, silliest little reasons . . .

ARTHUR: Go on!

ALA: I won't tell you. You always get mad.

ARTHUR: Oh God!

ALA: If you want, we'll never say another word about the whole thing. Is it all my fault?

ARTHUR (*goes up to* STOMIL *and* ELEANOR): Why are you all against me? What have I done to you? Mother, did you hear that?

ELEANOR: Ala, I warned you.

ARTHUR (*clinging to* ELEANOR): Mama, tell her she mustn't do such things. Do something, help me, I can't live like this. Tell her . . . How can she treat me like this . . . (*He bursts into tears.*)

ELEANOR (*tearing herself away from him*): Get away from me, you silly child.

ARTHUR (*repulsed, staggers to the center of the stage; tearfully*): I wanted to save you. I was so close . . . And now you've ruined it all. Ah, the world is evil, evil, evil.

ALA: Come to me, Arthur! (*She goes toward him.*) Oh, my poor boy, I feel so sorry for you.

ARTHUR (*shoving her away*): You! Sorry for me? You dare to pity me? I don't need anyone's pity. You don't know me yet . . . but you're going to now. All right.

You've rejected my idea. You've trampled me under-foot. (*To* ALA.) And you besmirched the noblest idea in all history, you goose! Oh! What blindness! You can't even begin to imagine who it is you've lost. And who did you do it with? With this half-witted punk, this garbage dumped out by our times. I'll go away, but I won't leave you behind in this world. You don't know what you're living for anyway. Where is he, your darling lover? Where's that rotten beer belly anyway? I'll fix that early bird's guts! (*He runs desperately around the room, looking blindly for something on the tables and on the sofa.*) The revolver! Where can it be? It's impossible to find anything with all this damned order! Mama, have you seen the revolver?

EDDIE *creeps up from behind, takes the revolver from his breast pocket, and, taking a wide swing, hits* ARTHUR *in the back of the neck with the butt.* ARTHUR *sinks to his knees.* EDDIE *tosses the revolver aside, pushes Arthur's head deftly forward so that it hangs down, clasps his hands and, raising himself on his tiptoes, swings his hands down on Arthur's head like an ax.* ARTHUR *falls over, hitting the floor with his forehead. This scene must look very realistic.*

ALA (*kneels beside* ARTHUR): Arthur!

ELEANOR (*kneels on the other side of* ARTHUR): Arthur! My son!

EDDIE (*steps aside, looks at his hands, with surprise*): Hm, that was hard.

ARTHUR (*slowly and softly, as though amazed*): Strange . . . everything's disappeared . . .

ALA: But I didn't want . . . It's not true!

EDDIE: Ha ha ha!

ARTHUR (*still with his face on the floor, very softly*): I loved you, Ala.

ALA: Why didn't you tell me before?

EDDIE: "I love you and you're sound asleep."

ELEANOR (*runs to* STOMIL *and shakes him*): Wake up. Your son is dying!

STOMIL (*opening his eyes*): Can't you people spare me anything?

He stands up with difficulty and leaning on ELEANOR *approaches* ARTHUR. ELEANOR, STOMIL *and* EUGENE *stand over him.* ALA *kneels.* EDDIE *to one side makes himself comfortable in an armchair.*

ARTHUR (*stretching out on the floor*): I wanted . . . I wanted . . . (*pause*).

ALA (*stands up; matter-of-factly*): He's dead.

EUGENE: Perhaps he's better off. He nearly murdered his uncle.

STOMIL: Forgive him. He wasn't happy.

EUGENE (*magnanimously*): Oh, I don't bear him any grudge. He can't hurt me now.

STOMIL: He tried to overcome indifference and mediocrity. He lived for reason, but lived too passionately. He died because his thought had betrayed his feelings.

EDDIE: He meant well, but he was too highstrung. His kind never gets old.

All turn toward EDDIE.

STOMIL: Hold your tongue, you scoundrel, and get out of my house. You ought to be glad to get off so easy.

EDDIE: Why should I leave? I'll say it again: he meant well. I'm staying.

STOMIL: Why?

EDDIE: It's my turn now. Now you're all going to listen
to me.

STOMIL: We listen? To you?

EDDIE: Sure, why not? You've seen that I pack a wicked
punch. Nothing to worry about so long as you keep
quiet and do what I say. You'll see. You won't have
to worry. I'm a regular guy. I like a joke, like a good
time. But get this: There's got to be order.

EUGENE: We're in for it now.

EDDIE: You know, you talk too much. Take my shoes off
for me, will you?

EUGENE: I submit to brute force. But I'll despise him in my
heart.

EDDIE: Go ahead and despise me, but now take my shoes
off, and quick.

EUGENE *kneels in front of him and takes his shoes off.*

STOMIL: I've always thought we were slaves of abstractions,
but that someday humanity would take its revenge.
Now I see that it's only Eddie.

ELEANOR: Maybe it won't be so bad. He certainly won't
mind if you diet.

EUGENE (*holding the shoes*): Should I shine them, sir?

EDDIE: No, you can have 'em. I'm changing anyway. (*He
stands up, takes off Arthur's jacket, puts it on and
looks at himself in the mirror.*) A little tight, but not
bad!

STOMIL: Come, Eleanor. We're only a poor old couple now.

EDDIE: Don't go too far, and be ready to come running when
I call.

ELEANOR: Are you coming with us, Ala?

ALA: I'm coming. He loved me, nobody can take that away
from me.

STOMIL (*to himself*): We may as well assume it was love.
ALA: Did you say something, Father?
STOMIL: Me? No.

> ELEANOR *and* STOMIL *go out, holding hands.* ALA *follows.* EDDIE *takes various poses and expressions before the mirror, thrusts out his lower jaw, puts one hand on his hip.* EUGENE *runs up and down with Eddie's shoes, finally stops beside* ARTHUR.

EUGENE: I've got the feeling, Arthur, my boy, that nobody needs you anymore.

> *He stands there meditating.* EDDIE *goes out and comes back with a tape recorder. Puts it on the table and plugs it in. Immediately the tango "La Cumparsita" resounds very loud and clear. It must be this tango and no other.*

EDDIE: Well, Uncle Eugene, would you like to dance?
EUGENE: Me? With you . . . Oh, all right, why not?

> EUGENE *puts down the shoes beside* ARTHUR. EDDIE *puts his arm around him. They take the proper position, wait out one measure and start dancing.* EDDIE *leads. They dance.* EUGENE *still has the red carnation in his buttonhole.* EDDIE *in Arthur's jacket that is too tight for him, his powerful arms protruding from the sleeves that are too short. He has taken* EUGENE *by the waist. They dance all the figures of the tango. The curtain falls. "La Cumparsita" is still heard. As the light goes on in the theater, the tune issues from numerous loudspeakers throughout the house.*

END

Rosencrantz

and

Guildenstern

are

Dead

by
Tom Stoppard

The first performance of *Rosencrantz and Guildenstern Are Dead* was given in a slightly shortened form on August 24, 1966 at Cranston Street Hall, Edinburgh, by the Oxford Theatre Group as part of the "fringe" of the Edinburgh Festival. The cast was as follows:

ROSENCRANTZ	David Marks
GUILDENSTERN	Clive Cable
THE PLAYER	Jules Roach
TRAGEDIANS	Ron Forfar, Nic Renton, Howard Daubney
HAMLET	John Dodgson
OPHELIA	Janet Watts
CLAUDIUS	Nick Elliot
GERTRUDE	Frances Morrow
POLONIUS	Walter Merricks

Directed by Brian Daubney

The first professional production was given on April 11, 1967 at the Old Vic Theatre, London, by the National Theatre Company. The cast was as follows:

ROSENCRANTZ	John Stride
GUILDENSTERN	Edward Petherbridge
THE PLAYER	Graham Crowden
ALFRED	Alan Adams
TRAGEDIANS	Oliver Cotton, Neil Fitzpatrick, Luke Hardy, Roger Kemp
HAMLET	John McEnery
OPHELIA	Caroline John
CLAUDIUS	Kenneth Mackintosh
GERTRUDE	Mary Griffiths
POLONIUS	Peter Cellier
HORATIO	David Hargreaves
FORTINBRAS	David Bailie
AMBASSADOR	David Ryall
1ST SOLDIER	Christopher Timothy
2ND SOLDIER	Denis de Marne

COURT AND ATTENDANTS
Petronella Barker, Margo Cunningham, Kay Gallie, David Belcher, Reginald Green, William Hobbs, Lennard Pearce, Ron Pember, Frederick Pyne

Directed by Derek Goldby

Designed by Desmond Heeley

The New York première of *Rosencrantz and Guildenstern Are Dead* was given on October 16, 1967 at the Alvin Theatre. The cast was as follows:

ROSENCRANTZ	Brian Murray
GUILDENSTERN	John Wood
THE PLAYER	Paul Hecht
ALFRED	Douglas Norwick
TRAGEDIANS	Roger Kemp, Dino Laudicina, B. J. DeSimone, Roy Lozano
HAMLET	Noel Craig
OPHELIA	Pat McAneny
CLAUDIUS	Roger Hamilton
GERTRUDE	Anne Meacham
POLONIUS	Ralph Drischell
SOLDIER	Alexander Courtney
HORATIO	Michael Holmes

COURTIERS, AMBASSADORS, SOLDIERS, AND ATTENDANTS
Walter Beery, Stephen Bernstein, Gaetano Bon Giovanni, Margaret Braidwood, Esther Buffler, Alexander Courtney, Elizabeth Eis, Elizabeth Franz, William Grannell, John Handy, Mary Hara, Carl Jacobs, Ed Marshall, Ted Pezzulo, Jonathan Reynolds

MUSICIANS Bruce Levine, Arthur Lora, Bernie Karl, Jack Knitzer

Directed by Derek Goldby

Designed by Desmond Heeley

ACT ONE

Two ELIZABETHANS *passing the time in a place without any visible character.*

They are well dressed—hats, cloaks, sticks and all.

Each of them has a large leather money bag.

GUILDENSTERN's *bag is nearly empty.*

ROSENCRANTZ's *bag is nearly full.*

The reason being: they are betting on the toss of a coin, in the following manner: GUILDENSTERN *(hereafter "*GUIL*") takes a coin out of his bag, spins it, letting it fall.* ROSENCRANTZ *(hereafter "*ROS*") studies it, announces it as "heads" (as it happens) and puts it into his own bag. Then they repeat the process. They have apparently been doing this for some time.*

The run of "heads" is impossible, yet ROS *betrays no surprise at all—he feels none. However, he is nice enough to feel a little embarrassed at taking so much money off his friend. Let that be his character note.*

GUIL *is well alive to the oddity of it. He is not worried about the money, but he is worried by the implications; aware but not going to panic about it—his character note.*

GUIL *sits.* ROS *stands (he does the moving, retrieving coins).*
GUIL *spins.* ROS *studies coin.*

ROS: Heads.

He picks it up and puts it in his bag. The process is repeated.

Heads.

Again.

Heads.

Again.

Heads.

Again.

Heads.

GUIL (*flipping a coin*): There is an art to the building up of suspense.

ROS: Heads.

GUIL (*flipping another*): Though it can be done by luck alone.

ROS: Heads.

GUIL: If that's the word I'm after.

ROS (*raises his head at* GUIL): Seventy-six—love.

> GUIL *gets up but has nowhere to go. He spins another coin over his shoulder without looking at it, his attention being directed at his environment or lack of it.*

Heads.

GUIL: A weaker man might be moved to re-examine his faith, if in nothing else at least in the law of probability. (*He slips a coin over his shoulder as he goes to look upstage.*)

ROS: Heads.

> GUIL, *examining the confines of the stage, flips over two more coins as he does so, one by one of course.* ROS *announces each of them as "heads."*

GUIL (*musing*): The law of probability, it has been oddly asserted, is something to do with the proposition that if six monkeys (*he has surprised himself*) . . . if six monkeys were . . .

ROS: Game?

GUIL: Were they?

ROS: Are you?

GUIL (*understanding*): Game. (*Flips a coin.*) The law of averages, if I have got this right, means that if six monkeys were thrown up in the air for long enough they would land on their tails about as often as they would land on their——

ROS: Heads. (*He picks up the coin.*)

GUIL: Which even at first glance does not strike one as a particularly rewarding speculation, in either sense, even without the monkeys. I mean you wouldn't *bet* on it. I mean *I* would, but *you* wouldn't. . . . (*As he flips a coin.*)

ROS: Heads.

GUIL: Would you? (*Flips a coin.*)

ROS: Heads.

Repeat.

Heads. (*He looks up at* GUIL—*embarrassed laugh.*) Getting a bit of a bore, isn't it?

GUIL (*coldly*): A bore?

ROS: Well . . .

GUIL: What about the suspense?

ROS (innocently): What suspense?

Small pause.

GUIL: It must be the law of diminishing returns. . . . I feel the spell about to be broken. (*Energizing himself somewhat. He takes out a coin, spins it high, catches it, turns it over on to the back of his other hand, studies the coin—and tosses it to* ROS. *His energy deflates and he sits.*)

Well, it was an even chance . . . if my calculations are correct.

ROS: Eighty-five in a row—beaten the record!

GUIL: Don't be absurd.

ROS: Easily!

GUIL (*angry*): Is that *it,* then? Is that ail?

ROS: What?

GUIL: A new record? Is that as far as you are prepared to go?

ROS: Well . . .

GUIL: No questions? Not even a pause?

ROS: You spun them yourself.

GUIL: Not a flicker of doubt?

ROS (*aggrieved, aggressive*): Well, I won—didn't I?

GUIL (*approaches him—quieter*): And if you'd lost? If they'd come down against you, eighty-five times, one after another, just like that?

ROS (*dumbly*): Eighty-five in a row? *Tails?*

GUIL: Yes! What would you think?

ROS (*doubtfully*): Well . . . . (*Jocularly.*) Well, I'd have a good look at your coins for a start!

GUIL (*retiring*): I'm relieved. At least we can still count on self-interest as a predictable factor. . . . I suppose it's the last to go. Your capacity for trust made me wonder if perhaps . . . you, alone . . . (*He turns on him suddenly, reaches out a hand.*) Touch.

> ROS *clasps his hand.* GUIL *pulls him up to him.*

GUIL (*more intensely*): We have been spinning coins together since—— (*He releases him almost as violently.*) This is not the first time we have spun coins!

ROS: Oh no—we've been spinning coins for as long as I remember.

GUIL: How long is that?

ROS: I forget. Mind you—eighty-five times!

GUIL: Yes?

ROS: It'll take some beating, I imagine.

GUIL: Is *that* what you imagine? Is that it? No *fear?*

ROS: Fear?

GUIL (*in fury—flings a coin on the ground*): *Fear!* The crack that might flood your brain with light!

ROS: Heads. . . . (*He puts it in his bag.*)

GUIL *sits despondently. He takes a coin, spins it, lets it fall between his feet. He looks at it, picks it up, throws it to* ROS, *who puts it in his bag.*

GUIL *takes another coin, spins it, catches it, turns it over on to his other hand, looks at it, and throws it to* ROS, *who puts it in his bag.*

GUIL *takes a third coin, spins it, catches it in his right hand, turns it over onto his left wrist, lobs it in the air, catches it with his left hand, raises his left leg, throws the coin up under it, catches it and turns it over on the top of his head, where it sits.* ROS *comes, looks at it, puts it in his bag.*

ROS: I'm afraid——

GUIL: So am I.

ROS: I'm afraid it isn't your day.

GUIL: I'm afraid it is.

Small pause.

ROS: Eighty-nine.

GUIL: It must be indicative of something, besides the redistribution of wealth. (*He muses.*) List of possible explanations.
One: I'm willing it. Inside where nothing shows, I am the essence of a man spinning double-headed coins, and betting against himself in private atonement for an unremembered past. (*He spins a coin at* ROS.)

ROS: Heads.

GUIL: Two: time has stopped dead, and the single experience of one coin being spun once has been repeated ninety times. . . . (*He flips a coin, looks at it, tosses it to* ROS.) On the whole, doubtful. Three: divine intervention, that is to say, a good turn from above concerning him, cf. children of Israel, or retribution from above concerning me, cf. Lot's wife. Four: a spectacular vindication of the principle that each individual coin spun individually (*he spins one*) is as likely to come down heads as tails and therefore should cause no surprise each individual time it does. (*It does. He tosses it to* ROS.)

ROS: I've never known anything like it!

GUIL: And a syllogism: One, he has never known anything like it. Two, he has never known anything to write home about. Three, it is nothing to write home about. . . . Home . . . What's the first thing you remember?

ROS: Oh, let's see. . . . The first thing that comes into my head, you mean?

GUIL: No—the first thing you remember.

ROS: Ah. (*Pause.*) No, it's no good, it's gone. It was a long time ago.

GUIL (*patient but edged*): You don't get my meaning. What is the first thing after all the things you've forgotten?

ROS: Oh I see. (*Pause.*) I've forgotten the question.

GUIL *leaps up and paces.*

GUIL: Are you happy?

ROS: What?

GUIL: Content? At ease?

ROS: I suppose so.

GUIL: What are you going to do now?

ROS: I don't know. What do you want to do?

GUIL: I have no desires. None. (*He stops pacing dead.*) There was
a messenger . . . that's right. We were sent for. (*He wheels at*
ROS *and raps out:*) Syllogism the second: One, probability
is a factor which operates within natural forces. Two,
probability is not operating as a factor. Three, we are now
within un-, sub- or supernatural forces. Discuss. (ROS *is*
suitably startled. Acidly.) Not too heatedly.

ROS: I'm sorry I——What's the matter with you?

GUIL: The scientific approach to the examination of
phenomena is a defence against the pure emotion of fear.
Keep tight hold and continue while there's time. Now—
counter to the previous syllogism: tricky one, follow me
carefully, it may prove a comfort. If we postulate, and we
just have, that within un-, sub- or supernatural forces *the*
probability is that the law of probability will not operate as
a factor, then we must accept that the probability of the
first part will not operate as a factor, in which case the law
of probability *will* operate as a factor within un-, sub- or
supernatural forces. And since it obviously hasn't been
doing so, we can take it that we are not held within un-, sub-
or supernatural forces after all; in all probability, that is.
Which is a great relief to me personally. (*Small pause.*)
Which is all very well, except that——(*He continues with*
tight hysteria, under control.) We have been spinning coins
together since I don't know when, and in all that time (if it
is all that time) I don't suppose either of us was more than

a couple of gold pieces up or down. I hope that doesn't sound surprising because its very unsurprisingness is something I am trying to keep hold of. The equanimity of your average tosser of coins depends upon a law, or rather a tendency, or let us say a probability, or at any rate a mathematically calculable chance, which ensures that he will not upset himself by losing too much nor upset his opponent by winning too often. This made for a kind of harmony and a kind of confidence. It related the fortuitous and the ordained into a reassuring union which we recognized as nature. The sun came up about as often as it went down, in the long run, and a coin showed heads about as often as it showed tails. Then a messenger arrived. We had been sent for. Nothing else happened. Ninety-two coins spun consecutively have come down heads ninety-two consecutive times . . . and for the last three minutes on the wind of a windless day I have heard the sound of drums and flute. . . .

ROS (*cutting his fingernails*): Another curious scientific phenomenon is the fact that the fingernails grow after death, as does the beard.

GUIL: What?

ROS (*loud*): Beard!

GUIL: But you're not dead.

ROS (*irritated*): I didn't say they *started* to grow after death! (*Pause, calmer.*) The fingernails also grow before birth, though *not* the beard.

GUIL: *What?*

ROS (*shouts*): Beard! What's the matter with you? (*Reflectively.*) The toenails, on the other hand, never grow at all.

GUIL (*bemused*): The toenails never grow at all?

ROS: Do they? It's a funny thing—I cut my fingernails all the time, and every time I think to cut them, they need cutting. Now, for instance. And yet, I never, to the best of my knowledge, cut my toenails. They ought to be curled under my feet by now, but it doesn't happen. I never think about them. Perhaps I cut them absent-mindedly, when I'm thinking of something else.

GUIL (*tensed up by this rambling*): Do you remember the first thing that happened today?

ROS (*promptly*): I woke up, I suppose. (*Triggered.*) Oh—I've got it now—that man, a foreigner, he woke us up——

GUIL: A messenger. (*He relaxes, sits.*)

ROS: That's it—pale sky before dawn, a man standing on his saddle to bang on the shutters—shouts—What's all the row about?! Clear off!—But then he called our names. You remember that—this man woke us up.

GUIL: Yes.

ROS: We were sent for.

GUIL: Yes.

ROS: That's why we're here. (*He looks round, seems doubtful, then the explanation.*) Travelling.

GUIL: Yes.

ROS (*dramatically*): It was urgent—a matter of extreme urgency, a royal summons, his very words: official business and no questions asked—lights in the stable-yard, saddle up and off headlong and hotfoot across the land, our guides outstripped in breakneck pursuit of our duty! Fearful lest we come too late!!

Small pause.

GUIL: Too late for what?

ROS: How do I know? We haven't got there yet.

GUIL: Then what are we doing here, I ask myself.

ROS: You might well ask.

GUIL: We better get on.

ROS: You might well think.

GUIL: We better get on.

ROS (*actively*): Right! (*Pause.*) On where?

GUIL: Forward.

ROS (*forward to footlights*): Ah. (*Hesitates.*) Which way do we——(*He turns round.*) Which way did we——?

GUIL: Practically starting from scratch. . . . An awakening, a man standing on his saddle to bang on the shutters, our names shouted in a certain dawn, a message, a summons . . . A new record for heads and tails. We have not been . . . picked out . . . simply to be abandoned . . . set loose to find our own way. . . . We are entitled to some direction. . . . I would have thought.

ROS (*alert, listening*): I say——! I say——

GUIL: Yes?

ROS: I can hear—I thought I heard—music.

> GUIL *raises himself.*

GUIL: Yes?

ROS: Like a band. (*He looks around, laughs embarrassedly, expiating himself.*) It sounded like—a band. Drums.

GUIL: Yes.

ROS (*relaxes*): It couldn't have been real.

GUIL: "The colours red, blue and green are real. The colour yellow is a mystical experience shared by everybody"— demolish.

ROS (*at edge of stage*): It must have been thunder. Like drums . . .

By the end of the next speech, the band is faintly audible.

GUIL: A man breaking his journey between one place and
   another at a third place of no name, character, population
   or significance, sees a unicorn cross his path and disappear.
   That in itself is startling, but there are precedents for
   mystical encounters of various kinds, or to be less extreme,
   a choice of persuasions to put it down to fancy; until—
   "My God," says a second man, "I must be dreaming, I
   thought I saw a unicorn." At which point, a dimension is
   added that makes the experience as alarming as it will ever
   be. A third witness, you understand, adds no further
   dimension but only spreads it thinner, and a fourth thinner
   still, and the more witnesses there are the thinner it gets and
   the more reasonable it becomes until it is as thin as reality,
   the name we give to the common experience. . . . "Look,
   look!" recites the crowd. "A horse with an arrow in its
   forehead! It must have been mistaken for a deer."

ROS (*eagerly*): I knew all along it was a band.

GUIL (*tiredly*): He knew all along it was a band.

ROS: Here they come!

GUIL (*at the last moment before they enter—wistfully*): I'm sorry
   it wasn't a unicorn. It would have been nice to have
   unicorns.

   The TRAGEDIANS *are six in number, including a small* BOY
   (ALFRED). *Two pull and push a cart piled with props and
   belongings. There is also a* DRUMMER, *a* HORN-PLAYER *and a*
   FLAUTIST. *The* SPOKESMAN (*"the* PLAYER"*) has no instrument.
   He brings up the rear and is the first to notice them.*

PLAYER: Halt!

The group turns and halts.

(*Joyously.*) An audience!

ROS *and* GUIL *half rise.*

Don't move!

They sink back. He regards them fondly.

Perfect! A lucky thing we came along.

ROS: For us?

PLAYER: Let us hope so. But to meet two gentlemen on the road––we would not hope to meet them off it.

ROS: No?

PLAYER: Well met, in fact, and just in time.

ROS: Why's that?

PLAYER: Why, we grow rusty and you catch us at the very point of decadence—by this time tomorrow we might have forgotten everything we ever knew. That's a thought, isn't it? (*He laughs generously.*) We'd be back where we started —improvising.

ROS: Tumblers, are you?

PLAYER: We can give you a tumble if that's your taste, and times being what they are. . . . Otherwise, for a jingle of coin we can do you a selection of gory romances, full of fine cadence and corpses, pirated from the Italian; and it doesn't take much to make a jingle—even a single coin has music in it.

They all flourish and bow, raggedly.

Tragedians, at your command.

ROS *and* GUIL *have got to their feet.*

ROS: My name is Guildenstern, and this is Rosencrantz.

GUIL *confers briefly with him.*

(*Without embarrassment.*) I'm sorry—*his* name's Guildenstern, and *I'm* Rosencrantz.

PLAYER: A pleasure. We've played to bigger, of course, but quality counts for something. I recognized you at once——

ROS: And who are we?

PLAYER: —as fellow artists.

ROS: I thought we were gentlemen.

PLAYER: For some of us it is performance, for others, patronage. They are two sides of the same coin, or, let us say, being as there are so many of us, the same side of two coins. (*Bows again.*) Don't clap too loudly—it's a very old world.

ROS: What is your line?

PLAYER: Tragedy, sir. Deaths and disclosures, universal and particular, denouements both unexpected and inexorable, transvestite melodrama on all levels including the suggestive. We transport you into a world of intrigue and illusion . . . clowns, if you like, murderers—we can do you ghosts and battles, on the skirmish level, heroes, villains, tormented lovers—set pieces in the poetic vein; we can do you rapiers or rape or both, by all means, faithless wives and ravished virgins—*flagrante delicto* at a price, but that comes under realism for which there are special terms. Getting warm, am I?

ROS (*doubtfully*): Well, I don't know. . . .

PLAYER: It costs little to watch, and little more if you happen to get caught up in the action, if that's your taste and times being what they are.

ROS: What are they?

PLAYER: Indifferent.

ROS: Bad?

PLAYER: Wicked. Now what precisely is your pleasure? (*He turns to the* TRAGEDIANS.) Gentlemen, disport yourselves.

The TRAGEDIANS *shuffle into some kind of line.*

There! See anything you like?

ROS (*doubtful, innocent*): What do they do?

PLAYER: Let your imagination run riot. They are beyond surprise.

ROS: And how much?

PLAYER: To take part?

ROS: To watch.

PLAYER: Watch what?

ROS: A private performance.

PLAYER: How private?

ROS: Well, there are only two of us. Is that enough?

PLAYER: For an audience, disappointing. For voyeurs, about average.

ROS: What's the difference?

PLAYER: Ten guilders.

ROS (*horrified*): Ten *guilders*!

PLAYER: I mean eight.

ROS: Together?

PLAYER: Each. I don't think you understand—

ROS: What are you *saying*?

PLAYER: What am I saying—seven.

ROS: Where have you *been*?

PLAYER: Roundabout. A nest of children carries the custom of the town. Juvenile companies, they are the fashion. But they cannot match our repertoire . . . we'll stoop to anything if that's your bent. . . .

He regards ROS *meaningfully but* ROS *returns the stare blankly.*

ROS: They'll grow up.

PLAYER (*giving up*): There's one born every minute. (*To* TRAGEDIANS:) On-ward!

The TRAGEDIANS *start to resume their burdens and their journey.* GUIL *stirs himself at last.*

GUIL: Where are you going?

PLAYER: Ha-alt!

They halt and turn.

Home, sir.

GUIL: Where from?

PLAYER: Home. We're travelling people. We take our chances where we find them.

GUIL: It was chance, then?

PLAYER: Chance?

GUIL: You found us.

PLAYER: Oh yes.

GUIL: You were looking?

PLAYER: Oh no.

GUIL: Chance, then.

PLAYER: Or fate.

GUIL: Yours or ours?

PLAYER: It could hardly be one without the other.

GUIL: Fate, then.

PLAYER: Oh yes. We have no control. Tonight we play to the court. Or the night after. Or to the tavern. Or not.

GUIL: Perhaps I can use my influence.

PLAYER: At the tavern?

GUIL: At the court. I would say I have some influence.

PLAYER: Would you say so?

GUIL: I have influence yet.

PLAYER: Yet what?

GUIL *seizes the* PLAYER *violently.*

GUIL: I have influence!

The PLAYER *does not resist.* GUIL *loosens his hold.*

(*More calmly.*) You said something—about getting caught up in the action——

PLAYER (*gaily freeing himself*): I did!—I did!—You're quicker than your friend. . . . (*Confidingly.*) Now for a handful of guilders I happen to have a private and uncut performance of *The Rape of the Sabine Women*—or rather woman, or rather Alfred——(*Over his shoulder.*) Get your skirt on, Alfred——

The BOY *starts struggling into a female robe.*

. . . and for eight you can participate.

GUIL *backs,* PLAYER *follows.*

. . . taking either part.

GUIL *backs.*

. . . or both for ten.

GUIL *tries to turn away,* PLAYER *holds his sleeve.*

. . . with encores——

GUIL *smashes the* PLAYER *across the face. The* PLAYER *recoils.* GUIL *stands trembling.*

(*Resigned and quiet*). Get your skirt off, Alfred. . . .

ALFRED *struggles out of his half-on robe.*

GUIL (*shaking with rage and fright*): It could have been—it didn't have to be *obscene*. . . . It could have been—a bird out of season, dropping bright-feathered on my shoulder. . . . It could have been a tongueless dwarf standing by the road to point the way. . . . I was *prepared*. But it's this, is it? No enigma, no dignity, nothing classical, portentous, only this —a comic pornographer and a rabble of prostitutes. . . .

PLAYER (*acknowledging the description with a sweep of his hat, bowing; sadly*): You should have caught us in better times. We were purists then. (*Straightens up.*) On-ward.

The PLAYERS *make to leave.*

ROS (*his voice has changed: he has caught on*): Excuse me!

PLAYER: Ha-alt!

They halt.

A-al-l-fred!

ALFRED *resumes the struggle. The* PLAYER *comes forward.*

ROS: You're not—ah—exclusively players, then?

PLAYER: We're inclusively players, sir.

ROS: So you give—exhibitions?

PLAYER: Performances, sir.

ROS: Yes, of course. There's more money in that, is there?

PLAYER: There's more trade, sir.

ROS: Times being what they are.

PLAYER: Yes.

ROS: Indifferent.

PLAYER: Completely.

ROS: You know I'd no idea——

PLAYER: No——

ROS: I mean, I've *heard* of—but I've never actually——

PLAYER: No.

ROS: I mean, what exactly do you *do*?

PLAYER: We keep to our usual stuff, more or less, only inside out. We do on stage the things that are supposed to happen off. Which is a kind of integrity, if you look on every exit being an entrance somewhere else.

ROS (*nervy, loud*): Well, I'm not really the type of man who— no, but don't hurry off—sit down and tell us about some of the things people ask you to do——

The PLAYER *turns away.*

PLAYER: On-ward!

ROS: Just a minute!

They turn and look at him without expression.

Well, all right—I wouldn't mind seeing—just an idea of the kind of—(*Bravely.*) What will you do for that? (*And tosses a single coin on the ground between them.*)

The PLAYER *spits at the coin, from where he stands.*

The TRAGEDIANS *demur, trying to get at the coin. He kicks and cuffs them back.*

On!

ALFRED *is still half in and out of his robe. The* PLAYER *cuffs him.*

(*To* ALFRED:) What are you playing at?

ROS *is shamed into fury.*

ROS: Filth! Disgusting—I'll report you to the authorities—*perverts*! I know your game all right, it's all filth!

The PLAYERS *are about to leave.* GUIL *has remained detached.*

GUIL (*casually*): Do you like a bet?

The TRAGEDIANS *turn and look interested. The* PLAYER *comes forward.*

PLAYER: What kind of bet did you have in mind?

GUIL *walks half the distance towards the* PLAYER, *stops with his foot over the coin.*

GUIL: Double or quits.

PLAYER: Well . . . heads.

GUIL *raises his foot. The* PLAYER *bends. The* TRAGEDIANS *crowd round. Relief and congratulations. The* PLAYER *picks up the coin.* GUIL *throws him a second coin.*

GUIL: Again?

Some of the TRAGEDIANS *are for it, others against.*

GUIL: Evens.

The PLAYER *nods and tosses the coin.*

GUIL: Heads.

It is. He picks it up.

Again.

GUIL *spins coin.*

PLAYER: Heads.

It is. PLAYER *picks up coin. He has two coins again. He spins one.*

GUIL: Heads.

It is. GUIL *picks it up. Then tosses it immediately.*

PLAYER (*fractional hesitation*): Tails.

But it's heads. GUIL *picks it up.* PLAYER *tosses down his last coin by way of paying up, and turns away.* GUIL *doesn't pick it up; he puts his foot on it.*

GUIL: Heads.

PLAYER: No!

Pause. The TRAGEDIANS *are against this.*

(*Apologetically.*) They don't like the odds.

GUIL (*lifts his foot, squats; picks up the coin still squatting; looks up*): You were right—heads. (*Spins it, slaps his hand on it, on the floor.*) Heads I win.

PLAYER: No.

GUIL (*uncovers coin*): Right again. (*Repeat.*) Heads I win.

PLAYER: No.

GUIL (*uncovers coin*): And right again. (*Repeat.*) Heads I win.

PLAYER: *No!*

He turns away, the TRAGEDIANS *with him.* GUIL *stands up, comes close.*

GUIL: Would you believe it? (*Stands back, relaxes, smiles.*) Bet me the year of my birth doubled is an odd number.

PLAYER: *Your* birth——!

GUIL: If you don't trust me don't bet with me.

PLAYER: Would you trust *me*?

GUIL: *Bet* me then.

PLAYER: My birth?

GUIL: Odd numbers you win.

PLAYER: You're on———

The TRAGEDIANS *have come forward, wide awake.*

GUIL: Good. Year of your birth. Double it. Even numbers I win, odd numbers I lose.

Silence. An awful sigh as the TRAGEDIANS *realize that any number doubled is even. Then a terrible row as they object. Then a terrible silence.*

PLAYER: We have no money.

GUIL *turns to him.*

GUIL: Ah. Then what *have* you got?

The PLAYER *silently brings* ALFRED *forward.* GUIL *regards* ALFRED *sadly.*

Was it for this?

PLAYER: It's the best we've got.

GUIL (*looking up and around*): Then the times are bad indeed.

The PLAYER *starts to speak, protestation, but* GUIL *turns on him viciously.*

The very *air* stinks.

The PLAYER *moves back.* GUIL *moves down to the footlights and turns.*

Come here, Alfred.

ALFRED *moves down and stands, frightened and small.*

(*Gently.*) Do you lose often?

ALFRED: Yes, sir.

GUIL: Then what could you have left to lose?

ALFRED: Nothing, sir.

Pause. GUIL *regards him.*

GUIL: Do you like being . . . an actor?

ALFRED: No, sir.

GUIL *looks around, at the audience.*

GUIL: You and I, Alfred—we could create a dramatic precedent here.

And ALFRED, *who has been near tears, starts to sniffle.*

Come, come, Alfred, this is no way to fill the theatres of Europe.

The PLAYER *has moved down, to remonstrate with* ALFRED. GUIL *cuts him off again.*

(*Viciously.*) Do you know any good plays?

PLAYER: Plays?

ROS (*coming forward, faltering shyly*): Exhibitions. . . .

GUIL: I thought you said you were actors.

PLAYER (*dawning*): Oh. Oh well, we *are*. We are. But there hasn't been much call——

GUIL: You lost. Well then—one of the Greeks, perhaps? You're familiar with the tragedies of antiquity, are you? The great homicidal classics? Matri, patri, fratri, sorrori, uxori and it goes without saying——

ROS: Saucy——

GUIL: —Suicidal—hm? Maidens aspiring to godheads——

ROS: And vice versa——

GUIL: Your kind of thing, is it?

PLAYER: Well, no, I can't say it is, really. We're more of the blood, love and rhetoric school.

GUIL: Well, I'll leave the choice to you, if there is anything to choose between them.

PLAYER: They're hardly divisible, sir—well, I can do you blood and love without the rhetoric, and I can do you blood and rhetoric without the love, and I can do you all three concurrent or consecutive, but I can't do you love and rhetoric without the blood. Blood is compulsory—they're all blood, you see.

GUIL: Is that what people want?

PLAYER: It's what we do. (*Small pause. He turns away.*)

>GUIL *touches* ALFRED *on the shoulder.*

GUIL (*wry, gentle*): Thank you; we'll let you know.

>*The* PLAYER *has moved upstage.* ALFRED *follows.*

PLAYER (*to* TRAGEDIANS): Thirty-eight!

ROS (*moving across, fascinated and hopeful*): Position?

PLAYER: Sir?

ROS: One of your—tableaux?

PLAYER: No, sir.

ROS: Oh.

PLAYER (*to the* TRAGEDIANS, *now departing with their cart, already taking various props off it*): Entrances there and there (*indicating upstage*).

>*The* PLAYER *has not moved his position for his last four lines. He does not move now.* GUIL *waits.*

GUIL: Well . . . aren't you going to change into your costume?

PLAYER: I never change out of it, sir.

GUIL: Always in character.

PLAYER: That's it.

Pause.

GUIL: Aren't you going to—come *on*?

PLAYER: I *am* on.

GUIL: But if you *are* on, you can't *come* on. *Can* you?

PLAYER: I *start* on.

GUIL: But it hasn't *started*. Go on. We'll look out for you.

PLAYER: I'll give you a wave.

He does not move. His immobility is now pointed, and getting awkward. Pause. ROS *walks up to him till they are face to face.*

ROS: Excuse me.

Pause. The PLAYER *lifts his downstage foot. It was covering* GUIL'S *coin.* ROS *puts his foot on the coin. Smiles.*

Thank you.

The PLAYER *turns and goes.* ROS *has bent for the coin.*

GUIL (*moving out*): Come on.

ROS: I say—that was lucky.

GUIL (*turning*): What?

ROS: It was tails.

He tosses the coin to GUIL *who catches it. Simultaneously— a lighting change sufficient to alter the exterior mood into interior, but nothing violent.*

And OPHELIA *runs on in some alarm, holding up her skirts— followed by* HAMLET.

OPHELIA *has been sewing and she holds the garment. They are both mute.* HAMLET, *with his doublet all unbraced, no hat upon his head, his stockings fouled, ungartered and down-gyved to his ankle, pale as his shirt, his knees knocking each other . . . and with a look so piteous, he takes her by the wrist and holds her hard, then he goes to the length of his arm, and with his other hand over his brow, falls to such perusal of her face as he would draw it. . . . At last, with a little shaking of his arm, and thrice his head waving up and down, he raises a sigh so piteous and profound that it does seem to shatter all his bulk and end his being. That done he lets her go, and with his head over his shoulder turned, he goes out backwards without taking his eyes off her . . . she runs off in the opposite direction.*

ROS *and* GUIL *have frozen.* GUIL *unfreezes first. He jumps at* ROS.

GUIL: Come on!

But a flourish—enter CLAUDIUS *and* GERTRUDE, *attended.*

CLAUDIUS: Welcome, dear Rosencrantz . . . (*he raises a hand at* GUIL *while* ROS *bows*—GUIL *bows late and hurriedly*) . . . and Guildenstern.

He raises a hand at ROS *while* GUIL *bows to him*—ROS *is still straightening up from his previous bow and halfway up he bows down again. With his head down, he twists to look at* GUIL, *who is on the way up.*

Moreover that we did much long to see you,
The need we have to use you did provoke
Our hasty sending.

ROS *and* GUIL *still adjusting their clothing for* CLAUDIUS's *presence.*

Something have you heard
Of Hamlet's transformation, so call it,

Sith nor th'exterior nor the inward man
Resembles that it was. What it should be,
More than his father's death, that thus hath put him,
So much from th'understanding of himself,
I cannot dream of. I entreat you both
That, being of so young days brought up with him
And sith so neighboured to his youth and haviour
That you vouchsafe your rest here in our court
Some little time, so by your companies
To draw him on to pleasures, and to gather
So much as from occasion you may glean,
Whether aught to us unknown afflicts him thus,
That opened lies within our remedy.

GERTRUDE: Good (*fractional suspense*) gentlemen . . .

They both bow.

He hath much talked of you,
And sure I am, two men there is not living
To whom he more adheres. If it will please you
To show us so much gentry and goodwill
As to expand your time with us awhile
For the supply and profit of our hope,
Your visitation shall receive such thanks
As fits a king's remembrance.

ROS: Both your majesties
Might, by the sovereign power you have of us,
Put your dread pleasures more into command
Than to entreaty.

GUIL: But we both obey,
And here give up ourselves in the full bent
To lay our service freely at your feet,
To be commanded.

CLAUDIUS: Thanks, Rosencrantz (*turning to* ROS *who is caught
unprepared, while* GUIL *bows*) and gentle Guildenstern
(*turning to* GUIL *who is bent double*).

GERTRUDE (*correcting*): Thanks Guildenstern (*turning to* ROS, *who bows as* GUIL *checks upward movement to bow too— both bent double, squinting at each other*) . . . and gentle Rosencrantz (*turning to* GUIL, *both straightening up—*GUIL *checks again and bows again*).

> And I beseech you instantly to visit
> My too much changed son. Go, some of you,
> And bring these gentlemen where Hamlet is.

Two ATTENDANTS *exit backwards, indicating that* ROS *and* GUIL *should follow.*

GUIL: Heaven make our presence and our practices
Pleasant and helpful to him.

GERTRUDE: Ay, amen!

ROS and GUIL *move towards a downstage wing. Before they get there,* POLONIUS *enters. They stop and bow to him. He nods and hurries upstage to* CLAUDIUS. *They turn to look at him.*

POLONIUS: The ambassadors from Norway, my good lord, are joyfully returned.

CLAUDIUS: Thou still hast been the father of good news.

POLONIUS: Have I, my lord? Assure you, my good liege,
I hold my duty as I hold my soul,
Both to my God and to my gracious King;
And I do think, or else this brain of mine
Hunts not the trail of policy so sure
As it hath used to do, that I have found
The very cause of Hamlet's lunacy. . . .

Exeunt—leaving ROS *and* GUIL.

ROS: I want to go home.

GUIL: Don't let them confuse you.

ROS: I'm out of my step here——

GUIL: We'll soon be home and high—dry and home—I'll——

ROS: It's all over my *depth*——

GUIL: —I'll hie you home and——

ROS: —out of my head——

GUIL: —dry you high and——

ROS (*cracking, high*): —over my step over my head body!—I tell you it's all stopping to a death, it's boding to a depth, stepping to a head, it's all heading to a dead stop——

GUIL (*the nursemaid*): There! . . . and we'll soon be home and dry . . . and *high* and dry. . . . (*Rapidly.*) Has it ever happened to you that all of a sudden and for no reason at all you haven't the faintest idea how to spell the word— "wife"—or "house"—because when you write it down you just can't remember ever having seen those letters in that order before . . . ?

ROS: I remember——

GUIL: Yes?

ROS: I remember when there were no questions.

GUIL: There were always questions. To exchange one set for another is no great matter.

ROS: Answers, yes. There were answers to everything.

GUIL: You've forgotten.

ROS (*flaring*): I haven't forgotten—how I used to remember my own name—and yours, oh *yes!* There were answers everywhere you *looked*. There was no question about it— people knew who I was and if they didn't they asked and I told them.

GUIL: You did, the trouble is, each of them is . . . plausible, without being instinctive. All your life you live so close to truth, it becomes a permanent blur in the corner of your eye, and when something nudges it into outline it is like being ambushed by a grotesque. A man standing in his saddle in the half-lit half-alive dawn banged on the shutters and called two names. He was just a hat and a cloak levitating in the grey plume of his own breath, but when he called we came. That much is certain—we came.

ROS: Well I can tell you I'm sick to death of it. I don't care one way or another, so why don't you make up your mind.

GUIL: We can't afford anything quite so arbitrary. Nor did we come all this way for a christening. All *that*—preceded us. But we are comparatively fortunate; we might have been left to sift the whole field of human nomenclature, like two blind men looting a bazaar for their own portraits. . . . At least we are presented with alternatives.

ROS: Well as from now——

GUIL: —But not choice.

ROS: You made me look ridiculous in there.

GUIL: I looked just as ridiculous as you did.

ROS (*an anguished cry*): Consistency is all I ask!

GUIL (*low, wry rhetoric*): Give us this day our daily mask.

ROS (*a dying fall*): I want to go home. (*Moves.*) Which way did we come in? I've lost my sense of direction.

GUIL: The only beginning is birth and the only end is death—if you can't count on that, what can you count on?

They connect again.

ROS: We don't owe anything to anyone.

GUIL: We've been caught up. Your smallest action sets off another somewhere else, and is set off by it. Keep an eye open, an ear cocked. Tread warily, follow instructions. We'll be all right.

ROS: For how long?

GUIL: Till events have played themselves out. There's a logic at work—it's all done for you, don't worry. Enjoy it. Relax. To be taken in hand and led, like being a child again, even without the innocence, a child—it's like being given a prize, an extra slice of childhood when you least expect it, as a prize for being good, or compensation for never having had one. . . . Do I contradict myself?

ROS: I can't remember. . . . What have we got to go on?

GUIL: We have been briefed. Hamlet's transformation. What do you recollect?

ROS: Well, he's changed, hasn't he? The exterior and inward man fails to resemble——

GUIL: Draw him on to pleasures—glean what afflicts him.

ROS: Something more than his father's death——

GUIL: He's always talking about us—there aren't two people living whom he dotes on more than us.

ROS: We cheer him up—find out what's the matter——

GUIL: Exactly, it's a matter of asking the right questions and giving away as little as we can. It's a game.

ROS: And then we can go?

GUIL: And receive such thanks as fits a king's remembrance.

ROS: I like the sound of that. What do you think he means by remembrance?

GUIL: He doesn't forget his friends.

ROS: Would you care to estimate?

GUIL: Difficult to say, really—some kings tend to be amnesiac, others I suppose—the opposite, whatever that is. . . .

ROS: Yes—but——

GUIL: Elephantine . . . ?

ROS: Not how long—how much?

GUIL: *Retentive*—he's a very retentive king, a royal retainer. . . .

ROS: What are you playing at?

GUIL: Words, words. They're all we have to go on.

Pause.

ROS: Shouldn't we be doing something—constructive?

GUIL: What did you have in mind? . . . A short, blunt human pyramid . . . ?

ROS: We could go.

GUIL: Where?

ROS: After him.

GUIL: Why? They've got us placed now—if we start moving around, we'll all be chasing each other all night.

Hiatus.

ROS (*at footlights*): How very intriguing! (*Turns.*) I feel like a spectator—an appalling business. The only thing that makes it bearable is the irrational belief that somebody interesting will come on in a minute. . . .

GUIL: See anyone?

ROS: No. You?

GUIL: No. (*At footlights.*) What a fine persecution—to be kept intrigued without ever quite being enlightened. . . . (*Pause.*) We've had no practice.

ROS: We could play at questions.

GUIL: What good would that do?

ROS: Practice!

GUIL: Statement! One—love.

ROS: Cheating!

GUIL: How?

ROS: I hadn't started yet.

GUIL: Statement. Two—love.

ROS: Are you counting that?

GUIL: What?

ROS: Are you counting that?

GUIL: Foul! No repetitions. Three—love. First game to . . .

ROS: I'm not going to play if you're going to be like that.

GUIL: Whose serve?

ROS: Hah?

GUIL: Foul! No grunts. Love—one.

ROS: Whose go?

GUIL: Why?

ROS: Why not?

GUIL: What for?

ROS: Foul! No synonyms! One—all.

GUIL: What in God's name is going on?

ROS: Foul! No rhetoric. Two—one.

GUIL: What does it all add up to?

ROS: Can't you guess?

GUIL: Were you addressing me?

ROS: Is there anyone else?

GUIL: Who?

ROS: How would I know?

GUIL: Why do you ask?

ROS: Are you serious?

GUIL: Was that rhetoric?

ROS: No.

GUIL: Statement! Two—all. Game point.

ROS: What's the matter with you today?

GUIL: When?

ROS: What?

GUIL: Are you deaf?

ROS: Am I dead?

GUIL: Yes or no?

ROS: Is there a choice?

GUIL: Is there a God?

ROS: Foul! No *non sequiturs,* three—two, one game all.

GUIL (*seriously*): What's your name?

ROS: What's yours?

GUIL: I asked you first.

ROS: Statement. One—love.

GUIL: What's your name when you're at home?

ROS: What's yours?

GUIL: When I'm at home?

ROS: Is it different at home?

GUIL: What home?

ROS: Haven't you got one?

GUIL: Why do you ask?

ROS: What are you driving at?

GUIL (*with emphasis*): What's your name?!

ROS: Repetition. Two—love. Match point to me.

GUIL (*seizing him violently*): WHO DO YOU THINK YOU ARE?

ROS: Rhetoric! Game and match! (*Pause.*) Where's it going to end?

GUIL: That's the question.

ROS: It's *all* questions.

GUIL: Do you think it matters?

ROS: Doesn't it matter to you ?

GUIL: Why should it matter?

ROS: What does it matter why?

GUIL (*teasing gently*): Doesn't it *matter* why it matters?

ROS (*rounding on him*): What's the *matter* with you?

   Pause.

GUIL: It doesn't matter.

ROS (*voice in the wilderness*): . . . What's the game?

GUIL: What are the rules?

   Enter HAMLET *behind, crossing the stage, reading a book—as he is about to disappear* GUIL *notices him.*

GUIL (*sharply*): Rosencrantz!

ROS (*jumps*): What!

HAMLET *goes. Triumph dawns on them, they smile.*

GUIL: There! How was that?

ROS: Clever!

GUIL: Natural?

ROS: Instinctive.

GUIL: Got it in your head?

ROS: I take my hat off to you.

GUIL: Shake hands.

They do.

ROS: Now I'll try you—Guil—!

GUIL: —Not yet—catch me unawares.

ROS: Right.

They separate. Pause. Aside to GUIL.

Ready?

GUIL (*explodes*): Don't be stupid.

ROS: Sorry.

Pause.

GUIL (*snaps*): Guildenstern!

ROS (*jumps*): What?

He is immediately crestfallen, GUIL *is disgusted.*

GUIL: Consistency is all I ask!

ROS (*quietly*): Immortality is all I seek. . . .

GUIL (*dying fall*): Give us this day our daily week. . . .

Beat.

ROS: Who was that?

GUIL: Didn't you know him?

ROS: He didn't know me.

GUIL: He didn't see you.

ROS: I didn't see him.

GUIL: We shall see. I *hardly* knew him, he's changed.

ROS: You could see that?

GUIL: Transformed.

ROS: How do you know?

GUIL: Inside and out.

ROS: I see.

GUIL: He's not himself.

ROS: He's changed.

GUIL: I could see that.

> *Beat.*

> Glean what afflicts him.

ROS: Me?

GUIL: Him.

ROS: How?

GUIL: Question and answer. Old ways are the best ways.

ROS: He's afflicted.

GUIL: You question, I'll answer.

ROS: He's not himself, you know.

GUIL: I'm him, you see.

> *Beat.*

ROS: Who am I then?

GUIL: You're yourself.

ROS: And he's you?

GUIL: Not a bit of it.

ROS: Are you afflicted?

GUIL: That's the idea. Are you ready?

ROS: Let's go back a bit.

GUIL: I'm afflicted.

ROS: I see.

GUIL: Glean what afflicts me.

ROS: Right.

GUIL: Question and answer.

ROS: How should I begin?

GUIL: Address me.

ROS: My dear Guildenstern!

GUIL (*quietly*): You've forgotten—haven't you?

ROS: My dear Rosencrantz!

GUIL (*great control*): I don't think you quite understand. What we are attempting is a hypothesis in which *I* answer for *him*, while *you* ask me questions.

ROS: Ah! Ready?

GUIL: You know what to do?

ROS: What?

GUIL: Are you stupid?

ROS: Pardon?

GUIL: Are you deaf?

ROS: Did you speak?

GUIL (*admonishing*): Not now——

ROS: Statement.

GUIL (*shouts*): Not now! (*Pause.*) If I had any doubts, or rather hopes, they are dispelled. What could we possibly have in common except our situation? (*They separate and sit.*) Perhaps he'll come back this way.

ROS: Should we go?

GUIL: Why?

> *Pause.*

ROS (*starts up. Snaps fingers*): Oh! You mean—you pretend to be *him,* and *I* ask you questions!

GUIL (*dry*): Very good.

ROS: You had me confused.

GUIL: I could see I had.

ROS: How should I begin?

GUIL: Address me.

> *They stand and face each other, posing.*

ROS: My honoured Lord!

GUIL: My dear Rosencrantz!

> *Pause.*

ROS: Am I pretending to be you, then?

GUIL: Certainly not. If you like. Shall we continue?

ROS: Question and answer.

GUIL: Right.

ROS: Right. My honoured lord!

GUIL: My dear fellow!

ROS: How are you?

GUIL: Afflicted!

ROS: Really? In what way?

GUIL: Transformed.

ROS: Inside or out?

GUIL: Both.

ROS: I see. (*Pause.*) Not much new there.

GUIL: Go into details. *Delve.* Probe the background, establish the situation.

ROS: So—so your uncle is the king of Denmark?!

GUIL: And my father before him.

ROS: His father before him?

GUIL: No, my father before him.

ROS: But surely——

GUIL: You might well ask.

ROS: Let me get it straight. Your father was king. You were his only son. Your father dies. You are of age. Your uncle becomes king.

GUIL: Yes.

ROS: Unorthodox.

GUIL: Undid me.

ROS: Undeniable. Where were you?

GUIL: In Germany.

ROS: Usurpation, then.

GUIL: He slipped in.

ROS: Which reminds me.

GUIL: Well, it would.

ROS: I don't want to be personal.

GUIL: It's common knowledge.

ROS: Your mother's marriage.

GUIL: He slipped in.

> *Beat.*

ROS (*lugubriously*): His body was still warm.

GUIL: So was hers.

ROS: Extraordinary.

GUIL: Indecent.

ROS: Hasty.

GUIL: Suspicious.

ROS: It makes you think.

GUIL: Don't think I haven't thought of it.

ROS: And with her husband's brother.

GUIL: They were close.

ROS: She went to him——

GUIL: —Too close——

ROS: —for comfort.

GUIL: It looks bad.

ROS: It adds up.

GUIL: Incest to adultery.

ROS: Would you go so far?

GUIL: Never.

ROS: To sum up: your father, whom you love, dies, you are his heir, you come back to find that hardly was the corpse cold before his young brother popped onto his throne and into his sheets, thereby offending both legal and natural practice. Now why exactly are you behaving in this extraordinary manner?

GUIL: I can't imagine! (*Pause.*) But all that is well known, common property. Yet he sent for us. And we did come.

ROS (*alert, ear cocked*): I say! I heard music——

GUIL: We're here.

ROS: —Like a band—I thought I heard a band.

GUIL: Rosencrantz . . .

ROS (*absently, still listening*): What?

 Pause, short.

GUIL (*gently wry*): Guildenstern . . .

ROS (*irritated by the repetition*): *What?*

GUIL: Don't you discriminate at all?

ROS (*turning dumbly*): Wha'?

 Pause.

GUIL: Go and see if he's there.

ROS: Who?

GUIL: There.

 ROS *goes to an upstage wing, looks, returns, formally making his report.*

ROS: Yes.

GUIL: What is he doing?

ROS *repeats movement.*

ROS: Talking.

GUIL: To himself?

ROS *starts to move.* GUIL *cuts in impatiently.*

Is he alone?

ROS: No.

GUIL: Then he's not talking to himself, is he?

ROS: Not *by* himself. . . . Coming this way, I think. (*Shiftily.*)
Should we go?

GUIL: Why? We're marked now.

HAMLET *enters, backwards, talking, followed by* POLONIUS,
upstage. ROS *and* GUIL *occupy the two downstage corners
looking upstage.*

HAMLET: . . . for you yourself, sir, should be as old as I am if
like a crab you could go backward.

POLONIUS (*aside*): Though this be madness, yet there is method
in it. Will you walk out of the air, my lord?

HAMLET: Into my grave.

POLONIUS: Indeed, that's out of the air.

HAMLET *crosses to upstage exit,* POLONIUS *asiding unintelli-
gibly until———*

My lord, I will take my leave of you.

HAMLET: You cannot take from me anything that I will more
willingly part withal—except my life, except my life, except
my life. . . .

POLONIUS (*crossing downstage*): Fare you well, my lord. (*To
ROS:*) You go to seek Lord Hamlet? There he is.

ROS (*to* POLONIUS): God save you sir.

POLONIUS *goes.*

GUIL (*calls upstage to* HAMLET): My honoured lord!

ROS: My most dear lord!

HAMLET *centred upstage, turns to them.*

HAMLET: My excellent good friends! How dost thou
Guildenstern? (*Coming downstage with an arm raised to*
ROS, GUIL *meanwhile bowing to no greeting.* HAMLET *corrects
himself. Still to* ROS:) Ah Rosencrantz!

*They laugh good-naturedly at the mistake. They all meet
midstage, turn upstage to walk,* HAMLET *in the middle, arm
over each shoulder.*

HAMLET: Good lads how do you both?

BLACKOUT

ACT TWO

HAMLET, ROS *and* GUIL *talking, the continuation of the previous scene. Their conversation, on the move, is indecipherable at first. The first intelligible line is* HAMLET's, *coming at the end of a short speech—see Shakespeare Act II, scene ii.*

HAMLET: S'blood, there is something in this more than natural, if philosophy could find it out.

A flourish from the TRAGEDIANS' *band.*

GUIL: There are the players.

HAMLET: Gentlemen, you are welcome to Elsinore. Your hands, come then. (*He takes their hands.*) The appurtenance of welcome is fashion and ceremony. Let me comply with you in this garb, lest my extent to the players (which I tell you must show fairly outwards) should more appear like entertainment than yours. You are welcome. (*About to leave.*) But my uncle-father and aunt-mother are deceived.

GUIL: In what, my dear lord?

HAMLET: I am but mad north north-west; when the wind is southerly I know a hawk from a handsaw.

POLONIUS *enters as* GUIL *turns away.*

POLONIUS: Well be with you gentlemen.

HAMLET (*to* ROS): Mark you, Guildenstern (*uncertainly to* GUIL) and you too; at each ear a hearer. That great baby you see there is not yet out of his swaddling clouts. . . . (*He takes* ROS *upstage with him, talking together.*)

720

POLONIUS: My Lord! I have news to tell you.

HAMLET (*releasing* ROS *and mimicking*): My lord, I have news to tell you. . . . When Roscius was an actor in Rome . . .

ROS *comes downstage to rejoin* GUIL.

POLONIUS (*as he follows* HAMLET *out*): The actors are come hither my lord.

HAMLET: Buzz, buzz.

Exeunt HAMLET *and* POLONIUS.

ROS *and* GUIL *ponder. Each reluctant to speak first.*

GUIL: Hm?

ROS: Yes?

GUIL: What?

ROS: I thought you . . .

GUIL: No.

ROS: Ah.

Pause.

GUIL: I think we can say we made some headway.

ROS: You think so?

GUIL: I think we can say that.

ROS: I think we can say he made us look ridiculous.

GUIL: We played it close to the chest of course.

ROS (*derisively*): "Question and answer. Old ways are the best ways"! He was scoring off us all down the line.

GUIL: He caught us on the wrong foot once or twice, perhaps, but I thought we gained some ground.

ROS (*simply*): He murdered us.

GUIL: He might have had the edge.

ROS (*roused*): Twenty-seven—three, and you think he might have had the edge?! He *murdered* us.

GUIL: What about our evasions?

ROS: Oh, our evasions were lovely. "Were you sent for?" he says. "My lord, we were sent for. . . ." I didn't know where to put myself.

GUIL: He had six rhetoricals——

ROS: It was question and answer, all right. Twenty-seven questions he got out in ten minutes, and answered three. I was waiting for you to *delve*. "When is he going to start *delving*?" I asked myself.

GUIL: —And two repetitions.

ROS: Hardly a leading question between us.

GUIL: We got his *symptoms,* didn't we?

ROS: Half of what he said meant something else, and the other half didn't mean anything at all.

GUIL: Thwarted ambition—a sense of grievance, that's my diagnosis.

ROS: Six rhetorical and two repetition, leaving nineteen, of which we answered fifteen. And what did we get in return? He's depressed! . . . Denmark's a prison and he'd rather live in a nutshell; some shadow-play about the nature of ambition, which never got down to cases, and finally one direct question which might have led somewhere, and led in fact to his illuminating claim to tell a hawk from a handsaw.

  Pause.

GUIL: When the wind is southerly.

ROS: And the weather's clear.

GUIL: And when it isn't he can't.

ROS: He's at the mercy of the elements. (*Licks his finger and holds it up—facing audience.*) Is that southerly?

They stare at audience.

GUIL: It doesn't *look* southerly. What made you think so?

ROS: I didn't *say* I think so. It could be northerly for all I know.

GUIL: I wouldn't have thought so.

ROS: Well, if you're going to be dogmatic.

GUIL: Wait a minute—we came from roughly south according to a rough map.

ROS: I see. Well, which way did we come in? (GUIL *looks round vaguely.*) Roughly.

GUIL (*clears his throat*): In the morning the sun would be easterly. I think we can assume that.

ROS: That it's morning?

GUIL: If it is, and the sun is over *there* (*his right as he faces the audience*) for instance, *that* (*front*) would be northerly. On the other hand, if it is not morning and the sun is over *there* (*his left*) . . . *that* . . . (*lamely*) would *still* be northerly. (*Picking up.*) To put it another way, if we came from down there (*front*) and it is morning, the sun would be up there (*his left*), and if it is actually over *there* (*his right*) and it's still morning, we must have come from up *there* (*behind him*), and if *that* is southerly (*his left*) and the sun is really over *there* (*front*), then it's the afternoon. However, if none of these is the case——

ROS: Why don't you go and have a look?

GUIL: Pragmatism?!—is that all you have to offer? You seem to have no conception of where we stand! You won't find the answer written down for you in the bowl of a compass

—I can tell you that. (*Pause.*) Besides, you can never tell this far north—it's probably dark out there.

ROS: I merely suggest that the position of the sun, if it is out, would give you a rough idea of the time; alternatively, the clock, if it is going, would give you a rough idea of the position of the sun. I forget which you're trying to establish.

GUIL: I'm trying to establish the direction of the wind.

ROS: There isn't any wind. *Draught,* yes.

GUIL: In that case, the origin. Trace it to its source and it might give us a rough idea of the way we came in—which might give us a rough idea of south, for further reference.

ROS: It's coming up through the floor. (*He studies the floor.*) That can't be south, can it?

GUIL: That's not a direction. Lick your toe and wave it around a bit.

ROS *considers the distance of his foot.*

ROS: No, I think you'd have to lick it for me.

Pause.

GUIL: I'm prepared to let the whole matter drop.

ROS: Or I could lick yours, of course.

GUIL: No thank you.

ROS: I'll even wave it around for you.

GUIL (*down* ROS's *throat*): What in God's name is the matter with you?

ROS: Just being friendly.

GUIL (*retiring*): Somebody might come in. It's what we're counting on, after all. Ultimately.

Good pause.

ROS: Perhaps they've all trampled each other to death in the rush. . . . Give them a shout. Something provocative. *Intrigue* them.

GUIL: Wheels have been set in motion, and they have their own pace, to which we are . . . condemned. Each move is dictated by the previous one—that is the meaning of order. If we start being arbitrary it'll just be a shambles: at least, let us hope so. Because if we happened, just happened to discover, or even suspect, that our spontaneity was part of their order, we'd know that we were lost. (*He sits.*) A Chinaman of the T'ang Dynasty—and, by which definition, a philosopher—dreamed he was a butterfly, and from that moment he was never quite sure that he was not a butterfly dreaming it was a Chinese philosopher. Envy him; in his two-fold security.

A good pause. ROS *leaps up and bellows at the audience.*

ROS: Fire!

GUIL *jumps up.*

GUIL: Where?

ROS: It's all right—I'm demonstrating the misuse of free speech. To prove that it exists. (*He regards the audience, that is the direction, with contempt—and other directions, then front again.*) Not a move. They should burn to death in their shoes. (*He takes out one of his coins. Spins it. Catches it. Looks at it. Replaces it.*)

GUIL: What was it?

ROS: What?

GUIL: Heads or tails?

ROS: Oh. I didn't look.

GUIL: Yes you did.

ROS: Oh, did I? (*He takes out a coin, studies it.*) Quite right—it rings a bell.

GUIL: What's the last thing you remember?

ROS: I don't wish to be reminded of it.

GUIL: We cross our bridges when we come to them and burn them behind us, with nothing to show for our progress except a memory of the smell of smoke, and a presumption that once our eyes watered.

> ROS *approaches him brightly, holding a coin between finger and thumb. He covers it with his other hand, draws his fists apart and holds them for* GUIL. GUIL *considers them. Indicates the left hand,* ROS *opens it to show it empty.*

ROS: No.

> *Repeat process.* GUIL *indicates left hand again.* ROS *shows it empty.*

Double bluff!

> *Repeat process—*GUIL *taps one hand, then the other hand, quickly.* ROS *inadvertently shows that both are empty.* ROS *laughs as* GUIL *turns upstage.* ROS *stops laughing, looks around his feet, pats his clothes, puzzled.*

> POLONIUS *breaks that up by entering upstage followed by the* TRAGEDIANS *and* HAMLET.

POLONIUS (*entering*): Come sirs.

HAMLET: Follow him, friends. We'll hear a play tomorrow.
(*Aside to the* PLAYER, *who is the last of the* TRAGEDIANS:) Dost thou hear me, old friend? Can you play *The Murder of Gonzago*?

PLAYER: Ay, my lord.

HAMLET: We'll ha't tomorrow night. You could for a need study a speech of some dozen or sixteen lines which I would set down and insert in't, could you not?

PLAYER: Ay, my lord.

HAMLET: Very well. Follow that lord, and look you mock him not.

The PLAYER *crossing downstage, notes* ROS *and* GUIL. *Stops.* HAMLET *crossing downstage addresses them without pause.*

HAMLET: My good friends, I'll leave you till tonight. You are welcome to Elsinore.

ROS: Good, my lord.

HAMLET *goes.*

GUIL: So you've caught up.

PLAYER (*coldly*): Not yet, sir.

GUIL: Now mind your tongue, or we'll have it out and throw the rest of you away, like a nightingale at a Roman feast.

ROS: Took the very words out of my mouth.

GUIL: You'd be *lost* for words.

ROS: You'd be tongue-tied.

GUIL: Like a mute in a monologue.

ROS: Like a nightingale at a Roman feast.

GUIL: Your diction will go to pieces.

ROS: Your lines will be cut.

GUIL: To dumbshows.

ROS: And dramatic pauses.

GUIL: You'll never *find* your tongue.

ROS: Lick your lips.

GUIL: Taste your tears.

ROS: Your breakfast.

GUIL: You won't know the difference.

ROS: There won't be any.

GUIL: We'll take the very words out of your mouth.

ROS: So you've caught on.

GUIL: So you've caught up.

PLAYER (*tops*): Not yet! (*Bitterly.*) You left us.

GUIL: Ah! I'd forgotten—you performed a dramatic spectacle on the way. Yes, I'm sorry we had to miss it.

PLAYER (*bursts out*): We can't look each other in the face! (*Pause, more in control.*) You don't understand the humiliation of it —to be tricked out of the single assumption which makes our existence viable—that somebody is *watching.* . . . The plot was two corpses gone before we caught sight of ourselves, stripped naked in the middle of nowhere and pouring ourselves down a bottomless well.

ROS: Is *that* thirty-eight?

PLAYER (*lost*): There we were—demented children mincing about in clothes that no one ever wore, speaking as no man ever spoke, swearing love in wigs and rhymed couplets, killing each other with wooden swords, hollow protestations of faith hurled after empty promises of vengeance—and every gesture, every pose, vanishing into the thin unpopulated air. We ransomed our dignity to the clouds, and the uncomprehending birds listened. (*He rounds on them.*) Don't you see?! We're *actors*—we're the opposite of people! (*They recoil nonplussed, his voice calms.*) Think, in your head, *now,* think of the most . . . *private* . . . *secret* . . . *intimate* thing you have ever done secure in the knowledge of its privacy. . . . (*He gives them—and the audience—a good pause.* ROS *takes on a shifty look.*) Are you thinking of it? (*He strikes with his voice and his head.*) *Well, I saw you do it!*

ROS *leaps up, dissembling madly.*

ROS: You never! It's a lie! (*He catches himself with a giggle in a vacuum and sits down again.*)

PLAYER: We're actors. . . . We pledged our identities, secure in the conventions of our trade, that someone would be watching. And then, gradually, no one was. We were caught, high and dry. It was not until the murderer's long soliloquy that we were able to look around; frozen as we were in profile, our eyes searched you out, first confidently, then hesitantly, then desperately as each patch of turf, each log, every exposed corner in every direction proved uninhabited, and all the while the murderous King addressed the horizon with his dreary interminable guilt. . . . Our heads began to move, wary as lizards, the corpse of unsullied Rosalinda peeped through his fingers, and the King faltered. Even then, habit and a stubborn trust that our audience spied upon us from behind the nearest bush, forced our bodies to blunder on long after they had emptied of meaning, until like runaway carts they dragged to a halt. No one came forward. No one shouted at us. The silence was unbreakable, it imposed itself upon us; it was obscene. We took off our crowns and swords and cloth of gold and moved silent on the road to Elsinore.

Silence. Then GUIL *claps solo with slow measured irony.*

GUIL: Brilliantly re-created—if these eyes could weep! . . . Rather strong on metaphor, mind you. No criticism—only a matter of taste. And so here you are—with a vengeance. That's a figure of speech . . . isn't it? Well let's say we've made up for it, for you may have no doubt whom to thank for your performance at the court.

ROS: We are counting on you to take him out of himself. You are the pleasures which we draw him on to—(*he escapes a fractional giggle but recovers immediately*) and by that I don't mean your usual filth; you can't treat royalty like people with normal perverted desires. They know nothing of that and you know nothing of them, to your mutual survival. So give him a good clean show suitable for all the family, or you can rest assured you'll be playing the tavern tonight.

GUIL: Or the night after.

ROS: Or not.

PLAYER: We already have an entry here. And always have had.

GUIL: You've played for him before?

PLAYER: Yes, sir.

ROS: And what's *his* bent?

PLAYER: Classical.

ROS: Saucy!

GUIL: What will you play?

PLAYER: *The Murder of Gonzago.*

GUIL: Full of fine cadence and corpses.

PLAYER: Pirated from the Italian. . . .

ROS: What is it about?

PLAYER: It's about a King and Queen. . . . .

GUIL: Escapism! What else?

PLAYER: Blood——

GUIL: ——Love and rhetoric.

PLAYER: Yes. (*Going.*)

GUIL: Where are you going?

PLAYER: I can come and go as I please.

GUIL: You're evidently a man who knows his way around.

PLAYER: I've been here before.

GUIL: We're still finding our feet.

PLAYER: I should concentrate on not losing your heads.

GUIL: Do you speak from knowledge?

PLAYER: Precedent.

GUIL: You've been here before.

PLAYER: And I know which way the wind is blowing.

GUIL: Operating on two levels, are we?! How clever! I expect
it comes naturally to you, being in the business so to speak.

The PLAYER's *grave face does not change. He makes to move
off again.* GUIL *for the second time cuts him off.*

The truth is, we value your company, for want of any
other. We have been left so much to our own devices—
after a while one welcomes the uncertainty of being left to
other people's.

PLAYER: Uncertainty is the normal state. You're nobody special.

He makes to leave again. GUIL *loses his cool.*

GUIL: But for God's sake what are we supposed to *do*?!

PLAYER: Relax. Respond. That's what people do. You can't go
through life questioning your situation at every turn.

GUIL: But we don't know what's going on, or what to do with
ourselves. We don't know how to *act*.

PLAYER: Act natural. You know why you're here at least.

GUIL: We only know what we're told, and that's little enough.
And for all we know it isn't even true.

PLAYER: For all anyone knows, nothing is. Everything has to be taken on trust; truth is only that which is taken to be true. It's the currency of living. There may be nothing behind it, but it doesn't make any difference so long as it is honoured. One acts on assumptions. What do you assume?

ROS: Hamlet is not himself, outside or in. We have to glean what afflicts him.

GUIL: He doesn't give much away.

PLAYER: Who does, nowadays?

GUIL: He's—melancholy.

PLAYER: Melancholy?

ROS: Mad.

PLAYER: How is he mad?

ROS: Ah. (*To* GUIL:) How is he mad?

GUIL: More morose than mad, perhaps.

PLAYER: Melancholy.

GUIL: Moody.

ROS: He has moods.

PLAYER: Of moroseness?

GUIL: Madness. And yet.

ROS: Quite.

GUIL: For instance.

ROS: He talks to himself, which might be madness.

GUIL: If he didn't talk sense, which he does.

ROS: Which suggests the opposite.

PLAYER: Of what?

Small pause.

GUIL: I think I have it. A man talking sense to himself is no madder than a man talking nonsense not to himself.

ROS: Or just as mad.

GUIL: Or just as mad.

ROS: And he does both.

GUIL: So there you are.

ROS: Stark raving sane.

Pause.

PLAYER: Why?

GUIL: Ah. (*To* ROS:) Why?

ROS: Exactly.

GUIL: Exactly what?

ROS: Exactly why.

GUIL: Exactly why *what*?

ROS: What?

GUIL: *Why?*

ROS: Why what, exactly?

GUIL: Why is he mad?!

ROS: *I* don't know!

Beat.

PLAYER: The old man thinks he's in love with his daughter.

ROS (*appalled*): Good God! We're out of our depth here.

PLAYER: No, no, no—*he* hasn't got a daughter—the old man thinks he's in love with *his* daughter.

ROS: The old man is?

PLAYER: Hamlet, in love with the old man's daughter, the old man thinks.

ROS: Ha! It's beginning to make sense! Unrequited passion!

The PLAYER *moves.*

GUIL: (*Fascist.*) Nobody leaves this room! (*Pause, lamely.*) Without a *very* good reason.

PLAYER: Why not?

GUIL: All this strolling about is getting too arbitrary by half— I'm rapidly losing my grip. From now on reason will prevail.

PLAYER: I have lines to learn.

GUIL: Pass!

The PLAYER *passes into one of the wings.* ROS *cups his hands and shouts into the opposite one.*

ROS: Next!

But no one comes.

GUIL: What did you expect?

ROS: Something . . . someone . . . nothing.

They sit facing front.

Are you hungry?

GUIL: No, are you?

ROS (*thinks*): No. You remember that coin?

GUIL: No.

ROS: I think I lost it.

GUIL: What coin?

ROS: I don't remember exactly.

> *Pause.*

GUIL: Oh, that coin . . . clever.

ROS: I can't remember how I did it.

GUIL: It probably comes natural to you.

ROS: Yes, I've got a show-stopper there.

GUIL: Do it again.

> *Slight pause.*

ROS: We can't afford it.

GUIL: Yes, one must think of the future.

ROS: It's the normal thing.

GUIL: To have one. One is, after all, having it all the time . . . now . . . and now . . . and now. . . .

ROS: It could go on for ever. Well, not for *ever,* I suppose. (*Pause.*) Do you ever think of yourself as actually *dead,* lying in a box with a lid on it?

GUIL: No.

ROS: Nor do I, really. . . . It's silly to be depressed by it. I mean one thinks of it like being *alive* in a box, one keeps forgetting to take into account the fact that one is *dead* . . . which should make all the difference . . . shouldn't it? I mean, you'd never *know* you were in a box, would you? It would be just like being *asleep* in a box. Not that I'd like to sleep in a box, mind you, not without any air—you'd wake up dead, for a start, and then where would you be? Apart from inside a box. That's the bit I don't like, frankly. That's why I don't think of it. . . .

GUIL *stirs restlessly, pulling his cloak round him.*

Because you'd be helpless, wouldn't you? Stuffed in a box like that, I mean you'd be in there for ever. Even taking into account the fact that you're dead, it isn't a pleasant thought. *Especially* if you're dead, really . . . *ask* yourself, if I asked you straight off—I'm going to stuff you in this box now, would you rather be alive or dead? Naturally, you'd prefer to be alive. Life in a box is better than no life at all. I expect. You'd have a chance at least. You could lie there thinking— well, at least I'm not dead! In a minute someone's going to bang on the lid and tell me to come out. (*Banging the floor with his fists.*) "Hey you, whatsyername! Come out of there!"

GUIL (*jumps up savagely*): You don't have to flog it to death!

Pause.

ROS: I wouldn't think about it, if I were you. You'd only get depressed. (*Pause.*) Eternity is a terrible thought. I mean, where's it going to end? (*Pause, then brightly.*) Two early Christians chanced to meet in Heaven. "Saul of Tarsus yet!" cried one. "What are *you* doing here?!" . . . "Tarsus-Schmarsus," replied the other, "I'm Paul already." (*He stands up restlessly and flaps his arms.*) They don't care. We count for nothing. We could remain silent till we're green in the face, they wouldn't come.

GUIL: Blue, red.

ROS: A Christian, a Moslem and a Jew chanced to meet in a closed carriage. . . . "Silverstein!" cried the Jew. "Who's your friend?" . . . "His name's Abdullah," replied the Moslem, "but he's no friend of mine since he became a convert." (*He leaps up again, stamps his foot and shouts into the wings.*) All right, we know you're in there! Come out talking! (*Pause.*) We have no control. None at all . . . (*He paces.*) Whatever became of the moment when one first knew about death? There must have been one, a moment, in childhood when it first occurred to you that you don't go on for ever. It must have been shattering—stamped into one's memory. And yet I can't remember it. It never occurred to me at all. What does one make of that? We must be born with an intuition of mortality. Before we know the words for it, before we know that there are words, out we come, bloodied and squalling with the knowledge that for all the compasses in the world, there's only one direction, and time is its only measure. (*He reflects, getting more desperate and rapid.*) A Hindu, a Buddhist and a lion-tamer chanced to meet, in a circus on the Indo-Chinese border. (*He breaks out.*) They're taking us for granted! Well, I won't stand for it! In future, notice will be taken. (*He wheels again to face into the wings.*) Keep out, then! I forbid anyone to enter! (*No one comes. Breathing heavily.*) That's better. . . .

Immediately, behind him a grand procession enters, principally CLAUDIUS, GERTRUDE, POLONIUS *and* OPHELIA. CLAUDIUS *takes* ROS's *elbow as he passes and is immediately deep in conversation: the context is Shakespeare Act III, scene i.* GUIL *still faces front as* CLAUDIUS, ROS, *etc., pass upstage and turn.*

GUIL: Death followed by eternity . . . the worst of both worlds. It *is* a terrible thought.

He turns upstage in time to take over the conversation with CLAUDIUS. GERTRUDE *and* ROS *head downstage.*

GERTRUDE: Did he receive you well?

ROS: Most like a gentleman.

GUIL (*returning in time to take it up*): But with much forcing of his disposition.

ROS (*a flat lie and he knows it and shows it, perhaps catching* GUIL's *eye*): Niggard of question, but of our demands most free in his reply.

GERTRUDE: Did you assay him to any pastime?

ROS: Madam, it so fell out that certain players
We o'erraught on the way: of these we told him
And there did seem in him a kind of joy
To hear of it. They are here about the court,
And, as I think, they have already order
This night to play before him.

POLONIUS: 'Tis most true
And he beseeched me to entreat your Majesties
To hear and see the matter.

CLAUDIUS: With all my heart, and it doth content me
To hear him so inclined.
Good gentlemen, give him a further edge
And drive his purpose into these delights.

ROS: We shall, my lord.

CLAUDIUS (*leading out procession*):
Sweet Gertrude, leave us, too,
For we have closely sent for Hamlet hither,
That he, as t'were by accident, may here
Affront Ophelia. . . .

  Exeunt CLAUDIUS *and* GERTRUDE.

ROS (*peevish*): Never a moment's peace! In and out, on and off, they're coming at us from all sides.

GUIL: You're never satisfied.

ROS: Catching us on the trot. . . . Why can't *we* go by *them*?

GUIL: What's the difference?

ROS: I'm going.

  ROS *pulls his cloak round him.* GUIL *ignores him. Without confidence* ROS *heads upstage. He looks out and comes back quickly.*

He's coming.

GUIL: What's he doing?

ROS: Nothing.

GUIL: He must be doing something.

ROS: Walking.

GUIL: On his hands?

ROS: No, on his feet.

GUIL: Stark naked?

ROS: Fully dressed.

GUIL: Selling toffee apples?

ROS: Not that I noticed.

GUIL: You could be wrong?

ROS: I don't think so.

> *Pause.*

GUIL: I can't for the life of me see how we're going to get into conversation.

> HAMLET *enters upstage, and pauses, weighing up the pros and cons of making his quietus.*

> ROS *and* GUIL *watch him.*

ROS: Nevertheless, I suppose one might say that this was a chance. . . . One might well . . . accost him. . . . Yes, it definitely looks like a chance to me. . . . Something on the lines of a direct informal approach . . . man to man . . . straight from the shoulder. . . . Now look here, what's it all about . . . sort of thing. Yes. Yes, this looks like one to be grabbed with both hands, I should say . . . if I were asked. . . . No point in looking at a gift horse till you see the whites of its eyes, etcetera. (*He has moved towards* HAMLET *but his nerve fails. He returns.*) We're overawed, that's our trouble. When it comes to the point we succumb to their personality. . . .

OPHELIA *enters, with prayerbook, a religious procession of one.*

HAMLET: Nymph, in thy orisons be all my sins remembered.

At his voice she has stopped for him, he catches her up.

OPHELIA: Good my lord, how does your honour for this many a day?

HAMLET: I humbly thank you—well, well, well.

They disappear talking into the wing.

ROS: It's like living in a public park!

GUIL: Very impressive. Yes, I thought your direct informal approach was going to stop this thing dead in its tracks there. If I might make a suggestion—shut up and sit down. Stop being perverse.

ROS (*near tears*): I'm not going to stand for it!

A FEMALE FIGURE, *ostensibly the* QUEEN, *enters.* ROS *marches up behind her, puts his hands over her eyes and says with a desperate frivolity.*

ROS: Guess who?!

PLAYER (*having appeared in a downstage corner*): Alfred!

ROS *lets go, spins around. He has been holding* ALFRED, *in his robe and blond wig.* PLAYER *is in the downstage corner still.* ROS *comes down to that exit. The* PLAYER *does not budge. He and* ROS *stand toe to toe.*

ROS: Excuse me.

The PLAYER *lifts his downstage foot.* ROS *bends to put his hand on the floor. The* PLAYER *lowers his foot.* ROS *screams and leaps away.*

PLAYER (*gravely*): I beg your pardon.

GUIL (*to* ROS): What did he do?

PLAYER: I put my foot down.

ROS: My hand was on the floor!

GUIL: You put your hand under his foot?

ROS: I——

GUIL: What for?

ROS: I thought—— (*Grabs* GUIL.) Don't leave me!

He makes a break for an exit. A TRAGEDIAN *dressed as a* KING *enters.* ROS *recoils, breaks for the opposite wing. Two cloaked* TRAGEDIANS *enter.* ROS *tries again but another* TRAGEDIAN *enters, and* ROS *retires to midstage. The* PLAYER *claps his hands matter-of-factly.*

PLAYER: Right! We haven't got much time.

GUIL: What are you doing?

PLAYER: Dress rehearsal. Now if you two wouldn't mind just moving back . . . there . . . good. . . . (*To* TRAGEDIANS:) Everyone ready? And for goodness' sake, remember what we're doing. (*To* ROS *and* GUIL:) We always use the same costumes more or less, and they forget what they are supposed to be *in* you see. . . . Stop picking your nose, Alfred. When Queens have to they do it by a cerebral process passed down in the blood. . . . Good. Silence! Off we go!

PLAYER-KING: Full thirty times hath Phoebus' cart——

PLAYER *jumps up angrily.*

PLAYER: No, no, no! Dumbshow first, your confounded majesty!

(*To* ROS *and* GUIL:) They're a bit out of practice, but they always pick up wonderfully for the deaths—it brings out the poetry in them.

GUIL: How nice.

PLAYER: There's nothing more unconvincing than an unconvincing death.

GUIL: I'm sure.

PLAYER *claps his hands.*

PLAYER: Act One—moves now.

The mime. Soft music from a recorder. PLAYER-KING *and* PLAYER-QUEEN *embrace. She kneels and makes a show of protestation to him. He takes her up, declining his head upon her neck. He lies down. She, seeing him asleep, leaves him.*

GUIL: What is the dumbshow for?

PLAYER: Well, it's a device, really—it makes the action that follows more or less comprehensible; you understand, we are tied down to a language which makes up in obscurity what it lacks in style.

The mime (continued)—enter another. He takes off the SLEEPER's *crown, kisses it. He has brought in a small bottle of liquid. He pours the poison in the* SLEEPER's *ear, and leaves him. The* SLEEPER *convulses heroically, dying.*

ROS: Who was that?

PLAYER: The King's brother and uncle to the Prince.

GUIL: Not exactly fraternal.

PLAYER: Not exactly avuncular, as time goes on.

The QUEEN *returns, makes passionate action, finding the* KING *dead. The* POISONER *comes in again, attended by two others (the two in cloaks). The* POISONER *seems to console with her. The dead body is carried away. The* POISONER *woos the* QUEEN *with gifts. She seems harsh awhile but in the end accepts his love. End of mime, at which point, the wail of a woman in torment and* OPHELIA *appears, wailing, closely followed by* HAMLET *in a hysterical state, shouting at her, circling her, both midstage.*

HAMLET: Go to, I'll no more on't; it hath made me mad!

She falls on her knees weeping.

I say we will have no more marriage! (*His voice drops to include the* TRAGEDIANS, *who have frozen.*) Those that are married already (*he leans close to the* PLAYER-QUEEN *and* POISONER, *speaking with quiet edge*) all but one shall live. (*He smiles briefly at them without mirth, and starts to back out, his parting shot rising again.*) The rest shall keep as they are. (*As he leaves,* OPHELIA *tottering upstage, he speaks into her ear a quick clipped sentence.*) To a nunnery, go.

He goes out. OPHELIA *falls on to her knees upstage, her sobs barely audible. A slight silence.*

PLAYER-KING: Full thirty times hath Phoebus' cart——

CLAUDIUS *enters with* POLONIUS *and goes over to* OPHELIA *and lifts her to her feet. The* TRAGEDIANS *jump back with heads inclined.*

CLAUDIUS: Love? His affections do not that way tend,
Or what he spake, though it lacked form a little,
Was not like madness. There's something
In his soul o'er which his melancholy sits on
Brood, and I do doubt the hatch and the
Disclose will be some danger; which for to
Prevent I have in quick determination thus set
It down: he shall with speed to England . . .

*Which carries the three of them—*CLAUDIUS, POLONIUS,

OPHELIA—*out of sight. The* PLAYER *moves, clapping his hands for attention.*

PLAYER: Gentle*men*! (*They look at him.*) It doesn't seem to be coming. We are not getting it at all. (*To* GUIL:) What did you think?

GUIL: What was I supposed to think?

PLAYER (*to* TRAGEDIANS): You're not getting across!

ROS *had gone halfway up to* OPHELIA; *he returns.*

ROS: That didn't look like love to me.

GUIL: Starting from scratch again . . .

PLAYER (*to* TRAGEDIANS): It was a *mess*.

ROS (*to* GUIL): It's going to be chaos on the night.

GUIL: Keep back—we're spectators.

PLAYER: Act Two! Positions!

GUIL: Wasn't that the end?

PLAYER: Do you call that an ending?—with practically everyone on his feet? My goodness no—over your dead body.

GUIL: How am I supposed to take that?

PLAYER: Lying down. (*He laughs briefly and in a second has never laughed in his life.*) There's a design at work in all art— surely you know that? Events must play themselves out to aesthetic, moral and logical conclusion.

GUIL: And what's that, in this case?

PLAYER: It never varies—we aim at the point where everyone who is marked for death dies.

GUIL: Marked?

PLAYER: Between "just desserts" and "tragic irony" we are given quite a lot of scope for our particular talent.

Generally speaking, things have gone about as far as they
can possibly go when things have got about as bad as they
reasonably get. (*He switches on a smile.*)

GUIL: Who decides?

PLAYER (*switching off his smile*): Decides? It is *written.*

> *He turns away.* GUIL *grabs him and spins him back violently.*

(*Unflustered.*) Now if you're going to be subtle, we'll miss
each other in the dark. I'm referring to oral tradition. So to
speak.

> GUIL *releases him.*

We're tragedians, you see. We follow directions—there is no
choice involved. The bad end unhappily, the good unluckily.
That is what tragedy means. (*Calling.*) Positions!

> *The* TRAGEDIANS *have taken up positions for the continuation
> of the mime: which in this case means a love scene, sexual
> and passionate, between the* QUEEN *and the* POISONER/KING.

PLAYER: Go!

> *The lovers begin. The* PLAYER *contributes a breathless
> commentary for* ROS *and* GUIL.

Having murdered his brother and wooed the widow—the
poisoner mounts the throne! Here we see him and his
queen give rein to their unbridled passion! She little
knowing that the man she holds in her arms——!

ROS: Oh, I say—here—really! You can't do that!

PLAYER: Why not?

ROS: Well, really—I mean, people want to be *entertained*—they
don't come expecting sordid and gratuitous filth.

PLAYER: You're wrong—they do! Murder, seduction and incest
—what do you want—*jokes?*

ROS: I want a good story, with a beginning, middle and end.

PLAYER (*to* GUIL): And you?

GUIL: I'd prefer art to mirror life, if it's all the same to you.

PLAYER: It's all the same to me, sir. (*To the grappling* LOVERS:)
All right, no need to indulge yourselves. (*They get up. To*
GUIL:) I come on in a minute. Lucianus, nephew to the
king! (*Turns his attention to the* TRAGEDIANS.) Next!

*They disport themselves to accommodate the next piece of
mime, which consists of the* PLAYER *himself exhibiting an
excitable anguish* (*choreographed, stylized*) *leading to an
impassioned scene with the* QUEEN (*cf. "The Closet Scene,"
Shakespeare Act III, scene iv*) *and a very stylized
reconstruction of a* POLONIUS *figure being stabbed behind the
arras* (*the murdered* KING *to stand in for* POLONIUS) *while the*
PLAYER *himself continues his breathless commentary for the
benefit of* ROS *and* GUIL.

PLAYER: Lucianus, nephew to the king . . . usurped by his uncle
and shattered by his mother's incestuous marriage . . . loses
his reason . . . throwing the court into turmoil and disarray
as he alternates between bitter melancholy and unrestricted
lunacy . . . staggering from the suicidal (*a pose*) to the
homicidal (*here he kills* "POLONIUS") . . . he at last confronts
his mother and in a scene of provocative ambiguity—(*a
somewhat oedipal embrace*) begs her to repent and recant——
(*He springs up, still talking.*) The King—(*he pushes forward
the* POISONER/KING) tormented by guilt—haunted by fear
—decides to despatch his nephew to England—and entrusts
this undertaking to two smiling accomplices—friends—
courtiers—to two spies——

He has swung round to bring together the POISONER/KING
and the two cloaked TRAGEDIANS; *the latter kneel and accept
a scroll from the* KING.

—giving them a letter to present to the English court——!
And so they depart—on board ship——

The two SPIES *position themselves on either side of the* PLAYER, *and the three of them sway gently in unison, the motion of a boat; and then the* PLAYER *detaches himself.*

—and they arrive——

One SPY *shades his eyes at the horizon.*

—and disembark—and present themselves before the English king——(*He wheels round.*) The English king——

An exchange of headgear creates the ENGLISH KING *from the remaining player—that is, the* PLAYER *who played the original murdered king.*

But where is the Prince? Where indeed? The plot has thickened—a twist of fate and cunning has put into their hands a letter that seals their deaths!

The two SPIES *present their letter; the* ENGLISH KING *reads it and orders their deaths. They stand up as the* PLAYER *whips off their cloaks preparatory to execution.*

Traitors hoist by their own petard?—or victims of the gods? —we shall never know!

The whole mime has been fluid and continuous but now ROS *moves forward and brings it to a pause. What brings* ROS *forward is the fact that under their cloaks the two* SPIES *are wearing coats identical to those worn by* ROS *and* GUIL, *whose coats are now covered by their cloaks.* ROS *approaches "his"* SPY *doubtfully. He does not quite understand why the coats are familiar.* ROS *stands close, touches the coat, thoughtfully. . . .*

ROS: Well, if it isn't——! No, wait a minute, don't tell me—it's a long time since—where was it? Ah, this is taking me back to—when was it? I know you, don't I? I never forget a face—(*he looks into the* SPY's *face*) . . . not that I know yours, that is. For a moment I thought—no, I don't know you, do I? Yes, I'm afraid you're quite wrong. You must have mistaken me for someone else.

GUIL *meanwhile has approached the other* SPY, *brow creased in thought.*

PLAYER (*to* GUIL): Are you familiar with this play?

GUIL: No.

PLAYER: A slaughterhouse—eight corpses all told. It brings out the best in us.

GUIL (*tense, progressively rattled during the whole mime and commentary*): You!—What do *you* know about *death*?

PLAYER: It's what the actors do best. They have to exploit whatever talent is given to them, and their talent is dying. They can die heroically, comically, ironically, slowly, suddenly, disgustingly, charmingly, or from a great height. My own talent is more general. I extract significance from melodrama, a significance which it does not in fact contain; but occasionally, from out of this matter, there escapes a thin beam of light that, seen at the right angle, can crack the shell of mortality.

ROS: Is that all they can do—die?

PLAYER: No, no—they kill beautifully. In fact some of them kill even better than they die. The rest die better than they kill. They're a team.

ROS: Which ones are which?

PLAYER: There's not much in it.

GUIL (*fear, derision*): Actors! The mechanics of cheap melodrama! That isn't *death*! (*More quietly.*) You scream and choke and sink to your knees, but it doesn't bring death home to anyone—it doesn't catch them unawares and start the whisper in their skulls that says—"One day you are going to die." (*He straightens up.*) You die so many times; how can you expect them to believe in your death?

PLAYER: On the contrary, it's the only kind they do believe.

They're conditioned to it. I had an actor once who was
condemned to hang for stealing a sheep—or a lamb, I forget
which—so I got permission to have him hanged in the
middle of a play—had to change the plot a bit but I thought
it would be effective, you know—and you wouldn't believe
it, he just *wasn't* convincing! It was impossible to suspend
one's disbelief—and what with the audience jeering and
throwing peanuts, the whole thing was a *disaster!*—he did
nothing but cry all the time—right out of character—just
stood there and cried. . . . Never again.

*In good humour he has already turned back to the mime: the
two* SPIES *awaiting execution at the hands of the* PLAYER, *who
takes his dagger out of his belt.*

Audiences know what to expect, and that is all that they
are prepared to believe in. (*To the* SPIES:) Show!

The SPIES *die at some length, rather well.*

The light has begun to go, and it fades as they die, and as
GUIL *speaks.*

GUIL: No, no, no . . . you've got it all wrong . . . you can't act
death. The *fact* of it is nothing to do with seeing it happen
—it's not gasps and blood and falling about—that isn't what
makes it death. It's just a man failing to reappear, that's all
—now you see him, now you don't, that's the only thing
that's real: here one minute and gone the next and never
coming back—an exit, unobtrusive and unannounced, a
disappearance gathering weight as it goes on, until, finally,
it is heavy with death.

The two SPIES *lie still, barely visible. The* PLAYER *comes
forward and throws the* SPIES' *cloaks over their bodies.* ROS
starts to clap, slowly.

BLACKOUT.

A second of silence, then much noise. Shouts . . . "The King rises!" . . . *"Give o'er the play!"* . . . *and cries for "Lights, lights, lights!"*

When the light comes, after a few seconds, it comes as a sunrise.

The stage is empty save for two cloaked figures sprawled on the ground in the approximate positions last held by the dead SPIES. *As the light grows, they are seen to be* ROS *and* GUIL, *and to be resting quite comfortably.* ROS *raises himself on his elbows and shades his eyes as he stares into the auditorium. Finally:*

ROS: That must be east, then. I think we can assume that.

GUIL: I'm assuming nothing.

ROS: No, it's all right. That's the sun. East.

GUIL (*looks up*): Where?

ROS: I watched it come up.

GUIL: No . . . it was light all the time, you see, and you opened your eyes very, very slowly. If you'd been facing back there you'd be swearing *that* was east.

ROS (*standing up*): You're a mass of prejudice.

GUIL: I've been taken in before.

ROS (*looks out over the audience*): Rings a bell.

GUIL: They're waiting to see what we're going to do.

ROS: Good old east.

GUIL: As soon as we make a move they'll come pouring in from every side, shouting obscure instructions, confusing us with ridiculous remarks, messing us about from here to breakfast and getting our names wrong.

ROS *starts to protest but he has hardly opened his mouth before:*

CLAUDIUS (*off stage—with urgency*): Ho, Guildenstern!

> GUIL *is still prone. Small pause.*

ROS AND GUIL: You're wanted. . . .

> GUIL *furiously leaps to his feet as* CLAUDIUS *and* GERTRUDE *enter. They are in some desperation.*

CLAUDIUS: Friends both, go join you with some further aid: Hamlet in madness hath Polonius slain, and from his mother's closet hath he dragged him. Go seek him out; speak fair and bring the body into the chapel. I pray you haste in this. (*As he and* GERTRUDE *are hurrying out.*) Come Gertrude, we'll call up our wisest friends and let them know both what we mean to do. . . .

> *They've gone.* ROS *and* GUIL *remain quite still.*

GUIL: Well . . .

ROS: Quite . . .

GUIL: Well, well.

ROS: Quite, quite. (*Nods with spurious confidence.*) Seek him out. (*Pause.*) Etcetera.

GUIL: Quite.

ROS: Well. (*Small pause.*) Well, that's a step in the right direction.

GUIL: You didn't like him?

ROS: Who?

GUIL: Good God, I hope more tears are shed for *us!* . . .

ROS: Well, it's *progress,* isn't it? Something positive. Seek him out. (*Looks round without moving his feet.*) Where does one begin . . . ? (*Takes one step towards the wings and halts.*)

GUIL: Well, that's a step in the right direction.

ROS: You think so? He could be anywhere.

GUIL: All right—you go that way, I'll go this way.

ROS: Right.

> *They walk towards opposite wings.* ROS *halts.*

No.

> GUIL *halts.*

You go this way—I'll go that way.

GUIL: All right.

> *They march towards each other, cross.* ROS *halts.*

ROS: Wait a minute.

> GUIL *halts.*

I think we should stick together. He might be violent.

GUIL: Good point. I'll come with you.

> GUIL *marches across to* ROS. *They turn to leave.* ROS *halts.*

ROS: No, I'll come with *you.*

GUIL: Right.

> *They turn, march across to the opposite wing.* ROS *halts.*
>
> GUIL *halts.*

ROS: I'll come with *you, my* way.

GUIL: All right.

> *They turn again and march across.* ROS *halts.* GUIL *halts.*

ROS: I've just thought. If we both go, he could come *here.* That would be stupid, wouldn't it?

GUIL: All right—I'll stay, you go.

ROS: Right.

GUIL *marches to midstage.*

I say.

GUIL *wheels and carries on marching back towards* ROS, *who starts marching downstage. They cross.* ROS *halts.*

I've just thought.

GUIL *halts.*

We ought to stick together; he might be violent.

GUIL: Good point.

>GUIL *marches down to join* ROS. *They stand still for a moment in their original positions.*

Well, at last we're getting somewhere.

Pause.

Of course, he might not come.

ROS (*airily*): Oh, he'll come.

GUIL: We'd have some explaining to do.

ROS: He'll come. (*Airily wanders upstage.*) Don't worry—take my word for it—(*Looks out—is appalled.*) He's coming!

GUIL: What's he doing?

ROS: Walking.

GUIL: Alone?

ROS: No.

GUIL: Not walking?

ROS: No.

GUIL: Who's with him?

ROS: The old man.

GUIL: Walking?

ROS: No.

GUIL: Ah. That's an opening if ever there was one. (*And is suddenly galvanized into action.*) Let him walk into the trap!

ROS: What trap?

GUIL: You stand there! Don't let him pass!

He positions ROS *with his back to one wing, facing* HAMLET'*s entrance.*

GUIL *positions himself next to* ROS, *a few feet away, so that they are covering one side of the stage, facing the opposite side.* GUIL *unfastens his belt.* ROS *does the same. They join the two belts, and hold them taut between them.* ROS'*s trousers slide slowly down.*

HAMLET *enters opposite, slowly, dragging* POLONIUS'*s body. He enters upstage, makes a small arc and leaves by the same side, a few feet downstage.*

ROS *and* GUIL, *holding the belts taut, stare at him in some bewilderment.*

HAMLET *leaves, dragging the body. They relax the strain on the belts.*

ROS: That was close.

GUIL: There's a limit to what two people can do.

They undo the belts: ROS *pulls up his trousers.*

ROS (*worriedly—he walks a few paces towards* HAMLET'*s exit*): He was dead.

GUIL: Of course he's dead!

ROS (*turns to* GUIL): Properly.

GUIL (*angrily*): Death's death, isn't it?

ROS *falls silent. Pause.*

Perhaps he'll come back this way.

ROS *starts to take off his belt.*

No, no, no!—if we can't learn by experience, what else have we got?

ROS *desists.*

Pause.

ROS: Give him a shout.

GUIL: I thought we'd been into all that.

ROS (*shouts*): Hamlet!

GUIL: Don't be absurd.

ROS (*shouts*): Lord Hamlet!

HAMLET *enters.* ROS *is a little dismayed.*

What have you done, my lord, with the dead body?

HAMLET: Compounded it with dust, whereto 'tis kin.

ROS: Tell us where 'tis, that we may take it thence and bear it to the chapel.

HAMLET: Do not believe it.

ROS: Believe what?

HAMLET: That I can keep your counsel and not mine own. Besides, to be demanded of a sponge, what replication should be made by the son of a king?

ROS: Take you me for a sponge, my lord?

HAMLET: Ay, sir, that soaks up the King's countenance, his rewards, his authorities. But such officers do the King best service in the end. He keeps them, like an ape, in the corner of his jaw, first mouthed, to be last swallowed. When he needs what you have gleaned, it is but squeezing you and, sponge, you shall be dry again.

ROS: I understand you not, my lord.

HAMLET: I am glad of it: a knavish speech sleeps in a foolish ear.

ROS: My lord, you must tell us where the body is and go with us to the King.

HAMLET: The body is with the King, but the King is not with the body. The King is a thing——

GUIL: A thing, my lord——?

HAMLET: Of nothing. Bring me to him.

> HAMLET *moves resolutely towards one wing. They move with him, shepherding. Just before they reach the exit,* HAMLET, *apparently seeing* CLAUDIUS *approaching from off stage, bends low in a sweeping bow.* ROS *and* GUIL, *cued by Hamlet, also bow deeply—a sweeping ceremonial bow with their cloaks swept round them.* HAMLET, *however, continues the movement into an about-turn and walks off in the opposite direction.* ROS *and* GUIL, *with their heads low, do not notice.*
>
> *No one comes on.* ROS *and* GUIL *squint upwards and find that they are bowing to nothing.*
>
> CLAUDIUS *enters behind them. At first words they leap up and do a double-take.*

CLAUDIUS: How now? What hath befallen?

ROS: Where the body is bestowed, my lord, we cannot get from him.

CLAUDIUS: But where is he?

ROS (*fractional hesitation*): Without, my lord; guarded to know your pleasure.

CLAUDIUS (*moves*): Bring him before us.

This hits ROS *between the eyes but only his eyes show it. Again his hesitation is fractional. And then with great deliberation he turns to* GUIL.

ROS: Ho! Bring in the lord.

Again there is a fractional moment in which ROS *is smug,* GUIL *is trapped and betrayed.* GUIL *opens his mouth and closes it.*

The situation is saved: HAMLET, *escorted, is marched in just as* CLAUDIUS *leaves.* HAMLET *and his* ESCORT *cross the stage and go out, following* CLAUDIUS.

Lighting changes to Exterior.

ROS (*moves to go*): All right, then?

GUIL (*does not move; thoughtfully*): And yet it doesn't seem enough; to have breathed such significance. Can that be all? And why us?—anybody would have done. And we have contributed nothing.

ROS: It was a trying episode while it lasted, but they've done with us now.

GUIL: Done what?

ROS: I don't pretend to have understood. Frankly, I'm not very interested. If they won't tell us, that's their affair. (*He wanders upstage towards the exit.*) For my part, I'm only glad that that's the last we've seen of him—(*And he glances off stage and turns front, his face betraying the fact that* HAMLET *is there.*)

GUIL: I knew it wasn't the end. . . .

ROS (*high*): What else?!

GUIL: We're taking him to England. What's he doing?

ROS *goes upstage and returns.*

ROS: Talking.

GUIL: To himself?

> ROS *makes to go,* GUIL *cuts him off.*

Is he alone?

ROS: No, he's with a soldier.

GUIL: Then he's not talking to himself, is he?

ROS: Not *by* himself. . . . Should we go?

GUIL: Where?

ROS: Anywhere.

GUIL: Why?

> ROS *puts up his head listening.*

ROS: There it is again. (*In anguish.*) All I ask is a change of ground!

GUIL (*coda*): Give us this day our daily round. . . .

> HAMLET *enters behind them, talking with a soldier in arms.* ROS *and* GUIL *don't look round.*

ROS: They'll have us hanging about till we're dead. At least. And the weather will change. (*Looks up.*) The spring can't last for ever.

HAMLET: Good sir, whose powers are these?

SOLDIER: They are of Norway, sir.

HAMLET: How purposed, sir, I pray you?

SOLDIER: Against some part of Poland.

HAMLET: Who commands them, sir?

SOLDIER: The nephew to old Norway, Fortinbras.

ROS: We'll be cold. The summer won't last.

GUIL: It's autumnal.

ROS (*examining the ground*): No leaves.

GUIL: Autumnal—nothing to do with leaves. It is to do with a certain brownness at the edges of the day. . . . Brown is creeping up on us, take my word for it. . . . Russets and tangerine shades of old gold flushing the very outside edge of the senses . . . deep shining ochres, burnt umber and parchments of baked earth—reflecting on itself and through itself, filtering the light. At such times, perhaps, coincidentally, the leaves might fall, somewhere, by repute. Yesterday was blue, like smoke.

ROS (*head up, listening*): I got it again then.

They listen—faintest sound of TRAGEDIANS' *band.*

HAMLET: I humbly thank you, sir.

SOLDIER: God by you, sir. (*Exit.*)

ROS *gets up quickly and goes to* HAMLET.

ROS: Will it please you go, my lord?

HAMLET: I'll be with you straight. Go you a little before.

HAMLET *turns to face upstage.* ROS *returns down.* GUIL *faces front, doesn't turn.*

GUIL: Is he there?

ROS: Yes.

GUIL: What's he doing?

ROS *looks over his shoulder.*

ROS: Talking.

GUIL: To himself?

ROS: Yes.

Pause. ROS *makes to leave.*

ROS: He *said* we can go. Cross my heart.

GUIL: I like to know where I am. Even if I don't know where I am, I like to know *that*. If we go there's no knowing.

ROS: No knowing what?

GUIL: If we'll ever come back.

ROS: We don't want to come back.

GUIL: That may very well be true, but do we want to go?

ROS: We'll be free.

GUIL: I don't know. It's the same sky.

ROS: We've come this far.

He moves towards exit. GUIL *follows him.*

And besides, anything could happen yet.

They go.

BLACKOUT

ACT THREE

Opens in pitch darkness.
Soft sea sounds.

After several seconds of nothing, a voice from the dark . . .

GUIL: Are you there?

ROS: Where?

GUIL (*bitterly*): A flying start. . . .

    Pause.

ROS: Is that you?

GUIL: Yes.

ROS: How do you know?

GUIL (*explosion*): Oh-for-God's-sake!

ROS: We're not finished, then?

GUIL: Well, we're here, aren't we?

ROS: Are we? I can't see a thing.

GUIL: You can still *think*, can't you?

ROS: I think so.

GUIL: You can still *talk*.

ROS: What should I say?

GUIL: Don't bother. You can *feel*, can't you?

ROS: Ah! There's life in me yet!

761

GUIL: What are you feeling?

ROS: A leg. Yes, it feels like my leg.

GUIL: How does it feel?

ROS: Dead.

GUIL: Dead?

ROS (*panic*): I can't feel a thing!

GUIL: Give it a pinch! (*Immediately he yelps.*)

ROS: Sorry.

GUIL: Well, that's cleared that up.

Longer pause: the sound builds a little and identifies itself—the sea. Ship timbers, wind in the rigging, and then shouts of sailors calling obscure but inescapably nautical instructions from all directions, far and near: A short list:

> Hard a larboard!
> Let go the stays!
> Reef down me hearties!
> Is that you, cox'n?
> Hel-llo! Is that you?
> Hard a port!
> Easy as she goes!
> Keep her steady on the lee!
> Haul away, lads!
> (*Snatches of sea shanty maybe.*)
> Fly the jib!
> Tops'l up, me maties!

When the point has been well made and more so.

ROS: We're on a boat. (*Pause.*) Dark, isn't it?

GUIL: Not for night.

ROS: No, not for *night.*

GUIL: Dark for day.

> *Pause.*

ROS: Oh yes, it's dark for *day*.

GUIL: We must have gone north, of course.

ROS: Off course?

GUIL: Land of the midnight sun, that is.

ROS: Of course.

> *Some sailor sounds.*
>
> *A lantern is lit upstage—in fact by* HAMLET.
>
> *The stage lightens disproportionately—*
>
> *Enough to see:*
>
> ROS *and* GUIL *sitting downstage.*
>
> *Vague shapes of rigging, etc., behind.*

I think it's getting light.

GUIL: Not for night.

ROS: This far north.

GUIL: Unless we're off course.

ROS (*small pause*): Of course.

> *A better light—Lantern? Moon? . . . Light.*
> *Revealing, among other things, three large man-sized casks on deck, upended, with lids. Spaced but in line. Behind and above—a gaudy striped umbrella, on a pole stuck into the deck, tilted so that we do not see behind it—one of those huge six-foot-diameter jobs. Still dim upstage.* ROS *and* GUIL *still facing front.*

ROS: Yes, it's lighter than it was. It'll be night soon. This far north. (*Dolefully.*) I suppose we'll have to go to sleep. (*He yawns and stretches.*)

GUIL: Tired?

ROS: No . . . I don't think I'd take to it. Sleep all night, can't
see a thing all day. . . . Those eskimos must have a quiet life.

GUIL: Where?

ROS: What?

GUIL: I thought you—— (*Relapses.*) I've lost all capacity for
disbelief. I'm not sure that I could even rise to a little
gentle scepticism.

Pause.

ROS: Well, shall we stretch our legs?

GUIL: I don't feel like stretching my legs.

ROS: I'll stretch them for you, if you like.

GUIL: No.

ROS: We could stretch each other's. That way we wouldn't have
to go anywhere.

GUIL (*pause*): No, somebody might come in.

ROS: In where?

GUIL: Out here.

ROS: In out here?

GUIL: On deck.

ROS *considers the floor: slaps it.*

ROS: Nice bit of planking, that.

GUIL: Yes, I'm very fond of boats myself. I like the way they're
—contained. You don't have to worry about which way to
go, or whether to go at all—the question doesn't arise,
because you're on a *boat*, aren't you? Boats are safe areas
in the game of tag . . . the players will hold their positions

until the music starts. . . . I think I'll spend most of my life on boats.

ROS: Very healthy.

ROS inhales with expectation, exhales with boredom. GUIL stands up and looks over the audience.

GUIL: One is free on a boat. For a time. Relatively.

ROS: What's it like?

GUIL: Rough.

ROS joins him. They look out over the audience.

ROS: I think I'm going to be sick.

GUIL licks a finger, holds it up experimentally.

GUIL: Other side, I think.

ROS goes upstage: Ideally a sort of upper deck joined to the downstage lower deck by short steps. The umbrella being on the upper deck. ROS pauses by the umbrella and looks behind it. GUIL meanwhile has been resuming his own theme —looking out over the audience——

Free to move, speak, extemporise, and yet. We have not been cut loose. Our truancy is defined by one fixed star, and our drift represents merely a slight change of angle to it: we may seize the moment, toss it around while the moments pass, a short dash here, an exploration there, but we are brought round full circle to face again the single immutable fact—that we, Rosencrantz and Guildenstern, bearing a letter from one king to another, are taking Hamlet to England.

By which time, ROS has returned, tiptoeing with great import, teeth clenched for secrecy, gets to GUIL, points surreptitiously behind him—and a tight whisper:

ROS: I say—*he's there!*

GUIL (*unsurprised*): What's he doing?

ROS: Sleeping.

GUIL: It's all right for him.

ROS: What is?

GUIL: He can sleep.

ROS: It's all right for him.

GUIL: He's got us now.

ROS: He can sleep.

GUIL: It's all done for him.

ROS: He's got us.

GUIL: And we've got nothing. (*A cry.*) All I ask is our common due!

ROS: For those in peril on the sea. . . .

GUIL: Give us this day our daily cue.

> *Beat, pause. Sit. Long pause.*

ROS (*after shifting, looking around*): What now?

GUIL: What do you mean?

ROS: Well, nothing is happening.

GUIL: We're on a boat.

ROS: I'm aware of that.

GUIL (*angrily*): Then what do you expect? (*Unhappily.*) We act on scraps of information . . . sifting half-remembered directions that we can hardly separate from instinct.

> ROS *puts a hand into his purse, then both hands behind his back, then holds his fists out.*

> GUIL *taps one fist.*

ROS *opens it to show a coin.*

He gives it to GUIL.

He puts his hand back into his purse. Then both hands behind his back, then holds his fists out.

GUIL *taps one.*

ROS *opens it to show a coin. He gives it to* GUIL.

Repeat.

Repeat.

GUIL *getting tense. Desperate to lose.*

Repeat.

GUIL *taps a hand, changes his mind, taps the other, and* ROS *inadvertently reveals that he has a coin in both fists.*

GUIL: You had money in both hands.

ROS (*embarrassed*): Yes.

GUIL: Every time?

ROS: Yes.

GUIL: What's the point of that?

ROS (*pathetic*): I wanted to make you happy.

   Beat.

GUIL: How much did he give you?

ROS: Who?

GUIL: The King. He gave us some money.

ROS: How much did he give you?

GUIL: I asked you first.

ROS: I got the same as you.

GUIL: He wouldn't discriminate between us.

ROS: How much did you get?

GUIL: The same.

ROS: How do you know?

GUIL: You just told me—how do *you* know?

ROS: He wouldn't discriminate between us.

GUIL: Even if he could.

ROS: Which he never could.

GUIL: He couldn't even be sure of mixing us up.

ROS: Without mixing us up.

GUIL (*turning on him furiously*): Why don't you say something original! No wonder the whole thing is so stagnant! You don't take me up on anything—you just repeat it in a different order.

ROS: I can't think of anything original. I'm only good in support.

GUIL: I'm sick of making the running.

ROS (*humbly*): It must be your dominant personality. (*Almost in tears.*) Oh, what's going to become of us!

And GUIL *comforts him, all harshness gone.*

GUIL: Don't cry . . . it's all right . . . there . . . there, I'll see we're all right.

ROS: But we've got nothing to go on, we're out on our own.

GUIL: We're on our way to England—we're taking Hamlet there.

ROS: What for?

GUIL: What for? Where have you been?

ROS: When? (*Pause.*) We won't know what to do when we get there.

GUIL: We take him to the King.

ROS: Will *he* be there?

GUIL: No—the king of England.

ROS: He's expecting us?

GUIL: No.

ROS: He won't know what we're playing at. What are we going to *say*?

GUIL: We've got a letter. You remember the letter.

ROS: Do I?

GUIL: Everything is explained in the letter. We count on that.

ROS: Is that it, then?

GUIL: What?

ROS: We take Hamlet to the English king, we hand over the letter—what then?

GUIL: There may be something in the letter to keep us going a bit.

ROS: And if not?

GUIL: Then that's it—we're finished.

ROS: At a loose end?

GUIL: Yes.

    Pause.

ROS: Are there likely to be loose ends? (*Pause.*) Who is the English king?

GUIL: That depends on when we get there.

ROS: What do you think it says?

GUIL: Oh . . . greetings. Expressions of loyalty. Asking of favours, calling in of debts. Obscure promises balanced by vague threats. . . . Diplomacy. Regards to the family.

ROS: And about Hamlet?

GUIL: Oh yes.

ROS: And us—the full background?

GUIL: I should say so.

Pause.

ROS: So we've got a letter which explains everything.

GUIL: You've got it.

ROS *takes that literally. He starts to pat his pockets, etc.*

What's the matter?

ROS: The letter.

GUIL: Have you got it?

ROS (*rising fear*): Have I? (*Searches frantically.*) Where would I have put it?

GUIL: You can't have lost it.

ROS: I must have!

GUIL: That's odd—I thought he gave it to me.

ROS *looks at him hopefully.*

ROS: Perhaps he did.

GUIL: But you seemed so sure it was *you* who hadn't got it.

ROS (*high*): It *was* me who hadn't got it!

GUIL: But if he gave it to me there's no reason why you should have had it in the first place, in which case I don't see what all the fuss is about you *not* having it.

ROS (*pause*): I admit it's confusing.

GUIL: This is all getting rather undisciplined. . . . The boat, the night, the sense of isolation and uncertainty . . . all these induce a loosening of the concentration. We must not lose control. Tighten up. Now. Either you have lost the letter or you didn't have it to lose in the first place, in which case the King never gave it to you, in which case he gave it to me, in which case I would have put it into my inside top pocket, in which case (*calmly producing the letter*) . . . it will be . . . here. (*They smile at each other.*) We mustn't drop off like that again.

Pause. ROS *takes the letter gently from him.*

ROS: Now that we have found it, why were we looking for it?

GUIL (*thinks*): We thought it was lost.

ROS: Something else?

GUIL: No.

Deflation.

ROS: Now we've lost the tension.

GUIL: What tension?

ROS: What was the last thing I said before we wandered off?

GUIL: When was that?

ROS (*helplessly*): I can't remember.

GUIL (*leaping up*): What a shambles! We're just not getting anywhere.

ROS (*mournfully*): Not even England. I don't believe in it anyway.

GUIL: What?

ROS: England.

GUIL: Just a conspiracy of cartographers, you mean?

ROS: I mean I don't believe it! (*Calmer.*) I have no image. I try

to picture us arriving, a little harbour perhaps . . . roads
. . . inhabitants to point the way . . . horses on the road . . .
riding for a day or a fortnight and then a palace and the
English king. . . . That would be the logical kind of thing.
. . . But my mind remains a blank. No. We're slipping off
the map.

GUIL: Yes . . . yes. . . . (*Rallying.*) But you don't believe anything
till it happens. And it *has* all happened. Hasn't it?

ROS: We drift down time, clutching at straws. But what good's
a brick to a drowning man?

GUIL: Don't give up, we can't be long now.

ROS: We might as well be dead. Do you think death could possibly
be a boat?

GUIL: No, no, no . . . Death is . . . not. Death isn't. You take
my meaning. Death is the ultimate negative. Not-being.
You can't not-be on a boat.

ROS: I've frequently not been on boats.

GUIL: No, no, no—what you've been is not on boats.

ROS: I wish I was dead. (*Considers the drop.*) I could jump over
the side. That would put a spoke in their wheel.

GUIL: Unless they're counting on it.

ROS: I shall remain on board. That'll put a spoke in their wheel.
(*The futility of it, fury.*) All right! We don't question, we
don't doubt. We perform. But a line must be drawn
somewhere, and I would like to put it on record that I have
no confidence in England. Thank you. (*Thinks about this.*)
And even if it's true, it'll just be another shambles.

GUIL: I don't see why.

ROS (*furious*): He won't know what we're talking about.—What
are we going to *say*?

GUIL: We say—Your majesty, we have arrived!

ROS (*kingly*): And who are you?

GUIL: We are Rosencrantz and Guildenstern.

ROS (*barks*): Never heard of you!

GUIL: Well, we're nobody special——

ROS (*regal and nasty*): What's your game?

GUIL: We've got our instructions——

ROS: First I've heard of it——

GUIL (*angry*): Let me finish—— (*Humble.*) We've come from Denmark.

ROS: What do you want?

GUIL: Nothing—we're delivering Hamlet——

ROS: Who's he?

GUIL (*irritated*): You've heard of *him*——

ROS: Oh, I've heard of him all right and I want nothing to do with it.

GUIL: But——

ROS: You march in here without so much as a by-your-leave and expect me to take in every lunatic you try to pass off with a lot of unsubstantiated——

GUIL: We've got a letter——

ROS *snatches it and tears it open.*

ROS (*efficiently*): I see . . . I see . . . well, this seems to support your story such as it is—it is an exact command from the king of Denmark, for several different reasons, importing Denmark's health and England's too, that on the reading of this letter, without delay, I should have Hamlet's head cut off——!

GUIL *snatches the letter.* ROS, *double-taking, snatches it back.*
GUIL *snatches it half back. They read it together, and separate.*

Pause.

They are well downstage looking front.

ROS: The sun's going down. It will be dark soon.

GUIL: Do you think so?

ROS: I was just making conversation. (*Pause.*) We're his *friends.*

GUIL: How do you know?

ROS: From our young days brought up with him.

GUIL: You've only got their word for it.

ROS: But that's what we depend on.

GUIL: Well, yes, and then again no. (*Airily.*) Let us keep things
in proportion. Assume, if you like, that they're going to
kill him. Well, he is a man, he is mortal, death comes to us
all, etcetera, and consequently he would have died anyway,
sooner or later. Or to look at it from the social point of
view—he's just one man among many, the loss would be
well within reason and convenience. And then again, what
is so terrible about death? As Socrates so philosophically
put it, since we don't know what death is, it is illogical to
fear it. It might be . . . very nice. Certainly it is a release
from the burden of life, and, for the godly, a haven and a
reward. Or to look at it another way—we are little men, we
don't know the ins and outs of the matter, there are wheels
within wheels, etcetera—it would be presumptuous of us to
interfere with the designs of fate or even of kings. All in all, I
think we'd be well advised to leave well alone. Tie up the
letter—there—neatly—like that.—They won't notice the
broken seal, assuming you were in character.

ROS: But what's the point?

GUIL: Don't apply logic.

ROS: He's done nothing to us.

GUIL: Or justice.

ROS: It's awful.

GUIL: But it could have been worse. I was beginning to think it was. (*And his relief comes out in a laugh.*)

Behind them HAMLET *appears from behind the umbrella. The light has been going. Slightly.* HAMLET *is going to the lantern.*

ROS: The position as I see it, then. We, Rosencrantz and Guildenstern, from our young days brought up with him, awakened by a man standing on his saddle, are summoned, and arrive, and are instructed to glean what afflicts him and draw him on to pleasures, such as a play, which unfortunately, as it turns out, is abandoned in some confusion owing to certain nuances outside our appreciation —which, among other causes, results in, among other effects, a high, not to say, homicidal, excitement in Hamlet, whom we, in consequence, are escorting, for his own good, to England. Good. We're on top of it now.

HAMLET *blows out the lantern. The stage goes pitch black. The black resolves itself to moonlight, by which* HAMLET *approaches the sleeping* ROS *and* GUIL. *He extracts the letter and takes it behind his umbrella; the light of his lantern shines through the fabric,* HAMLET *emerges again with a letter, and replaces it, and retires, blowing out his lantern.*

Morning comes.

ROS *watches it coming—from the auditorium. Behind him is a gay sight. Beneath the re-tilted umbrella, reclining in a deck-chair, wrapped in a rug, reading a book, possibly smoking, sits* HAMLET.

ROS *watches the morning come, and brighten to high noon.*

ROS: I'm assuming nothing. (*He stands up.* GUIL *wakes.*)
The position as I see it, then. That's west unless we're off
course, in which case it's night; the King gave me the same as
you, the King gave you the same as me; the King never gave
me the letter, the King gave you the letter, we don't know
what's in the letter; we take Hamlet to the English king, it
depending on when we get there who he is, and we hand
over the letter, which may or may not have something in it
to keep us going, and if not, we are finished and at a loose
end, if they have loose ends. We could have done worse. I
don't think we missed any chances. . . . Not that we're
getting much help. (*He sits down again. They lie down—
prone.*) If we stopped breathing we'd vanish.

*The muffled sound of a recorder. They sit up with
disproportionate interest.*

GUIL: Here we go.

ROS: Yes, but what?

They listen to the music.

GUIL (*excitedly*): Out of the void, finally, a sound; while on a
boat (admittedly) outside the action (admittedly) the perfect
and absolute silence of the wet lazy slap of water against
water and the rolling creak of timber—breaks; giving rise
at once to the speculation or the assumption or the hope
that something is about to happen; a pipe is heard. One of
the sailors has pursed his lips against a woodwind, his fingers
and thumb governing, shall we say, the ventages, whereupon,
giving it breath, let us say, with his mouth, it, the pipe,
discourses, as the saying goes, most eloquent music. A
thing like that, it could change the course of events.
(*Pause.*) Go and see what it is.

ROS: It's someone playing on a pipe.

GUIL: Go and find him.

ROS: And then what?

GUIL: I don't know—request a tune.

ROS: What for?

GUIL: Quick—before we lose our momentum.

ROS: Why!—something is happening. It had quite escaped my attention!

He listens: Makes a stab at an exit. Listens more carefully: Changes direction.

GUIL *takes no notice.*

ROS *wanders about trying to decide where the music comes from. Finally he tracks it down—unwillingly—to the middle barrel. There is no getting away from it. He turns to* GUIL *who takes no notice.* ROS, *during this whole business, never quite breaks into articulate speech. His face and his hands indicate his incredulity. He stands gazing at the middle barrel. The pipe plays on within. He kicks the barrel. The pipe stops. He leaps back towards* GUIL. *The pipe starts up again. He approaches the barrel cautiously. He lifts the lid. The music is louder. He slams down the lid. The music is softer. He goes back towards* GUIL. *But a drum starts, muffled. He freezes. He turns. Considers the left-hand barrel. The drumming goes on within, in time to the flute. He walks back to* GUIL. *He opens his mouth to speak. Doesn't make it. A lute is heard. He spins round at the third barrel. More instruments join in. Until it is quite inescapable that inside the three barrels, distributed, playing together a familiar tune which has been heard three times before, are the* TRAGEDIANS.

They play on.

ROS *sits beside* GUIL. *They stare ahead.*

The tune comes to an end.

Pause.

ROS: I thought I heard a band. (*In anguish.*) Plausibility is all I presume!

GUIL (*coda*): Call us this day our daily tune. . . .

The lid of the middle barrel flies open and the PLAYER's *head pops out.*

PLAYER: Aha! All in the same boat, then! (*He climbs out. He goes round banging on the barrels.*)

Everybody out!

Impossibly, the TRAGEDIANS *climb out of the barrels. With their instruments, but not their cart. A few bundles. Except* ALFRED. *The* PLAYER *is cheerful.*

(*To* ROS:) Where are we?

ROS: Travelling.

PLAYER: Of course, we haven't got there yet.

ROS: Are we all right for England?

PLAYER: You look all right to me. I don't think they're very particular in England. Al-l-fred!

ALFRED *emerges from the* PLAYER's *barrel.*

GUIL: What are you doing here?

PLAYER: Travelling. (*To* TRAGEDIANS:) Right—blend into the background!

The TRAGEDIANS *are in costume (from the mime): A King with crown,* ALFRED *as Queen, Poisoner and the two cloaked figures.*

They blend.

(*To* GUIL:) Pleased to see us? (*Pause.*) You've come out of it very well, so far.

GUIL: And you?

PLAYER: In disfavour. Our play offended the King.

GUIL: Yes.

PLAYER: Well, he's a second husband himself. Tactless, really.

ROS: It was quite a good play nevertheless.

PLAYER: We never really got going—it was getting quite interesting when they stopped it.

Looks up at HAMLET.

That's the way to travel. . . .

GUIL: What were you doing in there?

PLAYER: Hiding. (*Indicating costumes.*) We had to run for it just as we were.

ROS: Stowaways.

PLAYER: Naturally—we didn't get paid, owing to circumstances ever so slightly beyond our control, and all the money we had we lost betting on certainties. Life is a gamble, at terrible odds—if it was a bet you wouldn't take it. Did you know that any number doubled is even?

ROS: Is it?

PLAYER: We learn something every day, to our cost. But we troupers just go on and on. Do you know what happens to old actors?

ROS: What?

PLAYER: Nothing. They're still acting. Surprised, then?

GUIL: What?

PLAYER: Surprised to see us?

GUIL: I knew it wasn't the end.

PLAYER: With practically everyone on his feet. What do you make
of it, so far?

GUIL: We haven't got much to go on.

PLAYER: You speak to him?

ROS: It's possible.

GUIL: But it wouldn't make any difference.

ROS: But it's possible.

GUIL: Pointless.

ROS: It's allowed.

GUIL: Allowed, yes. We are not restricted. No boundaries have
been defined, no inhibitions imposed. We have, for the
while, secured, or blundered into, our release, for the while.
Spontaneity and whim are the order of the day. Other
wheels are turning but they are not our concern. We can
breathe. We can relax. We can do what we like and say
what we like to whomever we like, without restriction.

ROS: Within limits, of course.

GUIL: Certainly within limits.

> HAMLET *comes down to footlights and regards the audience.*
> *The others watch but don't speak.* HAMLET *clears his throat*
> *noisily and spits into the audience. A split second later he*
> *claps his hand to his eye and wipes himself. He goes back*
> *upstage.*

ROS: A compulsion towards philosophical introspection is his
chief characteristic, if I may put it like that. It does not
mean he is mad. It does not mean he isn't. Very often, it
does not mean anything at all. Which may or may not be a
kind of madness.

GUIL: It really boils down to symptoms. Pregnant replies,
mystic allusions, mistaken identities, arguing his father is

his mother, that sort of thing; intimations of suicide, forgoing of exercise, loss of mirth, hints of claustrophobia not to say delusions of imprisonment; invocations of camels, chameleons, capons, whales, weasels, hawks, handsaws—riddles, quibbles and evasions; amnesia, paranoia, myopia; day-dreaming, hallucinations; stabbing his elders, abusing his parents, insulting his lover, and appearing hatless in public—knock-kneed, droop-stockinged and sighing like a love-sick schoolboy, which at his age is coming on a bit strong.

ROS: And talking to himself.

GUIL: And talking to himself.

> ROS *and* GUIL *move apart together.*

Well, where has that got us?

ROS: He's the Player.

GUIL: His play offended the King——

ROS: —offended the King——

GUIL: —who orders his arrest——

ROS: —orders his arrest——

GUIL: —so he escapes to England——

ROS: On the boat to which he meets——

GUIL: Guildenstern and Rosencrantz taking Hamlet——

ROS: —who also offended the King——

GUIL: —and killed Polonius——

ROS: —offended the King in a variety of ways——

GUIL: —to England. (*Pause.*) That seems to be it.

> ROS *jumps up.*

ROS: Incidents! All we get is incidents! Dear God, is it too much to expect a little sustained action?!

And on the word, the PIRATES *attack. That is to say: Noise and shouts and rushing about. "Pirates."'*

Everyone visible goes frantic. HAMLET *draws his sword and rushes downstage.* GUIL, ROS *and* PLAYER *draw swords and rush upstage. Collision.* HAMLET *turns back up. They turn back down. Collision. By which time there is general panic right upstage. All four charge upstage with* ROS, GUIL *and* PLAYER *shouting:*

> At last!
> To arms!
> Pirates!
> Up there!
> Down there!
> To my sword's length!
> Action!

All four reach the top, see something they don't like, waver, run for their lives downstage:

HAMLET, *in the lead, leaps into the left barrel.* PLAYER *leaps into the right barrel.* ROS *and* GUIL *leap into the middle barrel. All closing the lids after them.*

*The lights dim to nothing while the sound of fighting continues. The sound fades to nothing. The lights come up. The middle barrel (*ROS's *and* GUIL's) *is missing.*

The lid of the right-hand barrel is raised cautiously, the heads of ROS *and* GUIL *appear.*

*The lid of the other barrel (*HAMLET's) *is raised. The head of the* PLAYER *appears.*

All catch sight of each other and slam down lids.

Pause.

Lids raised cautiously.

ROS (*relief*): They've gone. (*He starts to climb out.*) That was
close. I've never thought quicker.

They are all three out of barrels. GUIL *is wary and nervous.*
ROS *is light-headed. The* PLAYER *is phlegmatic. They note the
missing barrel.*

ROS *looks round.*

ROS: Where's——?

The PLAYER *takes off his hat in mourning.*

PLAYER: Once more, alone—on our own resources.

GUIL (*worried*): What do you mean? Where is he?

PLAYER: Gone.

GUIL: Gone where?

PLAYER: Yes, we were dead lucky there. If that's the word I'm
after.

ROS (*not a pick up*): Dead?

PLAYER: Lucky.

ROS (*he means*): Is he dead?

PLAYER: Who knows?

GUIL (*rattled*): He's not coming back?

PLAYER: Hardly.

ROS: He's dead then. He's dead as far as we're concerned.

PLAYER: Or we are as far as he is. (*He goes and sits on the floor
to one side.*) Not too bad, is it?

GUIL (*rattled*): But he can't—we're supposed to be—we've
got a *letter*—we're going to England with a letter for the
King——

PLAYER: Yes, that much seems certain. I congratulate you on the unambiguity of your situation.

GUIL: But you don't understand—it contains—we've had our instructions——the whole thing's pointless without him.

PLAYER: Pirates could happen to anyone. Just deliver the letter. They'll send ambassadors from England to explain. . . .

GUIL (*worked up*): Can't you see—the pirates left us home and high—dry and home—drome——(*Furiously.*) The pirates left us high and dry!

PLAYER (*comforting*): There . . .

GUIL (*near tears*): Nothing will be resolved without him. . . .

PLAYER: There . . . !

GUIL: We need Hamlet for our release!

PLAYER: There!

GUIL: What are we supposed to do?

PLAYER: This.

    He turns away, lies down if he likes. ROS *and* GUIL *apart.*

ROS: Saved again.

GUIL: Saved for what?

    ROS *sighs.*

ROS: The sun's going down. (*Pause.*) It'll be night soon. (*Pause.*) If that's west. (*Pause.*) Unless we've——

GUIL (*shouts*): Shut up! I'm sick of it! Do you think conversation is going to help us now?

ROS (*hurt, desperately ingratiating*): I—I bet you all the money I've got the year of my birth doubled is an odd number.

GUIL (*moan*): No-o.

ROS: *Your* birth!

GUIL *smashes him down.*

GUIL (*broken*): We've travelled too far, and our momentum has taken over; we move idly towards eternity, without possibility of reprieve or hope of explanation.

ROS: Be happy—if you're not even *happy* what's so good about surviving? (*He picks himself up.*) We'll be all right. I suppose we just go on.

GUIL: Go where?

ROS: To England.

GUIL: England! *That's* a dead end. I never believed in it anyway.

ROS: All we've got to do is make our report and that'll be that. Surely.

GUIL: I don't *believe* it—a shore, a harbour, say—and we get off and we stop someone and say—Where's the King?— And he says, Oh, you follow that road there and take the first left and—— (*Furiously.*) I don't believe any of it!

ROS: It doesn't sound very plausible.

GUIL: And even if we came face to face, what do we say?

ROS: We say—We've arrived!

GUIL (*kingly*): And who are you?

ROS: We are Guildenstern and Rosencrantz.

GUIL: Which is which?

ROS: Well, I'm—You're——

GUIL: What's it all about?——

ROS: Well, we were bringing Hamlet—but then some pirates——

GUIL: I don't begin to understand. Who are all these people, what's it got to do with me? You turn up out of the blue with some cock and bull story——

ROS (*with letter*): We have a letter——

GUIL (*snatches it, opens it*): A letter—yes—that's true. That's something . . . a letter . . . (*Reads.*) "As England is Denmark's faithful tributary . . . as love between them like the palm might flourish, etcetera . . . that on the knowing of this contents, without delay of any kind, should those bearers, Rosencrantz and Guildenstern, put to sudden death——"

He double-takes. ROS *snatches the letter.* GUIL *snatches it back.* ROS *snatches it half back. They read it again and look up.*

The PLAYER *gets to his feet and walks over to his barrel and kicks it and shouts into it.*

PLAYER: They've gone! It's all over!

One by one the PLAYERS *emerge, impossibly, from the barrel, and form a casually menacing circle round* ROS *and* GUIL, *who are still appalled and mesmerised.*

GUIL (*quietly*): Where we went wrong was getting on a boat. We can move, of course, change direction, rattle about, but our movement is contained within a larger one that carries us along as inexorably as the wind and current. . . .

ROS: They had it in for us, didn't they? Right from the beginning. Who'd have thought that we were so important?

GUIL: But why? Was it all for this? Who are we that so much should converge on our little deaths? (*In anguish to the* PLAYER:) Who are *we*?

PLAYER: You are Rosencrantz and Guildenstern. That's enough.

GUIL: No—it is not enough. To be told so little—to such an end— and still, finally, to be denied an explanation——

PLAYER: In our experience, most things end in death.

GUIL (*fear, vengeance, scorn*): Your experience!—*Actors!*

He snatches a dagger from the PLAYER'*s belt and holds the point at the* PLAYER'*s throat: the* PLAYER *backs and* GUIL *advances, speaking more quietly.*

I'm talking about death—and you've never experienced *that*. And you cannot *act* it. You die a thousand casual deaths—with none of that intensity which squeezes out life . . . and no blood runs cold anywhere. Because even as you die you know that you will come back in a different hat. But no one gets up after *death*—there is no applause—there is only silence and some second-hand clothes, and that's—*death*——

And he pushes the blade in up to the hilt. The PLAYER *stands with huge, terrible eyes, clutches at the wound as the blade withdraws: he makes small weeping sounds and falls to his knees, and then right down.*

While he is dying, GUIL, *nervous, high, almost hysterical, wheels on the* TRAGEDIANS——

If we have a destiny, then so had he—and if this is ours, then that was his—and if there are no explanations for us, then let there be none for him——

The TRAGEDIANS *watch the* PLAYER *die: they watch with some interest. The* PLAYER *finally lies still. A short moment of silence. Then the* TRAGEDIANS *start to applaud with genuine admiration. The* PLAYER *stands up, brushing himself down.*

PLAYER (*modestly*): Oh, come, come, gentlemen—no flattery—it was merely competent——

The TRAGEDIANS *are still congratulating him. The* PLAYER *approaches* GUIL, *who stands rooted, holding the dagger.*

PLAYER: What did you think? (*Pause.*) You see, it *is* the kind they do believe in—it's what is expected.

He holds his hand out for the dagger. GUIL *slowly puts the point of the dagger on to the* PLAYER's *hand, and pushes . . . the blade slides back into the handle. The* PLAYER *smiles, reclaims the dagger.*

For a moment you thought I'd—cheated.

ROS *relieves his own tension with loud nervy laughter.*

ROS: Oh, very good! *Very* good! Took me in completely—didn't he take you in completely—(*claps his hands*). Encore! Encore!

PLAYER (*activated, arms spread, the professional*): Deaths for all ages and occasions! Deaths by suspension, convulsion, consumption, incision, execution, asphyxiation and malnutrition—! Climactic carnage, by poison and by steel—! Double deaths by duel—! Show!—

ALFRED, *still in his Queen's costume, dies by poison: the* PLAYER, *with rapier, kills the* "KING" *and duels with a fourth* TRAGEDIAN, *inflicting and receiving a wound. The two remaining* TRAGEDIANS, *the two* "SPIES" *dressed in the same coats as* ROS *and* GUIL, *are stabbed, as before.*
And the light is fading over the deaths which take place right upstage.

(*Dying amid the dying—tragically; romantically.*) So there's an end to that—it's commonplace: light goes with life, and in the winter of your years the dark comes early. . . .

GUIL (*tired, drained, but still an edge of impatience; over the mime*): No . . . no . . . not for *us,* not like that. Dying is not romantic, and death is not a game which will soon be over . . . Death is not anything . . . death is not . . . It's the absence of presence, nothing more . . . the endless time of never coming back . . . a gap you can't see, and when the wind blows through it, it makes no sound. . . .

The light has gone upstage. Only GUIL *and* ROS *are visible as* ROS's *clapping falters to silence.*

Small pause.

ROS: That's it, then, is it?

No answer. He looks out front.

The sun's going down. Or the earth's coming up, as the fashionable theory has it.

Small pause.

Not that it makes any difference.

Pause.

What was it all about? When did it begin?

Pause. No answer.

Couldn't we just stay put? I mean no one is going to come on and drag us off. . . . They'll just have to wait. We're still young . . . fit . . . we've got years. . . .

Pause. No answer.

(*A cry.*) We've done nothing wrong! We didn't harm anyone. Did we?

GUIL: I can't remember.

ROS *pulls himself together.*

ROS: All right, then. I don't care. I've had enough. To tell you the truth, I'm relieved.

And he disappears from view. GUIL *does not notice.*

GUIL: Our names shouted in a certain dawn . . . a message . . . a summons . . . There must have been a moment, at the beginning, where we could have said—no. But somehow we missed it. (*He looks round and sees he is alone.*)

Rosen—?
Guil—?

He gathers himself.

Well, we'll know better next time. Now you see me, now you— (*and disappears*).

Immediately the whole stage is lit up, revealing, upstage, arranged in the approximate positions last held by the dead TRAGEDIANS, *the tableau of court and corpses which is the last scene of* Hamlet.

That is: The KING, QUEEN, LAERTES *and* HAMLET *all dead.* HORATIO *holds* HAMLET. FORTINBRAS *is there.*

So are two AMBASSADORS *from England.*

AMBASSADOR: The sight is dismal;
    and our affairs from England come too late.
    The ears are senseless that should give us hearing
    to tell him his commandment is fulfilled,
    that Rosencrantz and Guildenstern are dead.
    Where should we have our thanks?

HORATIO: Not from his mouth,
    had it the ability of life to thank you:
    He never gave commandment for their death.
    But since, so jump upon this bloody question,
    you from the Polack wars, and you from England,
    are here arrived, give order that these bodies
    high on a stage be placed to the view;
    and let me speak to the yet unknowing world
    how these things came about: so shall you hear
    of carnal, bloody and unnatural acts,
    of accidental judgments, casual slaughters,
    of deaths put on by cunning and forced cause,
    and, in this upshot, purposes mistook
    fallen on the inventors' heads: all this can I
    truly deliver.

But during the above speech, the play fades out, overtaken by dark and music.

American

Buffalo

by
David Mamet

American Buffalo was first produced by the Goodman Theatre Stage Two, Chicago, Illinois, and opened on November 23, 1975, with the following cast:

BOBBY	William H. Macy
TEACH	Bernard Erhard
DONNY	J. J. Johnston

This production was directed by Gregory Mosher; set by Michael Merritt; lighting by Robert Christen.

After a twelve-performance showcase at Stage Two, it re-opened at Chicago's St. Nicholas Theatre Company, with Mike Nussbaum in the role of TEACH.

In February, 1976, it was showcased at St. Clement's, New York, with the following cast:

BOBBY	J. T. Walsh
TEACH	Mike Kellin
DONNY	Michael Egan

This production was directed by Gregory Mosher; set by Akira Yoshimura; lighting by Gary Porto.

The New York Broadway production at the Ethel Barrymore Theatre opened on February 16, 1977, with the following cast:

BOBBY	John Savage
TEACH	Robert Duvall
DONNY	Kenneth McMillan

This production was directed by Ulu Grosbard; set by Santo Loquasto; lighting by Jules Fisher.

This play is dedicated to Mr. J. J. Johnston of Chicago, Illinois.

"Mine eyes have seen the glory of the coming of the Lord.
He is peeling down the alley in a black and yellow Ford."

Folk Tune.

THE CHARACTERS

DON DUBROW   A man in his late forties, the owner of
                  Don's Resale Shop

WALTER COLE
called TEACH   A friend and associate of Don

BOB   Don's gopher

THE SCENE

Don's Resale Shop. A junkshop.

THE TIME

.

One Friday. Act One takes place in the morning; Act Two
starts around 11:00 that night.

ACT I

Don's Resale Shop. Morning. DON *and* BOB *are sitting.*

DON: So?

> *Pause.*

So what, Bob?

> *Pause.*

BOB: I'm sorry, Donny.

> *Pause.*

DON: All right.

BOB: I'm sorry, Donny.

> *Pause.*

DON: Yeah.

BOB: Maybe he's still in there.

DON: If you think that, Bob, how come you're here?

BOB: I came in.

> *Pause.*

DON: You don't come in, Bob. You don't come in until you do a thing.

BOB: He didn't come out.

DON: What do I care, Bob, if he came out or not? You're s'posed to watch the guy, you watch him. Am I wrong?

BOB: I just went to the back.

DON: Why?

> *Pause.*

Why did you do that?

BOB: 'Cause he wasn't coming out the front.

DON: Well, Bob, I'm sorry, but this isn't good enough. If you want to do business . . . if we got a business deal, it isn't good enough. I want you to remember this.

BOB: I do.

DON: Yeah, *now* . . . but later, what?

> *Pause.*

Just one thing, Bob. Action counts.

> *Pause.*

Action talks and bullshit walks.

BOB: I only went around to see he's coming out the back.

DON: No, don't go fuck yourself around with these excuses.

> *Pause.*

BOB: I'm sorry.

DON: Don't tell me that you're sorry. I'm not mad at you.

BOB: You're not?

DON *(Pause)*: Let's clean up here.

> BOB *starts to clean up the debris around the poker table.*

The only thing I'm trying to teach you something here.

BOB: Okay.

DON: Now lookit Fletcher.

BOB: Fletch?

DON: Now, Fletcher is a standup guy.

BOB: Yeah.

DON: I don't *give* a shit. He is a fellow stands for something—

BOB: Yeah.

DON: You take him and you put him down in some strange town with just a nickel in his pocket, and by nightfall he'll have that town by the balls. This is not talk, Bob, this is action.

> *Pause.*

BOB: He's a real good card player.

DON: You're fucking A he is, Bob, and this is what I'm getting at. Skill. Skill and talent and the balls to arrive at your own *conclusions.*

The fucker won four hundred bucks last night.

BOB: Yeah?

DON: *Oh yeah.*

BOB: And who was playing?

DON: *Me* . . .

BOB: Uh-huh . . .

DON: And *Teach* . . .

BOB: (How'd Teach do?)*

DON: (Not too good.)

BOB: (No, huh?)

DON: (No.) . . . and Earl was here . . .

BOB: Uh-huh . . .

DON: And Fletcher.

BOB: *How'd* he do?

DON: He won four hundred bucks.

BOB: And who else won?

DON: Ruthie, she won.

BOB: She won, huh?

DON: Yeah.

BOB: She does okay.

DON: *Oh yeah* . . .

BOB: She's an okay card player.

DON: Yes, she is.

BOB: I like her.

DON: Fuck, I like her, too. (There's nothing wrong in that.)

---

* Some portions of the dialogue appear in parentheses, which serve to mark a slight change of outlook on the part of the speaker—perhaps a momentary change to a more introspective regard. —D.M.

BOB: (No.)

DON: I mean, she treats you right.

BOB: Uh-huh. How'd she do?

DON: She did okay.

>   *Pause.*

BOB: You win?

DON: I did all right.

BOB: Yeah?

DON: Yeah. I did okay. Not like *Fletch* . . .

BOB: No, huh?

DON: I mean, Fletcher, he plays *cards*.

BOB: He's real sharp.

DON: You're goddamn right he is.

BOB: I know it.

DON: Was he born that way?

BOB: Huh?

DON: I'm saying was he born that way or do you think he had to learn it?

BOB: Learn it.

DON: Goddamn right he did, and don't forget it.

Everything, Bobby: it's going to happen to you, it's *not* going to happen to you, the important thing is can you deal with it, and can you *learn* from it.

>   *Pause.*

And this is why I'm telling you to stand up. It's no different with you than with anyone else. Everything that I or Fletcher know we picked up on the street. That's all business is . . . common sense, experience, and talent.

BOB: Like when he jewed Ruthie out that pig iron.

DON: What pig iron?

BOB: That he got off her that time.

DON: When was this?

BOB: On the back of her truck.

DON: That wasn't, I don't think, her pig iron.

BOB: No?

DON: That was *his* pig iron, Bob.

BOB: Yeah?

DON: Yeah. He bought it off her.

>Pause.

BOB: Well, she was real mad at him.

DON: She was.

BOB: Yup.

DON: She was mad at him?

BOB: Yeah. That he stole her pig iron.

DON: He didn't steal it, Bob.

BOB: No?

DON: No.

BOB: She was *mad* at him . . .

DON: Well, that very well may be, Bob, but the fact remains that it was *business*. That's what business *is*.

BOB: What?

DON: People taking *care* of themselves. Huh?

BOB: No.

DON: 'Cause there's business and there's friendship, Bobby . . . there are many things, and when you walk around you *hear* a lot of things, and what you got to do is keep clear who your friends are, and who treated you like what. Or

else the rest is garbage, Bob, because I want to tell you
something.

BOB: Okay.

DON: Things are not always what they seem to be.

BOB: I know.

 Pause.

DON: There's lotsa people on this street, Bob, they want this
and they want that. Do anything to get it. You don't have
friends this life. . . . You want some breakfast?

BOB: I'm not hungry.

 Pause.

DON: *Never* skip breakfast, Bob.

BOB: Why?

DON: Breakfast . . . is the most important meal of the day.

BOB: I'm not hungry.

DON: It makes no earthly difference in the world. You know
how much nutritive benefits they got in coffee? Zero. Not
one thing. The stuff eats *you* up. You can't live on coffee,
Bobby. (And I've told you this before.) You cannot live on
cigarettes. You may feel *good,* you may feel *fine,* but something's getting overworked, and you are going to pay for it.

Now: What do you see me eat when I come in here every
day?

BOB: Coffee.

DON: Come on, Bob, don't fuck with me. I *drink* a little coffee . . . but what do I *eat?*

BOB: Yogurt.

DON: Why?

BOB: Because it's good for you.

DON: You're goddamn right. And it wouldn't kill you to take a
vitamin

BOB: They're too expensive.

DON: Don't worry about it. You should just take 'em.

BOB: I can't afford 'em.

DON: Don't worry about it.

BOB: You'll buy some for me?

DON: Do you need 'em?

BOB: *Yeah*.

DON: Well, then, I'll get you some. What do you *think*?

BOB: Thanks, Donny.

DON: It's for your own good. Don't thank *me* . . .

BOB: Okay.

DON: I just can't use you in here like a zombie.

BOB: I just went around the back.

DON: I don't care. Do you see? Do you see what I'm getting at?

> *Pause*.

BOB: Yeah.

> *Pause*.

DON: Well, we'll see.

BOB: I'm sorry, Donny.

DON: Well, we'll see.

TEACH *(appears in the doorway and enters the store)*: Good morning.

BOB: Morning, Teach.

TEACH *(walks around the store a bit in silence)*: Fuckin' Ruthie, fuckin' Ruthie, fuckin' Ruthie, fuckin' Ruthie, fuckin' Ruthie.

DON: What?

TEACH: Fuckin' *Ruthie* . . .

DON: . . . yeah?

TEACH: I come into the Riverside to get a cup of *coffee*, right? I sit down at the table Grace and Ruthie.

DON: Yeah.

TEACH: I'm gonna order just a cup of coffee.

DON: Right.

TEACH: So Grace and Ruthie's having breakfast, and they're done. *Plates . . . crusts* of stuff all over . . . So we'll shoot the shit.

DON: Yeah.

TEACH: Talk about the *game* . . .

DON: . . . yeah.

TEACH: . . . *so* on. Down I sit. "Hi, hi." I take a piece of toast off Grace's plate . . .

DON: . . . uh-huh . . .

TEACH: ︰. . and she goes "Help yourself."

Help myself.

I should help myself to half a piece of toast it's four slices for a quarter. I should have a nickel *every* time we're over at the game, I pop for coffee . . . cigarettes . . . a *sweet roll,* never say word.

"Bobby, see who wants what." Huh? A fucking *roast-beef* sandwich. *(To* BOB*)* Am I right? *(To* DON*)* Ahh, shit. We're sitting down, how many times do I pick up the check? But (No!) because I never go and make a big *thing* out of it—it's no big thing—and flaunt like "This one's on me" like some bust-out asshole, but I naturally assume that I'm with friends, and don't forget who's who when someone gets *behind* a half a yard or needs some help with (huh?) some fucking rent, or drops enormous piles of money at the track, or someone's *sick* or something . . .

DON *(to* BOB*):* This is what I'm talking about.

TEACH: Only (and I tell you this, Don). Only, and I'm not, I don't think, casting anything on anyone: from the mouth of a Southern bulldyke asshole ingrate of a vicious nowhere cunt can this trash come. *(To* BOB*)* And I take nothing back, and I know you're close with them.

BOB: With Grace and Ruthie?

TEACH: Yes.

BOB: (I like 'em.)

TEACH: I have always treated everybody more than fair, and never gone around complaining. Is this true, Don?

DON: Yup.

TEACH: Someone is *against* me, that's their problem . . . I can look out for myself, and I don't got to fuck around behind somebody's back, I don't like the way they're treating me. (Or pray some brick *safe* falls and hits them on the head, they're walking down the street.)

But to have that shithead turn, in one breath, every fucking sweet roll that I ever ate with them into *ground glass* (I'm wondering were they eating it and thinking "This guy's an idiot to blow a fucking *quarter* on his friends" . . .)

. . . this hurts me, Don.

This hurts me in a way I don't know what the fuck to do.

Pause.

DON: You're probably just upset.

TEACH: You're fuckin' A I'm upset. I am *very* upset, Don.

DON: They got their problems, too, Teach.

TEACH: *I* would like to have their problems.

DON: All I'm saying, nothing *personal* . . . they were probably, uh, *talking* about something.

TEACH: Then let them talk about it, then. No, I am sorry, Don, I cannot brush this off. They treat me like an asshole, they are an asshole.

Pause.

The only way to teach these people is to kill them.

Pause.

DON: You want some coffee?

TEACH: I'm not hungry.

DON: Come on, I'm sending Bobby to the Riverside.

TEACH: (Fuckin' joint . . .)

DON: Yeah.

TEACH: (They harbor *assholes* in there . . .)

DON: Yeah. Come on, Teach, what do you want? Bob?

BOB: Yeah?

DON *(to* TEACH*):* Come on, he's going anyway. *(To* BOB, *handing him a bill)* Get me a Boston, and go for the yogurt.

BOB: What kind?

DON: You know, plain, and, if they don't got it, uh, something else. And get something for yourself.

BOB: What?

DON: Whatever you want. But get something to *eat,* and whatever you want to drink, and get Teacher a coffee.

BOB: Boston, Teach?

TEACH: No.

BOB: What?

TEACH: Black.

BOB: Right.

DON: And something for yourself to eat. *(To* TEACH*)* He doesn't want to eat.

TEACH *(to* BOB*):* You got to eat (And this is what I'm saying at The Riverside.)

Pause.

BOB: (Black coffee.)

DON: And get something for yourself to eat. *(To* TEACH*)* What do you want to eat? An English muffin? *(To* BOB*)* Get Teach an English muffin.

TEACH: I don't want an English muffin.

DON: Get him an English muffin, and make sure they give you jelly.

TEACH: I don't want an English muffin.

DON: What do you want?

TEACH: I don't want anything.

BOB: Come on, Teach, eat something.

> *Pause.*

DON: You'll feel better you eat something, Teach.

> *Pause.*

TEACH *(to* BOB*)*: Tell 'em to give you an order of bacon, real dry, real crisp.

BOB: Okay.

TEACH: And tell the broad if it's for me she'll give you more.

BOB: Okay.

DON: Anything else you want?

TEACH: No.

DON: A cantaloupe?

TEACH: I never eat cantaloupe.

DON: No?

TEACH: It gives me the runs.

DON: Yeah?

TEACH: And tell him he shouldn't say anything to Ruthie.

DON: He wouldn't.

TEACH: No? No, you're right. I'm sorry, Bob.

BOB: It's okay.

TEACH: I'm upset.

BOB: It's okay, Teach.

>   *Pause.*

TEACH: Thank you.

BOB: You're welcome.

>   BOB *starts to exit.*

DON: And the plain if they got it.

BOB: I will. *(Exits.)*

DON: He wouldn't say anything.

TEACH: What the fuck do *I* care . . .

>   *Pause.*

Cunt.

>   *Pause.*

There is not one loyal bone in that bitch's body.

DON: How'd you finally do last night?

TEACH: This has nothing to do with that.

DON: No, I know. I'm just saying . . . for *talk* . .

TEACH: Last night? You were here, Don.

>   *Pause.*

How'd *you* do?

DON: Not well.

TEACH: Mmm.

DON: The only one won any money, Fletch and Ruthie.

TEACH *(Pause)*: Cunt had to win two hundred dollars.

DON: She's a good card player.

TEACH: She is *not* a good card player, Don. She is a mooch and she is a locksmith and she plays like a woman.

>   *Pause.*

Fletcher's a card player, I'll give him that. But *Ruthie* . . . I mean, *you* see how she fucking plays . . .

DON: Yeah.

TEACH: And always with that cunt on her shoulder.

DON: Grace?

TEACH: Yes.

DON: Grace is her partner.

TEACH: Then let her *be* her partner, then. (You see what I'm talking about?) Everyone, they're sitting at the table and then Grace is going to walk around . . . fetch an *ashtray* . . . go for *coffee* . . . this . . . and everybody's all they aren't going to hide their cards, and they're going to make a show how they don't hunch *over*, and like that. I don't give a shit. I say the broad's her fucking partner, and she walks in back of me I'm going to hide my hand.

DON: Yeah.

TEACH: And I say anybody doesn't's out of their mind.

    Pause.

We're talking about money for chrissake, huh? We're talking about cards. Friendship is friendship, and a wonderful thing, and I am all for it. I have never said different, and you know me on this point.

Okay.

But let's just keep it *separate* huh, let's just keep the two apart, and maybe we can deal with each other like some human beings.

    Pause.

This is all I'm saying, Don. I know you got a soft spot in your heart for Ruthie . . .

DON: . . . yeah?

TEACH: I know you like the broad and Grace and, Bob, I know he likes 'em too.

DON: (He likes 'em.)

TEACH: And I like 'em too. (I know, I know.) I m not averse to this. I'm not averse to sitting down. (I know we *will* sit down.) These things happen, I'm not saying that they don't . . . and yeah, yeah, yeah, I know I lost a bundle at the game and blah blah blah.

> *Pause.*

But all I ever ask (and I would say this to her face) is only she remembers who is who and not to go around with *her* or Gracie either with this attitude. "The Past is Past, and this is Now, and so Fuck You."

You see?

DON: Yes.

> *Long pause.*

TEACH: So what's new?

DON: Nothing.

TEACH: Same old shit, huh?

DON: Yup.

TEACH: You seen my hat?

DON: No. Did you leave it here?

TEACH: Yeah.

> *Pause.*

DON: You ask them over at The Riv?

TEACH: I left it here.

> *Pause.*

DON: Well, you left it here, it's here.

TEACH: You seen it?

DON: No.

> *Pause.*

TEACH: Fletch been in?

DON: No.

TEACH: Prolly drop in one or so, huh?

DON: Yeah, You know. You never know with Fletcher.

TEACH: No.

DON: He might drop in the *morning* . .

TEACH: Yeah.

DON: And then he might, he's gone for ten or fifteen days you never know he's gone.

TEACH: Yeah.

DON: Why?

TEACH: I want to talk to him.

DON *(Pause)*: Ruth would know.

TEACH: You sure you didn't seen my hat?

DON: I didn't see it. No.

> *Pause.*

Ruthie might know.

TEACH: (Vicious dyke.)

DON: Look in the john.

TEACH: It isn't in the john. I wouldn't leave it there.

DON: Do you got something up with Fletch?

TEACH: No. Just I have to talk to him.

DON: He'll probably show up.

TEACH: Oh yeah . . . *(Pause. Indicating objects on the counter)* What're *these*?

DON: Those?

TEACH: Yeah.

DON: They're from 1933.

TEACH: From the thing?

DON: Yeah.

Pause.

TEACH: Nice.

DON: They had a whole market in 'em. Just like anything. They license out the shit and everybody makes it.

TEACH: Yeah? (I knew that.)

DON: Just like now. They had *combs,* and *brushes* . . . you know, brushes with the thing on 'em . . .

TEACH: Yeah. I know. They had . . . uh . . . what? Clothing too, huh?

DON: I think. Sure. Everything. And there're guys they just collect the stuff.

TEACH: They got that much of it around?

DON: *Shit* yes. (It's not that long ago.) The thing, it ran two years, and they had (*I* don't know) all kinds of people every year they're buying everything that they can lay their hands on that they're going to take it back to Buffalo to give it, you know, to their aunt, and it mounts up.

TEACH: What does it go for?

DON: The compact?

TEACH: Yeah.

DON: Aah . . . (*You* want it?)

TEACH: No.

DON: Oh. I'm just asking. I mean, *you* want it . . .

TEACH: No. I mean somebody walks *in* here . . .

DON: Oh. Somebody walks *in* here . . . (This shit's fashionable . . .)

TEACH: (I don't doubt it.)

DON: . . . and they're gonna have to go like fifteen bucks.

TEACH: You're fulla shit.

DON: My word of honor.

TEACH: No shit.

DON: Everything like that.

TEACH: (A bunch of fucking thieves.)

DON: Yeah. Everything.

TEACH *(snorts)*: What a bunch of crap, huh?

DON: *Oh* yeah.

TEACH: Every goddamn thing.

DON: Yes.

TEACH: If I kept the stuff that I threw *out* . . .

DON: . . . yes.

TEACH: I would be a wealthy man today. I would be cruising on some European yacht.

DON: Uh-huh.

TEACH: (Shit my father used to keep in his *desk* drawer.)

DON: (My father, too.)

TEACH: (The *basement* . . .)

DON: (Uh-huh.)

TEACH: (Fuckin' toys in the back*yard*, for chrissake . . .)

DON: (Don't even talk about it.)

TEACH: It's . . . I don't know.

    Pause.

You want to play some gin?

DON: Maybe later.

TEACH: Okay.

    Pause.

I dunno.

    Pause.

Fucking *day* . . .

    Pause.

Fucking *weather* . . .

> *Pause.*

DON: You think it's going to rain?

TEACH: Yeah. I do. Later.

DON: Yeah?

TEACH: Well, *look* at it.

> BOB *appears, carrying a paper bag with coffee and foodstuffs in it.*

Bobby, Bobby, Bobby, Bobby, Bobby.

BOB: Ruthie isn't mad at you.

TEACH: She isn't?

BOB: No.

TEACH: How do you know?

BOB: I found out.

TEACH: How?

BOB: I talked to her.

TEACH: You talked to her.

BOB: Yes.

TEACH: I asked you you weren't going to.

BOB: Well, she asked me.

TEACH: What?

BOB: That were you over here.

TEACH: What did you tell her?

BOB: You were here.

TEACH: Oh. *(He looks at* DON.*)*

DON: What did you say to her, Bob?

BOB: Just Teach was here.

DON: And is she coming over here?

BOB: I don't think so. (They had the plain.)

DON *(to* TEACH*)*: So? (This is all right.)
(*To* BOB) All right, Bob.

   He looks at TEACH.

TEACH: That's all right, Bob. (*To self*) (Everything's all right to someone . . .)

   DON *takes bag and distributes contents to appropriate recipients.*

(*To* DON) You shouldn't eat that shit.

DON: Why?

TEACH: It's just I have a feeling about health foods.

DON: It's not health foods, Teach. It's only yogurt.

TEACH: That's not health foods?

DON: No. They've had it forever.

TEACH: Yogurt?

DON: Yeah. They used to joke about it on "My Little Margie." (*To* BOB) (Way before your time.)

TEACH: Yeah?

DON: Yeah.

TEACH: What the fuck. A little bit can't hurt you.

DON: It's *good* for you.

TEACH: Okay, okay. Each one his own opinion. (*Pause. To* BOB) Was Fletcher over there?

BOB: No.

DON: Where's my coffee?

BOB: It's not there?

DON: No.

   Pause.

BOB: I told 'em specially to put it in.

DON: Where *is* it?

BOB: They forgot it.

>   *Pause.*

> I'll go back and get it.

DON: Would you mind?

BOB: No.

>   *Pause.*

DON: You gonna get it?

BOB: Yeah.

>   *Pause.*

DON: What, Bob?

BOB: Can I talk to you?

>   *Pause.* DON *goes to* BOB.

DON: What is it?

BOB: I saw him.

DON: Who?

BOB: The guy.

DON: You saw the guy?

BOB: Yes.

DON: That I'm talking about?

BOB: Yes.

DON: Just now?

BOB: Yeah. He's going somewhere.

DON: He is.

BOB: Yeah. He's puttin' a suitcase in the car.

DON: The guy, or both of 'em?

BOB: Just him.

DON: He got in the car he drove off??

BOB: He's coming down the stairs . . .

DON: Yeah.

BOB: And he's got the suitcase . . .

> DON *nods.*

He gets in the car . . .

DON: Uh-huh . . .

BOB: He drives away.

DON: So where is she?

BOB: He's goin' to pick her up.

DON: What was he wearing?

BOB: Stuff. Traveling clothes.

DON: Okay.

> *Pause.*

Now you're talking. You see what I mean?

BOB: Yeah.

DON: All right.

BOB: And he had a coat, too.

DON: Now you're talking.

BOB: Like a raincoat.

DON: Yeah.

> *Pause.*

Good.

> *Pause.*

BOB: Yeah, he's gone.

DON: Bob, go get me that coffee, do you mind?

BOB: No.

DON: What did you get yourself to eat?

BOB: I didn't get anything.

DON: Well, get me my coffee, and get yourself something to eat, okay?

BOB: Okay. (Good.) *(Exits.)*

    Pause.

DON: How's your bacon?

TEACH: Aaaahh, they always fuck it up.

DON: Yeah.

TEACH: This time they fucked it up too burnt.

DON: Mmmm.

TEACH: You got to be breathing on their neck.

DON: Mmmm.

TEACH: Like a lot of things.

DON: Uh-huh.

TEACH: *Any* business . . .

DON: Yeah.

TEACH: You want it run right, *be* there.

DON: Yeah.

TEACH: Just like you.

DON: What?

TEACH: Like the shop.

DON: Well, no one's going to run it, I'm not here.

    Pause.

TEACH: No.

    Pause.

  You have to be here.

DON: Yeah.

TEACH: It's a one-man show.

DON: Uh-huh.

Pause.

TEACH: So what is this thing with the kid?

Pause.

I mean, is it anything, uh . . .

DON: It's nothing . . . *you* know . .

TEACH: Yeah.

Pause.

It's *what* . . . ?

DON: You know, it's just some *guy* we spotted.

TEACH: Yeah. Some *guy.*

DON: Yeah.

TEACH: (Some guy . . .)

DON: Yeah.

Pause.

What time is it?

TEACH: Noon.

DON: (Noon.) (Fuck.)

TEACH: What?

Pause.

DON: You parked outside?

TEACH: Yeah.

DON: Are you okay on the meter?

TEACH: Yeah. The broad came by already.

Pause.

DON: Good.

Pause.

TEACH: Oh, yeah, she came by.

DON: Good.

TEACH: You want to tell me what this thing is?

DON *(Pause)*: The thing?

TEACH: Yeah.

> *Pause.*

What is it?

DON: Nothing.

TEACH: No? What is it, jewelry?

DON: No. It's nothing.

TEACH: Oh.

DON: You know?

TEACH: Yeah.

> *Pause.*

Yeah. No. I don't know

> *Pause.*

Who am I, a *police*man . . . I'm making conversation, huh?

DON: Yeah.

TEACH: Huh?

> *Pause.*

'Cause you know I'm just asking for talk.

DON: Yeah. I know. Yeah, okay.

TEACH: And I can live without this.

DON *(reaches for phone)*: Yeah. I know. Hold on, I'll tell you.

TEACH: Tell me if you *want* to, Don.

DON: I want to, Teach.

TEACH: Yeah?
DON: Yeah.

> *Pause.*

TEACH: Well, I'd fucking *hope* so. Am I wrong?

DON: No. No. You're right.

TEACH: I *hope* so.

DON: No, hold on; I gotta make this call.

TEACH: Well, all right. So what is it, jewelry?

DON: No.

TEACH: What?

DON: Coins.

TEACH: (Coins.)

DON: Yeah. Hold on, I gotta make this call.

> DON *hunts for a card, dials telephone.*

(Into phone) Hello? This is Donny Dubrow. We were talking the other day. Lookit, sir, if I could get ahold of some of that stuff you were interested in, would you be interested in some of it?

> *Pause.*

Those *things* . . . *Old,* yeah.

> *Pause.*

Various pieces of various types.

> *Pause.*

Tonight. Sometime late. Are they *what* . . . ! ! ? ? Yes, but I don't *see* what kind of a question is that (at the prices we're talking about . . .)

> *Pause.*

No, hey, no, I understand *you* . . .

> *Pause.*

Sometime late.

> *Pause.*

One hundred percent.

> *Pause.*

I feel the same. All right. Good-bye. *(Hangs up.)* Fucking
asshole.

TEACH: Guys like that, I like to fuck their wives.

DON: I don't blame you.

TEACH: Fucking *jerk* . . .

DON: (I swear to God . . .)

TEACH: That guy's a collector?

DON: Who?

TEACH: The phone guy.

DON: Yeah.

TEACH: And the other guy?

DON: We spotted?

TEACH: Yeah.

DON: Him, too.

TEACH: So you hit him for his coins.

DON: Yeah.

TEACH: —And you got a buyer in the phone guy.

DON: (Asshole.)

TEACH: The thing is you're not sitting with the shit.

DON: No.

TEACH: The guy's an asshole or he's not, what do you care? It's
business.

    Pause.

DON: You're right.

TEACH: The guy with the suitcase, he's the mark.

DON: Yeah.

TEACH: How'd you find him?

DON: In here.

TEACH: Came in here, huh?

DON: Yeah.

TEACH: (No shit.)

Pause.

DON: He comes in here one day, like a week ago.

TEACH: For what?

DON: Just browsing. So he's looking in the case, he comes up and with this *buffalo-head* nickel . . .

TEACH: Yeah . . .

DON: From nine*teen*-something. (I don't know. I didn't even know it's there . . .)

TEACH: Uh-huh . . .

DON: . . . and he goes, "How much would that be?"

TEACH: Uh-huh . . .

DON: So I'm about to go, "Two bits," jerk that I am, but something tells me to shut up, so I go, "You tell me."

TEACH: Always good business.

DON: *Oh* yeah.

TEACH: How wrong can you go?

DON: That's what I mean, so then he thinks a minute, and he tells me he'll just *shop* a bit.

TEACH: Uh-huh . . . (*Stares out of window.*)

DON: And so he's *shopping* . . . What?

TEACH: Some cops.

DON: Where?

TEACH: At the corner.

DON: What are they doing?

TEACH: Cruising.

Pause.

DON: They turn the corner?

TEACH *(waits)*: *Yeah.*

> *Pause.*

DON: . . . And so he's shopping. And he's picking up a beat-up *mirror* . . . an old *kid's* toy . . . a *shaving* mug . . .

TEACH: . . . right . . .

DON: Maybe five, six things, comes to eight bucks. I get 'em and I put 'em in a box and then he tells me he'll go fifty dollars for the nickel.

TEACH: No.

DON: Yeah. So I tell him (get this), "Not a chance."

TEACH: (Took balls.)

DON: (Well, what-the-fuck . . .)

TEACH: (No, I mean it.)

DON: (I took a chance.)

TEACH: (You're goddamn right.)

> *Pause.*

DON *(shrugs)*: So I say, "Not a chance," he tells me eighty is his highest offer.

TEACH: (I knew it.)

DON: Wait. So I go, "Ninety-five."

TEACH: Uh-huh.

DON: We settle down on ninety, *takes* the nickel, leaves the box of shit.

TEACH: He pay for it?

DON: The box of shit?

TEACH: Yeah.

DON: No.

> *Pause.*

TEACH: And so what was the nickel?

DON: *I* don't know . . . some rarity.

TEACH: Ninety dollars for a nickel.

DON: Are you kidding, Teach? I bet it's worth five *times* that.

TEACH: Yeah, huh?

DON: Are you kidding me, the guy is going to come in here, he plunks down ninety bucks like nothing. *Shit* yeah.

    Pause.

TEACH: Well, what the fuck, it didn't cost you anything.

DON: That's not the point. The next day back he comes and he goes through the whole bit again. He looks at *this*, he looks at *that*, it's a nice *day* . . .

TEACH: Yeah . . .

DON: And he tells me he's the guy was in here yesterday and bought the buffalo off me and do I maybe have some other articles of interest.

TEACH: Yeah.

DON: And so I tell him, "Not offhand." He says that could I get in touch with him, I get some in, so I say "sure," he leaves his card, I'm s'posed to call him anything crops up.

TEACH: Uh-huh.

DON: He comes in here like I'm his fucking doorman.

TEACH: Mmmm.

DON: He takes me off my coin and will I call him if I find another one.

TEACH: Yeah.

DON: Doing me this favor by just coming in my shop.

TEACH: Yeah.

    Pause.

Some people never change.

DON: Like he has done me this big favor by just coming in my shop.

TEACH: Uh-huh. (You're going to get him now.)

DON: (You know I am.) So Bob, we kept a lookout on his place, and that's the shot.

TEACH: And who's the chick?

DON: What chick?

TEACH: You're asking Bob about.

DON: Oh yeah. The guy, he's married. I mean (*I* don't know.) We *think* he's married. They got two names on the bell. . . . Anyway, he's living with this chick, *you* know . . .

TEACH: What the hell.

DON: . . . and you should see this chick.

TEACH: Yeah, huh?

DON: She is a knockout. I mean, she is *real* nice-lookin', Teach.

TEACH: (Fuck *him* . . .)

DON: The other day, last Friday like a week ago, Bob runs in, lugs me out to look at 'em, they're going out on bicycles. The ass on this broad, un-be-fucking-lievable in these bicycling shorts sticking up in the air with these short handlebars.

TEACH: (Fuckin' *fruits* . . .)

    Pause.

DON: So that's it. We keep an eye on 'em. They both work. . . . (Yesterday he rode his bicycle to work.)

TEACH: He didn't.

DON: Yeah.

TEACH (*snorts*): (With the three-piece suit, huh?)

DON: I didn't see 'em. Bobby saw 'em.

    Pause.

And that's the shot. Earl gets me in touch the phone guy, he's this coin collector, and that's it.

TEACH: It fell in your lap.

DON: Yeah.

TEACH: You're going in tonight.

DON: It looks that way.

TEACH: And who's going in?

Pause.

DON: Bobby.

Pause.

He's a good kid, Teach.

TEACH: He's a great kid, Don. You know how I feel about the kid.

Pause.

I *like* him.

DON: He's doing good.

TEACH: I can see **that**.

Pause.

But I gotta say something here.

DON: What?

TEACH: Only this—and I don't think I'm *getting* at anything—

DON: What?

TEACH *(Pause)*: Don't send the kid in.

DON: I shouldn't send Bobby in?

TEACH: No. (Now, just wait a second.) Let's siddown on this. What are we saying here? Loyalty.

Pause.

You know how I am on this. This is great. This is admirable.

DON: What?

TEACH: This loyalty. This is swell. It turns my heart the things that you do for the kid.

DON: What do I do for him, Walt?

TEACH: Things. Things, you know what I mean.

DON: No. I don't do anything for him.

TEACH: In your mind you don't, but the things, I'm saying, that you actually go *do* for him. This is fantastic. All I mean, a guy can be too loyal, Don. Don't be dense on this. What are we saying here? Business.

I mean, the guy's got you're taking his high-speed blender and a Magnavox, you send the kid in. You're talking about a real *job* . . . they don't come in right away and know they been *had* . . .

You're talking maybe a safe, certainly a good lock or two, and you need a guy's looking for valuable shit, he's not going to mess with the stainless steel silverware, huh, or some digital clock.

   Pause.

We both know what we're saying here. We both know we're talking about some job needs more than the kid's gonna skin-pop go in there with a *crowbar* . . .

DON: I don't want you mentioning that.

TEACH: It slipped out.

DON: You know how I feel on that.

TEACH: Yes. And I'm sorry, Don. I admire that. All that I'm saying, don't confuse business with pleasure.

DON: But I don't want that talk, only, Teach.

   Pause.

You understand?

TEACH: I more than understand, and I apologize.

   Pause.

I'm sorry.

DON: That's the only thing.

TEACH: All right. But I tell you. I'm glad I said it.

DON: Why?

TEACH: 'Cause it's best for these things to be out in the open.

DON: But I don't want it in the open.

TEACH: Which is why I apologized.

> *Pause.*

DON: You know the fucking kid's clean. He's trying hard, he's working hard, and you leave him alone.

TEACH: Oh yeah, he's trying *real* hard.

DON: And he's no dummy, Teach.

TEACH: Far from it. All I'm saying, the job is beyond him. Where's the shame in this? This is not jacks, we get up to go home we give everything back. Huh? You want this fucked up?

> *Pause.*

All that I'm saying, there's the least *chance* something might fuck up, you'd get the law down, you would take the shot, and couldn't find the coins *whatever:* if you see the least chance, you cannot afford to take that chance! Don? *I* want to go in there and gut this motherfucker. Don? Where is the shame in this? You take care of him, *fine.* (Now this is loyalty.) But Bobby's got his own best interests, too. And you cannot afford (and simply as a *business* proposition) you cannot afford to take the chance.

(Pause. TEACH *picks up a strange object.)* What is this?

DON: That?

TEACH: Yes.

DON: It's a thing that they stick in dead pigs keep their legs apart all the blood runs out.

> TEACH *nods. Pause.*

TEACH: Mmmm.

Pause.

DON: I set it up with him.

TEACH: "You set it up with him." . . . You set it up and then you told him.

Long pause.

DON: I gave Earl ten percent.

TEACH: Yeah? for what?

DON: The connection.

TEACH: So ten off the top: forty-five, forty-five.

Pause.

DON: And Bobby?

TEACH: A hundred. A hundred fifty . . . we hit big . . . *whatever.*

DON: And *you* what?

TEACH: The *shot.* I *go,* I go *in* . . . I bring the stuff *back* (or wherever . . .)

Pause.

DON: And what do I do?

TEACH: You mind the fort.

Pause.

DON: Here?

TEACH: Well, yeah . . . this is the fort.

Pause.

DON: (You know, this is real classical money we're talking about.)

TEACH: I know it. You think I'm going to fuck with Chump Change?

Pause.

So tell me.

DON: Well, hold on a second. I mean, we're still talking.

TEACH: I'm sorry. I thought we were done talking.

DON: No.

TEACH: Well, then, let's talk some more. You want to bargain? You want to mess with the points?

DON: No. I just want to think for a second.

TEACH: Well, you think, but here's a helpful hint. Fifty percent of some money is better than ninety percent of some broken *toaster* that you're gonna have, you send the kid in. (Which is providing he don't trip the alarm in the *first* place . . .) Don? You don't even know what the *thing* is on this. Where he lives. They got alarms? What *kind* of alarms? What kind of *this* . . ? And what if (God forbid) the *guy* walks in? Somebody's nervous, whacks him with a table lamp—you wanna get touchy—and you can take your ninety dollars from the nickel shove it up your ass— the good it did you—and you wanna know *why*? (And I'm not *saying* anything . . .) because you didn't take the time to go first-class.

> BOB *re-enters with a bag.*

Hi, Bob.

BOB: Hi, Teach.

> *Pause.*

DON: You get yourself something to eat?

BOB: I got a piece of pie and a Pepsi.

> BOB *and* DON *extract foodstuffs and eat.*

DON: Did they charge you again for the coffee?

BOB: For your coffee?

DON: Yes.

BOB: They charged me this time. I don't know if they charged me last time, Donny.

DON: It's okay.

> *Pause.*

TEACH *(to* BOB*)*: How is it out there?

BOB: It's okay.

TEACH: Is it going to rain?

BOB: Today?

TEACH: Yeah.

BOB: I don't know.

> *Pause.*

TEACH: Well, what do you think?

BOB: It might.

TEACH: You think so, huh?

DON: Teach . . .

TEACH: What? I'm not saying anything.

BOB: What?

TEACH: I don't think I'm saying anything here.

> *Pause.*

BOB: It *might* rain.

> *Pause.*

I think *later.*

TEACH: How's your pie?

BOB: Real good.

TEACH *(holds up the dead-pig leg-spreader)*: You know what this is?

> *Pause.*

BOB: Yeah.

TEACH: What is it?

BOB: I know what it is.

TEACH: What?

BOB: I know.

Pause.

TEACH: Huh?

BOB: What?

TEACH: Things are what they are.

DON: Teach . . .

TEACH: What?

DON: We'll do this later.

BOB: I got to ask you something.

TEACH: Sure, that makes a difference.

DON: We'll just do it later.

TEACH: Sure.

BOB: Uh, Don?

DON: What?

> *Pause.*

BOB: I got to talk to you.

DON: Yeah? What?

BOB: I'm wondering on the thing that maybe I could have a little bit up front.

> *Pause.*

DON: Do you *need* it?

BOB: I don't *need* it . . .

DON: How much?

BOB: I was thinking that maybe you might let me have like fifty or something.

> *Pause.*

To sort of *have* . . .

TEACH: You got any cuff links?

DON: Look in the case. *(To* BOB*)* What do you need it for?

BOB: Nothing.

DON: Bob . . .

BOB: You can trust me.

DON: It's not a question of that. It's not a question I go around trusting you, Bob . . .

BOB: What's the question?

TEACH: Procedure.

DON: Hold on, Teach.

BOB: I got him all spotted.

> *Pause.*

TEACH: Who?

BOB: Some guy.

TEACH: Yeah?

BOB: Yeah.

TEACH: Where's he live?

BOB: Around.

TEACH: Where? Near here?

BOB: No.

TEACH: No?

BOB: He lives like on Lake Shore Drive.

TEACH: He does.

BOB: Yeah.

TEACH *(Pause)*: What have you got, a job cased?

BOB: I just went for coffee.

TEACH: But you didn't *get* the coffee.

> *Pause.*

Now, did you?

BOB: No.

TEACH: Why?

DON: Hold on, Teach. Bob . . .

BOB: What?

DON: You know what?

BOB: No.

DON: I was thinking, you know, we might hold off on this thing.

>*Pause.*

BOB: You wanna hold *off* on it?

DON: I was thinking that we might.

BOB: Oh.

DON: And, on the money, I'll give you . . . forty, you owe me twenty, and, for now, keep twenty for spotting the guy.

>*Pause.*

Okay?

BOB: Yeah.

>*Pause.*

You don't want me to do the job?

DON: That's what I *told* you. What am I telling you?

BOB: I'm not going to do it.

DON: Not *now*. We aren't going to do it now.

BOB: We'll do it later on?

DON *(shrugs)*: But I'm giving you twenty just for spotting the guy.

BOB: I need fifty, Donny.

DON: Well, I'm giving you forty.

BOB: You said you were giving me twenty.

DON: No, Bob, I did not. I said I was giving you forty, of *which* you were going to owe me twenty.

>*Pause.*

And you go *keep* twenty.

BOB: I got to give back twenty.

DON: That's the deal.

BOB: When?

DON: Soon. When you got it.

> *Pause.*

BOB: If I don't *get* it soon?

DON: Well, what do you call "soon"?

BOB: I don't know.

DON: Could you get it in a . . . day, or a couple of days or so?

BOB: Maybe. I don't *think* so. Could you let me have fifty?

DON: And you'll give me back thirty?

BOB: I could just give back the twenty.

DON: That's not the deal.

BOB: We could *make* it the deal.

> *Pause.*

Donny? We could *make* it the deal. Huh?

DON: Bob, lookit. Here it is: I give you fifty, next week you pay me back twenty-five.

> *Pause.*

You get to keep twenty-five, you pay me back twenty-five.

BOB: And what about the thing?

DON: Forget about it.

BOB: You tell me when you want me to do it.

DON: I don't know *that* I want you to do it. At this point.

> *Pause.*

You know what I mean?

> *Pause.*

BOB: No.

DON: I mean, I'm *giving* you twenty-five, and I'm saying forget the thing.

BOB: Forget it for me.

DON: Yes.

BOB: Oh.

> *Pause.*

Okay. Okay.

DON: You see what I'm talking about?

BOB: Yes.

DON: Like it never happened.

BOB: I know.

DON: So you see what I'm saying.

BOB: Yes.

> *Pause.*

I'm gonna go.

> *Pause.*

I'll see you later. *(Pause. He looks at* DON.*)*

DON: Oh. *(Reaches in pocket and hands bills to* BOB. *To* TEACH*)* You got two fives?

TEACH: No.

DON *(to* BOB*)*: I got to give you . . . thirty, you owe me back thirty.

BOB: You said you were giving me fifty.

DON: I'm sorry, I'm sorry, Bob, you're absolutely right. *(He gives* BOB *remainder of money.)*

> *Pause.*

BOB: Thank you.

> *Pause.*

I'll see you later, huh, Teach?

TEACH: I'll see you later, Bobby.

BOB: I'll see you, Donny.

DON: I'll see you later, Bob.

BOB: I'll come back later.

DON: Okay.

> BOB *starts to exit.*

TEACH: *See* you.

> *Pause.* BOB *is gone.*

You're only doing the right thing by him, Don.

> *Pause.*

Believe me.

> *Pause.*

It's best for everybody.

> *Pause.*

What's done is done.

> *Pause.*

So let's get started. On the thing. Tell me everything.

DON: Like what?

TEACH: . . . the *guy* . . . where does he *live* . . .

DON: Around the corner.

TEACH: Okay, and he's gone for the weekend.

DON: We don't know.

TEACH: Of course we know. Bob saw him coming out the door. The kid's not going to lie to you.

DON: Well, Bob just saw him coming *out* . . .

TEACH: He had a suitcase, Don, he wasn't going to the A&P . . . He's going for the weekend . . .

Pause.

Don, (Can you cooperate?) Can we get started? Do you want to tell me something about coins?

Pause.

DON: What about 'em?

TEACH: A crash course. What to look for. What to take. What to *not* take (. . . this they can trace) (that isn't *worth* nothing . . .)

Pause.

What looks like what but it's more *valuable* . . . *so* on . . .

DON: First off, I want that nickel back.

TEACH: Donny . . .

DON: No, I know, it's only a fuckin' nickel . . . I mean big deal, huh? But what I'm saying is I only want it back.

TEACH: You're going to get it back. I'm going in there for his coins, what am I going to take 'em all except your nickel? Wake up. Don, let's plan this out. The *spirit* of the thing?

Pause.

Let's not be loose on this. People are *loose,* people pay the price . . .

DON: You're right.

TEACH: (And I like you like a brother, Don.) So let's wake up on this.

Pause.

All right? A man, he walks in here, well-dressed . . . (With a briefcase?)

DON: (No.)

TEACH: All right. . . . comes into a junkshop looking for coins.

Pause.

He spots a valuable nickel hidden in a pile of shit. He farts around, he picks up this, he farts around, he picks up that.

DON: (He wants the nickel.)

TEACH: No shit. He goes to check out, he goes ninety on the nick.

DON: (He would of gone five times that.)

TEACH: (Look, don't kick yourself.) All right, we got a guy knows coins. Where does he keep his coin collection?

DON: Hidden.

TEACH: The man hides his coin collection, we're probably looking the guy has a *study* . . . I mean, he's not the kind of guy to keep it in the *basement* . . .

DON: No.

TEACH: So we're looking for a study.

DON: (A den.)

TEACH: And we're looking, for, he hasn't got a *safe* . . .

DON: Yeah . . . ?

TEACH: . . . he's probably going to keep 'em . . . where?

> *Pause.*

DON: I don't know. His desk drawer.

TEACH: (You open the middle, the rest of 'em pop out?)

DON: (Yeah.)

TEACH: (Maybe.) Which brings up a point.

DON: What?

TEACH: As we're moving the stuff tonight, we can go in like Gangbusters, huh? We don't care we wreck the joint up. So what else? We *take* it, or leave it?

DON: . . . well . . .

TEACH: I'm not talking *cash*, all I mean, what other stuff do we take . . . for our *trouble* . . .

> *Pause.*

DON: I don't know.

TEACH: It's hard to make up rules about this stuff.

DON: (You'll be in there under lots of pressure.)

TEACH: (Not so much.)

DON: (Come on, a little, anyway.)

TEACH: (That's only natural.)

DON: (Yeah.)

TEACH: (It would be unnatural I wasn't tense. A guy who isn't tense, I don't want him on my side.)

DON: (No.)

TEACH: (You know *why*?)

DON: (Yeah.)

TEACH: (Okay, then.) It's good to talk this stuff out.

DON: Yeah.

TEACH: You *have* to talk it out. Bad feelings, misunderstandings happen on a job. You can't get away from 'em, you have to deal with 'em. You want to quiz me on some coins? You want to show some coins to me? *List* prices . . . the blue book . . . ?

DON: You want to see the book?

TEACH: Sure.

DON *(hands large coin-book to* TEACH*)*: I just picked it up last week.

TEACH: Uh-hum.

DON: All the values aren't *current* . . .

TEACH: Uh-huh . . .

DON: *Silver* . . .

TEACH *(looking at book)*: Uh-huh . . .

DON: What's *rarity* . . .

TEACH: Well, that's got to be fairly steady, huh?

DON: I'm saying against what *isn't*.

TEACH: Oh.

DON: But the book gives you a general idea.

TEACH: You've been looking at it?

DON: Yeah.

TEACH: You got to have a feeling for your subject.

DON: The book can give you that.

TEACH: This is what I'm *saying* to you. One thing. Makes all the difference in the world.

DON: What?

TEACH: Knowing what the fuck you're talking about. And it's so rare, Don. *So* rare.

What do you think a 1929 S Lincoln-head penny with the wheat on the back is worth?

> DON *starts to speak.*

Ah! Ah! Ah! Ah! Ah! We got to know what *condition* we're talking about.

DON *(Pause)*: Okay. What condition?

TEACH: *Any* of 'em. You tell me.

DON: Well, pick one.

TEACH: Okay, I'm going to pick an easy one. Excellent condition 1929 S.

DON: It's worth . . . *about* thirty-six dollars.

TEACH: No.

DON: (More?)

TEACH: Well, guess.

DON: Just tell me is it more or less.

TEACH: What do you think?

DON: More.

TEACH: No.

DON: Okay, it's worth, I gotta say . . . eighteen-sixty.

TEACH: No.

DON: Then I give up.

TEACH: Twenty fucking cents.

DON: You're fulla shit.

TEACH: My mother's grave.

DON: Give me that fucking book. *(Business.)* Go beat that.

TEACH: This is what I'm saying, Don, you got to know what you're talking about.

DON: You wanna take the book?

TEACH: Naaa, *fuck* the book. What am I going to do, leaf through the book for hours on end? The important thing is to have the *idea* . . .

DON: Yeah.

TEACH: What was the other one?

DON: What other one?

TEACH: He stole off you.

DON: What do you mean what was it?

TEACH: The *date*, so on.

DON: How the fuck do *I* know?

TEACH *(Pause)*: When you looked it up.

DON: How are you getting in the house?

TEACH: The house?

DON: Yeah.

TEACH: Aah, you go in through a *window* they left open, something.

DON: Yeah.

TEACH: There's always something.

DON: Yeah. What else, if not the window.

TEACH: How the fuck do *I* know?

> *Pause.*

If not the window, something else.

DON: What?

TEACH: We'll see when we get there.

DON: Okay, all I'm asking, what it *might* be.

TEACH: Hey, you didn't warn us we were going to have a quiz . . .

DON: It's just a question.

TEACH: I know it.

> *Pause.*

DON: What is the answer?

TEACH: We're seeing when we get there.

DON: Oh. You can't answer me, Teach?

TEACH: You have your job, I have my job, Don. I am not here to smother you in theory. Think about it.

DON: I am thinking about it. I'd like you to answer my question.

TEACH: Don't push me, Don. Don't front off with me here. I am not other people.

DON: And just what does that mean?

TEACH: Just that nobody's perfect.

DON: They aren't.

TEACH: No.

> *Pause.*

DON: I'm going to have Fletch come with us.

TEACH: Fletch.

DON: Yes.

TEACH: You're having him *come* with us.

DON: Yes.

TEACH: Now you're kidding me.

DON: No.

TEACH: No? Then why do you say this?

DON: With Fletch.

TEACH: Yes.

DON: I want some depth.

TEACH: You want depth on the team.

DON: Yes, I do.

TEACH: So you bring in Fletch.

DON: Yes.

TEACH: 'Cause I don't play your games with you.

DON: We just might need him.

TEACH: We won't.

DON: We might, Teach.

TEACH: We don't need him, Don. We do not need this guy.

> DON *picks up phone.*

What? Are you *calling* him?

> DON *nods.*

DON: It's busy. *(Hangs up.)*

TEACH: He's probably talking on the phone.

DON: Yeah. He probably is.

TEACH: We don't need this guy, Don. We don't need him. I see
your point here, I do. So you're thinking I'm out there
alone, and you're worried I'll rattle, so you ask me how I go
in. I understand. I see this, I do. I could go in the second
floor, climb up a drainpipe. I could *this* . . .

> DON *dials phone again.*

He's talking, he's talking, for chrissake, give him a minute, huh?

> DON *hangs up phone.*

I am hurt, Don.

DON: I'm sorry, Teach.

TEACH: I'm not hurt for me.

DON: Who are you hurt for?

TEACH: Think about it.

DON: We can use somebody watch our rear.

TEACH: You keep your numbers down, you don't *have* a rear. You know what has rears? Armies.

DON: I'm just saying, something goes *wrong* . . .

TEACH: Wrong, wrong, you make your own right and wrong. Hey Biiig fucking deal. The shot is yours, no one's disputing that. We're talking business, let's *talk* business: you think it's good business call Fletch in? To help us.

DON: Yes.

TEACH: Well then okay.

> *Pause.*

Are you sure?

DON: Yeah.

TEACH: All right, if you're *sure* . . .

DON: I'm sure, Teach.

TEACH: Then, all right, then. That's all I worry about.

> *Pause.*

And you're probably right, we could use three of us on the job.

DON: Yeah.

TEACH: Somebody watch for the *cops* . . . work out a *signal* . . .

DON: Yeah.

TEACH: Safety in numbers.

DON: Yeah.

TEACH: Three-men jobs.

DON: Yeah.

TEACH: You, me, Fletcher.

DON: Yeah.

TEACH: A division of labor.

> *Pause.*

(Security. Muscle. Intelligence.) Huh?

DON: Yeah.

TEACH: This means, what, a traditional split. Am I right? We get ten off the top goes to Earl, and the rest, three-way split. Huh? That's what we got? Huh?

DON: Yeah.

TEACH: Well, that's what's right.

> *Pause.*

All right. Lay the shot out for me.

DON: For tonight?

TEACH: Yes.

DON: Okay.

> *Pause.*

I stay here on the phone . . .

TEACH: . . . yeah . . .

DON: . . . for Fletcher . . .

TEACH: Yeah.

DON: We meet, ten-thirty, 'leven, back here.

TEACH: (Back here, the three . . .)

DON: Yeah. And go in.

Pause.

Huh?

TEACH: Yeah. Where?

DON: Around the corner.

TEACH: Yeah.

Pause.

Are you mad at me?

DON: No.

TEACH: Do you want to play gin?

DON: Naaa.

TEACH: Then I guess I'll go home, take a nap, and rest up.
Come back here tonight and we'll take off this fucking fruit's
coins.

DON: Right.

TEACH: I feel like I'm trying to stay *up* to death . . .

DON: You ain't been to sleep since the game?

TEACH: *Shit* no (then that dyke cocksucker . . .)

DON: So go take a nap. You trying to kill yourself?

TEACH: You're right, and you do what you think is right, Don.

DON: I got to, Teach.

TEACH: You got to trust your instincts, right or wrong.

DON: I got to.

TEACH: I know it. I know you do.

Pause.

Anybody wants to get in touch with me, I'm over the hotel.

DON: Okay.

TEACH: I'm not the *hotel,* I stepped out for coffee, I'll be back
one minute.

DON: Okay.

TEACH: And I'll see you around eleven.

DON: O'*clock.*

TEACH: *Here.*

DON: Right.

TEACH: And don't worry about anything.

DON: I won't.

TEACH: I don't want to hear you're worrying about a god-damned thing.

DON: You won't, Teach.

TEACH: You're sure you want Fletch coming with us?

DON: Yes.

TEACH: All right, then, so long as you're sure.

DON: I'm sure, Teach.

TEACH: Then I'm going to see you tonight.

DON: Goddamn right you are.

TEACH: I am seeing you later.

DON: I know.

TEACH: Good-bye.

DON: Good-bye.

TEACH: I want to make one thing plain before I go, Don. I am not mad at you.

DON: I know.

TEACH: All right, then.

DON: You have a good nap.

TEACH: I will.

> TEACH *exits.*

DON: Fuckin' *business* . . .

> *Lights dim to black.*

ACT II

Don's Resale Shop. 11:15 that evening. The shop is darkened. DON *is alone. He is holding the telephone to his ear.*

DON: Great. Great great great great great.

Pause.

(*Cocksucking* fuckhead . . .)

Pause.

This is greatness.

DON hangs up phone. BOB appears in the door to the shop.

What are you doing here?

BOB: I *came* here.

DON: For what?

BOB: I got to talk to you.

DON: Why?

BOB: Business.

DON: Yeah?

BOB: I need some money.

DON: What for?

BOB: Nothing. I can pay for it.

DON: For what?

BOB: This guy. I found a coin.

DON: A coin?

BOB: A buffalo-head.

DON: Nickel?

BOB: Yeah. You want it?

Pause.

DON: What are you doing here, Bob?

BOB: I need money.

DON *picks up phone and dials. He lets it ring as he talks
to* BOB.

You want it?

DON: What?

BOB: My buffalo.

DON: Lemme look at it.

> *Pause.*

I got to look at it to know do I want it.

BOB: You don't know if you want it?

DON: I probably *want* it . . . what I'm saying, if it's *worth* anything.

BOB: It's a buffalo, it's worth something.

DON: The question is but what. It's just like everything else,
Bob. Like every other fucking thing. (*Pause. He hangs up
phone.)* Were you at The Riv?

BOB: Before.

DON: Is Fletch over there?

BOB: No.

DON: Teach?

BOB: No. Ruth and Gracie was there for a minute.

DON: What the fuck does that mean?

> *Pause.*

BOB: Nothing.

> *Pause.*

Only they were there.

> *Pause.*

I didn't *mean* anything . . . my nickel . . . I can tell you what
it is.

> *Pause.*

I can tell you what it is.

DON: What? What *date* it is? That don't mean shit.

BOB: No?

DON: Come *on*, Bobby? What's important in a coin . . .

BOB: . . . yeah?

DON: What *condition* it's in . . .

BOB: (Great.)

DON: . . . if you can (I don't know . . .) count the hair on the Indian, something. You got to look it up.

BOB: In the book?

DON: Yes.

BOB: Okay. And then you know.

DON: Well, no. What I'm saying, the book is like you use it like an *indicator* (I mean, right off with *silver* prices . . . so on . . .) *(He hangs up phone.)* Shit.

BOB: What?

DON: What do you want for the coin?

BOB: What it's worth only.

DON: Okay, we'll look it up

BOB: But you still don't know.

DON: But you got an idea, Bob. You got an idea you can *deviate* from.

    Pause.

BOB: The other guy went ninety bucks.

DON: He was a fuckin' sucker, Bob.

    Pause.

Am I a sucker? (Bob, I'm busy here. You see?)

BOB: Some coins are worth that.

DON: Oddities, Bob. Freak oddities of nature. What are we

talking about here? The silver? The silver's maybe three times face. You want fifteen cents for it?

BOB: No.

DON: So, okay. So what do you want for it?

BOB: What it's worth.

DON: Let me *see* it.

BOB: Why?

DON: To look in the goddamn . . . Forget it. Forget it. *Don't* let me see it.

BOB: But the book don't *mean* shit.

DON: The book gives us *ideas,* Bob. The book gives us a basis for *comparison.*

Look, we're human beings. We can *talk,* we can negotiate, we can *this* . . . you need money? What do you need?

Pause.

BOB: I *came* here . . .

Pause.

DON: What do you need, Bob?

Pause.

BOB: How come you're in here so late?

DON: We're gonna play cards.

BOB: Who?

DON: Teach and me and Fletcher.

TEACH *enters the store.*

What time is it?

TEACH: Fuck is *he* doing here?

DON: What fucking time is it?

TEACH: Where's Fletcher?

Pause.

Where's Fletcher?

BOB: Hi, Teach.

TEACH *(to* DON*)*: What is he doing here?

BOB: I came in.

DON: Do you know what time it is?

TEACH: What? I'm late?

DON: Damn right you're late.

TEACH: I'm fucked up since my watch broke.

DON: Your watch broke?

TEACH: I just told you that.

DON: When did your watch break?

TEACH: The fuck do *I* know?

DON: Well, you look at it. You want to know your watch broke, all you got to do is look at it.

> *Pause.*

TEACH: I don't have it.

DON: Why not?

TEACH: I took it off when it broke. (What do you *want* here?)

DON: You're going around without a watch.

TEACH: Yes. I am, Donny. What am I, you're my *keeper* all a sudden?

DON: I'm paying you to do a thing, Teach, I expect to know where you are when.

TEACH: Donny. You aren't paying me to do a thing. We are doing something together. I know we are. My watch broke, that is my concern. The *thing* is your and my concern. And the concern of Fletcher. You want to find a reason we should jump all over each other all of a sudden like we work in a *bloodbank*, fine. But it's not good business.

> *Pause.*

And so who knows what time it is offhand? Jerks on the radio? The phone broad?

Pause.

Now, I understand nerves.

DON: There's no fuckin' nerves involved in this. Teach.

TEACH: No, huh?

DON: No.

TEACH: Well, great. That's great, then. So what are we talking about? A little lateness? Some excusable fucking lateness? And a couple of guys they're understandably a bit excited?

Pause.

DON: I don't like it.

TEACH: Then *don't* like it, then. Let's do this. Let's everybody get a writ. I got a case. You got a case. Bobby—I don't know what the fuck *he's* doing here . . .

DON: Leave him alone.

TEACH: Now I'm picking on him.

DON: Leave him alone.

TEACH: What's he doing here?

DON: He came in.

BOB: I found a nickel.

TEACH: Hey, that's fantastic.

BOB: You want to see it?

TEACH: Yes, please let me see it.

BOB *(hands nickel, wrapped in cloth, to* TEACH*)*: I like 'em because of the art on it.

TEACH: Uh-huh.

BOB: Because it *looks* like something.

TEACH *(to* DON*)*: Is this worth anything?

BOB: We don't know yet.

TEACH: Oh.

BOB: We're going to look it up.

TEACH: Oh, what? Tonight?

BOB: I think so.

DON *(hangs up phone)*: Fuck.

TEACH: So where is he?

DON: How the fuck do I know?

TEACH: He said he'd be here?

DON: Yes, he did, Teach.

BOB: Fletcher?

TEACH: So where is he, then? And what's *he* doing here?

DON: Leave him alone. He'll leave.

TEACH: He's going to leave, huh?

DON: Yes.

TEACH: You're sure it isn't like the bowling league, Fletch doesn't show up, we just suit up Bobby, give him a shot, and *he* goes in?

> *Pause.*

Aaah, fuck. I'm sorry. I spoke in anger. I'm sorry, I'm sorry. (Everybody can make mistakes around here but me.) I'm sorry, Bob, I'm very sorry.

BOB: That's okay, Teach.

TEACH: All I meant to say, we'd give you a fuckin' suit, like in football . . .

> *Pause.*

and you'd (You know, like, whatever . . .) and *you'd* go in. *(Pause. To* DON*)* So what do you want me to do? Dress up and lick him all over? I said I was sorry, what's going on here. Huh? In the *first* place. I come in, I'm *late* . . . *he's* here . . .

> *Pause.*

DON: Bobby, I'll see you tomorrow, okay? *(He picks phone up and dials.)*

BOB: I need some money.

TEACH *(digging in pockets)*: What do you need?

BOB: I want to sell the *buffalo* nickel.

TEACH: I'll buy it myself.

BOB: We don't know what it's worth.

TEACH: What do you want for it?

BOB: Fifty dollars.

TEACH: You're outta your fuckin' mind.

> *Pause.*

Look. Here's a fin. Get lost. Okay?

> *Pause.*

BOB: It's worth more than that.

TEACH: How the fuck do you know that?

BOB: I think it is.

> *Pause.*

TEACH: Okay. You keep the fin like a loan. You *keep* the fuckin' nickel, and we'll call it a loan. Now go on. *(He hands nickel back to BOB.)*

DON *(hangs up phone)*: Fuck.

BOB: I need more.

TEACH *(to DON)*: Give the kid a couple of bucks.

DON: What?

TEACH: Give him some money.

DON: What for?

TEACH: The nickel.

> *Pause.*

BOB: We can look in the book tomorrow.

DON *(to* TEACH*)*: You bought the nickel?

TEACH: Don't worry about it. Give him some money. Get him out of here.

DON: How much?

TEACH: What? *I* don't care . . .

DON *(to* BOB*)*: How much . . . *(To* TEACH*)* What the fuck am I giving him money for?

TEACH: Just give it to him.

DON: What? Ten? *(Pause. Digs in pocket, hands bill to* BOB.*)* How is that, Bob? *(Pause. Hands additional bill to* BOB.*)* Okay?

BOB: We'll look it up.

DON: Okay. Huh? We'll see you tomorrow.

BOB: And we'll look it up.

DON: Yes.

BOB *(to* TEACH*)*: You should talk to Ruthie.

TEACH: Oh, I should, huh?

BOB: Yes.

TEACH: Why?

BOB: Because.

> *Pause.*

TEACH: I'll see you tomorrow, Bobby.

BOB: Good-bye, Teach.

TEACH: Good-bye.

DON: Good-bye, Bob.

BOB: Good-bye.

> *Pause.* BOB *exits.*

DON: Fuckin' *kid* . . .

TEACH: So where is Fletcher?

DON: Don't worry. He'll be here.

TEACH: The question is but when. Maybe his watch broke.

DON: Maybe it just did, Teach. Maybe his actual watch broke.

TEACH: And maybe mine didn't, you're saying? You wanna bet? You wanna place a little fucking wager on it? How much money you got in your pockets? I bet you all the money in your pockets against all the money in my pockets, I walk out that door right now, I come back with a broken watch.

    Pause.

DON: Calm down.

TEACH: I am calm. I'm just upset.

DON: I know.

TEACH: So where is he when I'm here?

DON: Don't worry about it.

TEACH: So who's going to worry about it then?

DON: (Shit.)

TEACH: This should go to prove you something.

DON: It doesn't prove anything. The guy's just late.

TEACH: Oh. And I wasn't?

DON: You were late, too.

TEACH: You're fuckin' A I was, and I got bawled out for it.

DON: He's late for a reason.

TEACH: I don't accept it.

DON: That's your privilege.

TEACH: And what was Bob doing here?

DON: He told you. He wanted to sell me the nickel.

TEACH: That's why he came here?

DON: Yes.

TEACH: To sell you the buffalo?

DON: Yes.

TEACH: Where did he get it?

DON: I think from some guy.

TEACH: Who?

>   *Pause.*

DON: I don't know.

>   *Pause.*

TEACH: Where's Fletcher?

DON: I don't know. He'll show up. *(Picks up phone and dials.)*

TEACH: He'll show up.

DON: Yes.

TEACH: He's not here now.

DON: No.

TEACH: You scout the guy's house?

DON: The guy? No.

TEACH: Well, let's do that, then. (He's not home. Hang up.)

DON *(hangs up phone)*: You wanna scout his house.

TEACH: Yeah.

DON: Why? Bob already saw him when he went off with the suitcase.

TEACH: Just to be sure, huh?

DON: Yeah. Okay.

TEACH: You bet. Now we call him up.

DON: We call the guy up.

TEACH: Yeah.

>   *Pause.*

DON: Good idea. *(He picks up phone. Hunts guy's number. Dials. To himself)* We can do this.

TEACH: This is planning. . . . This is preparation. If he answers . . .

DON *shhhhs* TEACH.

I'm telling you what to do if he answers.

DON: What?

TEACH: Hang up. (DON *starts to hang up phone.*) No. Don't hang up. Hang up now. Hang up *now*!

DON *hangs up phone.*

Now look: If he *answers* . . .

DON: . . . yeah?

TEACH: *Don't* arouse his fucking suspicions.

DON: All right.

TEACH: And the odds are he's not there, so when he answers just say you're calling for a wrong fucking *number*, something. Be simple.

Pause.

Give me the phone.

DON *hands* TEACH *the phone.*

Gimme the card.

DON *hands* TEACH *card.*

This is his number? 221—7834?

DON: Yeah.

TEACH *(snorts)*: All right. I dial, I'm calling for somebody named June, and we go interchange on number.

Pause.

We're gonna say like, "Is this 221—7834?"

DON: . . . yeah?

TEACH: And they go, "No." (I mean "—7843." It *is* —7834.)

So we go, very simply, "Is this 221—7843?" and they go "No," and right away the guy is home, we still haven't blown the shot.

DON: Okay.

> TEACH *picks up the phone and dials.*

TEACH *(into phone)*: Hi. Yeah. I'm calling . . . uh . . . is June there?

> *Pause.*

Well, is this 221—7843?

> *Pause.*

It is? Well, look I must of got the number wrong. I'm sorry.

> *He hangs up phone.*

(This is bizarre.) Read me that number.

DON: 221—7834.

TEACH: Right. *(Dials phone. Listens.)* Nobody home. See, this is careful operation . . . *(Pause. Hangs up.)* You wanna try it?

DON: No.

TEACH: I don't mind that you're careful, Don. This doesn't piss me off. What gets me mad, when you get loose.

DON: What do you mean?

TEACH: You know what I mean.

DON: No, I don't.

TEACH: Yes you do. I come in here. The kid's here.

DON: He doesn't know anything.

TEACH: He doesn't.

DON: No.

TEACH: What was he here for, then?

DON: Sell me the buffalo.

TEACH: Sell it tonight.

DON: Yeah.

TEACH: A valuable nickel.

DON: We don't know.

>   *Pause.*

TEACH: Where is Fletch?

DON: I don't know. *(Picks up phone and dials.)*

TEACH: He's not home. He's not home, Don. He's out.

DON *(into phone)*: Hello?

TEACH: He's in?

DON: This is Donny Dubrow.

TEACH: The Riv?

DON: I'm looking for Fletcher.

>   *Pause.*

>   Okay. Thank you. *(He hangs up.)*

TEACH: Cocksucker should be horsewhipped with a horsewhip.

DON: He'll show up.

TEACH: Fucking Riverside, too. (Thirty-seven cents for take-out coffee . . .)

DON: Yeah. *(Picks up phone.)*

TEACH: A lot of nerve you come in there for sixteen years. This is not free enterprise.

DON: No.

TEACH: You know what is free enterprise?

DON: No. What?

TEACH: The freedom . . .

DON: . . . yeah?

TEACH: Of the *Individual* . . .

DON: . . . yeah?

TEACH: To Embark on Any Fucking Course that he sees fit.

DON: Uh-huh . . .

TEACH: In order to secure his honest chance to make a profit. Am I so out of line on this?

DON: No.

TEACH: Does this make me a Commie?

DON: No.

TEACH: The country's *founded* on this, Don. You know this.

DON: Did you get a chance to take a nap?

TEACH: Nap nap nap nap nap. Big deal.

DON *(Pause)*: Yeah.

TEACH: Without this we're just savage shitheads in the wilderness.

DON: Yeah.

TEACH: Sitting around some vicious campfire. That's why *Ruthie* burns me up.

DON: Yeah.

TEACH: (Nowhere dyke . . .) And take those fuckers in the concentration camps. You think they went in there by *choice?*

DON: No.

TEACH: They were *dragged* in there, Don . . .

DON: . . . yeah.

TEACH: Kicking and screaming. *Gimme* that fucking phone.

   TEACH *grabs phone. Listens. Hangs up.*

   He's not home. I say *fuck* the cocksucker.

DON: He'll show up.

TEACH: You believe that?

DON: Yes.

TEACH: Then you are full of shit.

DON: Don't tell me that, Teach. Don't tell me I'm full of shit.

TEACH: I'm sorry. You want me to hold your hand? This is how you keep score. I mean, *we're* all here . . .

DON: Just, I don't want that talk.

TEACH: Don . . . I talk straight to you 'cause I respect you. It's kickass or kissass, Don, and I'd be lying if I told you any different.

DON: And what makes you such an authority on life all of a sudden?

TEACH: My life, Jim. And the way I've lived it.

> *Pause.*

DON: Now what does that mean, Teach?

TEACH: What does that mean?

DON: Yes.

TEACH: What does that *mean*?

DON: Yes.

TEACH: Nothing. Not a thing. All that I'm telling you, the shot is yours. It's one night only. Too many guys know. All I'm saying. Take your shot.

DON: Who knows?

TEACH: You and me.

DON: Yeah.

TEACH: Bob and Fletcher. Earl, the phone guy, Grace and Ruthie, maybe.

DON: Grace and Ruth don't know.

TEACH: Who *knows* they know or not, all that I'm telling you, it's not always so clear what's going on. Like Fletcher and the pig iron, that time.

DON: What was the shot on that?

TEACH: He stole some pig iron off Ruth.

DON: (I *heard* that . . .)

TEACH: That's a fact. A fact stands by itself. And we must face the facts and act on them. You better wake up, Don, right now, or things are going to fall around your *head*, and you are going to turn around to find he's took the joint off by himself.

DON: He would not do that.

TEACH: He would. He is an animal.

DON: He don't have the address.

TEACH: He doesn't know it.

DON: No.

TEACH: Now, that is wise. Then let us go and take what's ours.

DON: We have a deal with the man.

TEACH: With Fletcher.

DON: Yes.

TEACH: We had a deal with Bobby.

DON: What does that mean?

TEACH: Nothing.

DON: It don't.

TEACH: No.

DON: What did you mean by that?

TEACH: I didn't mean a thing.

DON: You didn't.

TEACH: No.

DON: You're full of shit, Teach.

TEACH: I am.

DON: Yes.

TEACH: Because I got the balls to face some facts?

Pause.

You scare me sometimes, Don.

DON: Oh, yeah?

TEACH: Yes. I don't want to go around with you here, things go down, we'll settle when we're done. We have a job to do here. Huh? Forget it. Let's go, come on.

DON: We're waiting for him.

TEACH: Fletcher.

DON: Yes.

TEACH: Why?

DON: Many reasons.

TEACH: Tell me one. You give me one good reason, why we're sitting here, and I'll sit down and never say a word. One reason. One. Go on. I'm listening.

DON: He knows how to get in.

Pause.

TEACH: Good night, Don. *(He starts to go for door.)*

DON: Where are you going?

TEACH: Home.

DON: You're going home.

TEACH: Yes.

DON: Why?

TEACH: You're fucking with me. It's all right.

DON: Hold on. You tell me how I'm fucking with you.

TEACH: Come *on*, Don.

DON: You asked me the one reason.

TEACH: You make yourself ridiculous.

DON: Yeah?

TEACH: Yeah.

DON: Then answer it.

TEACH: What is the question?

DON: Fletch knows how to get in.

TEACH: "Get in." That's your reason?

DON: Yes.

> *Pause.*

TEACH: What the fuck they live in Fort Knox? ("Get in.") *(Snorts.)* You break in a *window*, worse comes to worse you kick the fucking *back door* in. (What do you think this is, the Middle Ages?)

DON: What about he's got a safe?

TEACH: Biiiig fucking deal.

DON: How is that?

TEACH: You want to know about a safe?

DON: Yes.

TEACH: What you do, a *safe* . . . you find the combination.

DON: Where he wrote it down.

TEACH: Yes.

DON: What if he didn't write it down?

TEACH: He wrote it down. He's *gotta* write it down. What happens he forgets it?

DON: What happens he doesn't forget it?

TEACH: He's gotta forget it, Don. Human nature. The point being, even he *doesn't* forget it, *why* does he not forget it?

DON: Why?

TEACH: 'Cause he's got it *wrote down*.

> *Pause.*

That's why he *writes* it down.

> *Pause.*

Huh? Not because he's some fucking turkey can't even remember the combination to his own *safe* . . . but only in the event that (God forbid) he somehow *forgets* it . . . he's got it wrote down.

Pause.

This is common sense.

Pause.

What's the good keep the stuff in the safe, every time he wants to get at it he's got to write away to the manufacturer?

DON: Where does he write it?

TEACH: What difference? *Here* . . . We go in, I find the combination fifteen minutes, tops.

Pause.

There are only just so many places it could be. Man is a creature of habits. Man does not change his habits overnight. This is not like him. (And if he does, he has a very good reason.) Look, Don: You want to remember something (you write it down). Where do you put it?

Pause.

DON: In my wallet.

Pause.

TEACH: *Exactly!*

Pause.

Okay?

DON: What if he didn't write it down?

TEACH: He wrote it down.

DON: I know he did. But just, I'm saying, from *another* instance. Some made-up guy from my imagination.

TEACH: You're saying in the instance of some guy . . .

DON: (Some *other* guy . . .)

TEACH: . . . he didn't write it down?

Pause.

DON: Yes.

TEACH: Well, this is another thing.

Pause.

You *see* what I'm saying?

DON: Yeah.

TEACH: It's another matter. The guy, he's got the shit in the safe, he didn't write it *down* . .

Pause.

Don . . . ?

DON: Yes?

TEACH: How do you know he didn't write it down?

DON: (I'm, you know, making it up.)

Pause.

TEACH: Well, then, this is not based on *fact*.

Pause.

You *see* what I'm saying?

I can sit here and tell you *this*, I can tell you *that*, I can tell you any fucking thing you care to mention, but what is the point?

You aren't telling me he didn't write it down. All that you're saying, you can't *find* it. Which is only natural, as you don't know where to look. All I'm asking for a little trust here.

DON: I don't know.

TEACH: Then you know what? Fuck you. (All day long. Grace and Ruthie Christ) What am I standing here convincing you? What am I doing demeaning myself standing here pleading with you to protect your best interests? I can't believe this, Don. Somebody told me I'd do this for you . . . (For *anybody*) I'd call him a liar. (I'm coming in here to efface myself.) I am not Fletch, Don, no, and you should thank God and fall *down* I'm not. (You're coming in here all the time that "He's so good at cards . . . ") The man is a cheat, Don. He *cheats* at cards—Fletcher, the guy that you're waiting for.

DON: He cheats.

TEACH: Fucking A right, he does.

DON: Where do you get this?

> *Pause.*

You're full of shit, Walt. You're saying Fletch cheats at cards.

> *Pause.*

You've seen him. You've *seen* him he cheats.

> *Pause.*

You're *telling* me this?

TEACH: (The whatchamacallit is always the last to know.)

DON: Come on, Walt, I mean, forget with the job and all.

TEACH: You live in a world of your own, Don.

DON: Fletch cheats at cards.

TEACH: Yes.

DON: I don't believe you.

TEACH: Ah. You can't take the truth.

DON: No. I am sorry. I play in this fucking game.

TEACH: And you don't know what goes on.

DON: I leave Fletcher alone in my *store.* . . . He could take me off any time, day and night.

What are you telling me, Walt? This is nothing but poison, I don't want to hear it. *(Pause.)*

TEACH: And that is what you say.

DON: Yes. It is.

Pause.

TEACH: Think back, Donny. Last night. On one hand. You lost two hundred bucks.

Pause.

You got the straight, you stand pat. I go down before the draw.

DON: Yeah.

TEACH: He's got what?

DON: A flush.

TEACH: That is correct. How many did he take?

DON: What?

TEACH: How many did he take?

Pause.

DON: One?

TEACH: No. Two, Don. He took two.

Pause.

DON: Yeah. He took two on that hand.

TEACH: He takes two on your standing pat, you kicked him thirty bucks? He draws two, comes out with a *flush*?

DON *(Pause)*: Yeah?

TEACH: And spills his fucking Fresca?

DON: Yeah?

TEACH: Oh. You remember that?

DON *(Pause)*: Yeah.

TEACH: And we look down.

DON: Yeah.

TEACH: When we look back, he has come up with a king-high flush.

Pause.

After he has drawed two.

    Pause.

You're better than that, Don. You *knew* you had him beat, and you were right.

    Pause.

DON: It could happen.

TEACH: Donny . . .

DON: Yeah?

TEACH: He laid down five red cards. A heart flush to the king.

    Pause.

DON: Yeah?

TEACH: I swear to God as I am standing here that when I threw my hand in when you raised me out, that I folded the king of hearts.

    Pause.

DON: You never called him out.

TEACH: No.

DON: How come?

TEACH: (He don't got the address the guy?)

DON: I told you he didn't.

    Pause.

He's cheating, you couldn't say anything?

TEACH: It's not my responsibility, to cause bloodshed. I am not your keeper. You want to face facts, okay.

DON: I can't believe this, Teach.

TEACH: (Friendship is marvelous.)

DON: You couldn't say a word?

TEACH: I tell you now.

DON: He was cheating, you couldn't say anything?

TEACH: Don. Don, I see you're put out, you find out this guy is a cheat. . . .

DON: According to you.

TEACH: According to me, yes. I am the person it's usually according *to* when I'm talking. Have you noticed this? And I'm not crazed about it you're coming out I would lie to you on this. *Fuck* this. On anything. Wake up, Jim. I'm not the cheat. I know you're not mad at me, who are you mad at? Who fucked you up here, Don? Who's not here? Who?

DON: Ruth knows he cheats?

TEACH: Who is the bitch in league with?

DON: Him?

TEACH *(Pause)*: You know how much money they took from this game?

DON: Yeah?

TEACH: Well, I could be wrong.

DON: Don't fuck with me here, Teach.

TEACH: I don't fuck with my friends, Don. I don't fuck with my business associates. I am a businessman, I am here to do business, I am here to face facts.

(Will you open your eyes . . . ?) The kid comes in here, he has got a certain coin, it's like the one *you* used to have . . . the guy you brought in doesn't show, we don't know where *he* is.

    Pause.

Something comes down, some guy gets his house took off.

    Pause.

Fletcher, he's not showing up. All right. Let's say I don't know why. Let's say *you* don't know why. But I know that we're both better off. We are better off, Don.

    Pause.

What time is it?

DON: It's midnight.

> *Pause.*

TEACH: I'm going out there now. I'll need the address.

> TEACH *takes out revolver and begins to load it.*

DON: What's that?

TEACH: What?

DON: That.

TEACH: This "gun"?

DON: Yes.

TEACH: What does it look like?

DON: A gun.

TEACH: It *is* a gun.

DON *(rises and crosses to center)*: I don't like it.

TEACH: Don't look at it.

DON: I'm serious.

TEACH: So am I.

DON: We don't need a gun, Teach.

TEACH: I pray that we don't, Don.

DON: We don't, tell me why we need a gun.

TEACH: It's not a question do we *need* it . . . *Need* . . . Only that it makes me comfortable, okay? It helps me to relax.

> So, God forbid, something inevitable occurs and the choice is (And I'm *saying* "God forbid") it's either him or us.

DON: Who?

TEACH: The guy. I'm saying God forbid the *guy* (or somebody) comes in, he's got a knife . . . a cleaver from one of those magnetic *boards* . . . ?

DON: Yeah?

TEACH: . . . with the two *strips* . . . ?

DON: Yeah?

TEACH: And *whack,* and somebody is bleeding to death. This is all. Merely as a deterrent.

Pause.

All the preparation in the world does not mean *shit,* the path of some crazed lunatic sees you as an invasion of his personal domain. Guys go nuts, Don, *you* know this. Public *officials* . . . *Ax* murderers . . . all I'm saying, look out for your own.

DON: I don't like the gun.

TEACH: It's a personal thing, Don. A personal thing of mine. A silly personal thing. I just like to have it along. Is this so unreasonable?

DON: I don't want it.

TEACH: I'm not going without it.

DON: Why do you want it?

TEACH: Protection of me and my partner. Protection, deterrence. (We're only going around the fucking *corner* for chrissake . . .)

DON: I don't want it with.

TEACH: I can't step down on this, Don. I got to have it with. The light of things as they are.

DON: Why?

TEACH: Because of the way *things* are. (*He looks out window.*) Hold on a second.

DON: Fletcher?

TEACH: Cops.

DON: What are they doing?

TEACH: Cruising.

Pause.

DON: They turn the corner?

TEACH: Hold on.

    Pause.

Yes.

They have the right idea. Armed to the hilt. Sticks, Mace, knives . . . who knows *what* the fuck they got. They have the right idea. Social customs break down, next thing *everybody's* lying in the gutter.

    A knocking is heard at the door.

(Get down.) (Douse the light.)

DON: (Lemme see who it is . . .)

TEACH: Don't answer it.

BOB *(from behind door)*: Donny?

TEACH: (Great.)

DON: (It's Bobby.)

TEACH: (I know.)

BOB: Donny?

    Pause.

TEACH: (Don't let him in.)

DON: (He knows we're in here.)

TEACH: (So let him go away, then.)

BOB: I got to talk to you.

    DON *looks at* TEACH.

DON *(to BOB)*: What is it?

BOB: I can't come in?

TEACH: (Get him outta here.)

    Pause.

DON: Bob . . .

BOB: Yeah?

DON: We're busy here.

BOB: I got to talk to you.

> DON *looks at* TEACH.

TEACH: (Is he alone?)

DON: (I think.)

TEACH *(Pause)*: (Hold on.)

> TEACH *opens door and pulls* BOB *in.*

What, Bob? What do you want? You know we got work to do here, we don't need you to do it, so what are you doing here and what do you want?

BOB: To talk to Don.

TEACH: Well, Don does not want to talk to you.

BOB: I *got* to talk to him.

TEACH: You do not have to do anything, Bob. You do not have to do anything that we tell you that you have to do.

BOB: I got to talk to Donny. (*To* DON) Can I talk to you? (*Pause. To* DON.) I came here . . .

DON: . . . yeah?

BOB: . . . The Riverside?

DON: Yeah?

BOB: Grace and Ruthie . . . he's in the hospital. Fletch.

> *Pause.*

I only wanted to, like, *come* here. I know you guys are only playing *cards* this . . . now. I didn't want to disturb you like *up,* but they just I found out he was in the hospital and I came over here to . . . tell you.

> *Pause.*

TEACH: With what?

BOB: He got mugged.

TEACH: You're so full of shit.

BOB: I think some Mexicans.

TEACH *snorts.*

He did. He's in the hospital.

TEACH: You see this, Don?

DON: He's mugged?

BOB: Yeah, Grace, they just got back. They broke his jaw.

TEACH: They broke his jaw.

BOB: Yeah. Broke.

TEACH: And now he's in the hospital. Grace and Ruthie just got back. You thought that you'd come over.

BOB: Yeah.

TEACH: Well, how about this, Don? Here Fletch is in Masonic Hospital a needle in his arm, huh. How about this?

DON: How bad is he?

BOB: They broke his jaw.

DON: What else?

BOB: I don't know.

TEACH: Would you believe this if I told you this this afternoon?

DON: When did it happen, Bob?

BOB: Like before.

DON: Before, huh?

BOB: Yeah.

TEACH: How about this, Don?

BOB: We're going to see him tomorrow.

DON: When?

BOB: I don't know. In the morning.

DON: They got hours in the morning?

BOB: I guess so.

TEACH: Hey, thanks for coming here. You did real good in coming here.

BOB: Yeah?

TEACH *(to* DON*)*: He did real good in coming here, huh, Donny? *(To* BOB *)* We really owe you something.

BOB: What for?

TEACH: Coming here.

BOB: What?

TEACH: Something.

BOB: Like what?

DON: He don't know. He's saying that he thinks we owe you something, but right now he can't think what it is.

BOB: Thanks, Teach.

TEACH: It's okay, Bob.

> *Pause.* BOB *starts to exit.*

Stick around.

BOB: Okay. For a minute.

TEACH: What? You're busy?

BOB: I got, like, some things to do.

TEACH: Whaddaya got, a "date"?

BOB: No.

TEACH: What, then?

BOB: Business.

> *Pause.*

DON: Where did they take him, Bob?

> *Pause.*

BOB: Uh, Masonic.

DON: I don't think that they got hours start til after lunch.

BOB: Then we'll go then. I'm gonna go now.

TEACH: Hold on a second, Bob. I feel we should take care of you for coming here.

BOB: That's okay. I'll see you guys.

DON: Come here a minute, Bobby.

BOB: What, Donny?

DON: What's going on here?

BOB: Here?

DON: Yes.

   Pause.

BOB: Nothing.

DON: I'm saying what's happening, Bob?

BOB: I don't know.

DON: Where did you get that nickel from?

BOB: What nickel?

DON: You know what nickel, Bob, the nickel I'm talking about.

BOB: I got it off a guy

DON: What guy?

BOB: I met downtown.

TEACH: What was he wearing?

BOB: Things.

   Pause.

DON: How'd you get it off him, Bob?

BOB: We kinda talked.

   Pause.

DON: You know what, you look funny, Bob.

BOB: I'm late.

DON: It's after midnight, Bob. What are you late for?

BOB: Nothing.

DON *(very sadly)*: Jesus. Are you fucking with me here?

BOB: No.

DON: (Bobby.)

BOB: I'm not fucking with you, Donny.

>   *Pause.*

DON: Where's Fletcher?

>   *Pause.*

BOB: Masonic.

>   DON *goes to telephone and dials information.*

DON *(into phone)*: For Masonic Hospital, please.

BOB: . . . I *think* . . .

DON *(to* BOB*)*: What?

BOB: He might not be Masonic.

DON *(to phone)*: Thank you. *(Hangs up phone. To* BOB*)* Now, what?

BOB: He might not *be* there . . .

DON: You said he was there.

BOB: Yeah, I just, like, I *said* it. I really don't remember what they said, Ruthie.

TEACH: (Ruthie.)

BOB: . . . so I just . . . *said* Masonic.

DON: Why?

BOB: I thought of it.

>   *Pause.*

DON: Uh-huh. *(To phone)* Yes. I'm looking for a guy was just admitted. Fletcher Post.

>   *Pause.*

Just a short time ago.

>   *Pause.*

Thank you. *(Pause. To* BOB *and* TEACH*)* She's looking for it. *(To phone)* No?

BOB: (I told you . . .)

DON: You're sure?

>Pause.

Thank you. *(Hangs up phone. To* BOB*)* He's not there.

BOB: I told you.

TEACH: (What did I tell you, Don?)

DON: Where is he?

BOB: Somewhere else.

DON: (This makes me nuts . . .) Bobby . . .

BOB: Yeah?

>Pause.

They broke his jaw.

DON: Who?

BOB: Some spics. I don't know.

>TEACH *snorts.*

They did.

DON: Who?

TEACH: Yeah.

DON: Who is this "they," Bob, that you're talking about?

TEACH: Bob. . . .

BOB: . . . yeah?

TEACH: Who are these people you're talking about?

BOB: They broke his jaw.

TEACH: They took it in them all of a sudden they broke his jaw.

BOB: They didn't care it was him.

TEACH: No?

BOB: No, Teach.

TEACH: So who is it takes him out by accident. Huh? Grace and Ruthie?

BOB: They wouldn't do that.

TEACH: I'm not saying they would.

BOB *(to* DON*)*: What is he saying, Donny?

TEACH: Bob, Bob, Bob . . . what am I saying . . .

> *Pause.*

DON: Where's Fletch, Bobby?

BOB: Hospital.

TEACH: Aside from that.

BOB: All I know, that's the only place he is, Teach.

TEACH: Now, don't get smart with me, Bob, don't get smart with me, you young fuck, we've been sweating blood all day on this and I don't want your smart mouth on it (fuck around with Grace and Ruthie, and you come in here . . .), so all we want some answers. Do you understand?

> *Pause.*

I told you: Do you understand this?

DON: You better answer him.

BOB: I understand.

TEACH: Then let's make *this* clear: Loyalty does not mean *shit* a situation like this; I don't know what you and them are up to, and I do not *care*, but only you come clean with us.

BOB: He might of been a different hospital.

TEACH: Which one?

BOB: *Any* of 'em.

DON: So why'd you say "Masonic"?

BOB: I just thought of it.

TEACH: Okay. Okay. . . . Bob?

BOB: . . . yes?

TEACH: I want for you to tell us here and now (and for your own protection) what is going *on*, what is set *up* . . where *Fletcher* is . . . and everything you know.

DON *(sotto voce)*: (I can't believe this.)

BOB: I don't know anything.

TEACH: You don't, huh?

BOB: No.

DON: Tell him what you know, Bob.

BOB: I don't know it, Donny. Grace and Ruthie . . .

> TEACH *grabs a nearby object and hits* BOB *viciously on the side of the head.*

TEACH: Grace and Ruthie up your ass, you shithead; you don't fuck with us, *I'll* kick your fucking head in. (I don't give a shit . . .)

> *Pause.*

You *twerp* . . .

> *A pause near the end of which* BOB *starts whimpering.*

I don't give a shit. (Come in here with your fucking stories . . .)

> *Pause.*

Imaginary people in the hospital . .

> BOB *starts to cry.*

That don't mean shit to me, you fruit.

BOB: Donny . . .

DON: You brought it on yourself.

TEACH: Sending us out there . . who the fuck knows what . .

BOB: He's in the hospital.

DON: Which hospital?

BOB: I don't know.

TEACH: Well, then, you better make one up, and quick

DON: Bob . . .

TEACH: (Don't back down on this Don. Don't back down on me, here.)

DON: Bob . .

BOB: . . . yeah?

DON: You got to see our point here.

BOB *(whimpering)*: Yeah, I do.

DON: Now, we don't want to hit you

TEACH: (No.)

BOB: I know you don't.

TEACH: No.

DON: But you come in here .

BOB: . . . yeah . . .

DON: . . . the only one who knows the score . . .

BOB: Yeah . . . (My ear is bleeding. It's coming out my ear.) Oh, fuck, I'm real scared.

DON: (Shit.)

BOB: I don't feel good.

TEACH: (Fuckin' kid poops out on us . . .)

BOB: Don . . .

TEACH: Now what are we going to do with this?

DON: You know, we didn't want to do this to you, Bob.

BOB: I know . . .

DON: We didn't want to do this.

    Phone rings.

TEACH: (Great.)

DON *(to phone)*: What? What the fuck do *you* want?

TEACH: (It's the guy?)

DON: (It's Ruthie.) *(To phone)* Oh yeah, we heard about that, Ruth.

TEACH: (*She's* got a lot of nerve . . .)

DON *(to phone)*: From Bobby. Yeah. We'll *all* go.

Pause.

I thought he was at Masonic? Bobby. Well, okay, that's where we'll go then, Ruthie, we aren't going to go and see him at some hospital he isn't even *at* . . .

Pause.

Bobby's not here. I will. Okay. I will. Around eleven. Okay. *(He hangs up.)*

TEACH *(to* BOB*)*: And you owe me twenty bucks.

DON *(dialing)*: For Columbus Hospital, please.

TEACH: (Fuckin' medical costs . . .)

DON: Thank you.

TEACH *(singing softly to himself)*: ". . . and I'm never ever sick at sea."

DON: Yes. For Fletcher Post, please, he was just admitted?

Pause.

No. I only want to know is he all right, and when we go to see him.

Pause.

Thank you.

TEACH: What?

DON: She's looking. *(To phone)* Yes? Yeah. Thank you very much. Yes. You've been very kind. *(He hangs up phone.)*

TEACH: What is he, *in* there?

DON: Yeah.

TEACH: And they won't let us talk to him?

DON: His jaw is broke.

BOB: I feel funny.

TEACH: Your *ear* hurts.

DON: Bob, it hurts. Bob?

TEACH: I never felt quite right on this.

DON: Go tilt your head the other way.

TEACH I mean, we're fucked up here. We have not blown the shot, but we're fucked up.

DON: We are going to take you to the hospital.

TEACH: Yeah, yeah, we'll take you to the hospital, you'll get some *care*, this isn't a big deal.

DON: Bob, you fell downstairs, you hurt your ear.

TEACH: He understands?

DON: You understand? We're going to take you to the hospital, you fell downstairs.

TEACH *(at door)*: This fucking rain.

DON: You give 'em your right name, Bob, and you know what you can tell 'em. *(Reaches in pocket, thrusts money at* BOB.*)* You hold on to this, Bob. Anything you want inside the hospital.

BOB: I don't want to go to the hospital.

TEACH: You're going to the hospital, and that's the end of it.

BOB: I don't want to.

DON: You got to, Bob.

BOB: Why?

TEACH: You're fucked up, that's why.

BOB: I'm gonna do the job.

DON: We aren't going to do the job tonight, Bob.

TEACH: You got a hat or something keep my head dry?

DON: No.

BOB: I get to do the job.

TEACH: You shut up. You are going in the hospital.

DON: We aren't going to do the job tonight.

BOB: We do it sometime else.

DON: Yeah.

TEACH: He ain't going to do no job.

DON: Shut up.

TEACH: Just say he isn't going to do no job.

DON: It's done now.

TEACH: What?

DON: I'm saying, this is over.

TEACH: No, it's not, Don. It is not. He does no job.

DON: You leave the fucking kid alone.

TEACH: You want kids, you go have them. *I* am not your wife. *This* doesn't mean a thing to me. *I'm* in this. And it *isn't* over. This is for me, and this is my question:

> *Pause.*

Where did you get that coin?

BOB: What?

TEACH: Where'd you get that fucking nickel, if it all comes out now.

> *Pause.*

He comes in here, a fifty dollars for a nickel, where'd you get it?

BOB: Take me to the hospital.

> *Pause.*

TEACH: Where did you get that nickel? (I want you to watch this.)

Pause.

BOB: I bought it.

TEACH: (Mother Fucking Junkies.)

DON: Shut up.

TEACH: What are you saying that you bought that coin?

BOB: Yeah.

TEACH: Where?

BOB: A coin store.

Pause.

TEACH: You bought it in a coin store.

BOB: Yeah.

Pause.

TEACH: Why?

DON: Go get your car.

TEACH: What did you pay for it?

Pause.

What did you pay for it?

BOB: Fifty dollars.

TEACH: You buy a coin for fifty dollars, you come back here.

Pause.

Why?

DON: Go get your fucking car.

TEACH: Why would you do a thing like that?

BOB: I don't know.

TEACH: Why would you go do a thing like that?

BOB: For Donny.

Pause.

TEACH: You people make my flesh crawl.

DON: Bob, we're going to take you out of here.

TEACH: I can not take this anymore.

DON: Can you walk?

BOB: No.

DON: Go and get your car.

TEACH: I am not your nigger. I am not your wife.

DON: I'm through with you today.

TEACH: You are.

DON: Yes.

TEACH: Why?

  Pause.

DON: You have lamed this up real good.

TEACH: I did.

DON: Real good.

TEACH: I lamed it up.

BOB: He hit me.

DON: I know, Bob.

TEACH: Yes, I hit him. For his own good. For the good of all.

DON: Get out of here.

TEACH: "Get out of here"? And now you throw me out like *trash?* I'm doing this for *you.* What do I have to wreck this joint *apart?* He told you that he bought it in a *coin store.*

DON: I don't care.

TEACH: You don't *care?* (I cannot believe this.) You *believe* him?

DON: I don't *care.* I don't *care* anymore.

TEACH: You *fake.* You fucking *fake.* You fuck your friends. You *have* no friends. No *wonder* that you fuck this kid around.

DON: You shut your mouth.

TEACH: You seek your friends with *junkies.* You're a joke on this street, you and him.

DON: Get out.

TEACH: I do not go out, no.

BOB: (I eat shit.)

DON: You get out of here.

TEACH: I am not going anywhere. I have a piece of this.

DON: You have a piece of *shit,* you fucking lame. *(Advancing on him.)*

TEACH: (This from a man who has to buy his friends.)

DON: *I'll* tell you friends, *I'll* give you friends . . . (Still advancing.)

BOB: (Oh, fuck . . .)

DON: The stinking deals you come in here . . .

TEACH: You stay away from me . . .

DON: You stiff this one, you stiff that one . . . you come in here, you stick this poison in me . . . *(hitting him).*

TEACH: (Oh, Christ . . .)

BOB: (I eat shit.)

TEACH: (Oh, my God, I live with madmen.)

DON: All these years . . .

BOB: (A cause I missed him.)

DON *(advancing again)*: All these fucking years . . .

TEACH: (You're going to hit me.)

BOB: Donny . . .

DON: You make life of garbage.

BOB: Donny!

TEACH: (Oh, my God.)

BOB: I missed him.

DON *(stopping)*: What?

BOB: I got to tell you what a fuck I am.

DON: What?

BOB: I missed him.

DON: Who?

BOB: The guy.

DON: What guy?

BOB: The guy this morning.

DON: What guy?

BOB: With the suitcase.

DON *(Pause)*: You missed him?

BOB: I eat shit.

DON: What are you saying that you lied to me?

BOB: I eat shit.

TEACH: What is he saying?

    Pause.

DON: You're saying that you lied?

TEACH: What is he saying?

DON: You're saying you didn't see him with the suitcase?

TEACH: This kid is hysterical.

DON: You didn't see him?

TEACH: He's saying that he didn't see him?

DON: When he left this morning.

TEACH: He's saying that he lied?

BOB: I'm going to throw up.

TEACH: He's saying he didn't see the guy?

    Pause.

When he came out. I was in here. *Then* you saw him.
When he had the suitcase. *(Pause.)* Then.

> *Pause.*

You saw him *then*.

> *Pause.* BOB *shakes his head.*

My Whole Cocksucking Life.

> TEACH *picks up the dead-pig sticker and starts trashing
> the junkshop.*

The Whole Entire World.

There Is No Law.

There Is No Right And Wrong.

The World Is Lies.

There Is No Friendship.

Every Fucking Thing.

> *Pause.*

Every God-forsaken Thing.

DON: Calm down, Walt.

TEACH: We all live like the cavemen.

> *During the speech,* DON *tries to subdue* TEACH, *and
> finally does.*

DON: (Siddown.)

> *Pause.*

> TEACH *sits still.*

TEACH: I went on a limb for you.

> *Pause.*

You don't know what I go through. I put my dick on the
chopping block.

> *Pause.*

I hock my fucking watch . . .

> *Pause.*

I go out there. I'm out there every day.

Pause.

There is nothing out there.

Pause.

I fuck myself.

Pause.

DON: Are you all right?

TEACH: What?

DON: Are you all right.

TEACH: How the fuck do I know?

DON: You tire me out, Walt.

TEACH: What?

DON: I need a rest.

TEACH: This fucking day.

DON *(Pause)*: My shop's fucked up.

TEACH: I know.

DON: It's all fucked up.

Pause.

You fucked my shop up.

TEACH: Are you mad at me?

DON: What?

TEACH: Are you mad at me?

Pause.

DON: Come on.

TEACH: Are you?

DON: Go and get your car. Bob?

TEACH *(Pause)*: Tell me are you mad at me.

DON: No.

TEACH: You aren't?

DON: No.

> *Pause.*

TEACH: Good.

DON: You go and get your car.

TEACH: You got a hat?

DON: No.

TEACH: Do you have a piece of paper?

DON: Bob . . . ?

> TEACH *walks to counter, takes a piece of newspaper, and starts making himself a paper hat.*

TEACH: He's all right?

DON: Bob . . . ?

TEACH: Is he all right?

DON: Bob . . . ?

BOB *(waking up)*: What?

DON: Come on. We're taking you the hospital.

> TEACH *puts on paper hat and looks at self in window.*

TEACH: I look like a sissy.

DON: Go and get your car

> *Pause.*

TEACH: Can you get him to the door?

DON: Yeah.

> *Pause.*

TEACH: I'm going to get my car.

DON: You gonna honk?

TEACH: Yeah.

DON: Good.

TEACH: I'll honk the horn.

> *Pause.*

DON: Good.

> *Pause.*

TEACH: This fucking day, huh?

DON: Yeah.

TEACH: I know it. You should clean this place up.

DON: Yeah.

> *Pause.*

TEACH: Good. *(Exits.)*

DON: Bob.

BOB: What?

DON: Get up.

> *Pause.*

Bob. I'm sorry.

BOB: What?

DON: I'm sorry.

BOB: I fucked up.

DON: No. You did real good.

BOB: No.

DON: Yeah. You did real good.

> *Pause.*

BOB: Thank you.

DON: That's all right.

> *Pause.*

BOB: I'm sorry, Donny.

DON: That's all right.

> *Lights dim.*